D0914219

THE COMPLETE WORKS OF ROBERT BROWNING, VOLUME VIII

Drawing, by William Wetmore Story, 1869.

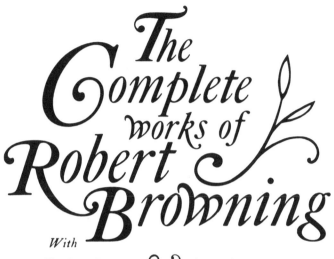

The Complete works of Robert Browning

With Variant Readings & Annotations

Volume VIII

BAYLOR UNIVERSITY
WACO, TEXAS
OHIO UNIVERSITY PRESS
ATHENS, OHIO
1988

Members of the Editorial Staff who have assisted in the preparation of Volume VIII:
John Berkey
Ashby Bland Crowder, Jr.
David R. Ewbank
Nathaniel Hart
W. Craig Turner

Ohio University Press books are printed on acid free paper. ∞
Copyright © 1988 by Ohio University Press and Baylor University
Library of Congress Catalog Card Number: 68-18389
ISBN 0-8214-0380-X
All rights reserved

Printed in the United States of America

CONTENTS

I CONTENTS

This edition of the works of Robert Browning is intended to be complete. It will comprise at least fourteen volumes and will contain:

1. The entire contents of the first editions of Browning's works, arranged in their chronological order of publication. (The poems included in *Dramatic Lyrics, Dramatic Romances and Lyrics,* and *Men and Women,* for example, appear in the order of their first publication rather than in the order in which Browning rearranged them for later publication.)

2. All prefaces and dedications which Browning is known to have written for his own works and for those of Elizabeth Barrett Browning.

3. The two prose essays that Browning is known to have published: the review of a book on Tasso, generally referred to as the "Essay on Chatterton," and the preface for a collection of letters supposed to have been written by Percy Bysshe Shelley, generally referred to as the "Essay on Shelley."

4. The front matter and the table of contents of each of the collected editions (1849, 1863, 1865, 1868, 1888-1889) which Browning himself saw through the press.

5. Poems published during Browning's lifetime but not collected by him.

6. Poems not published during Browning's lifetime which have come to light since his death.

7. John Forster's *Thomas Wentworth, Earl of Strafford,* to which Browning contributed significantly, though the precise extent of his contribution has not been determined.

8. Variants appearing in primary and secondary materials as defined in Section II below.

9. Textual emendations.

10. Informational and explanatory notes for each work.

II PRIMARY AND SECONDARY MATERIALS

Aside from a handful of uncollected short works, all of Browning's works but *Asolando* (1889) went through two or more editions during his lifetime. Except for *Pauline* (1833), *Strafford* (1837), and *Sordello* (1840), all the works published before 1849 were revised and corrected for the 1849 collection. *Strafford* and *Sordello* were revised and corrected for the collection of 1863, as were all the other works in that edition. Though no further poems were added in the collection of 1865, all the works were once again corrected and revised. The 1868 collection added a revised *Pauline* and *Dramatis Personae* (1864) to the other works, which were themselves again revised and corrected. The printing of the last edition of the *Poetical Works* over which Browning exercised control began in 1888, and the first eight volumes are dated thus on their title-pages. Volumes 9 through 16 of this first impression are dated 1889, and we have designated them 1889a to distinguish them from the second impression of all 16 volumes, which was begun and completed in 1889. Some of the earlier volumes of the first impression sold out almost immediately, and in preparation for a second impression, Browning revised and corrected the first ten volumes before he left for Italy in late August, 1889. The second impression, in which all sixteen volumes bear the date 1889 on their title-pages, consisted of a revised and corrected second impression of volumes 1-10, plus a second impression of volumes 11-16 altered by Browning in one instance. This impression we term 1889 (see section III below).

Existing manuscripts and editions are classified as either primary or secondary material. The primary materials include the following:

1. The manuscript of a work when such is known to exist.

2. Proof sheets, when known to exist, that contain authorial corrections and revisions.

3. The first and subsequent editions of a work that preserve evidence of Browning's intentions and were under his control.

4. The collected editions over which Browning exercised control:

1849—*Poems*. Two Volumes. London: Chapman and Hall.

1863—*The Poetical Works*. Three Volumes. London: Chapman and Hall.

1865—*The Poetical Works*. Three Volumes. London: Chapman and Hall.

1868—*The Poetical Works*. Six Volumes. London: Smith, Elder and Company. Reissued in stereotype impressions with varying title pages.

1888-1889—*The Poetical Works*. Sixteen Volumes. London: Smith, Elder and Company. Exists in numerous stereotype impressions, of which two are primary material:

1888-1889a—The first impression, in which volumes 1-8 are dated 1888 and volumes 9-16 are dated 1889.

1889—The corrected second impression of volumes 1-10 and a second impression of volumes 11-16 altered by Browning only as stated in section III below; all dated 1889 on the title pages.

5. The corrections in Browning's hand in the Dykes Campbell copy of 1888-1889a, and the manuscript list of corrections to that impression in the Brown University Library (see section III below).

Other materials (including some in the poet's handwriting) that affected the text are secondary. Examples are: the copy of the first edition of *Pauline* which contains annotations by Browning and John Stuart Mill; the copies of the first edition of *Paracelsus* which contain corrections in Browning's hand; a very early manuscript of *A Blot in the 'Scutcheon* which Browning presented to William Macready, but not the one from which the first edition was printed; informal lists of corrections that Browning included in letters to friends, such as the corrections to *Men and Women* he sent to D. G. Rossetti; Elizabeth Barrett's suggestions for revisions in *A Soul's Tragedy* and certain poems in *Dramatic Romances and Lyrics*; and the edition of *Strafford* by Emily Hickey for which Browning made suggestions.

The text and variant readings of this edition derive from collation of primary materials as defined above. Secondary materials are occasionally discussed in the notes and sometimes play a part when emendation is required.

III COPY-TEXT

The copy-text for this edition is Browning's final text: the first ten volumes of 1889 and the last six volumes of 1888-1889a, as described above. For this choice we offer the following explanation.

Manuscripts used as printer's copy for twenty of Browning's thirty-four book publications are known to exist; others may yet become available. These manuscripts, or, in their absence, the first editions of the works, might be considered as the most desirable copy-text. And this would be the case for an author who exercised little control over his text after the manuscript or first edition stage, or whose text clearly became corrupted in a succession of editions. To preserve the intention of such an author, one would have to choose an early text and emend it as evidence and judgment demanded.

With Browning, however, the situation is different, and our copy-text choice results from that difference. Throughout his life Browning continually revised his poetry. He did more than correct printer's errors and clarify previously intended meanings; his texts themselves remained fluid, subject to continuous alteration. As the manuscript which he submitted to his publisher was no doubt already a product of revision, so each subsequent edition under his control reflects the results of an ongoing process of creating, revising, and correcting. If we were to choose the manuscript (where extant) or first edition as copy-text, preserving Browning's intention would require extensive emendation to capture the additions, revisions, and alterations which Browning demonstrably made in later editions. By selecting Browning's final corrected text as our copy-text, emending it only to eliminate errors and the consequences of changing house-styling, we present his works in the form closest to that which he intended after years of revision and polishing.

But this is true only if Browning in fact exercised extensive control over the printing of his various editions. That he intended and attempted to do so is apparent in his comments and his practice. In 1855, demanding accuracy from the printers, he pointed out to his publisher Chapman, "I attach importance to the mere stops . . ." (DeVane and Knickerbocker, p. 83). There is evidence of his desire to control the details of his text as early as 1835, in the case of *Paracelsus*. The *Paracelsus* manuscript, now in the Forster and Dyce collection in the Victoria and Albert Museum Library, demonstrates a highly unconventional system of punctuation. Of particular note is Browning's unrestrained use of dashes, often in strings of two or three, instead of more precise or orthodox punctuation marks. It appears that this was done for its rhetorical effect. One sheet of Part 1 of the manuscript and all but the first and last sheets of Part 3 have had punctuation revised in pencil by someone other than Browning, perhaps J. Riggs, whose name appears three times in the margins of Part 3. In addition to these revisions, there are analogous punctuation revisions (in both pencil and ink) which appear to be in Browning's hand, and a few verbal alterations obviously in the poet's script.

A collation of the first edition (1835) with the manuscript reveals that a major restyling of punctuation was carried out before *Paracelsus* was published. However, the revisions incorporated into the first edition by no means slavishly follow the example set by the pencilled revisions of Parts 1 and 3 of the manuscript. Apparently the surviving manuscript was not used as printer's copy for the first edition. Browning may have submitted a second manuscript, or he may have revised extensively in proof. The printers may have carried out the revisions to punctuation, with or without the poet's point by point involvement. With the present evidence, we cannot be conclusive about the extent of Browning's control over the first edition of *Paracelsus*. It can be stated, however, in the light of the incompleteness of the pencilled revisions and the frequent lack of correspondence between the pencilled revisions and the lines as printed in 1835, that Browning himself may have been responsible for the punctuation of the first edition of *Paracelsus*. Certainly he was responsible for the frequent instances in the first and subsequent editions where the punctuation defies conventional rules, as in the following examples:

> What though
> It be so?—if indeed the strong desire
> Eclipse the aim in me?—if splendour break
> (Part I, ll. 329-331)

> I surely loved them—that last night, at least,
> When we . . . gone! gone! the better: I am saved
> (Part II, ll. 132-133)

> Of the body, even,)—what God is, what we are,
> (Part V, l. 642, 1849 reading)

The manuscripts of *Colombe's Birthday* (1844) and *Christmas-Eve and Easter-Day* (1850) were followed very carefully in the printing of the first editions. There are slight indications of minor house-styling, such as the spellings *colour* and *honour* for the manuscripts' *color* and *honor*. But the unorthodox punctuation, used to indicate elocutionary and rhetorical subtleties as well as syntactical relationships, is carried over almost unaltered from the manuscripts to the first editions. Similar evidence of Browning's painstaking attention to the smallest details in the printing of his poems can be seen in the manuscript and proof sheets of *The Ring and the Book* (1868-69). These materials reveal an interesting and significant pattern. It appears that Browning wrote swiftly, giving primary attention to wording and less to punctuation, being satisfied to use dashes to indicate almost any break in thought, syntax, or rhythm. Later, in the proof sheets for Books 1-6 of the poem and in the manuscript itself for Books 7-12, he changed the dashes to more specific and purposeful punctuation marks. The revised punctuation is what was printed, for the most part, in the first edition of *The Ring and the Book*; what further revisions there are conform to Browning's practice, though hardly to standard rules. Clearly Browning was in control of nearly every aspect of the published form of his works, even to the "mere stops."

Of still greater importance in our choice of copy-text is the substantial evidence that Browning took similar care with his collected editions. Though he characterized his changes for later editions as trivial and few in number, collations reveal thousands of revisions and corrections in each successive text. *Paracelsus*, for example, was extensively revised for the 1849 *Poems*; it was again reworked for the *Poetical Works* of 1863. *Sordello*, omitted in 1849, reappeared in 1863 with 181 new lines and short marginal glosses; Browning admitted only that it was "corrected throughout" (DeVane and Knickerbocker, p. 157). The poems of *Men and Women* (1855) were altered in numerous small but meaningful ways for both the 1863 and 1865 editions of the *Poetical Works* (See Allan C. Dooley, "The Textual Significance of Robert Browning's 1865 *Poetical Works*," *PBSA* 71 [1977], 212-18). Professor Michael Hancher, editor of Browning's correspondence with his publisher, George Smith, has cited evidence of the poet's close supervision of the 1868 collected edition ("Browning and the *Poetical Works* of 1888-1889," *Browning Newsletter*, Spring, 1971, 25-27). Mrs. Orr, writing of the same period in Browning's life, reports his resentment of those who garbled his text by misplacing his stops (*Life*, pp. 357-58).

There is plentiful and irrefutable evidence that Browning controlled, in the same meticulous way, the text of his last collected edition, that which we term 1888-1889. Hancher has summarized the relevant information:

> The evidence is clear that Browning undertook the 1888-1889 edition of his *Poetical Works* intent on controlling even the smallest minutiae of the text. Though he at one time considered supplying biographical and explanatory notes to the poems, he finally decided against such a scheme, concluding, in his letter to Smith of 12 November 1887, "I am correcting them carefully, and *that* must suffice." On 13 January 1888, he wrote, regarding the six-volume edition of his collected works published in 1868 which was to serve as the printer's copy for the final edition: "I have thoroughly corrected the six volumes of the Works, and can let you have them at once." . . . Browning evidently kept a sharp eye on the production of all sixteen of the volumes, including those later volumes. . . . Browning returned proof for Volume 3 on 6 May 1888, commenting, "I have had, as usual, to congratulate myself on the scrupulous accuracy of the Printers"; on 31 December he returned proofs of Volume 11, "corrected carefully"; and he returned "the corrected Proofs of Vol. XV" on 1 May 1889.

Throughout his long career, then, Browning continuously revised and corrected his works. Furthermore, his publishers took care to follow his directions exactly, accepting his changes and incorporating them into each successive edition. This is not to say that no one else had any effect whatsoever on Browning's text: Elizabeth Barrett made suggestions for revisions to *A Soul's Tragedy* and *Dramatic Romances and Lyrics*. Browning accepted some suggestions and rejected others, and those which he accepted we regard as his own. Mrs. Orr reports that Browning sent proof sheets to Joseph Milsand, a friend in France, for corrections (*Life*, p. 265), and that Browning accepted suggestions from friends and readers for the corrections of errors in his printed works. In some of the editions, there are slight evidences of minor house-styling in capitalization and the indication of quotations. But the evidence of Browning's own careful attention to revisions and corrections in both his manuscripts and proof sheets assures us that other persons played only a very minor role in the development of his text. We conclude that the vast majority of the alterations in the texts listed above as Primary Materials are Browning's own, and that only Browning's final corrected text, the result of years of careful work by the poet himself, reflects his full intentions.

The first impression of Browning's final collected edition (i.e., 1888-1889a) is not in and of itself the poet's final corrected text. By the spring of 1889 some of the early volumes of the first impression were already sold out, and by mid-August it was evident that a new one would be required. About this time James Dykes Campbell, Honorary Secretary of the London Browning Society, was informed by Browning that he was making further corrections to be incorporated into the new impression. According to Dykes Campbell, Browning had corrected the first ten volumes and offered to transcribe the corrections into Dykes Campbell's copy of 1888-1889a before leaving for Italy. The volumes altered in Browning's hand are now in the British Library and contain on the flyleaf of Volume 1 Dykes Campbell's note explaining precisely what happened. Of course, Dykes Campbell's copy was not the one used by the printer for the second impression. Nevertheless, these changes are indisputably Browning's and are those which, according to his own statement, he proposed to make in the new impression. This set of corrections carries, therefore, great authority.

Equally authoritative is a second set of corrections, also in Browning's hand, for part of 1888-1889a. In the poet's possession at the time of his death, this handwritten list was included in lot 179 of Sotheby, Wilkinson, and Hodge's auction of Browning materials in 1913; it is today located in the Brown University Library. The list contains corrections only for Volumes 4-10 of 1888-1889a. We know that Browning, on 26 July 1889, had completed and sent to Smith "the corrections for Vol. III in readiness for whenever you need them." By the latter part of August, according to Dykes Campbell, the poet had finished corrections for Volumes 1-10. Browning left for Italy on 29 August. The condition of the Brown University list does not indicate that it was ever used by the printer. Thus we surmise that the Brown list (completing the corrections through volume 10) may be the poet's copy of another list sent to his publisher. Whatever the case, the actual documents used by the printers—a set of marked volumes or handwritten lists—are not known to exist. A possible exception is a marked copy of *Red Cotton Night-Cap Country* (now in the Berg Collection of the New York Public Library) which seems to have been used by printers. Further materials used in preparing Browning's final edition may yet appear.

The matter is complicated further because neither set of corrections of 1888-1889a corresponds exactly to each other nor to the 1889 second impression. Each set contains corrections the other omits, and in a few cases the sets present alternative corrections of the same error. Our study of the Dykes Campbell copy of 1888-1889a reveals fifteen discrepancies between its corrections and the 1889 second impression. The Brown University list, which contains far fewer corrections, varies from the second impression in thirteen instances. Though neither of these sets of corrections was used by the printers, both are authoritative; we consider them legitimate textual variants, and record them as such. The lists are, of course, useful when emendation of the copy-text is required.

The value of the Dykes Campbell copy of 1888-1889a and the Brown University list is not that they render Browning's text perfect. The corrections to 1888-1889a must have existed in at least one other, still more authoritative form: the documents which Browning sent to his publisher. That this is so is indicated by the presence of required corrections in the second impression which neither the Dykes Campbell copy nor the Brown University list calls for. The significance of the existing sets of corrections is that they clearly indicate two important points: Browning's direct and active interest in the preparation of a corrected second impression of his final collected edition; and, given the high degree of correspondence between the two sets of corrections and the affected lines of the second impression, the concern of the printers to follow the poet's directives.

The second impression of 1888-1889 incorporated most of Browning's corrections to the first ten volumes of the first impression. There is no evidence whatever that any corrections beyond those which Browning sent to his publisher in the summer of 1889 were ever made. We choose, therefore, the 1889 corrected second impression of volumes 1-10 as copy-text for the works in those volumes. Corrections to the first impression were achieved by cutting the affected letters of punctuation out of the stereotype plates and pressing or soldering in the correct pieces of type. The corrected plates were then used for many copies, without changing the date on the title pages (except, of course, in volumes 17 [*Asolando*] and 18 [*New Poems*], added to the set by the publishers in 1894 and 1914 respectively). External evidence from publishers' catalogues and the advertisements bound into some volumes of 1889 indicate that copies of this impression were produced as late as 1913, although the dates on the title pages of volumes 1-16 remained 1889. Extensive plate deterioration is characteristic of the later copies, and use of the Hinman collator on early and late examples of 1889 reveals that the inserted corrections were somewhat fragile, some of them having decayed or disappeared entirely as the plates aged. (See Allan C. Dooley, "Browning's *Poetical Works* of 1888-1889," *SBHC* 7:1 [1978], 43-69.)

We do not use as copy-text volumes 11-16 of 1889, because there is no present evidence indicating that Browning exercised substantial control over this part of the second impression of 1888-1889. We do know that he made one correction, which he requested in a letter to Smith quoted by Hancher:

I have just had pointed out to [me] that an error, I supposed corrected, still is to be found in the 13th Volume—(Aristophanes' Apology) page 143, line 9, where the word should be Opora—without an i. I should like it altered, if that may be possible.

This correction was indeed made in the second impression. Our collations of copies of volumes 11-16 of 1889a and 1889 show no other intentional changes. The later copies do show, however, extensive type batter, numerous scratches, and irregular inking. Therefore our copy-text for the works in the last six volumes of 1888-1889 is volumes 11-16 of 1888-1889a.

IV VARIANTS

In this edition we record, with a very few exceptions discussed below, all variants from the copy-text appearing in the manuscripts and in the editions under Browning's control. Our purpose in doing this is two-fold.

1. We enable the reader to reconstruct the text of a work as it stood at the various stages of its development.

2. We provide the materials necessary to an understanding of how Browning's growth and development as an artist are reflected in his successive revisions to his works.

As a consequence of this policy our variant listings inevitably contain some variants that were not created by Browning; printer's errors and readings that may result from house-styling will appear occasionally. But the evidence that Browning assumed responsibility for what was printed, and that he considered and used unorthodox punctuation as part of his meaning, is so persuasive that we must record even the smallest and oddest variants. The following examples, characteristic of Browning's revisions, illustrate the point:

Pauline, 1. 700:
    1833: I am prepared—I have made life my own—
    1868: I am prepared: I have made life my own.
"Evelyn Hope," 1. 41:
    1855: I have lived, I shall say, so much since then,
    1865: I have lived (I shall say) so much since then,
"Bishop Blougram's Apology," 1. 267:
    1855: That's the first cabin-comfort I secure—
    1865: That's the first-cabin comfort I secure:
The Ring and the Book, Book 11 ("Guido"), 1. 1064:
    1869: What if you give up boys' and girls' fools'-play
    1872: What if you give up boy and girl fools'-play
    1889a: What if you give up boy-and-girl-fools' play

We have concluded that Browning himself is nearly always responsible for such changes. But even if he only accepted these changes (rather than originating them), their effect on syntax, rhythm, and meaning is so significant that they must be recorded in our variant listings.

The only variants we do not record are those which strongly appear to result from systematic house-styling. For example, Browning nowhere indicated that he wished to use typography to influence meaning, and our inference is that any changes in line-spacing, depth of paragraph indentation, and the like, were the responsibility of the printers of the various editions, not the poet himself. House-styling was also very probably the cause of certain variants in the apparatus of Browning's plays, including variants in stage directions which involve a change only in manner of statement, such as *Enter Hampden* instead of *Hampden enters*; variants in the printing of stage directions, such as *Aside* instead of *aside*, or [*Aside.*] instead of [*Aside*], or [*Strafford.*] instead of [*Strafford*]; variants in character designations, such as *Lady Carlisle* instead of *Car* or *Carlisle*. Browning also accepted current convention for indicating quotations (see section V below). Neither do we list changes in type face (except when used for emphasis), nor the presence or absence of a period at the end of the title of a work.

V ALTERATIONS TO THE COPY-TEXT

We have rearranged the sequence of works in the copy-text, so that they appear in the order of their first publication. This process involves the restoration to the original order of the poems included in *Dramatic Lyrics, Dramatic Romances and Lyrics,* and *Men and Women.* We realize, of course, that Browning himself was responsible for the rearrangement of these poems in the various collected editions; in his prefatory note for the 1888-1889 edition, however, he indicates that he desired a chronological presentation:

> The poems that follow are again, as before, printed in chronological order; but only so far as proves compatible with the prescribed size of each volume, which necessitates an occasional change in the distribution of its contents.

We would like both to indicate Browning's stated intentions about the placement of his poems and to present the poems in the order which suggests Browning's development as a poet. We have chosen, therefore, to present the poems in order of their first publication, with an indication in the notes as to their respective subsequent placement. We also include the tables of contents of the editions listed as Primary Materials above.

We have regularized or modernized the copy-text in the following minor ways:

1. We do not place a period at the end of the title of a work, though the copy-text does.

2. In some of Browning's editions, including the copy-text, the first word of each work is printed in capital letters. We have used the modern practice of capitalizing only the first letter.

3. The inconsistent use of both an ampersand and the word *and* has been regularized to the use of *and*.

4. We have eliminated the space between the two parts of a contraction; thus the copy-text's *it 's* is printed as *it's*, for example.

5. We uniformly place periods and commas within closing quotation marks.

6. We have employed throughout the modern practice of indicating quoted passages with quotation marks only at the beginning and end of the quotation. Throughout Browning's career, no matter which publisher or printer was handling his works, this matter was treated very inconsistently. In some of the poet's manuscripts and in most of his first editions, quotations are indicated by quotation marks only at the beginning and end. In the collected editions of 1863 and 1865, issued by Chapman and Hall, some quoted passages have quotation marks at the beginning of each line of the quotation, while others follow modern practice. In Smith, Elder's collected editions of 1868 and 1888-1889, quotation marks appear at the beginning of each line of a quotation. We have regularized and modernized what seems a matter of house-styling in both copy-text and variants.

The remaining way in which the copy-text is altered is emendation. Our policy is to emend the copy-text to eliminate apparent errors of either Browning or his printers. It is evident that Browning did make errors and overlook mistakes, as shown by the following example from "One Word More," the last poem in *Men and Women*. Stanza sixteen of the copy-text opens with the following lines:

What, there's nothing in the moon noteworthy?
Nay: for if that moon could love a mortal,
Use, to charm him (so to fit a fancy,
All her magic ('tis the old sweet mythos)
She . . .

Clearly the end punctuation in the third line is incorrect. A study of the various texts is illuminating. Following are the readings of the line in each of the editions for which Browning was responsible:

| MS: | fancy) | 1855: | fancy) | 1865: | fancy) | 1888: | fancy |
| P: | fancy) | 1863: | fancy) | 1868: | fancy) | 1889: | fancy, |

The omission of one parenthesis in 1888 was almost certainly a printer's error. Browning, in the Dykes Campbell copy corrections to 1888-1889a, missed or ignored the error. However, in the Brown University list of corrections, he indicated that *fancy* should be followed by a comma. This is the way the line appears in the corrected second impression of Volume 4, but the correction at best satisfies the demands of syntax only partially. Browning might have written the line:

> Use, to charm him, so to fit a fancy,

or, to maintain parallelism between the third and fourth lines:

> Use, to charm him (so to fit a fancy),

or he might simply have restored the earlier reading. Oversights of this nature demand emendation, and our choice would be to restore the punctuation of the manuscript through 1868. All of our emendations will be based, as far as possible, on the historical collation of the passage involved, the grammatical demands of the passage in context, and the poet's treatment of other similar passages. Fortunately, the multiple editions of most of the works provide the editor with ample textual evidence to make an informed and useful emendation.

All emendations to the copy-text are listed at the beginning of the Editorial Notes for each work. The variant listings for the copy-text also incorporate the emendations, which are preceded and followed there by the symbol indicating an editor's note.

VI APPARATUS

1. *Variants*. In presenting the variants from the copy-text, we list at the bottom of each page readings from the known manuscripts, proof sheets of the editions when we have located them, and the first and subsequent editions.

A variant is generally preceded and followed by a pickup and a drop word (example a). No note terminates with a punctuation mark unless the punctuation mark comes at the end of the line; if a variant drops or adds a punctuation mark, the next word is added (example b). If the normal pickup word has appeared previously in the same line, the note begins with the word preceding it. If the normal drop word appears subsequently in the line, the next word is added (example c). If a capitalized pickup word occurs within the line, it is accompanied by the preceding word (example d). No pickup or drop words, however, are used for any variant consisting of an internal change, for example a hyphen in a compounded word, an apostrophe, a tense change or a spelling change (example e). A change in capitalization within a line of poetry will be preceded by a pickup word, for which, within an entry containing other variants, the <> is suitable (example f). No drop word is used when the variant comes at the end of a line (example g). Examples from *Sordello* (all from Book 1 except c [2] which is from Book 4):

a. [611] *1840:*but that appeared *1863:*but this appeared

b. variant at end of line: [109] *1840:*intrigue:" *1863:* intrigue.

   variant within line: [82] *1840:*forests like *1863:*forests, like

c. [132] *1840:*too sleeps; but 1863:too sleeps: but [77] *1840:*that night by *1863:*that, night by night, *1888:*by night

d. [295] *1840:*at Padua to repulse the *1863:*at Padua who repulsed the

e. [284] *1840:*are *1863:*were [344] *1840:*dying-day, *1863:*dying day,

f. capitalization change with no other variants: [741] *1840:* retaining Will, *1863:*retaining will,

   with other variants: [843] *1840:*Was <> Him back! Why *1863:* Is <> back!" Why *1865:*him

g. [427] *1840:*dregs; *1863:*dregs.

Each recorded variant will be assumed to be incorporated in the next edition if there is no indication otherwise. This rule applies even in cases where the only change occurs in 1888-1889, although it means that the variant note duplicates the copy-text. A variant listing, then, traces the history of a line and brings it forward to the point where it matches the copy-text.

An editor's note always refers to the single word or mark of punctuation immediately preceding or following the comment, unless otherwise specified.

In Browning's plays, all character designations which happen to occur in variant listings are standardized to the copy-text reading. In listing variants in the plays, we ignore character designations unless the designation comes within a numbered line. In such a case, the variant is treated as any other word, and can be used as a pickup or drop word. When a character designation is used as a pickup word, however, the rule excluding capitalized pickup words (except at the beginning of a line) does not apply, and we do not revert to the next earliest uncapitalized pickup word.

2. *Line numbers.* Poetic lines are numbered in the traditional manner, taking one complete poetic line as one unit of counting. In prose passages the unit of counting is the type line of this edition.

3. *Table of signs in variant listings.* We have avoided all symbols and signs used by Browning himself. The following is a table of the signs used in the variant notes:

§ . . . §	Editor's note
< >	Words omitted
/	Line break
/ / , / / / , . . .	Line break plus one or more lines without internal variants

4. *Annotations.* In general principle, we have annotated proper names, phrases that function as proper names, and words or groups of words the full meaning of which requires factual, historical, or literary background. Thus we have attempted to hold interpretation to a minimum, although we realize that the act of selection itself is to some extent interpretative.

Notes, particularly on historical figures and events, tend to fullness and even to the tangential and unessential. As a result, some of the information provided may seem unnecessary to the scholar. On the other hand, it is not possible to assume that all who use this edition are fully equipped to assimilate unaided all of Browning's copious literary, historical, and mythological allusions. Thus we have directed our efforts toward a diverse audience.

Tables

1. *Manuscripts.* We have located manuscripts for the following of Browning's works; the list is chronological.
Paracelsus
    Forster and Dyce Collection,
    Victoria and Albert Museum, London
Colombe's Birthday
    New York Public Library
Christmas-Eve and Easter-Day
    Forster and Dyce Collection,
    Victoria and Albert Museum, London
"Love Among the Ruins"
    Lowell Collection,
    Houghton Library, Harvard University
"The Twins"
    Pierpont Morgan Library, New York
"One Word More"
    Pierpont Morgan Library, New York
Dramatis Personae
    Pierpont Morgan Library, New York
The Ring and the Book
    British Library, London
Balaustion's Adventure
    Balliol College Library, Oxford

Prince Hohenstiel-Schwangau
    Balliol College Library, Oxford
Fifine at the Fair
    Balliol College Library, Oxford
Red Cotton Night-Cap Country
    Balliol College Library, Oxford
Aristophanes' Apology
    Balliol College Library, Oxford
The Inn Album
    Balliol College Library, Oxford
Of Pacchiarotto, and How He Worked in Distemper
    Balliol College Library, Oxford
The Agamemnon of Aeschylus
    Balliol College Library, Oxford
La Saisaiz and The Two Poets of Croisic
    Balliol College Library, Oxford
Dramatic Idylls
    Balliol College Library, Oxford
Dramatic Idylls, Second Series
    Balliol College Library, Oxford
Jocoseria
    Balliol College Library, Oxford
Ferishtah's Fancies
    Balliol College Library, Oxford
Parleyings With Certain People of Importance in Their Day
    Balliol College Library, Oxford
Asolando
    Pierpont Morgan Library, New York

We have been unable to locate manuscripts for the following works, and request that persons with information about any of them communicate with us.

Pauline	*The Return of the Druses*
Strafford	*A Blot in the 'Scutcheon*
Sordello	*Dramatic Romances and Lyrics*
Pippa Passes	*Luria*
King Victor and King Charles	*A Soul's Tragedy*
"Essay on Chatterton"	"Essay on Shelley"
Dramatic Lyrics	*Men and Women*

2. *Editions referred to in Volume VII.* The following editions have been used in preparing the text and variants presented in this volume. The dates given below are used as symbols in the variant listings at the bottom of each page.

1868	*The Ring and the Book*. Volumes 1 and 2. Two Volumes. London: Smith, Elder and Company.
1869	*The Ring and the Book*. Volumes 3 and 4. Two Volumes, London: Smith, Elder and Company.
1872	*The Ring and the Book*. Four Volumes. London: Smith, Elder and Company.
1888	*The Poetical Works*. Volumes 1-8. London: Smith, Elder and Company.
1889a	*The Poetical Works*. Volumes 9-16. London: Smith, Elder and Company.
1889	*The Poetical Works*. Sixteen Volumes. London: Smith, Elder and Company. (second impression of 1888-1889a)

3. *Short titles and abbreviations.* The following short forms of reference have been used in notes for this edition:

Altick	*The Ring and the Book*, ed. Richard D. Altick. Baltimore: Penguin Books, 1971.
B	Browning
BrU	Browning's list of corrections located at Brown University
Cook	A.K. Cook. *A Commentary upon Browning's "The Ring and the Book."* Hamden, Connecticut: Archon Books, 1966 (first pub. 1920).
Corrigan	*Curious Annals: New Documents Relating to Browning's Roman Murder Story*, ed. and tr. Beatrice Corrigan. Toronto: University of Toronto Press, 1956.
DC	Browning's corrections in James Dykes Campbell's copy of 1888-1889a
DeVane, *Hbk.*	William Clyde DeVane. *A Browning Handbook*. New York: Appleton-Century Crofts, 1955.
DeVane and Knickerbocker	*New Letters of Robert Browning*, ed. William Clyde DeVane and Kenneth L. Knickerbocker. New Haven: Yale University Press, 1950.
EBB	Elizabeth Barrett Browning
Gest	*The Old Yellow Book*, ed. and tr. John Marshall Gest. Philadelphia: University of Pennsylvania Press, 1927.

Griffin and Minchin	W. H. Griffin and H. C. Minchin. *The Life of Robert Browning*. New York: Macmillan, 1910.
Heydon and Kelley	*Elizabeth Barrett Browning's Letters to Mrs. David Ogilvy*, ed. Peter N. Heydon and Philip Kelley. London: Murray, 1974.
Hodell	*The Old Yellow Book*, in facsimile, ed. and tr. Charles W. Hodell. Washington: The Carnegie Institution, 1908.
Hood, *Ltrs.*	*Letters of Robert Browning Collected by T. J. Wise*, ed. Thurman L. Hood. New Haven: Yale University Press, 1933.
Irvine and Honan	William Irvine and Park Honan. *The Book, the Ring, and the Poet*. New York: McGraw-Hill, 1974.
Landis and Freeman	*Letters of the Brownings to George Barrett*, ed. Paul Landis and Ronald E. Freeman. Urbana: University of Illinois Press, 1958.
Letters of EBB	*The Letters of Elizabeth Barrett Browning*, ed. F.G. Kenyon. 2 vols. New York: Macmillan, 1897.
New Poems	*New Poems by Robert Browning and Elizabeth Barrett Browning*, ed. F.G. Kenyon. New York: Macmillan, 1915.
Orr, *Hbk.*	Mrs. Sutherland Orr. *Handbook to the Works of Robert Browning*. New Edition. Revised and in Part Rewritten by F.G. Kenyon. New York: McMillan, 1915.
Orr, *Life*	Mrs. Sutherland Orr. *Life and Letters of Robert Browning*. Second Edition. London: Smith, Elder, 1891.
OYB	Browning's source for *The Ring and the Book*, in its original format.
OYB, E	*The Old Yellow Book*, ed. and tr. Charles W. Hodell. New York: E. P. Dutton (Everyman's Library), 1911.
P-C	*The Complete Works of Robert Browning*, ed. Charlotte Porter and Helen A. Clarke. New York: Thomas Y. Crowell, 1898.
RB-EBB, ed. Kintner	*The Letters of Robert Browning and Elizabeth Barrett Barrett*, 1845-1846, ed. Elvan Kintner. 2 vols. Cambridge, Mass.: The Belknap Press of Harvard University Press, 1969.

Story	William Wetmore Story. *Roba di Roma*. 2 vols. Boston and New York: Houghton, Mifflin and Co., 1887 (first published 1862).
Treves	Sir Frederick Treves. *The Country of The Ring and the Book*. London: Cassell and Company, 1913.
Vasari	Giorgio Vasari. *Lives of the Painters, Sculptors and Architects*, ed. and tr. A. B. Hinds. Intro. by William Gaunt. 4 vols. London: Dent (Everyman's Library), 1963.

Citations and quotations from the Bible refer to the King James Version.

Citations and quotations from Shakespeare refer to *The Riverside Shakespeare*, ed. G. B. Evans, et. al. Boston: Houghton Mifflin, 1974.

ACKNOWLEDGMENTS

For providing money and services which have made it possible for us to assemble the vast materials required for the preparation of this edition, the following institutions have our especial appreciation: the Ohio University Press, the Ohio University Library, the Ohio University English Department; Baylor University and the Armstrong Browning Library of Baylor University; the American Council of Learned Societies; the Kent State University Library and its Bibliographical and Textual Center, the Kent State University Research Council, the Kent State University English Department.

We also thank the following for making available to us materials under their care: the Armstrong Browning Library; the Balliol College Library, Oxford; the Beinecke Rare Book and Manuscript Library, Yale University, and its director Mr. H. W. Liebert; the British Library; the John Hay Library, Brown University; the Houghton Library, Harvard University; the Henry E. Huntington Library; the Department of Special Collections, Kent State University; Mr. E. V. Quinn; Mr. Philip Kelley; Mr. John Murray; the Library of the Victoria and Albert Museum.

We are also grateful to Professor Paul Murphy and Professor Bartolomeo Martello for their invaluable assistance in translation of Latin and Italian sources and passages, and to Victor Goedicke and The U.S. Naval Observatory for precisely dating the appearance of the new moon in April 1697.

The frontispiece is reproduced by permission of the Pierpont Morgan Library.

THE RING AND THE BOOK
Books V-VIII

Edited by Roma A. King, Jr. and Susan Crowl

THE RING AND THE BOOK

THE RING AND THE BOOK

1868-9

V

COUNT GUIDO FRANCESCHINI

Thanks, Sir, but, should it please the reverend Court,
I feel I can stand somehow, half sit down
Without help, make shift to even speak, you see,
Fortified by the sip of . . . why, 'tis wine,
5   Velletri,—and not vinegar and gall,
So changed and good the times grow! Thanks, kind Sir!
Oh, but one sip's enough! I want my head
To save my neck, there's work awaits me still.
How cautious and considerate . . . aie, aie, aie,
10   Nor your fault, sweet Sir! Come, you take to heart
An ordinary matter. Law is law.
Noblemen were exempt, the vulgar thought,
From racking; but, since law thinks otherwise,
I have been put to the rack: all's over now,
15   And neither wrist—what men style, out of joint:
If any harm be, 'tis the shoulder-blade,
The left one, that seems wrong i' the socket,—Sirs,
Much could not happen, I was quick to faint,
Being past my prime of life, and out of health.
20   In short, I thank you,—yes, and mean the word.
Needs must the Court be slow to understand
How this quite novel form of taking pain,
This getting tortured merely in the flesh,
Amounts to almost an agreeable change

---

§ MS in Department of Manuscripts of the British Library. P1868, CP1868, P1869, CP1869,
Ed. 1868-69, 1872, 1888, 1889 §
¹| MS:but should   *P1868:*but, should   ³| MS:to even § inserted above §
⁴| MS:wine *P1868:*wine,   ⁵| MS:Trebbian, § crossed out and replaced above by §
Velletri,—not hyssop, vinegar *P1868:*Velletri,—and not vinegar   ⁶| MS:kind sir!
*P1868:*kind Sir!   ⁷| MS:enough; I *P1868:*enough! I   ¹³| MS:racking, but
*1889a:*racking; but   ¹⁴| MS:now *P1868:*now,   ¹⁵| MS:wrist's
P1868:wrist   ¹⁷| MS:in *P1868:*i'   ¹⁸| MS:faint *P1868:*faint,   ²⁰| MS:short
I < > you, yes and *P1868:*you,—yes, and *P1889a:*short, I   ²³| MS:This being

²⁵ In my case, me fastidious, plied too much
With opposite treatment, used (forgive the joke)
To the rasp-tooth toying with this brain of mine,
And, in and out my heart, the play o' the probe.
Four years have I been operated on
³⁰ I' the soul, do you see—its tense or tremulous part—
My self-respect, my care for a good name,
Pride in an old one, love of kindred—just
A mother, brothers, sisters, and the like,
That looked up to my face when days were dim,
³⁵ And fancied they found light there—no one spot,
Foppishly sensitive, but has paid its pang.
That, and not this you now oblige me with,
That was the Vigil-torment, if you please!
The poor old noble House that drew the rags
⁴⁰ O' the Franceschini's once superb array
Close round her, hoped to slink unchallenged by,—
Pluck off these! Turn the drapery inside out
And teach the tittering town how scarlet wears!
Show men the lucklessness, the improvidence
⁴⁵ Of the easy-natured Count before this Count,
The father I have some slight feeling for,
Who let the world slide, nor foresaw that friends
Then proud to cap and kiss their patron's shoe,
Would, when the purse he left held spider-webs,
⁵⁰ Properly push his child to wall one day!
Mimic the tetchy humour, furtive glance,
And brow where half was furious, half fatigued,
O' the same son got to be of middle age,
Sour, saturnine,—your humble servant here,—
⁵⁵ When things go cross and the young wife, he finds
Take to the window at a whistle's bid,

tortured   *P1868:*This getting tortured   ²⁶| MS:With the opposite   *P1868:*With
opposite   ²⁸| MS:of   *P1868:*o'   ³⁰| MS:In   *P1868:*I'   ³²| MS:kindred—say,
*P1868:*kindred—just   ³³| MS:sisters and   *P1868:*sisters, and   ³⁴| MS:dim
*P1868:*dim,   ³⁵| MS:spot   *P1868:*spot,   ³⁶| MS:sensitive but   *P1868:*sensitive,
but   ³⁷| MS:not what you have just obliged me   *P1868:*not this you now oblige me
⁴⁰| MS:Of   *P1868:*O'   ⁴⁴| MS:Show up the   *P1868:*Show men the   ⁴⁸| MS:kiss
the patron's   *1889a:*kiss their patron's   ⁵¹| MS:furtive eye   *P1868:*furtive glance
*1889a:*glance,   ⁵²| MS:furious half   *1889a:*furious, half   ⁵³| MS:Of <> to his
middle age   *P1868:*O' <> to be of middle   ⁵⁶| MS:Takes   *P1868:*Take

And yet demurs thereon, preposterous fool!—
Whereat the worthies judge he wants advice
And beg to civilly ask what's evil here,
60 Perhaps remonstrate on the habit they deem
He's given unduly to, of beating her:
. . . Oh, sure he beats her—why says John so else,
Who is cousin to George who is sib to Tecla's self
Who cooks the meal and combs the lady's hair?
65 What! 'Tis my wrist you merely dislocate
For the future when you mean me martyrdom?
—Let the old mother's economy alone,
How the brocade-strips saved o' the seamy side
O' the wedding-gown buy raiment for a year?
70 —How she can dress and dish up—lordly dish
Fit for a duke, lamb's head and purtenance—
With her proud hands, feast household so a week?
No word o' the wine rejoicing God and man
The less when three-parts water? Then, I say,
75 A trifle of torture to the flesh, like yours,
While soul is spared such foretaste of hell-fire,
Is naught. But I curtail the catalogue
Through policy,—a rhetorician's trick,—
Because I would reserve some choicer points
80 O' the practice, more exactly parallel
(Having an eye to climax) with what gift,
Eventual grace the Court may have in store
I' the way of plague—what crown of punishments.
When I am hanged or headed, time enough

⁵⁷| MS:And he demurs < > fool, *P1868:*And yet demurs < > fool!— ⁵⁹| MS:ask
him what's the coil, *P1868:*ask what's evil here, ⁶¹| MS:her *P1889a:*her:
⁶²| MS: . . Oh *1889a:* . . . Oh ⁶³| MS:sib to Lucy's § crossed out and replaced
above by § Tecla's ⁶⁴| MS:That cooks *P1868:*Who cooks ⁶⁵| MS:What? 'Tis
my wrists *P1868:*wrist *1872:*What! 'Tis ⁶⁶| MS:martyrdom, *P1868:*martyrdom?
⁶⁸| MS:on *P1868:*o' ⁶⁹| MS:Of her wedding-gown buys *P1868:*O' the
wedding-gown buy *1889a:*wedding-grown § emended to § wedding-gown § see Editorial
Notes § ⁷²| MS:her fair hands *P1868:*her proud hands ⁷³| MS:of *P1868:*o'
⁷⁴| MS:three parts *P1868:*three-parts ⁷⁵| MS:like, this *P1868:*like yours,
⁷⁶| MS:foretastes *P1868:*foretaste ⁷⁷| MS:naught. If § crossed out and replaced
above by § But I curtail their catalogue *P1868:*naught < > curtail the catalogue
⁸⁰| MS:Of the practice, more exactly § last two words inserted above line § parallel,
*P1868:*O' < > parallel— *1872:*parallel ⁸¹| MS:gift *P1868:*gift, ⁸³| MS:In < >

⁸⁵ To prove the tenderness of only that,
Mere heading, hanging,—not their counterpart,
Not demonstration public and precise
That I, having married the mongrel of a drab,
Am bound to grant that mongrel-brat, my wife,
⁹⁰ Her mother's birthright-license as is just,—
Let her sleep undisturbed, i' the family style,
Her sleep out in the embraces of a priest,
Nor disallow their bastard as my heir!
Your sole mistake,—dare I submit so much
⁹⁵ To the reverend Court?—has been in all this pains
To make a stone roll down hill,—rack and wrench
And rend a man to pieces, all for what?
Why—make him ope mouth in his own defence,
Show cause for what he has done, the irregular deed,
¹⁰⁰ (Since that he did it, scarce dispute can be)
And clear his fame a little, beside the luck
Of stopping even yet, if possible,
Discomfort to his flesh from noose or axe—
For that, out come the implements of law!
¹⁰⁵ May it content my lords the gracious Court
To listen only half so patient-long
As I will in that sense profusely speak,
And—fie, they shall not call in screws to help!

I killed Pompilia Franceschini, Sirs;
¹¹⁰ Killed too the Comparini, husband, wife,
Who called themselves, by a notorious lie,
Her father and her mother to ruin me.
There's the irregular deed: you want no more

---

plague, my crown *P1868:*I' <> plague—my crown   ⁸⁶| MS:Just § crossed out and
replaced by § Mere <> counterpart *P1868:*counterpart,   ⁸⁷| MS:In demonstration
*P1868:*Not demonstration   ⁸⁹| MS:mongrel-brat my wife *P1868:*mongrel-brat, my
wife,   ⁹¹| MS:in *P1868:*i'   ⁹⁶| MS:hill, rack *CP1868:*hill,—rack
⁹⁹| MS:he did § crossed out and replaced above by § has   ¹⁰²| MS:yet if possible
*P1868:*yet, if possible,   ¹⁰³| MS:from rope § crossed out and replaced above by § noose
¹⁰⁴| MS:came <> of Law! *P1868:*come <> of law!   ¹⁰⁸| MS:in cord § crossed out
and replaced above by § screws   ¹⁰⁸⁻⁹| MS:§ marginal note *N.P.* indicates new ¶ §
P1868:§ no ¶ § *1889:*§ no ¶; emended to restore ¶; see Editorial Notes §   ¹⁰⁹| MS:killed
Pompilia Franceschini, Sirs, *P1868:*killed Pompilia Franceschini, Sirs;   ¹¹⁰| MS:the
Comparini, husband and wife, *P1868:*the Comparini, husband, wife,   ¹¹²| MS:and

Than right interpretation of the same,
115 And truth so far—am I to understand?
To that then, with convenient speed,—because
Now I consider,—yes, despite my boast,
There is an ailing in this omoplat
May clip my speech all too abruptly short,
120 Whatever the good-will in me. Now for truth!

I' the name of the indivisible Trinity!
Will my lords, in the plenitude of their light,
Weigh well that all this trouble has come on me
Through my persistent treading in the paths
125 Where I was trained to go,—wearing that yoke
My shoulder was predestined to receive,
Born to the hereditary stoop and crease?
Noble, I recognized my nobler still,
The Church, my suzerain; no mock-mistress, she;
130 The secular owned the spiritual: mates of mine
Have thrown their careless hoofs up at her call
"Forsake the clover and come drag my wain!"
There they go cropping: I protruded nose
To halter, bent my back of docile beast,
135 And now am whealed, one wide wound all of me,
For being found at the eleventh hour o' the day
Padding the mill-track, not neck-deep in grass:
—My one fault, I am stiffened by my work,
—My one reward, I help the Court to smile!

140 I am representative of a great line,
One of the first of the old families

---

mother <> me and mine. *P1868:*and her mother <> me. 114| MS:same
*P1868:*same, 116| MS:speed, because *P1868:*speed,—because 117| MS:boast
*P1868:*boast, 118| MS:ailing of § altered to § in 119| MS:abruptly short § crossed
out and replaced by § close, *1872:*abruptly short, 120| MS:good will
*P1868:*good-will 121| MS:§ marginal note *N.P.* § In *P1868:*I' 123| MS:Perpend
§ crossed out and replaced above by § Weigh well 128| MS:still *P1868:*still,
129| MS:mock-mistress she; *P1868:*mock-mistress, she; 130| MS:spiritual: careless
§ crossed out § mates 131| MS:Of § crossed out § <> call, *P1868:*call
134| MS:bent the back *P1868:*bent my back 136| MS:of *P1868:*o'
137| MS:Inside § crossed out and replaced above by § Padding 140| MS:§ marginal note
N.P. § 141| MS:first of noble families *P1868:*first of the old families

9

In Arezzo, ancientest of Tuscan towns.
When my worst foe is fain to challenge this,
His worst exception runs—not first in rank
145 But second, noble in the next degree
Only; not malice' self maligns me more.
So, my lord opposite has composed, we know,
A marvel of a book, sustains the point
That Francis boasts the primacy 'mid saints;
150 Yet not inaptly hath his argument
Obtained response from yon my other lord
In thesis published with the world's applause
—Rather 'tis Dominic such post befits:
Why, at the worst, Francis stays Francis still,
155 Second in rank to Dominic it may be,
Still, very saintly, very like our Lord;
And I at least descend from Guido once
Homager to the Empire, nought below—
Of which account as proof that, none o' the line
160 Having a single gift beyond brave blood,
Or able to do aught but give, give, give
In blood and brain, in house and land and cash,
Not get and garner as the vulgar may,
We became poor as Francis or our Lord.
165 Be that as it likes you, Sirs,—whenever it chanced
Myself grew capable anyway of remark,
(Which was soon—penury makes wit premature)
This struck me, I was poor who should be rich
Or pay that fault to the world which trifles not
170 When lineage lacks the flag yet lifts the pole:
On, therefore, I must move forthwith, transfer
My stranded self, born fish with gill and fin
Fit for the deep sea, now left flap bare-backed

146| MS:malice' self   P1868:malice 'self   1889a:malice' self   149| MS:That Francis
has the primacy of saints;   P1868:That Francis boasts the primacy 'mid saints;
152| MS:published mid the   P1868:published with the   153| MS:—Rather Saint
§ crossed out and replaced above by § 'tis   154| MS:worst, stays Francis § last two words
separately circled and line is followed by marginal note TR § Francis   P1868:worst, Francis
stays Francis   156| MS:our Lord,   P1868:our Lord;   157| MS:from a Guido
1889a:from Guido   159| MS:account some proof <> of   P1868:account as proof <>
o'   166| MS:remark   P1868:remark,   167| MS:Which was soon (penury
P1868:(Which was soon—penury   168| MS:who must be   P1868:who should be
171| MS:Therefore I must make move   1872:On, therefore, I must move   173| MS:sea,

In slush and sand, a show to crawlers vile
175   Reared of the low-tide and aright therein.
The enviable youth with the old name,
Wide chest, stout arms, sound brow and pricking veins,
A heartful of desire, man's natural load,
A brainful of belief, the noble's lot,—
180   All this life, cramped and gasping, high and dry
I' the wave's retreat,—the misery, good my lords,
Which made you merriment at Rome of late,—
It made me reason, rather—muse, demand
—Why our bare dropping palace, in the street
185   Where such-an-one whose grandfather sold tripe
Was adding to his purchased pile a fourth
Tall tower, could hardly show a turret sound?
Why Countess Beatrice, whose son I am,
Cowered in the winter-time as she spun flax,
190   Blew on the earthen basket of live ash,
Instead of jaunting forth in coach and six
Like such-another widow who ne'er was wed?
I asked my fellows, how came this about?
"Why, Jack, the suttler's child, perhaps the camp's,
195   Went to the wars, fought sturdily, took a town
And got rewarded as was natural.
She of the coach and six—excuse me there!
Why, don't you know the story of her friend?
A clown dressed vines on somebody's estate,
200   His boy recoiled from muck, liked Latin more,
Stuck to his pen and got to be a priest,
Till one day . . . don't you mind that telling tract

---

left to flap *P1868:*sea, now left flap   ¹⁷⁵| MS:therein,— *P1868:*therein.
¹⁸¹| MS:In *P1868:*I'   ¹⁸²| MS:made such merriment for Rome *P1868:*made you
merriment at Rome   ¹⁸⁴| MS:palace in *P1868:*palace, in   ¹⁸⁵| MS:such an one
*P1868:*such-an-one   ¹⁸⁶⁻⁸⁸| MS:Is adding to his three towered § crossed out and replaced
above by § turretted pile a fourth?/ Why *P1868:*Was adding to his purchased pile a fourth/
Tall tower, could hardly show a turret sound?/ Why   ¹⁹⁰| MS:earthen-basket
*CP1868:*earthen basket   ¹⁹¹| MS:coach and cape *P1868:*coach and six
¹⁹²| MS:such another's *CP1868:*such-another   ¹⁹⁴| MS:"Why, This, the suttler's
CP1868:"Why, Jack, the suttler's   ¹⁹⁷⁻⁹⁹| MS:and cape—excuse <> / A *P1868:*coach
and six <> / Why, don't you know the story of her friend? / A   ²⁰¹| MS:pen, soon got
*P1868:*pen and got   ²⁰²| MS:day . . don't *1889a:*day . . . don't

Against Molinos, the old Cardinal wrote?
He penned and dropped it in the patron's desk
205 Who, deep in thought and absent much of mind,
Licensed the thing, allowed it for his own;
Quick came promotion,—*suum cuique*, Count!
Oh, he can pay for coach and six, be sure!"
"—Well, let me go, do likewise: war's the word—
210 That way the Franceschini worked at first,
I'll take my turn, try soldiership."—"What, you?
The eldest son and heir and prop o' the house,
So do you see your duty? Here's your post,
Hard by the hearth and altar. (Roam from roof,
215 This youngster, play the gipsy out of doors,
And who keeps kith and kin that fall on us?)
Stand fast, stick tight, conserve your gods at home!"
"—Well then, the quiet course, the contrary trade!
We had a cousin amongst us once was Pope,
220 And minor glories manifold. Try the Church,
The tonsure, and,—since heresy's but half-slain
Even by the Cardinal's tract he thought he wrote,—
Have at Molinos!"—"Have at a fool's head!
You a priest? How were marriage possible?
225 There must be Franceschini till time ends—
That's your vocation. Make your brothers priests,
Paul shall be porporate, and Girolamo step
Red-stockinged in the presence when you choose,
But save one Franceschini for the age!
230 Be not the vine but dig and dung its root,
Be not a priest but gird up priesthood's loins,
With one foot in Arezzo stride to Rome,

203| MS:Against Molinos the   *P1868:*Against Molinos, the   205| MS:Who, much in
*P1868:*Who, deep in   208| MS:and cape, be   *P1868:*and six, be   209| MS:"Well
P1868:"—Well   211| MS:soldiership." "What   *P1868:*soldiership."—"What
212| MS:of   *P1868:*o'   214-16| MS:roof/ And who   *CP1868:*roof,/ This youngster,
play the gipsy out of doors,/ And who   *1889a:*gipsy   217| MS:stick firm, conserve your
home at   *P1868:*stick tight, conserve your gods at   218| MS:"Well <> trade—
P1868:"—Well <> trade!   220| MS:the Church—   *P1868:*the Church,
221| MS:tonsure—and, since   *P1868:*tonsure, and,—since   222| MS:the Cardinal's
book § crossed out and replaced above by § tract <> wrote,   *P1868:*wrote,—
225| MS:'till   *P1868:*till   227| MS:porporate and   *P1868:*porporate, and
228| MS:you please,   *P1868:*you choose,   229| MS:age.   *P1868:*age!

Spend yourself there and bring the purchase back!
Go hence to Rome, be guided!"

                                    So I was.
235 I turned alike from the hill-side zig-zag thread
     Of way to the table-land a soldier takes,
     Alike from the low-lying pasture-place
     Where churchmen graze, recline and ruminate,
     —Ventured to mount no platform like my lords
240 Who judge the world, bear brain I dare not brag—
     But stationed me, might thus the expression serve,
     As who should fetch and carry, come and go,
     Meddle and make i' the cause my lords love most—
     The public weal, which hangs to the law, which holds
245 By the Church, which happens to be through God himself.
     Humbly I helped the Church till here I stand,—
     Or would stand but for the omoplat, you see!
     Bidden qualify for Rome, I, having a field,
     Went, sold it, laid the sum at Peter's foot:
250 Which means—I settled home-accounts with speed,
     Set apart just a modicum should suffice
     To hold the villa's head above the waves
     Of weed inundating its oil and wine,
     And prop roof, stanchion wall o' the palace so
255 As to keep breath i' the body, out of heart
     Amid the advance of neighbouring loftiness—
     (People like building where they used to beg)—
     Till succoured one day,—shared the residue
     Between my mother and brothers and sisters there,

233| MS:back. *P1868:*back! *1872:*back *1889a:*back!   234| MS:guided!" So
*P1868:*guided!" § ¶ § So   239| MS:my Lords *P1868:*my lords   240| MS:world,
want § crossed out and replaced above by § bear <> not boast § crossed out and replaced
above by § brag—   243| MS:in *P1868:*i'   245| MS:the church, which happened
*P1868:*the Church, which happens   246| MS:the church *P1868:*the Church
247| MS:see. *P1868:*see!   248| MS:Bid § altered to § Bidden <> Rome, I having a field
*P1868:*for Rome, I, having a field,   249| MS:foot— *P1868:*foot: 251| MS:just
such modicum *P1868:*just a modicum   252| MS:To keep the Villa's *P1868:*the
villa's *1889a:*To hold the villa's   253| MS:weed § over illegible word §
254| MS:And prop roof, § last word and comma inserted above § the Palace stanchion wall of
§ last five words transposed to read § stanchion wall of the Palace *P1868:*o' the palace
255| MS:It should keep <> in the body, hold its own *P1868:*i' *1889a:*As to keep <>

260 Black-eyed babe Donna This and Donna That,
As near to starving as might decently be,
—Left myself journey-charges, change of suit,
A purse to put i' the pocket of the Groom
O' the Chamber of the patron, and a glove
265 With a ring to it for the digits of the niece
Sure to be helpful in his household,—then
Started for Rome, and led the life prescribed.
Close to the Church, though clean of it, I assumed
Three or four orders of no consequence,
270 —They cast out evil spirits and exorcise,
For example; bind a man to nothing more,
Give clerical savour to his layman's-salt,
Facilitate his claim to loaf and fish
Should miracle leave, beyond what feeds the flock,
275 Fragments to brim the basket of a friend—
While, for the world's sake, I rode, danced and gamed,
Quitted me like a courtier, measured mine
With whatsoever blade had fame in fence,
—Ready to let the basket go its round
280 Even though my turn was come to help myself,
Should Dives count on me at dinner-time
As just the understander of a joke
And not immoderate in repartee.
Utrique sic paratus, Sirs, I said,
285 "Here," (in the fortitude of years fifteen,
So good a pedagogue is penury)
"Here wait, do service,—serving and to serve!
And, in due time, I nowise doubt at all,

---

body, out of heart   260| MS:babe—Donna *P1868:*babe Donna   263| MS:in <>
groom *P1868:*i' <> Groom   264| MS:Of the chamber *P1868:*O' the Chamber
266| MS:in the § crossed out and replaced above by § his   268| MS:I crept § last two
words crossed out and replaced above by § Close   271| MS:example, bind
*P1868:*example; bind   272| MS:layman's salt *CP1868:*layman's-salt
274| MS:miracle find § crossed out and replaced above by § leave   278| MS:whatsoe'er
blade § inserted above § had mastery § crossed out and replaced above by § fame
*P1868:*whatsoever   279-84| MS:round/ Should Dives think of me at dinner-time./
Utrique <> said *P1868:*round/ Even though my turn was come to help myself,/ Should
Dives count on me at dinner-time/ As just the understander of a joke/ And not immoderate
in repartee./ *Utrique* <> *1889a:*///// <> said,   285| MS:the plenitude of
*CP1868:*the fortitude of   286| MS:So brisk a *P1868:*So good a   287| MS:wait I

14

The recognition of my service comes.
290 Next year I'm only sixteen. I can wait."

I waited thirty years, may it please the Court:
Saw meanwhile many a denizen o' the dung
Hop, skip, jump o'er my shoulder, make him wings
And fly aloft,—succeed, in the usual phrase.
295 Everyone soon or late comes round by Rome:
Stand still here, you'll see all in turn succeed.
Why, look you, so and so, the physician here,
My father's lacquey's son we sent to school,
Doctored and dosed this Eminence and that,
300 Salved the last Pope his certain obstinate sore,
Soon bought land as became him, names it now:
I grasp bell at his griffin-guarded gate,
Traverse the half-mile avenue,—a term,
A cypress, and a statue, three and three,—
305 Deliver message from my Monsignor,
With varletry at lounge i' the vestibule
I'm barred from who bear mud upon my shoe.
My father's chaplain's nephew, Chamberlain,—
Nothing less, please you!—courteous all the same,
310 —He does not see me though I wait an hour
At his staircase-landing 'twixt the brace of busts,
A noseless Sylla, Marius maimed to match,
My father gave him for a hexastich
Made on my birthday,—but he sends me down,
315 To make amends, that relic I prize most—

service < > serve,— *P1868:*wait, do service < > serve!   289| MS:of service. Fifteen
years! *P1868:*of my service comes.   292| MS:of *P1868:*o'   295| MS:by Rome,
*P1868:*by Rome: 296| MS:still there, you'll < > in their turn *P1868:*still here, you'll
< > in turn   297| MS:here *P1868:*here,   298| MS:son he sent *P1868:*son we sent
301| MS:And bought < > now; *CP1868:*Soon bought < > now: 303| MS:avenue, a
*P1868:*avenue,—a   304| MS:three and three, *P1868:*three and three,—
305| MS:my Monsignor *P1868:*my Monsignor,   306| MS:With the § crossed out § < >
in that vestibule *P1868:*i' the vestibule   307| MS:from, who *1889a:*from who
308| MS:nephew, Chamberlain, *P1868:*nephew, Chamberlain,—   311| MS:staircase
landing < > busts *P1868:*staircase-landing < > busts,   314| MS:birth-day < > down
*P1868:*down, *1889a:*birthday   315| MS:amends that *P1868:*amends, that

The unburnt end o' the very candle, Sirs,
Purfled with paint so prettily round and round,
He carried in such state last Peter's-day,—
In token I, his gentleman and squire,
320 Had held the bridle, walked his managed mule
Without a tittup the procession through.
Nay, the official,—one you know, sweet lords!—
Who drew the warrant for my transfer late
To the New Prisons from Tordinona,—he
325 Graciously had remembrance—"Francesc . . . ha?
His sire, now—how a thing shall come about!—
Paid me a dozen florins above the fee,
For drawing deftly up a deed of sale
When troubles fell so thick on him, good heart,
330 And I was prompt and pushing! By all means!
At the New Prisons be it his son shall lie,—
Anything for an old friend!" and thereat
Signed name with triple flourish underneath.
These were my fellows, such their fortunes now,
335 While I—kept fasts and feasts innumerable,
Matins and vespers, functions to no end
I' the train of Monsignor and Eminence,
As gentleman-squire, and for my zeal's reward
Have rarely missed a place at the table-foot
340 Except when some Ambassador, or such like,
Brought his own people. Brief, one day I felt
The tick of time inside me, turning-point
And slight sense there was now enough of this:
That I was near my seventh climacteric,
345 Hard upon, if not over, the middle life,

316| MS:of *P1868:*o'   318| MS:carried round the square last Peter's day
*P1868:*carried in such state last Peter's day   *CP1868:*last Peter's-day
322| MS:official,—none you   *CP1868:*official,—one you   324| MS:From Tordinona to
the Prisons New,   *P1868:*To the New Prisons from Tordinona,—he
325| MS:remembrance—"Francesc . . what?   *P1868:*remembrance—"Francesc . . ha?
*1889a:*remembrance—"Francesc . . . ha?   326| MS:now . . how <>
about!   *P1868:*now—how <> about!—   327| MS:fee *P1868:*fee,
330| MS:was brisk and   *P1868:*was prompt and   335| MS:And I *P1868:*While I
337| MS:In <> Eminence *P1868:*I' <> Eminence,   339| MS:missed my place
*P1868:*missed a place   340| MS:or the § crossed out and replaced above by § such
342| MS:of the time *CP1868:*of time   345| MS:over the *P1868:*over,

And, although fed by the east-wind, fulsome-fine
With foretaste of the Land of Promise, still
My gorge gave symptom it might play me false;
Better not press it further,—be content
³⁵⁰ With living and dying only a nobleman,
Who merely had a father great and rich,
Who simply had one greater and richer yet,
And so on back and back till first and best
Began i' the night; I finish in the day.
³⁵⁵ "The mother must be getting old," I said;
"The sisters are well wedded away, our name
Can manage to pass a sister off, at need,
And do for dowry: both my brothers thrive—
Regular priests they are, nor, bat-like, 'bide
³⁶⁰ 'Twixt flesh and fowl with neither privilege.
My spare revenue must keep me and mine.
I am tired: Arezzo's air is good to breathe;
Vittiano,—one limes flocks of thrushes there;
A leathern coat costs little and lasts long:
³⁶⁵ Let me bid hope good-bye, content at home!"
Thus, one day, I disbosomed me and bowed.

Whereat began the little buzz and thrill
O' the gazers round me; each face brightened up:
As when at your Casino, deep in dawn,
³⁷⁰ A gamester says at last, "I play no more,
Forego gain, acquiesce in loss, withdraw
Anyhow:" and the watchers of his ways,

---

the   ³⁴⁶| MS:And, fed although § circled with arrow indicating that word
should precede *fed* § < > East-wind   *P1868:*the east-wind   ³⁵⁰| MS:nobleman
*P1868:*nobleman,   ³⁵⁴| MS:in the night   *P1868:*i' the night   ³⁵⁷| MS:Can always
§ crossed out and replaced above by § manage to   ³⁵⁹| MS:bide   *P1868:*'bide
³⁶¹| MS:My old § crossed out and replaced above by following word § spare revenue may
§ crossed out and replaced above by § must   ³⁶²| MS:tired: the fields at home give air
§ crossed out and replaced above by following word § space to breathe,   *P1868:*tired: Arezzo's
air is good to breathe;   ³⁶³| MS:there,   *P1868:*there;   ³⁶⁴| MS:leathern-coat < >
long,   *P1868:*leathern-coat < > long: ³⁶⁵| MS:me give § crossed out and replaced
above by § bid hopes § *s* crossed out § up, die § last two words crossed out and replaced above
by word and comma § goodbye, < > home."   *P1868:*good-bye < > home!"   ³⁶⁶| MS:So
§ crossed out and replaced above by § Thus   ³⁶⁶⁻⁶⁷| MS:§ ¶ §   *P1868:*§ no ¶ §
1889:§ no ¶; emended to restore ¶; see Editorial Notes §   ³⁶⁸| MS:Of < > me: each < > up
*P1868:*O' < > me; < > up: ³⁷⁰| MS:last "I   *P1868:*last, "I   ³⁷²| MS:of the
§ crossed out and replaced above by following word § his game,   *P1868:*his ways,

A trifle struck compunctious at the word,
Yet sensible of relief, breathe free once more,
375 Break up the ring, venture polite advice—
"How, Sir? So scant of heart and hope indeed?
Retire with neither cross nor pile from play?—
So incurious, so short-casting?—give your chance
To a younger, stronger, bolder spirit belike,
380 Just when luck turns and the fine throw sweeps all?"
Such was the chorus: and its goodwill meant—
"See that the loser leave door handsomely!
There's an ill look,—it's sinister, spoils sport,
When an old bruised and battered year-by-year
385 Fighter with fortune, not a penny in poke,
Reels down the steps of our establishment
And staggers on broad daylight and the world,
In shagrag beard and doleful doublet, drops
And breaks his heart on the outside: people prate
390 'Such is the profit of a trip upstairs!'
Contrive he sidle forth, baulked of the blow
Best dealt by way of moral, bidding down
No curse but blessings rather on our heads
For some poor prize he bears at tattered breast,
395 Some palpable sort of kind of good to set
Over and against the grievance: give him quick!"

Whereon protested Paul, "Go hang yourselves!
Leave him to me. Count Guido and brother of mine,

374| MS:relief, draw § crossed out § breathe better at § last two words crossed out § free again,
P1868:free once more,   381| MS:chorus—and < > meant   P1868:chorus: and < >
meant—   383| MS:sinister, stops mirth, § last two words crossed out §   384| MS:old
bruised and § last two words inserted above line §   388| MS:and shabby doublet
P1868:and doleful doublet   389| MS:the door-sill § crossed out and replaced above by
word and colon § outside: 390| MS:"Such < > upstairs."   P1868:'Such < > upstairs!'
391| MS:Better he   P1868:Contrive he   392-94| MS:By < > bidding bless our heads/
For   P1868:Best dealt way < > bidding down/ No curse but blessings rather on our heads/
For   CP1868:Best dealt by way   395| MS:Some sort of palpable kind   P1868:Some
palpable sort of kind   396| MS:Over against < > give and quick!"   P1868:Over and
against < > give him quick!"   396-97| MS: § ¶ §   P1868: § no ¶ §   1889: § no ¶; emended
to restore ¶; see Editorial Notes §   397| MS:protested Paul "Go   P1868:protested Paul,

A word in your ear! Take courage, since faint heart
400 Ne'er won . . . aha, fair lady, don't men say?
There's a *sors*, there's a right Virgilian dip!
Do you see the happiness o' the hint? At worst,
If the Church want no more of you, the Court
No more, and the Camp as little, the ingrates,—come,
405 Count you are counted: still you've coat to back,
Not cloth of gold and tissue, as we hoped,
But cloth with sparks and spangles on its frieze
From Camp, Court, Church, enough to make a shine,
Entitle you to carry home a wife
410 With the proper dowry, let the worst betide!
Why, it was just a wife you meant to take!"

Now, Paul's advice was weighty: priests should know:
And Paul apprised me, ere the week was out,
That Pietro and Violante, the easy pair,
415 The cits enough, with stomach to be more,
Had just the daughter and exact the sum
To truck for the quality of myself: "She's young,
Pretty and rich: you're noble, classic, choice.
Is it to be a match?" "A match," said I.
420 Done! He proposed all, I accepted all,
And we performed all. So I said and did
Simply. As simply followed, not at first
But with the outbreak of misfortune, still
One comment on the saying and doing—"What?
425 No blush at the avowal you dared buy

"Go   399| MS:courage since   *1889a:*courage, since   402| MS:of   *P1868:*o'
403| MS:wants <> the Camp § crossed out §   *CP1868:*want   406| MS:we guessed,
*P1868:*we hoped,   407| MS:But showing § crossed out and replaced above by following
word § saving sparks   *P1868:*But cloth with sparks   410| MS:let their worst   *P1868:*let
the worst   411-12| MS:take!/ Deuce, ace, and rafle! Leave the cards to me!"/ Now
*P1868:*take!"/ § ¶ § Now   417| MS:myself: she's young,   *P1868:*myself: She's young,
*1872:*young   *1889a:*young,   418| MS:noble, classed and choice.   *P1868:*noble, classic,
choice.   419| MS:be a match?" "A match" said   *P1868:*be a match?" "A match," said
420| MS:proposed and § crossed out and replaced above by § all, <> all   *CP1868:*accepted
all,   421| MS:all. So I simply § crossed out §   422| MS:Simply, and thence followed
*P1868:*Simply. As simply followed   424| MS:This comment <> doing—"Beast,
*P1868:*One comment <> doing—"What?   425| MS:the avouching you   *P1868:*the

A girl of age beseems your granddaughter,
Like ox or ass? Are flesh and blood a ware?
Are heart and soul a chattel?"

                      Softly, Sirs!
Will the Court of its charity teach poor me
430   Anxious to learn, of any way i' the world,
Allowed by custom and convenience, save
This same which, taught from my youth up, I trod?
Take me along with you; where was the wrong step?
If what I gave in barter, style and state
435   And all that hangs to Franceschinihood,
Were worthless,—why, society goes to ground,
Its rules are idiot's-rambling. Honour of birth,—
If that thing has no value, cannot buy
Something with value of another sort,
440   You've no reward nor punishment to give
I' the giving or the taking honour; straight
Your social fabric, pinnacle to base,
Comes down a-clatter like a house of cards.
Get honour, and keep honour free from flaw,
445   Aim at still higher honour,—gabble o' the goose!
Go bid a second blockhead like myself
Spend fifty years in guarding bubbles of breath,
Soapsuds with air i' the belly, gilded brave,
Guarded and guided, all to break at touch
450   O' the first young girl's hand and first old fool's purse!
All my privation and endurance, all
Love, loyalty and labour dared and did,
Fiddle-de-dee!—why, doer and darer both,—
Count Guido Franceschini had hit the mark
455   Far better, spent his life with more effect,

---

avowal you   426| MS:A girl of age might be your grand-daughter § marked to indicate
that it should be transposed to read § age your grand-daughter might be   *P1868:*age beseems
your granddaughter,   429| MS:teach a man   *P1868:*teach poor me   430| MS:in
the world   *P1868:*i' the world,   432| MS:up I took?   *P1868:*up, I trod?
433| MS:me with < > step, I beg?   *P1868:*me along with < > step?   436| MS:Was < >
why society   *P1868:*Were < > why, society   437| MS:Honor   *P1868:*Honour
440| MS:reward to give nor punishment   *P1868:*reward nor punishment to give
441| MS:In < > honor   *P1868:*I' < > honour   444| MS:honor, keep that honor
*P1868:*honour, and keep honour   445| MS:honor   *P1868:*honour   448| MS:in
*P1868:*i'   449| MS:at a § crossed out §   450| MS:Of < > and old   *P1868:*O' < > and
first old   453| MS:Fiddle de dee   *P1868:*Fiddle-de-dee   455| MS:§ crowded

As a dancer or a prizer, trades that pay!
On the other hand, bid this buffoonery cease,
Admit that honour is a privilege,
The question follows, privilege worth what?
⁴⁶⁰ Why, worth the market-price,—now up, now down,
Just so with this as with all other ware:
Therefore essay the market, sell your name,
Style and condition to who buys them best!
"Does my name purchase," had I dared inquire,
⁴⁶⁵ "Your niece, my lord?" there would have been rebuff
Though courtesy, your Lordship cannot else—
"Not altogether! Rank for rank may stand:
But I have wealth beside, you—poverty;
Your scale flies up there: bid a second bid,
⁴⁷⁰ Rank too and wealth too!" Reasoned like yourself!
But was it to you I went with goods to sell?
This time 'twas my scale quietly kissed the ground,
Mere rank against mere wealth—some youth beside,
Some beauty too, thrown into the bargain, just
⁴⁷⁵ As the buyer likes or lets alone. I thought
To deal o' the square: others find fault, it seems:
The thing is, those my offer most concerned,
Pietro, Violante, cried they fair or foul?
What did they make o' the terms? Preposterous terms?
⁴⁸⁰ Why then accede so promptly, close with such
Nor take a minute to chaffer? Bargain struck,
They straight grew bilious, wished their money back,
Repented them, no doubt: why, so did I,

---

between lines 454 and 456 §   ⁴⁵⁶| MS:a singer or   *P1868:*a dancer or
⁴⁵⁷| MS:hand, halt § crossed out and replaced above by § bid this buffoonery stop,
*P1868:*buffoonery cease,   ⁴⁵⁸| MS:Admit nobility is *P1868:*Admit that honour is
⁴⁶¹| MS:With < > ware in the world: *P1868:*Just so with < > ware:
⁴⁶²| MS:Therefore consult § crossed out and replaced above by § essay
⁴⁶³| MS:conditions < > best!" *P1868:*condition < > best!   ⁴⁶⁵| MS:would be prompt
rebuff *P1868:*would have been rebuff   ⁴⁶⁸| MS:you, poverty; *CP1868:*you—poverty;
⁴⁶⁹| MS:second bid, *1889a:*second bid § emended to § bid, § see Editorial Notes §
⁴⁷²| MS:ground *P1868:*ground,   ⁴⁷⁶| MS:on < > fault, with me: § last two words
crossed out and replaced above by it seems: *P1868:*o'   ⁴⁷⁸| MS:they foul or fair?
*P1868:*they fair or foul?   ⁴⁷⁹| MS:of *P1868:*o'   ⁴⁸¹| MS:After § crossed out
and replaced above by following two words § Nor take a minute? § *?* crossed out § to
§ inserted above § chaffering? § *ing* crossed out § Afterward § crossed out §

So did your Lordship, if town-talk be true,
485 Of paying a full farm's worth for that piece
By Pietro of Cortona—probably
His scholar Ciro Ferri may have retouched—
You caring more for colour than design—
Getting a little tired of cupids too.
490 That's incident to all the folk who buy!
I am charged, I know, with gilding fact by fraud;
I falsified and fabricated, wrote
Myself down roughly richer than I prove,
Rendered a wrong revenue,—grant it all!
495 Mere grace, mere coquetry such fraud, I say:
A flourish round the figures of a sum
For fashion's sake, that deceives nobody.
The veritable back-bone, understood
Essence of this same bargain, blank and bare,
500 Being the exchange of quality for wealth,—
What may such fancy-flights be? Flecks of oil
Flirted by chapmen where plain dealing grates.
I may have dripped a drop—"My name I sell;
Not but that I too boast my wealth"—as they,
505 "—We bring you riches; still our ancestor
Was hardly the rapscallion folk saw flogged,
But heir to we know who, were rights of force!"
They knew and I knew where the backbone lurked
I' the writhings of the bargain, lords, believe!
510 I paid down all engaged for, to a doit,
Delivered them just that which, their life long,
They hungered in the hearts of them to gain—
Incorporation with nobility thus
In word and deed: for that they gave me wealth.
515 But when they came to try their gain, my gift,

484| MS:if the town-talk's true, *P1868:*if town-talk be true, 487| MS:scholar
Ciro Ferri may have § last two words inserted above § 489| MS:of Ledas too:
*CP1868:*of cupids too. 496-98| MS:flourish that deceives no one in the
world./ The *P1868:*flourish round the figures of a sum/ For fashion's sake, that deceives
nobody./ The 500| MS:wealth, *P1868:*wealth,— 503| MS:sell— *P1868:*sell;
505| MS:"We < > riches, still *P1868:*"—We < > riches; still 506| MS:rapscallion,
folks *1889a:* rapscallion folk 508| MS:back-bone *1889a:*backbone 509| MS:In
*P1868:*I' 510| MS:for to *P1868:*for, to 515| MS:gain my *P1868:*gain, my

Quit Rome and qualify for Arezzo, take
The tone o' the new sphere that absorbed the old,
Put away gossip Jack and goody Joan
And go become familiar with the Great,
520 Greatness to touch and taste and handle now,—
Why then,—they found that all was vanity,
Vexation, and what Solomon describes!
The old abundant city-fare was best,
The kindly warmth o' the commons, the glad clap
525 Of the equal on the shoulder, the frank grin
Of the underling at all so many spoons
Fire-new at neighbourly treat,—best, best and best
Beyond compare!—down to the loll itself
O' the pot-house settle,—better such a bench
530 Than the stiff crucifixion by my dais
Under the piecemeal damask canopy
With the coroneted coat of arms a-top!
Poverty and privation for pride's sake,
All they engaged to easily brave and bear,—
535 With the fit upon them and their brains a-work,—
Proved unendurable to the sobered sots.
A banished prince, now, will exude a juice
And salamander-like support the flame:
He dines on chestnuts, chucks the husks to help
540 The broil o' the brazier, pays the due baioc,
Goes off light-hearted: his grimace begins
At the funny humours of the christening-feast
Of friend the money-lender,—then he's touched
By the flame and frizzles at the babe to kiss!
545 Here was the converse trial, opposite mind:
Here did a petty nature split on rock

517| MS:of *P1868*:o'   520| MS:touch, and taste *P1868*:touch and taste
521| MS:Why, then *1889a*:Why then   522| MS:what Solomon found first. § last two
words crossed out and replaced above by § describes. *P1868*:describes!   524| MS:of
P1868:o'   527| MS:neighbourly feast § crossed out and replaced above by § treat
529| MS:On *P1868*:O'   531| MS:piece-meal velvet § crossed out and replaced
above by following word § damask canopy. *P1868*:canopy *1889a*:piecemeal
532| MS:coronetted *P1868*:coroneted   534| MS:bear *P1868*:bear,—
535| MS:brains a-fume, *P1868*:brains a-work,— *1872*:brains a-work, *1889a*:brains
a-work,—   540| MS:of *P1868*:o'   542| MS:christening feast
P1868:christening-feast   545| MS:mind. *P1868*:mind: 546| MS:petty soul

Of vulgar wants predestinate for such—
One dish at supper and weak wine to boot!
The prince had grinned and borne: the citizen shrieked,
550 Summoned the neighbourhood to attest the wrong,
Made noisy protest he was murdered,—stoned
And burned and drowned and hanged,—then broke away,
He and his wife, to tell their Rome the rest.
And this you admire, you men o' the world, my lords?
555 This moves compassion, makes you doubt my faith?
Why, I appeal to . . . sun and moon? Not I!
Rather to Plautus, Terence, Boccaccio's Book,
My townsman, frank Ser Franco's merry Tales.—
To all who strip a vizard from a face,
560 A body from its padding, and a soul
From froth and ignorance it styles itself,—
If this be other than the daily hap
Of purblind greed that dog-like still drops bone,
Grasps shadow, and then howls the case is hard!

565 So much for them so far: now for myself,
My profit or loss i' the matter: married am I:
Text whereon friendly censors burst to preach.
Ay, at Rome even, long ere I was left
To regulate her life for my young bride
570 Alone at Arezzo, friendliness outbroke
(Sifting my future to predict its fault)
"Purchase and sale being thus so plain a point,
How of a certain soul bound up, may-be,

---

§ crossed out and replaced above by § nature   551| MS:was murdered,— § inserted above §
stoned, P1868:stoned   552| MS: Burned, drowned P1868:And burned and drowned
553| MS:wife to P1868:wife, to   554| MS:of P1868:o'   555| MS:This § inserted
in margin § Moves your § crossed out §   556| MS:to . . sun 1889a:to . . . sun
558| MS:frank Ser Franco's § 's apparently added in revision § and his § last two words crossed
out and replaced above by § merry Tales, P1868:merry Tales,—   559| MS:And all who
know § crossed out and replaced by § strip P1868:To all   561| MS:itself,
P1868:itself,—   562| MS:daily case CP1868:daily hap   563| MS:Of human
§ crossed out and replaced above by § purblind greed that dog-like § inserted above § still lets
§ crossed out § drops the § crossed out § bone P1868:bone   564| MS:For the § last two
words crossed out and replaced above by § Grasps shadows § s crossed out § and then § inserted
above line § howls was never § last two words crossed out and replaced above by § the case so
§ crossed out and replaced above by § is hard? P1868:hard!   565| MS:myself
P1868:myself,   566| MS:in P1868:i'   567| MS:Whereupon friendly P1868:Text
whereon friendly   573| MS:up, belike § crossed out § may be, CP1868:may-be,

24

I' the barter with the body and money-bags?
575 From the bride's soul what is it you expect?"
Why, loyalty and obedience,—wish and will
To settle and suit her fresh and plastic mind
To the novel, not disadvantageous mould!
Father and mother shall the woman leave,
580 Cleave to the husband, be it for weal or woe:
There is the law: what sets this law aside
In my particular case? My friends submit
"Guide, guardian, benefactor,—fee, faw, fum,
The fact is you are forty-five years old,
585 Nor very comely even for that age:
Girls must have boys." Why, let girls say so then,
Nor call the boys and men, who say the same,
Brute this and beast the other as they do!
Come, cards on table! When you chaunt us next
590 Epithalamium full to overflow
With praise and glory of white womanhood,
The chaste and pure—troll no such lies o'er lip!
Put in their stead a crudity or two,
Such short and simple statement of the case
595 As youth chalks on our walls at spring of year!
No! I shall still think nobler of the sex,
Believe a woman still may take a man
For the short period that his soul wears flesh,
And, for the soul's sake, understand the fault
600 Of armour frayed by fighting. Tush, it tempts
One's tongue too much! I'll say—the law's the law:
With a wife I look to find all wifeliness,
As when I buy, timber and twig, a tree—
I buy the song o' the nightingale inside.

605 Such was the pact: Pompilia from the first

574| MS:In < > beside flesh § last two words crossed out and replaced above by three words §
with the body and money-bags— P1868:I' < > money-bags?
576| MS:obedience,—the wish P1868:obedience,—wish 578| MS:novel, not
disadvantageous P1868:novel, nor disadvantageous 1872:novel, not disadvantageous
579| MS:leave P1868:leave, 580| MS:woe. P1868:woe: 587| MS:men who say
as much § last two words crossed out and replaced above by two words § the same
P1868:men, who < > same, 589| MS:you recite § crossed out and replaced above by §
chaunt 591| MS:With praise and § last two words inserted above § glorifying § altered
to § glory 592| MS:lies with lip! P1868:lies o'er lip! 593| MS:two P1868:two,
598| MS:flesh P1868:flesh, 601| MS:law,— P1868:law: 604| MS:of P1868:o'

Broke it, refused from the beginning day
Either in body or soul to cleave to mine,
And published it forthwith to all the world.
No rupture,—you must join ere you can break,—
⁶¹⁰ Before we had cohabited a month
She found I was a devil and no man,—
Made common cause with those who found as much,
Her parents, Pietro and Violante,—moved
Heaven and earth to the rescue of all three.
⁶¹⁵ In four months' time, the time o' the parents' stay,
Arezzo was a-ringing, bells in a blaze,
With the unimaginable story rife
I' the mouth of man, woman and child—to-wit
My misdemeanour. First the lighter side,
⁶²⁰ Ludicrous face of things,—how very poor
The Franceschini had become at last,
The meanness and the misery of each shift
To save a soldo, stretch and make ends meet.
Next, the more hateful aspect,—how myself
⁶²⁵ With cruelty beyond Caligula's
Had stripped and beaten, robbed and murdered them,
The good old couple, I decoyed, abused,
Plundered and then cast out, and happily so,
Since,—in due course the abominable comes,—
⁶³⁰ Woe worth the poor young wife left lonely here!
Repugnant in my person as my mind,
I sought,—was ever heard of such revenge?
—To lure and bind her to so cursed a couch,
Such co-embrace with sulphur, snake and toad,
⁶³⁵ That she was fain to rush forth, call the stones
O' the common street to save her, not from hate

⁶¹⁵| MS:of *P1868*:o'   ⁶¹⁶| MS:Arezzo rang the changes, like § last four words crossed
out and replaced above by two words and comma § was a-ringing, bells bewitched § crossed
out and replaced above by § in a blaze,   ⁶¹⁸| MS:In < > child, to-wit *P1868*:I' < >
child—to-wit   ⁶¹⁹| MS:misdemeanour—first < > side *P1868*:misdemeanour. First
< > side,   ⁶²⁰| MS:Ludicrous aspect, § crossed out and replaced by following three
words § face of things, how § illegible word crossed out and replaced above by § very
P1868:things,—how   ⁶²⁸| MS:Plundered—and then *P1868*:Plundered and then
⁶³³| MS:—To bind—and bind § dash and last two words inserted above line § her to § illegible
erasure § *P1868*:—To lure and   ⁶³⁴| MS:Much § altered to § Such   ⁶³⁶| MS:Of

Of mine merely, but . . . must I burn my lips
With the blister of the lie? . . . the satyr-love
Of who but my own brother, the young priest,
640 Too long enforced to lenten fare belike,
Now tempted by the morsel tossed him full
I' the trencher where lay bread and herbs at best.
Mark, this yourselves say!—this, none disallows,
Was charged to me by the universal voice
645 At the instigation of my four-months' wife!—
And then you ask "Such charges so preferred,
(Truly or falsely, here concerns us not)
Pricked you to punish now if not before?—
Did not the harshness double itself, the hate
650 Harden?" I answer "Have it your way and will!"
Say my resentment grew apace: what then?
Do you cry out on the marvel? When I find
That pure smooth egg which, laid within my nest,
Could not but hatch a comfort to us all,
655 Issues a cockatrice for me and mine,
Do you stare to see me stamp on it? Swans are soft:
Is it not clear that she you call my wife,
That any wife of any husband, caught
Whetting a sting like this against his breast,—
660 Speckled with fragments of the fresh-broke shell,
Married a month and making outcry thus,—
Proves a plague-prodigy to God and man?
She married: what was it she married for,
Counted upon and meant to meet thereby?
665 "Love" suggests some one, "love, a little word
Whereof we have not heard one syllable."
So, the Pompilia, child, girl, wife, in one,

---

*P1868:*O'   637| MS:merely but *P1868:*merely, but   638| MS:lie? . . the
*1889a:*lie? . . . the   642| MS:In <> where the bread and herbs are best.
*P1868:*I' <> where lay bread and herbs at best.   647| MS:falsely, now concerns
*P1868:*falsely, here concerns   648| MS:before?—   *P1868:*before?—
650| MS:answer, "Have *CP1868:*answer "Have   655| MS:Issues § altered to § Issue
*P1868:*Issues   660| MS:Speckled § inserted above § With <> the fresh-broke
§ inserted above § *P1868:*with   667| MS:So the <> wife in *P1868:*So,

Wanted the beating pulse, the rolling eye,
The frantic gesture, the devotion due
670 From Thyrsis to Neæra! Guido's love—
Why not Provençal roses in his shoe,
Plume to his cap, and trio of guitars
At casement, with a bravo close beside?
Good things all these are, clearly claimable
675 When the fit price is paid the proper way.
Had it been some friend's wife, now, threw her fan
At my foot, with just this pretty scrap attached,
"Shame, death, damnation—fall these as they may,
So I find you, for a minute! Come this eve!"
680 —Why, at such sweet self-sacrifice,—who knows?
I might have fired up, found me at my post,
Ardent from head to heel, nor feared catch cough.
Nay, had some other friend's . . . say, daughter, tripped
Upstairs and tumbled flat and frank on me,
685 Bareheaded and barefooted, with loose hair
And garments all at large,—cried "Take me thus!
Duke So-and-So, the greatest man in Rome—
To escape his hand and heart have I broke bounds,
Traversed the town and reached you!"—then, indeed,
690 The lady had not reached a man of ice!
I would have rummaged, ransacked at the word
Those old odd corners of an empty heart
For remnants of dim love the long disused,
And dusty crumblings of romance! But here,
695 We talk of just a marriage, if you please—

---

the <> wife, in   670| MS:to Neæra: Guido's *CP1868:* to Neæra! Guido's
671| MS:provençal *1889a:*Provençal   672| MS:cap and *P1868:*cap, and
676| MS:her glove § crossed out §   677| MS:foot with just this scrap of note attached
*P1868:*foot, with just this pretty scrap attached,   678| MS:damnation—be these <>
may *P1868:*damnation—fall these <> may,   679| MS:So I gain you but a minute:
§ altered to § ! come § altered to § Come this eve!"— *P1868:*So I find you, for a <> eve!"
680| MS:—Why, for such *P1868:*—Why, at such   682| MS:Rosy from *P1868:*Ardent
from   683| MS:friend's . . say, daughter tripped *1889a:*friend's . . . say
687| MS:Duke So and So *P1868:*Duke So-and-So   689| MS:you!"—Then

The every-day conditions and no more;
Where do these bind me to bestow one drop
Of blood shall dye my wife's true-love-knot pink?
Pompilia was no pigeon, Venus' pet,
700 That shuffled from between her pressing paps
To sit on my rough shoulder,—but a hawk,
I bought at a hawk's price and carried home
To do hawk's service—at the Rotunda, say,
Where, six o' the callow nestlings in a row,
705 You pick and choose and pay the price for such.
I have paid my pound, await my penny's worth,
So, hoodwink, starve and properly train my bird,
And, should she prove a haggard,—twist her neck!
Did I not pay my name and style, my hope
710 And trust, my all? Through spending these amiss
I am here! 'Tis scarce the gravity of the Court
Will blame me that I never piped a tune,
Treated my falcon-gentle like my finch.
The obligation I incurred was just
715 To practise mastery, prove my mastership:—
Pompilia's duty was—submit herself,
Afford me pleasure, perhaps cure my bile.
Am I to teach my lords what marriage means,
What God ordains thereby and man fulfils
720 Who, docile to the dictate, treads the house?
My lords have chosen the happier part with Paul
And neither marry nor burn,—yet priestliness
Can find a parallel to the marriage-bond
In its own blessed special ordinance
725 Whereof indeed was marriage made the type:
The Church may show her insubordinate,

1889a:you!"—then   696| MS:every day CP1868:every-day   701| MS:hawk
P1868:hawk,   704| MS:of P1868:o'   707| MS:So hoodwink P1868:So,
hoodwink   708| MS:And should <> haggard,—twitch § crossed out and replaced above
by § twist her beak § crossed out § neck! P1868:And, should   710| MS:spending all
amiss P1868:spending these amiss   715| MS:To prove the § last two words crossed out
and replaced above by § practise mastery, of § crossed out and replaced above by two words §
prove my   716| MS:duty,—to submit P1868:duty was—submit   718| MS:my
Lords P1868:my lords   722| MS:priestliness, P1868:priestliness   726| MS:My
Lords, too have their § last five words crossed out and replaced above by five words § The

29

As marriage her refractory. How of the Monk
Who finds the claustral regimen too sharp
After the first month's essay? What's the mode
730 With the Deacon who supports indifferently
The rod o' the Bishop when he tastes its smart
Full four weeks? Do you straightway slacken hold
Of the innocents, the all-unwary ones
Who, eager to profess, mistook their mind?—
735 Remit a fast-day's rigour to the Monk
Who fancied Francis' manna meant roast quails,—
Concede the Deacon sweet society,
He never thought the Levite-rule renounced,—
Or rather prescribe short chain and sharp scourge
740 Corrective of such peccant humours? This—
I take to be the Church's mode, and mine.
If I was over-harsh,—the worse i' the wife
Who did not win from harshness as she ought,
Wanted the patience and persuasion, lore
745 Of love, should cure me and console herself.
Put case that I mishandle, flurry and fright
My hawk through clumsiness in sportsmanship,
Twitch out five pens where plucking one would serve—
What, shall she bite and claw to mend the case?
750 And, if you find I pluck five more for that,
Shall you weep "How he roughs the turtle there"?

Such was the starting; now of the further step.

Church may show her   727| MS:As wedlock § crossed out and replaced above by §
marriage <> the monk § crossed out and replaced above by § friar § crossed out and original
restored §   729| MS:month's fasting § crossed out and replaced above by § essay <> the
way § crossed out §   730| MS:the deacon   P1868:the Deacon   731| MS:The rule
§ crossed out and replaced above by § rod of   CP1868:o'   732| MS:hold,   P1868:hold
733| MS:all unwary   CP1868:all-unwary   734| MS:Who, made § crossed out and
replaced above by two words § eager to <> mind,—   P1868:mind?—   736| MS:quails,
1889a:quails,—   737| MS:society   CP1868:society,   738| MS:He never § inserted
above line § <> the levite-rule   P1868:the Levite-rule   740| MS:such peccant § inserted
above line §   741| MS:the Churches'   P1868:the Church's   742| MS:was over
§ inserted above § harsh <> in   CP1868:over-harsh <> i'   745| MS:love should <>
and repay § crossed out and replaced above by § console herself   P1868:love, should <>
herself.   746| MS:mishandle, fright and fury § last three words crossed out and replaced
above by three words § flurry and fright   749| MS:case,   P1868:case?   751| MS:he
treats § crossed out and replaced above by § roughs <> there?"   1889a:there"?

30

In lieu of taking penance in good part,
The Monk, with hue and cry, summons a mob
755 To make a bonfire of the convent, say,—
And the Deacon's pretty piece of virtue (save
The ears o' the Court! I try to save my head)
Instructed by the ingenuous postulant,
Taxes the Bishop with adultery, (mud
760 Needs must pair off with mud, and filth with filth)—
Such being my next experience. Who knows not—
The couple, father and mother of my wife,
Returned to Rome, published before my lords,
Put into print, made circulate far and wide
765 That they had cheated me who cheated them?
Pompilia, I supposed their daughter, drew
Breath first 'mid Rome's worst rankness, through the deed
Of a drab and a rogue, was by-blow bastard-babe
Of a nameless strumpet, passed off, palmed on me
770 As the daughter with the dowry. Daughter? Dirt
O' the kennel! Dowry? Dust o' the street! Nought more,
Nought less, nought else but—oh—ah—assuredly
A Franceschini and my very wife!
Now take this charge as you will, for false or true,—
775 This charge, preferred before your very selves
Who judge me now,—I pray you, adjudge again,
Classing it with the cheats or with the lies,
By which category I suffer most!
But of their reckoning, theirs who dealt with me
780 In either fashion,—I reserve my word,

752| MS:step: *P1868:*step. 755| MS:say— *P1868:*say,— 756| MS:virtue,—save
*P1868:*virtue (save 757| MS:the Court, I <> head,— *CP1868:*the Court! I <> head)
758| MS:ingenious *P1868:*ingenuous 759| MS:adultery,—mud *P1868:*adultery,
(mud 760| MS:and filth with filth, *CP1868:*and filth with filth)—
761| MS:experience: who <> not *P1868:*not— *1889a:*experience. Who
762| MS:wife *P1868:*wife, 765| MS:them, *P1868:*them? 767| MS:mid <>
rankness through *P1868:*'mid <> rankness, through 768| MS:rogue, the § crossed
out and replaced above by § was bye-blow *1889a:*by-blow 771| MS:Of the kennel. <>
of the street. Nought *P1868:*O' the kennel! <> o' the street! Nought 772| MS:but,
oh—ay— § inserted above line § assuredly *P1868:*but oh—ah—assuredly
776| MS:again *P1868:*again, 777| MS:§ crowded between lines 776 and 778 § with the
§ inserted above § cheats then § crossed out § or with the § inserted above § lies vow, § last word
crossed out § 778| MS:most: *P1868:*most! 779| MS:reckoning, those who

Justify that in its place; I am now to say,
Whichever point o' the charge might poison most,
Pompilia's duty was no doubtful one.
You put the protestation in her mouth
785 "Henceforward and forevermore, avaunt
Ye fiends, who drop disguise and glare revealed
In your own shape, no longer father mine
Nor mother mine! Too nakedly you hate
Me whom you looked as if you loved once,—me
790 Whom, whether true or false, your tale now damns,
Divulged thus to my public infamy,
Private perdition, absolute overthrow.
For, hate my husband to your hearts' content,
I, spoil and prey of you from first to last,
795 I who have done you the blind service, lured
The lion to your pitfall,—I, thus left
To answer for my ignorant bleating there,
I should have been remembered and withdrawn
From the first o' the natural fury, not flung loose
800 A proverb and a by-word men will mouth
At the cross-way, in the corner, up and down
Rome and Arezzo,—there, full in my face,
If my lord, missing them and finding me,
Content himself with casting his reproach
805 To drop i' the street where such impostors die.
Ah, but—that husband, what the wonder were!—
If, far from casting thus away the rag
Smeared with the plague his hand had chanced upon,
Sewn to his pillow by Locusta's wile,—

P1868:reckoning, theirs who ⁷⁸¹| MS:to urge, § last word crossed out and
replaced by § say, P1868:to say, ⁷⁸²| MS:Whichever point of § last two
words inserted above line § P1868:o' ⁷⁸⁶| MS:glare at me § last two words
crossed out § ⁷⁸⁸| MS:Nor § written over word, perhaps Not § < > mine: how nakedly
P1868:mine! Too nakedly ⁷⁹⁰| MS:Who, whether this your § inserted above line § tale
of yours § last two words crossed out § be true or false P1868:Whom, whether true or false,
your tale now damns, ⁷⁹¹| MS:Divulge it to P1868:Divulged thus to
⁷⁹⁵| MS:who had done P1868:who have done ⁷⁹⁶| MS:pit-fall 1889a:pitfall
⁷⁹⁹| MS:of P1868:o' ⁸⁰⁰| MS:byeword men should § crossed out and replaced above
by § will 1889a:by-word ⁸⁰⁵| MS:in < > imposters go § crossed out and replaced
above by § die. P1868:i' ⁸⁰⁶| MS:were— P1868:were!— ⁸⁰⁷| MS:If far
CP1868:If, far ⁸⁰⁸| MS: § crowded between 807 and 809 § plague, his < > upon
P1868:upon, 1889a:plague his ⁸⁰⁹| MS:by Locusta's craft,— CP1868:by Locusta's

⁸¹⁰ Far from abolishing, root, stem and branch,
The misgrowth of infectious mistletoe
Foisted into his stock for honest graft,—
If he repudiate not, renounce nowise,
But, guarding, guiding me, maintain my cause
⁸¹⁵ By making it his own, (what other way?)
—To keep my name for me, he call it his,
Claim it of who would take it by their lie,—
To save my wealth for me—or babe of mine
Their lie was framed to beggar at the birth—
⁸²⁰ He bid them loose grasp, give our gold again:
If he become no partner with the pair
Even in a game which, played adroitly, gives
Its winner life's great wonderful new chance,—
Of marrying, to-wit, a second time,—
⁸²⁵ Ah, if he did thus, what a friend were he!
Anger he might show,—who can stamp out flame
Yet spread no black o' the brand?—yet, rough albeit
In the act, as whose bare feet feel embers scorch,
What grace were his, what gratitude were mine!"
⁸³⁰ Such protestation should have been my wife's.
Looking for this, do I exact too much?
Why, here's the,—word for word, so much, no more,—
Avowal she made, her pure spontaneous speech
To my brother the Abate at first blush,

---

wile,—   ^{810|} MS:branch *P1868:*branch,   ^{812|} MS:graft, *P1868:*graft,—
^{813|}   MS: § crowded between lines 811 and 813 § He, repudiated not, renounced nowise,
*P1868:*If he, repudiate not, renounce nowise,   *1889a:*If he repudiate
^{814|}   MS:But guarding <> maintained   *P1868:*But, guarding <> maintain
^{815|}   MS:own, what <> way? *P1868:*own, (what <> way?)   ^{816|} MS:To <> he
called it *P1868:*—To <> he call it   ^{817|} MS:Claimed *P1868:*Claim
^{818|}   MS:or better, § crossed out §   ^{819|} MS:birth, *P1868:*birth—   ^{820|} MS:bade
<> give his gold *P1868:*bid <> give our gold   ^{821|} MS:Refused to be a partner
*P1868:*Refuse to become partner   *1872:*If he become no partner   ^{822|} MS:adroitly, gave
*P1868:*adroitly, gives   ^{823–25|} MS:The winner that great <> / Ah, did he do thus
*P1868:*Its winner life's great <> / Of marrying, to-wit, a second time,— / Ah *1889a:*/ /
Ah, if he did thus   ^{827|} MS:of <> yet rough *P1868:*o' <> yet, rough
^{828|}   MS:act as <> bare foot feels § last two words altered to following two words § feet feel
embers burn, *P1868:*act, as <> embers scorch,   ^{829|} MS:What deed were his
*P1868:*What grace were his   ^{832|} MS:for word so *1889a:*for word, so

33

835 Ere the good impulse had begun to fade:
So did she make confession for the pair,
So pour forth praises in her own behalf.
"Ay, the false letter," interpose my lords—
"The simulated writing,—'twas a trick:
840 You traced the signs, she merely marked the same,
The product was not hers but yours." Alack,
I want no more impulsion to tell truth
From the other trick, the torture inside there!
I confess all—let it be understood—
845 And deny nothing! If I baffle you so,
Can so fence, in the plenitude of right,
That my poor lathen dagger puts aside
Each pass o' the Bilboa, beats you all the same,—
What matters inefficiency of blade?
850 Mine and not hers the letter,—conceded, lords!
Impute to me that practice!—take as proved
I taught my wife her duty, made her see
What it behoved her see and say and do,
Feel in her heart and with her tongue declare,
855 And, whether sluggish or recalcitrant,
Forced her to take the right step, I myself
Was marching in marital rectitude!
Why who finds fault here, say the tale be true?
Would not my lords commend the priest whose zeal
860 Seized on the sick, morose or moribund,
By the palsy-smitten finger, made it cross
His brow correctly at the critical time?

835| MS:fade— *1889a:*fade: 838| MS:letter" interpose you here—   *P1868:*letter,"
interpose my lords—   840| MS:signs, you § crossed out and replaced above by § she
843| MS:the little trick <> there—   *P1868:*the other trick <> there!
845| MS:nothing,—if *P1868:*nothing! If   847| MS:lathen sword § altered to § dagger
848| MS:of <> same, *P1868:*o' <> same,—   849| MS:of arm? *P1868:*of blade?
851| MS:Impute to me § last two words written above § that practice,—take
*P1868:*practice!—take   854| MS:declare. *P1868:*declare,   855| MS:§ crowded
between lines 854 and 856 § whether ignorant § crossed out and replaced in right margin by §
sluggish   857| MS:Marching in mere marital rectitude, *P1868:*rectitude! *1872:*Was
marching in marital   858| MS:And who *1872:*Why, who *1889a:*Why who
860| MS:Siezes the *P1868:*Seized on the   861| MS:makes *P1868:*made

—Or answered for the inarticulate babe
At baptism, in its stead declared the faith,
865 And saved what else would perish unprofessed?
True, the incapable hand may rally yet,
Renounce the sign with renovated strength,—
The babe may grow up man and Molinist,—
And so Pompilia, set in the good path
870 And left to go alone there, soon might see
That too frank-forward, all too simple-straight
Her step was, and decline to tread the rough,
When here lay, tempting foot, the meadow-side,
And there the coppice rang with singing-birds!
875 Soon she discovered she was young and fair,
That many in Arezzo knew as much.
Yes, this next cup of bitterness, my lords,
Had to begin go filling, drop by drop,
Its measure up of full disgust for me,
880 Filtered into by every noisome drain—
Society's sink toward which all moisture runs.
Would not you prophesy—"She on whose brow is stamped
The note of the imputation that we know,—
Rightly or wrongly mothered with a whore,—
885 Such an one, to disprove the frightful charge,
What will she but exaggerate chastity,
Err in excess of wifehood, as it were,
Renounce even levities permitted youth,
Though not youth struck to age by a thunderbolt?

863| MS:Or answers   *P1868:*—Or answered   864| MS:in his § crossed out and replaced
above by § its <> declares   *P1868:*declared   865| MS:saves   *P1868:*saved
866| MS:yet   *P1868:*yet,   867| MS:strength,   *P1868:*strength,—   868| MS:up to a
§ last two words crossed out and replaced above by two words § man and
871| MS:simple-strait   *1889a:*simple-straight   872| MS:rough   *P1868:*rough,
874| MS:coppice called with singing-birds.   *P1868:*singing-birds!   *1872:*coppice rang with
876| MS:much,—   *1889a:*much.   879| MS:Its cavity § crossed out and replaced above
by § measure <> me   *P1868:*me,   880| MS:every fulsome drain—   *CP1868:*every
noisome drain—   882| MS:prophesy "She   *P1868:*prophesy—"She   883| MS:The
shame § crossed out and replaced above by § note <> know,   *P1868:*know,—
884| MS:whore,   *P1868:*whore,—   885| MS:one—to   *P1868:*one, to
886| MS:Will, could § last two words crossed out and replaced by § What will
887| MS:wifehood as   *P1868:*wifehood, as   888| MS:youth—   *P1868:*youth,
889| MS:Youth <> by shame the thunderbolt?   *P1868:*Though not youth <> by a

890 Cry 'wolf' i' the sheepfold, where's the sheep dares bleat,
Knowing the shepherd listens for a growl?"
So you expect. How did the devil decree?
Why, my lords, just the contrary of course!
It was in the house from the window, at the church
895 From the hassock,—where the theatre lent its lodge,
Or staging for the public show left space,—
That still Pompilia needs must find herself
Launching her looks forth, letting looks reply
As arrows to a challenge; on all sides
900 Ever new contribution to her lap,
Till one day, what is it knocks at my clenched teeth
But the cup full, curse-collected all for me?
And I must needs drink, drink this gallant's praise,
That minion's prayer, the other fop's reproach,
905 And come at the dregs to—Caponsacchi! Sirs,
I,—chin-deep in a marsh of misery,
Struggling to extricate my name and fame
And fortune from the marsh would drown them all,
My face the sole unstrangled part of me,—
910 I must have this new gad-fly in that face,
Must free me from the attacking lover too!
Men say I battled ungracefully enough—
Was harsh, uncouth and ludicrous beyond
The proper part o' the husband: have it so!
915 Your lordships are considerate at least—
You order me to speak in my defence
Plainly, expect no quavering tuneful trills
As when you bid a singer solace you,—
Nor look that I shall give it, for a grace,
920 *Stans pede in uno:*—you remember well

---

thunderbolt?   ⁸⁹⁰| MS:in the sheepfold where's <> bleat   *CP1868:*i' the sheepfold,
where's <> bleat,   ⁸⁹¹| MS:growl? *P1868:*growl?"   ⁸⁹³| MS:course,
*P1868:*course!   ⁸⁹⁶| MS:The staging <> space, *P1868:*Or staging <> space,—
⁸⁹⁹| MS:challenge, on *P1868:*challenge; on   ⁹⁰¹| MS:knocks my *P1868:*knocks at my
⁹⁰²| MS:me, *P1868:*me?   ⁹⁰³| MS:drink up this *P1868:*drink, drink this
⁹⁰⁵| MS:to—Caponsacchi: Sirs, *P1868:*to—Caponsacchi! Sirs,   ⁹⁰⁶| MS:I—chin deep
<> misery— *CP1868:*I,—chin deep <> misery, *1889a:*chin-deep   ⁹¹⁰| MS:in my
face, *P1868:*in that face,   ⁹¹¹| MS:Defend § crossed out and replaced by § Must free
⁹¹⁴| MS:of *P1868:*o'   ⁹¹⁷| MS:quavering, tuneful *P1868:*quavering tuneful
⁹¹⁸| MS:solace you, *P1868:*solace you,—   ⁹²⁰| MS:*uno,*—you *P1868:*uno: you

In the one case, 'tis a plainsong too severe,
This story of my wrongs,—and that I ache
And need a chair, in the other. Ask you me
Why, when I felt this trouble flap my face,
925   Already pricked with every shame could perch,—
When, with her parents, my wife plagued me too,—
Why I enforced not exhortation mild
To leave whore's-tricks and let my brows alone,
With mulct of comfits, promise of perfume?

930   "Far from that! No, you took the opposite course,
Breathed threatenings, rage and slaughter!" What you will!
And the end has come, the doom is verily here,
Unhindered by the threatening. See fate's flare
Full on each face of the dead guilty three!
935   Look at them well, and now, lords, look at this!
Tell me: if on that day when I found first
That Caponsacchi thought the nearest way
To his church was some half-mile round by my door,
And that he so admired, shall I suppose,
940   The manner of the swallows' come-and-go
Between the props o' the window over-head,—
That window happening to be my wife's,—
As to stand gazing by the hour on high,
Of May-eves, while she sat and let him smile,—
945   If I,—instead of threatening, talking big,
Showing hair-powder, a prodigious pinch,
For poison in a bottle,—making believe

921| MS:severe *P1868:*severe,   922| MS:that my limbs are § last three words crossed out
and replaced by § I ache   924| MS:That, when *P1868:*Why, when   925| MS:perch
*P1868:*perch,—   926| MS:And, with <> plague *P1868:*When, with <> plagued
927| MS:That I enforced some exhortation *P1868:*Why I enforced not exhortation
928| MS:whore's tricks <> alone *P1868:*whore's-tricks <> alone,   931| MS:Breathed
fire § crossed out and replaced above by the following word § rage and slaughter, threatened
her" . . . what *P1868:*Breathed threatenings, rage and slaughter!" What   932| MS:is
fallen § crossed out and followed by illegible word, apparently superimposed upon an earlier
word, also crossed out and the two replaced by § verily here,   934| MS:Three!
*P1868:*three!   935| MS:now, Lords *P1868:*now, lords   939| MS:so conceited,
shall I say, *P1868:*so admired, shall I suppose,   940| MS:swallows making nest
*P1868:*swallows' come-and-go   941| MS:of *P1868:*o'   943| MS:hour thereat
*P1868:*hour on high,   944| MS:sate *P1868:*sat   945| MS:If I, instead of

At desperate doings with a bauble-sword,
And other bugaboo-and-baby-work,—
950 Had, with the vulgarest household implement,
Calmly and quietly cut off, clean thro' bone
But one joint of one finger of my wife,
Saying "For listening to the serenade,
Here's your ring-finger shorter a full third:
955 Be certain I will slice away next joint,
Next time that anybody underneath
Seems somehow to be sauntering as he hoped
A flower would eddy out of your hand to his
While you please fidget with the branch above
960 O' the rose-tree in the terrace!"—had I done so,
Why, there had followed a quick sharp scream, some pain,
Much calling for plaister, damage to the dress,
A somewhat sulky countenance next day,
Perhaps reproaches,—but reflections too!
965 I don't hear much of harm that Malchus did
After the incident of the ear, my lords!
Saint Peter took the efficacious way;
Malchus was sore but silenced for his life:
He did not hang himself i' the Potter's Field
970 Like Judas, who was trusted with the bag
And treated to sops after he proved a thief.
So, by this time, my true and obedient wife
Might have been telling beads with a gloved hand;
Awkward a little at pricking hearts and darts
975 On sampler possibly, but well otherwise:
Not where Rome shudders now to see her lie.

---

threatening,—talking *P1868:*If I,—instead of threatening, talking   949| MS:With all
such bugaboo-and-baby-work,   *P1868:*And other bugaboo-and-baby work,—
950| MS:—Had *P1868:*Had   951| MS:bone, *1889a:*bone   952| MS:wife
*P1868:*wife,   954| MS:third, *P1868:*third: 955| MS:away the next, *P1868:*away
next joint,   960| MS:Of *P1868:*O'   964| MS:too:
*P1868:*too!   965| MS:of wrong that *P1868:*of harm that   966| MS:lords,
*P1868:*lords!   967| MS:way, *P1868:*way;   968| MS:but sobered for his life,
*P1868:*but silenced for his life: 969| MS:in < > field— *P1868:*i' < >
Field   970| MS:But Judas did, who *P1868:*Like Judas, who   971| MS:thief:
*P1868:*thief.   972| MS:So by this time my *P1868:*So, by this time, my
973| MS:hand *P1868:*hand;   975| MS:otherwise, *P1868:*otherwise:

I give that for the course a wise man takes;
I took the other however, tried the fool's,
The lighter remedy, brandished rapier dread
980 With cork-ball at the tip, boxed Malchus' ear
Instead of severing the cartilage,
Called her a terrible nickname, and the like,
And there an end: and what was the end of that?
What was the good effect o' the gentle course?
985 Why, one night I went drowsily to bed,
Dropped asleep suddenly, not suddenly woke,
But did wake with rough rousing and loud cry,
To find noon in my face, a crowd in my room,
Fumes in my brain, fire in my throat, my wife
990 Gone God knows whither,—rifled vesture-chest,
And ransacked money-coffer. "What does it mean?"
The servants had been drugged too, stared and yawned
"It must be that our lady has eloped!"
—"Whither and with whom?"—"With whom but the Canon's self?
995 One recognizes Caponsacchi there!"—
(By this time the admiring neighbourhood
Joined chorus round me while I rubbed my eyes)
" 'Tis months since their intelligence began,—
A comedy the town was privy to,—
1000 He wrote and she wrote, she spoke, he replied,
And going in and out your house last night
Was easy work for one . . . to be plain with you . . .
Accustomed to do both, at dusk and dawn

977| MS:takes, *P1868:*takes; 978| MS:tried, the fool's *P1868:*tried the fool's,
982| MS:like *1889a:*like, 984| MS:of *P1868:*o' 987| MS:rough shaking
and *P1868:*rough rousing and 989| MS:throat *1889a:*thoat § emended to §
throat § see Editorial Notes § 992| MS:yawned, *1872:*yawned 993| MS:our
Lady *P1868:*our lady 994| MS:"Whither <> whom?" With <> self,
P1868:—"Whither <> whom?"—"With <> self? 995| MS:there,—
*P1868:*there!"— 998| MS:'Tis months ago the intelligence began, *P1868:*" 'Tis
months since their intelligence began,— 999| MS:to, *P1868:*to,—
1002| MS:one . . to *1889a:*one . . . to 1003| MS:both at *P1868:*both, at

When you were absent,—at the villa, you know,
1005 Where husbandry required the master-mind.
Did not you know? Why, we all knew, you see!"
And presently, bit by bit, the full and true
Particulars of the tale were volunteered
With all the breathless zeal of friendship—"Thus
1010 Matters were managed: at the seventh hour of night" . . .
—"Later, at daybreak" . . . "Caponsacchi came" . . .
—"While you and all your household slept like death,
Drugged as your supper was with drowsy stuff" . . .
—"And your own cousin Guillichini too—
1015 Either or both entered your dwelling-place,
Plundered it at their pleasure, made prize of all,
Including your wife . . ."—"Oh, your wife led the way,
Out of doors, on to the gate . . ."—"But gates are shut,
In a decent town, to darkness and such deeds:
1020 They climbed the wall—your lady must be lithe—
At the gap, the broken bit . . ." —"Torrione, true!
To escape the questioning guard at the proper gate,
Clemente, where at the inn, hard by, 'the Horse,'
Just outside, a calash in readiness
1025 Took the two principals, all alone at last,
To gate San Spirito, which o'erlooks the road,
Leads to Perugia, Rome and liberty."
Bit by bit thus made-up mosaic-wise,

1004| MS:the Villa, you know— *P1868:*the villa, you know,   1009| MS:With the
breathless zealousness of *P1868:*With all the breathless zeal of   1010| MS:night" . . .
*P1868:*night" . . § emended to § night" . . . § see Editorial Notes §
1011| MS: . . "Later § over perhaps *then* §, at daybreak"—"Caponsacchi *P1868:*—"Later,
at daybreak" . . "Caponsacchi *1889a:*daybreak" . . . "Caponsacchi
1012-13| MS:§ crowded between lines 1011 and 1014 §   1012| MS:"While <> death
P1868:—"While <> death,   1013| MS:stuff," *P1868:*stuff" . . .
1014| MS: . . And <> too"— *P1868:*—"And <> too—   1016| MS:pleasure, and
prize and all, *P1868:*pleasure, made prize of all,   1017| MS:wife,—" "Oh <> way . . .
*P1868:*wife . . ."—"Oh <> way,   1018| MS:gate." "But <>
shut *P1868:*gate . . ."—"But <> shut,   1019| MS:town to
*P1868:*town, to   1020| MS:lithe . . . *P1868:*lithe—   1021| MS:gap and the
broken bit—" "Torrione, true," . . . *CP1868:*gap, the broken bit . ." —"Torrione, true!
*1889a:*gap, the broken bit . . ." —"Torrione   1022| MS:"To <> gate *P1868:*To <>
gate,   1023| MS:by, the Horse, *P1868:*by, 'the Horse,'   1024| MS:outside, the
Calash *P1868:*outside, a calash   1026| MS:To the gate <> road *CP1868:*To gate <>
road,   1027| MS:to Perugia; Rome *P1868:*to Perugia, Rome   1028| MS:made up

Flat lay my fortune,—tesselated floor,
1030 Imperishable tracery devils should foot
And frolic it on, around my broken gods,
Over my desecrated hearth.
                                So much
For the terrible effect of threatening, Sirs!

Well, this way I was shaken wide awake,
1035 Doctored and drenched, somewhat unpoisoned so.
Then, set on horseback and bid seek the lost,
I started alone, head of me, heart of me
Fire, and each limb as languid . . . ah, sweet lords,
Bethink you!—poison-torture, try persuade
1040 The next refractory Molinist with that! . . .
Floundered thro' day and night, another day
And yet another night, and so at last,
As Lucifer kept falling to find hell,
Tumbled into the court-yard of an inn
1045 At the end, and fell on whom I thought to find,
Even Caponsacchi,—what part once was priest,
Cast to the winds now with the cassock-rags.
In cape and sword a cavalier confessed,
There stood he chiding dilatory grooms,
1050 Chafing that only horseflesh and no team
Of eagles would supply the last relay,

CP1868:made-up   1029| MS:floor   P1868:floor,   1030| MS:Imperishable place
devils   P1868:Imperishable tracery devils   1031| MS:gods   CP1868:gods,
1032-34| MS:hearth, for ever more./ Well   P1868:hearth. So much/ For the terrible effect of
threatening, Sirs!/ Well   1033-34| MS:§ ¶ §   1889a:§ no ¶ §   1889:§ no ¶; emended to
restore ¶; see Editorial Notes §   1035| MS:drenched and somewhat <> so;
P1868:drenched, somewhat   1889a:so.   1036| MS:And, set <> bid § followed by
illegible erasure §   P1868:Then, set   1037| MS:Started   P1868:I started
1038| MS:each <> languid. .ah, my § crossed out and replaced above by § sweet
1889a:eaeh § emended to § each § see Editorial Notes § <> languid . . . ah
1039| MS:you,—poison-torture   P1868:you!—poison-torture <> persuade,
CP1868:persuade   1041| MS:night and another   P1868:night, and another
CP1868:night, another   1044| MS:the Court yard <> Inn   P1868:court-yard <> inn
1045| MS:And the <> on him I found   P1868:At the <> on whom I thought to find,
1046| MS:part was priest of yore   P1868:part once was priest,   1047| MS:cassock-rags,
P1868:cassock-rags: 1889a:cassock-rags.   1048| MS:a Cavalier confessed   P1868:a

Whirl him along the league, the one post more
Between the couple and Rome and liberty.
'Twas dawn, the couple were rested in a sort,
1055 And though the lady, tired,—the tenderer sex,—
Still lingered in her chamber,—to adjust
The limp hair, look for any blush astray,—
She would descend in a twinkling,—"Have you out
The horses therefore!"
                              So did I find my wife.
1060 Is the case complete? Do your eyes here see with mine?
Even the parties dared deny no one
Point out of all these points.
                              What follows next?
"Why, that then was the time," you interpose,
"Or then or never, while the fact was fresh,
1065 To take the natural vengeance: there and thus
They and you,—somebody had stuck a sword
Beside you while he pushed you on your horse,—
'Twas requisite to slay the couple, Count!"
Just so my friends say. "Kill!" they cry in a breath,
1070 Who presently, when matters grow to a head
And I do kill the offending ones indeed,—
When crime of theirs, only surmised before,
Is patent, proved indisputably now,—
When remedy for wrong, untried at the time,
1075 Which law professes shall not fail a friend,
Is thrice tried now, found threefold worse than null,—
When what might turn to transient shade, who knows?
Solidifies into a blot which breaks
Hell's black off in pale flakes for fear of mine,—

cavalier confessed,   1052| MS:more, *P1868:*more   1054| *1872:*Twas § space for
apostrophe remains § *1889a:*'Twas   1058| MS:have *P1868:*twinkling,—"Have
1059| MS:therefore!" So *P1868:*therefore!" § ¶ § So   1062| MS:Point out § inserted
above § of all § inserted above § <>points. What *P1868:*points. § ¶ § What
1063| MS:interpose *P1868:*interpose,   1064| MS:fresh *P1868:*fresh,
1068| MS:couple, Count! *P1868:*couple, Count!"   1069| MS:say—"Kill" they
*P1868:*say—"Kill!" they *1889a:*say. "Kill!" they   1073| MS:Are patent and proved
*CP1868:*Is patent, proved   1075| MS:Law makes profession shall *P1868:*Which law
professes shall   1076| MS:Are thrice *P1868:*Is thrice   1077| MS:who knew?

1080　Then, when I claim and take revenge—"So rash?"
　　　They cry—"so little reverence for the law?"

　　　Listen, my masters, and distinguish here!
　　　At first, I called in law to act and help:
　　　Seeing I did so, "Why, 'tis clear," they cry,
1085　"You shrank from gallant readiness and risk,
　　　Were coward: the thing's inexplicable else."
　　　Sweet my lords, let the thing be! I fall flat,
　　　Play the reed, not the oak, to breath of man.
　　　Only inform my ignorance! Say I stand
1090　Convicted of the having been afraid,
　　　Proved a poltroon, no lion but a lamb,—
　　　Does that deprive me of my right of lamb
　　　And give my fleece and flesh to the first wolf?
　　　Are eunuchs, women, children, shieldless quite
1095　Against attack their own timidity tempts?
　　　Cowardice were misfortune and no crime!
　　　—Take it that way, since I am fallen so low
　　　I scarce dare brush the fly that blows my face,
　　　And thank the man who simply spits not there,—
1100　Unless the Court be generous, comprehend
　　　How one brought up at the very feet of law
　　　As I, awaits the grave Gamaliel's nod
　　　Ere he clench fist at outrage,—much less, stab!
　　　—How, ready enough to rise at the right time,
1105　I still could recognise no time mature

---

*P1868:*who knows?　　1080| 　MS:Now, when <> rash?　*P1868:*Then, when <> rash?"
1081–82| 　MS:§ no ¶ §　*P1868:*§ ¶ §　　1083| 　MS:first, truce § crossed out and replaced above
by § I called <> help,　*P1868:*help:　　1084| 　MS:And seeing <> so, "why 'tis clear," you
§ crossed out and replaced above by § they　*P1868:*Seeing <> so, "Why, 'tis　　1085| 　MS:I
shrank from the gallant's　*CP1868:*"You shrank from gallant　　1086| 　MS:Was a
coward,—the　*P1868:*Were coward: the　　1087| 　MS:lords let it be so! I　*P1868:*lords, let
the thing be! I　　1088| 　MS:reed not the oak to the breath of man:　*P1868:*reed, not the
oak, to breath of man.　　1089| 　MS:Only,—inform my ignorance, say　*P1868:*Only,
inform my ignorance! Say　*1889a:*Only inform　　1092| 　MS:of the right of a lamb
*P1868:*of my right of lamb　　1094| 　MS:women and children shieldless　*P1868:*women,
children, shieldless　　1096| 　MS:crime—　*P1868:*crime!　　1097| 　MS:Take <> way,—
since　*P1868:*—Take <> way, since　　1101| 　MS:of Law　*P1868:*of law
1102| 　MS:await　*P1868:*awaits　　1103| 　MS:Ere I clench <> stab—　*P1868:*Ere he
clench <> stab!　　1104| 　MS:How　*P1868:*—How　　1105| 　MS:I still could § last two
words inserted above § recognized § final *d* crossed out § that § crossed out and replaced above
by § no time as § crossed out § immature　*P1868:*recognise no time mature

Unsanctioned by a move o' the judgment-seat,
So, mute in misery, eyed my masters here
Motionless till the authoritative word
Pronounced amercement. There's the riddle solved:
¹¹¹⁰ This is just why I slew nor her nor him,
But called in law, law's delegate in the place,
And bade arrest the guilty couple, Sirs!
We had some trouble to do so—you have heard
They braved me,—he with arrogance and scorn,
¹¹¹⁵ She, with a volubility of curse,
A conversancy in the skill of tooth
And claw to make suspicion seem absurd,
Nay, an alacrity to put to proof
At my own throat my own sword, teach me so
¹¹²⁰ To try conclusions better the next time,—
Which did the proper service with the mob.
They never tried to put on mask at all:
Two avowed lovers forcibly torn apart,
Upbraid the tyrant as in a playhouse scene,
¹¹²⁵ Ay, and with proper clapping and applause
From the audience that enjoys the bold and free.
I kept still, said to myself, "There's law!" Anon
We searched the chamber where they passed the night,
Found what confirmed the worst was feared before,
¹¹³⁰ However needless confirmation now—
The witches' circle intact, charms undisturbed

---

¹¹⁰⁶| MS:on judgment-seat, *P1868:*o' the judgment-seat, ¹¹⁰⁷| MS:And § crossed out
and replaced above by § So, muting § altered to § mute in § inserted above §
misery knew § crossed out and replaced by § eyed my masters still § crossed out
and replaced by § here, *P1868:*misery, eyed <> here ¹¹⁰⁸| MS:Was dumb § illegible
word § § last three words crossed out and replaced above by § Reticent till law's § last three
words crossed out and replaced by three words § Motionless till the authoritative voice
§ crossed out § ¹¹⁰⁹| MS:Declaring the § last two words crossed out and replaced above
by § Pronounce <> solved! *P1868:*pronounced <> solved: ¹¹¹¹| MS:in Law, her
delegates *P1868:*law, law's delegates *CP1868:*delegate ¹¹¹²| MS:couple there
*P1868:*couple, Sirs! ¹¹¹⁵| MS:She with *P1868:*She, with ¹¹¹⁶| MS:conversancy
with § crossed out and replaced above by § in ¹¹²⁰⁻²²| MS:time./ They <> all,
*P1868:*time,—/ Which did the proper service with the mob./ They <> all:
¹¹²³| MS:lovers, forcibly *P1868:*lovers forcibly ¹¹²⁴| MS:Accusing fate § last two
words crossed out and replaced above by § Upbraiding the husband *P1868:*Upbraid the
tyrant as ¹¹²⁷| MS:myself, "There's Law *P1868:*myself, "There's law

That raised the spirit and succubus,—letters, to-wit,
Love-laden, each the bag o' the bee that bore
Honey from lily and rose to Cupid's hive,—
1135 Now, poetry in some rank blossom-burst,
Now, prose,—"Come here, go there, wait such a while,
He's at the villa, now he's back again:
We are saved, we are lost, we are lovers all the same!"
All in order, all complete,—even to a clue
1140 To the drowsiness that happed so opportune—
No mystery, when I read "Of all things, find
What wine Sir Jealousy decides to drink—
Red wine? Because a sleeping-potion, dust
Dropped into white, discolours wine and shows."

1145 —"Oh, but we did not write a single word!
Somebody forged the letters in our name!—"
Both in a breath protested presently.
Aha, Sacchetti again!—"Dame,"—quoth the Duke,
"What meaneth this epistle, counsel me,
1150 I pick from out thy placket and peruse,
Wherein my page averreth thou art white
And warm and wonderful 'twixt pap and pap?"
"Sir," laughed the Lady, " 'tis a counterfeit!
Thy page did never stroke but Dian's breast,
1155 The pretty hound I nurture for thy sake:

1132| MS:to-wit *P1868:*to-wit,   1133| MS:of *P1868:*o'   1134| MS:hive,
*P1868:*hive,—   1135| MS:blossom-burst *P1868:*blossom-burst,
1136| MS:prose,—come *P1868:*prose,—"Come   1137| MS:the Villa *P1868:*the villa
1138| MS:same. *P1868:*same!"   1141| MS:mystery when < > things find
*P1868:*mystery, when < > things, find   1142| MS:wine § followed by illegible word
altered to § Sir   1144| MS:discolours it and *P1868:*discolours wine and
1144-45| MS: § no ¶ § *P1868:* § ¶ §   1148| MS:again,—"Dame < > the spouse § crossed out
and replaced above by § Duke, *P1868:*again!—"Dame   1149| MS:What this epistle meaneth,
counsel *CP1868:*What meaneth this epistle, counsel   1150| MS:pick this § crossed out §
from out § inserted above § < > peruse *P1868:*peruse,   1153| MS:"Sir," quoth § crossed
out and replaced above by following word § laughed the Lady " 'tis a counterfeit,
*P1868:*counterfeit! *1872:*the Lady, " 'tis   1154| MS:breast *P1868:*breast,
1155| MS:§ written in margin following line 1154 § Hound thou didst § illegible word
follows § me with: § last five words crossed out and replaced above by § I nurture for thy sake:

To lie were losel,—by my fay, no more!"
And no more say I too, and spare the Court.

Ah, the Court! yes, I come to the Court's self;
Such the case, so complete in fact and proof,
1160   I laid at the feet of law,—there sat my lords,
Here sit they now, so may they ever sit
In easier attitude than suits my haunch!
In this same chamber did I bare my sores
O' the soul and not the body,—shun no shame,
1165   Shrink from no probing of the ulcerous part,
Since confident in Nature,—which is God,—
That she who, for wise ends, concocts a plague,
Curbs, at the right time, the plague's virulence too:
Law renovates even Lazarus,—cures me!
1170   Cæsar thou seekest? To Cæsar thou shalt go!
Cæsar's at Rome: to Rome accordingly!

The case was soon decided: both weights, cast
I' the balance, vibrate, neither kicks the beam,
Here away, there away, this now and now that.
1175   To every one o' my grievances law gave
Redress, could purblind eye but see the point.
The wife stood a convicted runagate
From house and husband,—driven to such a course

1156| MS:Some § written in margin preceding line § The § crossed out § lie of a § crossed out §
1157| MS:Enough, I § last two words crossed out and replaced above by § And no more say I
too—and <> the gravity of the § last three words crossed out § Court: P1868:too, and <>
Court.   1157–58| MS:§ no ¶ §   P1868:§ ¶ §   1158| MS:the Court! Yes   P1868:the
Court! yes   1159| MS:proof   1889a:proof,   1160| MS:of Law <> Lords,
P1868:of law <> lords,   1161| MS:Here sat § altered to § sit they then § crossed out and
replaced above by § now, here § crossed out and replaced above by § so   1163| MS:did I
strip,— § crossed out § bare my § inserted above § sores,   P1868:sores   1164| MS:Of
P1868:O'   1165| MS:part   P1868:part,   1167| MS:plague   P1868:plague,
1168| MS:Curbs, § last word written over illegible word § at <> time, curb § crossed out § the
plague's § inserted above §   1171| MS:at Rome; to   1872:at Rome: to
1172| MS:N.P. § marginal notation § The <> both sides § crossed out and replaced above by §
weights,   P1868:The   1173| MS:In the balance vibrate   CP1868:I' the balance, vibrate
1175| MS:of <> Law   P1868:o' <> law   1176| MS:the same.   CP1868:the point.
1177| MS:My § crossed out and replaced above by § The <> runaway § way crossed out and

By what she somehow took for cruelty,
1180 Oppression and imperilment of life—
Not that such things were, but that so they seemed:
Therefore, the end conceded lawful, (since
To save life there's no risk should stay our leap)
It follows that all means to the lawful end
1185 Are lawful likewise,—poison, theft and flight.
As for the priest's part, did he meddle or make,
Enough that he too thought life jeopardized;
Concede him then the colour charity
Casts on a doubtful course,—if blackish white
1190 Or whitish black, will charity hesitate?
What did he else but act the precept out,
Leave, like a provident shepherd, his safe flock
To follow the single lamb and strayaway?
Best hope so and think so,—that the ticklish time
1195 I' the carriage, the tempting privacy, the last
Somewhat ambiguous accident at the inn,
—All may bear explanation: may? then, must!
The letters,—do they so incriminate?
But what if the whole prove a prank o' the pen,
1200 Flight of the fancy, none of theirs at all,
Bred of the vapours of my brain belike,
Or at worst mere exercise of scholar's-wit
In the courtly Caponsacchi: verse, convict?
Did not Catullus write less seemly once?
1205 Yet *doctus* and unblemished he abides.
Wherefore so ready to infer the worst?
Still, I did righteously in bringing doubts
For the law to solve,—take the solution now!

replaced above by § gate   1179| MS:By mine she P1868:By what she   1186| MS:the
Priest's P1868:the priest's   1187| MS:jeopardised, P1868:jeopardised;
1889a:jeopardized;   1194| MS:Best think § crossed out and replaced
by § hope < > think so, and that P1868:think so,—that   1195| MS:In P1868:I'
1199| MS:of P1868:o'   1201| MS:vapours of your brain P1868:vapours of my brain
1202| MS:scholar's wit CP1868:scholar's-wit   1203| MS:verse, forsooth?
P1868:verse, convict?   1205| MS:doctus P1868:*doctus*   1208| MS:now.

"Seeing that the said associates, wife and priest,
1210 Bear themselves not without some touch of blame
—Else why the pother, scandal and outcry
Which trouble our peace and require chastisement?
We, for complicity in Pompilia's flight
And deviation, and carnal intercourse
1215 With the same, do set aside and relegate
The Canon Caponsacchi for three years
At Civita in the neighbourhood of Rome:
And we consign Pompilia to the care
Of a certain Sisterhood of penitents
1220 I' the city's self, expert to deal with such."
Word for word, there's your judgment! Read it, lords,
Re-utter your deliberate penalty
For the crime yourselves establish! Your award—
Who chop a man's right-hand off at the wrist
1225 For tracing with forefinger words in wine
O' the table of a drinking-booth that bear
Interpretation as they mocked the Church!
—Who brand a woman black between the breasts
For sinning by connection with a Jew:
1230 While for the Jew's self—pudency be dumb!
You mete out punishment such and such, yet so
Punish the adultery of wife and priest!
Take note of that, before the Molinists do,
And read me right the riddle, since right must be!

1235 While I stood rapt away with wonderment,
Voices broke in upon my mood and muse.
"Do you sleep?" began the friends at either ear,

*P1868:*now!   1209| MS:Seeing   *CP1868:*"Seeing   1210| MS:without
touch   *P1868:*without some touch   1212| MS:trouble the peace /
*P1868:*trouble our peace   1219| MS:sisterhood   *CP1868:*certain Sisterhood   1220| MS:In
< > such.   *CP1868:*"I' < > such."   1221| MS:it, Lords,   *P1868:*it, lords,
1224| MS:right hand   *P1868:*right-hand   1226| MS:On < > drinking booth   *P1868:*O'
< > drinking-booth   1228| MS:Who   *P1868:*—Who   1229| MS:a Jew,   *P1868:*a
Jew: 1230| MS:self, . . pudency is dumb.   *P1868:*self—pudency   *CP1868:*pudency be
dumb!   1232| MS:priest.   *P1868:*priest!   1234| MS:And counsel me the cause,
since cause must   *P1868:*And read me the riddle, since right must   1234-35| MS:§ ¶ §
P1868:§ no ¶ §   *1889:*§ no ¶; emended to restore ¶; see Editorial Notes §   1235| MS:rapt
awhile with thoughts like these, § last five words crossed out and replaced above by § away
with wonderment,   1236| MS:muse,   *P1868:*muse.   1237| MS:you hear?" began

"The case is settled,—you willed it should be so—
None of our counsel, always recollect!
1240 With law's award, budge! Back into your place!
Your betters shall arrange the rest for you.
We'll enter a new action, claim divorce:
Your marriage was a cheat themselves allow:
Your erred i' the person,—might have married thus
1245 Your sister or your daughter unaware.
We'll gain you, that way, liberty at least,
Sure of so much by law's own showing. Up
And off with you and your unluckiness—
Leave us to bury the blunder, sweep things smooth!"
1250 I was in humble frame of mind, be sure!
I bowed, betook me to my place again.
Station by station I retraced the road,
Touched at this hostel, passed this post-house by,
Where, fresh-remembered yet, the fugitives
1255 Had risen to the heroic stature: still—
"That was the bench they sat on,—there's the board
They took the meal at,—yonder garden-ground
They leaned across the gate of,"—ever a word
O' the Helen and the Paris, with "Ha! you're he,
1260 The . . . much-commiserated husband?" Step
By step, across the pelting, did I reach
Arezzo, underwent the archway's grin,
Traversed the length of sarcasm in the street,
Found myself in my horrible house once more,
1265 And after a colloquy . . . no word assists!

<>ear *P1868:* you sleep?'' began <>ear,   1240| MS:budge! Back, Sir, to your
*P1868:*budge! Back into your   1244| MS:in <>married so *P1868:*i' <>married thus
1245| MS:unaware: *CP1868:*unaware.   1246| MS:you that way liberty at least
*P1868:*you, that way, liberty at least,   1247| MS:showing,—so, up *CP1868:*showing.
Up   1249| MS:to hide § crossed out and replaced above by § built the shame
§ crossed out and replaced above by § and sweep *P1868:*blunder, sweep
1250| MS:mind by this— *CP1868:*mind, be sure!   1251| MS:blowed, left § crossed out §
betook <>again, *CP1868:*again.   1255| MS:stature, still in mind *P1868:*stature:
still—   1257| MS:at, yonder *CP1868:*at,—yonder   1258| MS:of,—ever
*P1868:*of,''—ever   1259| MS:Of <>with—"Ha,—you're *P1868:*O' <>with "Ha!
you're   1260| MS:The . . much-commiserated husband?"—Step *P1868:*husband?''
Step *1889a:* The . . . much-commiserated   1265| MS:And a colloquy . . no word
assists . . *P1868:*And after a colloquy . . no word assists! *1889a:*colloquy . . . no

With the mother and the brothers, stiffened me
Straight out from head to foot as dead man does,
And, thus prepared for life as he for hell,
Marched to the public Square and met the world.
1270 Apologize for the pincers, palliate screws?
Ply me with such toy-trifles, I entreat!
Trust who has tried both sulphur and sops-in-wine!

I played the man as I best might, bade friends
Put non-essentials by and face the fact.
1275 "What need to hang myself as you advise?
The paramour is banished,—the ocean's width,
Or the suburb's length,—to Ultima Thule, say,
Or Proxima Civitas, what's the odds of name
And place? He's banished, and the fact's the thing.
1280 Why should law banish innocence an inch?
Here's guilt then, what else do I care to know?
The adulteress lies imprisoned,—whether in a well
With bricks above and a snake for company,
Or tied by a garter to a bed-post,—much
1285 I mind what's little,—least's enough and to spare!
The little fillip on the coward's cheek
Serves as though crab-tree cudgel broke his pate.
Law has pronounced there's punishment, less or more:
And I take note o' the fact and use it thus—

---

^{1266|} MS:the Mother <> Brothers   *P1868:*mother <> brothers   ^{1267|} MS:Strait <>
as a dead   *P1868:*as dead   *1889a:*Straight   ^{1268|} MS:And thus <> for hell, . . what
would you have?   *P1868:*And, thus <> for life as he for hell,   ^{1269|} MS:public square
*CP1868:*public Square   ^{1270|} MS:Apologise   *1889a:*Apologize   ^{1271|} MS:Poke
away § last two words crossed out and replaced above by § Ply me with such § crossed out and
replaced by § your § crossed out and *such* restored §   *P1868:*Play   *CP1868:*Ply
^{1272|} MS:both. Pray you, a § period and following three words crossed out and replaced
above by dash and following two words § —sulphur and sops of § crossed out and replaced
above by § in wine!   *P1868:*sulphur and sops-in-wine!   ^{1273|} MS:bade my friends
*P1868:*bade friends   ^{1276|} MS:The Paramour is banished,—banished the
*P1868:*paramour is banished,—the   ^{1278|} MS:of the § crossed out § name
^{1285|} MS:little when least's <> spare.   *P1868:*little,—least's spare!
^{1288|} MS:punishment less or more,   *P1868:*punishment, less or more: ^{1289|} MS:of

¹²⁹⁰ For the first flaw in the original bond,
I claim release. My contract was to wed
The daughter of Pietro and Violante. Both
Protest they never had a child at all.
Then I have never made a contract: good!
¹²⁹⁵ Cancel me quick the thing pretended one.
I shall be free. What matter if hurried over
The harbour-boom by a great favouring tide,
Or the last of a spent ripple that lifts and leaves?
The Abate is about it. Laugh who wins!
¹³⁰⁰ You shall not laugh me out of faith in law!
I listen, through all your noise, to Rome!"

                                    Rome spoke.

In three months letters thence admonished me,
"Your plan for the divorce is all mistake.
It would hold, now, had you, taking thought to wed
¹³⁰⁵ Rachel of the blue eye and golden hair,
Found swarth-skinned Leah cumber couch next day:
But Rachel, blue-eyed golden-haired aright,
Proving to be only Laban's child, not Lot's,
Remains yours all the same for ever more.
¹³¹⁰ No whit to the purpose is your plea: you err
I' the person and the quality—nowise
In the individual,—that's the case in point!
You go to the ground,— are met by a cross-suit
For separation, of the Rachel here,
¹³¹⁵ From bed and board,—she is the injured one,
You did the wrong and have to answer it.
As for the circumstance of imprisonment
And colour it lends to this your new attack,

*P1868:*o'   ¹²⁹⁰| MS:bond *P1868:*bond,   ¹²⁹⁷| MS:tide *P1868:*tide,
¹²⁹⁸| MS:lifts me and *P1868:*lifts and   ¹³⁰⁰| MS:in Law! *P1868:*in law!
¹³⁰¹| MS:listen through <> noise to Rome! / Rome spoke. *P1868:*listen, through <>
noise, to Rome!" / Rome spoke.   ¹³⁰²| MS:months, Brother Paul § last two words
crossed out and replaced above by two words § letters thence *P1868:*months letters
¹³⁰³| MS:mistake— *CP1868:*mistake.   ¹³⁰⁵| MS:hair *P1868:*hair,
¹³⁰⁸| MS:Proved to be § last two words inserted above § only *P1868:*Proving to be only
¹³⁰⁹| MS:same and forever *P1868:*same for ever   ¹³¹⁰| MS:plea: no fault § last two
words crossed out and replaced above by two words § you err   ¹³¹¹| MS:In *P1868:*I'
¹³¹⁴| MS:separation of your injured wife § last three words crossed out and replaced above by
three words § the Rachel here *P1868:*separation, of <> here,   ¹³¹⁸| MS:And the

Never fear, that point is considered too!
¹³²⁰ The durance is already at an end;
The convent-quiet preyed upon her health,
She is transferred now to her parents' house
—No-parents, when that cheats and plunders you,
But parentage again confessed in full,
¹³²⁵ When such confession pricks and plagues you more—
As now—for, this their house is not the house
In Via Vittoria wherein neighbours' watch
Might incommode the freedom of your wife,
But a certain villa smothered up in vines
¹³³⁰ At the town's edge by the gate i' the Pauline Way,
Out of eye-reach, out of ear-shot, little and lone,
Whither a friend,—at Civita, we hope,
A good half-dozen-hours' ride off,—might, some eve,
Betake himself, and whence ride back, some morn,
¹³³⁵ Nobody the wiser: but be that as it may,
Do not afflict your brains with trifles now.
You have still three suits to manage, all and each
Ruinous truly should the event play false.
It is indeed the likelier so to do,
¹³⁴⁰ That brother Paul, your single prop and stay,
After a vain attempt to bring the Pope
To set aside procedures, sit himself
And summarily use prerogative,
Afford us the infallible finger's tact

---

colour *CP1868:*And colour   ^{1319|} MS:too. *P1868:*too!   ^{1321|} MS:Convent-quiet
*P1868:*convent-quiet   ^{1323|} MS:—No-parents,—when that plagues § crossed out and
replaced above by § cheats *P1868:*—No-parents, when   ^{1324|} MS:parentage back
§ crossed out § again and ten times more § last four words crossed out and replaced above by §
confessed . . . in full, *P1868:*confessed in full,   ^{1326|} MS:for this *P1868:*for, this
^{1327|} MS:neighbours' eye § crossed out and replaced above by § watch   ^{1329|} MS:certain
little § crossed out § Villa, smothered *P1868:*villa smothered   ^{1330|} MS:in the Pauline
way, *P1868:*i' the Pauline Way,   ^{1332|} MS:at Civita we hope *P1868:*at Civita, we
hope,   ^{1333|} MS:And § crossed out § a § altered to § A <> six § crossed out and replaced
above by § half-dozen hours' ride distant § crossed out and replaced above by § off,—
*CP1868:*half-dozen-hours'   ^{1334|} MS:himself, and § inserted above line § whence slink
away § last two words crossed out and replaced above by § back *P1868:*whence ride back
^{1335|} MS:And § crossed out § nobody § altered to § Nobody the § crossed out and then restored §
wiser   ^{1337|} MS:have still § inserted above § three   ^{1338|} MS:event be wrong § last
two words crossed out and replaced above by two words § so prove. § last two words and

¹³⁴⁵ To disentwine your tangle of affairs,
Paul,—finding it moreover past his strength
To stem the irruption, bear Rome's ridicule
Of . . . since friends must speak . . . to be round with you . . .
Of the old outwitted husband, wronged and wroth,
¹³⁵⁰ Pitted against a brace of juveniles—
A brisk priest who is versed in Ovid's art
More than his Summa, and a gamesome wife
Able to act Corinna without book,
Beside the waggish parents who played dupes
¹³⁵⁵ To dupe the duper—(and truly divers scenes
Of the Arezzo palace, tickle rib
And tease eye till the tears come, so we laugh;
Nor wants the shock at the inn its comic force,
And then the letters and poetry—*merum sal!*)
¹³⁶⁰ —Paul, finally, in such a state of things,
After a brief temptation to go jump
And join the fishes in the Tiber, drowns
Sorrow another and a wiser way:
House and goods, he has sold all off, is gone,
¹³⁶⁵ Leaves Rome,—whether for France or Spain, who knows?
Or Britain almost divided from our orb.
You have lost him anyhow."
                    Now,—I see my lords
Shift in their seat,—would I could do the same!
They probably please expect my bile was moved
¹³⁷⁰ To purpose, nor much blame me: now, they judge,

---

period crossed out §   ¹³⁴⁷| MS:irruption of Rome's   *P1868:*irruption, bear Rome's
¹³⁴⁸| MS:speak . . to <> you. .   *1889a:*speak . . . to <> you . . .
¹³⁴⁹| MS:husband wronged   *P1868:*husband, wronged   ¹³⁵⁰| MS:juveniles
*P1868:*juveniles—   ¹³⁵¹| MS:who has studied § last two words crossed out and replaced
above by three words § is versed in   ¹³⁵²| MS:than A-Kempis § crossed out and replaced
above by two words § his Summa <> a sprightly § crossed out and replaced by § gamesome
¹³⁵⁴| MS:dupe   *P1868:*dupes   ¹³⁵⁶| MS:the Arezzo Palace tickle   *P1868:*the Arezzo
palace, tickle   ¹³⁵⁷| MS:teaze the § erased § eye <> laugh—   *CP1868:*tease <> laugh;
¹³⁵⁹| MS:poetry—*merum*   *P1868:*poetry—*merum*   ¹³⁶⁰| MS:—Paul finally
P1868:—Paul, finally   ¹³⁶⁴| MS:all § followed by illegible erasure § off
¹³⁶⁹| MS:And § crossed out and replaced above by § They <> please to expect   *P1868:*please
expect   ¹³⁷⁰| MS:purpose nor without reason § last two words crossed out and replaced
above by three words § much blame me: now, you conceive, § last two words crossed out and

53

The fiery titillation urged my flesh
Break through the bonds. By your pardon, no, sweet Sirs!
I got such missives in the public place;
When I sought home,—with such news, mounted stair
1375 And sat at last in the sombre gallery,
('Twas Autumn, the old mother in bed betimes,
Having to bear that cold, the finer-frame
Of her daughter-in-law had found intolerable—
The brother, walking misery away
1380 O' the mountain-side with dog and gun belike)
As I supped, ate the coarse bread, drank the wine
Weak once, now acrid with the toad's-head-squeeze,
My wife's bestowment,—I broke silence thus:
"Let me, a man, manfully meet the fact,
1385 Confront the worst o' the truth, end, and have peace!
I am irremediably beaten here,—
The gross illiterate vulgar couple,—bah!
Why, they have measured forces, mastered mine,
Made me their spoil and prey from first to last.
1390 They have got my name,—'tis nailed now fast to theirs,
The child or changeling is anyway my wife;
Point by point as they plan they execute,
They gain all, and I lose all—even to the lure
That led to loss,—they have the wealth again
1395 They hazarded awhile to hook me with,
Have caught the fish and find the bait entire:
They even have their child or changeling back
To trade with, turn to account a second time.
The brother presumably might tell a tale
1400 Or give a warning,—he, too, flies the field,

---

replaced above by two words § they judge, *P1868:*purpose, nor ¹³⁷¹| MS:The
titillation urged flesh break the bonds. *P1868:*The fiery titillation urged my
flesh ¹³⁷²| MS:By your pardon, no, lords! Nowise moved my bile. *P1868:*Break
through the bonds. By < > no, sweet Sirs! ¹³⁷⁵| MS:sombre room alone
*P1868:*sombre gallery, ¹³⁷⁷| MS:cold the *P1868:*cold, the ¹³⁸⁰| MS:On
*P1868:*O' ¹³⁸¹| MS:bread, and § inserted above § drank the weak § crossed out § wine
*P1868:*bread, drank ¹³⁸²| MS:toad's-head-squeeze *P1868:*toad's-head-squeeze,
¹³⁸³| MS:Of my wedded § crossed out § wife's < > I began § crossed out and replaced above by
three words and colon § broke silence thus: *P1868:*My wife's ¹³⁸⁵| MS:of *P1868:*o'
¹³⁸⁸| MS:force and mastered *P1868:*forces, mastered ¹³⁹⁰| MS:have gained § crossed
out and replaced above by § got ¹³⁹¹| MS:wife, *P1868:*wife; ¹³⁹⁹| MS:brother,
presumably *1889a:*brother presumably ¹⁴⁰⁰| MS:too flies *P1868:*too, flies

And with him vanish help and hope of help.
They have caught me in the cavern where I fell,
Covered my loudest cry for human aid
With this enormous paving-stone of shame.
1405 Well, are we demigods or merely clay?
Is success still attendant on desert?
Is this, we live on, heaven and the final state,
Or earth which means probation to the end?
Why claim escape from man's predestined lot
1410 Of being beaten and baffled?—God's decree,
In which I, bowing bruised head, acquiesce.
One of us Franceschini fell long since
I' the Holy Land, betrayed, tradition runs,
To Paynims by the feigning of a girl
1415 He rushed to free from ravisher, and found
Lay safe enough with friends in ambuscade
Who flayed him while she clapped her hands and laughed:
Let me end, falling by a like device.
It will not be so hard. I am the last
1420 O' my line which will not suffer any more.
I have attained to my full fifty years,
(About the average of us all, 'tis said,
Though it seems longer to the unlucky man)
—Lived through my share of life; let all end here,
1425 Me and the house and grief and shame at once.
Friends my informants,—I can bear your blow!"
And I believe 'twas in no unmeet match
For the stoic's mood, with something like a smile,
That, when morose December roused me next,
1430 I took into my hand, broke seal to read
The new epistle from Rome. "All to no use!
Whate'er the turn next injury take," smiled I,

1402| MS:the pitfall where I lie, *P1868:*the cavern where I fell, 1407| MS:this we live
on Heaven and the happy state *P1868:*this, we live on, heaven and the final state,
1409| MS:claim exc § crossed out and replaced above by § escape. 1411| MS:bowing a
bruised *P1868:*bowing bruised 1413| MS:betrayed, so runs the tale, *P1868:*betrayed,
tradition runs, 1416| MS:Was safe *P1868:*Lay safe 1418| MS:end falling
*CP1868:*end, falling 1420| MS:Of my race which *CP1868:*O' my line which
1422| MS:About *P1868:*(About 1423| MS:man, *P1868:*man) 1424| MS:Lived
P1868:—Lived 1425| MS:and my § crossed out and replaced above by § the <> and the
grief *P1868:*and grief 1432| MS:Whatever the turn this injury take" smiled I

"Here's one has chosen his part and knows his cue.
I am done with, dead now; strike away, good friends!
1435 Are the three suits decided in a trice?
Against me,—there's no question! How does it go?
Is the parentage of my wife demonstrated
Infamous to her wish? Parades she now
Loosed of the cincture that so irked the loin?
1440 Is the last penny extracted from my purse
To mulct me for demanding the first pound
Was promised in return for value paid?
Has the priest, with nobody to court beside,
Courted the Muse in exile, hitched my hap
1445 Into a rattling ballad-rhyme which, bawled
At tavern-doors, wakes rapture everywhere,
And helps cheap wine down throat this Christmas time,
Beating the bagpipes? Any or all of these!
As well, good friends, you cursed my palace here
1450 To its old cold stone face,—stuck your cap for crest
Over the shield that's extant in the Square,—
Or spat on the statue's cheek, the impatient world
Sees cumber tomb-top in our family church:
Let him creep under covert as I shall do,
1455 Half below-ground already indeed. Good-bye!
My brothers are priests, and childless so; that's well—
And, thank God most for this, no child leave I—
None after me to bear till his heart break
The being a Franceschini and my son!"

1460 "Nay," said the letter, "but you have just that!

---

*P1868:*Whate'er the turn next injury take," smiled I,   1433| MS:I have my § last three
words crossed out and replaced above by § Here's one has chosen his <> knows my § crossed
out and replaced by § his   1436| MS:question: how   *P1868:*question! How
1441| MS:To pay § crossed out and replaced above by § mulct me   1443| MS:the Priest
*P1868:*the priest   1444| MS:the Muse at Civi § last two words crossed out and replaced
above by two words § in exile   1445| MS:which bawled   *P1868:*which, bawled
1446| MS:At Tavern-doors wakes   *P1868:*tavern-doors, wakes   1448| MS:these,
*P1868:*these!   1451| MS:the household coat § last two words crossed out and replaced
above by following word § shield that shown you § last two words crossed out and replaced
above by § 's extant <> the square,—   *P1868:*the Square,—   1452| MS:cheek, that
§ over what appears an erasure § after age   *P1868:*cheek, the impatient world
1455| MS:below ground <> Good bye!   *P1868:*below-ground   *1868:*Good-bye!
1460| MS:"Nay" said the letter "But you do leave just   *P1868:*"Nay," said the letter, "but

56

A babe, your veritable son and heir—
Lawful,—'tis only eight months since your wife
Left you,—so, son and heir, your babe was born
Last Wednesday in the villa,—you see the cause
1465   For quitting Convent without beat of drum,
Stealing a hurried march to this retreat
That's not so savage as the Sisterhood
To slips and stumbles: Pietro's heart is soft,
Violante leans to pity's side,—the pair
1470   Ushered you into life a bouncing boy:
And he's already hidden away and safe
From any claim on him you mean to make—
They need him for themselves,—don't fear, they know
The use o' the bantling,—the nerve thus laid bare
1475   To nip at, new and nice, with finger-nail!"

Then I rose up like fire, and fire-like roared.
What, all is only beginning not ending now?
The worm which wormed its way from skin through flesh
To the bone and there lay biting, did its best,—
1480   What, it goes on to scrape at the bone's self,
Will wind to inmost marrow and madden me?
There's to be yet my representative,
Another of the name shall keep displayed
The flag with the ordure on it, brandish still
1485   The broken sword has served to stir a jakes?
Who will he be, how will you call the man?
A Franceschini,—when who cut my purse,
Filched my name, hemmed me round, hustled me hard

---

you have just   1461| MS:A son and heir § last four words crossed out and replaced above
by four words § A babe, your veritable   1464| MS:the Villa   *P1868:*the villa
1465| MS:drum   *P1868:*drum,   1474| MS:of the bantling,—the § written over a word
now illegible § nerve   *P1868:*o'   1476| MS:roared—   *P1868:*roared.
1477| MS:"What   *P1868:*What   1478| MS:the snake § crossed out and replaced above
by § worm   1479| MS:best,   *1889a:*best,—   1480| MS:self   *P1868:*self,
1481| MS:wind its way § last two words crossed out § to the inmost § inserted above line §
*CP1868:*to inmost   1483| MS:of my § crossed out and replaced above by § the
1485| MS:to bolt a   *P1868:*to stir a   1486| MS:man—   *P1868:*man?   1487| MS:A
Franceschini, when   *P1868:*A Franceschini,—when   1488| MS:round, and § crossed

As rogues at a fair some fool they strip i' the midst,
1490 When these count gains, vaunt pillage presently:—
But a Caponsacchi, oh, be very sure!
When what demands its tribute of applause
Is the cunning and impudence o' the pair of cheats,
The lies and lust o' the mother, and the brave
1495 Bold carriage of the priest, worthily crowned
By a witness to his feat i' the following age,—
And how this three-fold cord could hook and fetch
And land leviathan that king of pride!
Or say, by some mad miracle of chance,
1500 Is he indeed my flesh and blood, this babe?
Was it because fate forged a link at last
Betwixt my wife and me, and both alike
Found we had henceforth some one thing to love,
Was it when she could damn my soul indeed
1505 She unlatched door, let all the devils o' the dark
Dance in on me to cover her escape?
Why then, the surplusage of disgrace, the spilth
Over and above the measure of infamy,
Failing to take effect on my coarse flesh
1510 Seasoned with scorn now, saturate with shame,—
Is saved to instil on and corrode the brow,

out § hustled § illegible word §　　1489| MS:in the midst　P1868:i' the midst,
1490| MS:presently:　P1868:presently:—　　1491| MS:oh be very sure,　P1868:oh, be very
sure!　　1493| MS:and the § crossed out § impudence of　P1868:o'　　1494| MS:The lies
§ inserted above § And <> of　P1868:and <> o'　　1496| MS:in　CP1868:i'
1498| MS:that King of pride.　P1868:king of pride!　　1501| MS:because a link
§ indication that last two words are to be transposed to follow forged § was
§ crossed out and replaced above by § fate forged at　　1503| MS:Found at last
§ last two words crossed out § we had henceforth § inserted above §　　1504| MS:it
then § crossed out § when <> indeed　CP1868:indeed, § comma apparently added and then
crossed out §　　1505| MS:unlatched the door　P1868:unlatched door　　1506| MS:me
and § crossed out and replaced above by § to　　1507| MS:of shame § crossed out and
replaced above by § disgrace　　1508| MS:of agony § crossed out § infamy　P1868:infamy,
1509| MS:coarse clay § crossed out § flesh　　1510| MS:with venom § crossed out and
replaced above by § slander § crossed out and replaced by § scorn now, and § crossed out §
saturate <> shame,　P1868:shame,—　　1511| MS:brow　P1868:brow,

The baby-softness of my first-born child—
The child I had died to see though in a dream,
The child I was bid strike out for, beat the wave
1515 And baffle the tide of troubles where I swam,
So I might touch shore, lay down life at last
At the feet so dim and distant and divine
Of the apparition, as 'twere Mary's Babe
Had held, through night and storm, the torch aloft,—
1520 Born now in very deed to bear this brand
On forehead and curse me who could not save!
Rather be the town talk true, square's jest, street's jeer
True, my own inmost heart's confession true,
And he the priest's bastard and none of mine!
1525 Ay, there was cause for flight, swift flight and sure!
The husband gets unruly, breaks all bounds
When he encounters some familiar face,
Fashion of feature, brow and eyes and lips
Where he least looked to find them,—time to fly!
1530 This bastard then, a nest for him is made,
As the manner is of vermin, in my flesh:
Shall I let the filthy pest buzz, flap and sting,
Busy at my vitals and, nor hand nor foot
Lift, but let be, lie still and rot resigned?
1535 No, I appeal to God,—what says Himself,
How lessons Nature when I look to learn?
Why, that I am alive, am still a man
With brain and heart and tongue and right-hand too—
Nay, even with friends, in such a cause as this,

1512| MS:And § crossed out and replaced above by § The   1518| MS:babe 1889a:'twere
Mary's Babe   1521| MS:On the forehead P1868:On forehead   1522| MS:town-talk
true, the stree § last two words crossed out and replaced above by § square's P1868:true,
Square's 1889a:town talk true, square's   1524| MS:And he's priest's, bastard < >
mine,— P1868:priest's bastard < > mine! 1889a:And he the   1525| MS:sure,
P1868:sure!   1528| MS:feature, brow and § last two words inserted above § eyes and lips
and ch § last two words crossed out §   1529| MS:look P1868:looked
1531| MS:flesh— 1889a:flesh: 1534| MS:Lift but P1868:Lift, but   1535| MS:says
the Book § last two words crossed out and replaced above by § Himself,
1536| MS:lessons nature P1868:lessons Nature   1538| MS:right hand P1868:right-hand

¹⁵⁴⁰ To right me if I fail to take my right.
No more of law; a voice beyond the law
Enters my heart, *Quis est pro Domino?*

Myself, in my own Vittiano, told the tale
To my own serving-people summoned there:
¹⁵⁴⁵ Told the first half of it, scarce heard to end
By judges who got done with judgment quick
And clamoured to go execute her 'hest—
Who cried "Not one of us that dig your soil
And dress your vineyard, prune your olive-trees,
¹⁵⁵⁰ But would have brained the man debauched our wife,
And staked the wife whose lust allured the man,
And paunched the Duke, had it been possible,
Who ruled the land yet barred us such revenge!"
I fixed on the first whose eyes caught mine, some four
¹⁵⁵⁵ Resolute youngsters with the heart still fresh,
Filled my purse with the residue o' the coin
Uncaught-up by my wife whom haste made blind,
Donned the first rough and rural garb I found,
Took whatsoever weapon came to hand,
¹⁵⁶⁰ And out we flung and on we ran or reeled
Romeward. I have no memory of our way,
Only that, when at intervals the cloud
Of horror about me opened to let in life,
I listened to some song in the ear, some snatch
¹⁵⁶⁵ Of a legend, relic of religion, stray
Fragment of record very strong and old
Of the first conscience, the anterior right,

---

^{1540|} MS:fail to take my § last two words inserted above line § ^{1541|} MS:of the Law; a
*P1868:*of law; a ^{1542|} MS:heart, Quis est pro Domino? *P1868:*heart, *Quis est pro
Domino?* ^{1542–43|} MS:§ no ¶ § *P1868:*§ ¶ § ^{1545|} MS:scarce was heard
*P1868:*scarce heard ^{1547|} MS:hest— *P1868:*'hest— ^{1548|} MS:us who till
§ crossed out and replaced above by § dig your ground § crossed out and replaced above by §
soil *P1868:*us that dig ^{1552|} MS:possible *P1868:*possible, ^{1553|} MS:land and
§ crossed out and replaced above by § yet <> revenge." *P1868:*land, yet <> revenge!"
*1889a:*land yet ^{1554|} MS:I took § crossed out and replaced above by two words §
fixed on <> four, *1889a:*four ^{1556|} MS:of the § inserted above § *P1868:*o'
^{1557|} MS:Uncaught up <> wife when haste *P1868:*Uncaught-up <> wife whom haste
^{1561|} MS:Romeward, I *1889a:*Romeward. I ^{1562|} MS:that when *P1868:*that, when
^{1563|} MS:life *P1868:*life, ^{1566|} MS:Scrap § crossed out and replaced above by §

60

The God's-gift to mankind, impulse to quench
The antagonistic spark of hell and tread
1570   Satan and all his malice into dust,
Declare to the world the one law, right is right.
Then the cloud re-encompassed me, and so
I found myself, as on the wings of winds,
Arrived: I was at Rome on Christmas Eve.

1575   Festive bells—everywhere the Feast o' the Babe,
Joy upon earth, peace and good will to man!
I am baptized. I started and let drop
The dagger. "Where is it, His promised peace?"
Nine days o' the Birth-Feast did I pause and pray
1580   To enter into no temptation more.
I bore the hateful house, my brother's once,
Deserted,—let the ghost of social joy
Mock and make mouths at me from empty room
And idle door that missed the master's step,—
1585   Bore the frank wonder of incredulous eyes,
As my own people watched without a word,
Waited, from where they huddled round the hearth
Black like all else, that nod so slow to come.
I stopped my ears even to the inner call
1590   Of the dread duty, only heard the song
"Peace upon earth," saw nothing but the face
O' the Holy Infant and the halo there
Able to cover yet another face
Behind it, Satan's which I else should see.
1595   But, day by day, joy waned and withered off:
The Babe's face, premature with peak and pine,
Sank into wrinkled ruinous old age,
Suffering and death, then mist-like disappeared,

Fragment   1568| MS:The God's gift *P1868:*The God's-gift   1575| MS:Christmas
Eve,—everywhere < > of § next two words written above but without indication where they
are to go § festive bells *P1868:*Festive bells—everywhere < > o'   1576| MS:Joy on the
earth *P1868:*Joy upon earth   1577| MS:baptised *P1868:*baptized   1578| MS:it,
the § crossed out and replaced above by § his *P1868:*it, His   1579| MS:of *P1868:*o'
1581| MS:the horrible house *P1868:*the hateful house   1585| MS:eyes *P1868:*eyes,
1586| MS:word *P1868:*word,   1588| MS:come— *1889a:*come.   1590| MS:duty,
heard only the angel's song *P1868:*only the song *1872:*duty, only heard the
1592| MS:Of *P1868:*O'   1595| MS:off, *P1868:*off: 1596| MS:The babe's
*CP1868:*The Babe's   1598| MS:§ crowded between lines 1597 and 1599 §

And showed only the Cross at end of all,
1600 Left nothing more to interpose 'twixt me
And the dread duty: for the angels' song,
"Peace upon earth," louder and louder pealed
"O Lord, how long, how long be unavenged?"
On the ninth day, this grew too much for man.
1605 I started up—"Some end must be!" At once,
Silence: then, scratching like a death-watch-tick,
Slowly within my brain was syllabled,
"One more concession, one decisive way
And but one, to determine thee the truth,—
1610 This way, in fine, I whisper in thy ear:
Now doubt, anon decide, thereupon act!"

"That is a way, thou whisperest in my ear!
I doubt, I will decide, then act," said I—
Then beckoned my companions: "Time is come!"

1615 And so, all yet uncertain save the will
To do right, and the daring aught save leave
Right undone, I did find myself at last
I' the dark before the villa with my friends,
And made the experiment, the final test,
1620 Ultimate chance that ever was to be
For the wretchedness inside. I knocked, pronounced
The name, the predetermined touch for truth,
"What welcome for the wanderer? Open straight—"
To the friend, physician, friar upon his rounds,

1601-4| MS:duty,—louder and louder pealed/ "Shall sin's work ever thus be managed?"/
On <> day this <> man, *P1868*:duty,—for the angel's song,/ "Peace upon earth" louder
<> / <> unavenged?"/ On <> day, this <> man *CP1868*:earth," louder <> / "O
Lord, how long, how long be unavenged?"/ <> man.   1605| MS:be!" At once, § over
illegible erasure §   1606| MS:death-watch tick, *P1868*:death-watch-tick,
1607| MS:Plainly within *P1868*:Slowly within   1608| MS:One *P1868*:"One
1609| MS:one to <> truth, *P1868*:one, to <> truth,—   1610| MS:way in fine I
P1868:way, in fine, I   1611-12| MS:§ no ¶ § *P1868*:§ ¶ §   1612| MS:§ crowded
between lines 1611 and 1613 § ear— *P1868*:ear!   1614| MS:companions. "Time is
come—" *P1868*:companions: "Time is come!"   1615| MS:N.P. § marginal notation §
1616| MS:right and *P1868*:right, and   1618| MS:In <> Villa *P1868*:I' <> villa
1621| MS:knocked—pronounced *1889a*:knocked, pronounced   1623| MS:straight—

Traveller belated, beggar lame and blind?
No, but—"to Caponsacchi!" And the door
Opened.

          And then,—why, even then, I think,
I' the minute that confirmed my worst of fears,
Surely,—I pray God that I think aright!—
1630 Had but Pompilia's self, the tender thing
Who once was good and pure, was once my lamb
And lay in my bosom, had the well-known shape
Fronted me in the door-way,—stood there faint
With the recent pang perhaps of giving birth
1635 To what might, though by miracle, seem my child,—
Nay more, I will say, had even the aged fool
Pietro, the dotard, in whom folly and age
Wrought, more than enmity or malevolence,
To practise and conspire against my peace,—
1640 Had either of these but opened, I had paused.
But it was she the hag, she that brought hell
For a dowry with her to her husband's house,
She the mock-mother, she that made the match
And married me to perdition, spring and source
1645 O' the fire inside me that boiled up from heart
To brain and hailed the Fury gave it birth,—
Violante Comparini, she it was,
With the old grin amid the wrinkles yet,
Opened: as if in turning from the Cross,
1650 With trust to keep the sight and save my soul,
I had stumbled, first thing, on the serpent's head
Coiled with a leer at foot of it.
                  There was the end!
Then was I rapt away by the impulse, one

---

*P1868:*straight—"　　1625| 　MS:blind?— 　*1889a:*blind?　　1626| 　MS:but—to
Caponsacchi! And 　*P1868:*but—"to Caponsacchi!" And　　1627| 　MS:why even
*P1868:*why, even　　1628| 　MS:In <> fears 　*P1868:*I' <> fears,　　1629| 　MS:Surely . .
I <> aright . . 　*P1868:*Surely,—I <> aright!—　　1630| 　MS:Had poor § crossed out and
replaced above by § but　　1631| 　MS:my wife 　*P1868:*my lamb　　1632| 　MS:Had lain
§ last two words crossed out and replaced above by two words § And lay　　1634| 　MS:pang,
perhaps, of 　*1889a:*pang perhaps of　　1638| 　MS:Wrought more <> malevolence
*P1868:*Wrought, more <> malevolence,　　1639| 　MS:practice 　*1889a:*practise
1644| 　MS:perdition, she, § word and comma crossed out § spring and § inserted above § source
1645| 　MS:Of <> me, that 　*P1868:*O' <> me that　　1652| 　MS:at the foot of it. There

Immeasurable everlasting wave of a need
1655   To abolish that detested life. 'Twas done:
You know the rest and how the folds o' the thing,
Twisting for help, involved the other two
More or less serpent-like: how I was mad,
Blind, stamped on all, the earth-worms with the asp,
1660   And ended so.

                    You came on me that night,
Your officers of justice,—caught the crime
In the first natural frenzy of remorse?
Twenty miles off, sound sleeping as a child
On a cloak i' the straw which promised shelter first,
1665   With the bloody arms beside me,—was it not so?
Wherefore not? Why, how else should I be found?
I was my own self, had my sense again,
My soul safe from the serpents. I could sleep:
Indeed and, dear my lords, I shall sleep now,
1670   Spite of my shoulder, in five minutes' space,
When you dismiss me, having truth enough!
It is but a few days are passed, I find,
Since this adventure. Do you tell me, four?
Then the dead are scarce quiet where they lie,
1675   Old Pietro, old Violante, side by side
At the church Lorenzo,—oh, they know it well!
So do I. But my wife is still alive,
Has breath enough to tell her story yet,
Her way, which is not mine, no doubt at all.
1680   And Caponsacchi, you have summoned him,—
Was he so far to send for? Not at hand?

<> end. *P1868:*at foot of it. § ¶ § There <> end!   1654| MS:everlasting fire of a will
*P1868:*everlasting wave of a need   1656| MS:of the thing *P1868:*o' the thing,
1657| MS:help involved *P1868:*help, involved   1658| MS:serpent-like and I
*P1868:*serpent-like: how I   1659| MS:all, those earth-worms *P1868:*all, the
earth-worms   1660| MS:so. You *P1868:*so. § ¶ § You   1661| *P1868:*crime #followed
by punctuation illegibly crossed out §   1662| MS:remorse,— *P1868:*remorse?
1663| MS:Thirty miles *P1868:*Twenty miles   1664| MS:in *P1868:*i'
1668| MS:With my <> sleep. *CP1868:*My <> sleep: 1669| MS:now *P1868:*now,
1670| MS:space *P1868:*space,   1671| MS:enough. *P1868:*enough!
1672| MS:days ago, I *P1868:*days are passed, I   1673| MS:From this *CP1868:*Since
this   1674| MS:lie *P1868:*lie,   1675| MS:old Violante, at the church § last three
words crossed out § side by side   1681| MS:He, as is right will § last five words crossed

I thought some few o' the stabs were in his heart,
Or had not been so lavish: less had served.
Well, he too tells his story,—florid prose
¹⁶⁸⁵ As smooth as mine is rough. You see, my lords,
There will be a lying intoxicating smoke
Born of the blood,—confusion probably,—
For lies breed lies—but all that rests with you!
The trial is no concern of mine; with me
¹⁶⁹⁰ The main of the care is over: I at least
Recognize who took that huge burthen off,
Let me begin to live again. I did
God's bidding and man's duty, so, breathe free;
Look you to the rest! I heard Himself prescribe,
¹⁶⁹⁵ That great Physician, and dared lance the core
Of the bad ulcer; and the rage abates,
I am myself and whole now: I prove cured
By the eyes that see, the ears that hear again,
The limbs that have relearned their youthful play,
¹⁷⁰⁰ The healthy taste of food and feel of clothes
And taking to our common life once more,
All that now urges my defence from death.
The willingness to live, what means it else?
Before,—but let the very action speak!
¹⁷⁰⁵ Judge for yourselves, what life seemed worth to me
Who, not by proxy but in person, pitched
Head-foremost into danger as a fool
That never cares if he can swim or no—
So he but find the bottom, braves the brook.
¹⁷¹⁰ No man omits precaution, quite neglects

out § Was   ¹⁶⁸²| MS:of < > heart   P1868:o' < > heart,   ¹⁶⁸³| MS:lavish,—less
1889a:lavish: less   ¹⁶⁸⁶| MS:intoxicating fume   P1868:intoxicating smoke
¹⁶⁸⁸| MS:you,   P1868:you!   ¹⁶⁹¹| MS:Recognise   1889a:Recognize   ¹⁶⁹³| MS:so
breathe   CP1868:so, breathe   ¹⁶⁹⁴| MS:rest. I   P1868:rest! I   ¹⁶⁹⁶| MS:the bad
§ inserted above § < > the burning § crossed out § rage   ¹⁶⁹⁷| MS:and cured § crossed out
and replaced by § whole   ¹⁷⁰⁴| MS:the very § inserted above § < > speak—
P1868:speak!   ¹⁷⁰⁶| MS:Who not < > person pitched   P1868:Who, not < > person,
pitched   ¹⁷⁰⁷| MS:into the danger   CP1868:into danger   ¹⁷⁰⁸| MS:never thinks
§ crossed out and replaced above by § cares   ¹⁷⁰⁹| MS:but reach § crossed out and
replaced above by § find   ¹⁷¹⁰| MS:precautions   P1868:precaution

Secresy, safety, schemes not how retreat,
Having schemed he might advance. Did I so scheme?
Why, with a warrant which 'tis ask and have,
With horse thereby made mine without a word,
1715 I had gained the frontier and slept safe that night.
Then, my companions,—call them what you please,
Slave or stipendiary,—what need of one
To me whose right-hand did its owner's work?
Hire an assassin yet expose yourself?
1720 As well buy glove and then thrust naked hand
I' the thorn-bush. No, the wise man stays at home,
Sends only agents out, with pay to earn:
At home, when they come back,—he straight discards
Or else disowns. Why use such tools at all
1725 When a man's foes are of his house, like mine,
Sit at his board, sleep in his bed? Why noise,
When there's the *acquetta* and the silent way?
Clearly my life was valueless.

                      But now
Health is returned, and sanity of soul
1730 Nowise indifferent to the body's harm.
I find the instinct bids me save my life;
My wits, too, rally round me; I pick up
And use the arms that strewed the ground before,
Unnoticed or spurned aside: I take my stand,
1735 Make my defence. God shall not lose a life
May do Him further service, while I speak
And you hear, you my judges and last hope!

1711| MS:schemes he may retreat *P1868:*schemes not how retreat,   1714| MS:And the
horse *P1868:*With horse   1716| MS:Then my companions, call < > please,—
*CP1868:*Then, my companions,—call < > please,   1717| MS:stipendiary, what
*P1868:*stipendiary,—what   1721| MS:In *P1868:*I'   1722| MS:out with < > earn,
*P1868:*out with < > earn: *1889a:*Send, only   DC, BrU: Sends only *1889:*Sends only
1723| MS:back,—why, he *P1868:*back,—he   1726| MS:bed: why noise *CP1868:*bed?
Why noise,   1727| MS:acquetta *P1868:acquetta*   1728| MS:valueless: but
*P1868:*valueless. § ¶ § But   1731| MS:I have the < > life, *P1868:*I find the < > life;
1732| MS:me: I *P1868:*me; I   1734| MS:aside, I *P1868:*aside: I
1735| MS:defence, God *P1868:*defence. God   1737| MS:my Judges *P1868:*my judges

You are the law: 'tis to the law I look.
I began life by hanging to the law,
¹⁷⁴⁰ To the law it is I hang till life shall end.
My brother made appeal to the Pope, 'tis true,
To stay proceedings, judge my cause himself
Nor trouble law,—some fondness of conceit
That rectitude, sagacity sufficed
¹⁷⁴⁵ The investigator in a case like mine,
Dispensed with the machine of law. The Pope
Knew better, set aside my brother's plea
And put me back to law,—referred the cause
Ad judices meos,—doubtlessly did well.
¹⁷⁵⁰ Here, then, I clutch my judges,—I claim law—
Cry, by the higher law whereof your law
O' the land is humbly representative,—
Cry, on what point is it, where either accuse,
I fail to furnish you defence? I stand
¹⁷⁵⁵ Acquitted, actually or virtually,
By every intermediate kind of court
That takes account of right or wrong in man,
Each unit in the series that begins
With God's throne, ends with the tribunal here.

---

^{1738|} MS:the Law <> Law *P1868:*the law <> law ^{1739|} MS:the Law, *P1868:*the
law, ^{1740|} MS:the Law *P1868:*the law ^{1741|} MS:the Pope, supposed § crossed
out and replaced above by § you § crossed out § 'tis ^{1742|} MS:there § followed by two
illegible words, all replaced above by three words and comma § to stay proceedings,
^{1748|} MS:to Law *P1868:*to law ^{1750|} MS:then, I find § crossed out and replaced above
by § clutch <> law! *CP1868:*law— ^{1751|} MS:And § crossed out and replaced above by
word and comma § Cry, by the higher § inserted above § law of the land, and the higher law
§ last eight words crossed out and replaced above by four words § whereof § illegible word
crossed out § your § inserted above § law ^{1752|} MS:Whereof it is earth's § last five words
crossed out and replaced above by five words § Of the land is humbly representative,
*P1868:*O' <> representative,— ^{1753|} MS:Say § crossed out and replaced above by §
Come, on what single § crossed out § point is it § last two words inserted above § where both
make § last two words crossed out and replaced above by § either accuse, *CP1868:*Cry, on
^{1754|} MS:Fail I § indication that these two words are to be reversed in order § to make good
my § last three words crossed out and replaced above by two words § furnish you defences? I
§ crossed out and replaced above by § Who § crossed out and original reading restored §
*P1868:*defence? I ^{1755|} MS:Acquitted, or actually *CP1868:*Acquitted, actually
^{1756|} MS:But § crossed out and replaced above by § By ^{1758|} MS:that depends § crossed
out § begins ^{1759|} MS:From § crossed out and replaced above by § With God's throne, to
your own § last three words crossed out and replaced above by three words § ends with the

1760 God breathes, not speaks, his verdicts, felt not heard,
Passed on successively to each court I call
Man's conscience, custom, manners, all that make
More and more effort to promulgate, mark
God's verdict in determinable words,
1765 Till last come human jurists—solidify
Fluid result,—what's fixable lies forged,
Statute,—the residue escapes in fume,
Yet hangs aloft, a cloud, as palpable
To the finer sense as word the legist welds.
1770 Justinian's Pandects only make precise
What simply sparkled in men's eyes before,
Twitched in their brow or quivered on their lip,
Waited the speech they called but would not come.
These courts then, whose decree your own confirms,—
1775 Take my whole life, not this last act alone,
Look on it by the light reflected thence!
What has Society to charge me with?
Come, unreservedly,—favour none nor fear,—
I am Guido Franceschini, am I not?
1780 You know the courses I was free to take?
I took just that which let me serve the Church,
I gave it all my labour in body and soul
Till these broke down i' the service. "Specify?"
Well, my last patron was a Cardinal.

< > here— *CP1868:*here.　　　^{1760|}　MS:breathes the absolute § last two words crossed out
and replaced above by three words § not speaks his verdicts felt not heard—
*CP1868:*breathes, not speaks, his verdicts, felt not heard,　　　^{1761|}　MS:to the courts
*CP1868:*to each court　　　^{1762|}　MS:Man's § in margin § Conscience § altered to § conscience,
and § crossed out §　　　^{1763|}　MS:mark § written over illegible word §　　　^{1765|}　MS:human
law, § crossed out and replaced above by word and dash § jurists—　　　^{1766|}　MS:forged—
*CP1868:*forged,　　　^{1767|}　MS:Statutes,— the　*P1868:*Statute,—the　　　^{1768|}　MS:aloft in a
*CP1868:*aloft, a　　　^{1769|}　MS:words § final *s* erased §　　　^{1771|}　MS:What only § inserted
above line § sparkled in a million § last two words crossed out and replaced above by § men's
*P1868:*What simply sparkled　　　^{1772|}　MS:brows　*P1868:*brow　　　^{1776|}　MS:thence.
*P1868:*thence!　　　^{1778|}　MS:unreservedly, no favours, nor　*P1868:*unreservedly,—favour
nor　*1872:*favour none nor　　　^{1779|}　MS:am Guido Franceschini am　*P1868:*am Guido
Franceschini, am　　　^{1780|}　MS:take,　*P1868:*take?　　　^{1783|}　MS:in the service—
"specify?"　*CP1868:*i' the service. "Specify?"　　　^{1784|}　MS:a Cardinal　*P1868:*a Cardinal.

1785 I left him unconvicted of a fault—
Was even helped, by way of gratitude,
Into the new life that I left him for,
This very misery of the marriage,—he
Made it, kind soul, so far as in him lay—
1790 Signed the deed where you yet may see his name.
He is gone to his reward,—dead, being my friend
Who could have helped here also,—that, of course!
So far, there's my acquittal, I suppose.
Then comes the marriage itself—no question, lords,
1795 Of the entire validity of that!
In the extremity of distress, 'tis true,
For after-reasons, furnished abundantly,
I wished the thing invalid, went to you
Only some months since, set you duly forth
1800 My wrong and prayed your remedy, that a cheat
Should not have force to cheat my whole life long.
"Annul a marriage? 'Tis impossible!
Though ring about your neck be brass not gold,
Needs must it clasp, gangrene you all the same!"
1805 Well, let me have the benefit, just so far,
O' the fact announced,—my wife then is my wife,
I have allowance for a husband's right.
I am charged with passing right's due bound,—such acts
As I thought just, my wife called cruelty,
1810 Complained of in due form,—convoked no court
Of common gossipry, but took her wrongs—
And not once, but so long as patience served—

1785| MS:fault P1868:fault—   1786| MS:And even P1868:Was even
1794| MS:question, Lords, P1868:question, lords,   1797| MS:after-reasons furnished
abundantly P1868:after-reasons, furnished abundantly,   1798| MS:invalid and went
P1868:invalid, went   1800| MS:wrongs P1868:wrong   1801| MS:long,
CP1868:long.   1802| MS:impossible— CP1868:impossible!   1803| MS:Your ring
about the neck is brass not gold P1868:Though ring about your neck be brass not gold,
1804| MS:Must must still clasp P1868:Needs must it clasp   1806| MS:Of P1868:O'
1809| MS:thought justice, my P1868:thought just, my   1812| MS:once but

To the town's top, jurisdiction's pride of place,
To the Archbishop and the Governor.
1815 These heard her charge with my reply, and found
That futile, this sufficient: they dismissed
The hysteric querulous rebel, and confirmed
Authority in its wholesome exercise,
They, with directest access to the facts.
1820 "—Ay, for it was their friendship favoured you,
Hereditary alliance against a breach
I' the social order: prejudice for the name
Of Franceschini!"—So I hear it said:
But not here. You, lords, never will you say
1825 "Such is the nullity of grace and truth,
Such the corruption of the faith, such lapse
Of law, such warrant have the Molinists
For daring reprehend us as they do,—
That we pronounce it just a common case,
1830 Two dignitaries, each in his degree
First, foremost, this the spiritual head, and that
The secular arm o' the body politic,
Should, for mere wrongs' love and injustice' sake,
Side with, aid and abet in cruelty
1835 This broken beggarly noble,—bribed perhaps
By his watered wine and mouldy crust of bread—
Rather than that sweet tremulous flower-like wife
Who kissed their hands and curled about their feet
Looking the irresistible loveliness

---

*P1868:*once, but   1813| MS:the Town's   *P1868:*the town's   1820| MS:for they were
your § last three words crossed out and replaced above by three words § it was their friends
§ altered to § friendship and § crossed out § favoured § word crossed out, apparently *here*, and
replaced above by § you   1821| MS:Hereditary allies § altered to § alliance made § crossed
out and replaced above by § against a foe § crossed out § breach   1822| MS:In the social
§ inserted above §   *P1868:*I'   1823| MS:Of Franceschini."—So < > said   *P1868:*Of
Franceschini!"—So < > said: 1828| MS:do,   *CP1868:*do,—   1829| MS:it natural,
inform § uncertain; last two words crossed out and replaced above by three words § just a
common   1831| MS:First, beyond question, § last two words crossed out and replaced
above by word and comma § foremost, that § altered to § this   1832| MS:And this § crossed
out § the § altered to § The § followed by what appears to be § spiritual § crossed out and
replaced above by § secular arm   *P1868:*o'   1833| MS:Did, for mere § followed by word
blotted and crossed out so as to be illegible, replaced above by § wrong's   *P1868:*Should, for
1835| MS:broken, beggarly   *P1868:*broken beggarly   1837| MS:than poor § crossed out
and replaced above by two words § that sweet   1838| MS:That curled about his feet and
kissed their hands § altered to § that kissed their hands and curled about their feet

¹⁸⁴⁰ In tears that takes man captive, turns" . . . enough!
Do you blast your predecessors? What forbids
Posterity to trebly blast yourselves
Who set the example and instruct their tongue?
You dreaded the crowd, succumbed to the popular cry,
¹⁸⁴⁵ Or else, would nowise seem defer thereto
And yield to public clamour though i' the right!
You ridded your eye of my unseemliness,
The noble whose misfortune wearied you,—
Or, what's more probable, made common cause
¹⁸⁵⁰ With the cleric section, punished in myself
Maladroit uncomplaisant laity,
Defective in behaviour to a priest
Who claimed the customary partnership
I' the house and the wife. Lords, any lie will serve!
¹⁸⁵⁵ Look to it,—or allow me freed so far!

Then I proceed a step, come with clean hands
Thus far, re-tell the tale told eight months since.
The wife, you allow so far, I have not wronged,
Has fled my roof, plundered me and decamped
¹⁸⁶⁰ In company with the priest her paramour:
And I gave chase, came up with, caught the two
At the wayside inn where both had spent the night,
Found them in flagrant fault, and found as well,
By documents with name and plan and date,

---

*CP1868:*Who kissed   ¹⁸⁴⁰| MS:turns . . . enough! *P1868:*turns" . . . enough!
¹⁸⁴²| MS:yourselves?— *P1868:*yourselves   ¹⁸⁴³| MS:You § crossed out and replaced
above by § Who < > their speech— § word and dash crossed out and replaced above by §
tongue *P1868:*tongue?   ¹⁸⁴⁴| MS:"You *P1868:*You   ¹⁸⁴⁶| MS:clamour the
other way: *P1868:*clamour though i' the right!   ¹⁸⁴⁷| MS:rid < > of his unseemliness
*P1868:*ridded < > of my unseemliness,   ¹⁸⁴⁸| MS:misfortune brought disgrace,
*P1868:*misfortune wearied you,—   ¹⁸⁵⁰| MS:the priestly § crossed out and replaced
above by § cleric party, punished *P1868:*cleric section, punished   ¹⁸⁵¹| MS:The
maladroit and uncomplaisant man *P1868:*Maladroit uncomplaisant laity,
¹⁸⁵³| MS:Claiming the *P1868:*Who claimed the   ¹⁸⁵⁴| MS:In *P1868:*I'
¹⁸⁵⁵| MS:far. *P1868:*far!   ¹⁸⁵⁶| MS:come, with *P1868:*come with   ¹⁸⁵⁷| MS:far,
and tell you that tale eight < > since— *P1868:*far, re-tell the tale told eight < > since.
¹⁸⁵⁸| MS:That the wife, you allow I < > wronged so far, *CP1868:*The wife, you allow so
far, I < > wronged,   ¹⁸⁶¹| MS:That I pursued, § crossed out and replaced above by §
gave chase < > with and caught the pair *P1868:*And I gave chace < > with, caught
*CP1868:*the two *1889a:*chase   ¹⁸⁶³| MS:well *P1868:*well,   ¹⁸⁶⁴| MS:date

¹⁸⁶⁵ The fault was furtive then that's flagrant now,
Their intercourse a long established crime.
I did not take the license law's self gives
To slay both criminals o' the spot at the time,
But held my hand,—preferred play prodigy
¹⁸⁷⁰ Of patience which the world calls cowardice,
Rather than seem anticipate the law
And cast discredit on its organs,—you.
So, to your bar I brought both criminals,
And made my statement: heard their counter-charge,
¹⁸⁷⁵ Nay,—their corroboration of my tale,
Nowise disputing its allegements, not
I' the main, not more than nature's decency
Compels men to keep silence in this kind,—
Only contending that the deeds avowed
¹⁸⁸⁰ Would take another colour and bear excuse.
You were to judge between us; so you did.
You disregard the excuse, you breathe away
The colour of innocence and leave guilt black,
"Guilty" is the decision of the court,
¹⁸⁸⁵ And that I stand in consequence untouched,
One white integrity from head to heel.
Not guilty? Why then did you punish them?
True, punishment has been inadequate—
'Tis not I only, not my friends that joke,
¹⁸⁹⁰ My foes that jeer, who echo "inadequate"—
For, by a chance that comes to help for once,
The same case simultaneously was judged
At Arezzo, in the province of the Court
Where the crime had its beginning but not end.

---

*P1868:*date,   ¹⁸⁶⁷| MS:licence *P1868:*license   ¹⁸⁶⁸| MS:on *P1868:*o'
¹⁸⁷⁰| MS:patience that the *P1868:*patience which the   ¹⁸⁷²| MS:you— *1889a:*you.
¹⁸⁷³| MS:So to *P1868:*So, to   ¹⁸⁷⁴| MS:counter-charge *1872:*counter-charge,
¹⁸⁷⁵| MS:No,—their *P1868:*Nay,—their   ¹⁸⁷⁷| MS:In *P1868:*I'   ¹⁸⁷⁸| MS:kind,
*P1868:*kind,—   ¹⁸⁸⁴| MS:is then § crossed out § the sentence § crossed out and replaced
above by § decision <> Court. *P1868:*the court,   ¹⁸⁸⁵| MS:untouched
*P1868:*untouched,   ¹⁸⁸⁷| MS:If innocent, § last two words and comma crossed out and
replaced above by two words and question mark § Not guilty? why then § inserted above line §
*P1868:*guilty? Why   ¹⁸⁸⁹| MS:that gripe, *P1868:*that joke,   ¹⁸⁹²| MS:Half
§ crossed out § the § altered to § The same § inserted above §   ¹⁸⁹⁴| MS:had beginning

They then, deciding on but half o' the crime,
The effraction, robbery,—features of the fault
I never cared to dwell upon at Rome,—
What was it they adjudged as penalty
To Pompilia,—the one criminal o' the pair
1900 Amenable to their judgment, not the priest
Who is Rome's? Why, just imprisonment for life
I' the Stinche. There was Tuscany's award
To a wife that robs her husband: you at Rome—
Having to deal with adultery in a wife
1905 And, in a priest, breach of the priestly vow—
Give gentle sequestration for a month
In a manageable Convent, then release,
You call imprisonment, in the very house
O' the very couple, which the aim and end
1910 Of the culprits' crime was—just to reach and rest
And there take solace and defy me: well,—
This difference 'twixt their penalty and yours
Is immaterial: make your penalty less—
Merely that she should henceforth wear black gloves
1915 And white fan, she who wore the opposite—
Why, all the same the fact o' the thing subsists.
Reconcile to your conscience as you may,
Be it on your own heads, you pronounced but half
O' the penalty for heinousness like hers
1920 And his, that pays a fault at Carnival
Of comfit-pelting past discretion's law,
Or accident to handkerchief in Lent

---

*1889a:*had its beginning   1895| MS:of the crime *P1868:*o' the crime,   1899| MS:of
*P1868:*o'   1902| MS:In *P1868:*I'   1903| MS:at Rome *1889a:*at Rome—
1905| MS:And in a priest § last three words inserted above § <> vow, *P1868:*And, in a
priest, breach *1889a:*vow—   1907| MS:release *P1868:*release,
1908| MS:imprisonment in *P1868:*imprisonment, in   1909| MS:Of <> couple, the
sole aim *P1868:*O' *1889a:*couple, which the aim   1910| MS:was—there to
*1889a:*was—just to   1912| MS:twixt *P1868:*'twixt   1913| MS:less *P1868:*less—
1914| MS:should wear henceforth § indication that order of last two words should be
reversed §   1915| MS:And a white *P1868:*And white   1916| MS:of <> subsists:
*CP1868:*o' <> subsists.   1917| MS:may *P1868:*may,   1918| MS:pronounce one
half *CP1868:*pronounced one half *1889a:*pronounced but half   1919| MS:Of
*P1868:*O'   1920| MS:his, than for a <> carnival *CP1868:*his, that's for <> Carnival
*1872:*his, that pays a   1921| MS:discretion's play, *P1868:*discretion's law,

Which falls perversely as a lady kneels
Abruptly, and but half conceals her neck!
¹⁹²⁵ I acquiesce for my part: punished, though
By a pin-point scratch, means guilty: guilty means
—What have I been but innocent hitherto?
Anyhow, here the offence, being punished, ends.

Ends?—for you deemed so, did you not, sweet lords?
¹⁹³⁰ That was throughout the veritable aim
O' the sentence light or heavy,—to redress
Recognized wrong? You righted me, I think?
Well then,—what if I, at this last of all,
Demonstrate you, as my whole pleading proves,
¹⁹³⁵ No particle of wrong received thereby
One atom of right?—that cure grew worse disease?
That in the process you call "justice done"
All along you have nipped away just inch
By inch the creeping climbing length of plague
¹⁹⁴⁰ Breaking my tree of life from root to branch,
And left me, after all and every act
Of your interference,—lightened of what load?
At liberty wherein? Mere words and wind!
"Now I was saved, now I should feel no more
¹⁹⁴⁵ The hot breath, find a respite from fixed eye
And vibrant tongue!" Why, scarce your back was turned,
There was the reptile, that feigned death at first,
Renewing its detested spire and spire
Around me, rising to such heights of hate
¹⁹⁵⁰ That, so far from mere purpose now to crush

---

¹⁹²³| MS:That falls <> Lady kneels § crossed out and replaced above by § prays
*CP1868:*Which falls <> lady kneels   ¹⁹²⁴| MS:Abruptly and only half protects
§ crossed out and replaced above by § conceals her breast:—   *P1868:*Abruptly, and but half
<> her neck:—   *CP1868:*neck!   ¹⁹²⁵| MS:part,—punished   *1889a:*part: punished
¹⁹²⁹| MS:sweet Lords?   *P1868:*sweet lords?   ¹⁹³¹| MS:Of <> heavy, to   *CP1868:*O'
<> heavy,—to   ¹⁹³³| MS:what when I   *P1868:*what if I   ¹⁹³⁵| MS:of the § crossed
out §   ¹⁹³⁶| MS:right? that <> worst   *P1868:*right?—that <> worse
¹⁹³⁸| MS:All along § over erasure § just joint   *P1868:*just inch   ¹⁹³⁹| MS:By joint the
creeping § inserted above §   *P1868:*By inch the   ¹⁹⁴³| MS:wherein? Why, words
*P1868:*wherein? Mere words   ¹⁹⁴⁶| MS:tongue." Why   *P1868:*tongue!" Why
¹⁹⁴⁷| MS:reptile that <> first   *P1868:*reptile, that <> first,   ¹⁹⁵⁰| MS:That so

And coil itself on the remains of me,
Body and mind, and there flesh fang content,
Its aim is now to evoke life from death,
Make me anew, satisfy in my son
1955　The hunger I may feed but never sate,
Tormented on to perpetuity,—
My son, whom, dead, I shall know, understand,
Feel, hear, see, never more escape the sight
In heaven that's turned to hell, or hell returned
1960　(So rather say) to this same earth again,—
Moulded into the image and made one,
Fashioned of soul as featured like in face,
First taught to laugh and lisp and stand and go
By that thief, poisoner and adulteress
1965　I call Pompilia, he calls . . . sacred name,
Be unpronounced, be unpolluted here!
And last led up to the glory and prize of hate
By his . . . foster-father, Caponsacchi's self,
The perjured priest, pink of conspirators,
1970　Tricksters and knaves, yet polished, superfine,
Manhood to model adolescence by!
Lords, look on me, declare,—when, what I show,
Is nothing more nor less than what you deemed
And doled me out for justice,—what did you say?
1975　For reparation, restitution and more,—
Will you not thank, praise, bid me to your breasts
For having done the thing you thought to do,
And thoroughly trampled out sin's life at last?
I have heightened phrase to make your soft speech serve,

---

*P1868:*That, so　　1951|　MS:me　*P1868:*me,　　1952|　MS:mind and there feed § crossed
out and replaced above by § flesh　*P1868:*mind, and　　1959|　MS:In Heaven so turned to
Hell, or Hell　*P1868:*heaven that's turned to hell, or hell　　1960|　MS:So—rather say—to
<> again,　*P1868:*(So, rather, say) to <> again,—　*1889a:*(So rather say)
1967|　MS:of Hell　*P1868:*of hate　　1968|　MS:his . . foster-father <> self　*P1868:*self,
*1889a:*his . . . foster-father　　1969|　MS:conspirators　*P1868:*conspirators,
1971|　MS:by . . .　*1889a:*by!　　1972|　MS:when what I show　*P1868:*when, what I show,
1973|　MS:you thought § crossed out and replaced above by § deemed,　*P1868:*deemed
1975|　MS:Reparation <> and much more,—　*P1868:*For reparation <> and more,—
1979|　MS:Words you spoke, I respoke in heighted phrase. § entire line crossed out and
replaced above by nine words and two commas § I have heightened phrase, to make your

1980 Doubled the blow you but essayed to strike,
Carried into effect your mandate here
That else had fallen to ground: mere duty done,
Oversight of the master just supplied
By zeal i' the servant. I, being used to serve,
1985 Have simply . . . what is it they charge me with?
Blackened again, made legible once more
Your own decree, not permanently writ,
Rightly conceived but all too faintly traced.
It reads efficient, now, comminatory,
1990 A terror to the wicked, answers so
The mood o' the magistrate, the mind of law.
Absolve, then, me, law's mere executant!
Protect your own defender,—save me, Sirs!
Give me my life, give me my liberty,
1995 My good name and my civic rights again!
It would be too fond, too complacent play
Into the hands o' the devil, should we lose
The game here, I for God: a soldier-bee
That yields his life, exenterate with the stroke
2000 O' the sting that saves the hive. I need that life.
Oh, never fear! I'll find life plenty use
Though it should last five years more, aches and all!
For, first thing, there's the mother's age to help—
Let her come break her heart upon my breast,
2005 Not on the blank stone of my nameless tomb!
The fugitive brother has to be bidden back
To the old routine, repugnant to the tread,
Of daily suit and service to the Church,—

---

half-speech serve, *P1868:*your soft speech   ¹⁹⁸²| MS:to the ground *P1868:*to ground
¹⁹⁸⁴| MS:in the servant: I   *P1868:*i'   *1889a:*servant. I   ¹⁹⁸⁵| *P1868:*charged
*CP1868:*charge   ¹⁹⁸⁶| MS:Rewritten and § crossed out and replaced above by following
two words and comma § blackened again, made   ¹⁹⁸⁷| MS:permanently tr § crossed out §
¹⁹⁸⁸| MS:traced,—   *1889a:*traced.   ¹⁹⁹¹| MS:of the magistrate < > Law.
*P1868:*o' the magistrate < > law.   ¹⁹⁹²| MS:Absolve me then, Law's   *P1868:*Absolve,
then, me, law's   ¹⁹⁹⁷| MS:of   *P1868:*o'   ¹⁹⁹⁸| MS:here, I and § crossed out and
replaced above by § for   ²⁰⁰⁰| MS:Of < > life,   *P1868:*O'   *1889a:*life.
²⁰⁰²| MS:more aches   *P1868:*more, aches   ²⁰⁰⁴| MS:Let her § inserted above §
²⁰⁰⁶| MS:be called § crossed out and replaced above by § bidden   ²⁰⁰⁷| MS:the home and
friends he finds too hard to bear: § last nine words and colon crossed out and replaced above
by ten words and three commas § old routine, now bitter over much, § last four words and
comma crossed out § repugnant to the tread,   ²⁰⁰⁸| MS:Of customary § crossed out §

76

Thro' gibe and jest, those stones that Shimei flung!
2010 Ay, and the spirit-broken youth at home,
The awe-struck altar-ministrant, shall make
Amends for faith now palsied at the source,
Shall see truth yet triumphant, justice yet
A victor in the battle of this world!
2015 Give me—for last, best gift—my son again,
Whom law makes mine,—I take him at your word,
Mine be he, by miraculous mercy, lords!
Let me lift up his youth and innocence
To purify my palace, room by room
2020 Purged of the memories, lend from his bright brow
Light to the old proud paladin my sire
Shrunk now for shame into the darkest shade
O' the tapestry, showed him once and shrouds him now!
Then may we,—strong from that rekindled smile,—
2025 Go forward, face new times, the better day.
And when, in times made better through your brave
Decision now,—might but Eutopia be!—
Rome rife with honest women and strong men,
Manners reformed, old habits back once more,
2030 Customs that recognize the standard worth,—
The wholesome household rule in force again,
Husbands once more God's representative,
Wives like the typical Spouse once more, and Priests
No longer men of Belial, with no aim
2035 At leading silly women captive, but
Of rising to such duties as yours now,—
Then will I set my son at my right-hand

2009| MS: §written in margin following line 2008 §   2011| MS:altar-ministrant shall
P1868:altar-ministrant, shall   2015| MS:gift, my   1889a:gift—my
2017| MS:mercy, Lords! P1868:mercy, lords!   2023| MS:Of the tapestry, that
showed <> now. P1868:O' the tapestry, showed <> now!   2024| MS:Then we
may,—strong P1868:Then may we,—strong   2025| MS:day— P1868:day.
2026| MS:in days § crossed out and replaced above by § times   2027| MS:now,
may but Utopia be! P1868:now,—might but <> be!—   DC,BrU: Eutopia
1889:Utopia § emended to § Eutopia § see Editorial Notes §   2029| MS:back
again, P1868:back once more,   2035| MS:but end P1868:but   2036| MS:your
own, P1868:yours now,—   2037| MS:right hand P1868:right-hand

77

And tell his father's story to this point,
Adding "The task seemed superhuman, still
2040   I dared and did it, trusting God and law:
And they approved of me: give praise to both!"
And if, for answer, he shall stoop to kiss
My hand, and peradventure start thereat,—
I engage to smile "That was an accident
2045   I' the necessary process,—just a trip
O' the torture-irons in their search for truth,—
Hardly misfortune, and no fault at all."

2038| MS:fathers story once again   *P1868:*father's story to this point,   2040| MS:and
Law,   *P1868:*and law: 2041| MS:me, due praise to both!   *P1868:*me: give praise to
both!"   2043| MS:thereat,   *P1868:*thereat,—   2044| MS:to add "That   *P1868:*to
smile "That   2045| MS:In < > process, just a slip   *P1868:*I' < > process,—just a trip
2046| MS:Of < > truth,   *P1868:*O' < > truth,—   2047| MS:Hardly a
misfortune and < > all.   *CP1868:*Hardly misfortune, and < > all."

VI

GIUSEPPE CAPONSACCHI

Answer you, Sirs? Do I understand aright?
Have patience! In this sudden smoke from hell,—
So things disguise themselves,—I cannot see
My own hand held thus broad before my face
5   And know it again. Answer you? Then that means
Tell over twice what I, the first time, told
Six months ago: 'twas here, I do believe,
Fronting you same three in this very room,
I stood and told you: yet now no one laughs,
10   Who then . . . nay, dear my lords, but laugh you did,
As good as laugh, what in a judge we style
Laughter—no levity, nothing indecorous, lords!
Only,—I think I apprehend the mood:
There was the blameless shrug, permissible smirk,
15   The pen's pretence at play with the pursed mouth,
The titter stifled in the hollow palm
Which rubbed the eyebrow and caressed the nose,
When I first told my tale: they meant, you know,
"The sly one, all this we are bound believe!
20   Well, he can say no other than what he says.
We have been young, too,—come, there's greater guilt!
Let him but decently disembroil himself,
Scramble from out the scrape nor move the mud,—
We solid ones may risk a finger-stretch!"

2| MS:Hell,— P1868:hell,—   4| MS:My right § crossed out and replaced above by §
own hand   10| MS:then . . nay, good dear § written above good §   1889a:then . . .
nay   12| MS:Laughter—not § crossed out and replaced above by § no levity <>
indecorous, Lords. P1868:indecorous, lords!   13| MS:think I recognize § crossed out
and replaced above by § apprehend the   14| MS:blameless titter, § crossed out and
replaced above by § shrug   17| MS:nose P1868:nose,   18| MS:my story: they
P1868:my tale: they   22| MS:Decently let him disembroil P1868:Let him but decently
disembroil   23| MS:mud, P1868:mud,—   24| MS:finger's-stretch."
P1868:finger-stretch."   1889a:finger-stretch! § emended to § finger-stretch!" § see Editorial

25 And now you sit as grave, stare as aghast
    As if I were a phantom: now 'tis—"Friend,
    Collect yourself!"—no laughing matter more—
    "Counsel the Court in this extremity,
    Tell us again!"—tell that, for telling which,
30 I got the jocular piece of punishment,
    Was sent to lounge a little in the place
    Whence now of a sudden here you summon me
    To take the intelligence from just—your lips!
    You, Judge Tommati, who then tittered most,—
35 That she I helped eight months since to escape
    Her husband, was retaken by the same,
    Three days ago, if I have seized your sense,—
    (I being disallowed to interfere,
    Meddle or make in a matter none of mine,
40 For you and law were guardians quite enough
    O' the innocent, without a pert priest's help)—
    And that he has butchered her accordingly,
    As she foretold and as myself believed,—
    And, so foretelling and believing so,
45 We were punished, both of us, the merry way:
    Therefore, tell once again the tale! For what?
    Pompilia is only dying while I speak!
    Why does the mirth hang fire and miss the smile?
    My masters, there's an old book, you should con
50 For strange adventures, applicable yet,
    'Tis stuffed with. Do you know that there was once
    This thing: a multitude of worthy folk

Notes §   26| MS:'tis "Friend, P1868:'tis—"Friend,   27| MS:yourself"—no
CP1868:yourself!"—no   29| MS:that for P1868:that, for   33| MS:just your lips
P1868:just—your 1889a:lips!   34| MS:most, P1868:most,—   36| MS:husband
is retaken <> same P1868:husband, is <> same, 1889a:husband, was retaken
38| MS:I <> interfere P1868:(I <> interfere,   40| MS:and Law are
guardians P1868:and law were guardians CP1868:law were guardians   41| MS:Of the innocent
without <> help,— P1868:O' the innocent, without <> help)—
42| MS:accordingly P1868:accordingly,   43| MS:believed P1868:believed,—
44| MS:believing both § crossed out and replaced above by § it, P1868:believing so,
45| MS:way. P1868:way: 48| MS:What, shall the P1868:Why does the
49| MS:book you P1868:book, you   50| MS:adventures—applicable yet—
P1868:adventures, applicable yet,   52| MS:thing—a P1868:thing: a

Took recreation, watched a certain group
Of soldiery intent upon a game,—
55 How first they wrangled, but soon fell to play,
Threw dice,—the best diversion in the world.
A word in your ear,—they are now casting lots,
Ay, with that gesture quaint and cry uncouth,
For the coat of One murdered an hour ago!
60 I am a priest,—talk of what I have learned.
Pompilia is bleeding out her life belike,
Gasping away the latest breath of all,
This minute, while I talk—not while you laugh?

Yet, being sobered now, what is it you ask
65 By way of explanation? There's the fact!
It seems to fill the universe with sight
And sound,—from the four corners of this earth
Tells itself over, to my sense at least.
But you may want it lower set i' the scale,—
70 Too vast, too close it clangs in the ear, perhaps;
You'd stand back just to comprehend it more.
Well then, let me, the hollow rock, condense
The voice o' the sea and wind, interpret you
The mystery of this murder. God above!
75 It is too paltry, such a transference
O' the storm's roar to the cranny of the stone!

This deed, you saw begin—why does its end
Surprise you? Why should the event enforce
The lesson, we ourselves learned, she and I,
80 From the first o' the fact, and taught you, all in vain?
This Guido from whose throat you took my grasp,

55| MS:wrangled, and then fell *P1868*:wrangled, but soon fell   58| MS:with those
§ altered to § that gestures § altered to § gesture <> and uncouth cry, *P1868*:and cry uncouth,
60| MS:priest, talk *P1868*:priest,—talk   63| MS:while I tell—not <> laugh.
P1868:while I talk—not <> laugh?   63-64| MS:§ no ¶ §
P1868:§ ¶ §   65| MS:fact. *P1868*:fact!   67| MS:sound, from <>
this world *P1868*:sound,—from <> this earth   68| MS:least; *P1868*:least.
69| MS:in *P1868*:i'   70| MS:perhaps, *P1868*:perhaps;   71| MS:comprehend
the more; *P1868*:comprehend it more: *1889a*:more.   73| MS:of *P1868*:o'
74| MS:above *P1868*:above!   76| MS:Of *P1868*:O'   76-77| MS: § no ¶ §
P1868:§ ¶ §   77| MS:deed you *P1868*:deed, you   80| MS:of *P1868*:o'

Was this man to be favoured, now, or feared,
Let do his will, or have his will restrained,
In the relation with Pompilia? Say!
⁸⁵ Did any other man need interpose
—Oh, though first comer, though as strange at the work
As fribble must be, coxcomb, fool that's near
To knave as, say, a priest who fears the world—
Was he bound brave the peril, save the doomed,
⁹⁰ Or go on, sing his snatch and pluck his flower,
Keep the straight path and let the victim die?
I held so; you decided otherwise,
Saw no such peril, therefore no such need
To stop song, loosen flower, and leave path. Law,
⁹⁵ Law was aware and watching, would suffice,
Wanted no priest's intrusion, palpably
Pretence, too manifest a subterfuge!
Whereupon I, priest, coxcomb, fribble and fool,
Ensconced me in my corner, thus rebuked,
¹⁰⁰ A kind of culprit, over-zealous hound
Kicked for his pains to kennel; I gave place
To you, and let the law reign paramount:

---

^{82|} MS:this a § crossed out § man to be § inserted above § favor § altered to § favored and not
§ last two words crossed out and replaced above by following two words § now, or fear
§ altered to § feared, *P1868:*be favoured, now   ^{83|} MS:will or *P1868:*will, or
^{84|} MS:with Pompilia, say! *P1868:*with Pompilia?—say! *1889a:*with Pompilia? Say!
^{86|} MS:as new to § last two words crossed out and replaced by following two words § strange
at the   ^{87|} MS:As a § crossed out § fribble < > fool as § crossed out and replaced above
by § that's near   ^{88|} MS:To a § crossed out § knave < > who loves the *P1868:*who fears
the   ^{89|} MS:bound stop § crossed out and replaced above by § stay § crossed out and
replaced by § brave the danger § crossed out and replaced above by § peril, save
^{91|} MS:victim lie? *P1868:*victim die?   ^{92|} MS:so, you *P1868:*so; you
^{94|} MS:path: Law, *1889a:*path. Law   ^{97|} MS:subterfuge. *P1868:*subterfuge!
^{98|} MS:Whereupon I, the coxcomb < > and priest, *P1868:*Whereupon I, priest, coxcomb
< > and fool,   ^{99|} MS:Betook § crossed out and replaced above by § Ensconced me to
§ crossed out and replaced by § in   ^{100|} MS:over zealous *P1868:*over-zealous
^{101|} MS:kennel, and fit § last two words crossed out and replaced above by two words § I gave
place, *P1868:*kennel; I   DC, BrU: place *1889:*place   ^{102|} MS:You and § last two
words crossed out and replaced above by five words § To you, and let the < > paramount,

I left Pompilia to your watch and ward,
And now you point me—there and thus she lies!

105 Men, for the last time, what do you want with me?
Is it,—you acknowledge, as it were, a use,
A profit in employing me?—at length
I may conceivably help the august law?
I am free to break the blow, next hawk that swoops
110 On next dove, nor miss much of good repute?
Or what if this your summons, after all,
Be but the form of mere release, no more,
Which turns the key and lets the captive go?
I have paid enough in person at Civita,
115 Am free,—what more need I concern me with?
Thank you! I am rehabilitated then,
A very reputable priest. But she—
The glory of life, the beauty of the world,
The splendour of heaven, . . . well, Sirs, does no one move?
120 Do I speak ambiguously? The glory, I say,
And the beauty, I say, and splendour, still say I,
Who, priest and trained to live my whole life long
On beauty and splendour, solely at their source,
God,—have thus recognized my food in her,
125 You tell me, that's fast dying while we talk,
Pompilia! How does lenity to me,
Remit one death-bed pang to her? Come, smile!
The proper wink at the hot-headed youth
Who lets his soul show, through transparent words,

---

*P1868:*paramount: ¹⁰⁴⁻⁵| MS:§ no ¶ § *P1868:*§ ¶ § ¹⁰⁵| MS:time, what's your
want *P1868:*time, what do you want ¹⁰⁶| MS:it, you <> use *P1868:*it,—you
<> use, ¹⁰⁷| MS:me, at *P1868:*me?—at ¹¹⁰| MS:nor pay § crossed out and
replaced above by § miss much ¹¹⁰| MS:nor pay § crossed out and replaced above by §
miss much ¹¹⁶| MS:you,—I *P1868:*you! I ¹¹⁷| MS:reputable man. But she
*P1868:*reputable priest. But she— ¹²⁰| MS:glory I say *P1868:*glory, I say,
¹²¹| MS:beauty I say and splendour, I still say, *P1868:*beauty, I say, and splendour, still say
I, ¹²²| MS:I § written over by § Who, a priest, trained *1872:*Who, priest and trained
¹²³| MS:splendour solely *P1868:*splendour, solely ¹²⁴| MS:have thus § inserted
above § recognised <> her, *CP1868:*in one, *1868:*recognized *1872:*in her,
¹²⁵| MS:§ crowded between lines 124 and 126 § me is fast *P1868:*me, is *1872:*me, that's fast
¹²⁶| MS:Pompilia,—how do § altered to § does <> me *P1868:*me, *1872:*Pompilia! How
¹²⁷| MS:her? Come, smile! *1889:*her? Come smile! § emended to § Come, smile § see
Editorial Notes § ¹²⁹| MS:show thro' <> words *P1868:*show, through <> words,

130 The mundane love that's sin and scandal too!
You are all struck acquiescent now, it seems:
It seems the oldest, gravest signor here,
Even the redoubtable Tommati, sits
Chop-fallen,—understands how law might take
135 Service like mine, of brain and heart and hand,
In good part. Better late than never, law!
You understand of a sudden, gospel too
Has a claim here, may possibly pronounce
Consistent with my priesthood, worthy Christ,
140 That I endeavoured to save Pompilia?

                                    Then,
You were wrong, you see: that's well to see, though late:
That's all we may expect of man, this side
The grave: his good is—knowing he is bad:
Thus will it be with us when the books ope
145 And we stand at the bar on judgment-day.
Well then, I have a mind to speak, see cause
To relume the quenched flax by this dreadful light,
Burn my soul out in showing you the truth.
I heard, last time I stood here to be judged,
150 What is priest's-duty,—labour to pluck tares
And weed the corn of Molinism; let me
Make you hear, this time, how, in such a case,
Man, be he in the priesthood or at plough,
Mindful of Christ or marching step by step
155 With . . . what's his style, the other potentate

---

¹³⁰| MS:love, that's sin, and *P1868:*love that's sin and   ¹³³| MS:redoubtable
Tommati sits *P1868:*redoubtable Tommati, sits   ¹³⁴| MS:Chop fallen
*P1868:*Chop-fallen   ¹³⁵| MS:mine, in heart and brain and § indication that should be
transposed to read § mine in brain, and heart and *P1868:*mine, of brain and heart and
¹³⁶| MS:never, Lords! *P1868:*never, law! *1889a:*never, law § emended to § law! § see
Editorial Notes §   ¹³⁷| MS:sudden Gospel *P1868:*gospel   ¹³⁸| MS:Had <>
possibly declare *P1868:*Has <> possibly pronounce   ¹³⁹| MS:priesthood and worthy
Christ *P1868:*priesthood, worthy Christ,   ¹⁴⁰| MS:to help Pompilia? Then,
*P1868:*to save Pompilia? § ¶ § Then,   ¹⁴¹| MS:see though *P1868:*see, though
¹⁴²⁻⁴⁴| MS:man this side of the grave:/ Nay, thus *P1868:*man, this side/ The grave: his
good is—knowing he is bad:/ Thus   ¹⁴⁶| MS:then I *P1868:*then, I
¹⁴⁷| MS:flax, by <> light *P1868:*flax by <> light,   ¹⁵⁰| MS:priest's duty
*P1868:*priest's-duty   ¹⁵⁵| MS:With . . . what § altered to § what's may be § last two

Who bids have courage and keep honour safe,
Nor let minuter admonition tease?—
How he is bound, better or worse, to act.
Earth will not end through this misjudgment, no!
160 For you and the others like you sure to come,
Fresh work is sure to follow,—wickedness
That wants withstanding. Many a man of blood,
Many a man of guile will clamour yet,
Bid you redress his grievance,—as he clutched
165 The prey, forsooth a stranger stepped between,
And there's the good gripe in pure waste! My part
Is done; i' the doing it, I pass away
Out of the world. I want no more with earth.
Let me, in heaven's name, use the very snuff
170 O' the taper in one last spark shall show truth
For a moment, show Pompilia who was true!
Not for her sake, but yours: if she is dead,
Oh, Sirs, she can be loved by none of you
Most or least priestly! Saints, to do us good,
175 Must be in heaven, I seem to understand:
We never find them saints before, at least.
Be her first prayer then presently for you—
She has done the good to me . . .
                              What is all this?
There, I was born, have lived, shall die, a fool!
180 This is a foolish outset:—might with cause

---

words crossed out and replaced above by two words and comma § his style,   156| MS:bids
be simply brave and § last four words crossed out and replaced above by four words § have
courage and keep honorable § altered to § honor safe,   P1868:honour safe   CP1868:safe,
157| MS:teaze,—   P1868:teaze?—   1889a:tease?—   160| MS:come,
BrU:come   1889:come,   161| MS:work as sure will § crossed out and replaced above
by § to follow   P1868:work is sure to follow   163| MS:clamour here § crossed out § yet
P1868:clamour yet,   165| MS:stranger steps between   P1868:stranger stepped between,
166| MS:waste. My   P1868:waste! My   167| MS:in   P1868:i'   168| MS:with you
§ crossed out and replaced above by § earth.   169| MS:in God's § crossed out and replaced
above by § heaven's name   170| MS:Of <> one glimmer § crossed out and replaced
above by § last spark shall   P1868:O'   171| MS:true—   P1868:true!   173| MS:Oh,
sirs   P1868:Oh, Sirs   174| MS:priestly: saints to <> good   P1868:priestly! Saints to
CP1868:priestly! Saints, to <> good,   175| MS:understand—   P1868:understand:
176| MS:before at least;   P1868:before, at least.   178| MS:me . . § ¶ § What
1889a:me . . . § ¶ § What   179| MS:fool.   P1868:fool!   180| MS:outset:

Give colour to the very lie o' the man,
The murderer,—make as if I loved his wife,
In the way he called love. He is the fool there!
Why, had there been in me the touch of taint,
185 I had picked up so much of knaves'-policy
As hide it, keep one hand pressed on the place
Suspected of a spot would damn us both.
Or no, not her!—not even if any of you
Dares think that I, i' the face of death, her death
190 That's in my eyes and ears and brain and heart,
Lie,—if he does, let him! I mean to say,
So he stop there, stay thought from smirching her
The snow-white soul that angels fear to take
Untenderly. But, all the same, I know
195 I too am taintless, and I bare my breast.
You can't think, men as you are, all of you,
But that, to hear thus suddenly such an end
Of such a wonderful white soul, that comes
Of a man and murderer calling the white black,
200 Must shake me, trouble and disadvantage. Sirs,
Only seventeen!

                    Why, good and wise you are!
You might at the beginning stop my mouth:
So, none would be to speak for her, that knew.
I talk impertinently, and you bear,
205 All the same. This it is to have to do
With honest hearts: they easily may err,
But in the main they wish well to the truth.
You are Christians; somehow, no one ever plucked

---

might *P1868:*outset:—might   181| MS:of *P1868:*o'   183| MS:there:
*P1868:*there!   184| MS:been the <> taint in mine   *P1868:*been in me the <> taint,
185| MS:knaves' policy *CP1868:*knaves'-policy   189| MS:that I in   *P1868:*that I, i'
191| MS:him, I *P1868:*him! I   193| MS:soul the angels   *P1868:*soul that angels
195| MS:taintless and *P1868:*taintless, and   196| MS:men that § crossed out and
replaced above by § as   197| MS:suddenly, such *P1868:*suddenly such
200| MS:Shakes me, brings trouble *P1868:*Must shake me, trouble
201| MS:seventeen! Why <> are. *P1868:*seventeen! § ¶ § Why <> are!
202| MS:mouth, *CP1868:*mouth: 203| MS:So none <> her that   *P1868:*her, that
*CP1868:*So, none   204| MS:bear *CP1868:*bear,   206| MS:err *P1868:*err,
207| MS:truth: *P1868:*truth.   208| MS:somehow no   *P1868:*somehow, no

A rag, even, from the body of the Lord,
210 To wear and mock with, but, despite himself,
He looked the greater and was the better. Yes,
I shall go on now. Does she need or not
I keep calm? Calm I'll keep as monk that croons
Transcribing battle, earthquake, famine, plague,
215 From parchment to his cloister's chronicle.
Not one word more from the point now!

                                        I begin.
Yes, I am one of your body and a priest.
Also I am a younger son o' the House
Oldest now, greatest once, in my birth-town
220 Arezzo, I recognize no equal there—
(I want all arguments, all sorts of arms
That seem to serve,—use this for a reason, wait!)
Not therefore thrust into the Church, because
O' the piece of bread one gets there. We were first
225 Of Fiesole, that rings still with the fame
Of Capo-in-Sacco our progenitor:
When Florence ruined Fiesole, our folk
Migrated to the victor-city, and there
Flourished,—our palace and our tower attest,
230 In the Old Mercato,—this was years ago,
Four hundred, full,—no, it wants fourteen just.
Our arms are those of Fiesole itself,
The shield quartered with white and red: a branch
Are the Salviati of us, nothing more.
235 That were good help to the Church? But better still—
Not simply for the advantage of my birth
I' the way of the world, was I proposed for priest;
But because there's an illustration, late
I' the day, that's loved and looked to as a saint

209| MS:rag even from <> Lord   P1868:rag, even, from <> Lord   CP1868:the Lord,
210| MS:himself   P1868:himself,   212| MS:need   P1868:need or not
214| MS:plague   P1868:plague,   216| MS:now! I begin.   P1868:now! § ¶ § I begin.
217| MS:Yes I   P1868:Yes, I   218| MS:of   P1868:o'   220| MS:recognize
P1868:recognize   224| MS:Of   P1868:O'   226| MS:Of Capo in Sacco   P1868:Of
Capo-in-Sacco   230| MS:the Old Mercato; this <> ago   P1868:the old Mercato,—this
<> ago,   237| MS:In <> priest,   P1868:I' <> priest;   239| MS:In   P1868:I'

Still in Arezzo, he was bishop of,
        Sixty years since: he spent to the last doit
        His bishop's-revenue among the poor,
        And used to tend the needy and the sick,
        Barefoot, because of his humility.
²⁴⁵   He it was,—when the Granduke Ferdinand
        Swore he would raze our city, plough the place
        And sow it with salt, because we Aretines
        Had tied a rope about the neck, to hale
        The statue of his father from its base
²⁵⁰   For hate's sake,—he availed by prayers and tears
        To pacify the Duke and save the town.
        This was my father's father's brother. You see,
        For his sake, how it was I had a right
        To the self-same office, bishop in the egg,
²⁵⁵   So, grew i' the garb and prattled in the school,
        Was made expect, from infancy almost,
        The proper mood o' the priest; till time ran by
        And brought the day when I must read the vows,
        Declare the world renounced and undertake
²⁶⁰   To become priest and leave probation,—leap

---

²⁴⁰| MS:in Arezzo he < > of   *P1868:*in Arezzo, he < > of,   ²⁴²| MS:His Bishop's
revenue   *P1868:*His bishop's-revenue   ²⁴⁵| MS:was who § crossed out §,—when the
Great— § inserted above § Duke   *P1868:*was,—when the Granduke   ²⁴⁶| MS:city to the
ground   *P1868:*city, plough the place   ²⁴⁷| MS:sow the place § last two words crossed
out and replaced above by § it < > because our Aretines   *P1868:*because we
Aretines   ²⁵¹| MS:the wrath and   *P1868:*the Duke and   ²⁵³| MS:a chance
§ crossed out § right   ²⁵⁴| MS:Of § crossed out and replaced above by § To the < > office,
was § crossed out §   ²⁵⁵| MS:So, dressed § crossed out and replaced above by § draped
§ crossed out and replaced beside by § grew in the dress § crossed out and
replaced above by § garb and put into § last two words crossed out and replaced above by two
words § prattled in the path § crossed out § school   *P1868:*So, grew i' the < > school,
²⁵⁶| MS:Was § *And* written above *Was* § made profess § crossed out and replaced above by §
expect from < > almost   *P1868:*Was made expect, from < > almost,   ²⁵⁷| MS:of the
priest, till   *P1868:*o' the priest; till   ²⁵⁸| MS:And brought § inserted above § one day
needs § crossed out and replaced above by two words § when I must I § imperfectly erased §
read   *P1868:*brought the day   ²⁵⁹| MS:the obligation § crossed out and replaced above
by three words § world renounced and undertake   ²⁶⁰| MS:become § following four
words inserted above § priest and drop § crossed out § leave mere § crossed out § probation

Over the ledge into the other life,
Having gone trippingly hitherto up to the height
O'er the wan water. Just a vow to read!

I stopped short awe-struck. "How shall holiest flesh
265   Engage to keep such vow inviolate,
How much less mine? I know myself too weak,
Unworthy! Choose a worthier stronger man!"
And the very Bishop smiled and stopped my mouth
In its mid-protestation. "Incapable?
270   Qualmish of conscience? Thou ingenuous boy!
Clear up the clouds and cast thy scruples far!
I satisfy thee there's an easier sense
Wherein to take such vow than suits the first
Rough rigid reading. Mark what makes all smooth,
275   Nay, has been even a solace to myself!
The Jews who needs must, in their synagogue,
Utter sometimes the holy name of God,
A thing their superstition boggles at,
Pronounce aloud the ineffable sacrosanct,—
280   How does their shrewdness help them? In this wise;
Another set of sounds they substitute,
Jumble so consonants and vowels—how
Should I know?—that there grows from out the old
Quite a new word that means the very same—
285   And o'er the hard place slide they with a smile.
Giuseppe Maria Caponsacchi mine,
Nobody wants you in these latter days

---

²⁶¹| MS:life   *P1868:*life,   ²⁶³⁻⁶⁴| MS:§ no ¶ §   *P1868:*§ ¶ §   ²⁶⁵| MS:to keep
§ smudged, perhaps written over illegible word § the § crossed out § such
²⁶⁶| MS:mine,—I   *1889a:*mine? I   ²⁶⁷| MS:Unworthy!" § imperfectly erased § Choose
²⁶⁸| MS:stopped the mouth   *1872:*stopped my mouth   ²⁷¹| MS:far.   *P1868:*far!
²⁷³| MS:Wherein § inserted above § To § altered to § to take vows § *s* imperfectly erased §
²⁷⁵| MS:myself.   *P1868:*myself!   ²⁷⁶| MS:Blind § crossed out and replaced above by §
The Jews   ²⁸¹| MS:Another cognate word § last two words crossed out and replaced
above by following three words § set of sounds they   ²⁸²| MS:So jumble consonants
P1868: Jumble so consonants   ²⁸⁴| MS:new word § apparently written over a now
illegible word § that   ²⁸⁵| MS:over   *P1868:*o'er   ²⁸⁶| MS:Giuseppe—Maria

To prop the Church by breaking your back-bone,—
As the necessary way was once, we know,
290 When Diocletian flourished and his like.
That building of the buttress-work was done
By martyrs and confessors: let it bide,
Add not a brick, but, where you see a chink,
Stick in a sprig of ivy or root a rose
295 Shall make amends and beautify the pile!
We profit as you were the painfullest
O' the martyrs, and you prove yourself a match
For the cruelest confessor ever was,
If you march boldly up and take your stand
300 Where their blood soaks, their bones yet strew the soil,
And cry 'Take notice, I the young and free
And well-to-do i' the world, thus leave the world,
Cast in my lot thus with no gay young world
But the grand old Church: she tempts me of the two!'
305 Renounce the world? Nay, keep and give it us!
Let us have you, and boast of what you bring.
We want the pick o' the earth to practise with,
Not its offscouring, halt and deaf and blind
In soul and body. There's a rubble-stone
310 Unfit for the front o' the building, stuff to stow
In a gap behind and keep us weather-tight;
There's porphyry for the prominent place. Good lack!
Saint Paul has had enough and to spare, I trow,
Of ragged run-away Onesimus:
315 He wants the right-hand with the signet-ring

*P1868:*Giuseppe Maria   288| MS:back-bone *P1868:*back-bone,—   290| MS:When
martyrs § crossed out and replaced above by § Dioclesian flourished <> like,— *P1868:*like;
*1889a:*When Diocletian <> like.   291| MS:That business § crossed out and replaced
above by § building of   295| MS:Shall make amends and § last three words inserted
above line § beautify   296| MS:You profit *P1868:*We profit   297| MS:Of the
martyrs, prove <> match, I say, *P1868:*O' the martyrs, and you prove <> match
298| MS:cruellest *1889a:*cruelest   300| MS:soaks and their bones strew the place
§ crossed out and replaced above by § soil, *P1868:*soaks, their bones yet strew 302| MS:in
*P1868:*i'   304| MS:old Church, she <> two." *P1868:*old Church: she <> two!'
306| MS:you, to § crossed out and replaced above by § and   307| MS:of <> practice
*P1868:*o' <> practise   309| MS:body; there's *P1868:*body. There's   310| MS:of
*P1868:*o'   313| MS:spare, by this § crossed out and replaced above by § now,
*P1868:*spare, I trow,   315| MS:right hand <> signet ring *P1868:*right-hand <>

Of King Agrippa, now, to shake and use.
I have a heavy scholar cloistered up,
Close under lock and key, kept at his task
Of letting Fénelon know the fool he is,
320 In a book I promise Christendom next Spring.
Why, if he covets so much meat, the clown,
As a lark's wing next Friday, or, any day,
Diversion beyond catching his own fleas,
He shall be properly swinged, I promise him.
325 But you, who are so quite another paste
Of a man,—do you obey me? Cultivate
Assiduous that superior gift you have
Of making madrigals—(who told me? Ah!)
Get done a Marinesque Adoniad straight
330 With a pulse o' the blood a-pricking, here and there,
That I may tell the lady 'And he's ours!' "

So I became a priest: those terms changed all,
I was good enough for that, nor cheated so;
I could live thus and still hold head erect.
335 Now you see why I may have been before
A fribble and coxcomb, yet, as priest, break word
Nowise, to make you disbelieve me now.
I need that you should know my truth. Well, then,
According to prescription did I live,
340 —Conformed myself, both read the breviary
And wrote the rhymes, was punctual to my place

---

signet-ring   316| MS:Of King Agrippa now to   P1868:Of King Agrippa, now, to
317| MS:up   P1868:up,   319| MS:letting Leibnitz § crossed out and replaced above by §
Fenelon <> is   P1868:is,   1889a:Fénelon   320| MS:next spring.   P1868:next Spring.
321| MS:Why if   P1868:Why, if   322| MS:larks wing any § crossed out and replaced
above by § next   P1868:lark's   324| MS:promise you § crossed out and replaced above
by § him.   327| MS:Assiduous, that   1889a:Assiduous that   328| MS:madrigal
P1868:madrigals   330| MS:of <> a-pricking, if you dare,   P1868:o' <> a-pricking,
here and there,   331| MS:lady "And he's ours!"   P1868:lady, 'And he's ours!' "
1889a:lady 'And   334| MS:hold my head   P1868:hold head   335| MS:why I could have been till now   P1868:why I may have been
before   336| MS:coxcomb, and yet break my word   P1868:coxcomb, yet,
as priest, break word   337| MS:Nowise to   P1868:Nowise, to   338| MS:know
me true. Well   P1868:know my truth. Well   340| MS:Conformed myself,
exactly, said the mass § last four words crossed out and replaced above by four words §
both read the breviary   P1868:—Conformed   341| MS:punctual

I' the Pieve, and as diligent at my post
Where beauty and fashion rule. I throve apace,
Sub-deacon, Canon, the authority
For delicate play at tarocs, and arbiter
O' the magnitude of fan-mounts: all the while
Wanting no whit the advantage of a hint
Benignant to the promising pupil,—thus:
"Enough attention to the Countess now,
The young one; 'tis her mother rules the roast,
We know where, and puts in a word: go pay
Devoir to-morrow morning after mass!
Break that rash promise to preach, Passion-week!
Has it escaped you the Archbishop grunts
And snuffles when one grieves to tell his Grace
No soul dares treat the subject of the day
Since his own masterly handling it (ha, ha!)
Five years ago,—when somebody could help
And touch up an odd phrase in time of need,
(He, he!)—and somebody helps you, my son!
Therefore, don't prove so indispensable
At the Pieve, sit more loose i' the seat, nor grow
A fixture by attendance morn and eve!
Arezzo's just a haven midway Rome—
Rome's the eventual harbour,—make for port,
Crowd sail, crack cordage! And your cargo be
A polished presence, a genteel manner, wit
At will, and tact at every pore of you!
I sent our lump of learning, Brother Clout,
And Father Slouch, our piece of piety,

to my place § change in ink suggests last three words added in revision §   342| MS:In
P1868:I'   343| MS:Where Beauty and Fashion   P1868:Where beauty and fashion
345| MS:at Taro, and   P1868:at tarocs, and   346| MS:Of   P1868:O'
348| MS:thus   P1868:thus: 350| MS:roast   P1868:roast,   352| MS:to morrow
<>mass.   P1868:to-morrow <>mass!   353| MS:preach Passion week;
P1868:preach, Passion-week!   355| MS:Graciously § crossed out and replaced above by §
And snuffles   360| MS:son,   P1868:son!   362| MS:in   P1868:i'
363| MS:attendance night § crossed out and replaced above by § morn and day § crossed out
and replaced above by § eve: P1868:eve!   364| MS:haven midway, Rome   P1868:haven
midway Rome—   367| MS:A polished wit, § crossed out and replaced above by §
presence   368| MS:you.   P1868:you!   370| MS:And Father Slouch our

To see Rome and try suit the Cardinal.
Thither they clump-clumped, beads and book in hand,
And ever since 'tis meat for man and maid
How both flopped down, prayed blessing on bent pate
375   Bald many an inch beyond the tonsure's need,
Never once dreaming, the two moony dolts,
There's nothing moves his Eminence so much
As—far from all this awe at sanctitude—
Heads that wag, eyes that twinkle, modified mirth
380   At the closet-lectures on the Latin tongue
A lady learns so much by, we know where.
Why, body o' Bacchus, you should crave his rule
For pauses in the elegiac couplet, chasms
Permissible only to Catullus! There!
385   Now go to duty: brisk, break Priscian's head
By reading the day's office—there's no help.
You've Ovid in your poke to plaster that;
Amen's at the end of all: then sup with me!"

Well, after three or four years of this life,
390   In prosecution of my calling, I
Found myself at the theatre one night
With a brother Canon, in a mood and mind
Proper enough for the place, amused or no:
When I saw enter, stand, and seat herself
395   A lady, young, tall, beautiful, strange and sad.
It was as when, in our cathedral once,
As I got yawningly through matin-song,
I saw *facchini* bear a burden up,
Base it on the high-altar, break away
400   A board or two, and leave the thing inside
Lofty and lone: and lo, when next I looked,

*P1868:*And Father Slouch, our   371| MS:the Cardinal   *P1868:*the Cardinal.
373| MS:'tis mirth § crossed out and replaced above by § meat   376| MS:moony fools,
*P1868:*moony dolts,   378| MS:from stupid § crossed out and replaced above by
following two words § all this awe   380| MS:latin   *P1868:*Latin   382| MS:you
would crave   *P1868:*you should crave   385-87| MS:go do duty <> head,/ With Ovid in
<> that,   *CP1868:*head/ By reading the day's office—there's no help./ You've Ovid in <>
that;   *1889a:*go to duty   388| MS:me."   *P1868:*me!"   393| MS:no,   *P1868:*no:
396| MS:when in our Cathedral once   *P1868:*when, in our cathedral once,   398| MS:up
*P1868:*up,   399| MS:And base   *P1868:*Base   401| MS:lone, and   *P1868:*lone: and

There was the Rafael! I was still one stare,
When—"Nay, I'll make her give you back your gaze"—
Said Canon Conti; and at the word he tossed
405 A paper-twist of comfits to her lap,
And dodged and in a trice was at my back
Nodding from over my shoulder. Then she turned,
Looked our way, smiled the beautiful sad strange smile.
"Is not she fair? 'Tis my new cousin," said he:
410 "The fellow lurking there i' the black o' the box
Is Guido, the old scapegrace: she's his wife,
Married three years since: how his Countship sulks!
He has brought little back from Rome beside,
After the bragging, bullying. A fair face,
415 And—they do say—a pocketful of gold
When he can worry both her parents dead.
I don't go much there, for the chamber's cold
And the coffee pale. I got a turn at first
Paying my duty: I observed they crouched
420 —The two old frightened family spectres—close
In a corner, each on each like mouse on mouse
I' the cat's cage: ever since, I stay at home.
Hallo, there's Guido, the black, mean and small,
Bends his brows on us—please to bend your own
425 On the shapely nether limbs of Light-skirts there
By way of a diversion! I was a fool
To fling the sweetmeats. Prudence, for God's love!

402| MS:the Rafaelle. I <> stare   P1868:the Rafael! I <> stare,   403| MS:When "Nay
<> gaze"   1868:When—"Nay <> gaze"—   404| MS:Said Canon Conti, and
P1868:Said Canon Conti; and   405| MS:paper twist of comfits into her
P1868:paper-twist of comfits to her   409| MS:she lovely § crossed out § fair <> he,
P1868:he: 410| MS:lurking in <> of   P1868:lurking there i' <> o'
413| MS:brought nothing § crossed out and replaced above by § little back
414| MS:face—   P1868:face,   415| MS:pocketful   P1868:pocket-full   1889a:pocketful
417| MS:there for   P1868:there, for   418| MS:coffee's pale: I   P1868:coffee pale. I
419| MS:my devoir,—I observed how they   P1868:my duty,—I observed they   1872:duty: I
420| MS:old frightened § inserted above § family spectres, close   1872:spectres—close
422| MS:In <> since I   P1868:I' <> since, I   423| MS:black mean and § inserted
above § small man § crossed out §   P1868:black, mean and small,   425| MS:of
light-skirts   P1868:of Light-skirts   426| MS:diversion. I   P1868:diversion! I

To-morrow I'll make my peace, e'en tell some fib,
Try if I can't find means to take you there."

430 That night and next day did the gaze endure,
Burnt to my brain, as sunbeam thro' shut eyes,
And not once changed the beautiful sad strange smile.
At vespers Conti leaned beside my seat
I' the choir,—part said, part sung—*"In ex-cel-sis—*
435 All's to no purpose; I have louted low,
But he saw you staring—*quia sub*—don't incline
To know you nearer: him we would not hold
For Hercules,—the man would lick your shoe
If you and certain efficacious friends
440 Managed him warily,—but there's the wife:
Spare her, because he beats her, as it is,
She's breaking her heart quite fast enough—*jam tu*—
So, be you rational and make amends
With little Light-skirts yonder—*in secula*
445 *Secu-lo-o-o-o-rum.* Ah, you rogue! Every one knows
What great dame she makes jealous: one against one,
Play, and win both!"
                              Sirs, ere the week was out,
I saw and said to myself "Light-skirts hides teeth
Would make a dog sick,—the great dame shows spite
450 Should drive a cat mad: 'tis but poor work this—
Counting one's fingers till the sonnet's crowned.
I doubt much if Marino really be
A better bard than Dante after all.
'Tis more amusing to go pace at eve
455 I' the Duomo,—watch the day's last gleam outside

429-30| MS:§ no ¶ § *1889a:*§ ¶ §   430-32| MS:did that gaze endure,/ And <> smile:
*P1868:*did the gaze endure,/ Burnt to my brain, as sunbeam thro' shut eyes,/ And <>
smile.   433| MS:At Vespers *P1868:*At vespers   434| MS:In *P1868:*I'
435| MS:low *CP1868:*low,   438| MS:For Hercules, the *P1868:*For Hercules,—the
440| MS:warily, but *P1868:*warily,—but   441| MS:her as *P1868:*her, as
443| MS:So be *P1868:*So, be   444| MS:yonder *in* *P1868:*yonder—*in*
445| MS:*Secu-loooo-rum* *P1868:Secu-lo-o-o-o-rum*   446| MS:against one.
*P1868:*against one,   448| MS:myself "Light skirts *P1868:*myself
"Light-skirts   450| MS:To drive *P1868:*Should drive   455| MS:In
the Duomo, watch <> last glen § *glen* ends in illegible letter, perhaps crossed out §

Turn, as into a skirt of God's own robe,
Those lancet-windows' jewelled miracle,—
Than go eat the Archbishop's ortolans,
Digest his jokes. Luckily Lent is near:
460 Who cares to look will find me in my stall
At the Pieve, constant to this faith at least—
Never to write a canzonet any more."

So, next week, 'twas my patron spoke abrupt,
In altered guise. "Young man, can it be true
465 That after all your promise of sound fruit,
You have kept away from Countess young or old
And gone play truant in church all day long?
Are you turning Molinist?" I answered quick:
"Sir, what if I turned Christian? It might be.
470 The fact is, I am troubled in my mind,
Beset and pressed hard by some novel thoughts.
This your Arezzo is a limited world;
There's a strange Pope,—'tis said, a priest who thinks.
Rome is the port, you say: to Rome I go.
475 I will live alone, one does so in a crowd,
And look into my heart a little." "Lent
Ended,"—I told friends—"I shall go to Rome."

One evening I was sitting in a muse

outside   *P1868*:I' the Duomo,—watch <> last gleam outside   456| MS:Turn as
<> robe   *P1868*:Turn, as <> robe,   457| MS:lancet windows <> miracle,
P1868:lancet-windows' <> miracle,—   459| MS:near—   *P1868*:near:
461| MS:least   *P1868*:least—   462| MS:canzonet once more."   *P1868*:canzonet
any more."   462–63| MS:§ no ¶ §   *P1868*:§ ¶ §   463| MS:So next   *P1868*:So,
next   464| MS:guise, put on the § last three words plus two illegible letters crossed
out and replaced above by quotation marks and three words § "Young man, can
1889a:guise. "Young   466| MS:from the Countess   *P1868*:from
Countess   468| MS:answered him § crossed out § quick   *1889a*:quick:
472| MS:world,   *P1868*:world;   473| MS:a new Pope <> a man
that § crossed out and replaced above by § who   *CP1868*:a strange Pope <> a priest who
1872:thinks § period omitted; apparently printer's error §   *1889a*:thinks.
475| MS:alone, there, at § last two words crossed out § one can § crossed out and replaced
above by two words § does so in   476| MS:little there § crossed out § "Lent § change in
ink suggests last word added in revision §   477| MS:So § crossed out and replaced above
by word and quotation marks § "Ended" I told people § crossed out and replaced above by §
friends, "I   *P1868*:"Ended,"—I told friends,—"I   *1889a*:friends—"I   478| MS:Next

Over the opened "Summa," darkened round
480 By the mid-March twilight, thinking how my life
Had shaken under me,—broke short indeed
And showed the gap 'twixt what is, what should be,—
And into what abysm the soul may slip,
Leave aspiration here, achievement there,
485 Lacking omnipotence to connect extremes—
Thinking moreover . . . oh, thinking, if you like,
How utterly dissociated was I
A priest and celibate, from the sad strange wife
Of Guido,—just as an instance to the point,
490 Nought more,—how I had a whole store of strengths
Eating into my heart, which craved employ,
And she, perhaps, need of a finger's help,—
And yet there was no way in the wide world
To stretch out mine and so relieve myself,—
495 How when the page o' the Summa preached its best,
Her smile kept glowing out of it, as to mock
The silence we could break by no one word,—
There came a tap without the chamber-door,
And a whisper; when I bade who tapped speak out.
500 And, in obedience to my summons, last
In glided a masked muffled mystery,

---

§ crossed out and replaced above by § One <> in my § crossed out and replaced above by § a
480| MS:By the mid-March § last two words inserted above § twilight, looking at § last two
words crossed out and replaced above by two words § thinking how   481| MS:me, broke
P1868:me,—broke   482| MS:be, P1868:be,—   483| MS:And into § inserted above §
<> slip— P1868:slip,   484| MS:With aspiration P1868:Leave aspiration
485| MS:Lacking Omnipotence P1868:Lacking omnipotence   486| MS:moreover . .
oh 1889a:moreover . . . oh   488| MS:celibate from P1868:celibate, from
492| MS:And she perhaps need <> help P1868:And she, perhaps, need <> help,—
494| MS:myself— 1872:myself,—   495| MS:of the Summa spoke § crossed out and
replaced above by § preached its best P1868:o' <> best,   496| MS:kept speaking
louder § last two words crossed out and replaced above by four words § glowing out of it, as
497| MS:we should break <> word— P1868:we could break <> word,—
498| MS:came the tap P1868:came a tap   499| MS:And the whisper when <> out,
P1868:And a whisper, when 1889a:whisper; when <> out.   501| MS:masked, muffled

Laid lightly a letter on the opened book,
Then stood with folded arms and foot demure,
Pointing as if to mark the minutes' flight.

505 I took the letter, read to the effect
That she, I lately flung the comfits to,
Had a warm heart to give me in exchange,
And gave it,—loved me and confessed it thus,
And bade me render thanks by word of mouth,
510 Going that night to such a side o' the house
Where the small terrace overhangs a street
Blind and deserted, not the street in front:
Her husband being away, the surly patch,
At his villa of Vittiano.

                          "And you?"—I asked:
515 "What may you be?" "Count Guido's kind of maid—
Most of us have two functions in his house.
We all hate him, the lady suffers much,
'Tis just we show compassion, furnish help,
Specially since her choice is fixed so well.
520 What answer may I bring to cheer the sweet
Pompilia?"

                     Then I took a pen and wrote
"No more of this! That you are fair, I know:
But other thoughts now occupy my mind.
I should not thus have played the insensible
525 Once on a time. What made you,—may one ask,—

CP1868:masked muffled   502| MS:light   P1868:lightly   503| MS:arms, and
P1868:arms and   504–5| MS:§ no ¶ §   P1868:§ ¶ §   507| MS:Had just a heart
P1868:Had a warm heart   509| MS:me answer only § last two words crossed out and
replaced above by two words § render thanks by the § crossed out and replaced above by two
words § word of mouth   P1868:mouth,   510| MS:to that side of her house   P1868:to
such a side o' the house   511| MS:overhangs the street   P1868:overhangs a street
514| MS:of Vittiano. "And   P1868:of Vittiano. § ¶ § "And   515| MS:be?"— "Count
1889a:be?" "Count   518| MS:furnish aid,   1889a:furnish help,   519| MS:fixed on
you § last two words crossed out and replaced above by two words § so well.
520| MS:answer shall § crossed out and replaced above by § may   521| MS:Pompilia?"

Marry your hideous husband? 'Twas a fault,
And now you taste the fruit of it. Farewell."

"There!" smiled I as she snatched it and was gone—
"There, let the jealous miscreant,—Guido's self,
530 Whose mean soul grins through this transparent trick,—
Be baulked so far, defrauded of his aim!
What fund of satisfaction to the knave,
Had I kicked this his messenger down stairs,
Trussed to the middle of her impudence,
535 And set his heart at ease so! No, indeed!
There's the reply which he shall turn and twist
At pleasure, snuff at till his brain grow drunk,
As the bear does when he finds a scented glove
That puzzles him,—a hand and yet no hand,
540 Of other perfume than his own foul paw!
Last month, I had doubtless chosen to play the dupe,
Accepted the mock-invitation, kept
The sham appointment, cudgel beneath cloak,
Prepared myself to pull the appointer's self
545 Out of the window from his hiding-place
Behind the gown of this part-messenger
Part-mistress who would personate the wife.
Such had seemed once a jest permissible:

Then <> wrote. *P1868:*Pompilia?" § ¶ § Then *1889a:*wrote   527-28| MS:§ no ¶ §
P1868:§ ¶ §   528| MS:gone, *P1868:*gone—   529| MS:There—let the miserable
§ crossed out and replaced above by § jealous miscreant, Guido's self *P1868:*There, let <>
miscreant,— <> self,   530| MS:trick, *P1868:*trick,—   531| MS:aim: *P1868:*aim!
532| MS:Nor find the § last three words crossed out and replaced above by
three words § What fund of satisfaction and breathe free § last three words crossed
out and replaced above by three words and comma § to the fool, *P1868:*the knave,
533| MS:Did I kick this <> stairs *P1868:*Had I kicked this <>
stairs,   534| MS:impudence *P1868:*impudence,   535| MS:Setting his *1872:*And
set his   537| MS:drunk *P1868:*drunk,   539| MS:no hand— *P1868:*no hand,
540| MS:paw. *P1868:*paw!   541| MS:month I had probably § crossed out and replaced
above by § doubtless chosen *P1868:*month, I   542| MS:mock invitation
*CP1868:*mock-invitation   543| MS:apointment *P1868:*appointment
544| MS:And been prepared to *P1868:*Prepared myself to   545| MS:hiding place
*P1868:*hiding-place   546| MS:this the messenger *P1868:*this part-messenger
547| MS:And mistress *P1868:*Part-mistress   548| MS:That had been § crossed out and

Now I am not i' the mood."

　　　　　　　　　Back next morn brought
550　The messenger, a second letter in hand.
"You are cruel, Thyrsis, and Myrtilla moans
Neglected but adores you, makes request
For mercy: why is it you dare not come?
Such virtue is scarce natural to your age.
555　You must love someone else; I hear you do,
The Baron's daughter or the Advocate's wife,
Or both,—all's one, would you make me the third—
I take the crumbs from table gratefully
Nor grudge who feasts there. 'Faith, I blush and blaze!
560　Yet if I break all bounds, there's reason sure.
Are you determinedly bent on Rome?
I am wretched here, a monster tortures me:
Carry me with you! Come and say you will!
Concert this very evening! Do not write!
565　I am ever at the window of my room
Over the terrace, at the *Ave.* Come!"

I questioned—lifting half the woman's mask
To let her smile loose. "So, you gave my line
To the merry lady?" "She kissed off the wax,
570　And put what paper was not kissed away,
In her bosom to go burn: but merry, no!
She wept all night when evening brought no friend,
Alone, the unkind missive at her breast;
Thus Philomel, the thorn at her breast too,
575　Sings" . . . "Writes this second letter?" "Even so!

---

replaced above by § seemed　*P1868:*Such had　　　549| 　MS:Now, I <> in the mood. § ¶ §
Back next night § crossed out and replaced above by § morn came　*P1868:*i' the mood." <>
morn brought　*1889a:*Now I　　　554| 　MS:age:　*1889a:*age.　　　558| 　MS:from the table
*P1868:*from table　　　560| 　MS:sure:　*P1868:*sure.　*1868:*sure, *P1872:*sure.
562| 　MS:am miserable, a wretch tortures me—　*P1868:*am wretched here, a monster tortures
me:　　　563| 　MS:will—　*P1868:*will!　　　564| 　MS:Concert with me this evening. <>
write.　*P1868:*Concert this very evening! <> write!　　　566| 　MS:terrace at the Ave
*P1868:*terrace, at the *Ave*　　　566–67| 　MS:§ no ¶ §　*P1868:*§ ¶ §　　　568| 　MS:smile free.
"So you　*P1868:*smile loose. "So, you　　　569| 　MS:lady?"—"She <> wax　*P1868:*lady?"
"She <> wax,　　　570| 　MS:away　*P1868:*away,　　　571| 　MS:burn: there § crossed out §:
but　　　573| 　MS:unkind letter § crossed out and replaced above by § missive
574| 　MS:the sharp § crossed out §　　　575| 　MS:letter?"—Even　*P1868:*letter?" "Even

Then she may peep at vespers forth?"—"What risk
Do we run o' the husband?"—"Ah,—no risk at all!
He is more stupid even than jealous. Ah—
That was the reason? Why, the man's away!
580 Beside, his bugbear is that friend of yours,
Fat little Canon Conti. He fears him,
How should he dream of you? I told you truth:
He goes to the villa at Vittiano—'tis
The time when Spring-sap rises in the vine—
585 Spends the night there. And then his wife's a child:
Does he think a child outwits him? A mere child:
Yet so full grown, a dish for any duke.
Don't quarrel longer with such cates, but come!"
I wrote "In vain do you solicit me.
590 I am a priest: and you are wedded wife,
Whatever kind of brute your husband prove.
I have scruples, in short. Yet should you really show
Sign at the window . . . but nay, best be good!
My thoughts are elsewhere." "Take her that!"
                                                    "Again
595 Let the incarnate meanness, cheat and spy,
Mean to the marrow of him, make his heart
His food, anticipate hell's worm once more!
Let him watch shivering at the window—ay,
And let this hybrid, this his light-of-love
600 And lackey-of-lies,—a sage economy,—
Paid with embracings for the rank brass coin,—
Let her report and make him chuckle o'er

576| MS:Then you will come § last three words crossed out and replaced above by three
words § she may peek at Vespers forth § inserted above *Vespers* § ?" "What of the § last two
words crossed out § *P1868:*may peep at vespers   577| MS:of *P1868:*o'
579| MS:away— *P1868:*away!   580| MS:Beside his <> yours *P1868:*Beside, his <>
yours,   581| MS:him— *1889a:*him,   582| MS:truth— *1889a:*truth:
583| MS:the Villa at Vittiano: 'tis *P1868:*the villa at Vittiano—'tis   584| MS:when
spring-sap *P1868:*when Spring-sap   585| MS:child, *1889a:*child:
586| MS:child *P1868:*child: 587| MS:any Duke, *CP1868:*duke.
588–89| MS:§ no ¶ § *P1868:*§ ¶ §   589| MS:me: *P1868:*me.   590| MS:wife
*P1868:*wife,   591| MS:husband be. *P1868:*husband prove.   592| MS:scruples in
*P1868:*scruples, in   594| MS:elsewhere."—"Take her that!" § ¶ § —"Again
*1889a:*elsewhere," § emended to § elsewhere." § see Editorial Notes § "Take her that!" § ¶ §
"Again   595| MS:spy *P1868:*spy,   599| MS:this woman, this *P1868:*this hybrid,

---

101

The break-down of my resolution now,
And lour at disappointment in good time!
605   —So tantalize and so enrage by turns,
Until the two fall each on the other like
Two famished spiders, as the coveted fly
That toys long, leaves their net and them at last!"

And so the missives followed thick and fast
610   For a month, say,—I still came at every turn
On the soft sly adder, endlong 'neath my tread.
I was met i' the street, made sign to in the church,
A slip was found i' the door-sill, scribbled word
'Twixt page and page o' the prayer-book in my place.
615   A crumpled thing dropped even before my feet,
Pushed through the blind, above the terrace-rail,
As I passed, by day, the very window once.
And ever from corners would be peering up
The messenger, with the self-same demand
620   "Obdurate still, no flesh but adamant?
Nothing to cure the wound, assuage the throe
O' the sweetest lamb that ever loved a bear?"
And ever my one answer in one tone—
"Go your ways, temptress! Let a priest read, pray,
625   Unplagued of vain talk, visions not for him!
In the end, you'll have your will and ruin me!"

One day, a variation: thus I read:
"You have gained little by timidity.

this   604| MS:And take his disappointment <> time—   *P1868:*And lour at
disappointment <> time!   605| MS:So <> turns   *P1868:*—So <> turns,
607| MS:spiders on the   *P1868:*spiders, as the   608-9| MS:§ ¶ §   *P1868:*§ no ¶ §
1889: § no ¶; emended to restore ¶; see Editorial Notes §   611| MS:neath   *P1868:*'neath
612| MS:in   *P1868:*i'   613| MS:in the sill, a scribbled   *P1868:*i' the door-sill, scribbled
614| MS:Twixt leaf § crossed out and replaced above by § page <> of <> prayer book <>
place: *P1868:*'Twixt <> o' <> prayer-book   *1889a:*place.   615| MS:feet   *P1868:*feet,
616-17| MS:§ order of these lines reversed § passed by day the <> once/ <> terrace rail.
CP1868: § final order established § terrace-rail,/ <> passed, by day, the <> once.
619| MS:self-same soft demand   *P1868:*self-same demand   622| MS:Of   *P1868:*O'
623| MS:ever came my <> tone   *P1868:*ever my <> tone—   624| MS:temptress: let a
poor soul § last two words crossed out and replaced above by two words § priest read, pray
*P1868:*temptress! Let <> pray,   626| MS:Some day § last two words crossed out and
replaced above by three words § In the end, you'll draw me to my last § last four words crossed
out and replaced above by four words § have your will and <> me."   *P1868:*me!"
627| MS:read.   *P1868:*read: 628| MS:gained nothing § crossed out and replaced above

My husband has found out my love at length,
630 Sees cousin Conti was the stalking-horse,
And you the game he covered, poor fat soul!
My husband is a formidable foe,
Will stick at nothing to destroy you. Stand
Prepared, or better, run till you reach Rome!
635 I bade you visit me, when the last place
My tyrant would have turned suspicious at,
Or cared to seek you in, was . . . why say, where?
But now all's changed: beside, the season's past
At the villa,—wants the master's eye no more.
640 Anyhow, I beseech you, stay away
From the window! He might well be posted there."

I wrote—"You raise my courage, or call up
My curiosity, who am but man.
Tell him he owns the palace, not the street
645 Under—that's his and yours and mine alike.
If it should please me pad the path this eve,
Guido will have two troubles, first to get
Into a rage and then get out again.
Be cautious, though: at the *Ave!*"
                                    You of the Court!
650 When I stood question here and reached this point
O' the narrative,—search notes and see and say
If someone did not interpose with smile
And sneer, "And prithee why so confident

---

by § little   630| MS:stalking horse   *P1868:*stalking-horse,   631| MS:You are the
*P1868:*And you the   635| MS:me when   *P1868:*me, when   636| MS:suspicious to
*P1868:*suspicious at,   637| MS:in was . . why say where?   *P1868:*in, was <> say,
where?   *1889a:*was . . . why   638| MS:changed: he says the   *P1868:*changed: beside,
the   639| MS:the Villa   *P1868:*the villa   641| MS:there.   *P1868:*there."
641-42| MS:§ no ¶ §   *P1868:* § ¶ §   643| MS:curiosity who   *P1868:*curiosity, who
645| MS:that's mine and his and yours alike. § indication that should be transposed to read §
that's his and yours and mine   646| MS:eve   *P1868:*eve,   647| MS:Two § crossed
out §   649| MS:the Ave!" <> the Court!   *P1868:*the *Ave!*" <> court!   *1889a:*the
Court   651| MS:Of   *P1868:*O'   652| MS:someone <> with word   *P1868:*some
one <> with smile   *1889a:*someone   653| MS:sneer "And   *P1868:*sneer, "And

That the husband must, of all needs, not the wife,
655 Fabricate thus,—what if the lady loved?
What if she wrote the letters?''
                                    Learned Sir,
I told you there's a picture in our church.
Well, if a low-browed verger sidled up
Bringing me, like a blotch, on his prod's point,
660 A transfixed scorpion, let the reptile writhe,
And then said "See a thing that Rafael made—
This venom issued from Madonna's mouth!''
I should reply, "Rather, the soul of you
Has issued from your body, like from like,
665 By way of the ordure-corner!''
                                    But no less,
I tired of the same long black teasing lie
Obtruded thus at every turn; the pest
Was far too near the picture, anyhow:
One does Madonna service, making clowns
670 Remove their dung-heap from the sacristy.
"I will to the window, as he tempts,'' said I:
"Yes, whom the easy love has failed allure,
This new bait of adventure tempts,—thinks he.
Though the imprisoned lady keeps afar,
675 There will they lie in ambush, heads alert,
Kith, kin, and Count mustered to bite my heel.

654| MS:the Husband must of needs, and not the wife   P1868:the husband must, of all
needs, not the wife,   655| MS:the Lady   P1868:the lady   657| MS:our Church.
P1868:our church.   659| MS:me like § written over illegible word § a blotch on <>
point   P1868:me, like a blotch, on <> point,   661| MS:said "She <> Rafaelle
P1868:said, "She <> Rafael   1889a:said "See   662| MS:This creature issued
P1868:This venom issued <> mouth!''—   1872:mouth!''   665| MS:less   P1868:less,
666| MS:same black teazing   1872:same long black   1889a:teasing   668| MS:near
Madonna § crossed out and replaced above by § the picture   669| MS:service making folk
P1868:service, making clowns   671| MS:will go to <> tempts'' said   P1868:will to
<> tempts,'' said   672| MS:failed to lure,   P1868:failed allure,
673–75| MS:adventure may,—he thinks./ There <> ambush, all the brave, § last
three words crossed out and replaced above by two words and comma § heads alert,
P1868:thinks./ While the imprisoned lady keeps afar,/ There   1872:adventure
tempts,—thinks he./ Though the <> / There   676| MS:Mustering § altered to §
Mustered to match one man § last two words crossed out and replaced above by
two words § my heel,—Kith, kin, and Count. § indication that should be transposed
to read § Kith, kin and Count. Mustered to match my heel,—   P1868:and Count

No mother nor brother viper of the brood
Shall scuttle off without the instructive bruise!"

So I went: crossed street and street: "The next street's turn,
680 I stand beneath the terrace, see, above,
The black of the ambush-window. Then, in place
Of hand's throw of soft prelude over lute,
And cough that clears way for the ditty last,"—
I began to laugh already—"he will have
685 'Out of the hole you hide in, on to the front,
Count Guido Franceschini, show yourself!
Hear what a man thinks of a thing like you,
And after, take this foulness in your face!' "

The words lay living on my lip, I made
690 The one-turn more—and there at the window stood,
Framed in its black square length, with lamp in hand,
Pompilia; the same great, grave, griefful air
As stands i' the dusk, on altar that I know,
Left alone with one moonbeam in her cell,
695 Our Lady of all the Sorrows. Ere I knelt—
Assured myself that she was flesh and blood—
She had looked one look and vanished.
                              I thought—"Just so:
It was herself, they have set her there to watch—

---

mustered to bite my heel.   677| MS:No mother or brother § last three words inserted
above § < > them § altered to § the   P1868:mother nor brother   678| MS:bruise."
P1868:bruise!"   679| MS:So I < > street: "the < > turn   P1868:So,
I < > street: "The < > turn,   1889a:So I   680| MS:terrace, and above   P1868:terrace,
see, above,   681| MS:ambush window. Then, instead § crossed out § in place
P1868:ambush-window   682| MS:Of the hand's < > prelude on the lute   P1868:Of
hand's < > prelude over lute   1889a:lute,   686| MS:Count Guido Franceschini, and
show   P1868:Count Guido Franceschini, show   687| MS:Hear § crossed out and
replaced above by § Take § crossed out and original reading restored § < > man thinks of § last
two words crossed out and replaced above by § gives to § crossed out and original reading
restored §   688| MS:face!"   P1868:face!' "   690| MS:one turn   1889a:one-turn
692| MS:Pompilia, with the same grave griefful air   P1868:Pompilia; the same great, grave,
griefful air;   1868:air   693| MS:in < > on an altar   P1868:i' < > on altar
695| MS:of all § inserted above § the < > knelt . . .   P1868:knelt—   697| MS:vanished.

105

Stationed to see some wedding-band go by,
700 On fair pretence that she must bless the bride,
Or wait some funeral with friends wind past,
And crave peace for the corpse that claims its due.
She never dreams they used her for a snare,
And now withdraw the bait has served its turn.
705 Well done, the husband, who shall fare the worse!"
And on my lip again was—"Out with thee,
Guido!" When all at once she re-appeared;
But, this time, on the terrace overhead,
So close above me, she could almost touch
710 My head if she bent down; and she did bend,
While I stood still as stone, all eye, all ear.

She began—"You have sent me letters, Sir:
I have read none, I can neither read nor write;
But she you gave them to, a woman here,
715 One of the people in whose power I am,
Partly explained their sense, I think, to me
Obliged to listen while she inculcates
That you, a priest, can dare love me, a wife,
Desire to live or die as I shall bid,
720 (She makes me listen if I will or no)
Because you saw my face a single time.
It cannot be she says the thing you mean;
Such wickedness were deadly to us both:
But good true love would help me now so much—
725 I tell myself, you may mean good and true.
You offer me, I seem to understand,

§ ¶ § I said "Just *P1868:*vanished. § ¶ § I thought—"Just   699-700| MS:And wait
§ preceding two words crossed out and replaced above by three words § Stationed to see < >
by, § slash indicating division of line and following six words inserted above § On fair
pretence that she must § original line continues § and § crossed out § bless the bride,
701| MS:The bride, § last two words crossed out and replaced above by two words § Or wait,
some *P1868:*wait some   703| MS:snare *P1868:*snare,   705| MS:worse!
*P1868:*worse!"   706| MS:my very lip was *P1868:*my lip again was
707| MS:re-appeared *P1868:*re-appeared;   708| MS:But this time on *P1868:*But, this
time, on   712| MS:began "You *P1868:*began—"You   722| MS:mean,
*P1868:*mean;   723| MS:both *P1868:*both: 725| MS:may have meant it good.

Because I am in poverty and starve,
Much money, where one piece would save my life.
The silver cup upon the altar-cloth
730 Is neither yours to give nor mine to take;
But I might take one bit of bread therefrom,
Since I am starving, and return the rest,
Yet do no harm: this is my very case.
I am in that strait, I may not dare abstain
735 From so much of assistance as would bring
The guilt of theft on neither you nor me;
But no superfluous particle of aid.
I think, if you will let me state my case,
Even had you been so fancy-fevered here,
740 Not your sound self, you must grow healthy now—
Care only to bestow what I can take.
That it is only you in the wide world,
Knowing me nor in thought nor word nor deed,
Who, all unprompted save by your own heart,
745 Come proffering assistance now,—were strange
But that my whole life is so strange: as strange
It is, my husband whom I have not wronged
Should hate and harm me. For his own soul's sake,
Hinder the harm! But there is something more,
750 And that the strangest: it has got to be

*P1868:*may mean good and true.   727| MS:starve *P1868:*starve,   728| MS:money
when *P1868:*money, where   730| MS:take, *P1868:*take;   731| MS:I < > take
just one *P1868:*But I < > take one   733| MS:And do *P1868:*Yet do
734| MS:strait that I may not abstain *P1868:*strait, I *1872:*not dare abstain
735| MS:as will bring *P1868:*as would bring   737| MS:Not one superfluous
*P1868:*But no superfluous   738| MS:think if *P1868:*think, if   739| MS:been
fancy-fevered *P1868:*been so fancy-fevered   740| MS:you would § crossed out and
replaced above by § must grow sober now— *P1868:*grow healthy now—   742| MS:in
all the world, *P1868:*in the wide world,   743| MS:A stranger to me § last three words
crossed out and replaced above by three words § Knowing me not in thought, nor § inserted
above § word and § crossed out and replaced above by § nor *P1868:*Knowing me nor in
thought nor   744| MS:by her § crossed out and replaced above by § your own heart
*P1868:*heart,   745| MS:now, were *P1868:*now,—were   747| MS:is my *P1868:*is, my
748| MS:me,—for < > sake *P1868:*me. For < > sake,   749| MS:more. *P1868:*more,

Somehow for my sake too, and yet not mine,
—This is a riddle—for some kind of sake
Not any clearer to myself than you,
And yet as certain as that I draw breath,—
755   I would fain live, not die—oh no, not die!
My case is, I was dwelling happily
At Rome with those dear Comparini, called
Father and mother to me; when at once
I found I had become Count Guido's wife:
760   Who then, not waiting for a moment, changed
Into a fury of fire, if once he was
Merely a man: his face threw fire at mine,
He laid a hand on me that burned all peace,
All joy, all hope, and last all fear away,
765   Dipping the bough of life, so pleasant once,
In fire which shrivelled leaf and bud alike,
Burning not only present life but past,
Which you might think was safe beyond his reach.
He reached it, though, since that beloved pair,
770   My father once, my mother all those years,
That loved me so, now say I dreamed a dream
And bid me wake, henceforth no child of theirs,
Never in all the time their child at all.
Do you understand? I cannot: yet so it is.
775   Just so I say of you that proffer help:
I cannot understand what prompts your soul,
I simply needs must see that it is so,
Only one strange and wonderful thing more.
They came here with me, those two dear ones, kept

751| MS:too and § inserted above § yet *P1868*:too, and   753| MS:you *P1868*:you,
754| MS:breath, *P1868*:breath,—   757| MS:those two § crossed out and replaced above
by § dear Comparini called *P1868*:dear Comparini, called   758| MS:me, when
P1868:me; when   759| MS:wife; *P1868*:wife: 762| MS:man,—fire § transposed to
follow *threw* § thrilled § crossed out § his face and § crossed out § threw, § comma crossed out§
at mine § last two words added to follow *fire* § *P1868*:man: his <> mine,   763| MS:He
§ written over illegible word § <> hand at § crossed out and replaced above by § on <> peace
P1868:peace,   765| MS:life so <> once *P1868*:life, so <> once,   767| MS:past
P1868:past,   769| MS:it though, <> that Comparini pair *P1868*:it, though, <> that
beloved pair,   772| MS:wake become § crossed out and replaced above by § henceforth
P1868:wake, henceforth   774| MS:is: *P1868*:is.   775| MS:help *P1868*:help:

⁷⁸⁰ All the old love up, till my husband, till
His people here so tortured them, they fled.
And now, is it because I grow in flesh
And spirit one with him their torturer,
That they, renouncing him, must cast off me?
⁷⁸⁵ If I were graced by God to have a child,
Could I one day deny God graced me so?
Then, since my husband hates me, I shall break
No law that reigns in this fell house of hate,
By using—letting have effect so much
⁷⁹⁰ Of hate as hides me from that whole of hate
Would take my life which I want and must have—
Just as I take from your excess of love
Enough to save my life with, all I need.
The Archbishop said to murder me were sin:
⁷⁹⁵ My leaving Guido were a kind of death
With no sin,—more death, he must answer for.
Hear now what death to him and life to you
I wish to pay and owe. Take me to Rome!
You go to Rome, the servant makes me hear.
⁸⁰⁰ Take me as you would take a dog, I think,
Masterless left for strangers to maltreat:
Take me home like that—leave me in the house
Where the father and the mother are; and soon
They'll come to know and call me by my name,
⁸⁰⁵ Their child once more, since child I am, for all
They now forget me, which is the worst o' the dream—
And the way to end dreams is to break them, stand,
Walk, go: then help me to stand, walk and go!
The Governor said the strong should help the weak:

---

⁷⁸¹| MS:fled *P1868:*fled.   ⁷⁸⁴| MS:cast me off? *CP1868:*cast off me?
⁷⁸⁵| MS:child *CP1868:*child,   ⁷⁸⁷| MS:Then since *P1868:*Then, since
⁷⁸⁸| MS:hate *P1868:*hate,   ⁷⁸⁹| MS:By taking § crossed out and replaced above by §
using   ⁷⁹⁴| MS:sin. *P1868:*sin: ⁷⁹⁹| MS:me know. *P1868:*me hear.
⁸⁰³| MS:are, and *P1868:*are; and   ⁸⁹⁴| MS:name *P1868:*name,   ⁸⁰⁵| MS:more,
for § crossed out and replaced above by § since   ⁸⁰⁶| MS:of *P1868:*o'

109

810 You know how weak the strongest women are.
     How could I find my way there by myself?
     I cannot even call out, make them hear—
     Just as in dreams: I have tried and proved the fact.
     I have told this story and more to good great men,
815 The Archbishop and the Governor: they smiled.
     'Stop your mouth, fair one!'—presently they frowned,
     'Get you gone, disengage you from our feet!'
     I went in my despair to an old priest,
     Only a friar, no great man like these two,
820 But good, the Augustinian, people name
     Romano,—he confessed me two months since:
     He fears God, why then needs he fear the world?
     And when he questioned how it came about
     That I was found in danger of a sin—
825 Despair of any help from providence,—
     'Since, though your husband outrage you,' said he,
     'That is a case too common, the wives die
     Or live, but do not sin so deep as this'—
     Then I told—what I never will tell you—
830 How, worse than husband's hate, I had to bear
     The love,—soliciting to shame called love,—
     Of his brother,—the young idle priest i' the house
     With only the devil to meet there. 'This is grave—
     Yes, we must interfere: I counsel,—write
835 To those who used to be your parents once,
     Of dangers here, bid them convey you hence!'
     'But,' said I, 'when I neither read nor write?'
     Then he took pity and promised 'I will write.'
     If he did so,—why, they are dumb or dead:

810| MS:are— *P1868:*are.   814| MS:men *P1868:*men,   819| MS:two
*P1868:*two,   820| MS:the Augustine whom the people *P1868:*the Augustinian, people
822| MS:need *P1868:*needs   824| MS:of the sin *P1868:*of a sin—   825| MS:from
Providence,— *P1868:*from providence,—   826| MS:"Since <> you" said he
P1868:'Since <> you,' said he,   827| MS:"That *P1868:*'That   828| MS:this."
*P1868:*this'—   830| MS:hate I *P1868:*hate, I   832| MS:in *P1868:*i'
833| MS:there. "This *P1868:*there. 'This   835| MS:once *P1868:*once,
836| MS:here, and § crossed out § <> hence. *P1868:*hence!'   837| MS:"But," said I
"when <> write? *P1868:*'But,' said I, 'when <> write?'   838| MS:promised "I will
write." *P1868:*promised 'I will write.'   839| MS:why they are dumb, the same:

110

840 Either they give no credit to the tale,
    Or else, wrapped wholly up in their own joy
    Of such escape, they care not who cries, still
    I' the clutches. Anyhow, no word arrives.
    All such extravagance and dreadfulness
845 Seems incident to dreaming, cured one way,—
    Wake me! The letter I received this morn,
    Said—if the woman spoke your very sense—
    'You would die for me:' I can believe it now:
    For now the dream gets to involve yourself.
850 First of all, you seemed wicked and not good,
    In writing me those letters: you came in
    Like a thief upon me. I this morning said
    In my extremity, entreat the thief!
    Try if he have in him no honest touch!
855 A thief might save me from a murderer.
    'Twas a thief said the last kind word to Christ:
    Christ took the kindness and forgave the theft:
    And so did I prepare what I now say.
    But now, that you stand and I see your face,
860 Though you have never uttered word yet,—well, I know,
    Here too has been dream-work, delusion too,
    And that at no time, you with the eyes here,
    Ever intended to do wrong by me,
    Nor wrote such letters therefore. It is false,
865 And you are true, have been true, will be true.
    To Rome then,—when is it you take me there?
    Each minute lost is mortal. When?—I ask."

---

*P1868:*why, they are dumb, or dead: *CP1868:*dumb or dead: 842| MS:escape they <>
cries still *P1868:*escape, they <> cries, still   843| MS:In the clutches. Anyhow no
*P1868:*I' the clutches. Anyhow no   845| MS:Are incident <> way, *P1868:*Seems
incident <> way,—   848| MS:"You <> me:" I <> now. *P1868:*'You <> me:' I <>
now: 850| MS:all you *P1868:*all, you   853| MS:extremity; entreat
*P1868:*extremity, entreat   854| MS:touch, *P1868:*touch!   857| MS:the comfort
and <> the sin: *P1868:*the kindness and <> the theft: 859| MS:face *P1868:*face,
861| MS:There § altered to § Here   862| MS:At that <> eyes there, *P1868:*And that
<> eyes here,   864| MS:wrote the letters *P1868:*wrote such letters   865| MS:true,
true will be. *P1868:*true, will be true.   867| MS:Each § written over illegible word §
<> is precious § crossed out and replaced above by § mortal: when? I *P1868:*mortal.

I answered "It shall be when it can be.
I will go hence and do your pleasure, find
870 The sure and speedy means of travel, then
Come back and take you to your friends in Rome.
There wants a carriage, money and the rest,—
A day's work by to-morrow at this time.
How shall I see you and assure escape?"

875 She replied, "Pass, to-morrow at this hour.
If I am at the open window, well:
If I am absent, drop a handkerchief
And walk by! I shall see from where I watch,
And know that all is done. Return next eve,
880 And next, and so till we can meet and speak!"
"To-morrow at this hour I pass," said I.
She was withdrawn.
                         Here is another point
I bid you pause at. When I told thus far,
Someone said, subtly, "Here at least was found
885 Your confidence in error,—you perceived
The spirit of the letters, in a sort,
Had been the lady's, if the body should be
Supplied by Guido: say, he forged them all!
Here was the unforged fact—she sent for you,
890 Spontaneously elected you to help,
—What men call, loved you: Guido read her mind,
Gave it expression to assure the world

When?—I   868| MS:answered, "It <> be;   P1868:answered "It <> be.
869| MS:your will § crossed out and replaced above by § pleasure   871| MS:Return
§ crossed out and replaced above by two words § Come back   872| MS:and other means
§ last two words inserted above line and then crossed out § the rest,   P1868:rest,—
874| MS:and concert escape?"   P1868:and assure escape?"   875| MS:replied "Pass
P1868:replied, "Pass   876| MS:If I can stand there § last three words § crossed out and
replaced above by § am at the open § inserted above §   878| MS:And walk by, I <>
watch   P1868:And walk by! I <> watch,   879| MS:done; return   P1868:done. Return
880| MS:speak."   P1868:speak!"   1872:speak!'   1889a:speak!"   881| MS:pass" said
P1868:pass," said   883| MS:I make you <> at. When last I   P1868:I bid you at When
CP1868:I bid you <> at. When I   884| MS:said subtly "Here   P1868:said, subtly,
"Here   888| MS:say he <> all,   P1868:say, he <> all!   889| MS:fact she
P1868:fact—she   891| MS:What <> mind   P1868:—What <> mind,

The case was just as he foresaw: he wrote,
She spoke."
        Sirs, that first simile serves still,—
895 That falsehood of a scorpion hatched, I say,
Nowhere i' the world but in Madonna's mouth.
Go on! Suppose, that falsehood foiled, next eve
Pictured Madonna raised her painted hand,
Fixed the face Rafael bent above the Babe,
900 On my face as I flung me at her feet:
Such miracle vouchsafed and manifest,
Would that prove the first lying tale was true?
Pompilia spoke, and I at once received,
Accepted my own fact, my miracle
905 Self-authorized and self-explained,—she chose
To summon me and signify her choice.
Afterward,—oh! I gave a passing glance
To a certain ugly cloud-shape, goblin-shred
Of hell-smoke hurrying past the splendid moon
910 Out now to tolerate no darkness more,
And saw right through the thing that tried to pass
For truth and solid, not an empty lie:
"So, he not only forged the words for her
But words for me, made letters he called mine:
915 What I sent, he retained, gave these in place,
All by the mistress-messenger! As I
Recognized her, at potency of truth,
So she, by the crystalline soul, knew me,
Never mistook the signs. Enough of this—

894| MS:serves here,— *P1868:*serves still,— 896| MS:in <> mouth: *P1868:*i' <>
mouth. 897| MS:on, suppose *CP1868:*on! Suppose 899| MS:Rafaelle bent on
§ crossed out and replaced above by § above <> Babe *P1868:*Rafael <> Babe,
903| MS:received *P1868:*received, 905| MS:Self-authorised and self-explained, she
*P1868:*self-explained,—she *1889a:*Self-authorized 907| MS:oh, I *P1868:*oh! I
908| MS:cloud-shape—goblin shred *P1868:*cloud-shape, goblin shred
*CP1868:*cloud-shape goblin-shred 915| MS:place *P1868:*place,
916| MS:mistress-messenger: as *P1868:*mistress-messenger! As 917| MS:her at <>
truth *P1868:*her, at <> truth, 918| MS:she by <> soul knew me *P1868:*she, by <>
soul, knew me, 919| MS:Nor § altered § Never ever § crossed out and replaced above by §
mis took the mean man § last two words crossed out and replaced above by § signs. Enough of
this— § last three words and dash written above line § *P1868:*Never mistook

113

920 Let the wraith go to nothingness again,
Here is the orb, have only thought for her!"

"Thought?" nay, Sirs, what shall follow was not thought:
I have thought sometimes, and thought long and hard.
I have stood before, gone round a serious thing,
925 Tasked my whole mind to touch and clasp it close,
As I stretch forth my arm to touch this bar.
God and man, and what duty I owe both,—
I dare to say I have confronted these
In thought: but no such faculty helped here.
930 I put forth no thought,—powerless, all that night
I paced the city: it was the first Spring.
By the invasion I lay passive to,
In rushed new things, the old were rapt away;
Alike abolished—the imprisonment
935 Of the outside air, the inside weight o' the world
That pulled me down. Death meant, to spurn the ground,
Soar to the sky,—die well and you do that.
The very immolation made the bliss;
Death was the heart of life, and all the harm
940 My folly had crouched to avoid, now proved a veil
Hiding all gain my wisdom strove to grasp:
As if the intense centre of the flame
Should turn a heaven to that devoted fly
Which hitherto, sophist alike and sage,
945 Saint Thomas with his sober grey goose-quill,
And sinner Plato by Cephisian reed,
Would fain, pretending just the insect's good,

921| MS:her." *P1868:*her!" 921-22| MS:§ no ¶ § *P1868:*§ ¶ §
922| MS:"Thought"? Nay, sirs *P1868:*"Thought?" nay, Sirs 923| MS:sometimes and
*P1868:*sometimes, and 925| MS:close *P1868:*close, 926| MS:to grasp § crossed
out and replaced above by § touch <> bar: *P1868:*bar. 927| MS:both, *P1868:*both,—
930| MS:powerless all *P1868:*powerless, all 931| MS:first Spring: *P1868:*first
Spring. 932| MS:In the <> I bore § crossed out and replaced above by § was passively,
§ *ly* crossed out § to § obviously added in revision § *P1868:*By the <> I lay passive to,
933| MS:away. *P1868:*away; 934| MS:abolished the *P1868:*abolished—the
935| MS:weight of *P1868:*weight o' 936| MS:ground *P1868:*ground,
937| MS:Spring to *P1868:*Soar to 938| MS:bliss, *P1868:*bliss; 940| MS:a mask
§ crossed out § veil 941| MS:grasp. *P1868:*grasp: 944| MS:Whom hitherto
*P1868:*Which hitherto 945| MS:grey-goose quill *P1868:*grey goose quill,
*CP1868:*grey goose-quill, 946| MS:reed *P1868:*reed, 947| MS:the creature's
§ crossed out and replaced above by two words and comma § insect's good,

Whisk off, drive back, consign to shade again.
Into another state, under new rule
950 I knew myself was passing swift and sure;
Whereof the initiatory pang approached,
Felicitous annoy, as bitter-sweet
As when the virgin-band, the victors chaste,
Feel at the end the earthly garments drop,
955 And rise with something of a rosy shame
Into immortal nakedness: so I
Lay, and let come the proper throe would thrill
Into the ecstasy and outthrob pain.

I' the grey of dawn it was I found myself
960 Facing the pillared front o' the Pieve—mine,
My church: it seemed to say for the first time
"But am not I the Bride, the mystic love
O' the Lamb, who took thy plighted troth, my priest,
To fold thy warm heart on my heart of stone
965 And freeze thee nor unfasten any more?
This is a fleshly woman,—let the free
Bestow their life-blood, thou art pulseless now!"
See! Day by day I had risen and left this church
At the signal waved me by some foolish fan,
970 With half a curse and half a pitying smile
For the monk I stumbled over in my haste,
Prostrate and corpse-like at the altar-foot
Intent on his *corona*: then the church
Was ready with her quip, if word conduced,

950| MS:sure *P1868:*sure;   953| MS:chaste *P1868:*chaste,   954| MS:garments
fall § crossed out § drop *P1868:*drop,   956| MS:nakedness, so *P1868:*nakedness: so
957| MS:Helpless § crossed out and replaced above by § Lay and *P1868:*Lay, and
958| MS:and repay all pain. *P1868:*and outthrob pain.   958–59| MS:§ no ¶ §
P1868:§ ¶ §   959| MS:In <> dawn it was § last two words inserted above § I *P1868:*I'
960| MS:of *P1868:*o'   963| MS:Of who take § crossed out and replaced above by § took
thy <> troth, of § crossed out and replaced above by § my priest, § indication that last two
words should be transposed to come between *took* and *thy* and then restored to original
position § *P1868:*O'   964| MS:my stony § crossed out §   967| MS:now."
*P1868:*now!"   968| MS:See! day *P1868:*See! Day   969| MS:waved by any Donna's
fan *P1868:*waved me by some foolish fan,   971| MS:haste *P1868:*haste,
974| MS:Threw me a cheery word § last five words crossed out and replaced above by five
words § Was ready with her quip, if word there were § crossed out and replaced above by §

115

975 To quicken my pace nor stop for prating—"There!
Be thankful you are no such ninny, go
Rather to teach a black-eyed novice cards
Than gabble Latin and protrude that nose
Smoothed to a sheep's through no brains and much faith!"

980 That sort of incentive! Now the church changed tone—
Now, when I found out first that life and death
Are means to an end, that passion uses both,
Indisputably mistress of the man
Whose form of worship is self-sacrifice:

985 Now, from the stone lungs sighed the scrannel voice
"Leave that live passion, come be dead with me!"
As if, i' the fabled garden, I had gone
On great adventure, plucked in ignorance
Hedge-fruit, and feasted to satiety,

990 Laughing at such high fame for hips and haws,
And scorned the achievement: then come all at once
O' the prize o' the place, the thing of perfect gold,
The apple's self: and, scarce my eye on that,
Was 'ware as well o' the seven-fold dragon's watch.

995 Sirs, I obeyed. Obedience was too strange,—
This new thing that had been struck into me

---

came, *P1868:*word conduced,   975| MS:prating § *ing* crossed out and replaced above
by § ed § crossed out and original reading restored §   977| MS:black eyed
*P1868:*black-eyed   978| MS:Than patter § crossed out and replaced above by § gabble
latin *P1868:*gabble Latin   979| MS:faith"— *P1868:*faith!"   981| MS:out first
§ inserted above §   983| MS:man, *P1868:*man   984| MS:self-sacrifice
*P1868:*self-sacrifice— *1889a:*self-sacrifice: 985| MS:Now from *P1868:*Now, from
987| MS:if ere while § last two words crossed out § in the fabled § inserted above § garden, once
was dreamed § last three words crossed out and replaced above by three words § I had gone
*P1868:*if, i'   988| MS:Gone § crossed out § on § altered to § On the great adventure, I had
§ last two words crossed out § plucked *P1868:*On great adventure
989| MS:Hedge-fruit, so feasting § last two words crossed out and replaced above by two
words § and feasted   990| MS:With laughter § last two words crossed out and replaced
above by § Laughing at such high § inserted above §   991| MS:the achievement: then come
unawares § crossed out and replaced above by three words § all at once *P1868:*achievement
992| MS:On the prize of the place *P1868:*O' the prize o' the place   993| MS:The
wondrous § inserted above and then crossed out §   994| MS:Was ware <> of <>
dragon's watch § crossed out and replaced above line by illegible word which is crossed out
and original reading restored § *P1868:*Was 'ware <> o'   995| MS:strange,

By the look o' the lady,—to dare disobey
The first authoritative word. 'Twas God's.
I had been lifted to the level of her,
1000 Could take such sounds into my sense. I said
"We two are cognisant o' the Master now;
She it is bids me bow the head: how true,
I am a priest! I see the function here;
I thought the other way self-sacrifice:
1005 This is the true, seals up the perfect sum.
I pay it, sit down, silently obey."

So, I went home. Dawn broke, noon broadened, I—
I sat stone-still, let time run over me.
The sun slanted into my room, had reached
1010 The west. I opened book,—Aquinas blazed
With one black name only on the white page.
I looked up, saw the sunset: vespers rang:
"She counts the minutes till I keep my word
And come say all is ready. I am a priest.
1015 Duty to God is duty to her: I think
God, who created her, will save her too
Some new way, by one miracle the more,
Without me. Then, prayer may avail perhaps."
I went to my own place i' the Pieve, read
1020 The office: I was back at home again
Sitting i' the dark. "Could she but know—but know
That, were there good in this distinct from God's,
Really good as it reached her, though procured

---

*P1868:*strange,—   997| MS:of the lady, to *P1868:*o' the lady,—to   998| MS:word.
'Twas God's: *P1868:*word. 'Twas God's   1001| MS:We <> cognizant of <> now,
P1868:"We <> o' <> now; *1889a:*cognisant   1002| MS:It is she bids <> head: too
§ crossed out and replaced above by § how *1889a:*She it is bids   1003| MS:priest: I <>
function now: *P1868:*priest! I <> function here;   1004| MS:other was self-sacrifice,
*P1868:*other way self-sacrifice: 1007| MS:So I <> home, daw <> noon somehow
came, *P1868:*So, I <> home. Dawn <> noon broadened, I—   1008| MS:stone still let
*P1868:*stone-still, let   1010| MS:The West. I opened the book *P1868:*The west. I
opened book   1016| MS:God who <> her will *P1868:*God, who <> her, will
1018| MS:me. Then prayer *P1868:*me. Then, prayer   1019| MS:in *P1868:*i'
1021| MS:in *P1868:*i'   1022| MS:That were her good *P1868:*That, were there good
1023| MS:as she gained § last two words crossed out § it reached her § last two words inserted
above § though made gain § last two words crossed out § *P1868:*her, though

By a sin of mine,—I should sin: God forgives.
1025 She knows it is no fear withholds me: fear?
Of what? Suspense here is the terrible thing.
If she should, as she counts the minutes, come
On the fantastic notion that I fear
The world now, fear the Archbishop, fear perhaps
1030 Count Guido, he who, having forged the lies,
May wait the work, attend the effect,—I fear
The sword of Guido! Let God see to that—
Hating lies, let not her believe a lie!"

Again the morning found me. "I will work,
1035 Tie down my foolish thoughts. Thank God so far!
I have saved her from a scandal, stopped the tongues
Had broken else into a cackle and hiss
Around the noble name. Duty is still
Wisdom: I have been wise." So the day wore.

1040 At evening—"But, achieving victory,
I must not blink the priest's peculiar part,
Nor shrink to counsel, comfort: priest and friend—
How do we discontinue to be friends?
I will go minister, advise her seek
1045 Help at the source,—above all, not despair:
There may be other happier help at hand.
I hope it,—wherefore then neglect to say?"

There she stood—leaned there, for the second time,
Over the terrace, looked at me, then spoke:

1024| MS:mine, I < > sin—God   P1868:mine,—I < > sin: God   1026| MS:thing:
P1868:thing.   1030| MS:he who < > lies   P1868:he who, < > lies,
1031| MS:Must wait   P1868:May wait   1032| MS:sword as a priest may! Let
P1868:sword of Guido! Let   1033-34| MS:§ no ¶ §   P1868:§ ¶ §   1039| MS:Wisdom,
I < > wise. So the § inserted above §   P1868:Wisdom: I < > wise." So   1039-40| MS:§ no
¶ §   P1868:§ ¶ §   1040| MS:evening—But achieving § last two words inserted above §
"Victory, is now achieved. § last three words crossed out §   P1868:evening—"But, achieving
victory,   1042| MS:comfort . . priest   P1868:comfort: priest
1048| MS:stood—leaned there, § last two words and comma inserted above §

¹⁰⁵⁰ "Why is it you have suffered me to stay
Breaking my heart two days more than was need?
Why delay help, your own heart yearns to give?
You are again here, in the self-same mind,
I see here, steadfast in the face of you,—
¹⁰⁵⁵ You grudge to do no one thing that I ask.
Why then is nothing done? You know my need.
Still, through God's pity on me, there is time
And one day more: shall I be saved or no?"
I answered—"Lady, waste no thought, no word
¹⁰⁶⁰ Even to forgive me! Care for what I care—
Only! Now follow me as I were fate!
Leave this house in the dark to-morrow night,
Just before daybreak:—there's new moon this eve—
It sets, and then begins the solid black.
¹⁰⁶⁵ Descend, proceed to the Torrione, step
Over the low dilapidated wall,
Take San Clemente, there's no other gate
Unguarded at the hour: some paces thence
An inn stands; cross to it; I shall be there."

¹⁰⁷⁰ She answered, "If I can but find the way.

---

^{1052|} MS:help your *P1868:*help, your   ^{1053|} MS:here in the self same *P1868:*here, in
the self-same   ^{1054|} MS:see there stedfast <> you. *P1868:*see here, steadfast <>
you,—   ^{1055|} MS:grudge me § crossed out and replaced above by two words § to do no
one effort § crossed out and replaced above by § thing <> ask *P1868:*ask.
^{1058|} MS:no? *P1868:*no?"   ^{1058-59|} MS:§ ¶ §   *P1868:*§ no ¶ §
^{1059|} MS:answered—"Lady, § inserted above § Waste no precious § crossed out and replaced
above by following two words § thought, no word on me. § last two words and period crossed
out §   ^{1060|} MS:Even for pardon § last two words crossed out and replaced above by
three words and exclamation mark § to forgive me! Care   ^{1061|} MS:§ line crowded
between lines 1060 and 1062. Two illegible words followed by *descend hence,* all crossed
out § Only <> fate. *P1868:*fate!   ^{1062|} MS:§ first six words crossed out and then
restored § dark, to-morrow *P1868:*dark to-morrow   ^{1063|} MS:before day dawn: the
§ altered to § there's new crescent § inserted above and then crossed out § moon is now, § last
two words crossed out and replaced above by following two words and dash § this eve—
*P1868:*before daybreak:—there's   ^{1066|} MS:delapidated *P1868:*dilapidated
^{1069|} MS:stands; called the Steed: § last three words and colon crossed out and replaced above
by following three words and semi-colon § cross to it; <> there. *P1868:*there."

But I shall find it. Go now!"

I did go,
Took rapidly the route myself prescribed,
Stopped at Torrione, climbed the ruined place,
Proved that the gate was practicable, reached
1075 The inn, no eye, despite the dark, could miss,
Knocked there and entered, made the host secure:
"With Caponsacchi it is ask and have;
I know my betters. Are you bound for Rome?
I get swift horse and trusty man," said he.

1080 Then I retraced my steps, was found once more
In my own house for the last time: there lay
The broad pale opened Summa. "Shut his book,
There's other showing! 'Twas a Thomas too
Obtained,—more favoured than his namesake here,—
1085 A gift, tied faith fast, foiled the tug of doubt,—
Our Lady's girdle; down he saw it drop
As she ascended into heaven, they say:
He kept that safe and bade all doubt adieu.
I too have seen a lady and hold a grace."

1090 I know not how the night passed: morning broke;
Presently came my servant. "Sir, this eve—
Do you forget?" I started. "How forget?
What is it you know?" "With due submission, Sir,
This being last Monday in the month but one
1095 And a vigil, since to-morrow is Saint George,
And feast day, and moreover day for copes,
And Canon Conti now away a month,

1070| MS:answered "If P1868:answered, "If   1075| MS:inn no P1868:inn, no
1076| MS:the Host P1868:the host   1083| MS:favored P1868:favoured
1085| MS:gift tied <> doubt, P1868:gift, tied <> doubt,—   1086| MS:girdle, down
P1868:girdle; down   1087| MS:into Heaven P1868:into heaven
1089–91| MS:grace./ Presently P1868:grace."/ § ¶ § I know not how the night passed:
morning broke:/ Presently 1872:/ <> broke 1889a:/ <> broke;   1092| MS:started.
"How P1868:started.—"How 1889a:started. "How   1093| MS:know?" "With
P1868:know?"—"With 1889a:know?" "With   1094| MS:That being the last <>
month P1868:This being last <> month but one   1095–97| MS:a Vigil, and moreover

And Canon Crispi sour because, forsooth,
You let him sulk in stall and bear the brunt
1100 Of the octave . . . Well, Sir, 'tis important!"
                                        "True!
Hearken, I have to start for Rome this night.
No word, lest Crispi overboil and burst!
Provide me with a laic dress! Throw dust
I' the Canon's eye, stop his tongue's scandal so!
1105 See there's a sword in case of accident."
I knew the knave, the knave knew me.

                                 And thus
Through each familiar hindrance of the day
Did I make steadily for its hour and end,—
Felt time's old barrier-growth of right and fit
1110 Give way through all its twines, and let me go.
Use and wont recognized the excepted man,
Let speed the special service,—and I sped
Till, at the dead between midnight and morn,
There was I at the goal, before the gate,
1115 With a tune in the ears, low leading up to loud,
A light in the eyes, faint that would soon be flare,

---

day for copes,/ And   *P1868:*a vigil, since to-morrow is St. George,/ And feast day, and
moreover day for copes,/ And   *CP1868:*is Saint George,   1098| MS:And Canon Crispi
sore because   *P1868:*And Canon Crispi sour because   1100| MS:Of
. . the octave . . § last two words inserted above § <> important." § ¶ § "So I
see. § three words crossed out and replaced above by § "True."   *P1868:*Of the important!" §
¶ § "True!"   *1872:*important!" § ¶ § "True!   1101| MS:to go § crossed out and replaced
above by § start to § altered to § for Rome to-night: § crossed out and replaced above by two
words and period § this eve.   *P1868:*for Rome this night.   1102| MS:Lest Canon §
crossed out § Crispi break all bounds! § last three words crossed out and replaced above by
three words and exclamation point § overboil and burst!   1103| MS:Better § crossed out
§ provide § altered to § provide me with § last two words inserted above § <> dress—throw
*P1868:*dress! Throw   1104| MS:In <> eye and § crossed out § stop a § crossed out § his
tongue's § last two words inserted above § <> so.   *P1868:*I' <> eye, stop <> so!
1106| MS:knave, and § crossed out § the <> me. And   *P1868:*me § ¶ § And
1108| MS:hour at end,—   *P1868:*hour and end,—   1109| MS:of fit § written over illegi-
ble word § and wont § crossed out and replaced above by § right § indication that should be
transposed to read § of right and fit   1110| MS:Give way through all its twines, § last
four words inserted above § and let me go; through twist and twine § last four words crossed
out §   *1872:*go.   1111| MS:As § crossed out and replaced above by three words § Use
and wont recognizing § altered to § recognized <> man   *P1868:*man,   1116| MS:A
faint § inserted above and then crossed out § <> eyes, faint turned § last
two words crossed out and replaced above by five words § that faint

121

Ever some spiritual witness new and new
In faster frequence, crowding solitude
To watch the way o' the warfare,—till, at last,
1120 When the ecstatic minute must bring birth,
Began a whiteness in the distance, waxed
Whiter and whiter, near grew and more near,
Till it was she: there did Pompilia come:
The white I saw shine through her was her soul's,
1125 Certainly, for the body was one black,
Black from head down to foot. She did not speak,
Glided into the carriage,—so a cloud
Gathers the moon up. "By San Spirito,
To Rome, as if the road burned underneath!
1130 Reach Rome, then hold my head in pledge, I pay
The run and the risk to heart's content!" Just that,
I said,—then, in another tick of time,
Sprang, was beside her, she and I alone.

So it began, our flight thro' dusk to clear,
1135 Through day and night and day again to night
Once more, and to last dreadful dawn of all.
Sirs, how should I lie quiet in my grave
Unless you suffer me wring, drop by drop,
My brain dry, make a riddance of the drench
1140 Of minutes with a memory in each,
Recorded motion, breath or look of hers,

---

would soon be *P1868:*eyes, faint that would   1117| MS:Ever the § crossed out and
replaced above by § some   1118| MS:frequence crowding § written over illegible word §
the § crossed out § *P1868:*frequence, crowding   1119| MS:of the battle § crossed out and
replaced above by § warfare *P1868:*o'   1121| MS:ecstatic § written over illegible word §
1122| MS:more near *P1868:*more near,   1123| MS:there was Pompilia *P1868:*there
did Pompilia   1124| MS:the light § crossed out and replaced above by § white
1125| MS:body's vesture was *P1868:*body was   1129| MS:underneath;
*P1868:*underneath!   1130| MS:pledge I *P1868:*pledge, I   1131| MS:that
*CP1868:*that, *1889a:*that § emended to § that, § see Editorial Notes §   1134| MS:thro'
dark § written over by § dusk and day § last two words crossed out and replaced above by two
words § to clear,   1135| MS:Through day § last two words inserted above § And—night
and < > to the § crossed out § night once more § last two words crossed out § *P1868:*and
night and   1136| MS:Once more; § last two words and semi-colon inserted above § And
the last § inserted above § *P1868:*more, and to last   1141| MS:motion, speech § crossed

122

Which poured forth would present you one pure glass,
Mirror you plain,—as God's sea, glassed in gold,
His saints,—the perfect soul Pompilia? Men,
1145 You must know that a man gets drunk with truth
Stagnant inside him! Oh, they've killed her, Sirs!
Can I be calm?
Calmly! Each incident
Proves, I maintain, that action of the flight
For the true thing it was. The first faint scratch
1150 O' the stone will test its nature, teach its worth
To idiots who name Parian—coprolite.
After all, I shall give no glare—at best
Only display you certain scattered lights
Lamping the rush and roll of the abyss:
1155 Nothing but here and there a fire-point pricks
Wavelet from wavelet: well!
For the first hour
We both were silent in the night, I know:
Sometimes I did not see nor understand.
Blackness engulphed me,—partial stupor, say—
1160 Then I would break way, breathe through the surprise,
And be aware again, and see who sat
In the dark vest with the white face and hands.
I said to myself—"I have caught it, I conceive
The mind o' the mystery: 'tis the way they wake
1165 And wait, two martyrs somewhere in a tomb
Each by each as their blessing was to die;
Some signal they are promised and expect,—
When to arise before the trumpet scares:
So, through the whole course of the world they wait

---

out and replaced above by § breath   1143| MS:Mirror § written over illegible word § <>
sea, glassy gold, *P1868:*sea, glassed in gold,   1146| MS:him! Oh, the murder, his—
§ last three words crossed out and replaced above by four words § they've killed her, Sirs!
1147| MS:calm? § ¶ § Calmly—each *P1868:*calm? § ¶ § Calmly! Each   1150| MS:Of
*P1868:*O'   1151| MS:To fools who name the Parian coprolite. *P1868:*To idiots who
name Parian, coprolite. *1889a:*name Parian—coprolite.   1152| MS:no glass—at
*P1868:*no glare—at   1154| MS:abyss— *1889a:*abyss: 1156| MS:well,— § ¶ § For
*P1868:*well! § ¶ § For   1158| MS:understand, *P1868:*understand.   1161| MS:be
myself § crossed out and replaced above by § aware   1164| MS:of the mystery—'tis
*P1868:*mystery: 'tis *CP1868:*o'   1166| MS:their manner was *P1868:*their blessing was
1167| MS:expect *P1868:*expect, *1872:*expect,—   1168| MS:scares *P1868:*scares:

123

1170 The last day, but so fearless and so safe!
No other wise, in safety and not fear,
I lie, because she lies too by my side."
You know this is not love, Sirs,—it is faith,
The feeling that there's God, he reigns and rules
1175 Out of this low world: that is all; no harm!
At times she drew a soft sigh—music seemed
Always to hover just above her lips,
Not settle,—break a silence music too.

In the determined morning, I first found
1180 Her head erect, her face turned full to me,
Her soul intent on mine through two wide eyes.
I answered them. "You are saved hitherto.
We have passed Perugia,—gone round by the wood,
Not through, I seem to think,—and opposite
1185 I know Assisi; this is holy ground."
Then she resumed. "How long since we both left
Arezzo?" "Years—and certain hours beside."

It was at . . . ah, but I forget the names!
'Tis a mere post-house and a hovel or two;
1190 I left the carriage and got bread and wine
And brought it her. "Does it detain to eat?"
"They stay perforce, change horses,—therefore eat!
We lose no minute: we arrive, be sure!"
This was—I know not where—there's a great hill
1195 Close over, and the stream has lost its bridge,

1170| MS:last Day *P1868:*last day   1171| MS:other wise *P1868:*otherwise § emended
to § other wise § see Editorial Notes §   1172| MS:side. *P1868:*side."
1174| MS:feeling there's God, and He *P1868:*feeling that there's God, he
1177| MS:lips *1889a:*lips,   1178-79| MS:§ no ¶ § *P1868:* § ¶ §   1180| MS:head erect,
her face § last three words inserted above §   1182| MS:hitherto: *P1868:*hitherto.
1183| MS:passed Perugia, gone < > § illegible word altered to § wood *P1868:*passed
Perugia,—gone < > wood,   1184| MS:know Assisi, this *P1868:*know Assisi; this   1187| MS:Arezzo?"—"Years
*1889a:*Arezzo?" "Years   1187-88| MS:§ no ¶ § *P1868:*§ ¶ §   1188| MS:names,
*P1868:*names!   1189| MS:Tis < > two, *P1868:*'Tis < > two,— *1889a:*two;
1191| MS:her. "Does *P1868:*her.—"Does *1889a:*her. "Does   1192| MS:"They
P1868:"—They *1889a:*"They   1194| MS:She said—I *1889a:*This was—I

One fords it. She began—"I have heard say
Of some sick body that my mother knew,
'Twas no good sign when in a limb diseased
All the pain suddenly departs,—as if
1200 The guardian angel discontinued pain
Because the hope of cure was gone at last:
The limb will not again exert itself,
It needs be pained no longer: so with me,
—My soul whence all the pain is past at once:
1205 All pain must be to work some good in the end.
True, this I feel now, this may be that good,
Pain was because of,—otherwise, I fear!"

She said,—a long while later in the day,
When I had let the silence be,—abrupt—
1210 "Have you a mother?" "She died, I was born."
"A sister then?" "No sister." "Who was it—
What woman were you used to serve this way,
Be kind to, till I called you and you came?"
I did not like that word. Soon afterward—
1215 "Tell me, are men unhappy, in some kind
Of mere unhappiness at being men,
As women suffer, being womanish?
Have you, now, some unhappiness, I mean,
Born of what may be man's strength overmuch,
1220 To match the undue susceptibility,
The sense at every pore when hate is close?
It hurts us if a baby hides its face
Or child strikes at us punily, calls names
Or makes a mouth,—much more if stranger men

1196| MS:began "I   *P1868:*began—"I   1197| MS:knew   *P1868:*knew,   1198| MS:a
part § crossed out and replaced above by § limb   1200| MS:The guardian § inserted
above §   1204| MS:My   *P1868:*—My   1207| MS:fear."   *P1868:*fear!"
1207-8| MS:§ no ¶ §   *P1868:*§ ¶ §   1208| MS:day   *P1868:*day,   1209| MS:abrupt
*P1868:*abrupt—   1210| MS:mother?"—"She   *1889a:*mother?" "She
1211| MS:then?"—"No sister."—"Whom   *CP1868:*sister."—"Who   *1889a:*then?" "No
sister." "Who   1215| MS:"Tell men, are   *P1868:*"Tell me, are
1214| MS:afterward   *P1868:*afterward—   1217| MS:woman suffer being   *P1868:*women
suffer, being   1218| MS:you now some   *P1868:*you, now, some   1223| MS:Or a

¹²²⁵ Laugh or frown,—just as that were much to bear!
Yet rocks split,—and the blow-ball does no more,
Quivers to feathery nothing at a touch;
And strength may have its drawback weakness scapes."

Once she asked "What is it that made you smile,
¹²³⁰ At the great gate with the eagles and the snakes,
Where the company entered, 'tis a long time since?"
"—Forgive—I think you would not understand:
Ah, but you ask me,—therefore, it was this.
That was a certain bishop's villa-gate,
¹²³⁵ I knew it by the eagles,—and at once
Remembered this same bishop was just he
People of old were wont to bid me please
If I would catch preferment: so, I smiled
Because an impulse came to me, a whim—
¹²⁴⁰ What if I prayed the prelate leave to speak,
Began upon him in his presence-hall
—'What, still at work so grey and obsolete?
Still rocheted and mitred more or less?
Don't you feel all that out of fashion now?
¹²⁴⁵ I find out when the day of things is done!' "

At eve we heard the *angelus:* she turned—
"I told you I can neither read nor write.
My life stopped with the play-time; I will learn,
If I begin to live again: but you—
¹²⁵⁰ Who are a priest—wherefore do you not read

child   *P1868:*Or child   ^{1225|}   MS:bear: *P1868:*bear!   ^{1226|}   MS:Yet, rocks
*P1868:*Yet rocks   ^{1227|}   MS:Flying § crossed out and replaced above by § Quivers
^{1228|}   MS:And § added in margin § < > drawback weakness   *P1868:*drawback, weakness
*1889a:*drawback weakness   ^{1228–29|}   MS:§ no ¶ §   *P1868:*§ ¶ §   *1889a:*§ no ¶ §   *1889:*§ no
¶; emended to restore ¶; see Editorial Notes §   ^{1231|}   MS:entered,—'tis   *P1868:*entered,
'tis   ^{1232|}   MS:"Forgive   *P1868:*"—Forgive   ^{1234|}   MS:certain Bishop's
*P1868:*certain bishop's   ^{1236|}   MS:same Bishop was the same   *P1868:*bishop was just
he   ^{1238|}   MS:so I   *P1868:*so, I   ^{1239|}   MS:whim,   *P1868:*whim—
^{1242|}   MS:"What   *P1868:*—'What   ^{1243|}   MS:rochetted   *CP1868:*rocheted
^{1245|}   MS:done!"   *P1868:*done!' "   ^{1245–46|}   MS:§ no ¶ §   *P1868:*§ ¶ §
^{1246|}   MS:angelus   *P1868:angelus*   ^{1247|}   MS:write   *P1868:*write.
^{1248|}   MS:play-time: I will learn   *P1868:*play-time; I   *CP1868:*learn,   ^{1249|}   MS:If life
§ crossed out and replaced above by § I begin to live § last two words inserted above §

The service at this hour? Read Gabriel's song,
The lesson, and then read the little prayer
To Raphael, proper for us travellers!"
I did not like that, neither, but I read.

1255 When we stopped at Foligno it was dark.
The people of the post came out with lights:
The driver said, "This time to-morrow, may
Saints only help, relays continue good,
Nor robbers hinder, we arrive at Rome."
1260 I urged, "Why tax your strength a second night?
Trust me, alight here and take brief repose!
We are out of harm's reach, past pursuit: go sleep
If but an hour! I keep watch, guard the while
Here in the doorway." But her whole face changed,
1265 The misery grew again about her mouth,
The eyes burned up from faintness, like the fawn's
Tired to death in the thicket, when she feels
The probing spear o' the huntsman. "Oh, no stay!"
She cried, in the fawn's cry, "On to Rome, on, on—
1270 Unless 'tis you who fear,—which cannot be!"

We did go on all night; but at its close
She was troubled, restless, moaned low, talked at whiles
To herself, her brow on quiver with the dream:
Once, wide awake, she menaced, at arms' length
1275 Waved away something—"Never again with you!
My soul is mine, my body is my soul's:
You and I are divided ever more

1253| MS:travellers." *P1868:*travellers!"   1254–55| MS:§ no ¶ §   *P1868:*§ ¶ §
1257| MS:said "This <> to-morrow, night § crossed out §   *P1868:*said, "This
1258| MS:If § crossed out § saints § altered to § Saints only § inserted above line § help, and
§ crossed out §   1259| MS:And § crossed out and replaced above by § Nor robbers do not
§ last two words crossed out §   1260| *P1868:*urged,—"Why   *1889a:*urged, "Why
1261| MS:repose.   *P1868:*repose!   1262| MS:reach, and long § last two words
crossed out § pursuit, go   *P1868:*pursuit: go   1263| MS:hour, I   *P1868:*hour! I
1266| MS:faintness like   *P1868:*faintness, like   1267| MS:thicket when
*P1868:*thicket, when   1268| MS:of the huntsman. Oh, no stay!   *P1868:*o' the huntsman.
"Oh, no stay!"   1270–71| MS:§ no ¶ §   *P1868:*§ ¶ §   1271| MS:night, but
*P1868:*night; but   1273| MS:dream;   *P1868:*dream: 1274| MS:arms   *P1868:*arms'

In soul and body: get you gone!" Then I—
"Why, in my whole life I have never prayed!
1280 Oh, if the God, that only can, would help!
Am I his priest with power to cast out fiends?
Let God arise and all his enemies
Be scattered!" By morn, there was peace, no sigh
Out of the deep sleep.

                              When she woke at last,
1285 I answered the first look—"Scarce twelve hours more,
Then, Rome! There probably was no pursuit,
There cannot now be peril: bear up brave!
Just some twelve hours to press through to the prize:
Then, no more of the terrible journey!" "Then,
1290 No more o' the journey: if it might but last!
Always, my life-long, thus to journey still!
It is the interruption that I dread,—
With no dread, ever to be here and thus!
Never to see a face nor hear a voice!
1295 Yours is no voice; you speak when you are dumb;
Nor face, I see it in the dark. I want
No face nor voice that change and grow unkind."
That I liked, that was the best thing she said.

In the broad day, I dared entreat, "Descend!"
1300 I told a woman, at the garden-gate
By the post-house, white and pleasant in the sun,
"It is my sister,—talk with her apart!
She is married and unhappy, you perceive;
I take her home because her head is hurt;

1279-80| MS:§ crowded between lines 1278 and 1281 in a continuous line and divided between
prayed and *Oh* by slash §   1281| MS:fiends. *P1868:*fiends?   1283| MS:scattered!"
By morning there   *P1868:*scattered!" By morn, there   1284| MS:sleep; when <> last
*P1868:*sleep. § ¶ § When <> last,   1285| MS:look—"Not twelve   *P1868:*look—"Scarce
twelve   1287| MS:peril,—bear up brave,   *P1868:*peril: bear up brave!
1288| MS:Just the § crossed out and replaced above by § some <> prize—   *1889a:*prize:
1289| MS:Then no <> "Then   *P1868:*Then, no <> "Then,   1290| MS:more journey
*P1868:*more o' the journey   1291| MS:life-long, to be here and thus § last five words
crossed out §   1298-99| MS:§ no ¶ § *P1868:*§ ¶ §   1299| MS:day, "I dare entreat,
descend!"   *P1868:*day, I dared entreat, "Descend!"   1300| MS:woman, by the
*P1868:*woman, at the   1302| MS:Sister <> apart.   *P1868:*sister <> apart!

¹³⁰⁵ Comfort her as you women understand!"
So, there I left them by the garden-wall,
Paced the road, then bade put the horses to,
Came back, and there she sat: close to her knee,
A black-eyed child still held the bowl of milk,
¹³¹⁰ Wondered to see how little she could drink,
And in her arms the woman's infant lay.
She smiled at me "How much good this has done!
This is a whole night's rest and how much more!
I can proceed now, though I wish to stay.
¹³¹⁵ How do you call that tree with the thick top
That holds in all its leafy green and gold
The sun now like an immense egg of fire?"
(It was a million-leaved mimosa.) "Take
The babe away from me and let me go!"
¹³²⁰ And in the carriage "Still a day, my friend!
And perhaps half a night, the woman fears.
I pray it finish since it cannot last:
There may be more misfortune at the close,
And where will you be? God suffice me then!"
¹³²⁵ And presently—for there was a roadside-shrine—
"When I was taken first to my own church
Lorenzo in Lucina, being a girl,
And bid confess my faults, I interposed
'But teach me what fault to confess and know!'
¹³³⁰ So, the priest said—'You should bethink yourself:
Each human being needs must have done wrong!'
Now, be you candid and no priest but friend—

---

^{1306|} MS:So there <> garden wall, *P1868:*So, there <> garden-wall,
^{1308|} MS:sat,—close <> knee *P1868:*sat: close <> knee, ^{1310|} MS:Wondered
§ followed by illegible letter, perhaps *t*, perhaps crossed out § see *P1868:*Wondered to see
^{1314|} MS:now though *P1868:*now, though ^{1317|} MS:an immense § inserted above §
^{1319|} MS:go." *P1868:*go!" ^{1320|} MS:friend, *P1868:*friend! ^{1322|} MS:I wish it
over § last three words crossed out and replaced above by three words § pray it finish <> last.
*1889a:*last DC, BrU: last: *1889:*last: ^{1323|} MS:the end, § crossed out and replaced
above by § close, ^{1324|} MS:then! *P1868:*then!" ^{1325|} MS:roadside shrine—
*P1868:*roadside-shrine— ^{1328|} MS:And § in left margin § Bid § altered to § bid
^{1329|} MS:know.' *P1868:*know!' ^{1330|} MS:So the <> said "You *P1868:*So, the <>
said—'You ^{1332|} MS:Now, you be candid *P1868:*Now, be you candid

129

Were I surprised and killed here on the spot,
A runaway from husband and his home,
¹³³⁵ Do you account it were in sin I died?
My husband used to seem to harm me, not . . .
Not on pretence he punished sin of mine,
Nor for sin's sake and lust of cruelty,
But as I heard him bid a farming-man
¹³⁴⁰ At the villa take a lamb once to the wood
And there ill-treat it, meaning that the wolf
Should hear its cries, and so come, quick be caught,
Enticed to the trap: he practised thus with me
That so, whatever were his gain thereby,
¹³⁴⁵ Others than I might become prey and spoil.
Had it been only between our two selves,—
His pleasure and my pain,—why, pleasure him
By dying, nor such need to make a coil!
But this was worth an effort, that my pain
¹³⁵⁰ Should not become a snare, prove pain threefold
To other people—strangers—or unborn—
How should I know? I sought release from that—
I think, or else from,—dare I say, some cause
Such as is put into a tree, which turns
¹³⁵⁵ Away from the north wind with what nest it holds,—
The woman said that trees so turn: now, friend,
Tell me, because I cannot trust myself!
You are a man: what have I done amiss?"
You must conceive my answer,—I forget—
¹³⁶⁰ Taken up wholly with the thought, perhaps,
This time she might have said,—might, did not say—
"You are a priest." She said, "my friend."

                    Day wore,

---

¹³³³| MS:Were I to die, be killed *P1868:*Were I surprised and killed   ¹³³⁵| MS:you esteem § crossed out and replaced above by § account   ¹³³⁶| MS:not § following 1336 a line is drawn across page and in margin is written *insert,* second line down from 1336 is circled and joined to horizontal line by arrow § *P1868:*not . . .   ¹³³⁸| MS:§ this line preceded 1337 in unaltered MS § Not for § inserted above § < > and mere § crossed out §
¹³⁴⁰| MS:the Villa *P1868:*the villa   ¹³⁴²| MS:caught *P1868:*caught,
¹³⁴⁶| MS:selves *P1868:*selves,—   ¹³⁴⁸| MS:coil. *P1868:*coil!   ¹³⁴⁹| MS:effort that *P1868:*effort, that   ¹³⁵⁰| MS:snare, prove § inserted above §
¹³⁵⁵| MS:northwind < > nests *P1868:*nest *1872:*north wind   ¹³⁵⁶| MS:—The *P1868:*The   ¹³⁵⁷| MS:myself, *P1868:*myself!   ¹³⁶⁰| MS:thought perhaps *P1868:*thought, perhaps,   ¹³⁶²| MS:priest"—she *P1868:*priest." She

We passed the places, somehow the calm went,
Again the restless eyes began to rove
1365 In new fear of the foe mine could not see.
She wandered in her mind,—addressed me once
"Gaetano!"—that is not my name: whose name?
I grew alarmed, my head seemed turning too.
I quickened pace with promise now, now threat:
1370 Bade drive and drive, nor any stopping more.
"Too deep i' the thick of the struggle, struggle through!
Then drench her in repose though death's self pour
The plenitude of quiet,—help us, God,
Whom the winds carry!"

Suddenly I saw
1375 The old tower, and the little white-walled clump
Of buildings and the cypress-tree or two,—
"Already Castelnuovo—Rome!" I cried,
"As good as Rome,—Rome is the next stage, think!
This is where travellers' hearts are wont to beat.
1380 Say you are saved, sweet lady!" Up she woke.
The sky was fierce with colour from the sun
Setting. She screamed out "No, I must not die!
Take me no farther, I should die: stay here!
I have more life to save than mine!"

She swooned.
1385 We seemed safe: what was it foreboded so?
Out of the coach into the inn I bore
The motionless and breathless pure and pale

1364| MS:the restlessness, § altered to § restless the § crossed out § eyes that § crossed out and
replaced above by two words § began to roved § altered to § rove   1365| MS:foe I § crossed
out and replaced above by § mine < > see: 1889a:see.   1367| MS:"Gaetano!" That
P1868:"Gaetano!"—that   1368| MS:too: 1889a:too.   1369| MS:threat,
P1868:threat: 1370| MS:more, P1868:more.   1371| MS:Too much § crossed out
and replaced above by § deep in < > through— P1868:i' < > through!
1372| MS:Then steep § crossed out and replaced above by § drench   1373| MS:help now,
God, P1868:help us, God,   1374| MS:carry!" Suddenly P1868:carry!" § ¶ § Suddenly
1379| MS:travellers P1868:travellers'   1380| MS:sweet Lady!" Up she sprang § crossed
out and replaced above by § woke P1868:sweet lady < > woke.   1384| MS:mine." § ¶ §
She swooned: P1868:mine!" § ¶ § She swooned.   1385| MS:We were safe: why § altered
to § what was it I § crossed out § boded § altered to § foreboded P1868:We seemed safe
1387| MS:The motionless and § last two words inserted above and followed by two illegible
letters, crossed out § breathless burden, oh, the pure and § last five words crossed out and
replaced above by following word and comma § lady, pale P1868:breathless pure and pale

Pompilia,—bore her through a pitying group
And laid her on a couch, still calm and cured
1390 By deep sleep of all woes at once. The host
Was urgent "Let her stay an hour or two!
Leave her to us, all will be right by morn!"
Oh, my foreboding! But I could not choose.

I paced the passage, kept watch all night long.
1395 I listened,—not one movement, not one sigh.
"Fear not: she sleeps so sound!" they said: but I
Feared, all the same, kept fearing more and more,
Found myself throb with fear from head to foot,
Filled with a sense of such impending woe,
1400 That, at first pause of night, pretence of gray,
I made my mind up it was morn.—"Reach Rome,
Lest hell reach her! A dozen miles to make,
Another long breath, and we emerge!" I stood
I' the court-yard, roused the sleepy grooms. "Have out
1405 Carriage and horse, give haste, take gold!" said I.
While they made ready in the doubtful morn,—
'Twas the last minute,—needs must I ascend
And break her sleep; I turned to go.
                                        And there
Faced me Count Guido, there posed the mean man
1410 As master,—took the field, encamped his rights,
Challenged the world: there leered new triumph, there
Scowled the old malice in the visage bad

1388| MS:pitying crowd § crossed out § group   1389| MS:still calm § written over
illegible word, perhaps *cured* §   1390| MS:once. They § altered to § The Host
*P1868:*The host   1391| MS:two: *P1868:*two!   1393–94| MS:§ no ¶ § *P1868:*§ ¶ §
1396| MS:sound," they said—but *P1868:*sound!" they *1889a:*said: but   1399| MS:woe
*P1868:*woe,   1400| MS:That at *P1868:*That, at   1401| MS:morn. "Reach
*P1868:*morn.—"Reach   1403| MS:emerge." I *P1868:*emerge!" I   1404| MS:In the
court, aroused <> grooms, "Have *P1868:*I' the court-yard, roused <> grooms. "Have
1405| MS:Man § crossed out and replaced above by § carriage and horse, I gave § last two
words crossed out and replaced above by three words § give haste, take gold for diligence.
§ last two words crossed out and replaced above by two words and period § "said I.
*P1868:*gold!"—said *1889a:*gold!" said   1406| MS:There they stood ready <> morn.
*P1868:*While they made ready <> morn,—   1408| MS:And summon her § last two
words crossed out and replaced above by three words § break the sleep *P1868:*break
her sleep   1409| MS:there the mean man posed § indication that *posed* is to
be transposed to follow *there* §   1410| MS:As the master, took *P1868:*As

And black o' the scamp. Soon triumph suppled the tongue
A little, malice glued to his dry throat,
¹⁴¹⁵ And he part howled, part hissed . . . oh, how he kept
Well out o' the way, at arm's length and to spare!—
"My salutation to your priestship! What?
Matutinal, busy with book so soon
Of an April day that's damp as tears that now
¹⁴²⁰ Deluge Arezzo at its darling's flight?—
'Tis unfair, wrongs feminity at large,
To let a single dame monopolize
A heart the whole sex claims, should share alike:
Therefore I overtake you, Canon! Come!
¹⁴²⁵ The lady,—could you leave her side so soon?
You have not yet experienced at her hands
My treatment, you lay down undrugged, I see!
Hence this alertness—hence no death-in-life
Like what held arms fast when she stole from mine.
¹⁴³⁰ To be sure, you took the solace and repose
That first night at Foligno!—news abound
O' the road by this time,—men regaled me much,
As past them I came halting after you,

---

master,—took   ¹⁴¹³| MS:of the losel § crossed out and replaced above by § scamp.
Soon § inserted above § Triumph loosed § crossed out and replaced above by § suppled
*P1868:*o' <> triumph   ¹⁴¹⁵| MS:hissed . . oh   *1889a:*hissed . . . oh
¹⁴¹⁶| MS:of <> spare . . .   *P1868:*spare!—   *CP1868:*o'   ¹⁴¹⁷| MS:priestship,—
what?   *P1868:*priestship! What?   ¹⁴¹⁸| MS:soon § followed by illegible erasure,
perhaps question mark §   ¹⁴²⁰| MS:flight,—   *P1868:*flight?—   ¹⁴²¹| MS:'Tis
on behalf of our § last four words crossed out and replaced above by two words § unfair to
femininity at large   *P1868:*unfair, wrongs femininity at large,   ¹⁴²²⁻²³| MS:§ crowded
between lines 1421 and 1424 in one continuous line, separated between *monopolize*
and *A* by slash §   ¹⁴²²| MS:single Dame   *P1868:*single dame
¹⁴²³| MS:claims to share   *P1868:*claims, should share   ¹⁴²⁴| MS:Therefore § written in
left margin § <> you, Canon: Come!   *P1868:*you, Canon! Come!   ¹⁴²⁵| MS:The lady
*P1868:*The lady,   ¹⁴²⁷| MS:treatment, were § crossed out and replaced above by three
words § you lay down undrugged, last night, § last two words crossed out § I see,   *P1868:*see!
¹⁴²⁸| MS:alertness—and no death in life   *P1868:*alertness—hence no death-in-life
¹⁴²⁹| MS:held me fast   *P1868:*held arms fast   ¹⁴³⁰| MS:you had § crossed out and
replaced above by § took   ¹⁴³¹| MS:On § crossed out § the § altered to § The first <>
Foligno,—news   *P1868:*That first <> Foligno!—news   ¹⁴³²| MS:On the road, by <>
me with   *P1868:*O' the road by <> me much,   ¹⁴³³| MS:As post § altered to § past
by post I halted § last four words crossed out and replaced above by four

133

Vulcan pursuing Mars, as poets sing,—
1435 Still at the last here pant I, but arrive,
Vulcan—and not without my Cyclops too,
The Commissary and the unpoisoned arm
O' the Civil Force, should Mars turn mutineer.
Enough of fooling: capture the culprits, friend!
1440 Here is the lover in the smart disguise
With the sword,—he is a priest, so mine lies still.
There upstairs hides my wife the runaway,
His leman: the two plotted, poisoned first,
Plundered me after, and eloped thus far
1445 Where now you find them. Do your duty quick!
Arrest and hold him! That's done: now catch her!"

During this speech of that man,—well, I stood
Away, as he managed,—still, I stood as near
The throat of him,—with these two hands, my own,—
1450 As now I stand near yours, Sir,—one quick spring,
One great good satisfying gripe, and lo!
There had he lain abolished with his lie,
Creation purged o' the miscreate, man redeemed,
A spittle wiped off from the face of God!
1455 I, in some measure, seek a poor excuse

---

words § them I came halting   1434| MS:sing— *P1868:*sing,—   1435| MS:I but
*P1868:*I, but   1437| MS:and an arm or so *P1868:*and the unpoisoned arm
1438| MS:Of < > Force, in case, § last two words crossed out and replaced above by § should
Mars turn § inserted above § *P1868:*O'   1439| MS:fooling: here are the *P1868:*fooling:
capture the   1441| MS:With § written over perhaps *And* § < > still: *1889a:*still.
1442| MS:There in the house, my *P1868:*There upstairs hides my   1443| MS:His
love: the two were fain to poison first, *P1868:*His leman: the two plotted, poisoned first,
1444| MS:Plunder me after, § crossed out and replaced above by two words § next and
last of all § last two words crossed out § elope *P1868:*Plundered me after, and
eloped   1445| MS:duty now! *P1868:*duty quick!   1446| MS:Disarm § crossed
out and replaced above by § Arrest < > him: that's § followed by apparently one
word superimposed upon another, both crossed out, illegible, and replaced above
by § done *P1868:*him! That's   1446-47| MS:§ ¶ § *P1868:*§ no ¶ § *1889:*§ no ¶;
emended to restore ¶; see Editorial Notes §   1448| MS:still I *P1868:*still, I
1449| MS:him with < > hands my own *P1868:*him,—with < > hands, my own,—
1450| MS:stand to you, Sirs, you or you. *P1868:*stand near yours, Sir,—one quick
spring,   1451| MS:lo *P1868:*lo!   1453| MS:Creation had been purged of the
miscreate, *P1868:*Creation purged o' the miscreate, man redeemed,   1454| MS:God.
*P1868:*God!   1455| MS:I in < > measure seek § written over illegible word § my sake
§ uncertain; last two words crossed out and replaced above by two words § out some excuse

134

For what I left undone, in just this fact
That my first feeling at the speech I quote
Was—not of what a blasphemy was dared,
Not what a bag of venomed purulence
1460 Was split and noisome,—but how splendidly
Mirthful, how ludicrous a lie was launched!
Would Molière's self wish more than hear such man
Call, claim such woman for his own, his wife,
Even though, in due amazement at the boast,
1465 He had stammered, she moreover was divine?
She to be his,—were hardly less absurd
Than that he took her name into his mouth,
Licked, and then let it go again, the beast,
Signed with his slaver. Oh, she poisoned him,
1470 Plundered him, and the rest! Well, what I wished
Was, that he would but go on, say once more
So to the world, and get his meed of men,
The fist's reply to the filth. And while I mused,
The minute, oh the misery, was gone!
1475 On either idle hand of me there stood
Really an officer, nor laughed i' the least:
Nay, rendered justice to his reason, laid
Logic to heart, as 'twere submitted them
"Twice two makes four."
                              "And now, catch her!" he cried.
1480 That sobered me. "Let myself lead the way—

*P1868:*I, in <> measure, seek a poor excuse   1456| MS:what I did not § last two words
crossed out and replaced above by two words § left undone, in just § inserted above line § this
simple § crossed out § fact   1458| MS:was spoken, § word and comma crossed out and
replaced above by word and comma § dared,   1460| MS:Was broken § crossed out and
replaced above by § split   1461| MS:Mirthful, what ludicrousness § altered to § ludicrous
<> launched.   *P1868:*launched!   *1889a:*Mirthful, how ludicrous   1462| MS:Would
Momus self   *P1868:*Would Molière's self   1463| *1872:*wife   DC, BrU:wife,
*1889:*wife,   1464| MS:the chance,   *P1868:*the boast,   1465| MS:stammered she
<> divine: *P1868:*stammered, she <> divine?   1467| MS:mouth   *P1868:*mouth,
1468| MS:Licked and   *P1868:*Licked, and   1470| MS:Plundered and all the
*P1868:*Plundered him, and the   1471| MS:Was that   *P1868:*Was, that
1472| MS:That to   *P1868:*So to   1476| MS:in the least.   *P1868:*i'   *1872:*least
*1889a:*least: 1477| MS:They rendered   *1889a:*Nay, rendered   1478| MS:as if he
submitted   *P1868:*as 'twere submitted   1479| MS:her," he   *P1868:*her!"—he
*1889a:*her!" he   1480| MS:me "Let <> way   *P1868:*me. "Let <> way—

Ere you arrest me, who am somebody,
Being, as you hear, a priest and privileged,—
To the lady's chamber! I presume you—men
Expert, instructed how to find out truth,
1485 Familiar with the guise of guilt. Detect
Guilt on her face when it meets mine, then judge
Between us and the mad dog howling there!"
Up we all went together, in they broke
O' the chamber late my chapel. There she lay,
1490 Composed as when I laid her, that last eve,
O' the couch, still breathless, motionless, sleep's self,
Wax-white, seraphic, saturate with the sun
O' the morning that now flooded from the front
And filled the window with a light like blood.
1495 "Behold the poisoner, the adulteress,
—And feigning sleep too! Seize, bind!" Guido hissed.

She started up, stood erect, face to face
With the husband: back he fell, was buttressed there
By the window all a-flame with morning-red,
1500 He the black figure, the opprobrious blur
Against all peace and joy and light and life.
"Away from between me and hell!" she cried:
"Hell for me, no embracing any more!
I am God's, I love God, God—whose knees I clasp,
1505 Whose utterly most just award I take,

1481-82| MS:§ written in continuous line in top margin and separated between *somebody*
and *And* by slash § 1482| MS:And, as < > priest, and privileged—§ slash through dash
§ *P1868:*priest and privileged,— *1889a:*Being, as 1483| MS:the Lady's chamber; I
< > you men *P1868:*the lady's chamber! I < > you—men 1484| MS: find the truth;
*P1868:*find out truth, 1487| MS:there." *P1868:*there!" 1489| MS:On < > lay
*P1868:*O' < > lay, 1491| MS:On < > breathless motionless, all sleep, *P1868:*O' < >
breathless, motionless, sleep's self, 1492| MS:seraphic § written over partially erased,
illegible word § 1493| MS:Of *P1868:*O' 1494-95| MS:blood:/ So a saint lies at
dawn of Judgment day./ "Behold the poisoner, and § crossed out and replaced above by § the
*P1868:*blood./ "Behold 1496| MS:And < > bind!"—Guido *P1868:*—And
*1889a:*bind!" Guido 1499| MS:a-flame *1889a:*a flame § emended to § a-flame § see
Editorial Notes § 1500| MS:that § altered to § the opprobrious blot *P1868:*opprobrious
blur 1501| MS:all light and life and peace and joy § indication that should be
transposed to read § all peace and joy and light and life. 1502| MS:and Hell" she
*P1868:*hell!"—she *1889a:*hell! she 1503| MS:Hell < > no embraces any *P1868:*"Hell
< > no embracing any 1504| MS:love God, God— § inserted above § 1505| MS:I
take His utterly most just award *P1868:*Whose utterly most just award I take,

But bear no more love-making devils: hence!"
I may have made an effort to reach her side
From where I stood i' the door-way,—anyhow
I found the arms, I wanted, pinioned fast,
1510 Was powerless in the clutch to left and right
O' the rabble pouring in, rascality
Enlisted, rampant on the side of hearth
Home and the husband,—pay in prospect too!
They heaped themselves upon me. "Ha!—and him
1515 Also you outrage? Him, too, my sole friend,
Guardian and saviour? That I baulk you of,
Since—see how God can help at last and worst!"
She sprang at the sword that hung beside him, seized,
Drew, brandished it, the sunrise burned for joy
1520 O' the blade, "Die," cried she, "devil, in God's name!"
Ah, but they all closed round her, twelve to one
—The unmanly men, no woman-mother made,
Spawned somehow! Dead-white and disarmed she lay.
No matter for the sword, her word sufficed
1525 To spike the coward through and through: he shook,
Could only spit between the teeth—"You see?
You hear? Bear witness, then! Write down . . but no—
Carry these criminals to the prison-house,
For first thing! I begin my search meanwhile
1530 After the stolen effects, gold, jewels, plate,
Money and clothes, they robbed me of and fled,

1508| MS:in the doorway *P1868:*i' the door-way   1509| MS:arms I *P1868:*arms, I
1511| MS:Of *P1868:*O'   1512| MS:Enlisted, rampant § inserted above § <> hearth
§ slash inserted after *hearth* § and home § last two words crossed out § *P1868:*hearth
1513| MS:Home § inserted above § And the husband, with some § last two words
crossed out and replaced above by dash and two words § —fees in prospect of a
§ last two words crossed out and replaced above by word and period § too. fee.
*P1868:*and the husband,—pay in prospect too!   1514| MS:me—"Ha—and
*P1868:*me.—"Ha—and *1889a:*me. "Ha   1518| MS:sprung <> beside me,
seized *P1868:*beside him, seized *1889a:*sprang   1520| MS:On the
blade, "Die" cried *P1868:*O' the blade, "Die," cried   1521| MS:one, *1872:*one
1522| MS:men no *P1868:*men, no   1523| MS:somehow,—dead-white <>
lay,— *P1868:*somehow! Dead-white <> lay. *1889a:*lay   DC, BrU: lay. *1889:*lay.
1525| MS:shook *P1868:*shook,   1526| MS:spit throu § crossed out and replaced
above by § between   1527| MS:then: write <> but, no— *P1868:*then! Write
*1872:*but no—   1528| MS:prison-house *P1868:*prison-house,   1529| MS:thing: I
*P1868:*thing! I   1530| MS:For certain *P1868:*After the   1531| MS:clothes they

With no few amorous pieces, verse and prose,
I have much reason to expect to find."

When I saw that—no more than the first mad speech,
1535 Made out the speaker mad and a laughing-stock,
So neither did this next device explode
One listener's indignation,—that a scribe
Did sit down, set himself to write indeed,
While sundry knaves began to peer and pry
1540 In corner and hole,—that Guido, wiping brow
And getting him a countenance, was fast
Losing his fear, beginning to strut free
O' the stage of his exploit, snuff here, sniff there,—
Then I took truth in, guessed sufficiently
1545 The service for the moment. "What I say,
Slight at your peril! We are aliens here,
My adversary and I, called noble both;
I am the nobler, and a name men know.
I could refer our cause to our own Court
1550 In our own country, but prefer appeal
To the nearer jurisdiction. Being a priest,
Though in a secular garb,—for reasons good

<> fled: *P1868:*clothes, they *1872:*fled *1889a:*fled, 1533| MS:find. *P1868:*find."
1533-34| MS:§ no ¶ § *P1868:*§ ¶ § 1534| MS:saw, § comma crossed out and replaced
above by word and comma § that, no <> the first § written over illegible word §
speech *P1868:*saw, that,—no <> the first mad speech, *1872:*saw that—no
1535| MS:speaker fool § crossed out and replaced above by § mad 1536| MS:So § in
margin § Neither § altered to § neither <> next § written over illegible word § charge § followed
by illegible fragment; both crossed out and replaced above by § device 1537| MS:One
man's mere indignation *P1868:*One listener's indignation 1538| *1872:*down; set
*1889a:*down, set 1539| MS:And sundry *1889a:*While sundry 1540| MS:hole, as
Guido *P1868:*hole,—that Guido 1542| MS:fears *P1868:*fear 1543| MS:On <>
exploits <> there, *P1868:*O' <> exploit <> there,— 1544| MS:I took the truth in,
saw sufficiently *P1868:*in, guessed sufficiently *1872:*Then I took truth 1545| MS:the
minute "What *P1868:*the moment—"What *1872:*moment. "What 1546| MS:peril.
We <> here *P1868:*peril! We <> here, 1547| MS:and I, and noble *P1868:*and I,
called noble 1548| MS:I being § crossed out and replaced above by following two
words § am the nobler, a great § last two words crossed out and replaced above by following
two words § and a <> know: *P1868:*know. 1549| MS:own court *1889a:*own Court
1550| MS:country but § written over illegible word § *P1868:*country, but 1551| MS:To
another § crossed out and replaced above by following two words § the nearer jurisdiction:
being a priest *P1868:*jurisdiction. Being a priest, 1552| MS:garb for

I shall adduce in due time to my peers,—
I demand that the Church I serve, decide
1555 Between us, right the slandered lady there.
A Tuscan noble, I might claim the Duke:
A priest, I rather choose the Church,—bid Rome
Cover the wronged with her inviolate shield."

There was no refusing this: they bore me off,
1560 They bore her off, to separate cells o' the same
Ignoble prison, and, separate, thence to Rome.
Pompilia's face, then and thus, looked on me
The last time in this life: not one sight since,
Never another sight to be! And yet
1565 I thought I had saved her. I appealed to Rome:
It seems I simply sent her to her death.
You tell me she is dying now, or dead;
I cannot bring myself to quite believe
This is a place you torture people in:
1570 What if this your intelligence were just
A subtlety, an honest wile to work
On a man at unawares? 'Twere worthy you.
No, Sirs, I cannot have the lady dead!
That erect form, flashing brow, fulgurant eye,
1575 That voice immortal (oh, that voice of hers!)
That vision in the blood-red day-break—that
Leap to life of the pale electric sword
Angels go armed with,—that was not the last
O' the lady! Come, I see through it, you find—
1580 Know the manœuvre! Also herself said

---

*P1868:*garb,—for   1553| MS:peers. *P1868:*peers,—   1554| MS:demand Rome,
whose rule § last three words crossed out and replaced above by following three words § that
the Church   1555| MS:the murdered lady *P1868:*the slandered lady
1556| MS:noble I might choose § crossed out and replaced above by § claim *P1868:*noble, I
1557| MS:priest I rather invoke Rome § last two words crossed out and replaced above by §
choose the Church *P1868:*priest, I   1559| MS:off *P1868:*off,   1560| MS:of
*P1868:*o'   1562| MS:face then and thus looked *P1868:*face, then and thus, looked
1565| MS:her: I *P1868:*her. I   1567| MS:now or dead: *P1868:*now, or dead;
1568| MS:believe. *P1868:*believe   1572| MS:unawares: 'Twere *P1868:*unawares?
'Twere   1573| MS:dead— *P1868:*dead!   1574| MS:eye *P1868:*eye,
1579| MS:Of <> you see— *P1868:*O' <> you find—   1580| MS:manœuvre: also

I had saved her: do you dare say she spoke false?
Let me see for myself if it be so!
Though she were dying, a Priest might be of use,
The more when he's a friend too,—she called me
1585 Far beyond "friend." Come, let me see her—indeed
It is my duty, being a priest: I hope
I stand confessed, established, proved a priest?
My punishment had motive that, a priest
I, in a laic garb, a mundane mode,
1590 Did what were harmlessly done otherwise.
I never touched her with my finger-tip
Except to carry her to the couch, that eve,
Against my heart, beneath my head, bowed low,
As we priests carry the paten: that is why
1595 —To get leave and go see her of your grace—
I have told you this whole story over again.
Do I deserve grace? For I might lock lips,
Laugh at your jurisdiction: what have you
To do with me in the matter? I suppose
1600 You hardly think I donned a bravo's dress
To have a hand in the new crime; on the old,
Judgment's delivered, penalty imposed,
I was chained fast at Civita hand and foot—
She had only you to trust to, you and Rome,
1605 Rome and the Church, and no pert meddling priest
Two days ago, when Guido, with the right,
Hacked her to pieces. One might well be wroth;
I have been patient, done my best to help:
I come from Civita and punishment
1610 As friend of the Court—and for pure friendship's sake

---

*P1868:*manœuvre! Also   ¹⁵⁸¹| MS:her—do *P1868:*her: do   ¹⁵⁸³| MS:a priest
might bring § crossed out and replaced above by § be *1872:*a Priest   ¹⁵⁸⁷| MS:I am
confessed *P1868:*I stand confessed   ¹⁵⁹⁰| MS:otherwise; *P1868:*otherwise.
¹⁵⁹²| MS:couch that eve *P1868:*couch, that eve,   ¹⁵⁹⁶| MS:again— *P1868:*again.
¹⁵⁹⁷| MS:lips *P1868:*lips,   ¹⁵⁹⁸| MS:jurisdiction—what *P1868:*jurisdiction: what
¹⁶⁰¹| MS:the murder § crossed out and replaced above by following two words and
semi-colon § new crime;   ¹⁶⁰²| MS:delivered, punishment's § crossed out and replaced
above by § penalty's imposed, *P1868:*penalty imposed,   ¹⁶⁰⁶| MS:when Guido, for his
part, *P1868:*when Guido, with the right,   ¹⁶⁰⁷| MS:pieces: one < > wroth,
*P1868:*pieces. One < > wroth;   ¹⁶¹⁰| MS:the court *1889a:*the Court

Have told my tale to the end,—nay, not the end—
For, wait—I'll end—not leave you that excuse!

When we were parted,—shall I go on there?
I was presently brought to Rome—yes, here I stood
1615 Opposite yonder very crucifix—
And there sat you and you, Sirs, quite the same.
I heard charge, and bore question, and told tale
Noted down in the book there,—turn and see
If, by one jot or tittle, I vary now!
1620 I' the colour the tale takes, there's change perhaps;
'Tis natural, since the sky is different,
Eclipse in the air now; still, the outline stays.
I showed you how it came to be my part
To save the lady. Then your clerk produced
1625 Papers, a pack of stupid and impure
Banalities called letters about love—
Love, indeed,—I could teach who styled them so,
Better, I think, though priest and loveless both!
"—How was it that a wife, young, innocent,
1630 And stranger to your person, wrote this page?"—
"—She wrote it when the Holy Father wrote
The bestiality that posts thro' Rome,
Put in his mouth by Pasquin." "Nor perhaps
Did you return these answers, verse and prose,
1635 Signed, sealed and sent the lady? There's your hand!"
"—This precious piece of verse, I really judge,
Is meant to copy my own character,

1612| MS:Well, wait <> excuse. *P1868:*For, wait <> excuse!   1612-13| MS:§ no ¶ §
P1868:§ ¶ §   1615| MS:very Crucifix— *P1868:*very crucifix—   1616| MS:sate
*P1868:*sat   1619| MS:tittle I <> now. *P1868:*tittle, I <> now!   1620| MS:In
the colour I now give, there's <> perhaps— *P1868:*I' the colour the tale takes, there's
<> perhaps;   1621| MS:natural; since *P1868:*natural, since   1622| MS:still the
*P1868:*still, the   1625| MS:Papers—a *P1868:*Papers, a   1626| MS:about Love—
*P1868:*about love—   1627| MS:so *P1868:*so,   1629| MS:"How *P1868:*"—How
1630| MS:A stranger <> person wrote *P1868:*And stranger <> person, wrote
1632| MS:That pasquinade § crossed out and replaced above by § bestiality <> Rome,
to-day § crossed out § *P1868:*The bestiality   1633| MS:by Pasquin."—"Nor
*1889a:*by Pasquin." "Nor   1635| MS:lady: there's *P1868:*lady? There's
1636| MS:"This <> judge *P1868:*"—This *1889a:*judge,   1637| MS:characters,

A clumsy mimic; and this other prose,
Not so much even; both rank forgery:
1640 Verse, quotha? Bembo's verse! When Saint John wrote
The tract 'De Tribus,' I wrote this to match."
"—How came it, then, the documents were found
At the inn on your departure?"—"I opine,
Because there were no documents to find
1645 In my presence,—you must hide before you find.
Who forged them hardly practised in my view;
Who found them waited till I turned my back."
"—And what of the clandestine visits paid,
Nocturnal passage in and out the house
1650 With its lord absent? 'Tis alleged you climbed . . . ."
"—Flew on a broomstick to the man i' the moon!
Who witnessed or will testify this trash?"
"—The trusty servant, Margherita's self,
Even she who brought you letters, you confess,
1655 And, you confess, took letters in reply:
Forget not we have knowledge of the facts!"
"—Sirs, who have knowledge of the facts, defray
The expenditure of wit I waste in vain,
Trying to find out just one fact of all!
1660 She who brought letters from who could not write,
And took back letters to who could not read,—
Who was that messenger, of your charity?"
"—Well, so far favours you the circumstance
That this same messenger . . . how shall we say? . . .

142

¹⁶⁶⁵ *Sub imputatione meretricis*
Laborat,—which makes accusation null:
We waive this woman's: nought makes void the next.
Borsi, called Venerino, he who drove,
O' the first night when you fled away, at length
¹⁶⁷⁰ Deposes to your kissings in the coach,
—Frequent, frenetic . . ." "When deposed he so?"
"After some weeks of sharp imprisonment . . ."
"—Granted by friend the Governor, I engage—"
"—For his participation in your flight!
¹⁶⁷⁵ At length his obduracy melting made
The avowal mentioned . . ." "Was dismissed forthwith
To liberty, poor knave, for recompense.
Sirs, give what credit to the lie you can!
For me, no word in my defence I speak,
¹⁶⁸⁰ And God shall argue for the lady!"
                                                            So
Did I stand question, and make answer, still
With the same result of smiling disbelief,
Polite impossibility of faith
In such affected virtue in a priest;
¹⁶⁸⁵ But a showing fair play, an indulgence, even,
To one no worse than others after all—
Who had not brought disgrace to the order, played
Discreetly, ruffled gown nor ripped the cloth
In a bungling game at romps: I have told you, Sirs—

---

^{1666|} MS:makes witness § crossed out and replaced above by § accusation null: and void
§ last two words crossed out § ^{1667|} MS:woman's,—nought <> next
*P1868:*woman's:—nought <> next. *1889a:*woman's: nought ^{1668|} MS:drove
*P1868:*drove, ^{1669|} MS:On *P1868:*O' ^{1670|} MS:coach *P1868:*coach,
^{1671|} MS:Frequent, frenetic" . . . *P1868:*—Frequent, frenetic . . ."
^{1672|} MS:imprisonment" . . . *P1868:*imprisonment . . ." ^{1673|} MS:"Granted <>
engage"— *P1868:*"—Granted <> engage—" ^{1674|} MS:For <> flight, *P1868:*—For
<> flight! ^{1676-78|} MS:mentioned . . ." "Was <> forthwith./ Sirs *P1868:*mentioned
. . ." § emended to § . . ." § see Editorial Notes § "Was <> forthwith/ To liberty, poor
knave, for recompense./ Sirs ^{1679|} MS:speak: *P1868:*speak, ^{1680|} MS:'Tis
God shall answer § crossed out and replaced above by § argue <> Lady!" So
*P1868:*And God <> lady!" § ¶ § So ^{1684|} MS:such pretence at § last two words
crossed out and replaced above by § affected virtue on our part *P1868:*virtue in a
priest, *CP1868:*priest; ^{1685|} MS:indulgence even *P1868:*indulgence,
even, ^{1686|} MS:To me no *P1868:*To one no ^{1687-89|} MS:not disgraced
my order, ripped the cloth/ In *P1868:*not brought disgrace to the order, played/

If I pretended simply to be pure
Honest and Christian in the case,—absurd!
As well go boast myself above the needs
O' the human nature, careless how meat smells,
Wine tastes,—a saint above the smack! But once
1695 Abate my crest, own flaws i' the flesh, agree
To go with the herd, be hog no more nor less,
Why, hogs in common herd have common rights:
I must not be unduly borne upon,
Who just romanced a little, sowed wild oats,
1700 But 'scaped without a scandal, flagrant fault.
My name helped to a mirthful circumstance:
"Joseph" would do well to amend his plea:
Undoubtedly—some toying with the wife,
But as for ruffian violence and rape,
1705 Potiphar pressed too much on the other side!
The intrigue, the elopement, the disguise,—well charged!
The letters and verse looked hardly like the truth.
Your apprehension was—of guilt enough
To be compatible with innocence,
1710 So, punished best a little and not too much.
Had I struck Guido Franceschini's face,
You had counselled me withdraw for my own sake,
Baulk him of bravo-hiring. Friends came round,
Congratulated, "Nobody mistakes!
1715 The pettiness o' the forfeiture defines
The peccadillo: Guido gets his share:
His wife is free of husband and hook-nose,

Discreetly, ruffled gown nor ripped the cloth/ In   ¹⁶⁹³| MS:Of < > smells *P1868:*O'
< > smells,   ¹⁶⁹⁴| MS:tastes, a < > smack! but *P1868:*tastes,—a < > smack! But
¹⁶⁹⁵| MS:in *P1868:*i'   ¹⁶⁹⁷| MS:Why hogs < > rights— *P1868:*Why, hogs
*1889a:*rights: ¹⁶⁹⁸| MS:upon. *P1868:*upon,   ¹⁶⁹⁹| MS:Who had just < > sown
*1872:*Who just < > sowed   ¹⁷⁰⁰| MS:But found out in no scandal < > fault:
*P1868:*But 'scaped without a scandal < > fault.   ¹⁷⁰¹| MS:circumstance
*P1868:*circumstance: ¹⁷⁰²| MS:Joseph *P1868:*"Joseph"   ¹⁷⁰⁵| MS:pressed to
much < > side. *P1868:*pressed too much < > side!   ¹⁷⁰⁷| MS:verses looked less like
*P1868:*verse looked hardly like   ¹⁷⁰⁸| MS:was of *P1868:*was—of   ¹⁷¹⁰| MS:So
punished < > much— *P1868:*So, punished < > much.   ¹⁷¹¹| MS:Had I spat in
Guido < > face *P1868:*Had I struck Guido < > face,   ¹⁷¹⁴| MS:Congratulated
"Nobody mistakes that case, *P1868:*Congratulated, "Nobody mistakes!   ¹⁷¹⁵| MS:of
*P1868:*o'   ¹⁷¹⁷| MS:of him and the hook nose *P1868:*of husband and hook-nose,

The mouldy viands and the mother-in-law.
To Citiva with you and amuse the time,
1720 Travesty us '*De Raptu Helenæ*!'
A funny figure must the husband cut
When the wife makes him skip,—too ticklish, eh?
Do it in Latin, not the Vulgar, then!
Scazons—we'll copy and send his Eminence.
1725 Mind—one iambus in the final foot!
He'll rectify it, be your friend for life!"
Oh, Sirs, depend on me for much new light
Thrown on the justice and religion here
By this proceeding, much fresh food for thought!

1730 And I was just set down to study these
In relegation, two short days ago,
Admiring how you read the rules, when, clap,
A thunder comes into my solitude—
I am caught up in a whirlwind and cast here,
1735 Told of a sudden, in this room where so late
You dealt out law adroitly, that those scales,
I meekly bowed to, took my allotment from,
Guido has snatched at, broken in your hands,
Metes to himself the murder of his wife,
1740 Full measure, pressed down, running over now!
Can I assist to an explanation?—Yes,
I rise in your esteem, sagacious Sirs,
Stand up a renderer of reasons, not
The officious priest would personate Saint George

1718| MS:mother-in-law: *P1868*:mother-in-law. 1719| MS:time *P1868*:time,
1720| MS:Translating us "de Raptu Helenæ," *P1868*:Travesty us '*De Raptu Helenæ*!'
1721| MS:A doleful figure did the Husband *P1868*:A funny figure must the husband
1722| MS:wife made him *P1868*:wife makes him 1722| MS:then *P1868*:then!
1724| MS:copy for the Cardinal § last three words crossed out and replaced above by following
four words and dash § and send his Eminence— *P1868*:Eminence! *1889a*:Eminence.
1725| MS:foot— *P1868*:foot! 1726| MS:rectify and be *P1868*:rectify it, be
1729–30| MS:§ no ¶ § *P1868*:§ ¶ § 1731| MS:In my relegation *P1868*:In relegation
1732| MS:when clap *P1868*:when, clap, 1733| MS:into the solitude— *P1868*:into my
solitude— 1734| MS:here *P1868*:here, 1737| MS:bowed, § comma apparently
added in revision § and § crossed out § took <> my measure § crossed out and replaced above
by § allotment *P1868*:bowed to, took 1738| MS:has burst § reading not certain; crossed
out and replaced above by § snatched 1739| MS:And § crossed out § metes § altered to §
Metes to § inserted above § 1740| MS:now: *P1868*:now! 1744| MS:officious young

For a mock Princess in undragoned days.
What, the blood startles you? What, after all
The priest who needs must carry sword on thigh
May find imperative use for it? Then, there was
A Princess, was a dragon belching flame,
1750 And should have been a Saint George also? Then,
There might be worse schemes than to break the bonds
At Arezzo, lead her by the little hand,
Till she reached Rome, and let her try to live?
But you were law and gospel,—would one please
1755 Stand back, allow your faculty elbow-room?
You blind guides who must needs lead eyes that see!
Fools, alike ignorant of man and God!
What was there here should have perplexed your wit
For a wink of the owl-eyes of you? How miss, then,
1760 What's now forced on you by this flare of fact—
As if Saint Peter failed to recognize
Nero as no apostle, John or James,
Till someone burned a martyr, made a torch
O' the blood and fat to show his features by!
1765 Could you fail read this cartulary aright
On head and front of Franceschini there,
Large-lettered like hell's masterpiece of print,—
That he, from the beginning pricked at heart

---

§ crossed out and replaced above by following three words § priest would personate Saint
George too bold § last two words crossed out §   1745| MS:For the perished § uncertain;
last two words crossed out and replaced above by § a mock   1746| MS:blood sobers you
P1868:blood startles you   1748| MS:May have found imperative <> it? Then there
P1868:May find imperative   CP1868:it? Then, there   1749| MS:A Princess, § comma
apparently added in revision § and § crossed out and replaced above by § was a Dragon <>
flame   P1868:dragon <> flame,   1750| MS:also? Then   CP1868:also? Then,
1753| MS:reached Rome, began to § last two words crossed out and replaced above by
following three words § and let her try and § crossed out and replaced above by § to
1754| MS:were the law and the gospel   1872:were law and gospel   1759| MS:a-wink
<> you? How fail find § two words crossed out and replaced above by two words § miss then
P1868:a wink <> miss, then,   1761| MS:is Saint Paul had § last two words crossed out
and replaced above by § Peter <> recognise   1889a:recognize   1762| MS:as not the
mate of § last four words crossed out and replaced above by two words § no Apostle, James
nor John § indication that should be transposed to read § John nor James   P1868:no apostle,
John or James,   1764| MS:Of   P1868:O'   1766| MS:On the head <> there
P1868:On head <> there,   1767| MS:Large § written over illegible word § <> like

By some lust, letch of hate against his wife,
1770 Plotted to plague her into overt sin
And shame, would slay Pompilia body and soul,
And save his mean self—miserably caught
I' the quagmire of his own tricks, cheats and lies?
—That himself wrote those papers,—from himself
1775 To himself,—which, i' the name of me and her,
His mistress-messenger gave her and me,
Touching us with such pustules of the soul
That she and I might take the taint, be shown
To the world and shuddered over, speckled so?
1780 —That the agent put her sense into my words,
Made substitution of the thing she hoped,
For the thing she had and held, its opposite,
While the husband in the background bit his lips
At each fresh failure of his precious plot?
1785 —That when at the last we did rush each on each,
By no chance but because God willed it so—
The spark of truth was struck from out our souls—
Made all of me, descried in the first glance,
Seem fair and honest and permissible love
1790 O' the good and true—as the first glance told me
There was no duty patent in the world
Like daring try be good and true myself,
Leaving the shows of things to the Lord of Show

Hell's <> print, *P1868:*like hell's <> print,—   1769| MS:By some § inserted above §
lust, and § crossed out §   1771| MS:shame, should slay *P1868:*shame, would slay
1772| MS:self miserably *P1868:*self—miserably   1773| MS:In *P1868:*I'
1775| MS:himself,—in <> of her and me § indication that should be transposed to read § of
me and her, *P1868:*himself,—which, i'   1777| MS:Spotting both § crossed out and
replaced above by following two words § Touching us with those pustules *P1868:*with such
pustules   1779| MS:shuddered at o'er speckled *P1868:*shuddered over, speckled
1780| MS:That <> words *P1868:*—That <> words,   1781| MS:hoped *P1868:*hoped,
1782| MS:For the the thing *P1868:*For the thing   1784| MS:his precious § inserted
above § plot? plot hatched § last two words crossed out §   1785| MS:In that § crossed out
and replaced above by two words so crossed out as to be illegible § — § perhaps added in
revision § that § altered to § That when we did meet § crossed out § at the last—rush each on
each, § last four words apparently added in revision; indication that should be transposed to
read § when at the last we did rush   1787| MS:struck forth § crossed out § from out
§ inserted above § our souls *P1868:*souls—   1788| MS:me descried through § crossed
out § <> glance *P1868:*me, descried <> glance,   1790| MS:Of *CP1868:*O'
1791| MS:duty for me § last two words crossed out and replaced above by § patent in the wide

And Prince o' the Power of the Air. Our very flight,
1795 Even to its most ambiguous circumstance,
Irrefragably proved how futile, false . . .
Why, men—men and not boys—boys and not babes—
Babes and not beasts—beasts and not stocks and stones!—
Had the liar's lie been true one pin-point speck,
1800 Were I the accepted suitor, free o' the place,
Disposer of the time, to come at a call
And go at a wink as who should say me nay,—
What need of flight, what were the gain therefrom
But just damnation, failure or success?
1805 Damnation pure and simple to her the wife
And me the priest—who bartered private bliss
For public reprobation, the safe shade
For the sunshine which men see to pelt me by:
What other advantage,—we who led the days
1810 And nights alone i' the house,—was flight to find?
In our whole journey did we stop an hour,
Diverge a foot from straight road till we reached
Or would have reached—but for that fate of ours—
The father and mother, in the eye of Rome,
1815 The eye of yourselves we made aware of us
At the first fall of misfortune? And indeed
You did so far give sanction to our flight,
Confirm its purpose, as lend helping hand,
Deliver up Pompilia not to him
1820 She fled, but those the flight was ventured for.
Why then could you, who stopped short, not go on
One poor step more, and justify the means,

---

§ crossed out § world   1794| MS:The § altered to § And Prince of <> flight   P1868:And
Prince o' <> flight,   1795| MS:circumstance   P1868:circumstance,
1798| MS:stones— P1868:stones!—   1799| MS:speck   P1868:speck,
1800| MS:And I <> of P1868:Were I <> o'   1802| MS:nay, P1868:nay,—
1803| MS:gain thereby P1868:gain therefrom   1804| MS:failure and success
P1868:failure or success?   1806| MS:barter P1868:bartered
1807| MS:reprobation, at the last § last three words crossed out §   1808| MS:pelt you by:
CP1868:pelt me by: 1809| MS:advantage, we P1868:advantage,—we
1810| MS:in P1868:i'   1812| MS:from the strait P1868:from strait 1889a:straight
1816| MS:misfortune: and P1868:misfortune? And   1817| MS:flight P1868:flight,
1818| MS:purpose as <> hand P1868:purpose, as <> hand,   1820| MS:fled but <>
for: P1868:fled, but <> for.   1822| MS:means P1868:means,

148

Having allowed the end?—not see and say
"Here's the exceptional conduct that should claim
1825 To be exceptionally judged on rules
Which, understood, make no exception here"—
Why play instead into the devil's hands
By dealing so ambiguously as gave
Guido the power to intervene like me,
1830 Prove one exception more? I saved his wife
Against law: against law he slays her now:
Deal with him!

                    I have done with being judged.
I stand here guiltless in thought, word and deed,
To the point that I apprise you,—in contempt
1835 For all misapprehending ignorance
O' the human heart, much more the mind of Christ,—
That I assuredly did bow, was blessed
By the revelation of Pompilia. There!
Such is the final fact I fling you, Sirs,
1840 To mouth and mumble and misinterpret: there!
"The priest's in love," have it the vulgar way!
Unpriest me, rend the rags o' the vestment, do—
Degrade deep, disenfranchise all you dare—
Remove me from the midst, no longer priest
1845 And fit companion for the like of you—
Your gay Abati with the well-turned leg
And rose i' the hat-rim, Canons, cross at neck
And silk mask in the pocket of the gown,
Brisk Bishops with the world's musk still unbrushed

1823| MS:end,—not *P1868:*end?—not   1826| MS:Which understood make
*P1868:*Which, understood, make   1829| MS:intervene as I, *P1868:*intervene like me,
1830| MS:more: I *P1868:*more? I   1832| MS:him. I appeal § uncertain; written over
illegible word; both crossed out and replaced above by § have done *P1868:*him! § ¶ § I
1833| MS:deed *P1868:*deed,   1834| MS:you, in *P1868:*you,—in   1835| MS:Of
§ crossed out and replaced above by § For   1836| MS:Of < > Christ, *P1868:*O' < >
Christ,—   1841| MS:"The Priest's *P1868:*"The priest's   1842| MS:Punish that
§ two words crossed out and replaced above by two words § Unfrock me < > of
*P1868:*Unpriest me < > o'   1843| MS:disenfranchize all you can—
*P1868:*disenfranchize all you dare—   1844| MS:Unfrock § crossed out § < > from the §
crossed out and replaced above by § your midst *P1868:*from the midst
1846| MS:abbati *P1868:*Abbati *CP1868:*Abati   1847| MS:in < > canons
cross *P1868:*i' < > Canons, cross   1849| MS:Brisk bishops

1850   From the rochet; I'll no more of these good things:
There's a crack somewhere, something that's unsound
I' the rattle!

              For Pompilia—be advised,
Build churches, go pray! You will find me there,
I know, if you come,—and you will come, I know.
1855   Why, there's a Judge weeping! Did not I say
You were good and true at bottom? You see the truth—
I am glad I helped you: she helped me just so.

But for Count Guido,—you must counsel there!
I bow my head, bend to the very dust,
1860   Break myself up in shame of faultiness.
I had him one whole moment, as I said—
As I remember, as will never out
O' the thoughts of me,—I had him in arm's reach
There,—as you stand, Sir, now you cease to sit,—
1865   I could have killed him ere he killed his wife,
And did not: he went off alive and well
And then effected this last feat—through me!
Me—not through you—dismiss that fear! 'Twas you
Hindered me staying here to save her,—not
1870   From leaving you and going back to him
And doing service in Arezzo. Come,
Instruct me in procedure! I conceive—
In all due self-abasement might I speak—
How you will deal with Guido: oh, not death!
1875   Death, if it let her life be: otherwise

---

*1889a:*Brisk Bishops   ¹⁸⁵⁰| MS:rochet: I'll *P1868:*rochet; I'll   ¹⁸⁵¹| MS:a
wrong § crossed out and replaced above by § crack   ¹⁸⁵²| MS:In the rattle:
for *P1868:*I' the rattle! § ¶ § For   ¹⁸⁵³| MS:pray: you <> there
*P1868:*pray! You <> there,   ¹⁸⁵⁴| MS:come, I know: *P1868:*come,
I know.   ¹⁸⁵⁵| MS:a Judge in tears: did *P1868:*a Judge weeping! Did
¹⁸⁵⁶| MS:bottom: you *P1868:*bottom? You   ^{1857–58}| MS:§ no ¶ §
P1868:§ ¶ §   ¹⁸⁵⁸| MS:there— *P1868:*there!   ¹⁸⁵⁹| MS:dust *P1868:*dust,
¹⁸⁶⁰| MS:faultiness— *P1868:*faultiness.   ¹⁸⁶³| MS:Of *P1868:*O'   ¹⁸⁶⁸| MS:Me!
not <> dismiss <> fear—'twas *P1868:*Me—not <> fear! 'Twas *1889a:*dsimiss § emended
to § dismiss § see Editorial Notes §   ¹⁸⁷⁰| MS:leaving her and *P1868:*leaving you and
¹⁸⁷²| MS:procedure—I *P1868:*procedure! I   ¹⁸⁷⁵| MS:Death if *P1868:*Death, if

Not death,—your lights will teach you clearer! I
Certainly have an instinct of my own
I' the matter: bear with me and weigh its worth!
Let us go away—leave Guido all alone
1880   Back on the world again that knows him now!
I think he will be found (indulge so far!)
Not to die so much as slide out of life,
Pushed by the general horror and common hate
Low, lower,—left o' the very ledge of things,
1885   I seem to see him catch convulsively
One by one at all honest forms of life,
At reason, order, decency and use—
To cramp him and get foothold by at least;
And still they disengage them from his clutch.
1890   "What, you are he, then, had Pompilia once
And so forwent her? Take not up with us!"
And thus I see him slowly and surely edged
Off all the table-land whence life upsprings
Aspiring to be immortality,
1895   As the snake, hatched on hill-top by mischance,
Despite his wriggling, slips, slides, slidders down
Hill-side, lies low and prostrate on the smooth
Level of the outer place, lapsed in the vale:
So I lose Guido in the loneliness,
1900   Silence and dusk, till at the doleful end,
At the horizontal line, creation's verge,
From what just is to absolute nothingness—
Whom is it, straining onward still, he meets?

1876| MS:clearer—I   P1868:clearer! I   1878| MS:In   P1868:I'   1879| MS:away
§ followed by erasure perhaps of now §   1880| MS:now.   P1868:now!   1882| MS:life
P1868:life,   1884| MS:on   P1868:o'   1887| MS:use   P1868:use—
1888| MS:foothold there § crossed out and replaced by § by at least,   P1868:least;
1889| MS:clutch   P1868:clutch.   1890| MS:he then had   P1868:he, then, had
1895| MS:snake hatched <> mischance   P1868:snake, hatched <> mischance,
1896| MS:wriggling slips   CP1868:wriggling, slips   1897| MS:Hill-side and § crossed
out § is found § inserted above § low prostrate   P1868:Hill-side, is low and prostrate
CP1868:Hill-side, lies   1899| MS:loneliness   P1868:loneliness,   1900| MS:and
night § crossed out and replaced above by § dusk till <> end   P1868:dusk, till <> end,
1901| MS:the horizon's last § crossed out and replaced above by § line   P1868:the horizontal
line   1902-3| MS: § order reversed § Lo, what is this he meets that § crossed out § strains
onward § last four letters inserted above § still/ From   P1868:nothingness—/ Lo <> meets,

What other man deep further in the fate,
1905 Who, turning at the prize of a footfall
To flatter him and promise fellowship,
Discovers in the act a frightful face—
Judas, made monstrous by much solitude!
The two are at one now! Let them love their love
1910 That bites and claws like hate, or hate their hate
That mops and mows and makes as it were love!
There, let them each tear each in devil's-fun,
Or fondle this the other while malice aches—
Both teach, both learn detestability!
1915 Kiss him the kiss, Iscariot! Pay that back,
That smatch o' the slaver blistering on your lip,
By the better trick, the insult he spared Christ—
Lure him the lure o' the letters, Aretine!
Lick him o'er slimy-smooth with jelly-filth
1920 O' the verse-and-prose pollution in love's guise!
The cockatrice is with the basilisk!
There let them grapple, denizens o' the dark,
Foes or friends, but indissolubly bound,
In their one spot out of the ken of God
1925 Or care of man, for ever and ever more!

Why, Sirs, what's this? Why, this is sorry and strange!
Futility, divagation: this from me
Bound to be rational, justify an act
Of sober man!—whereas, being moved so much,

strains <> still?   *1872:/* Whom is it, straining onward still, he meets?   1905| MS:Who
turning at the comfort § crossed out and replaced above by § prize of a step § crossed out §
footfall   *CP1868:*Who, turning   1906| MS:Close behind § crossed out and replaced
above by § to comfort his and promised § altered to § promise fellowship   *P1868:*To flatter
him and fellowship,   1911| MS:love;   *P1868:*love!   1912| MS:devils'-fun
*P1868:*devil's-fun   1913| MS:fondle each § crossed out and replaced above by § this
1914| MS:Each § crossed out and replaced above by § Both teach each § crossed out and
replaced above by § both <> detestability.   *P1868:*detestability!   1916| MS:That burn
§ crossed out and replaced above by § smatch of <> lip—   *P1868:*o'   *1872:*lip,
1917| MS: § crowded between lines 1916 and 1918 §   1918| MS:Wile him the wile of
*CP1868:*Lure him the lure o'   1919| MS:with the jelly-filth   *P1868:*with jelly-filth
1920| MS:Of   *P1868:*O'   1922| MS:of   *P1868:*o'   1925| MS:Or the care
*CP1868:*Or care   1926| MS:and wrong, § crossed out and replaced above by § poor
§ crossed out § strange,—   *P1868:*strange!—   *1872:*strange!   1927| MS:Futility, and
§ crossed out §   1928| MS:justify the choice   *P1868:*justify an act   1929| MS:Of the

1930 I give you cause to doubt the lady's mind:
A pretty sarcasm for the world! I fear
You do her wit injustice,—all through me!
Like my fate all through,—ineffective help!
A poor rash advocate I prove myself.
1935 You might be angry with good cause: but sure
At the advocate,—only at the undue zeal
That spoils the force of his own plea, I think?
My part was just to tell you how things stand,
State facts and not be flustered at their fume.
1940 But then 'tis a priest speaks: as for love,—no!
If you let buzz a vulgar fly like that
About your brains, as if I loved, forsooth,
Indeed, Sirs, you do wrong! We had no thought
Of such infatuation, she and I:
1945 There are many points that prove it: do be just!
I told you,—at one little roadside-place
I spent a good half-hour, paced to and fro
The garden; just to leave her free awhile,
I plucked a handful of Spring herb and bloom:
1950 I might have sat beside her on the bench
Where the children were: I wish the thing had been,
Indeed: the event could not be worse, you know:
One more half-hour of her saved! She's dead now, Sirs!
While I was running on at such a rate,
1955 Friends should have plucked me by the sleeve: I went
Too much o' the trivial outside of her face
And the purity that shone there—plain to me,
Not to you, what more natural? Nor am I
Infatuated,—oh, I saw, be sure!

---

sober man, whereas   *P1868:*Of sober man!—whereas   1931| MS:world. I
*P1868:*world! I   1932| MS:me   *P1868:*me!   1933| MS:And my <> help.
*P1868:*Like my <> help!   1934| MS:myself—   *P1868:*myself.
1935| MS:cause—but   *P1868:*cause: but   1937| MS:That turns the   *P1868:*That spoils
the   1943| MS:wrong: we   *P1868:*wrong! We   1944| MS:infatuation she
*P1868:*infatuation, she   1944| MS:just—   *P1868:*just!   1946| MS:roadside place
*P1868:*roadside-place   1948| MS:garden, just   *P1868:*garden; just
1949| MS:spring <> and flower: *P1868:*Spring <> and bloom: 1950| MS:sate
*P1868:*sat   1953–55| MS:now./ Friends   *P1868:*now, Sirs!/ While I was running on at
such a rate,/ Friends   1956| MS:on   *P1868:*o'   1957| MS:shone thence—plain to
me   *P1868:*shone there—plain to me,   1959| MS:sure—   *P1868:*sure!

¹⁹⁶⁰ Her brow had not the right line, leaned too much,
Painters would say; they like the straight-up Greek:
This seemed bent somewhat with an invisible crown
Of martyr and saint, not such as art approves.
And how the dark orbs dwelt deep underneath,
¹⁹⁶⁵ Looked out of such a sad sweet heaven on me!
The lips, compressed a little, came forward too,
Careful for a whole world of sin and pain.
That was the face, her husband makes his plea,
He sought just to disfigure,—no offence
¹⁹⁷⁰ Beyond that! Sirs, let us be rational!
He needs must vindicate his honour,—ay,
Yet slinks, the coward, in a clown's disguise,
Away from the scene, endeavours to escape.
Now, had he done so, slain and left no trace
¹⁹⁷⁵ O' the slayer,—what were vindicated, pray?
You had found his wife disfigured or a corpse,
For what and by whom? It is too palpable!
Then, here's another point involving law:
I use this argument to show you meant
¹⁹⁸⁰ No calumny against us by that title
O' the sentence,—liars try to twist it so:
What penalty it bore, I had to pay
Till further proof should follow of innocence—
Probationis ob defectum,—proof?

---

^{1961|} MS:say—they <> strait-up Greek— *P1868:*say; they <> straight-up Greek:
^{1964|} MS:underneath *P1868:*underneath, ^{1965|} MS:me— *1889a:*me!
^{1966|} MS:lips compressed a little came <> too *P1868:*lips, compressed a little, came <>
too, ^{1967|} MS:pain: *P1868:*pain. ^{1968|} MS:face her <> plea *P1868:*face, her
<> plea, ^{1969|} MS:disfigure, no *P1868:*disfigure,—no ^{1970|} MS:that! Sirs
§ written over illegible word § <> rational. *P1868:*rational! ^{1972|} MS:And slinks
*P1868:*Yet shirks § emended to § slinks § see Editorial Notes § ^{1973|} MS:escape:
*P1868:*escape. ^{1974|} MS:Could he have done so, killed § crossed out and
replaced above by § slain *P1868:*Now, had he done ^{1975|} MS:Of *P1868:*O'
^{1977|} MS: § illegible word followed by *and,* both crossed out § for § altered to § For
^{1979|} MS:Friends use *P1868:*I use ^{1980|} MS:that act of yours § last two words crossed
out § *P1868:*that title ^{1981|} MS:Of § in margin § The § altered to § the *P1868:*O'
^{1982–84|} MS:pay/ *Probationis* *P1868:*pay/ Till further proof should follow of innocence—/

1985   How could you get proof without trying us?
      You went through the preliminary form,
      Stopped there, contrived this sentence to amuse
      The adversary. If the title ran
      For more than fault imputed and not proved,
1990   That was a simple penman's error, else
      A slip i' the phrase,—as when we say of you
      "Charged with injustice"—which may either be
      Or not be,—'tis a name that sticks meanwhile.
      Another relevant matter: fool that I am!
1995   Not what I wish true, yet a point friends urge:
      It is not true,—yet, since friends think it helps,—
      She only tried me when some others failed—
      Began with Conti, whom I told you of,
      And Guillichini, Guido's kinsfolk both,
2000   And when abandoned by them, not before,
      Turned to me. That's conclusive why she turned.
      Much good they got by the happy cowardice!
      Conti is dead, poisoned a month ago:
      Does that much strike you as a sin? Not much,
2005   After the present murder,—one mark more
      On the Moor's skin,—what is black by blacker still?
      Conti had come here and told truth. And so
      With Guillichini; he's condemned of course
      To the galleys, as a friend in this affair,
2010   Tried and condemned for no one thing i' the world,
      A fortnight since by who but the Governor?—
      The just judge, who refused Pompilia help
      At first blush, being her husband's friend, you know.
      There are two tales to suit the separate courts,
2015   Arezzo and Rome: he tells you here, we fled

Probationis   1985| MS:get it without *P1868:*get proof without   1988| MS:The
hate of the adversary *P1868:*The adversary   1989| MS:more,—the thing imputed < >
proved—   *P1868:*more than fault imputed < > proved,   1991| MS:in *P1868:*i'
1994| MS:am— *P1868:*am!   1995–97| MS:urge:/ She *P1868:*urge:/ It is not true,—yet,
since friends think it helps,—/ She   1997| MS:when the others *P1868:*when some
others   2003| MS:ago, *P1868:*ago: 2004| MS:sin? Not much— *P1868:*sin? Not
much,   2008| MS:With Guillichini, he's *P1868:*With Guillichini; he's
2009| MS:gallies *P1868:*galleys   2010| MS:in the world *P1868:*i' the world,
2011| MS:the Governor *P1868:*the Governor?—   2013| MS:her Husband's *P1868:*her
husband's   2014| MS:separate Courts, *P1868:*separate courts,   2015| MS:and

Alone, unhelped,—lays stress on the main fault,
The spiritual sin, Rome looks to: but elsewhere
He likes best we should break in, steal, bear off,
Be fit to brand and pillory and flog—
2020 That's the charge goes to the heart of the Governor:
If these unpriest me, you and I may yet
Converse, Vincenzo Marzi-Medici!
Oh, Sirs, there are worse men than you, I say!
More easily duped, I mean; this stupid lie,
2025 Its liar never dared propound in Rome,
He gets Arezzo to receive,—nay more,
Gets Florence and the Duke to authorize!
This is their Rota's sentence, their Granduke
Signs and seals! Rome for me henceforward—Rome,
2030 Where better men are,—most of all, that man
The Augustinian of the Hospital,
Who writes the letter,—he confessed, he says,
Many a dying person, never one
So sweet and true and pure and beautiful.
2035 A good man! Will you make him Pope one day?
Not that he is not good too, this we have—
But old,—else he would have his word to speak,
His truth to teach the world: I thirst for truth,
But shall not drink it till I reach the source.

2040 Sirs, I am quiet again. You see, we are

Rome: they tell you here we   *P1868:*and Rome: he tells you here, we   2016| MS:lay
*P1868:*lays   2017| MS:sin Rome   *P1868:*sin, Rome   2018| MS:They like best
*P1868:*He likes best   2019| MS:Be stuff § crossed out and replaced above by § fit < > flog
*P1868:*flog—   2021| MS:If you § crossed out and replaced above by § these < > me,
he § crossed out and replaced above by § you   2025| MS:The liar   *P1868:*Its liar
2026| MS:to affirm,—nay   *P1868:*to receive,—nay   2027| MS:authorise!
*1889a:*authorize!   2028| MS:is the Florence § last two words crossed out § Rota's
sentence, § word and comma inserted above line § which the Duke   *P1868:*is their
Rotas' sentence, their Granduke   *CP1868:*their Rota's   2029| MS:henceforward—
Rome   *P1868:*henceforward—Rome,   2030-32| MS:all that
monk/ Who   *P1868:*all, that man/ The Augustinian of the Hospital,/ Who
2034| MS:So good § crossed out and replaced above by § sweet   2037| MS:speak
*P1868:*speak,   2038| MS:And § crossed out and replaced above by following three
words § His truth to < > world: by § crossed out § < > truth   *P1868:*truth,

So very pitiable, she and I,
Who had conceivably been otherwise.
Forget distemperature and idle heat!
Apart from truth's sake, what's to move so much?
2045 Pompilia will be presently with God;
I am, on earth, as good as out of it,
A relegated priest; when exile ends,
I mean to do my duty and live long.
She and I are mere strangers now: but priests
2050 Should study passion; how else cure mankind,
Who come for help in passionate extremes?
I do but play with an imagined life
Of who, unfettered by a vow, unblessed
By the higher call,—since you will have it so,—
2055 Leads it companioned by the woman there.
To live, and see her learn, and learn by her,
Out of the low obscure and petty world—
Or only see one purpose and one will
Evolve themselves i' the world, change wrong to right:
2060 To have to do with nothing but the true,
The good, the eternal—and these, not alone
In the main current of the general life,
But small experiences of every day,
Concerns of the particular hearth and home:
2065 To learn not only by a comet's rush
But a rose's birth,—not by the grandeur, God—

2040| MS:again: you see we P1868:again. You CP1868:see, we   2041| MS:and I
P1868:and I,   2042| MS:otherwise: P1868:otherwise.   2043| MS:heat:
P1868:heat!   2045| MS:with God, P1868:with God;   2047| MS:ends P1868:ends,
2050| MS:passion, how P1868:passion; how   2051| MS:Who call § crossed out and
replaced above by § come   2054| MS:call, since < > so, P1868:call,—since < > so,—
2055| MS:it with what § last two words crossed out and replaced above by following two
words § companioned by the § written over illegible word §   2056| MS:live and see her
learn and < > by her P1868:live, and see her learn, and < > by her,   2057| MS:the
miserable petty P1868:the low obscure and petty   2058| MS:To only P1868:Or only
2059| MS:in P1868:i'   2061| MS:Good and § written over illegible word partially
erased § eternal—and these not P1868:The good, the eternal—and these, not
2063| MS:day P1868:day,   2064| MS:home. P1868:home: 2066| MS:rose's
apparition, not the splendor, God— P1868:rose's birth,—not by the grandeur, God,—

But the comfort, Christ. All this, how far away!
Mere delectation, meet for a minute's dream!—
Just as a drudging student trims his lamp,
2070 Opens his Plutarch, puts him in the place
Of Roman, Grecian; draws the patched gown close,
Dreams, "Thus should I fight, save or rule the world!"—
Then smilingly, contentedly, awakes
To the old solitary nothingness.
2075 So I, from such communion, pass content . . .

O great, just, good God! Miserable me!

2067| MS:the mercy, Christ *P1868:*the comfort, Christ   2068| MS:dream,
*P1868:*dream!—   2069| MS:lamp *P1868:*lamp,   2071| MS:Of Roman, Grecian,
draws *P1868:*Of Roman, Grecian; draws   2072| MS:Says "So should I fight, rule or
save the world" *P1868:*Dreams, "Thus should I fight, save or rule the world!"—
2073| MS:contentedly, returns *P1868:*contentedly, awakes   2074| MS:nothingness,
*CP1868:*nothingness.   2075| MS:As I *P1868:*So I   2076| MS:O great § written over
illegible word §

VII

POMPILIA

I am just seventeen years and five months old,
And, if I lived one day more, three full weeks;
'Tis writ so in the church's register,
Lorenzo in Lucina, all my names
5   At length, so many names for one poor child,
—Francesca Camilla Vittoria Angela
Pompilia Comparini,—laughable!
Also 'tis writ that I was married there
Four years ago: and they will add, I hope,
10   When they insert my death, a word or two,—
Omitting all about the mode of death,—
This, in its place, this which one cares to know,
That I had been a mother of a son
Exactly two weeks. It will be through grace
15   O' the Curate, not through any claim I have;
Because the boy was born at, so baptized
Close to, the Villa, in the proper church:
A pretty church, I say no word against,
Yet stranger-like,—while this Lorenzo seems
20   My own particular place, I always say.
I used to wonder, when I stood scarce high
As the bed here, what the marble lion meant,
With half his body rushing from the wall,
Eating the figure of a prostrate man—
25   (To the right, it is, of entry by the door)
An ominous sign to one baptized like me,
Married, and to be buried there, I hope.
And they should add, to have my life complete,
He is a boy and Gaetan by name—

---

²| MS:And, three <> weeks, if <> more; § indication that should be transposed to read §
And, if <> more, three <> weeks;   ¹⁵| MS:Of *P1869:*O' ¹⁶| MS:born and § crossed
out and replaced above by § at   ¹⁷| MS:the Villa, at § crossed out and replaced above by
one word § in <> church, *P1869:*church: ¹⁸| MS: § crowded between 17 and 19 §
Pretty and what I   *P1869:*A pretty church, I   ²⁵| MS:To <> door— *P1869:*(To <>
door)   ²⁷| MS:and even § crossed out and replaced above by following two words § to be

30   Gaetano, for a reason,—if the friar
Don Celestine will ask this grace for me
Of Curate Ottoboni: he it was
Baptized me: he remembers my whole life
As I do his grey hair.

                              All these few things
35   I know are true,—will you remember them?
Because time flies. The surgeon cared for me,
To count my wounds,—twenty-two dagger-wounds,
Five deadly, but I do not suffer much—
Or too much pain,—and am to die to-night.

40   Oh how good God is that my babe was born,
—Better than born, baptized and hid away
Before this happened, safe from being hurt!
That had been sin God could not well forgive:
He was too young to smile and save himself.
45   When they took, two days after he was born,
My babe away from me to be baptized
And hidden awhile, for fear his foe should find,—
The country-woman, used to nursing babes,
Said "Why take on so? where is the great loss?
50   These next three weeks he will but sleep and feed,
Only begin to smile at the month's end;
He would not know you, if you kept him here,
Sooner than that; so, spend three merry weeks
Snug in the Villa, getting strong and stout,
55   And then I bring him back to be your own,
And both of you may steal to—we know where!"

---

³⁰| MS:the monk § crossed out § friar   ³²| MS:Of the § crossed out §   ³³| MS:me
and § crossed out and replaced above by colon and word § : he remembers all § crossed out § my
whole § inserted above line §   ³⁴| MS: § indication that new ¶ is to follow *hair*. §
³⁹| MS:Or § in margin § too <> and shall § crossed out and replaced above by two words §
am to <> to-night, § comma crossed out and replaced by period § they say § last two words
crossed out §   ⁴⁰| MS:§ marginal note that new ¶ begins § good God was § crossed out
and replaced above by § is   ⁴¹| MS:and sent § crossed out and replaced above by § hid
⁴⁵| MS:took,—two <> born,—   *P1869:*took, two <> born,   ⁴⁹| MS:so? Where
*P1869:*so? where   ⁵⁰| MS:All § crossed out and replaced by § These   ⁵⁴| MS:the
Villa getting   *P1869:*the Villa, getting   ⁵⁵| MS:him back § inserted above line § to be

160

The month—there wants of it two weeks this day!
Still, I half fancied when I heard the knock
At the Villa in the dusk, it might prove she—
60 Come to say "Since he smiles before the time,
Why should I cheat you out of one good hour?
Back I have brought him; speak to him and judge!"
Now I shall never see him; what is worse,
When he grows up and gets to be my age,
65 He will seem hardly more than a great boy;
And if he asks "What was my mother like?"
People may answer "Like girls of seventeen"—
And how can he but think of this and that,
Lucias, Marias, Sofias, who titter or blush
70 When he regards them as such boys may do?
Therefore I wish someone will please to say
I looked already old though I was young;
Do I not . . . say, if you are by to speak . . .
Look nearer twenty? No more like, at least,
75 Girls who look arch or redden when boys laugh,
Than the poor Virgin that I used to know
At our street-corner in a lonely niche,—
The babe, that sat upon her knees, broke off,—
Thin white glazed clay, you pitied her the more:
80 She, not the gay ones, always got my rose.

How happy those are who know how to write!
Such could write what their son should read in time,
Had they a whole day to live out like me.
Also my name is not a common name,
85 "Pompilia," and may help to keep apart
A little the thing I am from what girls are.

---

§ crossed out and then restored § < > own again § crossed out § ,   61| MS:good day
§ crossed out and replaced above by § hour?   66| MS:my mother § both words over
illegible erasure §   67| MS:People will say § last two words crossed out and replaced
above by two words § may answer "Like most § inserted above line and then crossed out §
< > seventeen years § crossed out §"—   P1869:answer "Like girls of   70| MS:he looks
at § last two words crossed out and replaced above by § regards   71| MS:someone
P1869:some one   1889a:someone   73| MS:not . . say § are by § inserted above line §
to speak . .   1889a:not . . . say < > speak . . .   77| MS:in her § last word crossed out
and replaced above by § a   79| MS:more,   P1869:more: 81| MS: § marginal note

But then how far away, how hard to find
Will anything about me have become,
Even if the boy bethink himself and ask!
90 No father that he ever knew at all,
Nor ever had—no, never had, I say!
That is the truth,—nor any mother left,
Out of the little two weeks that she lived,
Fit for such memory as might assist:
95 As good too as no family, no name,
Not even poor old Pietro's name, nor hers,
Poor kind unwise Violante, since it seems
They must not be my parents any more.
That is why something put it in my head
100 To call the boy "Gaetano"—no old name
For sorrow's sake; I looked up to the sky
And took a new saint to begin anew.
One who has only been made saint—how long?
Twenty-five years: so, carefuller, perhaps,
105 To guard a namesake than those old saints grow,
Tired out by this time,—see my own five saints!

On second thoughts, I hope he will regard
The history of me as what someone dreamed,
And get to disbelieve it at the last:
110 Since to myself it dwindles fast to that,
Sheer dreaming and impossibility,—
Just in four days too! All the seventeen years,
Not once did a suspicion visit me
How very different a lot is mine
115 From any other woman's in the world.
The reason must be, 'twas by step and step
It got to grow so terrible and strange.
These strange woes stole on tiptoe, as it were,
Into my neighbourhood and privacy,

that new ¶ begins §   87| MS:away, and § crossed out and replaced above by § how
91| MS:say— P1869:say!   96| MS:name,—nor P1869:name, nor   97| MS:Poor
§ in margin § Kind P1869:Poor kind   101| MS:sake; but § crossed out § < > to § written
over perhaps § at   104| MS:years—so P1869:years: so   106| MS:own four saints
P1869:own five saints   107| MS: § marginal note that new ¶ begins §   109| MS:it
all at last: P1869:it at the last: 112| MS:Just § written over illegible erasure §
114| MS:How very § inserted above line §   117| MS:strange: 1872:strange.

¹²⁰ Sat down where I sat, laid them where I lay;
And I was found familiarised with fear,
When friends broke in, held up a torch and cried
"Why, you Pompilia in the cavern thus,
How comes that arm of yours about a wolf?
¹²⁵ And the soft length,—lies in and out your feet
And laps you round the knee,—a snake it is!"
And so on.

Well, and they are right enough,
By the torch they hold up now: for first, observe,
I never had a father,—no, nor yet
¹³⁰ A mother: my own boy can say at least
"I had a mother whom I kept two weeks!"
Not I, who little used to doubt . . . *I* doubt
Good Pietro, kind Violante, gave me birth?
They loved me always as I love my babe
¹³⁵ (—Nearly so, that is—quite so could not be—)
Did for me all I meant to do for him,
Till one surprising day, three years ago,
They both declared, at Rome, before some judge
In some Court where the people flocked to hear,
¹⁴⁰ That really I had never been their child,
Was a mere castaway, the careless crime
Of an unknown man, the crime and care too much
Of a woman known too well,—little to these,
Therefore, of whom I was the flesh and blood:
¹⁴⁵ What then to Pietro and Violante, both
No more my relatives than you or you?
Nothing to them! You know what they declared.

So with my husband,—just such a surprise,

---

^{120|}   MS:Sate <> sate <> lay;   *P1869:*Sat <> sat   *1869:*lay,   *1872:*lay;
^{125|}   MS:And that soft   *P1869:*And the soft   ^{127|}   MS:§ marginal note that new ¶
begins after *on.* § <> enough   *P1869:*enough,   ^{128|}   MS:up thus § last word crossed out
and replaced above by § now   ^{131|}   MS:weeks"—   *P1869:*weeks!"   ^{132|}   MS:Not
I—who little § inserted above line § doubt . . *I*   *P1869:*Not I, who   *1889a:*doubt . . . *I*
^{135|}   MS:—Nearly <> be—   *P1869:*(—Nearly <> be—)   ^{138|}   MS:at Rome, here to
§ last two words crossed out and replaced above by § before   ^{139|}   MS:some court
*P1889a:*some Court   ^{144-46|}   MS: § crowded between lines 143 and 147 in continuous line
with breaks indicated following *blood*: and *both*.§   ^{147|}   MS:them,—you   *P1869:*them!

163

Such a mistake, in that relationship!
150 Everyone says that husbands love their wives,
Guard them and guide them, give them happiness;
'Tis duty, law, pleasure, religion: well,
You see how much of this comes true in mine!
People indeed would fain have somehow proved
155 He was no husband: but he did not hear,
Or would not wait, and so has killed us all.

Then there is . . . only let me name one more!
There is the friend,—men will not ask about,
But tell untruths of, and give nicknames to,
160 And think my lover, most surprise of all!
Do only hear, it is the priest they mean,
Giuseppe Caponsacchi: a priest—love,
And love me! Well, yet people think he did.
I am married, he has taken priestly vows,
165 They know that, and yet go on, say, the same,
"Yes, how he loves you!" "That was love"—they say,
When anything is answered that they ask:
Or else "No wonder you love him"—they say.
Then they shake heads, pity much, scarcely blame—
170 As if we neither of us lacked excuse,
And anyhow are punished to the full,
And downright love atones for everything!
Nay, I heard read out in the public Court
Before the judge, in presence of my friends,
175 Letters 'twas said the priest had sent to me,
And other letters sent him by myself,

You   148| MS:§ marginal note that new ¶ begins §   151| MS:guide and § crossed
out and replaced above by § them, give <> happiness,   *P1869:*happiness;
152| MS:duty, and § last word crossed out §   156-57| MS:§ ¶ §   *P1869:*§ no ¶ §   *1889:*§ no
¶; emended to restore ¶; see Editorial Notes §   157| MS:is . . only <> more—
*P1869:*more!   *1889a:*is . . . only   165| MS:that and   *P1869:*that, and
166| MS:say   *P1869:*say,   167| MS:ask—   *P1869:*ask: 168| MS:say: *P1869:*say.
*1872:*say   *1889a:*say.   169| MS:much, and § crossed out § scarcely   172| MS:And
§ crossed out and replaced above by a word erased beyond recognition; original restored §
173| MS:read out <> public court   *P1869:*read-out   *1889a:*read out <> public Court
174| MS:Before the § last word crossed out and replaced above by § a § last word crossed out
and original reading restored §   175| MS:the man had   *P1869:*the priest had

We being lovers!
   Listen what this is like!
When I was a mere child, my mother . . . that's
Violante, you must let me call her so
180 Nor waste time, trying to unlearn the word . . .
She brought a neighbour's child of my own age
To play with me of rainy afternoons;
And, since there hung a tapestry on the wall,
We two agreed to find each other out
185 Among the figures. "Tisbe, that is you,
With half-moon on your hair-knot, spear in hand,
Flying, but no wings, only the great scarf
Blown to a bluish rainbow at your back:
Call off your hound and leave the stag alone!"
190 "—And there are you, Pompilia, such green leaves
Flourishing out of your five finger-ends,
And all the rest of you so brown and rough:
Why is it you are turned a sort of tree?"
You know the figures never were ourselves
195 Though we nicknamed them so. Thus, all my life,—
As well what was, as what, like this, was not,—
Looks old, fantastic and impossible:
I touch a fairy thing that fades and fades.
—Even to my babe! I thought, when he was born,
200 Something began for once that would not end,
Nor change into a laugh at me, but stay
For evermore, eternally quite mine.
Well, so he is,—but yet they bore him off,
The third day, lest my husband should lay traps
205 And catch him, and by means of him catch me.
Since they have saved him so, it was well done:

177| MS:§ marginal indication that new ¶ follows *lovers!* § 178| MS:mother . . that's
*1889a:*mother . . . that's 180| MS:word, . . . *1889a:*word . . . 182| MS:of
§ written over *on* § 186| MS:hair-knot, bold § crossed out § 187| MS:Flying,
without § crossed out and replaced above by two words § but no 188| MS:a bluish
§ inserted above line § 190| MS:"And § altered to § "—And 196| MS:what was as
*P1869:*what was, as 198| MS:§ crowded between lines 197 and 199 § fades all day § last
two words crossed out § and fades. 200| MS:end *P1869:*end, 202| MS:ever more
*P1869:*evermore 206| MS:It < > done: since < > so, § indication that should be

165

Yet thence comes such confusion of what was
With what will be,—that late seems long ago,
And, what years should bring round, already come,
210 Till even he withdraws into a dream
As the rest do: I fancy him grown great,
Strong, stern, a tall young man who tutors me,
Frowns with the others "Poor imprudent child!
Why did you venture out of the safe street?
215 Why go so far from help to that lone house?
Why open at the whisper and the knock?"

Six days ago when it was New Year's-day,
We bent above the fire and talked of him,
What he should do when he was grown and great.
220 Violante, Pietro, each had given the arm
I leant on, to walk by, from couch to chair
And fireside,—laughed, as I lay safe at last,
"Pompilia's march from bed to board is made,
Pompilia back again and with a babe,
225 Shall one day lend his arm and help her walk!"
Then we all wished each other more New Years.
Pietro began to scheme—"Our cause is gained;
The law is stronger than a wicked man:
Let him henceforth go his way, leave us ours!
230 We will avoid the city, tempt no more
The greedy ones by feasting and parade,—

transposed to § Since <> so, It <> done: *P1869:*so, it   208| MS:be,—that § inserted
above line § lately § altered to § late   209| MS:should bring § inserted above line §
211| MS:grown tall § last word crossed out § great,   212| MS:a tall § inserted above line §
<> who may § last word crossed out § tutor § altered to § tutors   213| MS:chides with
<> imprudent one § crossed out and replaced above by § child!"   *P1869:*Frowns with <>
child!   214-16| MS:§ crowded between 213 and 217 in continuous line with indication
that breaks follow *street?* and *house?* §   216-17| MS:§ ¶ §   *1889a:*§ no ¶ §   *1889:*§ no ¶;
emended to restore ¶; see Editorial Notes §   217| MS:Four days § altered to § Six days <>
Year's eve § crossed out and replaced by § Day   *P1869:*Year's-day   219| MS:great:
*P1869:*great.   222| MS:By § crossed out and replaced above by § And the fireside <>
laughed as <> last   *P1869:*And fireside <> laughed, as <> last,   224| MS:back again
§ inserted above line § <> babe besides § crossed out § ,   225| MS:and let § crossed out
and replaced above by § help   231| MS:greedy ones § inserted above line § by our § crossed

166

Live at the other villa, we know where,
Still farther off, and we can watch the babe
Grow fast in the good air; and wood is cheap
235 And wine sincere outside the city gate.
I still have two or three old friends will grope
Their way along the mere half-mile of road,
With staff and lantern on a moonless night
When one needs talk: they'll find me, never fear,
240 And I'll find them a flask of the old sort yet!"
Violante said "You chatter like a crow:
Pompilia tires o' the tattle, and shall to bed:
Do not too much the first day,—somewhat more
To-morrow, and, the next, begin the cape
245 And hood and coat! I have spun wool enough."
Oh what a happy friendly eve was that!

And, next day, about noon, out Pietro went—
He was so happy and would talk so much,
Until Violante pushed and laughed him forth
250 Sight-seeing in the cold,—"So much to see
I' the churches! Swathe your throat three times!" she cried,
"And, above all, beware the slippery ways,
And bring us all the news by supper-time!"
He came back late, laid by cloak, staff and hat,
255 Powdered so thick with snow it made us laugh,
Rolled a great log upon the ash o' the hearth,
And bade Violante treat us to a flask,
Because he had obeyed her faithfully,

---

out §   232| MS:other Villa   *P1869:*other villa   233| MS:the child § crossed out and
replaced above by § babe   236-38| MS:grope/ With   *P1869:*grope/ Their way along
the mere half-mile of road,/ With   240| MS:yet."   *P1869:*yet!"   242| MS:of < >
to-bed: *P1869:*o'   *1872:*to bed: 245| MS:coat; I   *P1869:*coat! I
247| MS:§ marginal note that new ¶ begins §   248| MS:§ crowded between 247 and 249 §
much   *P1869:*much,   249| MS:Because § crossed out and replaced in margin by § Until
251| MS:In § altered to § I' < > times,—she § altered to § times!" she   252| MS:And.
above   *P1869:*And, above   253| MS:§ added in right margin with arrow indicating its
place in text § suppertime!"   *P1869:*supper-time!"   255| MS:§ crowded between 254
and 256 §   256| MS:of § altered to § o'   257| MS:bade Violante bring down wine
§ last three words crossed out and replaced above by five words § treat us to a flask
*P1869:*flask,   258| MS:§ in margin following and separated from line 257 by slash §

Gone sight-see through the seven, and found no church
260 To his mind like San Giovanni—"There's the fold,
And all the sheep together, big as cats!
And such a shepherd, half the size of life,
Starts up and hears the angel"—when, at the door,
A tap: we started up: you know the rest.

265 Pietro at least had done no harm, I know;
Nor even Violante, so much harm as makes
Such revenge lawful. Certainly she erred—
Did wrong, how shall I dare say otherwise?—
In telling that first falsehood, buying me
270 From my poor faulty mother at a price,
To pass off upon Pietro as his child.
If one should take my babe, give him a name,
Say he was not Gaetano and my own,
But that some other woman made his mouth
275 And hands and feet,—how very false were that!
No good could come of that; and all harm did.
Yet if a stranger were to represent
"Needs must you either give your babe to me
And let me call him mine for evermore,
280 Or let your husband get him"—ah, my God,
That were a trial I refuse to face!
Well, just so here: it proved wrong but seemed right
To poor Violante—for there lay, she said,

259| MS:He had § last two words crossed out § gone § altered to § Gone sight-see § last two
words inserted above line § <> the whole § crossed out §   260-64| MS:like San
Giovanni—when at the door § following *Giovanni*, three words inserted above line § "There's
the fold/ § lines 261-63 follow in right hand margin with arrow indicating their place in
text § <> cats,/ // A <> the dreadful § crossed out §   *P1869:*like San Giovanni—"There's
the fold,/ <> cats!/ // A   265| MS:§ marginal note that new ¶ begins §
268| MS:wrong,—how   *P1869:*wrong, how   271| MS:child: *1872:*child.
276| MS:come thence § crossed out and replaced above by two words § of that <>
harm must have § last two words crossed out and replaced above by § did   277| MS:yet
did § crossed out and replaced above by § if a stranger say—Or give him me § last five
words crossed out and replaced above by three words § were to represent
278| MS:§ follows in margin and separated from 277 by slash §   279| MS:§ crowded
between 278 and 280 § evermore   *P1869:*ever more,   *1872:*evermore,   283| MS:To

168

My poor real dying mother in her rags,
285 Who put me from her with the life and all,
Poverty, pain, shame and disease at once,
To die the easier by what price I fetched—
Also (I hope) because I should be spared
Sorrow and sin,—why may not that have helped?
290 My father,—he was no one, any one,—
The worse, the likelier,—call him—he who came,
Was wicked for his pleasure, went his way,
And left no trace to track by; there remained
Nothing but me, the unnecessary life,
295 To catch up or let fall,—and yet a thing
She could make happy, be made happy with,
This poor Violante,—who would frown thereat?

Well, God, you see! God plants us where we grow.
It is not that because a bud is born
300 At a wild briar's end, full i' the wild beast's way,
We ought to pluck and put it out of reach
On the oak-tree top,—say "There the bud belongs!"
She thought, moreover, real lies were lies told
For harm's sake; whereas this had good at heart,
305 Good for my mother, good for me, and good
For Pietro who was meant to love a babe,

---

poor § last word inserted above line § 284| MS:rags *P1869:*rags, 288| MS:Also,
I hope, because § altered to § Also (I hope) because 293| MS:Leaving § crossed out
and replaced above by two words § And left < > by: there *P1869:*by; there
294| MS:Nor infant § last two words crossed out and replaced above by two words §
Nothing but me, the pitiable § last word crossed out and replaced above by one
word § unnecessary life *P1869:*life, 298| MS:§ marginal note that new ¶ begins § see!
God puts § crossed out and replaced above by § plants 299| MS:that,—suppose,—a
*P1869:*that, because a *1889a:*that because 300| MS:a wild § inserted above line § < >
in the wild beast's § last two words crossed out and replaced above by one word § creatures'
way,— *P1869:*i' the wild beast's way, 302| MS:oak-tree- § word and hyphen inserted
above line § top, and § crossed out § —say, "there § altered to "There the rose shall wave. §
last two words and period crossed out and replaced above by § belongs!" *P1869:*oak-tree top
303| MS:More over, she thought real § indication that should be transposed and altered to §
She thought Moreover, real lies were—lies *P1869:*thought, moreover *1889a:*were lies
304| MS:had only § last word crossed out § 306| MS:§ first word crossed out beyond
recognition § for § altered to § For < > who was meant to § last three words inserted above
line § loved § altered to § love a babes § altered to § babe so much § last two words crossed

And needed one to make his life of use,
Receive his house and land when he should die.
Wrong, wrong and always wrong! how plainly wrong!
310 For see, this fault kept pricking, as faults do,
All the same at her heart: this falsehood hatched,
She could not let it go nor keep it fast.
She told me so,—the first time I was found
Locked in her arms once more after the pain,
315 When the nuns let me leave them and go home,
And both of us cried all the cares away,—
This it was set her on to make amends,
This brought about the marriage—simply this!
Do let me speak for her you blame so much!
320 When Paul, my husband's brother, found me out,
Heard there was wealth for who should marry me,
So, came and made a speech to ask my hand
For Guido,—she, instead of piercing straight
Through the pretence to the ignoble truth,
325 Fancied she saw God's very finger point,
Designate just the time for planting me
(The wild-briar slip she plucked to love and wear)
In soil where I could strike real root, and grow,
And get to be the thing I called myself:
330 For, wife and husband are one flesh, God says,
And I, whose parents seemed such and were none,
Should in a husband have a husband now,

out § *P1869:*babe,   308| MS:And have § last two words crossed out and replaced above by § Receive his goods § crossed out and replaced above by § house   309| MS:always wrong! How § altered to § how plainly wrong,— § altered to § wrong!— *P1869:*plainly wrong!   311| MS:heart,—the falsehood there found § last two words crossed out and replaced above by word and comma § hatched, *P1869:*heart,—this a *1889a:*heart: this   318| MS:simply this— *P1869:*simply this!   319| MS:§ crowded between 318 and 320 §   321| MS:was money § crossed out and replaced above by § wealth < > should make § crossed out and replaced above by § marry me, wife § crossed out §   322| MS:So came *P1869:*So, came   323| MS:of seeing clear § last two words crossed out and replaced above by two words § piercing straight   326| MS:Designate just § inserted above line § the very minute § last two words crossed out and replaced above by § time < > me, *1889a:*me   327| MS:The wild briar § last word inserted above line § < > had § crossed out § < > wear, § comma altered to §) *P1869:*wild briar's slip *CP1869:*wild briar-slip *1889a:*wild-briar slip   331| MS:seeming § altered to § seemed such and § inserted above line §

Find nothing, this time, but was what it seemed,
—All truth and no confusion any more.
335 I know she meant all good to me, all pain
To herself,—since how could it be aught but pain
To give me up, so, from her very breast,
The wilding flower-tree-branch that, all those years,
She had got used to feel for and find fixed?
340 She meant well: has it been so ill i' the main?
That is but fair to ask: one cannot judge
Of what has been the ill or well of life,
The day that one is dying,—sorrows change
Into not altogether sorrow-like;
345 I do see strangeness but scarce misery,
Now it is over, and no danger more.
My child is safe; there seems not so much pain.
It comes, most like, that I am just absolved,
Purged of the past, the foul in me, washed fair,—
350 One cannot both have and not have, you know,—
Being right now, I am happy and colour things.
Yes, everybody that leaves life sees all
Softened and bettered: so with other sights:
To me at least was never evening yet
355 But seemed far beautifuller than its day,
For past is past.

There was a fancy came,
When somewhere, in the journey with my friend,
We stepped into a hovel to get food;
And there began a yelp here, a bark there,—

---

³³³| MS:Find § in margin § Nothing but was § last two words crossed out § , this time, but
§ last word inserted above line § the thing § crossed out and replaced above by § fact
*P1869:*but was what it   ³³⁴| MS:—Find § crossed out and replaced above by § All
³³⁶| MS:pain, DC,BrU:pain *1889:*pain   ³³⁷| MS:Giving me *P1869:*To give me
³³⁸| MS:Its wilding § inserted above line § *P1869:*The wilding   ³⁴²| MS: § crowded
between 341 and 343 §   ³⁴⁹| MS:past, the black wiped clean § last three words crossed
out and replaced above by three words § foul in me   ³⁵¹| MS:Being set § crossed out §
right now § inserted above line §   ³⁵²| *P1869:*every body *1872:*everybody
³⁵⁶| MS: § marginal note that new ¶ begins after *past.* §   ³⁵⁹| MS:Which § crossed out

171

³⁶⁰ Misunderstanding creatures that were wroth
And vexed themselves and us till we retired.
The hovel is life: no matter what dogs bit
Or cats scratched in the hovel I break from,
All outside is lone field, moon and such peace—
³⁶⁵ Flowing in, filling up as with a sea
Whereon comes Someone, walks fast on the white,
Jesus Christ's self, Don Celestine declares,
To meet me and calm all things back again.

Beside, up to my marriage, thirteen years
³⁷⁰ Were, each day, happy as the day was long:
This may have made the change too terrible.
I know that when Violante told me first
The cavalier—she meant to bring next morn,
Whom I must also let take, kiss my hand—
³⁷⁵ Would be at San Lorenzo the same eve
And marry me,—which over, we should go
Home both of us without him as before,
And, till she bade speak, I must hold my tongue,
Such being the correct way with girl-brides,
³⁸⁰ From whom one word would make a father blush,—
I know, I say, that when she told me this,
—Well, I no more saw sense in what she said
Than a lamb does in people clipping wool;
Only lay down and let myself be clipped.
³⁸⁵ And when next day the cavalier who came—
(Tisbe had told me that the slim young man
With wings at head, and wings at feet, and sword

---

and replaced above by § And   ³⁶¹| MS:we gave way § last two words crossed out and
replaced above by word and period § retired.   ³⁶⁴| MS:and space § crossed out §
³⁶⁷| MS:the Savior's § last two words crossed out and replaced above by § Jesus Christ's self,
Don Celestine affirms § last word crossed out and replaced above by § asserts,   *P1869:*self,
Don Celestine declares,   ³⁶⁹| MS: § marginal note that new ¶ begins §
³⁷⁰| MS:And § crossed out and replaced above by § Were < > long—   *P1869:*long:
³⁷³| MS:cavalier,—she < > next day § crossed out and replaced above by § morn,
*1889a:*cavalier—she   ³⁷⁴| MS:hand,—   *1889a:*hand—   ³⁸⁰| MS:And § crossed
out and replaced above by two words § From whom one word fit to § last two words
crossed out and replaced above by one word § would make my § crossed out and replaced
above by § a   ³⁸¹| MS: § crowded between 380 and 382 §   ³⁸³| MS:wool—
*P1869:*wool;   ³⁸⁵| MS:came   *1889a:*came—   ³⁸⁶| MS:the tall § crossed out

172

Threatening a monster, in our tapestry,
Would eat a girl else,—was a cavalier)
390 When he proved Guido Franceschini,—old
And nothing like so tall as I myself,
Hook-nosed and yellow in a bush of beard,
Much like a thing I saw on a boy's wrist,
He called an owl and used for catching birds,—
395 And when he took my hand and made a smile—
Why, the uncomfortableness of it all
Seemed hardly more important in the case
Than,—when one gives you, say, a coin to spend,—
Its newness or its oldness; if the piece
400 Weigh properly and buy you what you wish,
No matter whether you get grime or glare!
Men take the coin, return you grapes and figs.
Here, marriage was the coin, a dirty piece
Would purchase me the praise of those I loved:
405 About what else should I concern myself?

So, hardly knowing what a husband meant,
I supposed this or any man would serve,
No whit the worse for being so uncouth:
For I was ill once and a doctor came
410 With a great ugly hat, no plume thereto,
Black jerkin and black buckles and black sword,
And white sharp beard over the ruff in front,
And oh so lean, so sour-faced and austere!—

---

and replaced above by § slim   391| MS: § crowded between 390 and 392 §
*1889a:*myself   DC, BrU: myself,   *1889:*myself,   396| MS:of it § inserted above
line §   398| MS:Than, when < > spend,   *P1869:*Than,—when < > spend,—
399| MS:Dirty § crossed out and replaced above by two words § The newness or shiny
§ crossed out and replaced by two words § its oldness; of the weight aright be well § last four
words crossed out and replaced above by § piece   400| MS:§ follows in margin and
separated from 399 by slash §   401| MS:Wh § crossed out § No § over illegible erasure §
< > grime with gold § last two words crossed out and replaced above by § or glare:
*P1869:*glare!   402| MS:take it and § last two words crossed out and replaced above by §
the coin   404| MS:loved—   *P1869:*loved: 406| MS:§ marginal note that new ¶
begins § < > meant   *P1869:*meant,   411| MS:A § crossed out § black § altered to § Black
cloak § crossed out and replaced above by § jerkin and black habit § crossed out and replaced
above by § buckles   413| MS:sour-faced and austere § last two words crossed out and
replaced above by words illegibly erased, and original restored § austere,   *P1869:*austere!—

173

Who felt my pulse, made me put out my tongue,
415 Then oped a phial, dripped a drop or two
Of a black bitter something,—I was cured!
What mattered the fierce beard or the grim face?
It was the physic beautified the man,
Master Malpichi,—never met his match
420 In Rome, they said,—so ugly all the same!

However, I was hurried through a storm,
Next dark eve of December's deadest day—
How it rained!—through our street and the Lion's-mouth
And the bit of Corso,—cloaked round, covered close,
425 I was like something strange or contraband,—
Into blank San Lorenzo, up the aisle,
My mother keeping hold of me so tight,
I fancied we were come to see a corpse
Before the altar which she pulled me toward.
430 There we found waiting an unpleasant priest
Who proved the brother, not our parish friend,
But one with mischief-making mouth and eye,
Paul, whom I know since to my cost. And then
I heard the heavy church-door lock out help
435 Behind us: for the customary warmth,
Two tapers shivered on the altar. "Quick—
Lose no time!" cried the priest. And straightway down

414| MS:pulse, and § crossed out § <> me show § crossed out and replaced below by two
words § put out   415| MS:oped a a phial   P1869:oped a phial   417| MS:mattered
the white § crossed out and replaced above by § fierce <> the sour § crossed out and replaced
above by § grim   418| MS:physick   CP1869:physic   419| MS:never yet was § last
two words crossed out and replaced by two words § met his   420| MS:they say § crossed
out and replaced above by § said   421| MS:§ marginal note that new ¶ begins §
424| MS:covered up § crossed out § close   P1869:close,   429| MS:toward;
P1869:toward.   430| MS:found yesterday's § crossed out and replaced above by two
words § waiting an unpleasant priest § written over perhaps man §   431| MS:Waiting,
§ crossed out and replaced above by two words § That proved <> parish priest § last word
crossed out §   P1869:Who proved   432| MS:with foe-like face § last two words crossed
out and replaced above by two words § mischief-making mouth and fierce § last word crossed
out § eye   P1869:eye,   437| MS:time!"—cried the priest—And   P1869:priest. And

From . . . what's behind the altar where he hid—
Hawk-nose and yellowness and bush and all,
440 Stepped Guido, caught my hand, and there was I
O' the chancel, and the priest had opened book,
Read here and there, made me say that and this,
And after, told me I was now a wife,
Honoured indeed, since Christ thus weds the Church,
445 And therefore turned he water into wine,
To show I should obey my spouse like Christ.
Then the two slipped aside and talked apart,
And I, silent and scared, got down again
And joined my mother who was weeping now.
450 Nobody seemed to mind us any more,
And both of us on tiptoe found our way
To the door which was unlocked by this, and wide.
When we were in the street, the rain had stopped,
All things looked better. At our own house-door,
455 Violante whispered "No one syllable
To Pietro! Girl-brides never breathe a word!"
"—Well treated to a wetting, draggle-tails!"
Laughed Pietro as he opened—"Very near
You made me brave the gutter's roaring sea
460 To carry off from roost old dove and young,
Trussed up in church, the cote, by me, the kite!
What do these priests mean, praying folk to death
On stormy afternoons, with Christmas close

*1889a:*time!" cried   438| MS:From—what's   *P1869:*From . . what's   *1889a:*From
. . . what's   439| MS:Hawk nose <>all—   *P1869:*Hawk-nose <>all,
440| MS:Stepped Guido—caught my hand—and   *P1869:*Stepped Guido, caught my hand,
and   441| MS:On § altered to § O' <>chancel and   *P1869:*chancel, and
444| MS:Honoured in this, that Christ   *P1869:*Honoured indeed, since Christ
445| MS:turned once water   *P1869:*turned he water   449| MS:was sobbing § crossed
out and replaced above by § weeping now;   *P1869:*now.   450| MS:§ crowded between
449 and 451 §   452| MS:this, lay wide—   *P1869:*this, and wide.   453| MS:And we
<>street: the   *P1869:*When we <>street, the   454| MS:house-door
*P1869:*house-door,   456| MS:To Pietro, girl-brides   *P1869:*To Pietro! Girl-brides
458| MS:opened—"very   *P1869:*opened—"Very   460| MS:And carry   *P1869:*To carry
461| MS:kite: *P1869:*kite!   463| MS:stormy winter nights § last two words crossed out

To wash our sins off nor require the rain?"
465 Violante gave my hand a timely squeeze,
Madonna saved me from immodest speech,
I kissed him and was quiet, being a bride.

When I saw nothing more, the next three weeks,
Of Guido—"Nor the Church sees Christ" thought I:
470 "Nothing is changed however, wine is wine
And water only water in our house.
Nor did I see that ugly doctor since
That cure of the illness: just as I was cured,
I am married,—neither scarecrow will return."

475 Three weeks, I chuckled—"How would Giulia stare,
And Tecla smile and Tisbe laugh outright,
Were it not impudent for brides to talk!"—
Until one morning, as I sat and sang
At the broidery-frame alone i' the chamber,—loud
480 Voices, two, three together, sobbings too,
And my name, "Guido," "Paolo," flung like stones
From each to the other! In I ran to see.
There stood the very Guido and the priest
With sly face,—formal but nowise afraid,—
485 While Pietro seemed all red and angry, scarce
Able to stutter out his wrath in words;
And this it was that made my mother sob,
As he reproached her—"You have murdered us,
Me and yourself and this our child beside!"
490 Then Guido interposed "Murdered or not,
Be it enough your child is now my wife!

---

and replaced above by § afternoons   467-68| MS:§ ¶ §   1889a:§ no ¶ §   1889:§ no ¶;
emended to restore ¶; see Editorial Notes §   468| MS:more the < > weeks   P1869:more,
the < > weeks,   469| MS:sees Christ" said § crossed out and replaced above by §
thought   473| MS:The cure   1889a:That cure   474| MS:return.   P1869:return."
475| MS:§ marginal note that new ¶ begins § Three whole § crossed out § weeks did I
chuckle—"Gigia would § last two words crossed out and replaced above by § How would
Gigia   P1869:Three weeks, I chuckled— < > Guilia   476| MS:outright
P1869:outright,   478| MS:Until § inserted above line § One morning, as § inserted above
line § I sate   P1869:Until one < > sat   482| MS:other:§ altered to § ! In
483| MS:the Priest   P1869:the priest   484| MS:With the fox § crossed out and replaced

176

I claim and come to take her." Paul put in,
"Consider—kinsman, dare I term you so?—
What is the good of your sagacity
Except to counsel in a strait like this?
I guarantee the parties man and wife
Whether you like or loathe it, bless or ban.
May spilt milk be put back within the bowl—
The done thing, undone? You, it is, we look
For counsel to, you fitliest will advise!
Since milk, though spilt and spoilt, does marble good,
Better we down on knees and scrub the floor,
Than sigh, 'the waste would make a syllabub!'
Help us so turn disaster to account,
So predispose the groom, he needs shall grace
The bride with favour from the very first,
Not begin marriage an embittered man!"
He smiled,—the game so wholly in his hands!
While fast and faster sobbed Violante—"Ay,
All of us murdered, past averting now!
O my sin, O my secret!" and such like.

Then I began to half surmise the truth;
Something had happened, low, mean, underhand,
False, and my mother was to blame, and I
To pity, whom all spoke of, none addressed:
I was the chattel that had caused a crime.
I stood mute,—those who tangled must untie
The embroilment. Pietro cried "Withdraw, my child!

---

by § sly   492| MS:in— P1869:in,   493| MS:kinsman, shall I dare address § last
four words crossed out and replaced above by five words and question mark § dare I name
you so?— P1869:dare I term you   494| MS:the good § crossed out and replaced above
by a word erased beyond recognition; original restored § of your sagacity § altered to
sagaciousness § and the original restored §   498| MS:be poured § crossed out and
replaced above by § put back into § crossed out and replaced above by § within
500| MS:advise; P1869:advise!   501| MS:spoilt, makes § crossed out and replaced
above by § does marble clean § crossed out and replaced above by § good,   502| MS:What
of § last two words crossed out and replaced above by § Better   503| MS:syllabub'!
P1869:syllabub!'   504| MS:turn the matter § last two words crossed out and replaced
above by § disaster   505| MS:the Groom he P1869:the groom, he   506| MS:The
Bride P1869:The bride   508| MS:hands!— P1869:hands!   509| MS:sobbed
Violante—"Ay— P1869:sobbed Violante—"Ay,   510| MS:now,— P1869:now!
511| MS:secret!"—and P1869:secret!" and   512| MS:§ marginal note that new ¶
begins § truth— P1869:truth;   515| MS:addressed; P1869:addressed:
517| MS:must untwine § crossed out and replaced above by § untie   518| MS:cried

She is not helpful to the sacrifice
520 At this stage,—do you want the victim by
While you discuss the value of her blood?
For her sake, I consent to hear you talk:
Go, child, and pray God help the innocent!"

I did go and was praying God, when came
525 Violante, with eyes swollen and red enough,
But movement on her mouth for make-believe
Matters were somehow getting right again.
She bade me sit down by her side and hear.
"You are too young and cannot understand,
530 Nor did your father understand at first.
I wished to benefit all three of us,
And when he failed to take my meaning,—why,
I tried to have my way at unaware—
Obtained him the advantage he refused.
535 As if I put before him wholesome food
Instead of broken victual,—he finds change
I' the viands, never cares to reason why,
But falls to blaming me, would fling the plate
From window, scandalize the neighbourhood,
540 Even while he smacks his lips,—men's way, my child!
But either you have prayed him unperverse
Or I have talked him back into his wits:

"Retire § crossed out and replaced above by § Withdraw   519| MS:not privy § crossed out
and replaced above by § helpful   520| MS:stage,—when § crossed out and replaced above
by § do < > victim well § crossed out § by   521| MS:§ crowded between 520 and 522 §
523| MS:innocent!"   1889a:innocent! § emended to § innocent!" § see Editorial Notes §
524| MS:§ marginal note that new ¶ begins § praying God § inserted above line § when there
§ crossed out § came   525| MS:Violante with < > enough but still § last two words
crossed out §   P1869:Violante, with enough,   526| MS:mouth meant § crossed out §
for a smi § last two words crossed out and replaced above by § make-believe
527| MS:again: P1869:again.   528| MS:And told § last two words crossed out and
replaced above by two words § She bade me to § crossed out § sit down § inserted above line §
529| MS:understand—   P1869:understand,   533-35| MS:unaware—/ As
P1869:unaware—/ Obtained him the advantage he refused./ As   536| MS:he smells
§ crossed out and replaced above by § finds   537| MS:§ crowded between 536 and 538 §
539| MS:§ crowded between 538 and 540 §   542| MS:have reasoned § crossed out and
replaced above by § talked him back § over illegible erasure § < > wits,   P1869:wits:

And Paolo was a help in time of need,—
Guido, not much—my child, the way of men!
545 A priest is more a woman than a man,
And Paul did wonders to persuade. In short,
Yes, he was wrong, your father sees and says;
My scheme was worth attempting: and bears fruit,
Gives you a husband and a noble name,
550 A palace and no end of pleasant things.
What do you care about a handsome youth?
They are so volatile, and tease their wives!
This is the kind of man to keep the house.
We lose no daughter,—gain a son, that's all:
555 For 'tis arranged we never separate,
Nor miss, in our grey time of life, the tints
Of you that colour eve to match with morn.
In good or ill, we share and share alike,
And cast our lots into a common lap,
560 And all three die together as we lived!
Only, at Arezzo,—that's a Tuscan town,
Not so large as this noisy Rome, no doubt,
But older far and finer much, say folk,—
In a great palace where you will be queen,
565 Know the Archbishop and the Governor,
And we see homage done you ere we die.
Therefore, be good and pardon!"—"Pardon what?
You know things, I am very ignorant:
All is right if you only will not cry!"

570 And so an end! Because a blank begins

547| MS:says— *P1869:*says;   548| MS:attempting—and *P1869:*attempting: and
551-53| MS:§ crowded between 550 and 554 and in margin; lines divided as they are in text §
552| MS:teaze *1889a:*tease   555| MS:we do not § last two words crossed out and
replaced above by § never separate *P1869:*separate,   556| MS:miss in <> life the
*P1869:*miss, in <> life, the   557| MS:eve like rosy § last two words crossed out and
replaced above by three words § to match with   559| MS:And § in margin § cast all three
§ last two words crossed out and replaced above by § our   560| MS:And all three § last
two words inserted above line § <> lived before § crossed out §— *P1869:*lived!
561| MS:that famed § crossed out and replaced above by § 's a <> town— *P1869:*town,
563| MS:older far § inserted above line § and finer much § inserted above line § <> folks,—
*1889a:*folk,—   564| MS:a fine § crossed out and replaced above by § great <> queen
*P1869:*queen,   565| MS:§ crowded between 564 and 566 §   568| MS:ignorant,
*P1869:*ignorant: 569| MS:cry." *P1869:*cry!"   570| MS:§ marginal note that new

From when, at the word, she kissed me hard and hot,
And took me back to where my father leaned
Opposite Guido—who stood eyeing him,
As eyes the butcher the cast panting ox
⁵⁷⁵ That feels his fate is come, nor struggles more,—
While Paul looked archly on, pricked brow at whiles
With the pen-point as to punish triumph there,—
And said "Count Guido, take your lawful wife
Until death part you!"

All since is one blank,
⁵⁸⁰ Over and ended; a terrific dream.
It is the good of dreams—so soon they go!
Wake in a horror of heart-beats, you may—
Cry "The dread thing will never from my thoughts!"
Still, a few daylight doses of plain life,
⁵⁸⁵ Cock-crow and sparrow-chirp, or bleat and bell
Of goats that trot by, tinkling, to be milked;
And when you rub your eyes awake and wide,
Where is the harm o' the horror? Gone! So here.
I know I wake,—but from what? Blank, I say!
⁵⁹⁰ This is the note of evil: for good lasts.
Even when Don Celestine bade "Search and find!
For your soul's sake, remember what is past,
The better to forgive it,"—all in vain!
What was fast getting indistinct before,
⁵⁹⁵ Vanished outright. By special grace perhaps,

¶ begins § end—because   *P1869:*end! Because   ⁵⁷¹| MS:hot   *P1869:*hot,
⁵⁷²| MS:father sat   *P1869:*father leaned   ⁵⁷³| MS:Opposite Guido,—who was eyeing
§ last two words crossed out and replaced above by two words § stood o'er him,—eyed,
*P1869:*Opposite Guido—who stood eyeing him,   ⁵⁷⁴| MS:butcher some § crossed out
and replaced above by § the cast panting § crossed out, replaced above by § prostrate § crossed
out and original reading restored §   ⁵⁷⁵| MS:is fallen § crossed out and replaced above
by § come   ⁵⁷⁸| MS:said "Count Guido take your lawful § inserted above line § wife
again § crossed out §   *1869:*said "Count Guido, take   ⁵⁷⁹| MS:§ marginal note that new
¶ begins after *you!"* §   ⁵⁸⁰| MS:ended,—a <> dream—   *P1869:*ended; a <> dream.
⁵⁸¹| MS:dreams that thus § last two words crossed out and replaced above by § —so soon
⁵⁸³| MS:Cry, "The   *1889a:*Cry "The   ⁵⁸⁶| MS:milked,   *P1869:*milked;
⁵⁸⁸| MS:Why, where's the harm o' the § last three words inserted above line §   *P1869:*Where
is the   ⁵⁸⁹| MS:say.   *P1869:*say!   ⁵⁹⁰| MS:evil—it § crossed out and replaced
above by two words § for good lasts. not § crossed out §   *P1869:*evil: for   ⁵⁹¹| MS:when

Between that first calm and this last, four years
Vanish,—one quarter of my life, you know.
I am held up, amid the nothingness,
By one or two truths only—thence I hang,
600   And there I live,—the rest is death or dream,
All but those points of my support. I think
Of what I saw at Rome once in the Square
O' the Spaniards, opposite the Spanish House:
There was a foreigner had trained a goat,
605   A shuddering white woman of a beast,
To climb up, stand straight on a pile of sticks
Put close, which gave the creature room enough:
When she was settled there he, one by one,
Took away all the sticks, left just the four
610   Whereon the little hoofs did really rest,
There she kept firm, all underneath was air.
So, what I hold by, are my prayer to God,
My hope, that came in answer to the prayer,
Some hand would interpose and save me—hand
615   Which proved to be my friend's hand: and,—blest bliss,—
That fancy which began so faint at first,
That thrill of dawn's suffusion through my dark,
Which I perceive was promise of my child,

Don Celestine bade § over illegible erasure §   598| MS:up amid that § crossed out and
replaced above by § the nothingness   *P1869:*up, amid the nothingness,   600| MS:death
and § crossed out and replaced above by § or dream—   *P1869:*dream,   603| MS:the
Spaniards opposite the § inserted above line §   *P1869:*the Spaniards, opposite
605| MS:of a thing § crossed out and replaced by § beast,   606| MS:up, and § crossed
out § stand straight § inserted above line §   612| MS:are the § crossed out and replaced
above by § my prayers § *s* erased §   613| MS:The § crossed out and replaced above by §
With § crossed out and replaced in margin by § My hope that came in § last three words
crossed out and replaced above by three words § which § followed by two illegible words, all
three crossed out and original reading restored §   614| MS:That § crossed out and
replaced in margin by § Some <> save, one day,— § last two words crossed out and replaced
above by two words § me—that § crossed out § —hand   *P1869:*save me—hand
615| MS:and, the § crossed out and replaced above by dash and word § —best bliss,—
1889a:—blest bliss,—   616| MS:Even in § last two words crossed out § that § altered to §
That fancy that began § last two words crossed out and replaced above by § which all
§ crossed out § began § last two words crossed out and replaced above by three words § which
all § crossed out § began § placed immediately above same word which was first crossed out
and then marked for restoration §   617| MS:—That § written over partly erased,
illegible word § of that star's dawning § last three words crossed out and replaced above by
two words § dawn's beginning § crossed out § suffusion   618| MS:which § in margin §

The light his unborn face sent long before,—
⁶²⁰ God's way of breaking the good news to flesh.
That is all left now of those four bad years.
Don Celestine urged "But remember more!
Other men's faults may help me find your own.
I need the cruelty exposed, explained,
⁶²⁵ Or how can I advise you to forgive?"
He thought I could not properly forgive
Unless I ceased forgetting,—which is true:
For, bringing back reluctantly to mind
My husband's treatment of me,—by a light
⁶³⁰ That's later than my life-time, I review
And comprehend much and imagine more,
And have but little to forgive at last.
For now,—be fair and say,—is it not true
He was ill-used and cheated of his hope
⁶³⁵ To get enriched by marriage? Marriage gave
Me and no money, broke the compact so:
He had a right to ask me on those terms,
As Pietro and Violante to declare
They would not give me: so the bargain stood:
⁶⁴⁰ They broke it, and he felt himself aggrieved,
Became unkind with me to punish them.
They said 'twas he began deception first,
Nor, in one point whereto he pledged himself,

I now § crossed out §   ⁶²⁰| MS:§ crowded between 619 and 621 §   ⁶²²| MS:Don
Celestine § followed by an illegibly blotted word, perhaps *urged* over *said*, and immediately
above B has written § urged <> more—   *P1869:*more!   ⁶²³| MS:may point us to § last
three words crossed out and replaced above by three words § help me find <> own—
*P1869:*own.   ⁶²⁴| MS:cruelties exposed, § inserted above line § explained,
some § crossed out §   *P1869:*cruelty   ⁶²⁵| MS:advise you to § last
two words inserted above line § forgive? them all? § last two words and question
mark crossed out § "   ⁶²⁷| MS:he was right § crossed out § which is true:
⁶²⁹| MS:treatment of me § last two words inserted above line §   ⁶³¹| MS:and
forgive the § last two words crossed out and replaced by § imagine   ⁶³²| MS:§ crowded
between 631 and 633 §   ⁶³⁷| MS:terms   *P1869:*terms,   ⁶³⁸| MS:And § crossed out
and replaced above by § As <> to refuse § crossed out §   ⁶³⁹| MS:§ crowded between 638
and 640 § give § followed by illegible word, crossed out and replaced above by § me: so, the
*P1869:*so the   ⁶⁴⁰| MS:They § two words illegibly crossed out and replaced below by
two words § broke it   ⁶⁴¹| MS:unkind to § altered to § with   ⁶⁴³| MS:And § crossed
out and replaced by § Nor, in all things § last two words crossed out and replaced above by

Kept promise: what of that, suppose it were?
645 Echoes die off, scarcely reverberate
For ever,—why should ill keep echoing ill
And never let our ears have done with noise?
Then my poor parents took the violent way
To thwart him,—he must needs retaliate,—wrong,
650 Wrong, and all wrong,—better say, all blind!
As I myself was, that is sure, who else
Had understood the mystery: for his wife
Was bound in some sort to help somehow there.
It seems as if I might have interposed,
655 Blunted the edge of their resentment so,
Since he vexed me because they first vexed him;
"I will entreat them to desist, submit,
Give him the money and be poor in peace,—
Certainly not go tell the world: perhaps
660 He will grow quiet with his gains."

                                        Yes, say
Something to this effect and you do well!
But then you have to see first: I was blind.
That is the fruit of all such wormy ways,
The indirect, the unapproved of God:
665 You cannot find their author's end and aim,
Not even to substitute your good for bad,

---

two words § one point   644| MS:Broke § crossed out and replaced above by § Kept
promise—what *P1869:*promise: what   645| MS:off, do not § last two words crossed out
and replaced by § scarcely   646| MS:keep making §crossed out and replaced above by §
echoing ill,   DC,BrU:ill   *1889:*ill   650| MS:Wrong, and § inserted above line § <>
blind!— *P1869:*blind!   652| MS:mystery,—for, § word and comma inserted above
line § his *P1869:*mystery: for his   654| MS:§ crowded between 653 and 655 §
655| MS:And turn § two words crossed out and replaced in margin by § Blunted the drift
§ crossed out and replaced below by § edge of all § crossed out § their argument § crossed out
and replaced above by § resentment so,   656| MS:Say § crossed out and replaced in
margin by § Since, me he vexed since § crossed out and replaced below by § because
*P1869:*Since he vexed me because   659| MS:world; perhaps *P1869:*world: perhaps
660| MS:§ marginal note that new ¶ begins with *Yes* § <> say— § dash crossed out §
661| MS:§ crowded between 660 and 662 § well— *P1869:*well!   662| MS:see and
§ crossed out and replaced by § first: I   663| MS:such hidden § crossed out and replaced
above by § wormy   664| MS:of God,— *P1869:*of God: 665| MS:You § crossed
out and then restored §   666| MS:Not § inserted in margin § Even to § crossed
out and replaced above by § to substitute your § altered to § our § original reading

183

Your straight for the irregular; you stand
Stupefied, profitless, as cow or sheep
That miss a man's mind, anger him just twice
670   By trial at repairing the first fault.
Thus, when he blamed me, "You are a coquette,
A lure-owl posturing to attract birds,
You look love-lures at theatre and church,
In walk, at window!"—that, I knew, was false:
675   But why he charged me falsely, whither sought
To drive me by such charge,—how could I know?
So, unaware, I only made things worse.
I tried to soothe him by abjuring walk,
Window, church, theatre, for good and all,
680   As if he had been in earnest: that, you know,
Was nothing like the object of his charge.
Yes, when I got my maid to supplicate
The priest, whose name she read when she would read
Those feigned false letters I was forced to hear
685   Though I could read no word of,—he should cease
Writing,—nay, if he minded prayer of mine,
Cease from so much as even pass the street
Whereon our house looked,—in my ignorance
I was just thwarting Guido's true intent;
690   Which was, to bring about a wicked change

---

restored § < > bad. *P1869:* Not even < > bad,   667| MS:Your § altered to §
Our § original reading restored § open for the irregular; you § crossed out and apparently
replaced above by illegible word and then original reading restored §   *1889a:* Your
straight for   669| MS:a man's § inserted above line § mind; anger
1889a: mind, anger   674| MS:window—" that < > false—   *P1869:* window!"—that < >
false: 676-77| MS:§ originally one line § charge,—so, unaware, § last two words replaced
above line by four words and question mark § how could I know?/ So, unaware < > worse—
P1869: worse.   680| MS:earnest—that, you know, § crossed out and then restored §
P1869: earnest: that   682| MS:to pray for me § last three words crossed out and replaced
above by § supplicate   683| MS:That he § crossed out and replaced above by two words
and comma § The priest,   684| MS:those feigned, false § last two words inserted above
line § letters to me § last two words crossed out § I was therefore § inserted above line and
crossed out §   *P1869:* feigned false   687| MS:Cease from § inserted above line § so
much even as § indication that order of last two words should be reversed § pass down
§ crossed out §   689| MS:intent   *P1869:* intent;   690| MS:§ crowded between 689
and 691 § was to < > wicked § followed by illegible word crossed out §   *P1869:* was, to

Of sport to earnest, tempt a thoughtless man
To write indeed, and pass the house, and more,
Till both of us were taken in a crime.
He ought not to have wished me thus act lies,
695   Simulate folly: but,—wrong or right, the wish,—
I failed to apprehend its drift. How plain
It follows,—if I fell into such fault,
He also may have overreached the mark,
Made mistake, by perversity of brain,
700   I' the whole sad strange plot, the grotesque intrigue
To make me and my friend unself ourselves,
Be other man and woman than we were!
Think it out, you who have the time! for me,—
I cannot say less; more I will not say.
705   Leave it to God to cover and undo!

Only, my dulness should not prove too much!
—Not prove that in a certain other point
Wherein my husband blamed me,—and you blame,

691| MS:§ immediately following and separated from 690 by slash §   692| MS:The
priest § in margin and crossed out § My friend should write § last four words crossed out and
replaced below by three words and comma § To write indeed   693| MS:a temp § last
word crossed out and replaced by § crime.   695| MS:Simulate guilt § crossed out and
replaced above by word and comma § folly,—but, wrong or right of him § last two words
crossed out § , the wish,   P1869:but,—wrong < > wish,—   1889a:folly: but
696| MS:to take the measure § last three words crossed out and replaced above by three words
and period § apprehend its drift. Why then § last two words crossed out and replaced by two
words § How plain   698| MS:Why § crossed out and replaced above by two words § He
also may not he § last two words crossed out § < > over reached himself, § crossed out and
replaced above by two words and comma § the mark,   699| MS:Made § inserted in
margin § Mistaken § altered to § mistake   700| MS:In the whole sad strange § last two
words inserted above line § plot, from first to last, § last four words crossed out § this same
intrigue   1872:I' < > the grotesque intrigue   703| MS:me   P1869:me,—
704| MS:cannot will § crossed out § say less, I will not say more; § indication that should be
transposed to § less; more I < > say   P1869:say.   705| MS:and forgive § crossed out §
705–6| MS:§ ¶ §   1869:§ no ¶ §   1889:§ no ¶; emended to restore ¶; see Editorial Notes §
706| MS:dullness does § crossed out and replaced above by § should not prove at all § last two
words crossed out § too much,   P1869:much!   707| MS:—Not prove § inserted in
margin § That § altered to § that < > certain single § crossed out and replaced above by § other
point § followed by slash apparently inserted in revision to indicate end of line § —wherein
§ crossed out § P1869:point   708| MS:Wherein § inserted in margin § My < > blamed
me, § inserted above line § and you also § crossed out §   P1869:Wherein my < > me,—and

If I interpret smiles and shakes of head,—
710   I was dull too. Oh, if I dared but speak!
Must I speak? I am blamed that I forwent
A way to make my husband's favour come.
That is true: I was firm, withstood, refused . . .
—Women as you are, how can I find the words?

715   I felt there was just one thing Guido claimed
I had no right to give nor he to take;
We being in estrangement, soul from soul:
Till, when I sought help, the Archbishop smiled,
Inquiring into privacies of life,
720   —Said I was blameable—(he stands for God)
Nowise entitled to exemption there.
Then I obeyed,—as surely had obeyed
Were the injunction "Since your husband bids,
Swallow the burning coal he proffers you!"
725   But I did wrong, and he gave wrong advice
Though he were thrice Archbishop,—that, I know!—
Now I have got to die and see things clear.
Remember I was barely twelve years old—
A child at marriage: I was let alone
730   For weeks, I told you, lived my child-life still
Even at Arezzo, when I woke and found

---

⁷⁰⁹| MS:interpret smiles and § last two words written above line § <> head,/ § obviously
added in revision to indicate end of line § aright,— § crossed out §   P1869:head,—
⁷¹⁰| MS:§ continuous with 709 § I did so very wrong § last four words crossed out and
replaced above by four words § was dull too,—oh <> dared but § inserted above line §
P1869:dull too. Oh   ⁷¹²| MS:way had § crossed out and replaced above by § to made
§ altered to § make   ⁷¹⁴| MS:are, I cannot § last two words crossed out and replaced
above by § how can I   ⁷¹⁵| MS:§ marginal note that new ¶ begins § felt that § crossed
out § <> was just § inserted above line §   ⁷¹⁶| MS:take—   P1869:take;
⁷¹⁷| MS:We § inserted in margin § Being § altered to § being in § inserted above line § such
§ crossed out § <> soul,—   P1869:soul: ⁷¹⁸| MS:Till the Archbishop said § crossed out
and replaced above by § help, when <> help,   P1869:Till, when <> help, the <>
smiled,   ⁷²⁰| MS:That I was wholly wrong § last two words crossed out and replaced
above by § blamable <> God—)   P1869:—Said I <> God)   ⁷²¹| MS:there,—
P1869:there.   ⁷²³| MS:bids,—   P1869:bids,   ⁷²⁴| MS:he gives his wife § last three
words crossed out and replaced above by two words § proffers you!   ⁷²⁵| MS:wrong, for
P1869:wrong, and   ⁷²⁶| MS:that I say § crossed out and replaced above by § know
P1869:that, I know!—   ⁷²⁷| MS:things plain § crossed out § clear—
⁷³⁰| MS:child-life § over erasure §   ⁷³¹| MS:when I woke Even § inserted above line § at
Arezzo, and found first § crossed out; indication that should be transposed to § Even at Arezzo,

First . . . but I need not think of that again—
Over and ended! Try and take the sense
Of what I signify, if it must be so.
735 After the first, my husband, for hate's sake,
Said one eve, when the simpler cruelty
Seemed somewhat dull at edge and fit to bear,
"We have been man and wife six months almost:
How long is this your comedy to last?
740 Go this night to my chamber, not your own!"
At which word, I did rush—most true the charge—
And gain the Archbishop's house—he stands for God—
And fall upon my knees and clasp his feet,
Praying him hinder what my estranged soul
745 Refused to bear, though patient of the rest:
"Place me within a convent," I implored—
"Let me henceforward lead the virgin life
You praise in Her you bid me imitate!"
What did he answer? "Folly of ignorance!
750 Know, daughter, circumstances make or mar
Virginity,—'tis virtue or 'tis vice.
That which was glory in the Mother of God
Had been, for instance, damnable in Eve
Created to be mother of mankind.
755 Had Eve, in answer to her Maker's speech
'Be fruitful, multiply, replenish earth'—
Pouted 'But I choose rather to remain
Single'—why, she had spared herself forthwith
Further probation by the apple and snake,

---

when I woke and   732| MS:There § crossed out and replaced in margin by § First . .
but <> that now § crossed out § again—   *1889a:*First . . . but   735| MS:Know then
that when § last four words crossed out § After the first § word not clear so repeated more
legibly under line §   737| MS:somewhat dulled § altered to § dull <> and fit to § last two
words inserted above line § bearable § altered to § bear,   738| MS:wife six months § last
two words inserted above line § almost a year   § last two words crossed out § :
744| MS:him spare now § last two words crossed out and replaced above by § hinder
749| MS:answer?—"Folly   *P1869:*answer? "Folly   752| MS:was a § crossed out §
753| MS:been—for instance—damnable   *P1869:*been, for instance, damnable
754| MS:be Mother of Man § altered to § mankind. Had Eve § last two words crossed out §
*P1869:*be mother   755| MS:Had Eve § last two words inserted in margin § In § altered
to § in <> her Maker's first command § last two words crossed out § speech   758| MS:A
virgin § last two words crossed out and replaced above by word and comma § Single, Why,—

187

760 Been pushed straight out of Paradise! For see—
  If motherhood be qualified impure,
  I catch you making God command Eve sin!
  —A blasphemy so like these Molinists',
  I must suspect you dip into their books."
765 Then he pursued " 'Twas in your covenant!"

  No! There my husband never used deceit.
  He never did by speech nor act imply
  "Because of our souls' yearning that we meet
  And mix in soul through flesh, which yours and mine
770 Wear and impress, and make their visible selves,
  —All which means, for the love of you and me,
  Let us become one flesh, being one soul!"
  He only stipulated for the wealth;
  Honest so far. But when he spoke as plain—
775 Dreadfully honest also—"Since our souls
  Stand each from each, a whole world's width between,
  Give me the fleshly vesture I can reach
  And rend and leave just fit for hell to burn!"—
  Why, in God's name, for Guido's soul's own sake
780 Imperilled by polluting mine,—I say,
  I did resist; would I had overcome!

  My heart died out at the Archbishop's smile;
  —It seemed so stale and worn a way o' the world,
  As though 'twere nature frowning—"Here is Spring,

she *P1869:*'Single'—why, she   ⁷⁶¹| MS:If Motherhood *P1869:*If motherhood
⁷⁶²| MS:sin— *P1869:*sin!   ⁷⁶³| MS:A < > Molinists' *P1869:*—A < > Molinists',
⁷⁶⁶| MS:§ marginal note that new ¶ begins §   ⁷⁶⁷| MS:by word § crossed out and
replaced above by § speech or deed § crossed out and replaced above by § act *P1869:*speech
nor act   ⁷⁶⁸| MS:Pompilia, for the § last three words crossed out and replaced above by
four words § Because of our souls' < > that we § inserted above line §   ⁷⁶⁹| MS:mix in
soul § last two words inserted above line § < > flesh, which § inserted above line § your
§ altered to § yours soul § crossed out § and mine   ⁷⁷⁰| MS:impress, and § inserted above
line § make § one or more words illegibly crossed out § these visible § written above §
⁷⁷¹| MS:the absolute § crossed out §   ⁷⁷⁶| MS:from each, the § crossed out and replaced
above by § a   ⁷⁷⁷| MS:fleshly *P1869:*fleshy *1889a:*fleshly   ⁷⁷⁹| MS:name,
and § crossed out and replaced above by § for   ⁷⁸⁰| MS:say *P1869:*say,
⁷⁸¹| MS:resist,—would *P1869:*resist; would   ⁷⁸²| MS:§ marginal note that new ¶
begins §   ⁷⁸³| MS:so worn and stale a § indication that should be transposed to read § so
stale and worn a way of § altered to § o'   ⁷⁸⁴| MS:'twere Nature *P1869:*'twere nature

785 The sun shines as he shone at Adam's fall,
The earth requires that warmth reach everywhere:
What, must your patch of snow be saved forsooth
Because you rather fancy snow than flowers?"
Something in this style he began with me.
790 Last he said, savagely for a good man,
"This explains why you call your husband harsh,
Harsh to you, harsh to whom you love. God's Bread!
The poor Count has to manage a mere child
Whose parents leave untaught the simplest things
795 Their duty was and privilege to teach,—
Goodwives' instruction, gossips' lore: they laugh
And leave the Count the task,—or leave it me!"
Then I resolved to tell a frightful thing.
"I am not ignorant,—know what I say,
800 Declaring this is sought for hate, not love.
Sir, you may hear things like almighty God.
I tell you that my housemate, yes—the priest
My husband's brother, Canon Girolamo—
Has taught me what depraved and misnamed love
805 Means, and what outward signs denote the sin,
For he solicits me and says he loves,
The idle young priest with nought else to do.
My husband sees this, knows this, and lets be.
Is it your counsel I bear this beside?"
810 "—More scandal, and against a priest this time!
What, 'tis the Canon now?"—less snappishly—
"Rise up, my child, for such a child you are,
The rod were too advanced a punishment!
Let's try the honeyed cake. A parable!
815 'Without a parable spake He not to them.'
There was a ripe round long black toothsome fruit,
Even a flower-fig, the prime boast of May:

785| MS:at Adam's birth § crossed out and replaced above by § fall,   786| MS:warmth
be § crossed out and replaced above by § reach everywhere,—   P1869:everywhere:
789| MS:§ crowded between 788 and 790 § me—   P1869:me.   799| MS:say   P1869:say,
802| MS:housemate, yes § inserted above line § the young § crossed out §   805| MS:Means
and   P1869:Means, and   808| MS:sees and § crossed out and replaced above by word
and comma § this, knows this and   P1869:knows this, and   810| MS:— § added in
margin § More scandal and   P1869:scandal, and   811| MS:now?"—Less   P1869:now?"

And, to the tree, said . . . either the spirit o' the fig,
Or, if we bring in men, the gardener,
820 Archbishop of the orchard—had I time
To try o' the two which fits in best: indeed
It might be the Creator's self, but then
The tree should bear an apple, I suppose,—
Well, anyhow, one with authority said
825 'Ripe fig, burst skin, regale the fig-pecker—
The bird whereof thou art a perquisite!'
'Nay,' with a flounce, replied the restif fig,
'I much prefer to keep my pulp myself:
He may go breakfastless and dinnerless,
830 Supperless of one crimson seed, for me!'
So, back she flopped into her bunch of leaves.
He flew off, left her,—did the natural lord,—
And lo, three hundred thousand bees and wasps
Found her out, feasted on her to the shuck:
835 Such gain the fig's that gave its bird no bite!
The moral,—fools elude their proper lot,
Tempt other fools, get ruined all alike.
Therefore go home, embrace your husband quick!
Which if his Canon brother chance to see,
840 He will the sooner back to book again."

So, home I did go; so, the worst befell:

—less 818| MS:said . . either <> of § altered to § o' 1889a:said . . . either
819| MS:gardener P1869:gardener, 821| MS:of § altered to § o' 826| MS:That
bird whereof you § crossed out and replaced above by § thou are § altered to § art P1869:The
bird 827| MS:'Nay' with a flounce replied P1869:'Nay,' with a flounce, replied
828| MS:keep my seeds § crossed out and replaced above by § pulp my own § altered to §
myself, P1869:myself: 829| MS:go down § crossed out § 830| MS:of a single
§ last two words crossed out and replaced above by two words § one crimson <> me.'
P1869:me!' 831| MS:So back <> leaves, P1869:So, back <> leaves.
832| MS:He flew off, § last two words and comma added above line § <> the § followed by
totally obliterated word § 834| MS:shuck,— P1869:shuck: 837| MS:alike,
P1869:alike. 838| MS:home, and kiss § last two words crossed out and replaced above
by § embrace <> husband's § altered to § husband hand § crossed out § quick, P1869:quick!
839| MS:The better § last two words crossed out and replaced above by § Which if his Canon
§ inserted above line § <> see P1869:see, 840| MS:Who § crossed out and replaced
above by two words § He the sooner will back § indication that should be transposed to read §
He will the sooner back to Breviary § crossed out and replaced above by § book
841| MS:§ marginal note that new ¶ begins § So home <> go,—so the <> befell—

190

So, I had proof the Archbishop was just man,
And hardly that, and certainly no more.
For, miserable consequence to me,
845 My husband's hatred waxed nor waned at all,
His brother's boldness grew effrontery soon,
And my last stay and comfort in myself
Was forced from me: henceforth I looked to God
Only, nor cared my desecrated soul
850 Should have fair walls, gay windows for the world.
God's glimmer, that came through the ruin-top,
Was witness why all lights were quenched inside:
Henceforth I asked God counsel, not mankind.

So, when I made the effort, freed myself,
855 They said—"No care to save appearance here!
How cynic,—when, how wanton, were enough!"
—Adding, it all came of my mother's life—
My own real mother, whom I never knew,
Who did wrong (if she needs must have done wrong)
860 Through being all her life, not my four years,
At mercy of the hateful: every beast
O' the field was wont to break that fountain-fence,
Trample the silver into mud so murk
Heaven could not find itself reflected there.

---

*P1869:*So, home <> go; so, the <> befell: 842| MS:So I *P1869:*So, I
843| MS:more— *P1869:*more.   844| MS:As the utter § last three words crossed out and replaced above by two words § For, miserable   848| MS:henceforth I cared for § last two words crossed out and replaced above by two words § looked to   849| MS:Only, nor for the § last three words crossed out and replaced above by three words § nor cared my
850| MS:So much as wonder how § last five words crossed out and replaced above by six words § Should hope fair walls, gay windows for the world— *P1869:*world.
851| MS:thro' *P1869:*through   852| MS:witness whenceforth all was black § last four words crossed out and replaced above by five words § why all the lights were quenched inside.
*P1869:*inside: 853| MS:mankind: *P1869:*mankind.   854| MS:§ marginal note that new ¶ begins § effort, saved myself *1889a:*effort, freed myself,   855| MS:Then said *P1869:*They said   859| MS:did wrong—if <> wrong— *P1869:*did wrong (if <> wrong)   860| MS:Through lying § altered to § being   861| MS:hateful,—every *1889a:*hateful: every   862| MS:Of § altered to § O'   864| MS:there,— *1889a:*there.

⁸⁶⁵ Now they cry "Out on her, who, plashy pool,
Bequeathed turbidity and bitterness
To the daughter-stream where Guido dipt and drank!"

Well, since she had to bear this brand—let me!
The rather do I understand her now,
⁸⁷⁰ From my experience of what hate calls love,—
Much love might be in what their love called hate.
If she sold . . . what they call, sold . . . me her child—
I shall believe she hoped in her poor heart
That I at least might try be good and pure,
⁸⁷⁵ Begin to live untempted, not go doomed
And done with ere once found in fault, as she.
Oh and, my mother, it all came to this?
Why should I trust those that speak ill of you,
When I mistrust who speaks even well of them?
⁸⁸⁰ Why, since all bound to do me good, did harm,
May not you, seeming as you harmed me most,
Have meant to do most good—and feed your child
From bramble-bush, whom not one orchard-tree
But drew bough back from, nor let one fruit fall?
⁸⁸⁵ This it was for you sacrificed your babe?
Gained just this, giving your heart's hope away
As I might give mine, loving it as you,
If . . . but that never could be asked of me!

There, enough! I have my support again,

---

^{865|} MS:her, the § crossed out and replaced above by § who, plashy § written over illegible word § ^{866|} MS:That lends § last two words crossed out and replaced above by § Bequeathed ^{867|} MS:dips § altered to § dipt and drinks! § altered to § drank!
^{867–68|} MS:§ ¶ § *1889a:*§ no ¶ § *1889:*§ no ¶; emended to restore ¶; see Editorial Notes § ^{868|} MS:this, why not I? § comma and last three words crossed out and replaced above by § brand—let me! ^{869|} MS:now,— *1889a:*now, ^{871|} MS:§ crowded between 870 and 871 § hate— *P1869:*hate. ^{872|} MS:Why § crossed out and replaced in margin by § If she sold . . what <> sold . . me *1889a:*sold . . . what <> sold . . . me ^{873|} MS:§ crowded between 872-74 § ^{878|} MS:you *P1869:*you, ^{879|} MS:speaks even § inserted above margin § ^{883|} MS:bramble-bushes § altered to § bramble-bush, whom each § crossed out and replaced above by § not one ^{884|} MS:But § inserted above line § Drew § altered to § drew back its § crossed out § bough from *P1869:*drew-back bough from *1889a:*drew bough back from § ^{885|} MS:sacrificed even me, § last two words crossed out and replaced above by § your babe, *P1869:*babe? ^{886|} MS:hearts' hope *P1869:*heart's hope ^{888|} MS:If . . but *1889a:*If . . . but ^{889|} MS:§ marginal

890　Again the knowledge that my babe was, is,
　　　Will be mine only. Him, by death, I give
　　　Outright to God, without a further care,—
　　　But not to any parent in the world,—
　　　So to be safe: why is it we repine?
895　What guardianship were safer could we choose?
　　　All human plans and projects come to nought:
　　　My life, and what I know of other lives,
　　　Prove that: no plan nor project! God shall care!

　　　And now you are not tired? How patient then
900　All of you,—Oh yes, patient this long while
　　　Listening, and understanding, I am sure!
　　　Four days ago, when I was sound and well
　　　And like to live, no one would understand.
　　　People were kind, but smiled "And what of him,
905　Your friend, whose tonsure the rich dark-brown hides?
　　　There, there!—your lover, do we dream he was?
　　　A priest too—never were such naughtiness!
　　　Still, he thinks many a long think, never fear,
　　　After the shy pale lady,—lay so light
910　For a moment in his arms, the lucky one!"
　　　And so on: wherefore should I blame you much?
　　　So we are made, such difference in minds,
　　　Such difference too in eyes that see the minds!
　　　That man, you misinterpret and misprise—
915　The glory of his nature, I had thought,
　　　Shot itself out in white light, blazed the truth
　　　Through every atom of his act with me:
　　　Yet where I point you, through the crystal shrine,

---

note that new ¶ begins § enough—I　*P1869:*enough! I　　⁸⁹⁰|　MS:Again § in left margin §
The　*P1869:*the　　⁸⁹⁶|　MS:nought,　*1889a:*nought:　　⁸⁹⁷|　MS:life and　*P1869:*life,
and　　⁸⁹⁸|　MS:that,—no < > project,—God　*P1869:*that: no < > project! God
⁸⁹⁹|　MS:§ marginal note that new ¶ begins § now, you　*P1869:*now you　　⁹⁰²|　MS:ago
when　*P1869:*ago, when　　⁹⁰⁵|　MS:tonsure, the < > dark brown　*P1869:*dark-brown
*1889a:*tonsure the　　⁹⁰⁶|　MS:There, there,—your　*P1869:*There, there!—your
⁹⁰⁸|　MS:Still he　*P1869:*Still, he　　⁹¹²|　MS:So men are　*P1869:*So we are
⁹¹⁴|　MS:That man you used to jest with and　*P1869:*That man, you misinterpret and
⁹¹⁵|　MS:The essence § crossed out and replaced above by § glory　　⁹¹⁸|　MS:you through

Purity in quintessence, one dew-drop,
920   You all descry a spider in the midst.
One says "The head of it is plain to see,"
And one, "They are the feet by which I judge,"
All say, "Those films were spun by nothing else."

Then, I must lay my babe away with God,
925   Nor think of him again, for gratitude.
Yes, my last breath shall wholly spend itself
In one attempt more to disperse the stain,
The mist from other breath fond mouths have made,
About a lustrous and pellucid soul:
930   So that, when I am gone but sorrow stays,
And people need assurance in their doubt
If God yet have a servant, man a friend,
The weak a saviour and the vile a foe,—
Let him be present, by the name invoked,
935   Giuseppe-Maria Caponsacchi!

There,
Strength comes already with the utterance!
I will remember once more for his sake
The sorrow: for he lives and is belied.
Could he be here, how he would speak for me!

940   I had been miserable three drear years

---

the chrystal shrine   *P1869:*you, through the crystal shrine,   920| MS:all would find a
*P1869:*all descry a   921| MS:says,—"Admit § crossed out § the § altered to § The head
of it § last two words inserted above line §   923| MS:those § altered to § Those
924| MS:§ marginal note that new paragraph begins § Then I will § crossed out and replaced
above by § must < > God   *P1869:*Then, I < > God,   925| MS:gratitude—
*P1869:*gratitude.   *1872:*again for   *1889a:*again, for   926| MS:last breath § crossed out
and replaced above by word illegibly erased; original restored §   *1872:*Yes my   *1889a:*Yes,
my   928| MS:from foul § crossed out and replaced above by § other breath foolish
§ crossed out and replaced above by § fond < > made   *P1869:*made,   929| MS:soul,
*P1869:*soul: 931| MS:And someone § crossed out and replaced above by word illegibly
erased and followed by § people needs § altered to § need < > in his § crossed out and replaced
above by § their   932| MS:servant, in the world § last three words crossed out and
replaced above by three words and comma § man a friend,   933| MS:and the world
§ crossed out and replaced above by § vile a man,— § word crossed out and replaced above
by § foe   934| MS:present, invoked by the name § indication that should be transposed
to § present, by the name invoked   *P1869:*invoked,   935| MS:§ marginal note that new ¶
begins with *There* §   938| MS:The old woe § last two words crossed out and replaced
above by § sorrow,—for   *P1869:*sorrow: for   939| MS:Had § crossed out and replaced

194

In that dread palace and lay passive now,
When I first learned there could be such a man.
Thus it fell: I was at a public play,
In the last days of Carnival last March,
945 Brought there I knew not why, but now know well.
My husband put me where I sat, in front;
Then crouched down, breathed cold through me from behind,
Stationed i' the shadow,—none in front could see,—
I, it was, faced the stranger-throng beneath,
950 The crowd with upturned faces, eyes one stare,
Voices one buzz. I looked but to the stage,
Whereon two lovers sang and interchanged
"True life is only love, love only bliss:
I love thee—thee I love!" then they embraced.
955 I looked thence to the ceiling and the walls,—
Over the crowd, those voices and those eyes,—
My thoughts went through the roof and out, to Rome
On wings of music, waft of measured words,—
Set me down there, a happy child again
960 Sure that to-morrow would be festa-day,
Hearing my parents praise past festas more,
And seeing they were old if I was young,
Yet wondering why they still would end discourse
With "We must soon go, you abide your time,

---

above by § Could he been § crossed out and replaced above by § be here how   *P1869:*here, how
939-40| MS:§ ¶ §   *1889a:*§ no ¶ §   *1889:*§ no ¶; emended to restore ¶; see Editorial Notes §
941| MS:and lay passive § last two words over illegible erasures §   942| MS:there was
§ crossed out and replaced above by § would be such a § inserted above line § man. alive. § word
and period crossed out §   943| MS:at the theatre, § last two words and comma crossed
out § a public play,   944| MS:§ crowded between 943 and 945 § the first § written over
by § last   945| MS:know well:§ crossed out and then restored §   *P1869:*well.
946| MS:front—   *P1869:*front;   948| MS:in § altered to § i'   949| MS:§ crowded
between 948 and 950 § I it was faced the strangers poured beneath,   *P1869:*I, it was, faced the
stranger-throng beneath,   950| MS:Of § crossed out § the § altered to § The < > stare
*P1869:*stare,   952| MS:sang: and § crossed out and replaced above by § they   *P1869:*sang
and   953| MS:only love, and § crossed out § love is § crossed out and replaced above by §
only bliss.   *P1869:*bliss: 954| MS:thee I love:" then   *P1869:*thee I love!" then
956| MS:§ crowded between 955 and 957 §   957| MS:and soared § crossed out and
replaced above by two words § out, reached § crossed out § to   958| MS:music, and
§ crossed out and replaced above by § waft   959| MS:there again, a < > child,
*P1869:*there, a < > child again,   960| MS:to-morrow was some § uncertain; last two
words crossed out and replaced above by two words § would be   964| MS:you must

965 And,—might we haply see the proper friend
    Throw his arm over you and make you safe!"

    Sudden I saw him; into my lap there fell
    A foolish twist of comfits, broke my dream
    And brought me from the air and laid me low,
970 As ruined as the soaring bee that's reached
    (So Pietro told me at the Villa once)
    By the dust-handful. There the comfits lay:
    I looked to see who flung them, and I faced
    This Caponsacchi, looking up in turn.
975 Ere I could reason out why, I felt sure,
    Whoever flung them, his was not the hand,—
    Up rose the round face and good-natured grin
    Of one who, in effect, had played the prank,
    From covert close beside the earnest face,—
980 Fat waggish Conti, friend of all the world.
    He was my husband's cousin, privileged
    To throw the thing: the other, silent, grave,
    Solemn almost, saw me, as I saw him.

    There is a psalm Don Celestine recites,
985 "Had I a dove's wings, how I fain would flee!"
    The psalm runs not "I hope, I pray for wings,"—
    Not "If wings fall from heaven, I fix them fast,"—
    Simply "How good it were to fly and rest,
    Have hope now, and one day expect content!
990 How well to do what I shall never do!"
    So I said "Had there been a man like that,
    To lift me with his strength out of all strife
    Into the calm, how I could fly and rest!

---

§ crossed out §   967| MS:§ marginal note that new ¶ begins § fell § over illegible word §
969| MS:brought me § inserted above line §   973| MS:them, thus § crossed out and
replaced above by § and   977| MS:good natured   P1869:good-natured
978| MS:Of him who   1872:Of one who   979| MS:face,— § over illegible erasure §
980| MS:world—   P1869:world.   984| MS:§ marginal note that new ¶ begins §
987| MS:if they § crossed out and replaced above by § wings < > them fast § crossed out §
here,"—   P1869:them fast,"—   988| MS:good a thing § last two words crossed out and
replaced above by two words § it were   989| MS:§ crowded between 988 and 990 §
content—   P1869:content!   993| MS:how I would fly   P1869:how I could fly

I have a keeper in the garden here
995 Whose sole employment is to strike me low
If ever I, for solace, seek the sun.
Life means with me successful feigning death,
Lying stone-like, eluding notice so,
Forgoing here the turf and there the sky.
1000 Suppose that man had been instead of this!"

Presently Conti laughed into my ear,
—Had tripped up to the raised place where I sat—
"Cousin, I flung them brutishly and hard!
Because you must be hurt, to look austere
1005 As Caponsacchi yonder, my tall friend
A-gazing now. Ah, Guido, you so close?
Keep on your knees, do! Beg her to forgive!
My cornet battered like a cannon-ball.
Good-bye, I'm gone!"—nor waited the reply.

1010 That night at supper, out my husband broke,
"Why was that throwing, that buffoonery?
Do you think I am your dupe? What man would dare
Throw comfits in a stranger lady's lap?
'Twas knowledge of you bred such insolence

994| MS:here § over illegible erasure §   996| MS:If ever § inserted above line § I look up
§ last two words crossed out § for solace, to § imperfectly erased and replaced above by two
words § seek the sun. or star. § last two words and period crossed out §   P1869:ever I, for
999| MS:the garden § crossed out and replaced above by two words § grass and
P1869:the turf and   1000| MS:Suppose this man <> of that!"   P1869:Suppose that
man <> of this!"   1001| MS:§ marginal note that new ¶ begins § ear   P1869:ear,
1003| MS:Cousin, I hit you § last two words crossed out and replaced above by two words §
flung them <> hard—   P1869:hard!   1004| MS:hurt to look so grave § last two words
crossed out and replaced above by § austere,   P1869:hurt, to <> austere
1005| MS:Grave § crossed out § as § altered to § As the § crossed out § Caponsacchi, yon § altered
to § yonder, tall § crossed out and then restored § my tall § last two lines written above line §
friend,   P1869:As Caponsacchi yonder, my tall friend   1006| MS:you there too? § last
two words crossed out § so close?   1007-8| MS:§ crowded between 1006 and 1009 in
continuous line separated by slash between forgive! and My §   1009| MS:gone!—we left
the theatre § last four words crossed out § nor waited the reply.   1010| MS:§ marginal
note that new ¶ begins § broke—   P1869:broke,   1011| MS:Why is § altered to § was that
comfit § crossed out § throwing, that § comma and word inserted above line §
1014| MS:'Twas § inserted in margin § <> you has § crossed out § bred that § crossed out and

1015 In Caponsacchi; he dared shoot the bolt,
Using that Conti for his stalking-horse.
How could you see him this once and no more,
When he is always haunting hereabout
At the street-corner or the palace-side,
1020 Publishing my shame and your impudence?
You are a wanton,—I a dupe, you think?
O Christ, what hinders that I kill her quick?"
Whereat he drew his sword and feigned a thrust.

All this, now,—being not so strange to me,
1025 Used to such misconception day by day
And broken-in to bear,—I bore, this time,
More quietly than woman should perhaps;
Repeated the mere truth and held my tongue.

Then he said, "Since you play the ignorant,
1030 I shall instruct you. This amour,—commenced
Or finished or midway in act, all's one,—
'Tis the town-talk; so my revenge shall be.
Does he presume because he is a priest?
I warn him that the sword I wear shall pink
1035 His lily-scented cassock through and through,
Next time I catch him underneath your eaves!"

But he had threatened with the sword so oft
And, after all, not kept his promise. All

---

replaced above by § such   1015| MS:In Caponsacchi,—he dared play § crossed out and replaced above by § shoot the fool § crossed out and replaced above by § bolt,   P1869:In Caponsacchi; he   1016| MS:Using § inserted above line § That § altered to § that creature § crossed out §   1017| MS:How did § crossed out and replaced above by § could < > more P1869:more,   1018| MS:hereabouts   P1869:hereabout   1020| MS:Telling in the town § last four words crossed out and replaced above by § Publishing my shame, § crossed out § and § inserted above line §   1023| MS:§ crowded between 1022 and 1024 § 1024| MS:§ marginal note that new ¶ begins §   1025| MS:Used with § crossed out and replaced above by § to   1026| MS:broken in   P1869:broken-in   1027| MS:than a wife § last two words crossed out and replaced above by § woman < > perhaps— P1869:perhaps;   1028| MS:my peace § crossed out §   1029| MS:§ marginal note that new ¶ begins § said—"Since   P1869:said, "Since   1030| MS:amour,—begun § crossed out §   1031| MS:Or ended § crossed out and replaced above by § finished 1033| MS:§ crowded between 1032 and 1034 §   1036-37| MS:§ ¶ § 1889a:§ no ¶ § 1889: § no ¶; emended to restore ¶; see Editorial Notes §   1037| MS:threatened me § crossed

I said was "Let God save the innocent!
1040 Moreover death is far from a bad fate.
I shall go pray for you and me, not him;
And then I look to sleep, come death or, worse,
Life." So, I slept.

There may have elapsed a week,
When Margherita,—called my waiting-maid,
1045 Whom it is said my husband found too fair—
Who stood and heard the charge and the reply,
Who never once would let the matter rest
From that night forward, but rang changes still
On this the threat and that the shame, and how
1050 Good cause for jealousy cures jealous fools,
And what a paragon was this same priest
She talked about until I stopped my ears,—
She said, "A week is gone; you comb your hair,
Then go mope in a corner, cheek on palm,
1055 Till night comes round again,—so, waste a week
As if your husband menaced you in sport.
Have not I some acquaintance with his tricks?
Oh no, he did not stab the serving-man
Who made and sang the rhymes about me once!
1060 For why? They sent him to the wars next day.
Nor poisoned he the foreigner, my friend
Who wagered on the whiteness of my breast,—
The swarth skins of our city in dispute:

---

out § with the § inserted above §   1039| MS:was—"Let   P1869:was, "Let   1889a:was
"Let   1040| MS:Moreover, death   1889a:Moreover death   1043| MS:Life."
§ inserted in margin § So I did § crossed out and replaced above by § slept. § marginal note that
new ¶ begins § week   P1869:So, I < > week,   1046| MS:§ crowded between 1045 and
1047 §   1048| MS:forward rang the changes   P1869:forward but rang changes
CP1869:forward, but   1049| MS:this the threat and < > the charge § crossed out and
replaced above by § shame   P1869:this the thrust § emended to § threat § see Editorial
Notes §   1050| MS:A cause < > fools, § written over illegible word §   P1869:Good cause
1051| MS:this poor § crossed out and replaced above by § young § crossed out and replaced
above by § same   1053| MS:said "A   P1869:said, "A   1055| MS:so waste
P1869:so, waste   1056| MS:menaced for a § last two words crossed out and replaced
above by two words § you in   1057| MS:Have § over illegible erasure §
1059| MS:Who made and § last two words inserted above § once,—   P1869:once!
1061| MS:friend, 1889a:friend   1063| MS:The brownness § uncertain; crossed out,
blotted, and altered to § swarth skins of the § crossed out and replaced above by § our < >

For, though he paid me proper compliment,
1065   The Count well knew he was besotted with
Somebody else, a skin as black as ink,
(As all the town knew save my foreigner)
He found and wedded presently,—'Why need
Better revenge?'—the Count asked. But what's here?
1070   A priest that does not fight, and cannot wed,
Yet must be dealt with! If the Count took fire
For the poor pastime of a minute,—me—
What were the conflagration for yourself,
Countess and lady-wife and all the rest?
1075   The priest will perish; you will grieve too late:
So shall the city-ladies' handsomest
Frankest and liberalest gentleman
Die for you, to appease a scurvy dog
Hanging's too good for. Is there no escape?
1080   Were it not simple Christian charity
To warn the priest be on his guard,—save him
Assured death, save yourself from causing it?
I meet him in the street. Give me a glove,
A ring to show for token! Mum's the word!"

1085   I answered "If you were, as styled, my maid,
I would command you: as you are, you say,
My husband's intimate,—assist his wife
Who can do nothing but entreat 'Be still!'
Even if you speak truth and a crime is planned,
1090   Leave help to God as I am forced to do!
There is no other help, or we should craze,

---

dispute,— _P1869:_dispute: ¹⁰⁶⁴| MS:For though _P1869:_For, though
¹⁰⁶⁵| MS:For he who then § last four words crossed out and replaced in margin and below by
six words § The Count well knew, he was < > with the fool § last two words crossed out §
¹⁰⁶⁶| MS:§ crowded between 1065 and 1067 § Somebody with § crosssed out and replaced
above by § else, a soul as _P1869:_a skin as   ¹⁰⁶⁶⁻⁶⁸| MS:ink,/ He _P1869:_ink,/ (As all
the town knew save my foreigner)/ He   ¹⁰⁷⁰| MS:priest—that < > fight § over illegible
erasure, crossed out and restored § _P1869:_priest, that _1889a:_priest that
¹⁰⁷³| MS:yourself? § question mark erased § _P1869:_yourself,   ¹⁰⁷⁴| MS:§ crowded
between 1073 and 1075 § —Countess _P1869:_Countess   ¹⁰⁷⁵| MS:The Priest
_P1869:_The priest   ¹⁰⁸⁵| MS:§ marginal note that new line begins § I answered—"If < >
maid— _P1869:_answered, "If < > maid, _1889a:_answered "If   ¹⁰⁸⁶| MS:you,—as
_P1869:_you: as   ¹⁰⁸⁸| MS:entreat 'be _P1869:_entreat 'Be   ¹⁰⁹¹| MS:no other

Seeing such evil with no human cure.
Reflect that God, who makes the storm desist,
Can make an angry violent heart subside.
1095 Why should we venture teach Him governance?
Never address me on this subject more!"

Next night she said "But I went, all the same,
—Ay, saw your Caponsacchi in his house,
And come back stuffed with news I must outpour.
1100 I told him 'Sir, my mistress is a stone:
Why should you harm her for no good you get?
For you do harm her—prowl about our place
With the Count never distant half the street,
Lurking at every corner, would you look!
1105 'Tis certain she has witched you with a spell.
Are there not other beauties at your beck?
We all know, Donna This and Monna That
Die for a glance of yours, yet here you gaze!
Go make them grateful, leave the stone its cold!'
1110 And he—oh, he turned first white and then red,
And then—'To her behest I bow myself,
Whom I love with my body and my soul:
Only a word i' the bowing! See, I write
One little word, no harm to see or hear!
1115 Then, fear no further!' This is what he wrote.
I know you cannot read,—therefore, let me!
'My idol!' " . . .

But I took it from her hand

§ crossed out and then restored § course, or 1872:other cause, or 1889a:other help, or
1093| MS:the sun § altered to § storm arise § crossed out § desist,   1097| MS:§ marginal
note that new ¶ begins § said—"But P1869:said, "But 1889a:said "But   1098| MS:saw
the § crossed out and replaced above by § your   1102| MS:harm why § smeared and
crossed out and replaced above by § her < > about this § crossed out and replaced above by §
our   1105| MS:certain you have § last two words crossed out and replaced above by two
words § she has witched him § crossed out and replaced above by § you
1110| MS:§ crowded between 1109 and 1111 §   1111| MS:myself— P1869:myself,
1112| MS:§ crowded between 1111 and 1113 § soul— P1869:soul: 1113| MS:Only, a
< > bowing. See P1869:bowing! See 1872:Only a   1114| MS:One only § crossed out
and replaced above by § little < > hear,— P1869:hear!   1117| MS:" 'My idol'!" . . .
§ marginal note that new ¶ begins § but § altered to § But P1869:" 'My idol!' ". . . .
§ ¶ § But CP1869:" 'My idol!' ". . . . § ¶ § But 1889a:" 'My idol!' " . . .

And tore it into shreds. "Why, join the rest
Who harm me? Have I ever done you wrong?
1120 People have told me 'tis you wrong myself:
Let it suffice I either feel no wrong
Or else forgive it,—yet you turn my foe!
The others hunt me and you throw a noose!"

She muttered "Have your wilful way!" I slept.

1125 Whereupon . . . no, I leave my husband out!
It is not to do him more hurt, I speak.
Let it suffice, when misery was most,
One day, I swooned and got a respite so.
She stooped as I was slowly coming to,
1130 This Margherita, ever on my trace,
And whispered—"Caponsacchi!"

                              If I drowned,
But woke afloat i' the wave with upturned eyes,
And found their first sight was a star! I turned—
For the first time, I let her have her will,
1135 Heard passively,—"The imposthume at such head,
One touch, one lancet-puncture would relieve,—
And still no glance the good physician's way
Who rids you of the torment in a trice!
Still he writes letters you refuse to hear.

1118| MS:shreds—"Why join P1869:shreds. "Why 1872:shreds. "Why, join
1119| MS:you hurt? § crossed out and replaced above by § wrong?   1120| MS:myself,—
P1869:myself: 1121| MS:suffice I do not § last two words uncertain, crossed out and
replaced above by § either feel my § crossed out and replaced above by § no
1122| MS:it,—here are § last two words crossed out and replaced above by § yet you, the same,
§ last two words and comma crossed out and replaced above by § turn
1124| MS:§ marginal note that new ¶ begins § muttered "Have P1869:muttered, "Have
1889a:muttered "Have   1125| MS:Whereupon . . no § over illegible erasure § < > out!
1889a:Whereupon . . . no < > out § emended to § out! § see Editorial Notes §
1126| MS:§ crowded between 1125 and 1127 §   1128| MS:One § over illegible erasure §
Day § crossed out and then restored § and § crossed out § < > got a § inserted above line §
respite thus, P1869:respite so.   1130| MS: § crowded between 1129 and 1131 §
1131| MS:whispered—"Caponsacchi!" § marginal note that new ¶ begins § If
1132| MS:in § altered to § i' < > eyes P1869:eyes,   1136| MS:One little § crossed out and
replaced above by two words § touch, one   1138| MS:Would § crossed out and replaced
above by § Who   1139| MS:letters that § crossed out § you hate § crossed out and replaced

¹¹⁴⁰ He may prevent your husband, kill himself,
So desperate and all fordone is he!
Just hear the pretty verse he made to-day!
A sonnet from Mirtillo. '*Peerless fair . . .*'
All poetry is difficult to read,
¹¹⁴⁵ —The sense of it is, anyhow, he seeks
Leave to contrive you an escape from hell,
And for that purpose asks an interview.
I can write, I can grant it in your name,
Or, what is better, lead you to his house.
¹¹⁵⁰ Your husband dashes you against the stones;
This man would place each fragment in a shrine:
You hate him, love your husband!"

                              I returned
"It is not true I love my husband,—no,
Nor hate this man. I listen while you speak,
¹¹⁵⁵ —Assured that what you say is false, the same:
Much as when once, to me a little child,
A rough gaunt man in rags, with eyes on fire,
A crowd of boys and idlers at his heels,
Rushed as I crossed the Square, and held my head
¹¹⁶⁰ In his two hands, 'Here's she will let me speak!
You little girl, whose eyes do good to mine,
I am the Pope, am Sextus, now the Sixth;
And that Twelfth Innocent, proclaimed to-day,
Is Lucifer disguised in human flesh!

---

above by § refuse   ¹¹⁴⁰| MS:He will § crossed out and replaced above by § may <>
himself— *P1869:*himself,   ¹¹⁴¹| MS:he.   *P1869:*he!   ¹¹⁴²| MS:§ crowded
between 1141 and 1143 § to-day—   *P1869:*to-day!   ¹¹⁴³| MS:A Sonnet <> fair, . . .'
*P1869:*A sonnet <> fair . . .'   ¹¹⁴⁴| MS:§ inserted in margin with arrow indicating its
place in text §   ¹¹⁴⁵| MS: anyhow, that he seeks § òver illegible erasure §
*P1869:*anyhow, he   ¹¹⁴⁶| MS:to direct § crossed out and replaced above by § contrive you
how to § last two words crossed out and replaced above by § an escape this § crossed out and
replaced above by § from   ^{1148–49}| MS:§ crowded between 1147 and 1150 in continuous
line separated by / between *name,* and *Or* §   ¹¹⁵²| MS:Yet § crossed out § you § altered
to§ You <> him, and § crossed out § <> husband!" § marginal note that new ¶ begins § I
returned,   *1889a:*returned   ¹¹⁵³| MS:is untrue § altered to § not true
¹¹⁵⁴| MS:Nor love § crossed out and replaced above by § hate   ¹¹⁵⁷| MS:rags with
*P1869:*rags, with   ¹¹⁵⁹| MS:square § altered to § Square   ¹¹⁶⁰| MS:With § crossed
out and replaced above by § In his   ¹¹⁶²| MS:the Pope, am Sextus, Come § crossed out

203

¹¹⁶⁵ The angels, met in conclave, crowned me!'—thus
He gibbered and I listened; but I knew
All was delusion, ere folk interposed
'Unfasten him, the maniac!' Thus I know
All your report of Caponsacchi false,
¹¹⁷⁰ Folly or dreaming; I have seen so much
By that adventure at the spectacle,
The face I fronted that one first, last time:
He would belie it by such words and thoughts.
Therefore while you profess to show him me,
¹¹⁷⁵ I ever see his own face. Get you gone!"

"—That will I, nor once open mouth again,—
No, by Saint Joseph and the Holy Ghost!
On your head be the damage, so adieu!"

And so more days, more deeds I must forget,
¹¹⁸⁰ Till . . . what a strange thing now is to declare!
Since I say anything, say all if true!
And how my life seems lengthened as to serve!
It may be idle or inopportune,
But, true?—why, what was all I said but truth,
¹¹⁸⁵ Even when I found that such as are untrue

---

and replaced above by § now the   ^{1165|}   MS:The angels told § crossed out and replaced
above by four words § met in conclave, crowned <> thus he gibbered on § last three words
crossed out §   ^{1166|}   MS:gibbered past § crossed out and replaced above by § and
^{1167|}   MS:folks   *1889a:*folk   ^{1168|}   MS:maniac,'—thus   *P1869:*maniac!' Thus
^{1169|}   MS:All this report   *P1869:*All your report   ^{1170|}   MS:dreaming: I
*P1869:*dreaming; I   ^{1172|}   MS:time;   *P1869:*time: ^{1173|}   MS:thoughts:
*P1869:*thoughts.   ^{1176|}   MS:§ marginal note that new ¶ begins §   ^{1178|}   MS:head be
the damage, § note above to transpose *be* to follow *damage* § and so § inserted above §
*P1869:*damage, so   ^{1178-79|}   MS:§ ¶ §   *P1869:*§ no ¶ §   *1889:*§ no ¶; emended to restore
¶; see Editorial Notes   ^{1169|}   MS:days, and § crossed out and replaced above by § more
^{1180|}   MS:Till . . what <> thing I am to   *P1869:*thing now is to   *1889a:*"Till . . . what
^{1181|}   MS:all,—if best. § last two words and dash crossed out and replaced above by two
words, colon and dash § if true:—   *P1869:*all if true!   ^{1182|}   MS:And § over illegible
erasure § <> life is lengthened   *P1869:*life seems lengthened <> serve   *CP1869:*serve!
^{1184|}   MS:true?—Why, what is it I say § last four words crossed out and replaced above by
four words § was all I said true?—why   ^{1185|}   MS:Even though § crossed out and replaced

204

Could only take the truth in through a lie?
Now—I am speaking truth to the Truth's self:
God will lend credit to my words this time.

It had got half through April. I arose
1190 One vivid daybreak,—who had gone to bed
In the old way my wont those last three years,
Careless until, the cup drained, I should die.
The last sound in my ear, the over-night,
Had been a something let drop on the sly
1195 In prattle by Margherita, "Soon enough
Gaieties end, now Easter's past: a week,
And the Archbishop gets him back to Rome,—
Everyone leaves the town for Rome, this Spring,—
Even Caponsacchi, out of heart and hope,
1200 Resigns himself and follows with the flock."
I heard this drop and drop like rain outside
Fast-falling through the darkness while she spoke:
So had I heard with like indifference,
"And Michael's pair of wings will arrive first
1205 At Rome, to introduce the company,
And bear him from our picture where he fights
Satan,—expect to have that dragon loose
And never a defender!"—my sole thought
Being still, as night came, "Done, another day!
1210 How good to sleep and so get nearer death!"—
When, what, first thing at daybreak, pierced the sleep

---

above by § when   1186| MS:Can § altered to § Could   1187| MS:to Him § crossed
out § the truth's § altered to § Truth's self— *P1869:*self: 1189| MS:§ marginal note
that new ¶ begins § Then § crossed out § it § altered to § It had got half § inserted above
line § thro' *P1869:*through   1191| MS:won't § over illegible erasure § < > years—
*P1869:*years,   1193| MS:last word § altered to § sound   1195| MS:In the § crossed
out § prattle of § crossed out and replaced above by § by Margherita "Soon *P1869:*of
Margherita, "Soon   1196| MS:The § crossed out § gaieties § altered to § Gaieties
1198| MS:the City for < > spring,— *P1869:*the town for < > Spring,—   1201| MS:rain
outside § crossed out and then restored § that fall— § crossed out §   1202| MS:§ crowded
between 1201 and 1203 § Fast § preceded by illegibly crossed out word §
1203| MS:indifference *P1869:*indifference,   1205| MS:§ crowded between 1204 and
1206 § *P1869:*At Rome to *1872:*At Rome, to   1206| MS:Bearing him *P1869:*Will
bear him *1872:*And bear him   1208| MS:a defence § altered to § defender!"—my only
§ crossed out and replaced above by § sole thought was still § last two words crossed out §
1209| MS:§ crowded between 1208 and 1210 §   1211| MS:day break, woke § crossed out
and replaced above by § pierced *P1869:*daybreak *1872:*day-break *1889a:*daybreak

With a summons to me? Up I sprang alive,
Light in me, light without me, everywhere
Change! A broad yellow sunbeam was let fall
1215 From heaven to earth,—a sudden drawbridge lay,
Along which marched a myriad merry motes,
Mocking the flies that crossed them and recrossed
In rival dance, companions new-born too.
On the house-eaves, a dripping shag of weed
1220 Shook diamonds on each dull grey lattice-square,
As first one, then another bird leapt by,
And light was off, and lo was back again,
Always with one voice,—where are two such joys?—
The blessed building-sparrow! I stepped forth,
1225 Stood on the terrace,—o'er the roofs, such sky!
My heart sang, "I too am to go away,
I too have something I must care about,
Carry away with me to Rome, to Rome!
The bird brings hither sticks and hairs and wool,
1230 And nowhere else i' the world; what fly breaks rank,
Falls out of the procession that befits
From window here to window there, with all
The world to choose,—so well he knows his course?
I have my purpose and my motive too,
1235 My march to Rome, like any bird or fly!
Had I been dead! How right to be alive!
Last night I almost prayed for leave to die,
Wished Guido all his pleasure with the sword
Or the poison,—poison, sword, was but a trick,

1213| MS:me,—everywhere *P1869:*me, everywhere   1214| MS:broad yellow § inserted
above line § sun-beam *1889a:*sunbeam   1218| MS:new born *P1869:*new-born
1219| MS:the house § inserted above line § outside § crossed out §   1220| MS:on my
§ crossed out and replaced above by § each   1221| MS:bird § followed by two words
heavily crossed out, uncertain, the second perhaps being *there* §   1226| MS:sang "I
*P1869:*sang, "I   1230| MS:in § altered to § i'   1234-35| MS:§ originally one line §
purpose in my march to Rome. § altered to § purpose § crossed out and then restored § and
my motive too § last four words inserted above line § / For my march to Rome, like any bird
or fly! § last five words added in margin § *P1869:*too,/ My < > Rome, like
1237| MS:die— *P1869:*die,   1238| MS:Let § crossed out and replaced above by § Wished
have § crossed out and replaced above by § all   1239| MS:poison,—it was all a harmless
§ last five words crossed out and replaced above by five words § poison, sword, was but a

1240 Harmless, may God forgive him the poor jest!
My life is charmed, will last till I reach Rome!
Yesterday, but for the sin,—ah, nameless be
The deed I could have dared against myself!
Now—see if I will touch an unripe fruit
1245 And risk the health I want to have and use!
Not to live, now, would be the wickedness,—
For life means to make haste and go to Rome
And leave Arezzo, leave all woes at once!"

Now, understand here, by no means mistake!
1250 Long ago had I tried to leave that house
When it seemed such procedure would stop sin;
And still failed more the more I tried—at first
The Archbishop, as I told you,—next, our lord
The Governor,—indeed I found my way,
1255 I went to the great palace where he rules,
Though I knew well 'twas he who,—when I gave
A jewel or two, themselves had given me,
Back to my parents,—since they wanted bread,
They who had never let me want a nosegay,—he
1260 Spoke of the jail for felons, if they kept
What was first theirs, then mine, so doubly theirs,
Though all the while my husband's most of all!
I knew well who had spoke the word wrought this:
Yet, being in extremity, I fled

---

trick— *P1869:*trick,   1240| MS:§ crowded between 1239 and 1241 § Harmless—may
*P1869:*Harmless, may   1241| MS:life was charmed *P1869:*life is charmed
1244| MS:Now,—see <> fruit, *P1869:*Now—see   DC, BrU: fruit *1889:*fruit
1247| MS:to Rome, *P1869:*to Rome   1248| MS:And § inserted in margin § Leave
§ altered to § leave this § crossed out § Arezzo, and § crossed out and replaced above by § leave
1249| MS:§ marginal note that new ¶ begins § Now understand here, and § crossed out and
replaced above by two words § by no <> mistake!— *P1869:*Now, understand <> mistake!
1251| MS:sin, *P1869:*sin;   1252| MS:tried; at *P1869:*tried—at   1253| MS:The
Archbishop, I have told *P1869:*The Archbishop, as I told   1255| MS:he dwells
§ crossed out § lives § crossed out §   1258| MS:parents, when § crossed out and replaced
above by § —since   1260| MS:felons—who should § last two words crossed out and
replaced above by§ if they keep § altered to § kept   1261| MS:mine, theirs doubly so
§ indication that last three words should be transposed to read § so doubly theirs,
1262| MS:§ crowded between 1261 and 1263 § Yet all the *P1869:*Though all the
1263| MS:this— *P1869:*this: 1264| MS:extremity, I sought § crossed out §

¹²⁶⁵ To the Governor, as I say,—scarce opened lip
When—the cold cruel snicker close behind—
Guido was on my trace, already there,
Exchanging nod and wink for shrug and smile,
And I—pushed back to him and, for my pains
¹²⁷⁰ Paid with . . . but why remember what is past?
I sought out a poor friar the people call
The Roman, and confessed my sin which came
Of their sin,—that fact could not be repressed,—
The frightfulness of my despair in God:
¹²⁷⁵ And, feeling, through the grate, his horror shake,
Implored him, "Write for me who cannot write,
Apprise my parents, make them rescue me!
You bid me be courageous and trust God:
Do you in turn dare somewhat, trust and write
¹²⁸⁰ 'Dear friends, who used to be my parents once,
And now declare you have no part in me,
This is some riddle I want wit to solve,
Since you must love me with no difference.
Even suppose you altered,—there's your hate,
¹²⁸⁵ To ask for: hate of you two dearest ones
I shall find liker love than love found here,
If husbands love their wives. Take me away
And hate me as you do the gnats and fleas,
Even the scorpions! How I shall rejoice!'
¹²⁹⁰ Write that and save me!" And he promised—wrote

---

^{1265|} MS:To § inserted in margin § The § altered to § the   ^{1268|} MS:§ crowded between
lines 1267 and 1269 §   ^{1269|} MS:And I, pushed < > and for   *P1869:*And I—pushed < >
and, for my pains, *1889a:*pains   ^{1270|} MS:with . . but *1889a:*with . . . but
^{1271|} MS:I went at last to § last four words crossed out and replaced above by two words §
sought out a poor § inserted above line § priest, a § last two words crossed out § friar § over
perhaps *man* § they § crossed out and replaced above by two words § the people
^{1272|} MS:sin—which *P1869:*sin which   ^{1273|} MS:that much could *P1869:*that fact
could   ^{1274|} MS:§ crowded between 1273 and 1275 § in God:— *P1869:*in God:
^{1276|} MS:Entreated § crossed out and replaced above by two words § Implored him "Write for
*P1869:*him, "Write for   ^{1277|} MS:Inform § crossed out and replaced above by § Apprise
^{1279|} MS:somewhat, and just this § last three words crossed out and replaced above by § trust
and write   ^{1282|} MS:solve *P1869:*solve,   ^{1283|} MS:difference,—
*P1869:*difference.   ^{1285|} MS:§ crowded between 1284 and 1286 § I ask *P1869:*To ask
^{1288|} MS:fleas— *P1869:*fleas,   ^{1289|} MS:scorpions—how *P1869:*scorpions! How

Or did not write; things never changed at all:
He was not like the Augustinian here!
Last, in a desperation I appealed
To friends, whoever wished me better days,
1295 To Guillichini, that's of kin,—"What, I—
Travel to Rome with you? A flying gout
Bids me deny my heart and mind my leg!"
Then I tried Conti, used to brave—laugh back
The louring thunder when his cousin scowled
1300 At me protected by his presence: "You—
Who well know what you cannot save me from,—
Carry me off! What frightens you, a priest?"
He shook his head, looked grave—"Above my strength!
Guido has claws that scratch, shows feline teeth;
1305 A formidabler foe than I dare fret:
Give me a dog to deal with, twice the size!
Of course I am a priest and Canon too,
But . . by the bye . . though both, not quite so bold
As he, my fellow-Canon, brother-priest,
1310 The personage in such ill odour here
Because of the reports—pure birth o' the brain!

1291-93| MS:write; I § crossed out and replaced above by § things < > all./ Last in < >
I cried § crossed out and replaced above by § appealed   P1869:all:/ He was not like
the Augustinian here!/ Last, in   1294| MS:whoever § over erasure §
1295| MS:The Guillichini   P1869:To Guillichini   1296| MS:you, § comma
erased and replaced by question mark § There's § crossed out § a § altered to § A
1298| MS:Then I tried § last two words inserted above line § Conti, that § crossed out and
replaced above by § used to try § crossed out and replaced above by word and dash § brave—
laugh 1300| MS:presence—"You—   P1869:presence: "You—   1301| MS:§ crowded
between 1300 and 1302 § Who § followed by word illegibly crossed out § best
know   P1869:Who well know   1302| MS:off,—what   P1869:off! What
1304| MS:has a long § last two words crossed out and replaced above by two words §
claws that reach § altered to § scratch, pulls many wires § last three words crossed out
and replaced above by three words § shows feline teeth,—   P1869:teeth;
1305| MS:formidabler man § crossed out and replaced above by § foe < > dare § followed by
illegible erasure § fret— § over illegible word §   P1869:fret: 1307| MS:too   P1869:too,
1308| MS:bye . . not quite so bold, though both, § indication that last five words should be
transposed to read § though both, not quite so bold,   1309| MS:As the one § last two
words crossed out and replaced above by two words § he, my fellow § over perhaps man §
1311| MS:pure calumny § crossed out and replaced above by two words § fumes of § last two
words crossed out and replaced by three words § birth o' the brain—   1872:brain!

Our Caponsacchi, he's your true Saint George
To slay the monster, set the Princess free,
And have the whole High-Altar to himself:
¹³¹⁵ I always think so when I see that piece
I' the Pieve, that's his church and mine, you know:
Though you drop eyes at mention of his name!"

That name had got to take a half-grotesque
Half-ominous, wholly enigmatic sense,
¹³²⁰ Like any by-word, broken bit of song
Born with a meaning, changed by mouth and mouth
That mix it in a sneer or smile, as chance
Bids, till it now means nought but ugliness
And perhaps shame.

     —All this intends to say,
¹³²⁵ That, over-night, the notion of escape
Had seemed distemper, dreaming; and the name,—
Not the man, but the name of him, thus made
Into a mockery and disgrace,—why, she
Who uttered it persistently, had laughed,
¹³³⁰ "I name his name, and there you start and wince
As criminal from the red tongs' touch!"—yet now,
Now, as I stood letting morn bathe me bright,
Choosing which butterfly should bear my news,—
The white, the brown one, or that tinier blue,—
¹³³⁵ The Margherita, I detested so,
In she came—"The fine day, the good Spring time!

---

^{1312|} MS:he's your § altered to § our *P1869:*he's your ^{1314|} MS:§ line in right margin
with arrow indicating its place in text § ^{1315–16|} MS:§ crowded in continuous line
between 1313 and 1317 separated by slash between *piece* and *I'* § ^{1318|} MS:§ marginal
note that new ¶ begins § ^{1320|} MS:bye-word *1889a:*by-word ^{1321|} MS:meaning
changed *P1869:*meaning, changed ^{1323|} MS:Lends, till *P1869:*Bids, till
^{1324|} MS:shame: § marginal note that new ¶ begins § —All *P1869:*shame. § ¶ § —All
^{1325|} MS:over night *P1869:*over-night ^{1326|} MS:Had seemed § crossed out and
replaced above by § been *P1869:*Had seemed ^{1327|} MS:but that name of his, remade
*P1869:*but the name of him, thus made ^{1328–29|} MS:§ originally one line § it cried
§ crossed out and replaced above by eight words § persistently would laugh./ "I name his
name, and § insertion ends and original line continues § there *P1869:*persistently, had
laughed,/ "I ^{1334|} MS:one or *P1869:*one, or ^{1335|} MS:§ crowded between 1334
and 1336 § That Margherita I *P1869:*The Margherita, I ^{1336|} MS:good time of
§ crossed out § Spring! § indication that should be transposed to read § good Spring time!

What, up and out at window? That is best.
No thought of Caponsacchi?—who stood there
All night on one leg, like the sentry crane,
1340 Under the pelting of your water-spout—
Looked last look at your lattice ere he leave
Our city, bury his dead hope at Rome.
Ay, go to looking-glass and make you fine,
While he may die ere touch one least loose hair
1345 You drag at with the comb in such a rage!"

I turned—"Tell Caponsacchi he may come!"⟡

"Tell him to come? Ah, but, for charity,
A truce to fooling! Come? What,—come this eve?
Peter and Paul! But I see through the trick!
1350 Yes, come, and take a flower-pot on his head,
Flung from your terrace! No joke, sincere truth?"

How plainly I perceived hell flash and fade
O' the face of her,—the doubt that first paled joy,
Then, final reassurance I indeed
1355 Was caught now, never to be free again!
What did I care?—who felt myself of force
To play with silk, and spurn the horsehair-springe.

"But—do you know that I have bade him come,

1337| MS:out the § crossed out and replaced above by § at < > is good too § last two words
crossed out §   1341| MS:His § crossed out and replaced above by § Looked
1342| MS:dead hopes at Rome? P1869:hope 1872:at Rome.   1346| MS:§ marginal
note that new ¶ begins §   1347| MS:§ marginal note that new ¶ begins § come? Ah, now
§ altered to § but   1348| MS:fooling! Come? and § crossed out and replaced above by
word, comma and dash § What,—   1349| MS:trick— 1872:trick!   1350| MS:head
1872:head,   1351| MS:joke, all sincere?" § two words crossed out and replaced above by
two words § sincere truth?"   1352| MS:§ marginal note that new ¶ begins § perceived each
§ crossed out and replaced above by § hell   1353| MS:On < > that first § inserted above
line § dashed the § crossed out § joy, P1869:O' < > first paled joy,   1354| MS:The final
P1869:Then-final CP1869:Then, final   1355| MS:Was springed § crossed out § caught
now § inserted above line §   1357| MS:with the fetter, § word and comma crossed out
and replaced above by two words § silk, and < > horsehair springe.
P1869:horsehair-springe. 1872:with silk   1358-64| MS:§ with exception of omitted
1363, written in right margin with arrow indicating placement in text §
1358| MS:§ marginal note that new ¶ begins § come— P1869:come,

And in your own name? I presumed so much,
1360 Knowing the thing you needed in your heart.
But somehow—what had I to show in proof?
He would not come: half-promised, that was all,
And wrote the letters you refused to read.
What is the message that shall move him now?"

1365 "After the Ave Maria, at first dark,
I will be standing on the terrace, say!"

"I would I had a good long lock of hair
Should prove I was not lying! Never mind!"

Off she went—"May he not refuse, that's all—
1370 Fearing a trick!"

I answered, "He will come."
And, all day, I sent prayer like incense up
To God the strong, God the beneficent,
God ever mindful in all strife and strait,
Who, for our own good, makes the need extreme,
1375 Till at the last He puts forth might and saves.
An old rhyme came into my head and rang
Of how a virgin, for the faith of God,

1359| MS:name?—I <> much P1869:name? I <> much,   1362-64| MS:all./ What
P1869:all,/ And wrote the letters you refused to read./ What   1365| MS:§ marginal
note that new ¶ begins § —After P1869:After   1366| MS:say!
1872:say!"   1367-68| MS:§ marginal note that new ¶ begins; crowded
between 1366 and 1369 in continuous line separated by / between hair and Should §
1368-69| MS:§ no ¶ § P1869:§ ¶ §   1370| MS:trick!" I answered—"He P1869:trick!"
§ ¶ § I answered, "He   1371| MS:§ marginal note that new ¶ begins § And that § crossed
out and replaced above by § all day I P1869:And, all day, I   1372| MS:strong § over
illegible word § , God the strong and merciful, § last three words crossed out and replaced
above by word and comma § beneficent,   1373| MS:ever present § crossed out and
replaced above by § mindful in all § crossed out and then restored § kind of § last two words
crossed out and replaced above by two words § strife and straits § altered to § strait,
1374| MS:good makes us § altered to § the need Him much § last two words crossed out and
replaced above by § extreme, P1869:good, makes   1375| MS:Then § crossed out and
replaced above by § Till <> last He § inserted above § puts forth His § crossed out
1376| MS:and sang P1869:and rang   1377| MS:a Virgin P1869:a virgin

Hid herself, from the Paynims that pursued,
In a cave's heart; until a thunderstone,
1380 Wrapped in a flame, revealed the couch and prey
And they laughed—"Thanks to lightning, ours at last!"
And she cried "Wrath of God, assert His love!
Servant of God, thou fire, befriend His child!"
And lo, the fire she grasped at, fixed its flash,
1385 Lay in her hand a calm cold dreadful sword
She brandished till pursuers strewed the ground,
So did the souls within them die away,
As o'er the prostrate bodies, sworded, safe,
She walked forth to the solitudes and Christ:
1390 So should I grasp the lightning and be saved!

And still, as the day wore, the trouble grew
Whereby I guessed there would be born a star,
Until at an intense throe of the dusk,
I started up, was pushed, I dare to say,
1395 Out on the terrace, leaned and looked at last
Where the deliverer waited me: the same
Silent and solemn face, I first descried
At the spectacle, confronted mine once more.

So was that minute twice vouchsafed me, so

1378| MS:the paynims *P1869:*the Paynims   1379| MS:In a § followed by word possibly
woods, altered, crossed out, blotted and replaced above by § cave's heart until a thunderbolt
§ altered to § thunderstone *P1869:*heart; until < > thunderstone,   1380| MS:flame—
revealed < > prey; *P1869:*flame, revealed < > prey: *1889a:*prey   1381| MS:laughed—
"Thank § altered to § Thanks the § crossed out and replaced above by § to
1382-84| MS:cried "Wrath § replaces word illegibly crossed out and blotted § of God, befriend
His child!"/ And *P1869:*of God, assert His love!/ Servant of God, thou fire, befriend
His child!"/ And *1872:*cried, "Wrath *1889a:*cried "Wrath   1385| MS:cold § over
perhaps *and* § dreadful point § crossed out §   1386| MS:the earth § crossed out
and replaced above by § ground,   1387| MS:the hearts § crossed out and
replaced above by § souls < > die at once, *P1869:*die away,   1388| MS:safe
*P1869:*safe,   1389| MS:solitudes and § crossed out and replaced above by § of Christ:
*P1869:*solitudes and Christ: 1390| MS:So shall I *P1869:*So should I
1391| MS:§ marginal note that new ¶ begins §   1392| MS:Whereby § over illegible word
§ you know § last two words crossed out and replaced above by § I guessed there will
§ crossed out and replaced above by § would   1393| MS:at one last § last two words
crossed out and replaced above by § an < > of the § inserted above line §
1396| MS:me—the *P1869:*me: the   1397| MS:Silent grave and § last two words crossed
out and replaced above by § and < > face, before revealed § last two words crossed out and
replaced above by three words § I first descried   1399| MS:§ marginal note that new ¶

213

1400 The manhood, wasted then, was still at watch
To save me yet a second time: no change
Here, though all else changed in the changing world!

I spoke on the instant, as my duty bade,
In some such sense as this, whatever the phrase.

1405 "Friend, foolish words were borne from you to me;
Your soul behind them is the pure strong wind,
Not dust and feathers which its breath may bear:
These to the witless seem the wind itself,
Since proving thus the first of it they feel.
1410 If by mischance you blew offence my way,
The straws are dropt, the wind desists no whit,
And how such strays were caught up in the street
And took a motion from you, why inquire?
I speak to the strong soul, no weak disguise.
1415 If it be truth,—why should I doubt it truth?—
You serve God specially, as priests are bound,
And care about me, stranger as I am,
So far as wish my good,—that miracle
I take to intimate He wills you serve
1420 By saving me,—what else can He direct?
Here is the service. Since a long while now,
I am in course of being put to death:
While death concerned nothing but me, I bowed
The head and bade, in heart, my husband strike.

---

begins § was that § inserted above line §   1400| MS:manhood wasted then was
*P1869:*manhood, wasted then, was   1401| MS:time, no *P1869:*time: no
1402| MS:Here, and § crossed out and replaced above by § though   1403| MS:§ marginal
note that new ¶ begins § bade— *P1869:*bade,   1404| MS:phrase. § over illegible
erasure §   1404-5| MS:§ no ¶ § *1889a:*§ ¶ §   1405| MS:"—Friend *P1869:*"Friend
1406| MS:wind— *P1869:*wind,   1407| MS:bear,— *P1869:*bear:
1408-9| MS:§ originally one line § These to the witless § last four words inserted in left
margin § Seem § altered to § seem the wind § last two words inserted above line § itself/
since § altered to § Since proving thus § last two words inserted above line §
1414| MS:no mean § uncertain; crossed out and replaced above by § weak
1418| MS:wish me § altered to § my well § crossed out and replaced above by § good
1420| MS:can I § crossed out and replaced above by § he *P1869:*can He

¹⁴²⁵ Now I imperil something more, it seems,
Something that's truelier me than this myself,
Something I trust in God and you to save.
You go to Rome, they tell me: take me there,
Put me back with my people!"

He replied—
¹⁴³⁰ The first word I heard ever from his lips,
All himself in it,—an eternity
Of speech, to match the immeasurable depth
O' the soul that then broke silence—"I am yours."

So did the star rise, soon to lead my step,
¹⁴³⁵ Lead on, nor pause before it should stand still
Above the House o' the Babe,—my babe to be,
That knew me first and thus made me know him,
That had his right of life and claim on mine,
And would not let me die till he was born,
¹⁴⁴⁰ But pricked me at the heart to save us both,
Saying "Have you the will? Leave God the way!"
And the way was Caponsacchi—"mine," thank God!
He was mine, he is mine, he will be mine.

No pause i' the leading and the light! I know,
¹⁴⁴⁵ Next night there was a cloud came, and not he:

---

¹⁴²⁷| MS:Which I relie up § crossed out and replaced above by four words § Something I trust
in   ¹⁴²⁹| MS:people!" § marginal note that new ¶ begins § He   ¹⁴³⁰| MS:ever
break § crossed out § from him § crossed out and replaced above by § his
¹⁴³²| MS:speech, immeasurable § crossed out and replaced above by five words § to span the
unfathomable depths § last five words crossed out and replaced below by four words § to
match the immeasurable depths of soul § last two words crossed out §   <i>1872:</i>depth
¹⁴³³| MS:Of § altered to § O' that § crossed out and replaced above by § the soul that § crossed
out and then restored §   ¹⁴³⁴| MS:§ marginal note that new ¶ begins § step—
P1869:step,   ¹⁴³⁵| MS:it should § inserted above line §   ¹⁴³⁶| MS:the house <>
be—   <i>P1869:</i>the House <> be,   ¹⁴³⁷| MS:§ crowded between 1436 and 1438 §
¹⁴³⁸| MS:rights § altered to § right <> mine   P1869:mine,   ¹⁴³⁹| MS:born
P1869:born,   ¹⁴⁴¹| MS:will, § altered to § ?—leave § altered to § Leave   P1869:will? Leave
¹⁴⁴³| MS:§ crowded between 1442 and 1444 §   ¹⁴⁴⁴| MS:§ marginal note that new ¶
begins § in   <i>P1869:</i>i'   ¹⁴⁴⁵| MS:a cloud § inserted above line § <> he—   <i>P1869:</i>he:

215

But I prayed through the darkness till it broke
And let him shine. The second night, he came.

"The plan is rash; the project desperate:
In such a flight needs must I risk your life,
1450   Give food for falsehood, folly or mistake,
Ground for your husband's rancour and revenge"—
So he began again, with the same face.
I felt that, the same loyalty—one star
Turning now red that was so white before—
1455   One service apprehended newly: just
A word of mine and there the white was back!

"No, friend, for you will take me! 'Tis yourself
Risk all, not I,—who let you, for I trust
In the compensating great God: enough!
1460   I know you: when is it that you will come?"

"To-morrow at the day's dawn." Then I heard
What I should do: how to prepare for flight
And where to fly.

          That night my husband bade
"—You, whom I loathe, beware you break my sleep

---

¹⁴⁴⁷⁻⁴⁸| MS:§ originally one line § shine. He said— § last two words crossed out and replaced
above by five words and period § The second night, he came./ § original line continues;
marginal note that new ¶ begins § "The plan is rash; the project desperate,
*P1869:*desperate: ¹⁴⁴⁹| MS:flight must needs be § crossed out and replaced above by § I
§ indication that order of last three words be transposed to § needs must I risk of § crossed out
and replaced above by § your   ¹⁴⁵⁰| MS:Give § inserted above line § Food for man's
§ crossed out § lying, folly *P1869:*food for falsehood, folly   ¹⁴⁵²| MS:§ crowded
between 1451 and 1453 § again with *P1869:*again, with   ¹⁴⁵³| MS:that—the <>
loyalty,—one *P1869:*that, the <> loyalty—one   ¹⁴⁵⁴| MS:before,— *P1869:*before—
¹⁴⁵⁶| MS:was § followed by word illegibly crossed out §   ¹⁴⁵⁷| MS:§ marginal note that
new ¶ begins §   ¹⁴⁵⁸| MS:That § uncertain; crossed out § risks § altered to § Risk all
§ inserted above line §   ¹⁴⁵⁹| MS:enough— *P1869:*enough!   ¹⁴⁶⁰| MS:We
understand each other § last four words crossed out and replaced above by seven words § I
know you: when is it that   ¹⁴⁶¹| MS:§ marginal note that new ¶ begins § —"Tomorrow
<> day § altered to § day's break § crossed out and replaced above by § dawn
¹⁴⁶²⁻⁶³| MS:§ originally one line § do. § altered to § do: how to prepare for flight/ And where
to fly. § last nine words inserted above line; marginal note that new ¶ begins § That
¹⁴⁶⁴| MS:loathe, let me not lose one wink § last six words crossed out and replaced above by
five words and exclamation point § because you break my sleep! *P1869:*sleep

1465 This whole night! Couch beside me like the corpse
I would you were!" The rest you know, I think—
How I found Caponsacchi and escaped.

And this man, men call sinner? Jesus Christ!
Of whom men said, with mouths Thyself mad'st once,
1470 "He hath a devil"—say he was Thy saint,
My Caponsacchi! Shield and show—unshroud
In Thine own time the glory of the soul
If aught obscure,—if ink-spot, from vile pens
Scribbling a charge against him—(I was glad
1475 Then, for the first time, that I could not write)—
Flirted his way, have flecked the blaze!

For me,
'Tis otherwise: let men take, sift my thoughts
—Thoughts I throw like the flax for sun to bleach!
I did pray, do pray, in the prayer shall die,
1480 "Oh, to have Caponsacchi for my guide!"
Ever the face upturned to mine, the hand
Holding my hand across the world,—a sense
That reads, as only such can read, the mark
God sets on woman, signifying so
1485 She should—shall peradventure—be divine;

1465| MS:Of § crossed out § <>night, lie § imperfectly erased and replaced above by § couch
*P1869:*night! Couched *CP1869:*night! Couch   1468| MS:§ marginal note that new ¶
begins § man, they § crossed out and replaced above by § men <> sinner? Jesus Christ,
*P1869:*sinner? Jesus Christ!   1472| MS:One day § last two words crossed out § In
§ inserted above line § thine § altered to § Thine <> the splendour § crossed out and replaced
above by § glory   1473| MS:obscure,—if § crossed out and replaced above by § some
§ crossed out and original restored §   1474| MS:against him § inserted above line §
1476| MS:way, has <> the white § crossed out and replaced above by § blaze! § marginal note
that new ¶ begins § For *CP1869:*way, have   1477| MS:otherwise,—let men take, and
§ crossed out § <> thoughts! *P1869:*otherwise: let <> thoughts   1478| MS:the grain
the § last two words crossed out and replaced above by two words § flax for sun shall § crossed
out and replaced above by § to bleach: *P1869:*bleach!   1479| MS:did think, do think, in
the thought now § crossed out and replaced above by § shall die— *P1869:*die, *1872:*did
pray, do pray, in the prayer shall   1480| MS:That to <> friend— § word and dash
crossed out § guide, *1872:*"Oh, to <> guide!"   1482| MS:sense § over illegible
word §   1483| MS:To see § last two words crossed out and replaced above by two words
and comma § That reads, as only § inserted above § such men only see § last three words
crossed out and replaced above by two words § can read   1485| MS:They § crossed out
and replaced above by § She should be, § word and comma crossed out and replaced above

217

Yet 'ware, the while, how weakness mars the print
And makes confusion, leaves the thing men see,
—Not this man sees,—who from his soul, re-writes
The obliterated charter,—love and strength
1490 Mending what's marred. "So kneels a votarist,
Weeds some poor waste traditionary plot
Where shrine once was, where temple yet may be,
Purging the place but worshipping the while,
By faith and not by sight, sight clearest so,—
1495 Such way the saints work,"—says Don Celestine.
But I, not privileged to see a saint
Of old when such walked earth with crown and palm,
If I call "saint" what saints call something else—
The saints must bear with me, impute the fault
1500 To a soul i' the bud, so starved by ignorance,
Stinted of warmth, it will not blow this year
Nor recognize the orb which Spring-flowers know.
But if meanwhile some insect with a heart
Worth floods of lazy music, spendthrift joy—
1505 Some fire-fly renounced Spring for my dwarfed cup,
Crept close to me, brought lustre for the dark,
Comfort against the cold,—what though excess
Of comfort should miscall the creature—sun?
What did the sun to hinder while harsh hands

---

by dash § shall hereafter § crossed out and replaced above by § peradventure be, divine—
*P1869:*peradventure—be divine;   1488| MS:man,—who < > his own soul   *1872:*man
sees,—who < > his soul   1489| MS:obliterated glory § crossed out and replaced above
by § charter   1490| MS:marred,—so   *P1869:*marred: "So   *1872:*marred. "So
1491| MS:plot § over illegible word §   1492| MS:Where § illegible word crossed out and
replaced above by two words § shrine once < > yet shall § crossed out and replaced above
by § may   1493| MS:place but § inserted above line § < > while.   *P1869:*while,
1494| MS:§ crowded between 1493 and 1495 § so,   *CP1869:*so,—   1495| MS:says Don
Celestine—   *P1869:*says Don Celestine.   1499| MS:§ illegibly crossed out but inserted
above § Saintship must bear with me—impute   *P1869:*The saints must bear with me, impute
1500| MS:in § altered to § i' < > so dwarfed § crossed out and replaced above by § starved
1502| MS:Nor understand § crossed out and replaced above by § justify § crossed out and
replaced above by § recognize < > which spring-flowers bless § crossed out § know:
*P1869:*which Spring-flowers know.   1503| MS:meanwhile an § crossed out and replaced
above by § some < > heart—   *P1869:*heart   1505| MS:One § altered to § Some < > my
starved § crossed out and replaced above by § dwarfed   1506| MS:me with lustre < > dark

218

Petal by petal, crude and colourless,
Tore me? This one heart gave me all the Spring!

Is all told? There's the journey: and where's time
To tell you how that heart burst out in shine?
Yet certain points do press on me too hard.
Each place must have a name, though I forget:
How strange it was—there where the plain begins
And the small river mitigates its flow—
When eve was fading fast, and my soul sank,
And he divined what surge of bitterness,
In overtaking me, would float me back
Whence I was carried by the striding day—
So,—"This grey place was famous once," said he—
And he began that legend of the place
As if in answer to the unspoken fear,
And told me all about a brave man dead,
Which lifted me and let my soul go on!
How did he know too,—at that town's approach
By the rock-side,—that in coming near the signs
Of life, the house-roofs and the church and tower,
I saw the old boundary and wall o' the world
Rise plain as ever round me, hard and cold,

---

*P1869:*dark,   *1872:*me, brought lustre   1510| MS:crude, blank, § word and commas crossed out and replaced above by § and   1511| MS:heart brought me   *1872:*heart gave me   1511–12| MS:§ ¶ §   *1889a:*§ no ¶ §   *1889:*§ no ¶; emended to restore ¶; see Editorial Notes §   1512–14| MS:§ lines inserted in left margin §   1512| MS:§ totally obliterated in binding of MS §   1513| MS:tell each point where that <> burst in   *P1869:*tell you how that <> burst out in   1514| MS:hard—   *P1869:*hard.   1515| MS:forget— *P1869:*forget: 1516| MS:where the § crossed out and replaced above by § bare § crossed out and original restored §   1517–18| MS:the mute § crossed out and replaced above by § small <> / § squeezed into right hand margin § And it § crossed out and replaced above by § eve was fading § over illegible word §   *P1869:*When eve   1519| MS:divined the § crossed out and replaced above by § In overtaking fast § crossed out and replaced above by § me 1521| MS:carried till § crossed out and replaced above by § by the striding § inserted above line § day—broke dawn— § last two words crossed out §   1522| MS:And § crossed out and replaced in margin by § So   1524| MS:fear—   *P1869:*fear,   1525| MS:§ crowded between 1524 and 1526 §   1526| MS:Which § crossed out and then restored § 1527| MS:How could § crossed out and replaced above by § did he know too, § word and comma inserted above line § —at that old § crossed out §   1528| MS:the world § crossed out§   1529| MS:§ crowded between 1528 and 1530 §   1530| MS:walls of life § last two words crossed out §   *P1869:*wall   1531| MS:around   *P1869:*round

As if the broken circlet joined again,
Tightened itself about me with no break,—
As if the town would turn Arezzo's self,—
1535   The husband there,—the friends my enemies,
All ranged against me, not an avenue
To try, but would be blocked and drive me back
On him,—this other, . . . oh the heart in that!
Did not he find, bring, put into my arms
1540   A new-born babe?—and I saw faces beam
Of the young mother proud to teach me joy,
And gossips round expecting my surprise
At the sudden hole through earth that lets in heaven.
I could believe himself by his strong will
1545   Had woven around me what I thought the world
We went along in, every circumstance,
Towns, flowers and faces, all things helped so well!
For, through the journey, was it natural
Such comfort should arise from first to last?
1550   As I look back, all is one milky way;
Still bettered more, the more remembered, so
Do new stars bud while I but search for old,

1532| MS:again *P1869:*again,   1533| *P1869:*Frightened *CP1869:*Tightened
1534| MS:§ crowded between 1533 and 1535 § self; *P1869:*self,—
1535| MS:there,—even § crossed out § the Parents too § last two words crossed out §
1536| MS:Ranged, § crossed out § all § altered to § All ranged § inserted above line §
1537| MS:I try but *P1869:*try, but *1872:*To try   1538-39| MS:§ originally one line §
this brought and § last two words crossed out and replaced above by § other, . . oh the heart
in that!/ How did he find, bring, § original line continues § put *P1869:*that!/ Did not he
*1889a:*other, . . . oh   1540| MS:new born babe—and I found § crossed out and replaced
above by § saw faces round § crossed out § *P1869:*new-born babe?—and
1541-42| MS:§ originally one line § the young § inserted above line § mother proud to teach me
joy— § last five words inserted above line § / § original line continues § and § altered to § And
gossips round § inserted below line § engaging § crossed out and replaced above by § expecting
*P1869:*joy,/ And   1543| MS:hole burst § crossed out § through earth § inserted above
line §   1545| MS:had worn § crossed out and replaced above by § woven
1546| MS:circumstance— *P1869:*circumstance,   1547| MS:things went so well.
*P1869:*things helped so well!   1548| MS:For through the journey,—was *P1869:*For,
through the journey, was   1550| MS:one galaxy § crossed out § milky § altered to § Milky
way *P1869:*milky way;   1551| MS:remembered, still § crossed out §   1552| MS:Do
§ inserted in left margin § New § altered to § new <> bud out § crossed out § while I but

And fill all gaps i' the glory, and grow him—
Him I now see make the shine everywhere.

1555   Even at the last when the bewildered flesh,
The cloud of weariness about my soul
Clogging too heavily, sucked down all sense,—
Still its last voice was, "He will watch and care;
Let the strength go, I am content: he stays!"

1560   I doubt not he did stay and care for all—
From that sick minute when the head swam round,
And the eyes looked their last and died on him,
As in his arms he caught me, and, you say,
Carried me in, that tragical red eve,
1565   And laid me where I next returned to life
In the other red of morning, two red plates
That crushed together, crushed the time between,
And are since then a solid fire to me,—
When in, my dreadful husband and the world
1570   Broke,—and I saw him, master, by hell's right,
And saw my angel helplessly held back
By guards that helped the malice—the lamb prone,
The serpent towering and triumphant—then
Came all the strength back in a sudden swell,

---

§ inserted above line § < > for the § crossed out §   ¹⁵⁵³| MS:in < > and all § crossed
out § *P1869:*i'   ¹⁵⁵⁴| MS:He at the last § last three words crossed out and replaced
above by three words § I now see makes *P1869:*Him I < > make   ^{1554–55}| MS:§ ¶ §
P1869:§no ¶ *1889:*§ no ¶; emended to restore ¶; see Editorial Notes §
¹⁵⁵⁷| MS:Clogging all § crossed out §   ¹⁵⁵⁸| MS:was—"He < > care, *P1869:*was, "He
< > care;   ¹⁵⁵⁹| MS:go, and he § last two words crossed out and replaced above by two
words § I am   ^{1559–60}| MS:§ ¶ § *P1869:*§ no ¶ § *1889:*§ no ¶; emended to restore ¶;
see Editorial Notes §   ¹⁵⁶¹| MS:when the § inserted above line §   ¹⁵⁶²| MS:And
my § crossed out and replaced above by § the   ¹⁵⁶³| MS:me in his § last two words
inserted above line § arms § indication that last three words are to be transposed to follow
As § , and, so § crossed out § *P1869:*me and *1872:*me, and   ¹⁵⁶⁷| MS:together, and §
crossed out § crushed the § crossed out and then restored §   ¹⁵⁶⁸| MS:me,
*P1869:*me,—   ¹⁵⁶⁹| MS:in my *P1869:*in, my   ¹⁵⁷⁰| MS:him, stand triumphant
there § last three words crossed out and replaced above by four words § master, by hell's
right,   ¹⁵⁷¹| MS:And my good angel § last two words inserted above line § < >
helplessly held *P1869:*And saw my angel   ¹⁵⁷²| MS:that did § crossed out and
replaced above by § helped his bidding § crossed out and replaced above by § malice—the

I did for once see right, do right, give tongue
The adequate protest: for a worm must turn
If it would have its wrong observed by God.
I did spring up, attempt to thrust aside
That ice-block 'twixt the sun and me, lay low
1580 The neutralizer of all good and truth.
If I sinned so,—never obey voice more
O' the Just and Terrible, who bids us—"Bear!"
Not—"Stand by, bear to see my angels bear!"
I am clear it was on impulse to serve God
1585 Not save myself,—no—nor my child unborn!
Had I else waited patiently till now?—
Who saw my old kind parents, silly-sooth
And too much trustful, for their worst of faults,
Cheated, brow-beaten, stripped and starved, cast out
1590 Into the kennel: I remonstrated,
Then sank to silence, for,—their woes at end,
Themselves gone,—only I was left to plague.
If only I was threatened and belied,
What matter? I could bear it and did bear;
1595 It was a comfort, still one lot for all:
They were not persecuted for my sake
And I, estranged, the single happy one.
But when at last, all by myself I stood

Lamb *P1869:*helped the malice—the lamb   1575| MS:right, act § crossed out and
replaced above by § do right, and make § last two words crossed out and replaced above by §
give   1576| MS:protest,—for *P1869:*protest: for   1579| MS:twixt *P1869:*'twixt
1581| MS:If I did wrong § last two words crossed out and replaced above by § sinned so
1582| MS:Of *P1869:*O'   1583| MS:by, § next word illegibly crossed out and replaced
above by § see, unmoved, my § crossed out and replaced above by word illegibly crossed out
and original restored § *P1869:*by, bear to see my   1585-86| MS:§ originally one line §
my § altered to § myself,—no—nor my child unborn! § last five words inserted above line §
had § altered to § Had I waited else § indication that order of last two words should be
reversed § patiently § added below line § till now? *P1869:*unborn!/ Had <> now?—
1587| MS:I who § crossed out § had seen my *P1869:*Who saw my   1588| MS:And all
§ crossed out § too much § inserted above line §   1590| MS:Into § over illegible word §
the kennel,—I *P1869:*kennel: I   1591| MS:silence; for, their *P1869:*silence, for,—their
1592| MS:They had § altered to § Themselves gone, only *P1869:*gone,—only
1593| MS:So only § inserted above line § I was beaten and cursed, § last three words crossed
out § <> belied— *P1869:*If only <> belied,   1594| MS:matter? Myself § crossed out
and replaced above by § I <> bear— *P1869:*bear;   1595| MS:comfort, still § inserted
above line § <> for us § crossed out § all, *P1869:*all: 1596-98| MS:§ originally one
line § Got me § last two words crossed out and replaced above by § They were not persecuted

Obeying the clear voice which bade me rise,
1600 Not for my own sake but my babe unborn,
And take the angel's hand was sent to help—
And found the old adversary athwart the path—
Not my hand simply struck from the angel's, but
The very angel's self made foul i' the face
1605 By the fiend who struck there,—that I would not bear,
That only I resisted! So, my first
And last resistance was invincible.
Prayers move God; threats, and nothing else, move men!
I must have prayed a man as he were God
1610 When I implored the Governor to right
My parents' wrongs: the answer was a smile.
The Archbishop,—did I clasp his feet enough,
Hide my face hotly on them, while I told
More than I dared make my own mother know?
1615 The profit was—compassion and a jest.
This time, the foolish prayers were done with, right
Used might, and solemnized the sport at once.
All was against the combat: vantage, mine?

---

for my sake and I estranged, § last three words inserted below line; original line continues §
the single and § crossed out § happy one. § last word and period inserted above line § / But
when at last, all by myself I stood § last nine words in right margin §   *P1869:*sake/ And I,
estranged   1599| MS:the voice of God which   *P1869:*the clear voice which
1601| MS:Taking the   *P1869:*And take   1602| MS:I found <> adversary in § crossed
out and replaced above by § athwart   *P1869:*And found   1604| MS:in § altered to § i'
1605| MS:who spat there <> bear—   *P1869:*who struck there <> bear,
1606| MS:That only § inserted above line § I resisted; and so my first/And last § arrow
indicating that last two words form beginning of next line §   *P1869:*resisted! So my
*CP1869:*resisted! So, my   1607| MS:Resistance was invincible. It would seem. § last
three words and period crossed out §   *P1869:*And last resistance   1608| MS:move God,
threats move men and nothing else— § indication that last three words should follow
threats §   *P1869:*move God; threats, and <> else, move men!   1609| MS:prayed such
prayer § last two words crossed out and replaced above by two words § a man as he were §
last two words inserted above line § God deserves § crossed out §   1613| MS:them, hotly
§ indication that last word should be transposed to follow *face* §   1614| MS:dared to
§ crossed out § <> my own § inserted above line § <> know?— *P1869:*know?
1615| MS:Weep my brain dry. As well have prayed the winds. § line crossed out and replaced
above by § The profit was—compassion and a joke. *P1869:*a jest.   1616| MS:the
foolish § inserted above line § <> right/ used § altered to § Used might, § arrow indicating
that last two words should form beginning of next line §   1617| MS:§ remaining line
written in right margin §   1618| MS:—All <> the trial, my § last two words crossed
out and replaced above by § combat—vantage, mine, § altered to § ?   *P1869:*All <> combat:

223

The runaway avowed, the accomplice-wife,
1620 In company with the plan-contriving priest?
Yet, shame thus rank and patent, I struck, bare,
At foe from head to foot in magic mail,
And off it withered, cobweb-armoury
Against the lightning! 'Twas truth singed the lies
1625 And saved me, not the vain sword nor weak speech!

You see, I will not have the service fail!
I say, the angel saved me: I am safe!
Others may want and wish, I wish nor want
One point o' the circle plainer, where I stand
1630 Traced round about with white to front the world.
What of the calumny I came across,
What o' the way to the end?—the end crowns all.
The judges judged aright i' the main, gave me
The uttermost of my heart's desire, a truce
1635 From torture and Arezzo, balm for hurt,
With the quiet nuns,—God recompense the good!
Who said and sang away the ugly past.
And, when my final fortune was revealed,
What safety while, amid my parents' arms,
1640 My babe was given me! Yes, he saved my babe:

---

vantage   1619| MS:The avowed runaway, the accomplice caught § altered to §
accomplice-wife   P1869:The runaway avowed, the accomplice-wife,   1620| MS:priest,
§ altered to § ?—   P1869:priest?   1621-23| MS:My shame was § crossed out and replaced
above by § thus rank and patent, in full show/ § illegible word § in proof/The foe, I fight
with? § last six words and question mark written above line; original line continues §
Cobweb armory § all preceding crossed out and replaced by three new lines written on
reverse of preceding page § My shame <> patent, I fought § crossed out and replaced above
by § struck/ With § crossed out and replaced above by § At a foe <> mail—/ <>
withered—cobweb-armoury   P1869:Yet, shame <> / At foe <> mail,/<> withered,
cobweb-armoury   1624| MS:lightning, § altered to § lightning! God's § crossed out and
replaced above by § 'Twas   1625| MS:sword and weak   P1869:sword nor weak
1625-26| MS:§ no ¶ §   P1869:§ ¶ §   1626| MS:fail—   P1869:fail!   1627| MS:me:
and § crossed out §   1629| MS:of § altered to § o'   1631| MS:§crowded between
1630 and 1632 §   1632| MS:of <> end, § altered to § end?—the end, crowns all:
P1869:o' <> all. CP1869:end?—the end crowns   1633| MS:in § altered to § i' the end
§ crossed out and replaced above by § main   1634| MS:desire,—a   P1869:desire, a
1635| MS:From Arezzo and the torture, balm for hurt   P1869:From torture and Arezzo, balm
1872:hurt,   1637| MS:Who sang and said away <> past—   P1869:Who said
and sang away <> past.   1640| MS:me,—yes <> babe—   P1869:me!

It would not have peeped forth, the bird-like thing,
Through that Arezzo noise and trouble: back
Had it returned nor ever let me see!
But the sweet peace cured all, and let me live
¹⁶⁴⁵ And give my bird the life among the leaves
God meant him! Weeks and months of quietude,
I could lie in such peace and learn so much—
Begin the task, I see how needful now,
Of understanding somewhat of my past,—
¹⁶⁵⁰ Know life a little, I should leave so soon.
Therefore, because this man restored my soul,
All has been right; I have gained my gain, enjoyed
As well as suffered,—nay, got foretaste too
Of better life beginning where this ends—
¹⁶⁵⁵ All through the breathing-while allowed me thus,
Which let good premonitions reach my soul
Unthwarted, and benignant influence flow
And interpenetrate and change my heart,
Uncrossed by what was wicked,—nay, unkind.
¹⁶⁶⁰ For, as the weakness of my time drew nigh,
Nobody did me one disservice more,
Spoke coldly or looked strangely, broke the love
I lay in the arms of, till my boy was born,
Born all in love, with nought to spoil the bliss
¹⁶⁶⁵ A whole long fortnight: in a life like mine
A fortnight filled with bliss is long and much.
All women are not mothers of a boy,

Yes <> babe:　　　　¹⁶⁴¹| MS:thing　CP1869:thing,　　　¹⁶⁴²| MS:trouble,—back
P1869:trouble: back　　　¹⁶⁴⁵⁻⁴⁷| MS:§ originally two lines § bird § over illegible erasure §
the life among the leaves/ § last three words inserted above line § God meant him! Weeks
and § inserted above line § months, § end of original first line § Of quietude—/ <> lie
in such peace § last three words inserted above line §　P1869:/ months of quietude,//
¹⁶⁴⁹| MS:understanding all § crossed out and replaced above by two words § somewhat of my
difficult § crossed out §　　　¹⁶⁵¹| MS:§ crowded between 1650 and 1652 §　　　¹⁶⁵⁴| MS:Of
a better　P1869:Of better　　　¹⁶⁵⁵| MS:thus　P1869:thus,　　　¹⁶⁵⁷| MS:Unthwarted, all
benignant　P1869:Unthwarted, and benignant　　　¹⁶⁵⁹| MS:unkind—　P1869:unkind.
¹⁶⁶¹| MS:did me § inserted above line § one disservice to me § last two words crossed out §
more　P1869:more,　　　¹⁶⁶⁴| MS:the joy　P1869:the bliss　　　¹⁶⁶⁶| MS:with joy is

Though they live twice the length of my whole life,
And, as they fancy, happily all the same.
1670 There I lay, then, all my great fortnight long,
As if it would continue, broaden out
Happily more and more, and lead to heaven:
Christmas before me,—was not that a chance?
I never realized God's birth before—
1675 How He grew likest God in being born.
This time I felt like Mary, had my babe
Lying a little on my breast like hers.
So all went on till, just four days ago—
The night and the tap.

                              Oh it shall be success
1680 To the whole of our poor family! My friends
. . . Nay, father and mother,—give me back my word!
They have been rudely stripped of life, disgraced
Like children who must needs go clothed too fine,
Carry the garb of Carnival in Lent.
1685 If they too much affected frippery,
They have been punished and submit themselves,
Say no word: all is over, they see God
Who will not be extreme to mark their fault
Or He had granted respite: they are safe.

1690 For that most woeful man my husband once,
Who, needing respite, still draws vital breath,

---

*P1869:*with bliss is   1668| MS:life   *P1869:*life,   1670| MS:lay then <> long
*P1869:*lay, then <> long,   1672| MS:Happily all the way § last three words crossed out
and replaced above by three words and comma § more and more, <> Heaven:
*P1869:*heaven: 1673| MS:that good chance? *P1869:*that a chance?
1675| MS:How he   *1872:*How He   1678| MS:till just   *P1869:*till, just
1679| MS:tap. § marginal note that new ¶ begins § O <> success! *P1869:*success
*1889a:*tap. § ¶ § Oh   1680| MS:friends—   *P1869:*friends   1681| MS: . . Nay <>
mother, let § crossed out and replaced above by § give me say this once— § last three words
and dash crossed out and replaced above by four words and dash § back my own § crossed
out § word—   *P1869:*word! *1889a:* . . . Nay   1683| MS:go garbed § crossed out and
replaced above by § clothed   1684| MS:in Lent,   *P1869:*in Lent: *1889a:*in Lent.
1687| MS:they with § crossed out and replaced above by § see   1684| MS:Or he
*P1869:*Or He   1689–90| MS:§ ¶ §   *1889a:*§ no ¶ §   *1889:*§ no ¶; emended to restore ¶;

I—pardon him? So far as lies in me,
I give him for his good the life he takes,
Praying the world will therefore acquiesce.
1695 Let him make God amends,—none, none to me
Who thank him rather that, whereas strange fate
Mockingly styled him husband and me wife,
Himself this way at least pronounced divorce,
Blotted the marriage-bond: this blood of mine
1700 Flies forth exultingly at any door,
Washes the parchment white, and thanks the blow.
We shall not meet in this world nor the next,
But where will God be absent? In His face
Is light, but in His shadow healing too:
1705 Let Guido touch the shadow and be healed!
And as my presence was importunate,—
My earthly good, temptation and a snare,—
Nothing about me but drew somehow down
His hate upon me,—somewhat so excused
1710 Therefore, since hate was thus the truth of him,—
May my evanishment for evermore
Help further to relieve the heart that cast
Such object of its natural loathing forth!
So he was made; he nowise made himself:
1715 I could not love him, but his mother did.
His soul has never lain beside my soul:
But for the unresisting body,—thanks!
He burned that garment spotted by the flesh.
Whatever he touched is rightly ruined: plague
1720 It caught, and disinfection it had craved

see Editorial Notes §   1695| MS:none—none *P1869:*none, none   1700| MS:door—
*P1869:*door,   1704| MS:light,—but *P1869:*light, but   1706| MS:importunate,
*P1869:*importunate,—   1707| MS:snare, *P1869:*snare,—   1713| MS:forth:
*P1869:*forth!   1716| MS:soul, *P1869:*soul;   DC, BrU:soul: *1889:*soul:
1717| MS:thanks— *P1869:*thanks!   1718| MS:flesh! *1889a:*flesh.
1719| MS:ruined—plague *P1869:*ruined: plague   1720| MS:caught and

Still but for Guido; I am saved through him
So as by fire; to him—thanks and farewell!

Even for my babe, my boy, there's safety thence—
From the sudden death of me, I mean: we poor
1725 Weak souls, how we endeavour to be strong!
I was already using up my life,—
This portion, now, should do him such a good,
This other go to keep off such an ill!
The great life; see, a breath and it is gone!
1730 So is detached, so left all by itself
The little life, the fact which means so much.
Shall not God stoop the kindlier to His work,
His marvel of creation, foot would crush,
Now that the hand He trusted to receive
1735 And hold it, lets the treasure fall perforce?
The better; He shall have in orphanage
His own way all the clearlier: if my babe
Outlived the hour—and he has lived two weeks—
It is through God who knows I am not by.
1740 Who is it makes the soft gold hair turn black,
And sets the tongue, might lie so long at rest,
Trying to talk? Let us leave God alone!
Why should I doubt He will explain in time
What I feel now, but fail to find the words?
1745 My babe nor was, nor is, nor yet shall be
Count Guido Franceschini's child at all—
Only his mother's, born of love not hate!
So shall I have my rights in after-time.
It seems absurd, impossible to-day;

_P1869:_caught, and   1722| MS:fire: to   _1869:_fire; to   1725| MS:strong—
_P1869:_strong!   1726| MS:life, _P1869:_life,—   1728| MS:ill, _P1869:_ill!
1729| MS:life,—see _P1869:_life; see   1731| MS:much, _P1869:_much.
1733| MS:creation foot _P1869:_creation, foot   1736| MS:better, He have in
_P1869:_better; He shall have in   1738| MS:Lives out the   _P1869:_Outlive the
_1872:_Outlived   1744| MS:now but < > words—   _P1869:_now, but < > words?
1746| MS:Count Franceschini's _P1869:_Count Guido Franceschini's   1747| MS:hate?—
_P1869:_hate!   1748| MS:after time. _P1869:_after-time.   1750| MS:else not < >

¹⁷⁵⁰ So seems so much else, not explained but known!

Ah! Friends, I thank and bless you every one!
No more now: I withdraw from earth and man
To my own soul, compose myself for God.

Well, and there is more! Yes, my end of breath
¹⁷⁵⁵ Shall bear away my soul in being true!
He is still here, not outside with the world,
Here, here, I have him in his rightful place!
'Tis now, when I am most upon the move,
I feel for what I verily find—again
¹⁷⁶⁰ The face, again the eyes, again, through all,
The heart and its immeasurable love
Of my one friend, my only, all my own,
Who put his breast between the spears and me.
Ever with Caponsacchi! Otherwise
¹⁷⁶⁵ Here alone would be failure, loss to me—
How much more loss to him, with life debarred
From giving life, love locked from love's display,
The day-star stopped its task that makes night morn!
O lover of my life, O soldier-saint,
¹⁷⁷⁰ No work begun shall ever pause for death!
Love will be helpful to me more and more
I' the coming course, the new path I must tread—
My weak hand in thy strong hand, strong for that!
Tell him that if I seem without him now,
¹⁷⁷⁵ That's the world's insight! Oh, he understands!
He is at Civita—do I once doubt
The world again is holding us apart?
He had been here, displayed in my behalf
The broad brow that reverberates the truth,
¹⁷⁸⁰ And flashed the word God gave him, back to man!
I know where the free soul is flown! My fate
Will have been hard for even him to bear:
Let it confirm him in the trust of God,

---

known. *1872:*else, not <> known!   ^{1765|} MS:failure—loss *P1869:*failure, loss
^{1772|} MS:tread, *1889a:*tread—   ^{1778|} MS:here, unfurled in *P1869:*here,
displayed in   ^{1779|} MS:truth *P1869:*truth,   ^{1782|} MS:bear— *P1869:*bear:

Showing how holily he dared the deed!
1785 And, for the rest,—say, from the deed, no touch
Of harm came, but all good, all happiness,
Not one faint fleck of failure! Why explain?
What I see, oh, he sees and how much more!
Tell him,—I know not wherefore the true word
1790 Should fade and fall unuttered at the last—
It was the name of him I sprang to meet
When came the knock, the summons and the end.
"My great heart, my strong hand are back again!"
I would have sprung to these, beckoning across
1795 Murder and hell gigantic and distinct
O' the threshold, posted to exclude me heaven:
He is ordained to call and I to come
Do not the dead wear flowers when dressed for God?
Say,—I am all in flowers from head to foot!
1800 Say,—not one flower of all he said and did,
Might seem to flit unnoticed, fade unknown,
But dropped a seed, has grown a balsam-tree
Whereof the blossoming perfumes the place
At this supreme of moments! He is a priest;
1805 He cannot marry therefore, which is right:
I think he would not marry if he could.
Marriage on earth seems such a counterfeit,
Mere imitation of the inimitable:
In heaven we have the real and true and sure.
1810 'Tis there they neither marry nor are given
In marriage but are as the angels: right,
Oh how right that is, how like Jesus Christ
To say that! Marriage-making for the earth,
With gold so much,—birth, power, repute so much,
1815 Or beauty, youth so much, in lack of these!
Be as the angels rather, who, apart,
Know themselves into one, are found at length

1784| MS:deed: *P1869:*deed! 1790| MS:last,— *P1869:*last— 1796| MS:heaven—
*P1869:*heaven: 1802| MS:seed has *1872:*seed, has 1810| MS:In heaven
§ crossed out and replaced above by two words § 'Tis there 1813| MS:earth
*P1869:*earth, 1815| MS:much in < > these: *P1869:*much, in < > these!

230

Married, but marry never, no, nor give
In marriage; they are man and wife at once
1820 When the true time is: here we have to wait
Not so long neither! Could we by a wish
Have what we will and get the future now,
Would we wish aught done undone in the past?
So, let him wait God's instant men call years;
1825 Meantime hold hard by truth and his great soul,
Do out the duty! Through such souls alone
God stooping shows sufficient of His light
For us i' the dark to rise by. And I rise.

1818| MS:Married but *P1869:*Married, but   1819| MS:marriage, then are
*P1869:*marriage; they are   1820| MS:wait— *P1869:*wait   1824| MS:So let <>
years, *P1869:*So, let <> years;   1826| MS:duty: through *CP1869:*duty! Through

VIII

DOMINUS HYACINTHUS DE ARCHANGELIS

PAUPERUM PROCURATOR

Ah, my Giacinto, he's no ruddy rogue,
Is not Cinone? What, to-day we're eight?
Seven and one's eight, I hope, old curly-pate!
—Branches me out his verb-tree on the slate,
⁵   *Amo -as -avi -atum -are -ans,*
Up to *-aturus,* person, tense, and mood,
Quies me *cum subjunctivo* (I could cry)
And chews Corderius with his morning crust!
Look eight years onward, and he's perched, he's perched
¹⁰ Dapper and deft on stool beside this chair,
Cinozzo, Cinoncello, who but he?
—Trying his milk-teeth on some crusty case
Like this, papa shall triturate full soon
To smooth Papinianian pulp!
                It trots
¹⁵ Already through my head, though noon be now,
Does supper-time and what belongs to eve.
Dispose, O Don, o' the day, first work then play!
—The proverb bids. And "then" means, won't we hold
Our little yearly lovesome frolic feast,
²⁰ Cinuolo's birth-night, Cinicello's own,
That makes gruff January grin perforce!
For too contagious grows the mirth, the warmth
Escaping from so many hearts at once—

---

§ At a number of lines in MS of Book 8 B did not underline the Latin, although all these passages are properly italicized in the first edition. The MS lines are: 516, 590, 904, 906, 909, 918, 919, 925, 926, 931, 933, 936, 947, 949, 950, 952, 960, 1010, 1013, 1186, 1209, 1211, 1274, 1283 (first two words), 1286, 1310, 1409, 1515, (first two words), 1622, 1637, 1639, 1641, 1643, 1644, 1653, 1659, 1661, 1668 (first word), 1678, 1679, 1687 (first two words), 1689, 1690, 1691, 1692, 1695, 1697, 1698, 1708, 1736. §
⁶| MS:to *aturus* <> tense, and   *P1869:*to—*aturus* <> tense, and   ⁷| MS:me *P1869:me* § emended to § me § see Editorial Notes §   ⁹| MS:he's perched, he's perched, *1872:*he's perched, he's perched   ¹²| MS:milk teeth *P1869:*milk-teeth ¹⁴| MS:smooth Papinian pulp! § ¶ § In truth, it *CP1869:*smooth Papinianian pulp! § ¶ § It   ¹⁶| MS:supper time *P1869:*supper-time   ¹⁹| MS:feast *P1869:*feast, ²⁰| MS:Cinozzo's § crossed out and replaced above by § Cinuolo's birth night

When the good wife, buxom and bonny yet,
25 Jokes the hale grandsire,—such are just the sort
To go off suddenly,—he who hides the key
O' the box beneath his pillow every night,—
Which box may hold a parchment (someone thinks)
Will show a scribbled something like a name
30 "Cinino, Ciniccino," near the end,
"To whom I give and I bequeath my lands,
Estates, tenements, hereditaments,
When I decease as honest grandsire ought."
Wherefore—yet this one time again perhaps—
35 Shan't my Orvieto fuddle his old nose!
Then, uncles, one or the other, well i' the world,
May—drop in, merely?—trudge through rain and wind,
Rather! The smell-feasts rouse them at the hint
There's cookery in a certain dwelling-place!
40 Gossips, too, each with keepsake in his poke,
Will pick the way, thrid lane by lantern-light,
And so find door, put galligaskin off
At entry of a decent domicile
Cornered in snug Condotti,—all for love,
45 All to crush cup with Cinucciatolo!
                                        Well,
Let others climb the heights o' the court, the camp!
How vain are chambering and wantonness,
Revel and rout and pleasures that make mad!
Commend me to home-joy, the family board,
50 Altar and hearth! These, with a brisk career,
A source of honest profit and good fame,
Just so much work as keeps the brain from rust,

_P1869:_Cinuolo's birth-night   26| MS:As go   _P1869:_To go   27| MS:night—
_P1869:_night,—   28| _P1869:_some one   _1889a:_someone   29| MS:That § crossed out
and replaced in left margin by § May shows   _P1869:_Will show   33| MS:grandsire
should § crossed out and replaced above by § ought:"   _1872:_ought."   34| MS:again
perchance § altered to § perhaps   35| MS:Sha'n't   _1889a:_Shan't   38| MS:smell
feasts rouze   _P1869:_smell-feasts rouse   39| MS:certain domicile § crossed out §
dwelling-place: _P1869:_dwelling-place!   41| MS:pick their § altered to § the
42| MS:so reach § crossed out and replaced above by § find door § crossed out and then
restored §   43| MS:a comfortable house § last two words crossed out §   45| MS:All
§ inserted in margin § To § altered to § to <> a § crossed out §   52| MS:the heart

Just so much play as lets the heart expand,
Honouring God and serving man,—I say,
55   These are reality, and all else,— fluff,
Nutshell and naught,—thank Flaccus for the phrase!
Suppose I had been Fisc, yet bachelor!

Why, work with a will, then! Wherefore lazy now?
Turn up the hour-glass, whence no sand-grain slips
60   But should have done its duty to the saint
O' the day, the son and heir that's eight years old!
Let law come dimple Cinoncino's cheek,
And Latin dumple Cinarello's chin,
The while we spread him fine and toss him flat
65   This pulp that makes the pancake, trim our mass
Of matter into Argument the First,
Prime Pleading in defence of our accused,
Which, once a-waft on paper wing, shall soar,
Shall signalize before applausive Rome
70   What study, and mayhap some mother-wit,
Can do toward making Master fop and Fisc
Old bachelor Bottinius bite his thumb.

Now, how good God is! How falls plumb to point
This murder, gives me Guido to defend
75   Now, of all days i' the year, just when the boy
Verges on Virgil, reaches the right age
For some such illustration from his sire,
Stimulus to himself! One might wait years
And never find the chance which now finds me!

---

§ crossed out and replaced above by § brain   ^{55|} MS:reality—and   *P1869:*reality, and
^{57|} MS:Suppose I had § written over word, perhaps *were* § the § crossed out and replaced
above by § been Fisc, and § crossed out and replaced above by § yet   ^{58|} MS:§ new ¶
noted in margin §   ^{59|} MS:hourglass whence no sandgrain *P1869:*hour-glass, whence
no sand-grain   ^{69|} MS:signalise *1889a:*signalize   ^{71|} MS:towards making
Master fribble § uncertain; crossed out and replaced above by § fop *P1869:*toward
^{72|} MS:Old bachelor § last two words inserted in margin § <> thumb. nail to the blood.
§ last four words and period crossed out §   ^{72–73|} MS:§ ¶ § *P1869:*§ no ¶ § *1889:*
§ no ¶; emended to restored ¶; see Editorial Notes §   ^{75|} MS:Now—of <> year—just
*P1869:*Now, of <> year, just   ^{76|} MS:Virges on Virgil—reaches *P1869:*Verges on

235

⁸⁰ The fact is, there's a blessing on the hearth,
A special providence for fatherhood!
Here's a man, and what's more, a noble, kills
—Not sneakingly but almost with parade—
Wife's father and wife's mother and wife's self
⁸⁵ That's mother's self of son and heir (like mine!)
—And here stand I, the favoured advocate,
Who pluck this flower o' the field, no Solomon
Was ever clothed in glorious gold to match,
And set the same in Cinoncino's cap!
⁹⁰ I defend Guido and his comrades—I!
Pray God, I keep me humble: not to me—
Non nobis, Domine, sed tibi laus!
How the fop chuckled when they made him Fisc!
We'll beat you, my Bottinius, all for love,
⁹⁵ All for our tribute to Cinotto's day.
Why, 'sbuddikins, old Innocent himself
May rub his eyes at the bustle,—ask "What's this
Rolling from out the rostrum, as a gust
O' the *Pro Milone* had been prisoned there,
¹⁰⁰ And rattled Rome awake?" Awaken Rome,
How can the Pope doze on in decency?
He needs must wake up also, speak his word,
Have his opinion like the rest of Rome,
About this huge, this hurly-burly case:
¹⁰⁵ He wants who can excogitate the truth,
Give the result in speech, plain black and white,
To mumble in the mouth and make his own

Virgil, reaches   ⁸⁰| MS:hearth— *P1869:*hearth,   ⁸⁷| MS:plucks § altered
to § pluck   ⁸⁹| MS:in Cinarello's § crossed out and replaced above by §
Cinoncino's   ⁹¹| MS:§ crowded between 90-92 § I hope § crossed out and replaced in
margin by § Pray God I   *P1869:*Pray God, I   ⁹³| MS:§ inserted in right margin with
arrow indicating place in text §   ⁹⁵| MS:day!   *1889a:*day.   ⁹⁸| MS:a gust § written
over illegible word §   ¹⁰⁰| MS:awake?" If § crossed out § Rome § followed by marking,
perhaps punctuation mark, illegibly crossed out § awaken § altered to § Awaken § indication
that order of last two words should be reversed §   ¹⁰²| MS:also, say § crossed out and
replaced above by § speak his say § crossed out and replaced above by § word,
¹⁰³| MS:Give § crossed out and replaced above by § Have <> of Rome   *P1869:*of Rome,
¹⁰⁴| MS:huge, and § crossed out and replaced above by § this hurly burly case—
*P1869:*hurly-burly case: ¹⁰⁶| MS:in speech, § inserted above line § plain words § crossed

—A little changed, good man, a little changed!
No matter, so his gratitude be moved,
110 By when my Giacintino gets of age,
Mindful of who thus helped him at a pinch,
Archangelus *Procurator Pauperum*—
And proved Hortensius *Redivivus!*
                              Whew!
To earn the *Est-est*, merit the minced herb
115 That mollifies the liver's leathery slice,
With here a goose-foot, there a cock's-comb stuck,
Cemented in an element of cheese!
I doubt if dainties do the grandsire good:
Last June he had a sort of strangling . . . bah!
120 He's his own master, and his will is made.
So, liver fizz, law flit and Latin fly
As we rub hands o'er dish by way of grace!
May I lose cause if I vent one word more
Except,—with fresh-cut quill we ink the white,—
125 *P-r-o-pro Guidone et Sociis.* There!

Count Guido married—or, in Latin due,
What? *Duxit in uxorem?*—commonplace!
Tædas jugales iniit, subiit,—ha!
He underwent the matrimonial torch?
130 *Connubio stabili sibi junxit,*—hum!
In stable bond of marriage bound his own?

---

out § <> white *P1869:*white,   108| MS:man, a little changed!— *P1869:*man, a little
changed!   109-10| MS:§ crowded between 108-11 §   109| MS:moved,—
*P1869:*moved,   112| MS:§ crowded between lines 111-13 §   113| MS:proved
Hortensius Redivivus! § ¶ § Come § crossed out §   116| MS:goose-foot *1872:*goose foot
*1889a:*goose-foot   117| MS:cheese— *P1869:*cheese!   118-20| MS:§ in right
margin with arrow indicating place in text §   119| MS:a sort of § last two words inserted
above line § strangling seizure § crossed out § . . . . . . bah! *P1869:*strangling . . . bah!
121| MS:So, § inserted in margin § How shall the § last three words crossed out and replaced
above by two words and comma § liver fizz, Law <> and the § crossed out § *P1869:*law
123| MS:if I say § crossed out and replaced above by § vent   124| MS:§ crowded between
123-25 § Except § inserted in margin § Thus then § last two words crossed out §   126| MS:
§ marginal note that new ¶ begins § in Latin, say § comma and last word crossed out and
replaced above by § due,   127| MS:What? § inserted in margin § *uxorem?*—which sounds
§ last two words crossed out §   128| MS:*iniit—subiit,*—ha! *P1869:iniit, subiit,*—ha!
131| MS:bound he § crossed out § his § over perhaps *was* § own— *P1869:*own?

That's clear of any modern taint: and yet . . .

Virgil is little help to who writes prose.
He shall attack me Terence with the dawn,
135   Shall Cinuccino! Mum, mind business, Sir!

Thus circumstantially evolve we facts,
Ita se habet ideo series facti:
He wedded,—ah, with owls for augury!
Nupserat, heu sinistris avibus,
140   One of the blood Arezzo boasts her best,
Dominus Guido, nobili genere ortus,
Pompiliæ . . .

          But the version afterward!
Curb we this ardour! Notes alone, to-day,
The speech to-morrow and the Latin last:
145   Such was the rule in Farinacci's time.
Indeed I hitched it into verse and good.
Unluckily, law quite absorbs a man,
Or else I think I too had poetized.
"Law is the pork substratum of the fry,
150   Goose-foot and cock's-comb are Latinity,"—
And in this case, if circumstance assist,
We'll garnish law with idiom, never fear!
Out-of-the-way events extend our scope:
For instance, when Bottini brings his charge,
155   "That letter which you say Pompilia wrote,—
To criminate her parents and herself
And disengage her husband from the coil,—

133| MS:§ crowded between 132-34; § marginal note that new ¶ begins § prose—
*P1869:*prose.   135-36| MS:§ ¶ §   *P1869:*§ no ¶ §   *1889:*§ no ¶; emended to restore ¶; see
Editorial Notes §   138| MS:ah, the § crossed out and replaced above by § with owls
was § crossed out and replaced above by § for   142| MS:Pompiliæ . . . § marginal
note that new ¶ begins § But the Latin § crossed out and replaced above by § version
143| MS:today, *P1869:*to-day,   144| MS:the version § crossed out and replaced above
by § Latin last— *P1869:*last: 145| MS:time, *P1869:*time.   146| MS:§ crowded
between 145-49 § good: *P1869:*good.   147-48| MS:§ written in right margin §
147| MS:man *P1869:*man,   148| MS:poetized: *P1869:*poetized.   149| MS:of the
dish § crossed out §   150| MS:cock's comb *P1869:*cock's-comb   152| MS:garnish
all § crossed out and replaced above by § law   153| MS:extend the § crossed out and
replaced above by § our   154| MS:charge *P1869:*charge,   155| MS:—"That <>

That, Guido Franceschini wrote, say we:
Because Pompilia could nor read nor write,
160 Therefore he pencilled her such letter first,
Then made her trace in ink the same again."
—Ha, my Bottini, have I thee on hip?
How will he turn this and break Tully's pate?
"*Existimandum*" (don't I hear the dog!)
165 "*Quod Guido designaverit elementa*
Dictæ epistolæ, quæ fuerint
(Superinducto ab ea calamo)
Notata atramento"—there's a style!—
"*Quia ipsa scribere nesciebat.*" Boh!
170 Now, my turn! Either, *Insulse!* (I outburst)
Stupidly put! Inane is the response,
Inanis est responsio, or the like—
To-wit, that each of all those characters,
Quod singula elementa epistolæ,
175 Had first of all been traced for her by him,
Fuerant per eum prius designata,
And then, the ink applied a-top of that,
Et deinde, superinducto calamo,
The piece, she says, became her handiwork,
180 *Per eam, efformata, ut ipsa asserit.*
Inane were such response! (a second time:)
Her husband outlined her the whole, forsooth?
Vir ejus lineabat epistolam?
What, she confesses that she wrote the thing,
185 *Fatetur eam scripsisse,* (scorn that scathes!)
That she might pay obedience to her lord?
Ut viro obtemperaret, apices

---

wrote, *P1869:*"That *1889a:*wrote,—   158| MS:wrote, we say— § indication that order
of last two words should be reversed § *P1869:*we: 160| MS:her the § crossed out
and replaced by § such   161| MS:trace the <> again in ink." § transposed to § trace in
ink the <> again."   163| MS:this nor break *1872:*this and break
164| MS:dog?) *P1869:*dog!)   170| MS:turn! Either, "*Insulse!*" § quotation marks
imperfectly erased § —I outburst, *P1872:*turn! Either, *Insulse!* (I outburst)
171| MS:put! Inane was § crossed out and replaced above by § is   179| MS:handiwork,
*P1869:*handiwork,   184| MS:So, she <> thing— *P1869:*What, she <> thing,
185| MS:*scripsisse,* (§ there follows an obliterated word, perhaps *in* §   186| MS:lord,

(Here repeat charge with proper varied phrase)
Eo designante, ipsaque calamum
190 *Super inducente?* By such argument,
Ita pariter, she seeks to show the same,
(Ay, by Saint Joseph and what saints you please)
Epistolam ostendit, medius fidius,
No voluntary deed but fruit of force!
195 *Non voluntarie sed coacte scriptam!*
That's the way to write Latin, friend my Fisc!
Bottini is a beast, one barbarous:
Look out for him when he attempts to say
"Armed with a pistol, Guido followed her!"
200 Will not I be beforehand with my Fisc,
Cut away phrase by phrase from underfoot!
Guido Pompiliam—Guido thus his wife
Following with igneous engine, shall I have?
Armis munitus igneis persequens—
205 *Arma sulphurea gestans,* sulphury arms,
Or, might one style a pistol—popping-piece?
Armatus breviori sclopulo?
We'll let him have been armed so, though it make
Somewhat against us: I had thought to own—
210 Provided with a simple travelling-sword,
Ense solummodo viatorio
Instructus: but we'll grant the pistol here:
Better we lost the cause than lacked the gird
At the Fisc's Latin, lost the Judge's laugh!
215 It's Venturini that decides for style.
Tommati rather goes upon the law.
So, as to law,—

Ah, but with law ne'er hope

---

*P1869:*lord?   191| MS:*pariter*—She § over illegible word § <> same   *P1869:*pariter,
she <> same,   192| MS:Ay <> please,   *P1869:*(Ay <> please)   194| MS:force,
*P1869:*force!   199| MS:her"! *P1869:*her!"   203| MS:shall I say § crossed out and
replaced above by § have?   205| MS:*gestans*—sulphury arms—   *P1869:gestans,*
sulphury arms,   206| MS:Or—might <> popping-piece   *P1869:*Or, might <>
popping-piece?   210| MS:travelling-sword   *P1869:*travelling-sword,   214| MS:the
Fisk's Latin, with § uncertain; crossed out and replaced above by § lost   215| MS:that
observes on § last two words crossed out and replaced above by two words § decides for
216| MS:§ crowded between lines 215-17 §   217| MS:Then § crossed out and replaced in

240

To level the fellow,—don't I know his trick!
How he draws up, ducks under, twists aside!
220 He's a lean-gutted hectic rascal, fine
As pale-haired red-eyed ferret which pretends
'Tis ermine, pure soft snow from tail to snout.
He eludes law by piteous looks aloft,
Lets Latin glance off as he makes appeal
225 To saint that's somewhere in the ceiling-top:
Do you suppose I don't conceive the beast?
Plague of the ermine-vermin! For it takes,
It takes, and here's the fellow Fisc, you see,
And Judge, you'll not be long in seeing next!
230 Confound the fop—he's now at work like me:
Enter his study, as I seem to do,
Hear him read out his writing to himself!
I know he writes as if he spoke: I hear
The hoarse shrill throat, see shut eyes, neck shot-forth,
235 —I see him strain on tiptoe, soar and pour
Eloquence out, nor stay nor stint at all—
Perorate in the air, then quick to press
With the product! What abuse of type and sheet!
He'll keep clear of my cast, my logic-throw,
240 Let argument slide, and then deliver swift
Some bowl from quite an unguessed point of stand—
Having the luck o' the last word, the reply!
A plaguy cast, a mortifying stroke:

---

margin by § So, as to law,—ah but   *P1869:*law,— § ¶ § Ah, but   221| MS:As the
§ crossed out § <> ferret, which   *P1869:*ferret which   225| MS:—To the saint <>
ceiling-top,—   *P1869:*To   *1872:*To saint   *1889a:*ceiling-top: 226| MS:§ crowded
between 225-27 § MS:suppose that I don't see the   *1872:*suppose I don't conceive the
227| MS:ermine-vermine, for it takes—   *P1869:*ermine-vermin! For it takes,
228| MS:The trick § last two words crossed out and replaced above by § It takes—and
*P1869:*It takes, and   230| MS:Follow § crossed out and replaced above by § Confound
the fellow § crossed out and replaced above by § fop—he's now § inserted above line §
232| MS:himself—   *P1869:*himself!   235| MS:—They say § crossed out and replaced
above by §—I see he strains § altered to § strain <> soars § altered to § soar and pours § altered
to § pour   *P1869:*see him strain   236| MS:stays § altered to § stay nor stints § altered to §
stint   237| MS:Perorates § altered to § Perorate in § over illegible word § <> air, and all
in § last two words crossed out and replaced above by two words § so, to press! § over illegible
erasure §   *P1869:*press   *1872:*air, then quick to   238| MS:§ crowded between 237-39 §
product: what <> type is here!   *P1869:*product! What   *1872:*type and sheet!
239| MS:logics's throw, § altered to § logic-throw,   240| MS:argument run § crossed out
and replaced above by § slide   241| MS:stand,—   *P1869:*stand—   243| MS:stroke,

You face a fellow—cries "So, there you stand?
²⁴⁵   But I discourteous jump clean o'er your head!
You take ship-carpentry for pilotage,
Stop rat-holes, while a sea sweeps through the breach,—
Hammer and fortify at puny points?
Do, clamp and tenon, make all tight and safe!
²⁵⁰   'Tis here and here and here you ship a sea,
No good of your stopped leaks and littleness!"

Yet what do I name "little and a leak"?
The main defence o' the murder's used to death,
By this time, dry bare bones, no scrap we pick:
²⁵⁵   Safer I worked the new, the unforeseen,
The nice by-stroke, the fine and improvised
Point that can titillate the brain o' the Bench
Torpid with over-teaching, long ago!
As if Tommati (that has heard, reheard
²⁶⁰   And heard again, first this side and then that—
Guido and Pietro, Pietro and Guido, din
And deafen, full three years, at each long ear)
Don't want amusement for instruction now,
Won't rather feel a flea run o'er his ribs,
²⁶⁵   Than a daw settle heavily on his head!

---

*P1869:*stroke: ²⁴⁵| MS:But § over illegible word §   ²⁴⁶| MS:You act § crossed out and replaced above by § play ship-carpenter, not pilot now § crossed out and replaced above by § so,—   *1872:*You take ship-carpentry for pilotage,   ²⁴⁷| MS:sea-sweeps <>
breach—   *P1869:*sea sweeps <> breach,—   ²⁴⁸| MS:points! *1889a:*points?
²⁴⁹| MS:safe, *P1869:*safe!   ²⁵⁰| MS:and here and here § last two words inserted above line §   ²⁵¹| MS:littleness! *P1869:*littleness!"   ²⁵¹⁻⁵²| MS:§ no ¶ § *P1869:*§ ¶ §
²⁵²| MS:leak?" *1889a:*leak"?   ²⁵³| MS:murder's known by now, § last three words and comma crossed out and replaced above by three words and comma § used to death,
²⁵⁴| MS:§ crowded between 253-55 § scrap to pick— *P1869:*pick: *1872:*scrap we pick:
²⁵⁵| MS:worked at the usual § crossed out and replaced below by two words § new, the
unforseen *P1869:*unforeseen *1872:*worked the   ²⁵⁶| MS:bye-stroke <> improvised,
*1872:*improvised *1889a:*by-stroke   ²⁵⁷| MS:Points *P1869:*Point
²⁵⁸| MS:over-teaching, by this time! *P1869:*time! *1872:*over-teaching, long ago!
²⁵⁹| MS:if Tommati, that *1872:*if Tommati (that   ²⁶⁰| MS:again, now § crossed out and replaced above by § first <> and now § crossed out and replaced above by § then that,—
*1872:*that—   ²⁶¹| MS:and Guido din *1872:*and Guido, din   ²⁶²| MS:And deafen these § crossed out § <> years, with the case § last three words crossed out and replaced above by four words § at each long ear, *P1869:*ear,— *1872:*ear)
²⁶³| MS:now— *P1869:*now,   ²⁶⁴| MS: flea skip § crossed out and replaced above by § run   ²⁶⁵| MS:Than an owl § last two words crossed out and replaced above by two

242

Oh I was young and had the trick of fence,
Knew subtle pass and push with careless right—
My left arm ever quiet behind back,
With dagger ready: not both hands to blade!
270   Puff and blow, put the strength out, Blunderbore!
There's my subordinate, young Spreti, now,
Pedant and prig,—he'll pant away at proof,
That's his way!

            Now for mine—to rub some life
Into one's choppy fingers this cold day!
275   I trust Cinuzzo ties on tippet, guards
The precious throat on which so much depends!
Guido must be all goose-flesh in his hole,
Despite the prison-straw: bad Carnival
For captives! no sliced fry for him, poor Count!

280   Carnival-time,—another providence!
The town a-swarm with strangers to amuse,
To edify, to give one's name and fame
In charge of, till they find, some future day,
Cintino come and claim it, his name too,
285   Pledge of the pleasantness they owe papa—
Who else was it cured Rome of her great qualms,
When she must needs have her own judgment?—ay,
When all her topping wits had set to work,

---

words § a daw < > his pate § crossed out and replaced above by § head!   ²⁶⁶| MS:Oh, I
*1889a:*Oh I   ²⁶⁸| MS:The left < > quietly < > back   *1872:*My left < > quiet < >
back,   ²⁶⁹| MS:With the dagger in't: not   *1872:*With dagger ready: not
²⁷¹| MS:That's my < > young Spreti now,   *P1869:*young Spreti, now,   *1872:*There's my
²⁷³| MS:way! § marginal note that new ¶ begins §   ²⁷⁵| MS:trust Cinuzzo puts
§ crossed out and replaced above by § ties on cloak and cape § last three words crossed out and
replaced above by two words and punctuation § tippet, guards   ²⁷⁶| MS:§ crowded
between 275-77 §   ²⁷⁷| MS:must show § crossed out § < > hole   *P1869:*hole,
²⁷⁸| MS:bad carnival   *P1869:*bad Carnival   ²⁷⁹| MS:No < > poor dog!   *P1869:*no
< > poor Count!   ²⁸⁰| MS:§ marginal note that new ¶ begins § providence!—
*P1869:*providence!   ²⁸²| MS:name to § erased §   ²⁸³| MS:until § altered to § till
< > day   *P1869:*day,   ²⁸⁵| MS:the gratitude § crossed out and replaced above by §
pleasantness < > Papa!—   *P1869:*papa—   ²⁸⁶| MS:Asks § crossed out § Who it
§ altered to § else was it, cured < > qualms?   *P1869:*qualms,   *1872:*it cured
²⁸⁷| MS:judgment,—ay,   *P1869:*judgment?—ay   *1872:*ay,   ²⁸⁸| MS:Since all

Pronounced already on the case: mere boys,
290   Twice Cineruggiolo's age with half his sense,
As good as tell me, when I cross the court,
"Master Arcangeli!" (plucking at my gown)
"We can predict, we comprehend your play,
We'll help you save your client." Tra-la-la!
295   I've travelled ground, from childhood to this hour,
To have the town anticipate my track?
The old fox takes the plain and velvet path,
The young hound's predilection,—prints the dew,
Don't he, to suit their pulpy pads of paw?
300   No! Burying nose deep down i' the briery bush,
Thus I defend Count Guido.

                                   Where are we weak?
First, which is foremost in advantage too,
Our murder,—we call, killing,—is a fact
Confessed, defended, made a boast of: good!
305   To think the Fisc claimed use of torture here,
And got thereby avowal plump and plain
That gives me just the chance I wanted,—scope
Not for brute-force but ingenuity,
Explaining matters, not denying them!
310   One may dispute,—as I am bound to do,
And shall,—validity of process here:
Inasmuch as a noble is exempt
From torture which plebeians undergo
In such a case: for law is lenient, lax,
315   Remits the torture to a nobleman
Unless suspicion be of twice the strength

---

*1872:*When all   289| MS:boys—   *P1869:*boys,   290| MS:age and half his
sense—   *P1869:*sense,   *1872:*age with half   291| MS:tell § followed by word illegibly
crossed out and replaced above by § me   292| MS:"Master Arcangeli!"—plucking < >
gown—   *P1869:*"Master Arcangeli!" (plucking < > gown)   293| MS:predict, we
understand § crossed out and replaced above by § comprehend   295| MS:childhood till
this hour   *P1869:*hour,   *1872:*childhood to this   296| MS:track!   *1889a:*track?
297| MS:plain, the § comma and last word crossed out and replaced above by § and < > path
*P1869:*path,   300| MS:bush   *P1869:*bush,   301| MS:Thus I § crossed out and
replaced above by § we   *P1869:*Thus I   302| MS:is foremost § over illegible erasure §
303| MS:The § crossed out and replaced in margin by § Our < > fact.   *P1869:*fact
305| MS:here   *P1869:*here,   309| MS:them.   *P1869:*them!   310| MS:do,—
*P1869:*do,   311| MS:of the § crossed out §   314| MS:is very clear § last two words

Attaches to a man born vulgarly:
We don't card silk with comb that dresses wool.
Moreover 'twas severity undue
320 In this case, even had the lord been lout.
What utters, on this head, our oracle,
Our Farinacci, my Gamaliel erst,
In those immortal "Questions"? This I quote:
"Of all the tools at Law's disposal, sure
325 That named *Vigiliarum* is the best—
That is, the worst—to whoso needs must bear:
Lasting, as it may do, from some seven hours
To ten; (beyond ten, we've no precedent;
Certain have touched their ten, but, bah, they died!)
330 It does so efficaciously convince,
That,—speaking by much observation here,—
Out of each hundred cases, by my count,
Never I knew of patients beyond four
Withstand its taste, or less than ninety-six
335 End by succumbing: only martyrs four,
Of obstinate silence, guilty or no,—against
Ninety-six full confessors, innocent
Or otherwise,—so shrewd a tool have we!"
No marvel either: in unwary hands,
340 Death on the spot is no rare consequence:
As indeed all but happened in this case
To one of ourselves, our young tough peasant-friend

---

crossed out and replaced above by § lenient, lax   *P1869:*lax,   318| MS:dresses flax.
*P1869:*dresses wool.   319| MS:Moreover, 'twas undue severity § indication that order of
last two words should be reversed §   *1889a:*Moreover 'twas   322| MS:My § crossed out
and replaced in margin by § Our   323| MS:immortal "Questions"? What I § last two
words over illegible erasure §   *1872:*immortal "Questions"? This I
324| MS:disposal—sure   *P1869:*disposal, sure   326| MS:whoso has to bear:
*1872:*whoso needs must bear: 328| MS:ten,—beyond ten, there's § crossed out and
replaced above by § we've no precedent—   *P1869:*ten, (beyond <> precedent;   *1872:*ten;
(beyond   329| MS:§ crowded between 328-30 § ten but, bah—they died—   *P1869:*bah,
they died!)   *1889a:*ten, but   330| MS:convince   *1872:*convince,   333| MS:Never
have § crossed out § I known § altered to § knew   334| MS:That could § last two words
crossed out § withstand § altered to § Withstand its taste § last two words inserted above line §
—or   *P1869:*taste, or   335| MS:That § crossed out § ended § altered to § End by
succumbing: only § inserted above line §   340| MS:consequence.   *P1869:*consequence:

245

The accomplice called Baldeschi: they were rough,
Dosed him with torture as you drench a horse,
345 Not modify your treatment to a man:
So, two successive days he fainted dead,
And only on the third essay, gave up,
Confessed like flesh and blood. We could reclaim,—
Blockhead Bottini giving cause enough!
350 But no,—we'll take it as spontaneously
Confessed: we'll have the murder beyond doubt.
Ah, fortunate (the poet's word reversed)
Inasmuch as we know our happiness!
Had the antagonist left dubiety,
355 Here were we proving murder a mere myth,
And Guido innocent, ignorant, absent,—ay,
Absent! He was—why, where should Christian be?—
Engaged in visiting his proper church,
The duty of us all at Christmas-time,
360 When Caponsacchi, the seducer, stung
To madness by his relegation, cast
About him and contrived a remedy
In murder: since opprobrium broke afresh,
By birth o' the babe, on him the imputed sire,
365 He it was quietly sought to smother up
His shame and theirs together,—killed the three,
And fled—(go seek him where you please to search)—
Just at the time when Guido, touched by grace,
Devotions ended, hastened to the spot,
370 Meaning to pardon his convicted wife,

343| MS:called Baldeschi,—they *P1869:*called Baldeschi: they   344| MS:horse
*P1869:*horse,   345| MS:man, *P1869:*man: 346| MS:So two *P1869:*So, two
347| MS:up *P1869:*up,   349| MS:The § crossed out § blockhead § altered to § Blockhead
Bottini § inserted above line § < > enough! But no! § last two words crossed out §
350| MS:But no,— § inserted in margin § < > as confessed § crossed out §
351| MS:§ crowded between 350-52 § murder § followed by illegible erasure §
352| MS:Ah fortunate *P1869:*Ah, fortunate   354| MS:left a shade of doubt § last three
words crossed out § dubiety *P1869:*left dubiety,   356| MS:absent, ay
*P1869:*absent,—ay,   358| MS:Church, *P1869:*church,   359| *P1869:*at
Christmas-time; *1872:*at Christmas-time,   362| MS:remedy: *1872:*remedy
363| MS:To stave off the opprobrium broke-afresh, *P1869:*off what opprobrium broke
afresh, *1872:*To murder: since opprobrium   364| MS:By the birth *1872:*By birth
365| MS:He came and quietly *1872:*He it was quietly   366| MS:three *P1869:*three,
368| MS:the moment, Guido *1872:*the time when Guido   370| MS:wife— *P1869:*wife,

"Neither do I condemn thee, go in peace!"—
And thus arrived i' the nick of time to catch
The charge o' the killing, though great-heartedly
He came but to forgive and bring to life.
375 Doubt ye the force of Christmas on the soul?
"Is thine eye evil because mine is good?"

So, doubtless, had I needed argue here
But for the full confession round and sound!
Thus might you wrong some kingly alchemist,—
380 Whose concern should not be with showing brass
Transmuted into gold, but triumphing,
Rather, about his gold changed out of brass,
Not vulgarly to the mere sight and touch,
But in the idea, the spiritual display,
385 The apparition buoyed by winged words
Hovering above its birth-place in the brain,—
Thus would you wrong this excellent personage
Forced, by the gross need, to gird apron round,
Plant forge, light fire, ply bellows,—in a word,

372| MS:And you § crossed out and replaced above by two words § Who thus _1872:_And
thus   373| MS:The § inserted in margin § charged § altered to § charge with § crossed
out § o' § apparently added in revision § the killing, who § crossed out and replaced above
by § though great heartedly _P1869:_great-heartedly   374| MS:He § inserted in margin §
Came rather § crossed out and replaced above by § but <> life: _P1869:_came <> life.
376–77| MS:§ no ¶ § _P1869:_§ ¶ §   377| MS:had we § crossed out and replaced above
by § I   378| MS:But § B over illegible letter §   379| MS:Thus § crossed out and
replaced above by § So would you have the § crossed out and replaced above by § some <>
alchemist— _P1869:_Thus would <> alchemist,— _1872:_Thus might you wrong some
380| MS:Whose business § crossed out and replaced above by § concern <> with proving
clay § crossed out § brass _1872:_with showing brass   381| MS:Transmutable to gold,
but triumphing _P1869:_triumphing, _1872:_Transmuted into gold   382| MS:Rather,
above his <> of clay § crossed out § _1872:_Rather, about his   383| MS:the gross §
crossed out and replaced above by § mere <> touch _P1869:_touch,   385| MS:Proud
apparition _1872:_The apparition   386| MS:brain— _P1869:_brain,—
387| MS:Here would you have this _1872:_Thus would you wrong this
388| MS:Forced by the vulgar § crossed out and replaced above by two words § gross need
to tie § crossed out and replaced above by § gird <> round _P1869:_Forced, by <> need,
to <> round,   389| MS:light coal § crossed out and replaced above by § fire

390 Demonstrate: when a faulty pipkin's crack
May disconcert you his presumptive truth!
Here were I hanging to the testimony
Of one of these poor rustics—four, ye gods!
Whom the first taste of friend the Fiscal's cord
395 May drive into undoing my whole speech,
Undoing, on his birthday,—what is worse,—
My son and heir!

        I wonder, all the same,
Not so much at those peasants' lack of heart;
But—Guido Franceschini, nobleman,
400 Bear pain no better! Everybody knows
It used once, when my father was a boy,
To form a proper, nay, important point
I' the education of our well-born youth,
That they took torture handsomely at need,
405 Without confessing in this clownish guise.
Each noble had his rack for private use,
And would, for the diversion of a guest,
Bid it be set up in the yard of arms,
And take thereon his hour of exercise,—
410 Command the varletry stretch, strain their best,
While friends looked on, admired my lord could smile
'Mid tugging which had caused an ox to roar.

390| MS:Demonstrate—when *1872:*Demonstrate: when   391| MS:disconcert you
§ inserted above line § his whole § crossed out §   392| MS:Here might § crossed out and
replaced above by § were   393| MS:poor animals § crossed out and replaced above by §
rustics—there are five § last three words crossed out and replaced above by three words and
punctuation § four, ye gods!   395-97| MS:Might twist § crossed out and replaced above
by § drive into unsaying § crossed out and replaced above by § undoing <> speech,—/
Shaming truth so! § ¶ § I   *P1869:*speech,   *1872:*May drive <> / Undoing, on his
birthday,—what is worse,—/ My son and heir! § ¶ § I   398| MS:Not so much § last
two words inserted above line § at those wretched animals § last two words crossed out §
399| MS:But—Guido to confess, a § last three words crossed out and replaced above by §
Franceschini   402| MS:proper, an § altered to § nay   403| MS:our noble § crossed
out and replaced above by § well-born youth *P1869:*youth,   404| MS:To take § inserted
above line § the torture dumbly § crossed out and replaced above by § handsomely *1872:*That
they took torture   405| MS:guise: *P1869:*guise.   406| MS:Each noble § inserted
above line § had a rack built § crossed out § for his § crossed out §   *P1869:*had his rack
407| MS:guest *P1869:*guest,   409| MS:And § crossed out and replaced in margin
by § To take <> exercise, *P1869:*exercise,— *1872:*And take   410| MS:stretch,
and § crossed out § <> best *P1869:*best,   412| MS:caused a lout § crossed

Men are no longer men!

—And advocates
No longer Farinacci, let us add,
415   If I one more time fly from point proposed!
So, *Vindicatio,*—here begins the speech!—
Honoris causa; thus we make our stand:
Honour in us had injury, we prove.
Or if we fail to prove such injury
420   More than misprision of the fact,—what then?
It is enough, authorities declare,
If the result, the deed in question now,
Be caused by confidence that injury
Is veritable and no figment: since,
425   What, though proved fancy afterward, seemed fact
At the time, they argue shall excuse result.
That which we do, persuaded of good cause
For what we do, hold justifiable!—
So casuists bid: man, bound to do his best,
430   They would not have him leave that best undone
And mean to do his worst,—though fuller light
Show best was worst and worst would have been best.
Act by the present light!—they ask of man.

out and replaced above by § ox   *P1869:*caused an ox   413| MS:longer men—
§ marginal note that new ¶ begins § And, § over *not* § advocates   *P1869:*men! § ¶ § —And
advocates   414| MS:longer Farinacci, one might § last two words crossed out and
replaced above by two words § let men add,   *1872:*let us add,   416| MS:So—
Vindicatio <> the same!,—   *P1869:*So, *Vindicatio* <> same!—   *1872:*the speech!—
417| *P1869:*causa; so we   *1872:*causa; thus we   418| MS:Honor <> we shall rove.
*P1869:*Honour   *1872:*we prove.   423| MS:Were § crossed out and replaced above by § Be
<> confidence such injury   *P1869:*confidence that injury   424| MS:Were § over *Was* §
veritable <> figment,—why,   *P1869:*Is veritable <> figment: since,   425| MS:This
§ crossed out and replaced in margin by § What   426| MS:time, I trow § last two words
inserted above line § and shall excuse whatever ensues § last two words crossed out and
replaced above by § result.   *P1869:*time, they argue shall   427| MS:persuaded there is
§ last two words crossed out and replaced above by two words § of good   428| MS:Do,
hold § over illegible word §   429| MS:The casuists   *1889a:*So casuists
430| MS:You § crossed out and replaced in margin by § They   431| MS:And § over
perhaps *So* § meaning § altered to § mean to do the § inserted above line § worst   *1872:*do
his worst   432| MS:and worst was best. Let man   *P1869:*and worst would have
been best.   433| MS:light, they ask no more.   *P1869:*ask of man.   *1872:*light!—they

Ultra quod hic non agitur, besides
435 It is not anyway our business here,
De probatione adulterii,
To prove what we thought crime was crime indeed,
Ad irrogandam pœnam, and require
Its punishment: such nowise do we seek:
440 *Sed ad effectum*, but 'tis our concern,
Excusandi, here to simply find excuse,
Occisorem, for who did the killing-work,
Et ad illius defensionem, (mark
The difference) and defend the man, just that!
445 *Quo casu levior probatio*
Exuberaret, to which end far lighter proof
Suffices than the prior case would claim:
It should be always harder to convict,
In short, than to establish innocence.
450 Therefore we shall demonstrate first of all
That Honour is a gift of God to man
Precious beyond compare: which natural sense
Of human rectitude and purity,—
Which white, man's soul is born with,—brooks no touch:

434| MS:*agitur*—beside *P1869:agitur*, besides   435| MS:here *P1869:*here,
436| MS:*adulterii* *P1869:adulterii*,   438| MS:*pœnam*, § two words illegibly crossed
out §   439| MS:§word illegibly crossed out § at our mode of § last four words crossed
out § Its § added above line § punishment: which § crossed out and replaced above by § such
no-wise *P1869:*nowise   440| MS:*effectum*—but tis our concern *P1869:effectum*,
but 'tis our concern,   441| MS:*Excusandi*—to § crossed out and replaced above by §
here <> excuse *P1869:Excusandi*, here <> excuse,   442| MS:did the § inserted
above line § killing-deed § crossed out and replaced by § killing-work *P1869:*killing-work,
443| MS:*defensionem*,—mark *P1869:defensionem*, (mark   444| MS:difference!,—I
§ crossed out and replaced above by § We defend § next two, perhaps three, words illegibly
crossed out and replaced above by three words § ourselves: just that *P1869:*difference!)
and defend the man, just that. *1872:*difference) and <> that!   446| MS:*Exuberaret*,—
to *P1869:Exuberaret*, to   448-49| MS:§ crowded between 447-50 in continuous
line divided by / between *convict*, and *In* § than to establish § crossed out and then
restored; written above line and crossed out is the partial word § demons
450| MS:shall establish § crossed out and replaced below by § demonstrate
451| MS:That Honor is the § crossed out and replaced above by § a *P1869:*That Honour
452| MS:compare,—the § crossed out and replaced above by § which *1872:*compare: which
453| MS:§ crowded between 452-54 §   454| MS:The § crossed out and replaced in
margin by § Which <> with, bears no specks: § crossed out and replaced above by § touch:

455   Therefore, the sensitivest spot of all,
Wounded by any wafture breathed from black,
Is,—honour within honour, like the eye
Centred i' the ball,—the honour of our wife.
Touch us o' the pupil of our honour, then,
460   Not actually,—since so you slay outright,—
But by a gesture simulating touch,
Presumable mere menace of such taint,—
This were our warrant for eruptive ire
"To whose dominion I impose no end."

465   (Virgil, now, should not be too difficult
To Cinoncino,—say, the early books.
Pen, truce to further gambols! *Poscimur!*)

Nor can revenge of injury done here
To the honour proved the life and soul of us,
470   Be too excessive, too extravagant:
Such wrong seeks and must have complete revenge.
Show we this, first, on the mere natural ground:
Begin at the beginning, and proceed
Incontrovertibly. Theodoric,
475   In an apt sentence Cassiodorus cites,

---

*P1869:*with, brooks no touch: *1872:*with,—brooks   455| MS:And that § last two words crossed out and replaced in margin by § Therefore the <> spot § over illegible erasure § *P1869:*Therefore, the   456| MS:Woundable by a wafture § next four words illegibly crossed out and replaced above by three words and comma § breathed from black, *1872:*Wounded by any wafture   457| MS:That's gross § last two words crossed out; followed by illegible erasure § Is   458| MS:honor of his § crossed out and replaced above by § our wife: *P1869:*honour <> wife.   459| MS:Touch him § crossed out and replaced above by § us <> of his § crossed out and replaced above by § our
460| MS:actually—since so § inserted above line § you slay him § crossed out § outright,— § over illegible word § *P1869:*actually,—since   462| MS:Presumably the menace *P1869:*Presumable mere menace   463| MS:This—this is § dash and last two words crossed out and replaced above by § mere   464| MS:end—" *P1869:*end."
464-65| MS:§ no ¶ § *P1869:*§ ¶ § *1889a:*§ no ¶ § *1889:*§ no ¶; emended to restore ¶; see Editorial Notes §   466| MS:To Cinincino, not § crossed out and replaced above by § —say <> books. . . . *1872:*books.   467-68| MS:§ no ¶ § *P1869:*§ ¶ §
469| MS:§ crowded between 468-70 §   470| MS:extravagant, *1869:*extravagant:
471| MS:It's needs § last two words crossed out and replaced in margin and above by § Such wrong seeks and needs § crossed out §   472| MS:ground. *P1869:*ground:

Propounds for basis of all household law—
I hardly recollect it, but it ends,
"Bird mates with bird, beast genders with his like,
And brooks no interference." Bird and beast?
480 The very insects . . . if they wive or no,
How dare I say when Aristotle doubts?
But the presumption is they likewise wive,
At least the nobler sorts; for take the bee
As instance,—copying King Solomon,—
485 Why that displeasure of the bee to aught
Which savours of incontinency, makes
The unchaste a very horror to the hive?
Whence comes it bees obtain their epithet
Of *castæ apes*, notably "the chaste"?
490 Because, ingeniously saith Scaliger,
(The young sage,—see his book of Table-talk)
"Such is their hatred of immodest act,
They fall upon the offender, sting to death."
I mind a passage much confirmative
495 I' the Idyllist (though I read him Latinized)
"Why" asks a shepherd, "is this bank unfit
For celebration of our vernal loves?"
"Oh swain," returns the instructed shepherdess,
"Bees swarm here, and would quick resent our warmth!"

476| MS:Propounds this § crossed out § for the § crossed out § basis of all § inserted above
line § household-law: *P1869:*household law— 477| MS:§ crowded between 476-78 §
ends— *P1869:*ends, 479| MS:interference:" bird and beast, § altered to § ? say I?
§ last two words and question mark crossed out § *1872:*interference." Bird
482| MS:they marry to § last two words crossed out and replaced above by two words §
likewise wive, 483| MS:sorts, for < > Bee *P1869:*sorts; for < > bee
486| MS:That savors *1872:*Which savors 487| MS:unchaste men the § last two
words crossed out and replaced above by two words § a very horror of § crossed out
and replaced above by § to 488| MS:it they § crossed out and replaced above by §
bees obtain their § altered to § the epithet, *P1869:*epithet *1872:*obtain their epithet
489| MS:Are *castæ apes*? Styled § crossed out and replaced above by § notably *P1869:*Of
castæ 490| MS:Because ingeniously saith Scaliger— *P1869:*Because, ingeniously
saith Scaliger, 491| MS:§ crowded between 490-92 § The young one—see < > of
Table-talk— *P1869:*(The < > of Table-talk) *1872:*young sage,—see 492| MS:act
*P1869:*act, 493| MS:death. *P1869:*death." 495| MS:the Idyllist—though < >
him Latinized— *P1869:*the idyllist (though < > him Latinized) *CP1869:*the Idyllist
496| MS:shepherd "is *P1869:*shepherd, "is 497| MS:our spring-time § crossed out
and replaced above by § vernal 498| MS:"Oh Swain < > the wiser shepherdess,

252

⁵⁰⁰ Only cold-blooded fish lack instinct here,
Nor gain nor guard connubiality:
But beasts, quadrupedal, mammiferous,
Do credit to their beasthood: witness him
That Ælian cites, the noble elephant,
⁵⁰⁵ (Or if not Ælian, somebody as sage)
Who seeing, much offence beneath his nose,
His master's friend exceed in courtesy
The due allowance to his master's wife,
Taught them good manners and killed both at once,
⁵¹⁰ Making his master and the world admire.
Indubitably, then, that master's self,
Favoured by circumstance, had done the same
Or else stood clear rebuked by his own beast.
Adeo, ut qui honorem spernit, thus,
⁵¹⁵ Who values his own honour not a straw,—
Et non recuperare curat, nor
Labours by might and main to salve its wound,
Se ulciscendo, by revenging him,
Nil differat a belluis, is a brute,
⁵²⁰ *Quinimo irrationabilior*
Ipsismet belluis, nay, contrariwise,
Much more irrational than brutes themselves,
Should be considered, *reputetur!* How?
If a poor animal feel honour smart,
⁵²⁵ Taught by blind instinct nature plants in him,
Shall man,—confessed creation's master-stroke,
Nay, intellectual glory, nay, a god,

P1869:"Oh swain   1872:the instructed shepherdess,   ⁵⁰²| MS:beasts, the § crossed
out§quadrupedal   ⁵⁰³| MS:him,   1872:him   ⁵⁰⁶| MS:seeing much   1872:seeing,
much   ⁵⁰⁸| MS:to the § altered to § that master's   P1872:to his master's
⁵⁰⁹| MS:manners, § comma crossed out § and § inserted above line § killing § altered to §
killed < > once   P1869:once,   ⁵¹⁰| MS:and all men admire.   1872:and the world
admire.   ⁵¹¹| MS:Indubitably then that < > self   P1869:Indubitably, then, that
1872:self,   ⁵¹⁴| MS:*spernit,*—thus   P1869:*spernit,* thus,   ⁵¹⁵| MS:honor
P1869:honour   ⁵¹⁶| MS:*non curat recuperare* § transposed to § *recuperare curat*—nor
P1869:*curat,* nor   ⁵¹⁷| MS:to cure its   CP1869:to salve its   ⁵¹⁸| MS:*ulciscendo,*—
by   P1869:*ulciscendo,* by   ⁵¹⁹| MS:*belluis,*—is a brute,—   P1869:*belluis,* is a brute,
⁵²⁰| MS:*irrationabilior,*   P1869:*irrationabilior*   ⁵²¹| MS:*belluis,*—but contrariwise
P1869:*belluis,* nay, contrariwise   CP1869:contrariwise,   ⁵²²| MS:As § crossed out and
replaced in margin by § Much < > than beasts § altered to § brutes   ⁵²⁶| MS:master
piece, § crossed out and replaced above by § -stroke   ⁵²⁷| MS:glory, nay § over illegible

Nay, of the nature of my Judges here,—
Shall man prove the insensible, the block,
530 The blot o' the earth he crawls on to disgrace?
(Come, that's both solid and poetic!) Man
Derogate, live for the low tastes alone,
Mean creeping cares about the animal life?
Absit such homage to vile flesh and blood!

535   (May Gigia have remembered, nothing stings
Fried liver out of its monotony
Of richness, like a root of fennel, chopped
Fine with the parsley: parsley-sprigs, I said—
Was there need I should say "and fennel too"?
540 But no, she cannot have been so obtuse!
To our argument! The fennel will be chopped.)

From beast to man next mount we—ay, but, mind,
Still mere man, not yet Christian,—that, in time!
Not too fast, mark you! 'Tis on Heathen grounds
545 We next defend our act: then, fairly urge—
If this were done of old, in a green tree,
Allowed in the Spring rawness of our kind,
What may be licensed in the Autumn dry
And ripe, the latter harvest-tide of man?
550 If, with his poor and primitive half-lights,
The Pagan, whom our devils served for gods,
Could stigmatise the breach of marriage-vow

word §   531| MS:poetic!) Shall man   *P1869:*poetic)—man   *1872:*poetic!) Man
532-35| MS:alone?— § marginal note that new ¶ begins § May   *P1869:*alone,/ Mean creeping
cares about the animal life?/ § ¶ § May   *1872://Absit,* such homage to vile flesh and blood!/
§ ¶ and indented line § (May   *1889a:Absit* such   536| MS:The § crossed out and
replaced in margin by § Fried   537| MS:richness like   *1872:*richness, like
538| MS:parsley-sprigs I   *P1869:*parsley-sprigs, I   539| MS:§ crowded between 538-40 §
too?"   *1889a:*too"?   541| MS:be found.   *P1869:*be chopped.   *1872:*chopped.)
542| MS:§ marginal note that new ¶ begins §   543| MS:Still § added in margin § Mere
§ altered to § mere man, the § crossed out § not   544| MS:fast, meanwhile: § last word
crossed out and replaced above by two words and exclamation mark § mark you! 'tis
*P1869:*you! 'Tis   545| MS:fairly add § crossed out § urge   *P1869:*urge—
546| MS:tree   *P1869:*tree,   548| *P1869:*dry,   *1872:*dry   549| MS:latter
harvest-tide § over illegible erasure §   550| MS:If—with < > half-lights—   *P1869:*If,
with < > half-lights,   551| MS:The natural Pagan, devils   *P1869:*The Pagan, whom

As that which blood, blood only might efface,—
Absolve the husband, outraged, whose revenge
555 Anticipated law, plied sword himself,—
How with the Christian in full blaze of noon?
Shall not he rather double penalty,
Multiply vengeance, than, degenerate,
Let privilege be minished, droop, decay?
560 Therefore set forth at large the ancient law!
Superabundant the examples be
To pick and choose from. The Athenian Code,
Solon's, the name is serviceable,—then,
The Laws of the Twelve Tables, that fifteenth,—
565 "Romulus" likewise rolls out round and large;
The Julian; the Cornelian; Gracchus' Law:
So old a chime, the bells ring of themselves!
Spreti can set that going if he please,
I point you, for my part, the belfry plain,
570 Intent to rise from dusk, *diluculum*,
Into the Christian day shall broaden next.

First, the fit compliment to His Holiness
Happily reigning: then sustain the point—
All that was long ago declared as law
575 By the natural revelation, stands confirmed
By Apostle and Evangelist and Saint,—
To-wit—that Honour is man's supreme good.

---

our devils   553| MS:only could efface— *P1869:*only might efface,—   556| MS:of
day? *1872:*of noon?   558| MS:degenerate *P1869:*degenerate,
561| MS:Superabundant are § crossed out § the instances § crossed out and replaced above by §
examples   562| MS:from—The *P1869:*from. The   565| MS:Romulus likewise
< > out well § crossed out and replaced above by § round and § over illegible erasure § large.
P1869:"Romulus" likewise *1889a:*large   DC,BrU:large; *1889:*large;   566| MS:The
Julian Law § crossed out § , the § over illegible erasure § Cornelian, Gracchus' statute
§ uncertain; crossed out § Law: *P1869:*The Julian; the Cornelian; Gracchus' Law:
569| MS:point out the belfry, for my part, § indication that should be transposed to read §
point you, § word and comma written above § for my part, the belfry out. *P1869:*out,
*1872:*belfry plain,   571| MS:day will § altered to § shall broaden round § crossed out §
572| MS:§ marginal note that new ¶ begins §   573| MS:reigning,—then < > point,
*P1869:*reigning: then < > point—   574| MS:All § added in margin § That § altered to §
that which § crossed out §   575| MS:the early Revelation, is § crossed out and replaced
above by § stands *1872:*the natural revelation   577| MS:that Honor is the supreme
good: *P1869:*To wit *1869:*To-wit—that Honour < > good. *1872:*is man's supreme

255

Why should I baulk Saint Jerome of his phrase?
Ubi honor non est, where no honour is,
580 *Ibi contemptus est;* and where contempt,
Ibi injuria frequens; and where that,
The frequent injury, *ibi et indignatio;*
And where the indignation, *ibi quies*
Nulla: and where there is no quietude,
585 Why, *ibi*, there, the mind is often cast
Down from the heights where it proposed to dwell,
Mens a proposito sæpe dejicitur.
And naturally the mind is so cast down,
Since harder 'tis, *quum difficilius sit,*
590 *Iram cohibere,* to coerce one's wrath,
Quam miracula facere, than work miracles,—
So Gregory smiles in his First Dialogue.
Whence we infer, the ingenuous soul, the man
Who makes esteem of honour and repute,
595 Whenever honour and repute are touched
Arrives at term of fury and despair,
Loses all guidance from the reason-check:
As in delirium or a frenzy-fit,

579| MS:*est*—where <> is—   *P1869:est*, where <> is,   580| MS:*est*—and   *P1869:est;*
and   581| MS:*frequens*—and   *P1869:frequens;* and   582| MS:*indignatio,*
P1869:indignatio;   583| MS:the § over illegible word §   584| MS:*Nulla,* and <>
quietude,   *P1869:Nulla;* and   *1872:Nulla:* and   *1889a:*quietude   DC,BrU:quietude,
*1889:*quietude,   588| MS:naturally so § crossed out and replaced above by five words § in
§ crossed out § the mind is so   589| MS:§ added in margin following 587 §
590–91| MS:§ originally one line § Iram cohibere—to § last three words inserted above line §
<> one's anger § crossed out and replaced below by § wrath/ *Quam miracula facere*— § last
three words inserted above line §   *P1869:cohibere,* to <> wrath,/ <> *facere,* than
592| MS:Saint Gregory saith § crossed out and replaced above by § smiles in his First
Dialogue: *1872:*his First Dialogue.   *1889a:*So Gregory   593| MS:We formulate to this
§ last four words crossed out and replaced above by four words § Whence we draw § crossed
out § inference § altered to § infer   594| MS:Which § crossed out and replaced in margin
by § Who   595| MS:Whenever in § crossed out; followed by word illegibly crossed out §
honor § followed by word illegibly erased § offence, § crossed out and replaced above by four
words § and repute are touched,   *P1869:*honour   DC,BrU:touched   *1889:*touched
596| MS:Arrived § altered to § Arrives at the § crossed out §   597| MS:Loses § over illegible
erasure § <> reason light § crossed out § -check,   *P1869:*reason-check: 598| MS:Like
a § last two words crossed out and replaced above by two words § As in delirious § altered to §
delirium man, one frenetic § last three words crossed out § or   *P1869:*delirium, or

Nor fury nor despair he satiates,—no,
600 Not even if he attain the impossible,
O'erturn the hinges of the universe
To annihilate—not whoso caused the smart
Solely, the author simply of his pain,
But the place, the memory, *vituperii*,
605 O' the shame and scorn: *quia*,—says Solomon,
(The Holy Spirit speaking by his mouth
In Proverbs, the sixth chapter near the end)
—Because, the zeal and fury of a man,
Zelus et furor viri, will not spare,
610 *Non parcet*, in the day of his revenge,
In die vindictæ, nor will acquiesce,
Nec acquiescet, through a person's prayers,
Cujusdam precibus,—nec suscipiet,
Nor yet take, *pro redemptione*, for
615 Redemption, *dona plurium*, gifts of friends,
Mere money-payment to compound for ache.
Who recognizes not my client's case?
Whereto, as strangely consentaneous here,
Adduce Saint Bernard in the Epistle writ
620 To Robertulus, his nephew: "Too much grief,
Dolor quippe nimius non deliberat,

1872:delirium or   599| MS:Nor § inserted in margin § Fury § altered to § fury and
§ crossed out and replaced above by § nor <> he cannot § crossed out § satiate § altered to §
satiates,—no—   *P1869*:no,   600| MS:attained § altered to § attain
601| MS:O'er-turned § altered to § O'er-turn   *P1869*:O'erturn   602| MS:not the author
of his § followed by illegible word; last five words crossed out and replaced above by three
words § whoso caused the   603| MS:§ crowded between 602-4 § pain   *P1869*:pain,
604| MS:memory of his shame and scorn § last five words crossed out § *vituperii*
P1869:memory, *vituperii*,   605| MS:And *vituperii* § uncertain; last two words crossed
out and replaced above by five words and colon § O' the shame and scorn: *quia*
608| MS:man   *P1869*:man,   611| MS:acquiesce   *P1869*:acquiesce,
612| MS:prayers   *P1869*:prayers,   613| MS:*sucipiet*   *P1869*:*sucipiet*,
614| MS:Nor will § crossed out and replaced above by § yet   615| MS:friends—
P1869:friends,   616| MS:§ crowded between 615-17 § Nor money-payment   *P1869*:ache
CP1869:ache.   *1872*:Mere money-payment   617| MS:not our client § altered to §
client's here? § last word and question mark crossed out §   *P1869*:not my client's
618| MS:consentaneous § followed by an illegible erasure § here,   619| MS:That of
§ last two words crossed out and replaced in margin by § Confer § altered to § Conduce Saint
P1869:Adduce Saint   620| MS:To Robert § altered to § Robertulus, his nephew: since
excessive § last two words crossed out and replaced above by two words § too much

Does not excogitate propriety,
Non verecundatur, nor knows shame at all,
Non consulit rationem, nor consults
625 Reason, *non dignitatis metuit*
Damnum, nor dreads the loss of dignity;
Modum et ordinem, order and the mode,
Ignorat, it ignores:" why, trait for trait,
Was ever portrait limned so like the life?
630 (By Cavalier Maratta, shall I say?
I hear he's first in reputation now.)
Yes, that of Samson in the Sacred Text
That's not so much the portrait as the man!
Samson in Gaza was the antetype
635 Of Guido at Rome: observe the Nazarite!
Blinded he was,—an easy thing to bear:
Intrepidly he took imprisonment,
Gyves, stripes and daily labour at the mill:
But when he found himself, i' the public place,
640 Destined to make the common people sport,
Disdain burned up with such an impetus
I' the breast of him that, all the man one fire,
Moriatur, roared he, let my soul's self die,
Anima mea, with the Philistines!
645 So, pulled down pillar, roof, and death and all,
Multosque plures interfecit, ay,
And many more he killed thus, *moriens,*
Dying, *quam vivus,* than in his whole life,

---

*P1869:*nephew: Too   *1872:*nephew: "Too   622| MS:not § followed by word illegibly crossed out §   626| MS:dignity, *CP1869:*dignity;   627| MS:*ordinem*—order and the § inserted above § mode   *P1869:ordinem,* order <> mode,   628| MS:*Ignorat*—it ignores: why *P1869:Ignorat,* it *1872:*ignores:" why   629| MS:Was § over illegible erasure §   630-31| MS:§ crowded between 629-32 in continuous line divided by / between *say?* and *I* § By Frederic Barroccio, shall   *P1869:*(By Cavalier Marratta, shall   632-34| MS:the Sacred Text!/ Sampson   *P1869:*the Sacred Text:/ That's not so much the portrait as the man!/ Sampson   *1889a:*the Sacred Text/ That's   635| MS:Of Guido in the Villa: such § last four words crossed out and replaced above by four words § at Rome: for, note the Nazarite—   *P1869:*the Nazarite!   *1872:*at Rome: observe the   636| MS:bear, *1872:*bear: 637| MS:he took § over perhaps *bore* §   638| MS:Gyves, § added in margin § Stripes and the § crossed out §   *P1869:*Gyves, stripes   642| MS:all of him one § crossed out and replaced above by § was fire,   *P1869:*him on fire,   *1872:*all the man one fire,   645| MS:So pulled <> death thereby § crossed out § and all   *P1869:*So, pulled <> all,   646| MS:*interfecit,*—ay,   *P1869:interfecit,* ay,   648| MS:In dying   *P1869:*Dying

Occiderat, he ever killed before.
650 Are these things writ for no example, Sirs?
One instance more, and let me see who doubts!
Our Lord Himself, made all of mansuetude,
Sealing the sum of sufferance up, received
Opprobrium, contumely and buffeting
655 Without complaint: but when He found Himself
Touched in His honour never so little for once,
Then outbroke indignation pent before—
"*Honorem meum nemini dabo!*" "No,
My honour I to nobody will give!"
660 And certainly the example so hath wrought,
That whosoever, at the proper worth,
Apprises worldly honour and repute,
Esteems it nobler to die honoured man
Beneath Mannaia, than live centuries
665 Disgraced in the eye o' the world. We find Saint Paul
No recreant to this faith delivered once:
"Far worthier were it that I died," cries he,
Expedit mihi magis mori, "than
That anyone should make my glory void,"
670 *Quam ut gloriam meam quis evacuet!*
See, *ad Corinthienses:* whereupon
Saint Ambrose makes a comment with much fruit,
Doubtless my Judges long since laid to heart,

649| MS:before? *P1869:*before.   651| MS:more—and *P1869:*more, and
652| MS:Our Lord Himself, made up § last two words inserted above line § of   *1872:*made
all of   655| MS:when he § inserted above line §   *CP1869:*when He   656| MS:once—
*P1869:*once,   658| MS:*dabo—*" cried, § word crossed out § "No,   *P1869:dabo!*" "No,
659| MS:give"!   *P1869:*give!"   660| MS:wrought   *CP1869:*wrought,
662| MS:Apprises worldly § inserted above line § <> and a good § last two words crossed out §
663| MS:Esteems far better § last two words crossed out and replaced above by three words § it
nobler to die an § crossed out §   667| MS:"Far better § crossed out and replaced above by §
worthier   668| MS:*mori,* than   *P1869:mori,* "than   669| MS:That any § altered
to § anyone man § crossed out § <> my glory § altered to § glorying void—   *P1869:*my glory
void,"   671| MS:*ad Corinthienses*—whereupon   *P1869:ad Corinthienses:* whereupon
672| MS:makes the § crossed out and replaced above by § a comment which § crossed out §
with much § inserted above line §   673| MS:my Judges studied § crossed out § long ago,

So I desist from bringing forward here.
675 (I can't quite recollect it.)

Have I proved
Satis superque, both enough and to spare,
That Revelation old and new admits
The natural man may effervesce in ire,
O'erflood earth, o'erfroth heaven with foamy rage,
680 At the first puncture to his self-respect?
Then, Sirs, this Christian dogma, this law-bud
Full-blown now, soon to bask the absolute flower
Of Papal doctrine in our blaze of day,—
Bethink you, shall we miss one promise-streak,
685 One doubtful birth of dawn crepuscular,
One dew-drop comfort to humanity,
Now that the chalice teems with noonday wine?
Yea, argue Molinists who bar revenge—
Referring just to what makes out our case!
690 Under old dispensation, argue they,
The doom of the adulterous wife was death,
Stoning by Moses' law. "Nay, stone her not,
Put her away!" next legislates our Lord;
And last of all, "Nor yet divorce a wife!"
695 Ordains the Church, "she typifies ourself,
The Bride no fault shall cause to fall from Christ."

---

§ last word and comma crossed out and replaced above by § since   674-75| MS:So I desist
here—have I proved my point? § altered to § So I desist from bringing forward here—/ (I can't
quite recollect it) § followed by two or more words, the last of which is perhaps *demanding,*
so heavily marked out as to be illegible § have I proved *P1869:*it.) § ¶ § Have *1872:*here./
676| MS:*superque,* ample § crossed out and replaced below by two words § both enough
678| MS:effervese in rage § crossed out and replaced above by § ire *P1869:*effervesce
679| MS:foamy ire, § altered to § rage,   681| MS:Then § over illegible word § < >
dogma, this § inserted above line § budding § crossed out § law § altered to § law-bud
682| MS:Full-blown and now to § transposed to § Full-blown now and to *P1869:*now, soon
to   684| MS:you,—shall *P1869:*you, shall   686| MS:One budding § inserted
above § comfort to humanity, in the bud,— § last three words and comma crossed out §
*P1869:*One dew-drop comfort   687| MS:the rosy § crossed out § < > with noonday
§ inserted above §   689| MS:case— *P1869:*case!   692| MS:by Moses law *P1869:*by
Moses' law.   693| MS:Divorce § crossed out § Put her away," next *P1869:*away!" next
694| MS:wife, *P1869:*wife!"   695| MS:the Pope § crossed out and replaced above by §
Church—She typifies the Church § last two words crossed out and replaced above by §
ourself, *P1869:*the Church, "she   696| MS:Christ's § crossed out and replaced above
by § The < > fall away § crossed out and replaced above by two words § from Christ."

Then, as no jot nor tittle of the Law
Has passed away—which who presumes to doubt?
As not one word of Christ is rendered vain—
700   Which, could it be though heaven and earth should pass?
—Where do I find my proper punishment
For my adulterous wife, I humbly ask
Of my infallible Pope,—who now remits
Even the divorce allowed by Christ in lieu
705   Of lapidation Moses licensed me?
The Gospel checks the Law which throws the stone,
The Church tears the divorce-bill Gospel grants:
Shall wives sin and enjoy impunity?
What profits me the fulness of the days,
710   The final dispensation, I demand,
Unless Law, Gospel and the Church subjoin
"But who hath barred thee primitive revenge,
Which, like fire damped and dammed up, burns more fierce?
Use thou thy natural privilege of man,
715   Else wert thou found like those old ingrate Jews,
Despite the manna-banquet on the board,
A-longing after melons, cucumbers,
And such like trash of Egypt left behind!"

(There was one melon had improved our soup:

698| MS:doubt?— *P1869:*doubt?   699| MS:is rendered § over illegible erasure § vain,—
*P1869:*vain—   700| MS:Which could not be though Heaven and earth were blank,—
*P1869:*Which, could it be though heaven and earth should pass?   701| MS:And as the
Pope § last four words crossed out and replaced above by four words § —Where do I find
702| MS:ask, *CP1869:*ask   703| MS:infallible Pope who *CP1869:*infallible Pope—
who *1869:*infallible Pope,—who   705| MS:Of the § crossed out § <> licensed erst
§ crossed out and replaced above by § me?   706| MS:the Law would throw the
*P1869:*the Law which throws the   707| MS:The Church denies § crossed out and
replaced above by two words § tears the divorce § altered to § divorce-bill the § crossed out §
<> grants,— *P1869:*grants, *1872:*grants: 708| MS:§ crowded between 707-9 § There
stands my wife, enjoys impunity! *P1869:*The wife sins and enjoys *1872:*Shall wives sin
and enjoy impunity?   711| MS:subjoin § over *unite* §   712| MS:barred thy § altered
to § the natural § crossed out and replaced above by § primitive   713| MS:Should, like a
§ crossed out § fire restricted § crossed out and replaced above by four words § damped and
dammed up, burn more *P1869:*Which, like <> burns   714| MS:§ crowded between
713-15 § thou the natural *P1869:*thou thy natural   715| MS:those old § inserted above §
ungrate § altered to § ingrate Jews *P1869:*ingrate Jews,   716| MS:the Christian § crossed
out and replaced above by § manna—   717| MS:cucumbers *1872:*cucumbers,
718| MS:And the good fare of <> behind." *P1869:*And such like trash of <> behind!"
718-19| MS:§ no ¶ § *1872:* § ¶ §   719| MS:melon, had improved the § crossed out and

But did not Cinoncino need the rind
        To make a boat with? So I seem to think.)

        Law, Gospel and the Church—from these we leap
        To the very last revealment, easy rule
        Befitting the well-born and thorough-bred
725   O' the happy day we live in, not the dark
        O' the early rude and acorn-eating race.
        "Behold," quoth James, "we bridle in a horse
        And turn his body as we would thereby!"
        Yea, but we change the bit to suit the growth,
730   And rasp our colt's jaw with a rugged spike
        We hasten to remit our managed steed
        Who wheels round at persuasion of a touch.
        Civilization bows to decency,
        The acknowledged use and wont: 'tis manners,—mild
735   But yet imperative law,—which make the man.
        Thus do we pay the proper compliment
        To rank, and what society of Rome
        Hath so obliged us by its interest,
        Taken our client's part instinctively,
740   As unaware defending its own cause.
        What *dictum* doth Society lay down
        I' the case of one who hath a faithless wife?
        Wherewithal should the husband cleanse his way?

---

replaced above by § our soup,   *1872:*melon had <> soup: 722| MS:§ note that new ¶
begins §   723| MS:the very § inserted above § <> revealment, light and § last two words
crossed out § easy rule   724| MS:thoroughly bred   *P1869:*thorough-bred
725| MS:the better day, § last two words and comma crossed out and replaced above by five
words, comma and dash § happy days we live in,—not our sires,   *P1869:*in,—not the dark
*1872:*in, not   726| MS:The early   *P1869:*O' the early   728| MS:thereby;"
*P1869:*thereby!"   730| MS:rasp the colt's   *P1869:*rasp our colt's
731| MS:remit the managed   *P1869:*remit our managed   734| MS:wont, the
manners   *1872:*wont: 'tis manners   735| MS:man—   *P1869:*man.
737| MS:rank, that good § crossed out and replaced above by § choice society   *P1869:*rank,
and that society   DC,BrU:and what society   *1889:*and that society § emended to § and
what society § see Editorial Notes §   738| MS:That § crossed out § hath § altered to §
Hath so § inserted above §   739| MS:instinctively   *P1869:*instinctively,
742| MS:of him § crossed out and replaced above by § one   743| MS:the Husband

Be patient and forgive? Oh, language fails,—
745 Shrinks from depicturing his turpitude!
For if wronged husband raise not hue and cry,
Quod si maritus de adulterio non
Conquereretur, he's presumed a—foh!
Presumitur leno: so, complain he must.
750 But how complain? At your tribunal, lords?
Far weightier challenge suits your sense, I wot!
You sit not to have gentlemen propose
Questions gentility can itself discuss.
Did not you prove that to our brother Paul?
755 The Abate, *quum judicialiter*
Prosequeretur, when he tried the law,
Guidonis causam, in Count Guido's case,
Accidit ipsi, this befell himself,
Quod risum moverit et cachinnos, that
760 He moved to mirth and cachinnation, all
Or nearly all, *fere in omnibus*
Etiam sensatis et cordatis, men
Strong-sensed, sound-hearted, nay, the very Court,
Ipsismet in judicibus, I might add,
765 *Non tamen dicam.* In a cause like this,
So multiplied were reasons *pro* and *con,*
Delicate, intertwisted and obscure,
That Law refused loan of a finger-tip
To unravel, re-adjust the hopeless twine,

---

*P1869:*the husband   744–47| MS:fails—/ § crowded between 744-45 § For < > cry—
*P1869:*fails—/ Shrinks from depicturing his punishment!/ For < > cry,/ *Quod*
*1872:*fails,—/ Shrinks < > his turpitude!//   748| MS:*Conqueretur*—he's
P1869:Conquereretur, he's   749| MS:so complain he must—   *P1869:*so, complain
he must.   750| MS:Lords?   *P1869:*lords?   751| MS:weightier business § crossed
out and replaced above by § challenge   752| MS:not here that gentlemen   *P1869:*not
to have gentlemen   753| MS:discuss: *P1869:*discuss.   756| MS:law   *P1869:*law,
758| MS:*Ipsi accidit* § transposed to § *Accidit ipsi*   761| MS:all—*fere   P1869:*all, *fere*
763| MS:sound-hearted, —nay, the very § inserted above § Court   *P1869:*sound-hearted, nay
< > Court,   764| MS:*Non tamen dicam* § crossed out and replaced above by § *Ipsismet*
in judicibus,—I might say § crossed out and replaced above by § add,—   *P1869: judicibus,* I
< > add,   765| MS:*Ipsismet* § crossed out and replaced above by § *Non tamen*
766| MS:pro and con,   *P1869:pro* and *con,*   768| MS:That law were shamed to lend a
*1872:*That Law refused loan of a   769| MS:readjust < > hopless   *P1869:*hopeless

263

⁷⁷⁰ Since, half-a-dozen steps outside Law's seat,
There stood a foolish trifler with a tool
A-dangle to no purpose by his side,
Had clearly cut the embroilment in a trice.
Asserunt enim unanimiter
⁷⁷⁵ *Doctores,* for the Doctors all assert
That husbands, *quod mariti,* must be held
Viles, cornuti reputantur, vile,
Fronts branching forth a florid infamy,
Si propriis manibus, if with their own hands,
⁷⁸⁰ *Non sumunt,* they fail straight to take revenge,
Vindictam, but expect the deed be done
By the Court—*expectant illam fieri*
Per judices, qui summopere rident, which
Gives an enormous guffaw for reply,
⁷⁸⁵ *Et cachinnantur.* For he ran away,
Deliquit enim, just that he might 'scape
The censure of both counsellors and crowd,
Ut vulgi et doctorum evitaret
Censuram, and lest so he superadd
⁷⁹⁰ To loss of honour ignominy too,
Et sic ne istam quoque ignominiam
Amisso honori superadderet.
My lords, my lords, the inconsiderate step
Was—we referred ourselves to Law at all!
⁷⁹⁵ Twit me not with "Law else had punished you!"

---

*1872:*re-adjust   ⁷⁷⁰| MS:While, half a dozen steps outside the Court,
*P1869:*half-a-dozen < > the court,   *1872:*outside Law's seat,   ⁷⁷²| MS:It § altered to §
A-dangle < > side   *P1869:*side,   ⁷⁷³| MS:Had fitly § uncertain; crossed out and replaced
above by § cleanly cut the tangle in   *P1869:*Had clearly   *1872:*the embroilment in
⁷⁷⁵| MS:assert, § over possibly *agree,* §   DC,BrU: assert   *1889:*assert, § emended to §
assert § see Editorial Notes §   ⁷⁷⁷| MS:vile   *1872:*vile,   ⁷⁷⁸| MS:And branching
*1872:*Fronts branching   ⁷⁷⁹| MS:hands   *1869:*hands,   ⁷⁸⁰| MS:they take not
straightway revenge,   *1872:*they fail straightway take revenge,   *1889a:*fail straight to take
⁷⁸¹| MS:*Vindictam*—but < > the deed § over illegible word §   *P1869:Vindictam,* but
⁷⁸³| MS:*Per judices—qui* < > *rident,*—which   *P1869:judices, qui* < > *rident,* which
⁷⁸⁴| MS:reply   *P1869:*reply,   ⁷⁸⁶| MS:scape   *P1869:*'scape   ⁷⁸⁷| MS:both
Counselors and crowd   *P1869:*both counsellors and crowd,   ⁷⁸⁸| MS:*et Doctorum*
1889a:et doctorum   ⁷⁹⁰| MS:honour, § followed by word inserted above and
then erased § ignominy too   *P1869:*honour ignominy too,   ⁷⁹¹| MS:Still worse §
crossed out §   ⁷⁹⁴| MS:Was. that § crossed out § —we   *P1869:*Was—we
⁷⁹⁵| MS:with—"Law < > you,"—   *P1869:*with, "Law < > you!"   *1889a:*with "Law

Each punishment of the extra-legal step,
To which the high-born preferably revert,
Is ever for some oversight, some slip
I' the taking vengeance, not for vengeance' self.
⁸⁰⁰ A good thing, done unhandsomely, turns ill;
And never yet lacked ill the law's rebuke.
For pregnant instance, let us contemplate
The luck of Leonardus,—see at large
Of Sicily's Decisions sixty-first.
⁸⁰⁵ This Leonard finds his wife is false: what then?
He makes her own son snare her, and entice
Out of the town walls to a private walk
Wherein he slays her with commodity.
They find her body half-devoured by dogs:
⁸¹⁰ Leonard is tried, convicted, punished, sent
To labour in the galleys seven years long:
Why? For the murder? Nay, but for the mode!
Malus modus occidendi, ruled the Court,
An ugly mode of killing, nothing more!
⁸¹⁵ Another fructuous sample,—see *"De Re*
Criminali," in Matthæus' divine piece.
Another husband, in no better plight,
Simulates absence, thereby tempts his wife;
On whom he falls, out of sly ambuscade,
⁸²⁰ Backed by a brother of his, and both of them
Armed to the teeth with arms that law had blamed.

---

⁷⁹⁶| MS:punishment for § crossed out and replaced above by § of <> step   *P1869:*step,
⁷⁹⁷| MS:the genteel § uncertain; crossed out and replaced above by § high-born <> revert
*P1869:*revert,   ⁷⁹⁸| MS:oversight, some fault § crossed out §   ⁷⁹⁹| MS:In § altered
to § I' <> self: *P1869:*self.   ⁸⁰⁰| MS:thing done unhandsomely turns ill,   *P1869:*ill;
*1872:*thing, done unhandsomely, turns   ⁸⁰¹| MS:the Law's   *P1869:*the law's
⁸⁰²| MS:For pregnant § inserted above line §   ⁸⁰⁴| MS:sixty-first: *P1869:*sixty-first.
⁸⁰⁵| MS:This Leonard § over illegible word §   ⁸⁰⁷| MS:town-walls <> private
place § crossed out § walk: *P1869:*walk,   *1889a:*walk   ⁸⁰⁸| MS:commodity;
*P1869:*commodity.   ⁸⁰⁹| MS:dogs.   *P1869:*dogs: ⁸¹⁰| MS:tried,
condemned § altered to § convicted, and § crossed out § punished   ⁸¹¹| MS:gallies
*P1869:*galleys   ⁸¹²| MS:Why, § altered to § ? for § altered to § For   ⁸¹⁵| MS:sample,
see   *P1869:*sample,—see   ⁸¹⁶| MS:in Matthaeus' masterpiece § altered to §
divine piece: *P1869:*piece.   ⁸¹⁷| MS:husband in <> plight   *P1869:*husband, in
<> plight,   ⁸¹⁸| MS:tempts the wife,   *P1869:*wife;   *1872:*tempts his wife;
⁸¹⁹| MS:of an § altered to § sly   ⁸²¹| MS:law forbade.   *P1869:*law had blamed.

Nimis dolose, overwilily,
Fuisse operatum, did they work,
Pronounced the law: had all been fairly done
825   Law had not found him worthy, as she did,
Of four years' exile. Why cite more? Enough
Is good as a feast—(unless a birthday-feast
For one's Cinuccio) so, we finish here.
My lords, we rather need defend ourselves
830   Inasmuch as, for a twinkling of an eye,
We hesitatingly appealed to law,—
Than need deny that, on mature advice,
We blushingly bethought us, bade revenge
Back to its simple proper private way
835   Of decent self-dealt gentlemanly death.
Judges, here is the law, and here beside,
The testimony! Look to it!
                         Pause and breathe!
So far is only too plain; we must watch:
Bottini will scarce hazard an attack
840   Here: best anticipate the fellow's play
And guard the weaker places—warily ask,
What if considerations of a sort,
Reasons of a kind, arise from out the strange
Peculiar unforeseen new circumstance
845   Of this our (candour owns) abnormal act,

822| MS:overwilily *1869:*overwilily,   823| MS:*operatum,* was his work *P1869:*was
it worked, *1872:operatum,* did they work,   824| MS:the Law *P1869:*the law
825| MS:Law § over illegible word §   826| MS:Of § inserted in margin § Four § altered to §
four whole § crossed out §   827| MS:birthday feast *P1869:*birthday-feast
828| MS:one's Cinuccio: so we'll finish here) *P1869:*so, we'll *1872:*one's Cinuccio) so, we
finish here.   829| MS:In fine—we *P1869:*My lords, we   830| MS:Inasmuch as
§ squeezed in § , for one § crossed out and replaced above by § a < > eye *1872:*eye,
831| MS:hesitated § altered to § hesitatingly and § crossed out §   832| MS:Rather than
that § crossed out and replaced above by § deny, on more mature advice *P1869:*deny that, on
mature advice, *1872:*Than need deny   833| MS:us, took ourselves *P1869:*us, bade
revenge   834| MS:to the simple *1872:*to its simple   836| MS:Judges, there is the
Law—and what beside? *P1869:*the law, and this beside, *1872:*Judges, here is < > and here
beside,   837| MS:testimony. Look *P1869:*testimony! Look   838| MS:watch,
*1872:*watch: 840| MS:Here: let's anticipate < > play, *1889a:*Here: best   DC,BrU:play
*1889:*play   843| MS:kind arise < > strange, *P1869:*kind, arise < > strange
844| MS:Peculiar, unforeseen, new *P1869:*Peculiar unforseen new
845| MS:our—candour owns—abnormal *P1869:*our (candour owns) abnormal

To bar the right of us revenging so?
"Impunity were otherwise your meed:
Go slay your wife and welcome,"—may be urged,—
"But why the innocent old couple slay,
850   Pietro, Violante? You may do enough,
Not too much, not exceed the golden mean:
Neither brute-beast nor Pagan, Gentile, Jew,
Nor Christian, no nor votarist of the mode,
Is justified to push revenge so far."

855   No, indeed? Why, thou very sciolist!
The actual wrong, Pompilia seemed to do,
Was virtual wrong done by the parents here—
Imposing her upon us as their child—
Themselves allow: then, her fault was their fault,
860   Her punishment be theirs accordingly!
But wait a little, sneak not off so soon!
Was this cheat solely harm to Guido, pray?
The precious couple you call innocent,—
Why, they were felons that Law failed to clutch,
865   *Qui ut fraudarent*, who that they might rob,
Legitime vocatos, folk law called,
Ad fidei commissum, true heirs to the Trust,
Partum supposuerunt, feigned this birth,
Immemores reos factos esse, blind
870   To the fact that, guilty, they incurred thereby,
Ultimi supplicii, hanging or what's worse.

846| MS:May bar <> so,   *P1869:*To bar <> so?   847| MS:The impunity <>
otherwise our meed?   *P1869:*otherwise your meed: *1869:*"Impunity
848| MS:welcome,—may   *P1869:*welcome,"—may   849| MS:But   *P1869:*"But
852| MS:nor pagan   *P1869:*nor Pagan   853| MS:mode   *P1869:*mode,
854| MS:Were free at all to <> far!   *P1869:*far!"   *1872:*Was justified to   *1889a:*Is justified
854-55| MS:§ no ¶ §   *P1869:*§ ¶ §   856| MS:wrong Pompilia <> do   *P1869:*wrong,
Pompilia <> do,   857| MS:here   *P1869:*here—   864| MS:are   *CP1869:*were
*P1869:*that law   *1889a:*that Law   865| MS:*fraudarent*—who <> rob
P1869:fraudarent, who <> rob,   866| MS:*vocatos*—folks law called   *P1869:vocatos*,
folks law called,   *1889a:*folk   867| MS:*commissum*—true   *P1869:commissum*, true
868| MS:*supposuerunt*—feigned <> birth   *P1869:supposuerunt*, feigned <> birth,
869| MS:*esse*—blind   *P1869:esse*, blind   870| MS:thereby   *P1869:*thereby,
871| MS:*supplicii*—hanging or aught worse.   *P1869:supplicii*, hanging   *1872:*or what's

Do you blame us that we turn Law's instruments,
Not mere self-seekers,—mind the public weal,
Nor make the private good our sole concern?
875 That having—shall I say—secured a thief,
Not simply we recover from his pouch
The stolen article our property,
But also pounce upon our neighbour's purse
We opportunely find reposing there,
880 And do him justice while we right ourselves?
He owes us, for our part, a drubbing say,
But owes our neighbour just a dance i' the air
Under the gallows: so, we throttle him.
That neighbour's Law, that couple are the Thief,
885 We are the over ready to help Law—
Zeal of her house hath eaten us up: for which,
Can it be, Law intends to eat up us,
Crudum Priamum, devour poor Priam raw,
('Twas Jupiter's own joke) with babes to boot,
890 *Priamique pisinnos*, in Homeric phrase?
Shame!—and so ends my period prettily.

But even,—prove the pair not culpable,
Free as unborn babe from connivance at,
Participation in, their daughter's fault:
895 Ours the mistake. Is that a rare event?
Non semel, it is anything but rare,
In contingentia facti, that by chance,
Impunes evaserunt, go scot-free,
Qui, such well-meaning people as ourselves,

worse. 872| MS:instruments 1872:instruments, 879| MS:there § over *here* §
*P1869:*there, 881| MS:say,—*P1869:*say, 882| MS:He owes *P1869:*But owes
883| MS:the gallows-tree: we strangle § crossed out and replaced above by § throttle
*P1869:*the gallows: so we 1872:so, we 884| MS:The neighbor's Law, the couple
1872:That neighbor's Law, that couple 885| MS:over-ready 1872:over ready
887| MS:be Law <> us— *P1869:*be, Law <> us, 888| MS:raw *P1869:*raw,
889| MS:'Twas <> joke, with his § crossed out § *P1869:*('Twas <> joke) with
890| MS:*pisinnos*—in *P1869:pisinnos*, in 891| MS:end the period *P1869:*ends
*1889a:*ends my period 892| MS:§ marginal notation that new ¶ begins § pair
unculpable, *P1869:*pair not culpable, 894| MS:in their *P1869:*in, their
898| MS:scot-free *P1869:*scot-free, 899| MS:*Qui—such* <> ourselves *P1869:Qui*,

⁹⁰⁰ *Justo dolore moti,* who aggrieved
With cause, *apposuerunt manus,* lay
Rough hands, *in innocentes,* on wrong heads.
Cite we an illustrative case in point:
Mulier Smirnea quædam, good my lords,
⁹⁰⁵ A gentlewoman lived in Smyrna once,
Virum et filium ex eo conceptum, who
Both husband and her son begot by him
Killed, *interfecerat, ex quo,* because,
Vir filium suum perdiderat, her spouse
⁹¹⁰ Had been beforehand with her, killed her son,
Matrimonii primi, of a previous bed.
Deinde accusata, then accused,
Apud Dolabellam, before him that sat
Proconsul, *nec duabus cædibus*
⁹¹⁵ *Contaminatam liberare,* nor
To liberate a woman doubly-dyed
With murder, *voluit,* made he up his mind,
Nec condemnare, nor to doom to death,
Justo dolore impulsam, one impelled
⁹²⁰ By just grief; *sed remisit,* but sent her up
Ad Areopagum, to the Hill of Mars,
Sapientissimorum judicum
Cœtum, to that assembly of the sage
Paralleled only by my judges here;

---

such <> ourselves,   ⁹⁰¹| MS:with justice § crossed out §   ⁹⁰²| MS:hands *in innocentes* on   *P1869:*hands, *in innocentes,* on   ⁹⁰⁴| MS:*quædam*—good *P1869:quædam,* good   ⁹⁰⁵| MS:once *P1869:*once,   ⁹⁰⁷| MS:son that he begot *P1869:*son begot by him, *1889a:*him   ⁹⁰⁸| MS:*quo* because, *P1869:quo,* because, ⁹¹⁰| MS:son *P1869:*son,   ⁹¹²| MS:*accusata,*—then accused *P1869:accusata,* then accused.   ⁹¹³| MS:before § followed by illegible erasure; perhaps *that* §   ⁹¹⁵| MS:*Contaminatam liberare,*—nor *P1869:Comtaminatam liberare,* nor *1872:Contaminatam*   ⁹¹⁶| MS:liberate one hu § last two words crossed out § ⁹¹⁷| MS:murder—*voluit*—made <> mind *P1869:*murder, *voluit,* made <> mind, ⁹¹⁸| MS:*condemnare*—nor condemn § crossed out and replaced above by two words § to doom to death *P1869:condemnare,* nor <> death,   ⁹¹⁹| MS:*impulsam* one *P1869:impulsam,* one   ⁹²⁰| MS:grief, *sed* <> sent up *P1869:*sent her up *1889a:*grief; *sed*   ⁹²³| MS:*Cœtum,*—to that § over possibly *the* § assemblies § altered to § assembly *P1869:Cœtum,* to   ⁹²⁴| MS:Only to be § last two words crossed out § paralleled § altered to § Paralleled § with indication that order of the two words be

925   *Ubi, cognito de causa,* where, the cause
      Well weighed, *responsum est,* they gave reply,
      Ut ipsa et accusator, that both sides
      O' the suit, *redirent,* should come back again,
      Post centum annos, after a hundred years,
930   For judgment; *et sic,* by which sage decree,
      Duplici parricidio rea, one
      Convicted of a double parricide,
      Quamvis etiam innocentem, though in truth
      Out of the pair, one innocent at least
935   She, *occidisset,* plainly had put to death,
      Undequaque, yet she altogether 'scaped,
      Evasit impunis. See the case at length
      In Valerius, fittingly styled *Maximus,*
      That eighth book of his Memorable Facts.
940   Nor Cyriacus cites beside the mark:
      Similiter uxor quæ mandaverat,
      Just so, a lady who had taken care,
      Homicidium viri, that her lord be killed,
      Ex denegatione debiti,
945   For denegation of a certain debt,
      Matrimonialis, he was loth to pay,
      Fuit pecuniaria mulcta, was
      Amerced in a pecuniary mulct,
      Punita, et ad pœnam, and to pains,
950   *Temporalem,* for a certain space of time,
      In monasterio, in a convent.

                    (Ay,

---

reversed § by my Judges *P1869:*only by my judges   925| MS:where the   *P1869:*where,
the   926| MS:*est,*—they <> reply   *P1869:est,* they <> reply,   928| MS:*redirent*
should <> again   *P1869:redirent,* should <> again,   929| MS:*annos* after § over
perhaps *an* §   *P1869:annos,* after   930| MS:judgment, *et*   *CP1869:*judgment; *et*
931| MS:*rea*—one   *P1869:rea,* one   932| MS:parricide   *P1869:*parricide,
934| MS:One <> least out <> pair   *P1869:*Out <> pair, one <> least
935| MS:She *occidisset*   *P1869:*She, *occidisset*   936| MS:scaped   *P1869:*'scaped,
938| MS:In Valerius—fittingly <> *Maximus*—   *P1869:*In Valerius, fittingly <> *Maximus,*
940| MS:§ initial illegible erasure § mark—   *P1869:*mark: 941| MS:*mandaverat*
P1869:mandaverat,   942| MS:so a <> care   *P1869:*so, a <> care,   943| MS:*viri*
that <> killed   *P1869:viri,* that <> killed,   944| MS:*debiti*   *P1869:debiti,*
945| MS:debt   *P1869:*debt,   946| MS:*Matrimonialis* he   *P1869:Matrimonialis,*
he   947| MS:*mulcta,*—was   *P1869:mulcta* was   948| MS:mulct   *P1869:*mulct,
949| MS:pains *P1869:*pains,   951| MS:convent: ay,   *P1869:*convent. § ¶ § Ay,

In monasterio! He mismanages
In with the ablative, the accusative!
I had hoped to have hitched the villain into verse
955   For a gift, this very day, a complete list
O' the prepositions each with proper case,
Telling a story, long was in my head.
"What prepositions take the accusative?
Ad to or at—*who saw the cat?*—down to
960   *Ob,* for, because of, *keep her claws off!"* Tush!
Law in a man takes the whole liberty:
The muse is fettered: just as Ovid found!)

And now, sea widens and the coast is clear.
What of the dubious act you bade excuse?
965   Surely things broaden, brighten, till at length
Remains—so far from act that needs defence—
Apology to make for act delayed
One minute, let alone eight mortal months
Of hesitation! "Why procrastinate?"
970   (Out with it my Bottinius, ease thyself!)
"Right, promptly done, is twice right: right delayed
Turns wrong. We grant you should have killed your wife,
But killed o' the moment, at the meeting her
In company with the priest: then did the tongue

1872:(Ay,   952| MS:monasterio—how he manages   *P1869:monasterio!* How
*1872:*manages,   *1889a:monasterio!* He mismanages   954| MS:hitched him into
*P1869:*hitched the villain into   955| MS:gift this <> day a   *P1869:*gift, this <> day, a
957| MS:story long <> head—   *P1869:*story, long <> head.   958| MS:What
1889a:"What   959| MS:who saw the cat?—down   *P1869:who saw the cat?*—down
960-62| MS:for, or because of, keep her claws off! Ah,/ The <> fettered,—just <> found!
*P1869:*for, because of, *keep her claws off!* Ah,/ Law in a man takes the whole liberty!//
1872:// <> fettered: just <> found!)   *1889a:*off!" Tush/ <> liberty://   963| MS:now,
sky brightens § last two words crossed out and replaced above by two words § sea widens <>
clear—   *P1869:*clear.   964-66| MS:the murky § crossed out and replaced above by §
dubious <> bade we cleanse § last two words crossed out and replaced above by two words §
be plain?/ Remains   *P1869:*bade excuse?/ Surely things brighten, brighten, till at length/
Remains   *1889a:/* <> things broaden, brighten, till <> //   969-71| MS:hesitation.
"Why procrastinate?/ "Right   *P1869:*hesitation! "Why procrastinate?"/ (Out with it my
Bottinius, ease thyself!)/ "Right   972| MS:you might § crossed out and replaced above
by § should   973| MS:But on the moment,—at   *P1869:*moment, at   *1872:*But killed
o' the   974| MS:with the § inserted above § priest,—then   *P1869:*priest: then

271

⁹⁷⁵ O' the Brazen Head give license, 'Time is now!'
Wait to make mind up? 'Time is past' it peals.
Friend, you are competent to mastery
O' the passions that confessedly explain
An outbreak: you allow an interval,
⁹⁸⁰ And then break out as if time's clock still clanged.
You have forfeited your chance, and flat you fall
Into the commonplace category
Of men bound to go softly all their days,
Obeying Law."
           Now, which way make response?
⁹⁸⁵ What was the answer Guido gave, himself?
—That so to argue came of ignorance
How honour bears a wound. "For, wound," said he,
"My body, and the smart soon mends and ends:
While, wound my soul where honour sits and rules,
⁹⁹⁰ Longer the sufferance, stronger grows the pain,
Being *ex incontinenti*, fresh as first."
But try another tack, urge common sense
By way of contrast: say—Too true, my lords!
We did demur, awhile did hesitate:
⁹⁹⁵ Since husband sure should let a scruple speak
Ere he slay wife,—for his own safety, lords!

---

^{975|} MS:licence, "Time <> now"! *P1869:*'Time <> now!' *1889a:*license
^{976|} MS:You make your mind up: "Time is past" it clangs § crossed out and replaced above
by § peals. *P1869:*up: 'Time is past' it *1872:*Wait to make mind up? 'Time
^{978|} MS:confessedly excuse *P1869:*confessedly explain   ^{979|} MS:An out-break,—yet
allow *P1869:*outbreak *1872:*outbreak: you allow   ^{980|} MS:And then § inserted in
margin § Break § altered to § break   ^{983|} MS:days *P1869:*days,   ^{984|} MS:Obeying
law." Now <> make rispost? *P1869:*" § ¶ § Now <> make response? *1889a:*Law
^{986|} MS:That <> came § over illegible word § *P1869:*—That   ^{987|} MS:a wound: for
wound, said *P1869:*a wound: "For, wound," said *1889a:*a wound. "For
^{988|} MS:"My <> smart is worst at first— *P1869:*"My <> first: *1872:*smart soon mends
and ends: ^{989|} MS:While, § word and comma inserted in margin § Wound <> where
my § crossed out § *P1869:*While, wound   ^{990|} MS:pain,— *P1869:*pain,
^{991|} MS:'Tis *ex incontinenti*—fresh as first. *P1869:*'Tis *ex incontinenti,* fresh as first."
*1872:*Being *ex*   ^{992|} MS:tack—calm common *P1869:*tack, calm common
*1872:*tack, urge common   ^{993|} MS:contrast—as—too <> lords— *P1869:*contrast:
as—Too <> lords! *P1872:*contrast: say—Too   ^{994|} MS:demur, did hesitate awhile:
§indication to change word order to § demur, awhile did hesitate: ^{995|} MS:Yet
husband <> let each scruple *P1869:*let a scruple *1872:*Since husband

Carpers abound in this misjudging world:
Moreover, there's a nicety in law
That seems to justify them should they carp.
1000 Suppose the source of injury a son,—
Father may slay such son yet run no risk:
Why graced with such a privilege? Because
A father so incensed with his own child,
Or must have reason, or believe he has:
1005 *Quia semper*, seeing that in such event,
Presumitur, the law is bound suppose,
Quod capiat pater, that the sire must take,
Bonum consilium pro filio,
The best course as to what befits his boy,
1010 Through instinct, *ex instinctu*, of mere love,
Amoris, and, *paterni*, fatherhood;
Quam confidentiam, which confidence,
Non habet, law declines to entertain,
De viro, of the husband: where finds he
1015 An instinct that compels him love his wife?
Rather is he presumably her foe.
So, let him ponder long in this bad world
Ere do the simplest act of justice.

                                                    But
Again—and here we brush Bottini's breast—
1020 Object you, "See the danger of delay!

997| MS:world, *P1869:*world. *1872:*world: 999| MS:carp: *1872:*carp.
1000| MS:son, *P1869:*son,—   1005| MS:*semper*—seeing *P1869:semper*, seeing
1006| MS:*Presumiter*—the <> suppose   *P1869:Presumiter*, the <> suppose,
1007| MS:*pater*—that <> take   *P1869:pater*, that <> take,   1008| MS:*filio*
P1869:filio,   1009| MS:boy.   *P1869:*boy,   1010| MS:instinct—ex instinctu—
of <> love   *P1869:*instinct, *ex instinctu*, of <> love,   1011| MS:And
fatherhood—*Amoris paterni* § last four words crossed out § *Amoris*, and, *paterni*,
fatherhood. *P1869:*fatherhood;   1012| MS:*confidentiam*—which confidence
P1869:confidentiam, which confidence,   1013| MS:*habet*—law <> entertain
P1869:habet, law <> entertain,   1014| MS:*viro* of the husband—where has he
P1869:viro, of the husband: where *1872:*where finds he   1016| MS:foe: *1872:*foe.
1017| MS:So let *P1869:*So, let   1018| MS:Ere he the <> justice do. *P1869:*Ere do
the <> justice. § ¶ § But   1020| MS:you. "See <> delay: *P1869:*you, "See <> delay!

Suppose a man murdered my friend last month:
Had I come up and killed him for his pains
In rage, I had done right, allows the law:
I meet him now and kill him in cold blood,
¹⁰²⁵ I do wrong, equally allows the law:
Wherein do actions differ, yours and mine?"
In plenitudine intellectus es?
Hast thy wits, Fisc? To take such slayer's life,
Returns it life to thy slain friend at all?
¹⁰³⁰ Had he stolen ring instead of stabbing friend,—
To-day, to-morrow or next century,
Meeting the thief, thy ring upon his thumb,
Thou justifiably hadst wrung it thence:
So, couldst thou wrench thy friend's life back again,
¹⁰³⁵ Though prisoned in the bosom of his foe,
Why, law would look complacent on thy wrath.
Our case is, that the thing we lost, we found:
The honour, we were robbed of eight months since,
Being recoverable at any day
¹⁰⁴⁰ By death of the delinquent. Go thy ways!
Ere thou hast learned law, will be much to do,
As said the gaby while he shod the goose.

Nay, if you urge me, interval was none!
From the inn to the villa—blank or else a bar
¹⁰⁴⁵ Of adverse and contrarious incident
Solid between us and our just revenge!
What with the priest who flourishes his blade,
The wife who like a fury flings at us,
The crowd—and then the capture, the appeal

---

^{1021|} MS:man has killed my *P1869:*man murdered my ^{1023|} MS:rage—I < > right—
allows *P1869:*rage, I < > right, allows ^{1025|} MS:And do wrong—equally *P1869:*I
do wrong, equally ^{1027|} MS:§ crowded between 1026-28 § ^{1030|} MS:friend
*P1869:*friend,— ^{1031|} MS:century *P1869:*century, ^{1034|} MS:So couldst < >
again *P1869:*So, couldst < > again, ^{1035|} MS:his § over illegible erasure § foe
*P1869:*foe, *1889a:*foe. § emended to § foe, § see Editorial Notes § ^{1036|} MS:thy rush.
*1872:*thy wrath. ^{1037|} MS:is that *P1869:*is, that ^{1040|} MS:delinquent, Go thy
ways, *P1869:*delinquent. Go thy ways! ^{1041|} MS:thou § followed by illegible erasure §
^{1042|} MS:the rustic while < > goose! *P1869:*goose. *1872:*the gaby while
^{1042-43|} MS:§ no ¶ § *P1869:*§ ¶ § *1889a:*§ no ¶ § *1889:*§ no ¶; emended to restore ¶; see
Editorial Notes § ^{1043|} MS:But, if *P1869:*Nay, if ^{1046|} MS:revenge.

1050   To Rome, the journey there, the jaunting thence
       To shelter at the House of Convertites,
       The visits to the Villa, and so forth,
       Where was one minute left us all this while
       To put in execution that revenge
1055   We planned o' the instant?—as it were, plumped down
       O' the spot, some eight months since, which round sound egg,
       Rome, more propitious than our nest, should hatch!
       Object not, "You reached Rome on Christmas-eve,
       And, despite liberty to act at once,
1060   Waited a whole and indecorous week!"
       Hath so the Molinism, the canker, lords,
       Eaten to our bone? Is no religion left?
       No care for aught held holy by the Church?
       What, would you have us skip and miss those Feasts
1065   O' the Natal Time, must we go prosecute
       Secular business on a sacred day?
       Should not the merest charity expect,
       Setting our poor concerns aside for once,
       We hurried to the song matutinal
1070   I' the Sistine, and pressed forward for the Mass
       The Cardinal that's Camerlengo chaunts,
       Then rushed on to the blessing of the Hat
       And Rapier, which the Pope sends to what prince
       Has done most detriment to the Infidel—
1075   And thereby whetted courage if 'twere blunt?

---

*P1869:*revenge!   1050| MS:there, the journey thence,   *1889a:*the jaunting thence
1051| MS:The shelter *1889a:*To shelter   1052| MS:visit *P1869:*visits
1054| MS:revenge,— *P1869:*revenge   1055| MS:Believe, dear Lords,—we <> instant,
plumped *P1869:*We <> instant?—as it were, plumped down   1056| MS:Down, a
sound egg, o' <> months hence, *P1869:*A round sound <> months since, *1872:*O'
<> since, which round sound egg,   1057| MS:hatch? *P1869:*hatch!
1058| MS:Remark not—you arrive § crossed out and replaced above by two words § reach
Rome on Christmas-night § crossed out and replaced above by § eve, *P1869:*Object not,
"You reach *CP1869:*reached   1060| MS:Wait a full week—indecorous delay!
*P1869:*delay!" *CP1869:*"Waited a week *1872:*a whole and indecorous week!"
1061| MS:the Molinism canker *P1869:*the Molinism-canker *1872:*the Molinism, the
canker   1062| MS:to the bone *1889a:*to our bone   1063| MS:church § altered to §
Church   1070| MS:forward to § altered to § for   1073| MS:what Prince
*CP1869:*prince   1075| MS:whet our courage *1872:*whetted courage

275

Meantime, allow we kept the house a week,
Suppose not we were idle in our mew!
Picture us raging here and raving there—
" 'Money?' I need none. 'Friends?' The word is null.
¹⁰⁸⁰ Restore the white was on that shield of mine
Borne at" . . . wherever might be shield to bear.
"I see my grandsire, he who fought so well
At" . . . here find out and put in time and place,
Or else invent the fight his grandsire fought:
¹⁰⁸⁵ "I see this! I see that!"

(See nothing else,
Or I shall scarce see lamb's fry in an hour!
What to the uncle, as I bid advance
The smoking dish? "Fry suits a tender tooth!
Behoves we care a little for our kin—
¹⁰⁹⁰ You, Sir,—who care so much for cousinship
As come to your poor loving nephew's feast!"
He has the reversion of a long lease yet—
Land to bequeath! He loves lamb's fry, I know!)

Here fall to be considered those same six
¹⁰⁹⁵ Qualities; what Bottini needs must call
So many aggravations of our crime,

---

¹⁰⁷⁶| MS:Meantime, suppose we *P1869:*Meantime, allow we   ¹⁰⁷⁷| MS:our cage:
*P1869:*our mew: *1872:*mew!   ¹⁰⁷⁸| MS:Picture Count Guido raging <> and there—
*1872:*Picture us raging <> and raving there—   ¹⁰⁷⁹| MS:"Money?" I <> none—
"Friends? The *P1869:*" 'Money?' I <> 'Friends?' The *1872:*none. 'Friends
¹⁰⁸⁰| MS:Match me the *1872:*Restore the   ¹⁰⁸¹| MS:Born at . . wherever
P1869:"Borne at" . . wherever *CP1869:*bear; *1872:*bear. *1889a:*at" . . . wherever
¹⁰⁸²| MS:I see *P1869:*"I see   ¹⁰⁸³| MS:At . . here <> out, put in the time and place
*P1869:*At" . . here <> out and put in time *1872:*place, *1889a:*At" . . . here
¹⁰⁸⁴| MS:Of what might be a fight his grandsire found, *P1869:*grandsire fought,
*CP1869:*fought; *1872:*Or else invent the fight   ¹⁰⁸⁵| MS:I see this—I see that—see to
it all, *P1869:*"I <> that" § ¶ § See *1869:*that—" § ¶ § See *1872:*this! I see that!" § ¶ § (See
nothing else,   ¹⁰⁸⁶| MS:hour: *P1869:*Or shall I scarce <> hour! *CP1869:*Or I shall
scarce   ¹⁰⁸⁷| MS:I'll say § crossed out and replaced above by § nod to *P1869:*—Nod to
*1872:*What to   ¹⁰⁸⁸| MS:dish—"Sir, for your tender teeth! *P1869:*dish, "This, for
*1872:*dish? "Fry suits a tender tooth!   ¹⁰⁸⁹| MS:us <> kin *P1869:*kin— *1872:*we
¹⁰⁹⁰| MS:You, Sir, who *P1869:*You, Sir,—who   ¹⁰⁹¹| MS:come for your <> feast!
*P1869:*come to your <> feast!"   ¹⁰⁹³| MS:He may bequeath! He <> know!
*P1869:*Land to bequeath! He *1872:*know!)   ¹⁰⁹⁵| MS:Qualities, what

276

Parasite-growth upon mere murder's back.
We summarily might dispose of such
By some off-hand and jaunty fling, some skit—
1100 "So, since there's proved no crime to aggravate,
A fico for your aggravations, Fisc!"
No,—handle mischief rather,—play with spells
Were meant to raise a spirit, and laugh the while
We show that did he rise we stand his match!
1105 Therefore, first aggravation: we made up—
Over and above our simple murderous selves—
A regular assemblage of armed men,
Coadunatio armatorum,—ay,
Unluckily it was the very judge
1110 That sits in judgment on our cause to-day
Who passed the law as Governor of Rome:
"Four men armed,"— though for lawful purpose, mark!
Much more for an acknowledged crime,—"shall die."
We five were armed to the teeth, meant murder too?
1115 Why, that's the very point that saves us, Fisc!
Let me instruct you. Crime nor done nor meant,—
You punish still who arm and congregate:
For wherefore use bad means to a good end?
Crime being meant not done,—you punish still
1120 The means to crime, whereon you haply pounce,
Though accident have baulked them of effect.
But crime not only compassed but complete,
Meant and done too? Why, since you have the end,

---

*P1869:*Qualities; what ¹⁰⁹⁷| MS:back: *P1869:*back. ¹⁰⁹⁹| MS:fling—some
*P1869:*fling, some ¹¹⁰⁴| MS:that had he risen we are his *P1869:*that did he rise we
*1889a:*we stand his ¹¹⁰⁵| MS:Therefore—First *P1869:*Therefore, first
¹¹⁰⁶| MS:murdering *1872:*murderous ¹¹⁰⁷| MS:men *P1869:*men,
¹¹⁰⁹| MS:very Judge *P1869:*very judge ¹¹¹⁰| MS:Who sits *1889a:*That sits
¹¹¹¹| MS:That passed *1889a:*Who passed ¹¹¹²| MS:armed—though < > mark—
*P1869:*mark! *CP1869:*armed,"—though ¹¹¹³| MS:crime—shall *P1869:*crime,—shall
*CP1869:*crime,—"shall ¹¹¹⁷| MS:You § over perhaps *We* § < > congregate
*P1869:*congregate: ¹¹¹⁸| MS:For why have used bad *1889a:*For wherefore use bad
¹¹¹⁹| MS:Crime being § inserted above § < > done, you *P1869:*done,—you
¹¹²⁰| MS:Those means to crime you < > pounce upon *P1869:*The means to crime, you < >
upon, *1872:*crime, whereon you < > pounce, ¹¹²¹| MS:Though circumstances have
baulked you of their end: *1872:*Though accident have < > end. *1889a:*baulked them of
effect. ¹¹²²| MS:complete? *P1869:*complete, ¹¹²³| MS:end *P1869:*end,

Be that your sole concern, nor mind those means
1125 No longer to the purpose! Murdered we?
(—Which, that our luck was in the present case,
Quod contigisse in præsenti casu,
Is palpable, *manibus palpatum est—*)
Make murder out against us, nothing else!
1130 Of many crimes committed with a view
To one main crime, Law overlooks the less,
Intent upon the large. Suppose a man
Having in view commission of a theft,
Climbs the town-wall: 'tis for the theft he hangs,
1135 In case he stands convicted of such theft:
Law remits whipping, due to who clomb wall
Through bravery or wantonness alone,
Just to dislodge a daw's nest, plant a flag.
So I interpret you the manly mind
1140 Of him about to judge both you and me,—
Our Governor, who, being no Fisc, my Fisc,
Cannot have blundered on ineptitude!

Next aggravation,—that the arms themselves
Were specially of such forbidden sort
1145 Through shape or length or breadth, as, prompt, Law plucks
From single hand of solitary man,
Making him pay the carriage with his life:

1124| MS:concern nor *P1869:*concern, nor 1125| MS:purpose: murdered
*P1869:*purpose! Murdered 1126| MS:—Which *P1869:*(—Which 1127| MS:*casu*
P1869:casu, 1128| MS:palpable—*manibus* <> *est—* *P1869:*palpable, *manibus* <>
est—) 1129| MS:nothing more! *P1869:*nothing less! *1889a:*nothing else!
1130| MS:Are many *P1869:*Of many 1131| MS:crime, you overlook the less
*P1869:*less, *1872:*crime, Law overlooks the 1134-36| MS:town-wall: you § crossed out §
<> hangs,/ Remit the whipping due <> climbs *P1869:*hangs,/ Remitted
*CP1869:*hangs,/ Suppose you can convict him of such theft,/ Remitted *1872:*/ In case he
stands convicted of <> theft: / Law remits whipping, <> clomb 1137| MS:For
bravery *1872:*Through bravery 1138| MS:nest and no more. *1872:*nest or plant flag.
*1889a:*nest, plant a flag. 1139-41| MS:mind/ O' the Governor, my Fisc, who, being no
babe § indication to transpose to § O' the Governor, who <> babe, my fisc, *P1869:*mind/ Of
him the Judge shall judge both you and me,—/ O' *1872://* Our Governor <> no Fisc, my
1889a:/ <> him about to judge both <> / 1142| MS:ineptitude. *P1869:*ineptitude!
1142-43| MS:§ no ¶ § *P1869:*§ ¶ § *1889a:*§ no ¶ § *1889:*§ no ¶; emended to restore ¶; see
Editorial Notes § 1145| MS:prompt, law *1872:*prompt, Law 1147| MS:And

Delatio armorum, arms against the rule,
Contra formam constitutionis, of
1150 Pope Alexander's blessed memory.
Such are the poignards with the double prong,
Horn-like, when tines make bold the antlered buck,
Each prong of brittle glass—wherewith to stab
And break off short and so let fragment stick
1155 Fast in the flesh to baffle surgery:
Such being the Genoese blade with hooked edge
That did us service at the villa here.
Sed parcat mihi tam eximius vir,
But,—let so rare a personage forgive,—
1160 Fisc, thy objection is a foppery!
Thy charge runs that we killed three innocents:
Killed, dost see? Then, if killed, what matter how?
By stick or stone, by sword or dagger, tool
Long or tool short, round or triangular—
1165 Poor slain folk find small comfort in the choice!
Means to an end, means to an end, my Fisc!
Nature cries out, "Take the first arms you find!"
Furor ministrat arma: where's a stone?
Unde mî lapidem, where darts for me?
1170 *Unde sagittas?* But subdue the bard

---

makes him   *1872:*Making him   1148| MS:*armorum*—arms <> rule   *P1869:armorum,*
arms <> rule,   1149| MS:*constitutionis* of   *P1869:consitutionis,* of   1151| MS:the
poniard of § crossed out and replaced above by § with   *P1869:*poignard   *1872:*is   *1889a:*are
the poignards   1153| MS:And all of brittle § inserted above § glass—for man to stab
*1872:*And made of <> glass—wherewith to   *1889a:*Each prong of   1156| MS:And such
the <> with hooks at edge   *1872:*Such being the <> with hooked edge
1158–59| MS:§ crowded between 1157-60 in continuous line § *Sed—parcat* <> *eximius vir—/*
But, let so choice § crossed out and replaced above by § rare forgive,   *P1869:Sed—parcat* <>
eximius vir,//   *1872:/* But, —let <> forgive,—   1160| MS:foppery.   *P1869:*foppery!
1161| MS:charge is—that   *P1869:*charge runs, that   *1872:*runs that   1162| MS:Killed,
do you see: if killed—what <> how?—   *P1869:*Killed, dost see? Then, if killed, what
*1889a:*how?   1163| MS:stick and stone, by sword and dagger, tools   *P1869:*stick or
stone, by sword or dagger, tool   1164| MS:tools   *P1869:*tool   1165| MS:Poor folks,
they find no comfort in a choice!   *P1869:*find small comfort   *1872:*Poor slain folks find <>
in the choice!   *1889a:*folk   1167| MS:out "Take   *1889a:*out, "Take
1169| MS:*lapidem,*—or § crossed out § where my § crossed out § darts? § question mark
altered to § for   *P1869:lapidem,* where   1170| MS:*sagittas?* § next two words illegibly
crossed out, perhaps *Best restrain* and replaced above by two words § But subdue

And rationalize a little. Eight months since,
Had we, or had we not, incurred your blame
For letting 'scape unpunished this bad pair?
I think I proved that in last paragraph!
1175 Why did we so? Because our courage failed.
Wherefore? Through lack of arms to fight the foe:
We had no arms or merely lawful ones,
An unimportant sword and blunderbuss,
Against a foe, pollent in potency,
1180 The *amasius*, and our vixen of a wife.
Well then, how culpably do we gird loin
And once more undertake the high emprise,
Unless we load ourselves this second time
With handsome superfluity of arms,
1185 Since better is "too much" than "not enough,"
And *"plus non vitiat,"* too much does no harm,
Except in mathematics, sages say.
Gather instruction from the parable!
At first we are advised—"A lad hath here
1190 Seven barley loaves and two small fishes: what
Is that among so many?" Aptly asked:
But put that question twice and, quite as apt,
The answer is "Fragments, twelve baskets full!"

And, while we speak of superabundance, fling

---

^{1171|} MS:rationalise a little: eight *P1869:*rationalize *1872:*little. Eight
^{1172|} MS:Had we or <> not incurred *P1869:*Had we, or <> not, incurred
^{1173–75|} MS:letting § over illegible word § scape <> / Why *P1869:*'scape <> / I think I
proved that in last paragraph!/ Why ^{1176|} MS:Wherefore? Thro' <> of means to <>
foe, *P1869:*Wherefore? Through <> of arms to <> foe: ^{1179|} MS:Against that foe
*P1869:*Against a foe ^{1181|} MS:culpably we gird our loins *P1869:*culpably do we
gird loin ^{1182|} MS:once again attempt the *P1869:*once more undertake the
^{1183|} MS:we load § over illegible word, perhaps *arm* § ^{1185|} MS:better say "too <>
enough, *P1869:*enough," *1872:*better is "too ^{1186|} MS:*vitiat"*—too-much <>
harm *P1869:vitiat,"* too much <> harm, ^{1187|} MS:mathematics, people say.
*P1869:*mathematics, sages say. ^{1189|} MS:we hear § crossed out and replaced above by
two words § are advised— "A lad among us hath § last three words crossed out and
replaced above by two words § hath here ^{1190|} MS:Seven barley § inserted above § <>
fishes—what is that § last two words crossed out § *P1869:*fishes: what ^{1191|} MS:Is that
§ last two words inserted in margin § <> many? —Aptly *P1869:*many?" Aptly
^{1192|} MS:apt *1889a:*apt, ^{1193|} MS:answer were "Fragments—twelve baskets ful § last
two words perhaps intended to be *basketsful* § *P1869:*answer is "Fragments, twelve <>
full!" ^{1193–94|} MS:§ no ¶ § *P1869:*§ ¶ § *1889a:*§ no ¶ § *1889:*§ no ¶; emended to
restore ¶; see Editorial Notes § ^{1194|} MS:superabunce, here § altered to § Sirs,

¹¹⁹⁵ We word by the way to fools who cast their flout
On Guido—"Punishment were pardoned him,
But here the punishment exceeds offence:
He might be just, but he was cruel too!"
Why, grant there seems a kind of cruelty
¹²⁰⁰ In downright stabbing people he could maim,
(If so you stigmatize the stern and strict)
Still, Guido meant no cruelty—may plead
Transgression of his mandate, over-zeal
O' the part of his companions: all he craved
¹²⁰⁵ Was, they should fray the faces of the folk,
Merely disfigure, nowise make them die.
Solummodo fassus est, he owns no more,
Dedisse mandatum, than that he desired,
Ad sfrisiandum, dicam, that they hack
¹²¹⁰ And hew, i' the customary phrase, his wife,
Uxorem tantum, and no harm beside.
If his instructions then be misconceived,
Nay, disobeyed, impute you blame to him?
Cite me no Panicollus to the point,
¹²¹⁵ As adverse! Oh, I quite expect his case—
How certain noble youths of Sicily
Having good reason to mistrust their wives,

---

*P1869:*superabundance, fling   ^{1195|} MS:A word < > fools that cast *1872:*We word
< > fools who cast   ^{1196–1201|} MS:On Guido—"Punishment exceeds offence,/ You might
be just but you were cruel here."/ If < > stigmatise < > strict, *P1869:*offence:/ < > cruel
too!"// *1872:*On Guido—"Punishment were pardoned him,/ "But here the punishment
exceeds offense:/ He might be just, but he was cruel too!"/ Why grant there seems a kind of
cruelty/ In downright stabbing people he could maim,/ (If < > strict) *1889a:*///// < >
stigmatize   ^{1202|} MS:Still, he is not without excuse—may *1872:*Still, Guido meant no
cruelty—may   ^{1204|} MS:On *P1869:*O'   ^{1205–7|} MS:Was—they < > of the three/
Solummodo < > *est*—he < > more *P1869:*Was, they < > three:/ *Solummodo* < > *est,* he
< > more, *1872:*of the folk,/ Merely disfigure, nowise make them die./ *Solummodo*
^{1208|} MS:desired *P1869:*desired,   ^{1210|} MS:wife *P1869:*wife,
^{1211|} MS:*tantum*—and *P1869:*tantum,* and   ^{1212|} MS:If our instructions
*P1869:*If his instructions   ^{1213|} MS:Nay, § inserted in margin § Disobeyed § altered
to § disobeyed < > to us? *P1869:*to him?   ^{1214|} MS:point *P1869:*point,

Killed them and were absolved in consequence:
While others who had gone beyond the need
1220 By mutilation of each paramour—
As Galba in the Horatian satire grieved
—These were condemned to the galleys, cast for guilt
Exceeding simple murder of a wife.
But why? Because of ugliness, and not
1225 Cruelty, in the said revenge, I trow!
Ex causa abscissionis partium;
Qui nempe id facientes reputantur
Naturæ inimici, man revolts
Against them as the natural enemy.
1230 Pray, grant to one who meant to slit the nose
And slash the cheek and slur the mouth, at most,
A somewhat more humane award than these
Obtained, these natural enemies of man!
Objectum funditus corruit, flat you fall,
1235 My Fisc! I waste no kick on you, but pass.

Third aggravation: that our act was done—
Not in the public street, where safety lies,
Not in the bye-place, caution may avoid,
Wood, cavern, desert, spots contrived for crime,—
1240 But in the very house, home, nook and nest,
O' the victims, murdered in their dwelling-place,
In domo ac habitatione propria,

1218| MS:consequence. *P1869:*consequence: 1220| MS:of the paramour—
*P1869:*paramour   *1872:*of each paramour—   1221| MS:(As <> Horatian
§ inserted above § satire had to § last two words crossed out § grieve § altered to §
grieved) *P1869:*(So Galba   *1872:*As Galba <> grieved   1222| MS:These
<> gallies, as for   *P1869:*—These <> galleys   *1872:*galleys, cast for
1224| MS:ugliness and   *P1869:*ugliness, and   1225| MS:Cruelty in   *P1869:*Cruelty,
in   1226| MS:*partium—*   *P1869:partium;*   1228| MS:*inimici,*—man
P1869:inimici, man   1229-34| MS:Against such as <> enemy—/ Is this mere § last
three words crossed out and replaced above by two words § Allow our slitting nose and
slashing cheek/ A <> these!/ *Objectum*   *P1869:*enemy./ Pray, grant to one who meant
to slit the nose/ And slash the cheek and slur the mouth, at most,/ A <>   *1872:*Against
them as <> /// <> these/ Obtained, these natural enemies of man!//
1234| MS:*corruit:* flat   *P1869:corruit,* flat   1235| MS:My fisc <> you but
*P1869:*My Fisc   *1872:*you, but   1236| MS:§ marginal note that new ¶ begins §
done   *P1869:*done—   1237| MS:street where lies   *P1869:*street, where <> lies,
1239| MS:crime,   *P1869:*crime,—   1240-42| MS:in our victims very home and/ *In*

Where all presumably is peace and joy.
The spider, crime, pronounce we twice a pest
1245 When, creeping from congenial cottage, she
Taketh hold with her hands, to horrify
His household more, i' the palace of the king.
All three were housed and safe and confident.
Moreover, the permission that our wife
1250 Should have at length *domum pro carcere*,
Her own abode in place of prison—why,
We ourselves granted, by our other self
And proxy Paolo: did we make such grant,
Meaning a lure?—elude the vigilance
1255 O' the jailor, lead her to commodious death,
While we ostensibly relented?

                              Ay,
Just so did we, nor otherwise, my Fisc!
Is vengeance lawful? We demand our right,
But find it will be questioned or refused
1260 By jailor, turnkey, hangdog,—what know we?
Pray, how is it we should conduct ourselves?
To gain our private right—break public peace,
Do you bid us?—trouble order with our broils?
Endanger . . shall I shrink to own . . ourselves?—
1265 Who want no broken head nor bloody nose
(While busied slitting noses, breaking heads)
From the first tipstaff that may interfere!

<> *propria*   *P1869:*in the very house, home, nook and/ O' the victim, murdered
in her dwelling-place,/ *In* <> *propria,*   *1869:*victims <> in their dwelling-place,/
1243| MS:is confidence. § word and period crossed out § peace and joy.   1244| MS:spider,
crime, § commas crossed out and then restored § seems twice a noxious § last four words
crossed out and replaced above by four words § pronounce we twice a   1245| MS:When,
leaving § crossed out and replaced above by § creeping   1246| MS:hands and houseth so
§ last two words crossed out and replaced above by § horrifies   *P1869:*hands, to horrify
1247| MS:His household so, § last three words inserted in margin § I'   *P1869:*household
more, i'   1250| MS:*carcere*   *P1869:carcere,*   1252| MS:ranted by   *P1869:*granted,
by   1253| MS:make the grant,   *P1869:*make such grant,   1254| MS:lure,—elude
*P1869:*lure?—elude   1256| MS:relented? § ¶ § —Ay,   *P1869:*relented? § ¶ § Ay,
1259| MS:And find <> questioned and refused   *P1869:*But find <> questioned or refused
1260-62| MS:we?/ To   *P1869:*we?/ Pray, how is it we should conduct ourselves?/ To
1265-67| MS:nose/ From <> tipstaff shall please interfere!   *P1869:*nose/ (While busied
slitting noses, breaking heads)/ From   *1872://* From <> tipstaff that may interfere!

Nam quicquid sit, for howsoever it be,
An de consensu nostro, if with leave
1270   Or not, *a monasterio,* from the nuns,
Educta esset, she had been led forth,
Potuimus id dissimulare, we
May well have granted leave in pure pretence,
Ut aditum habere, that thereby
1275   An entry we might compass, a free move
Potuissemus, to her easy death,
Ad eam occidendam. Privacy
O' the hearth, and sanctitude of home, say you?
Shall we give man's abode more privilege
1280   Than God's?—for in the churches where He dwells,
In quibus assistit Regum Rex, by means
Of His essence, *per essentiam,* all the same,
Et nihilominus, therein, *in eis,*
Ex justa via delinquens, whoso dares
1285   To take a liberty on ground enough,
Is pardoned, *excusatur:* that's our case—
Delinquent through befitting cause. You hold,
To punish a false wife in her own house
Is graver than, what happens every day,
1290   To hale a debtor from his hiding-place
In church protected by the Sacrament?
To this conclusion have I brought my Fisc?

1268| MS:*sit*—for <> be   *P1869:sit,* for <> be,   1269| MS:*nostro*—if   *P1869:nostro,*
if   1270| MS:not—*a monasterio* from the nuns   *P1869:*not, *a monasterio,* from the
nuns,   1271| MS:*esset*—she <> forth   *P1869:esset,* she <> forth,
1274| MS:*habere,* that to have   *P1869:habere,* that thereby   1275| MS:entry,
potuissemus, gain § last two words crossed out § we might compass by the move
*P1869:*compass, a free move   1276| MS:*Potuissemus*—to <> death,
P1869:Potuissemus, to <> death,   1279| MS:Then you give   *P1869:*Would you
*1872:*Shall we give   1280| MS:Than God's—for <> dwells   *P1869:*Than God's—for
<> dwells,   1281| MS:*assistit Regum Rex*—by   *P1869:assistit Regum Rex,* by
1282| MS:essence *per essentiam*—yet no less   *P1869:*essence, *per essentiam,* all the same,
1283| MS:*nihilominus*—therein   *P1869:nihilominus,* therein   1284| MS:*delinquens*—
who makes bold   *P1869:delinquens,* whoso dares   1285| MS:on fitting cause
*P1869:*on ground enough,   1286| MS:pardoned *excusatur*   *P1869:*pardoned, *excusatur*
1287| MS:through a fitting cause. You say   *P1869:*through befitting cause. You hold,
1290| MS:hiding place   *P1869:*hiding-place   1292| MS:my Fisc!   *P1869:*my Fisc?

Foxes have holes, and fowls o' the air their nests;
Praise you the impiety that follows, Fisc?
1295 Shall false wife yet have where to lay her head?
"Contra Fiscum definitum est!" He's done!
"Surge et scribe," make a note of it!
—If I may dally with Aquinas' word.

Or in the death-throe does he mutter still,
1300 Fourth aggravation, that we changed our garb,
And rusticized ourselves with uncouth hat,
Rough vest and goatskin wrappage; murdered thus
Mutatione vestium, in disguise,
Whereby mere murder got complexed with wile,
1305 Turned *homicidium ex insidiis?* Fisc,
How often must I round thee in the ears—
All means are lawful to a lawful end?
Concede he had the right to kill his wife:
The Count indulged in a travesty; why?
1310 *De illa ut vindictam sumeret,*
That on her he might lawful vengeance take,
Commodius, with more ease, *et tutius,*
And safelier: wants he warrant for the step?
Read to thy profit how the Apostle once
1315 For ease and safety, when Damascus raged,
Was let down in a basket by the wall

1293-96| MS:holes—and < > o' the air § last three words inserted above § < > nests—/ What follows—I shall let the Fisc declare—/ *"Contra fiscum* < > done, *P1869:*holes, and < > nests;/ Praise you the impiety that follows, Fisc?/ Shall false wife yet have where to lay her head?/ *"Contra Fiscum* < > *1872:///* done!   1297| MS:§ crowded between 1296-99 § *scribe!"* —make *P1869:scribe,"* make   1298| MS:§ inserted in margin § 1298-99| MS:§ no ¶ § *P1869:*§ ¶ §   1299| MS:still? *1872:*still,   1301| MS:uncouth cloak § followed by illegible word, both crossed out and replaced above by § hat 1302| MS:Rough hat § crossed out and replaced above by § vest   1303| MS:*vestium—* in *P1869:vestiium,* in *CP1869:vestium*   1304| MS:wile *P1869:*wile, 1305| MS:Turns < > *insidiis.* Fisc, *P1869:*Turned *1872:insidiis?* Fisc, 1308| MS:wife,— *P1869:*wife: 1309| MS:travesty, so *P1869:*travesty; why? 1310| MS:*sumeret P1869:sumeret,*   1311| MS:That he on her might vengeance take thereby *P1869:*That on her he might lawful vengeance take,   1312| MS:*Commodius et tutius,* with more ease *P1869:Commodius,* with more ease, *et tutius,*   1313| MS:And safety: wants *P1869:*And safelier: wants   1314| MS:how the § inserted above § Apostle Paul § crossed out §   1315| MS:ease, for safety, in § crossed out and replaced above by § when < > raged § over illegible word §,   1316| MS:wall, *1889a:*wall

To 'scape the malice of the governor
(Another sort of Governor boasts Rome!)
—Many are of opinion,—covered close,
1320 Concealed with—what except that very cloak
He left behind at Troas afterward?
I shall not add a syllable: Molinists may!

Well, have we more to manage? Ay, indeed!
Fifth aggravation, that our wife reposed
1325 *Sub potestate judicis,* beneath
Protection of the judge,—her house was styled
A prison, and his power became its guard
In lieu of wall and gate and bolt and bar.
This is a tough point, shrewd, redoubtable:
1330 Because we have to supplicate that judge
Shall overlook wrong done the judgment-seat.
Now, I might suffer my own nose be pulled,
As man: but then as father . . . if the Fisc
Touched one hair of my boy who held my hand
1335 In confidence he could not come to harm
Crossing the Corso, at my own desire,
Going to see those bodies in the church—
What would you say to that, Don Hyacinth?
This is the sole and single knotty point:
1340 For, bid Tommati blink his interest,
You laud his magnanimity the while:
But baulk Tommati's office,—he talks big!
"My predecessors in the place,—those sons

1317-19| MS:governor/ —Many <> covered too, *P1869:*governor/ (Another sort of
Governor boasts Rome!)/ —Many <> covered close, 1320| MS:with what
*1869:*with—what 1322-23| MS:§ no ¶ § *P1869:*§ ¶ § *1872:*§ no ¶ § *1889:*§ no ¶;
emended to restore ¶; see Editorial Notes § 1323| MS:indeed. *P1869:*indeed!
1329| MS:redoubtable. *P1869:*redoubtable: 1330| MS:to call upon § last two words
crossed out and replaced above by § supplicate the judge *1889a:*supplicate that judge
1331| MS:To § crossed out § overlook § altered to § Overlook wrong § crossed out and replaced
above by § insult <> judgment-seat; *P1869:*Shall overlook wrong done the judgment-seat.
1332| MS:pulled *P1869:*pulled, 1333| MS:man—but <> father . . if *1889a:*man:
but <> father . . . if 1336-38| MS:the Corso at <> desire—/ —What *P1869:*the
Corso, at <> desire,/ Going to see those bodies in the church—/ What
1340| MS:interest— *P1869:*interest, 1342| MS:big— *P1869:*big! 1343| MS:My
Predecessors <> place—those *P1869:*"My Predecessors <> place,—those *CP1869:*My

286

O' the prophets that may hope succeed me here,—
1345   Shall I diminish their prerogative?
Count Guido Franceschini's honour!—well,
Has the Governor of Rome none?"

                    You perceive,
The cards are all against us. Make a push,
Kick over table, as shrewd gamesters do!
1350   We, do you say, encroach upon the rights,
Deny the omnipotence o' the Judge forsooth?
We, who have only been from first to last
Intending that his purpose should prevail,
Nay more, at times, anticipating it
1355   At risk of his rebuke?

                But wait awhile!
Cannot we lump this with the sixth and last
Of the aggravations—that the Majesty
O' the Sovereign here received a wound? to-wit,
Læsa Majestas, since our violence
1360   Was out of envy to the course of law,
In odium litis? We cut short thereby
Three pending suits, promoted by ourselves
I' the main,—which worsens crime, *accedit ad*
Exasperationem criminis!

1365   Yes, here the eruptive wrath with full effect!
How, did not indignation chain my tongue,

---

predecessors   ¹³⁴⁴| MS:"Of < > me there,—   *P1869:*O' < > me here,—
¹³⁴⁵| MS:prerogative?"   *P1869:*prerogative?   ¹³⁴⁷| MS:none?" Brief, *P1869:*none?"
§ ¶ § You perceive,   ¹³⁴⁸| MS:us: make *P1869:*us. Make   ¹³⁴⁹| MS:as our
gamesters do: *P1869:*do! *1872:*as shrewd gamesters do!   ¹³⁵²| MS:We who
*P1869:*We, who   ¹³⁵³| MS:Intent his mind and purpose *P1869:*Intent on that his
purpose *1872:*Intending that his purpose   ¹³⁵⁴| MS:Even, though, at < >
anticipating both *P1869:*Nay, more, at *1872:*anticipating it *1889a:*Nay more
¹³⁵⁵| MS:of a rebuke . . . but < > awhile . . *P1869:*rebuke? § ¶ § But < > awhile!
*P1872:*of his rebuke? § ¶ § But   ¹³⁵⁸| MS:received an impious wound, *P1869:*received a
wound, to-wit, *1872:*wound? to-wit,   ¹³⁵⁹| MS:*Læsa as,* for our *P1869:Læsa*
Majestas, since our   ¹³⁶⁰| MS:law *P1869:*law,   ¹³⁶¹| MS:*litis:* we
P1869:litis? We   ^{1364–65}| MS:§ no ¶ § *P1869:*§ ¶ §   ¹³⁶⁵| MS:Yes,—here
*P1869:*Yes, here   ¹³⁶⁶| MS:How—did < > tongue *P1869:*tongue— *1872:*How, did

Could I repel this last, worst charge of all!
(There is a porcupine to barbacue;
Gigia can jug a rabbit well enough,
1370 With sour-sweet sauce and pine-pips; but, good Lord,
Suppose the devil instigate the wench
To stew, not roast him? Stew my porcupine?
If she does, I know where his quills shall stick!
Come, I must go myself and see to things:
1375 I cannot stay much longer stewing here.)
Our stomach . . . I mean, our soul is stirred within,
And we want words. We wounded Majesty?
Fall under such a censure, we?—who yearned
So much that Majesty dispel the cloud
1380 And shine on us with healing on her wings,
That we prayed Pope *Majestas'* very self
To anticipate a little the tardy pack,
Bell us forth deep the authoritative bay
Should start the beagles into sudden yelp
1385 Unisonous,—and, Gospel leading Law,
Grant there assemble in our own behoof
A Congregation, a particular Court,
A few picked friends of quality and place,
To hear the several matters in dispute,—
1390 Causes big, little and indifferent,
Bred of our marriage like a mushroom-growth,—
All at once (can one brush off such too soon?)
And so with laudable despatch decide
Whether we, in the main (to sink detail)
1395 Were one the Pope should hold fast or let go.

<> tongue,   1367| MS:last worst *P1869:*last, worst   1368-75| MS:barbacue—/ I
<> here) *P1869:*barbacue;/ § adds lines 1369-74 § *1872://////* <> here.)
1376| MS:stomach . . I <> soul—is *1872:*soul is *1889a:*stomach . . . I
1378| MS:we,—who *1872:*we?—who   1380| MS:healing in its wings, *P1869:*healing
on its *1872:*on her wings,   1381| MS:We prayed the Pope—*Majestas'* very self—
*P1869:*the Pope, *Majestas'* <> self, *1872:*That we prayed Pope <> self
1382| MS:pack § over illegible word, perhaps *herd* §,   1389| MS:Should hear <>
dispute, *P1869:*To hear *1889a:*dispute,—   1391| MS:mushroom-growth,
*1889a:*mushroom-growth,—   1392| MS:once—can <> soon?— *P1869:*once (can <>
soon?)   1393| MS:so decide with <> dispatch § transposed to § so with <> dispatch
decide   1394| MS:main—to <> detail— *P1869:*main (to <> detail)   1395| MS:the
Church should hold up or cast down,— *P1869:*hold fast or let go. *1872:*the Pope should

288

"What, take the credit from the Law?" you ask?
Indeed, we did! Law ducks to Gospel here:
Why should Law gain the glory and pronounce
A judgment shall immortalize the Pope?
1400 Yes: our self-abnegating policy
Was Joab's—we would rouse our David's sloth,
Bid him encamp against a city, sack
A place whereto ourselves had long laid siege,
Lest, taking it at last, it take our name
1405 Nor be styled *Innocentinopolis.*
But no! The modesty was in alarm,
The temperance refused to interfere,
Returned us our petition with the word
"Ad judices suos," "Leave him to his Judge!"
1410 As who should say "Why trouble my repose?
Why consult Peter in a simple case,
Peter's wife's sister in her fever-fit
Might solve as readily as the Apostle's self?
Are my Tribunals posed by aught so plain?
1415 Hath not my Court a conscience? It is of age,
Ask it!"

We do ask,—but, inspire reply
To the Court thou bidst me ask, as I have asked—
Oh thou, who vigilantly dost attend
To even the few, the ineffectual words
1420 Which rise from this our low and mundane sphere

1396–98| MS:And—"take/ Why P1869:"What, take < > / Why CP1869:ask?/ Indeed, we
did! Law ducks to Gospel here./ Why   1398–99| MS:§ crowded between 1396-1400 in
continuous line, divided by / between *pronounce* and *The judgment* §   1399| MS:The
judgment P1869:A judgment   1401| MS:rouze P1869:rouse   1405| MS:And be
not *Innocentinopolis*. 1872:Nor be styles *Innocentinopolis*.   1406| MS:But—the
P1869:But no! The   1407| MS:The holiness refused P1869:The temperance refused
1409| MS:*suos*"—"Leave P1869:*suos*," "Leave   1410| MS:say—"Why 1872:say
"Why   1411| MS:in a case might solve P1869:in a simple case CP1869:case,
1412–14| MS:fever-fit?/ Are my Tribunals so incompetent, § last two words and comma crossed
out and replaced above by five words § posed by aught so plain? P1869:fever-fit/ Might
solve as readily as the Apostle's self/ Are   1415| MS:conscience,—It P1869:conscience?
It   1416–18| MS:it!" We do § over illegible erasure § < > reply,/ Oh < > vigilantly
§ followed by two words crossed out, the first illegibly, the second being *ear* § dost attend
P1869:it!" § ¶ § We < > reply/ To the court thou bidst me ask, as I have asked—/ Oh
CP1869:/ < > the Court < > /   1419| MS:To these § crossed out and replaced above

Up to thy region out of smoke and noise,
Seeking corroboration from thy nod
Who art all justice—which means mercy too,
In a low noisy smoky world like ours
¹⁴²⁵ Where Adam's sin made peccable his seed!
We venerate the father of the flock,
Whose last faint sands of life, the frittered gold,
Fall noiselessly, yet all too fast, o' the cone
And tapering heap of those collected years:
¹⁴³⁰ Never have these been hurried in their flow,
Though justice fain would jog reluctant arm,
In eagerness to take the forfeiture
Of guilty life: much less shall mercy sue
In vain that thou let innocence survive,
¹⁴³⁵ Precipitate no minim of the mass
O' the all-so precious moments of thy life,
By pushing Guido into death and doom!

(Our Cardinal engages to go read
The Pope my speech, and point its beauties out.
¹⁴⁴⁰ They say, the Pope has one half-hour, in twelve,
Of something like a moderate return
Of the intellectuals,—never much to lose!
If I adroitly plant this passage there,
The Fisc will find himself forestalled, I think,
¹⁴⁴⁵ Though he stand, beat till the old ear-drum break!
—Ah, boy of my own bowels, Hyacinth,

---

by § even my few, my ineffectual   *P1869:*even the few, the ineffectual   ¹⁴²¹| MS:To thy
pure region   *P1869:*Up to thy region   ¹⁴²³| MS:too   *CP1869:*too,
¹⁴²⁵| MS:seed.   *P1869:*seed!   ¹⁴²⁶| MS:Oh, § crossed out and replaced in margin by §
We venerable § altered to § venerate the § inserted above §   ¹⁴²⁸| MS:noiselessly yet
<> fast, the cone   *P1869:*noiselessly, yet <> fast, o' the   ¹⁴²⁹| MS:O' the tapering
§ inserted above § <> years,—   *CP1869:*And tapering   *1889a:*years: ¹⁴³⁰| MS:flow
*P1869:*flow,   ¹⁴³¹| MS:§ crowded between 1430-32 § When justice fain had jogged
reluctant   *P1869:*Though justice fain would jog reluctant   ¹⁴³²| MS:By eagerness
*P1869:*In eagerness   ¹⁴³⁵⁻³⁷| MS:mass/ By   *P1869:*mass/ O' the all-so precious
moments of the life/ By   *CP1869:*/ <> life,/   ¹⁴³⁷⁻³⁸| MS:§ no ¶ §   *P1869:*§ ¶ §
¹⁴³⁸⁻⁴⁰| MS:engages read my speech—/ They <> the Pope § inserted above § <> half-hour
in the § crossed out § twelve   *P1869:*speech:/ They <>   *CP1869:*half-hour, in twelve,
*1872:*engages to go read/ The Pope my speech, and point its beauties out./ They
¹⁴⁴²| MS:lose!—   *1889a:*lose!   ¹⁴⁴³| MS:If he adroitly   *P1869:*If I adroitly
¹⁴⁴⁵| MS:stand, knock § crossed out and replaced above by § beat

290

Wilt ever catch the knack, requite the pains
Of poor papa, become proficient too
I' the how and why and when, the time to laugh,
1450 The time to weep, the time, again, to pray,
And all the times prescribed by Holy Writ?
Well, well, we fathers can but care, but cast
Our bread upon the waters!)
　　　　　　　　　　　　In a word,
These secondary charges go to ground,
1455 Since secondary, and superfluous,—motes
Quite from the main point: we did all and some,
Little and much, adjunct and principal,
Causa honoris. Is there such a cause
As the sake of honour? By that sole test try
1460 Our action, nor demand if more or less,
Because of the action's mode, we merit blame
Or may-be deserve praise! The Court decides.
Is the end lawful? It allows the means:
What we may do, we may with safety do,
1465 And what means "safety" we ourselves must judge.
Put case a person wrongs me past dispute:
If my legitimate vengeance be a blow,
Mistrusting my bare arm can deal that blow,
I claim co-operation of a stick;

1447| MS:knack,—requite *1872:*knack, requite   1449| MS:when—the *1872:*when, the
1451| MS:times described § altered to § prescribed in Holy *P1869:*prescribed by Holy
1452| MS:can but trust § crossed out and replaced above by § hope § crossed out and replaced
by § care   1453| MS:Our § inserted in margin; followed by word crossed out, perhaps
His § <> waters—) § ¶ § In a word *P1869:*waters!) § ¶ § In a word,   1454| MS:ground
*P1869:*ground,   1455| MS:secondary, and § crossed out and replaced above by word
illegibly erased and replaced by § so superfluous,—motes § over illegible word §
*1872:*secondary, and superfluous   1456| MS:point,—we *P1869:*point: we
1457| MS:principal *P1869:*principal,   1458| MS:*honoris:* is <> a thing § crossed out §
cause *P1869:honoris.* Is   1459| MS:honour? Try § crossed out § by § altered to § By
1460| MS:The § crossed out and replaced above by § Our action, here: § crossed out § <> less
*P1869:*less,   1461| MS:mode we *P1869:*mode, we   1462| MS:praise:—the <>
decides— *P1869:*praise. The <> decides.   1463| MS:means. *P1869:*means:
*1872:*praise! The   1464| MS:What we may do we must § crossed out and replaced by §
may *1872:*What we may do, we   1466| MS:§ crowded between 1465-67 § a man has
wronged me *P1869:*a person wrongs me   1467| MS:vengeance is a *P1869:*vengeance
be a   1468| MS:can fitly strike § last two words crossed out and replaced above by three
words § deal the same, *1872:*deal that blow,   1469| MS:cooperation <> a club

1470   Doubtful if stick be tough, I crave a sword;
      Diffident of ability in fence,
      I fee a friend, a swordsman to assist:
      Take one—he may be coward, fool or knave:
      Why not take fifty?—and if these exceed
1475   I' the due degree of drubbing, whom accuse
      But the first author of the aforesaid wrong
      Who put poor me to such a world of pains?
      Surgery would have just excised a wart;
      The patient made such pother, struggled so
1480   That the sharp instrument sliced nose and all.
      Taunt us not that our friends performed for pay!
      Ourselves had toiled for simple honour's sake:
      But country clowns want dirt they comprehend,
      The piece of gold! Our reasons, which suffice
1485   Ourselves, be ours alone; our piece of gold
      Be, to the rustic, reason he approves!
      We must translate our motives like our speech,
      Into the lower phrase that suits the sense
      O' the limitedly apprehensive. Let

---

§ crossed out § stick *P1869:*co-operation < > stick;   ¹⁴⁷⁰| MS:Doubtful the stick < >
sword, *P1869:*Doubtful if stick < > sword;   ¹⁴⁷¹| MS:ability § over illegible erasure §
to fence, *P1869:*ability in fence,   ¹⁴⁷²| MS:I take a friend, § last two words inserted
above § a swordsman shall § crossed out and replaced above by § may assist:§ punctuation
obviously added in revision § me—take § last two words crossed out § *P1869:*I fee a friend a
swordsman to assist: ¹⁴⁷³| MS:Take § inserted in margin § One—who may turn out
§ last two words crossed out and replaced above by § be < > knave— *P1869:*one
*1872:*one—he may < > knave: ¹⁴⁷⁵| MS:drubbing, whose § altered to § whom the fault
§ last two words crossed out §   ¹⁴⁷⁶| MS:the aforesaid § inserted above §
¹⁴⁷⁷| MS:Has put *P1869:*Who put   ¹⁴⁷⁸| MS:A § crossed out § surgeon § altered to §
Surgery wants to § last two words crossed out and replaced above by two words § would have
¹⁴⁷⁹| MS:patient makes a § last two words crossed out and replaced above by two words §
made such   ¹⁴⁸⁰| MS:instrument cuts § first altered and then crossed out and replaced
above by § slices   ¹⁴⁸²| MS:For us—enough the simple < > sake— *P1869:*us, enough
were simple < > sake: *1872:*Ourselves, the simple < > sake sufficed: *1889a:*Ourselves
had toiled for simple < > sake: ¹⁴⁸³| MS:For country clowns—the dirt *P1869:*Give
country clowns the *1872:*But country clowns want dirt   ¹⁴⁸⁴| MS:gold: our reasons
which *P1869:*gold! Our reasons, which   ¹⁴⁸⁵| MS:Ourselves be *P1869:*Ourselves,
be   ¹⁴⁸⁶| MS:Be to the rustic reason and to spare: *P1869:*Be, to the rustic, reason
< > spare! *1872:*reason he approves!   ¹⁴⁸⁷| MS:speech *1872:*speech,
¹⁴⁸⁸| MS:phase may suit the *P1869:*phase that suits the   ¹⁴⁸⁹| MS:Of the limitedly
intelli § last word crossed out § apprehensive, let *P1869:*O' < > apprehensive. Let

292

1490 Each level have its language! Heaven speaks first
To the angel, then the angel tames the word
Down to the ear of Tobit: he, in turn,
Diminishes the message to his dog,
And finally that dog finds how the flea
1495 (Which else, importunate, might check his speed)
Shall learn its hunger must have holiday
By application of his tongue or paw:
So many varied sorts of language here,
Each following each with pace to match the step,
1500 *Haud passibus æquis!*

　　　　　　　Talking of which flea,
Reminds me I must put in special word
For the poor humble following,—the four friends,
Sicarii, our assassins caught and caged.
Ourselves are safe in your approval now:
1505 Yet must we care for our companions, plead
The cause o' the poor, the friends (of old-world faith)
Who lie in tribulation for our sake.
Pauperum Procurator is my style:
I stand forth as the poor man's advocate:
1510 And when we treat of what concerns the poor,
Et cum agatur de pauperibus,
In bondage, *carceratis,* for their sake,
In eorum causis, natural piety,
Pietas, ever ought to win the day,

1490| MS:language: heaven *P1869:*language! Heaven　　　　1492| MS:of Tobit,—he
*P1869:*of Tobit: he　　　1494| MS:finally the § altered to § that dog to the first § last three
words crossed out and replaced above by three words § finds how the　　　1495| MS:Which
<> speed, *P1869:*(Which <> speed)　　　1496-99| MS:learn his hunger <> holiday,—/
Each *P1869:*learn its hunger <> / How many varied sorts of language here,/ Each
*1872:*holiday,/ By application of his tongue or paw:/ So many <> / Each
DC,BrU:holiday *1889:*holiday　　　1500| MS:*æquis.* Talking <> flea, *P1869:æquis!* § ¶ §
Talking <> flea *1872:*flea,　　　1503| MS:assassins in your charge: *P1869:*charge.
*1872:*assassins caught and caged.　　　1504| MS:now,— *P1869:*now:　　　1506| MS:poor,
—the friends of old-world faith *P1869:*poor, the friends (of old-world faith)
1507-9| MS:Who are in <> sake./ I <> advocate, *P1869:/ Pauperum Procurator*
is my style:/ I <> advocate: *1872:*Who lie in <> //　　　1510| MS:poor
*P1869:*poor,　　　1511| MS:*pauperibus P1869:pauperibus,*　　　1512| MS:bondage
carceratis—for § crossed out § <> sake *P1869:*bondage, *carceratis,* for <> sake,
1513| MS:piety *P1869:*piety,　　　1514| MS:*Pietas* ever <> day *P1869:Pietas,* ever <>

¹⁵¹⁵   *Triumphare debet, quia ipsi sunt,*
        Because those very paupers constitute,
        Thesaurus Christi, all the wealth of Christ.
        Nevertheless I shall not hold you long
        With multiplicity of proofs, nor burn
¹⁵²⁰   Candle at noon-tide, clarify the clear.
        There beams a case refulgent from our books—
        Castrensis, Butringarius, everywhere
        I find it burn to dissipate the dark.
        'Tis this: a husband had a friend, which friend
¹⁵²⁵   Seemed to him over-friendly with his wife
        In thought and purpose,—I pretend no more.
        To justify suspicion or dispel,
        He bids his wife make show of giving heed,
        Semblance of sympathy—propose, in fine,
¹⁵³⁰   A secret meeting in a private place.
        The friend, enticed thus, finds an ambuscade,
        To-wit, the husband posted with a pack
        Of other friends, who fall upon the first
        And beat his love and life out both at once.
¹⁵³⁵   These friends were brought to question for their help;
        Law ruled "The husband being in the right,
        Who helped him in the right can scarce be wrong"—
        Opinio, an opinion every way,
        Multum tenenda cordi, heart should hold!
¹⁵⁴⁰   When the inferiors follow as befits
        The lead o' the principal, they change their name,

---

day,   ^{1515|} MS:*sunt* *P1869:sunt,*   ^{1516|} MS:very poor do constitute *P1869:*very
paupers constitute,   ^{1517|} MS:*Thesaurus Christi.* all *P1869:Thesaurus Christi,* all
^{1521|} MS:beams § over illegible erasure § <> from § over *in* §   ^{1523|} MS:dark;
*P1869:*dark.   ^{1525|} MS:him more than § last two words crossed out and replaced above
by word and hyphen§ over-   ^{1526|} MS:purpose,—we pretend *P1869:*purpose,—I
pretend   ^{1531|} MS:friend enticed thus finds *P1869:*friend, enticed thus, finds
^{1534-36|} MS:once./ Law *P1869:*once./ These friends were brought to question for their
help./ Law *1872:/* <> help;//   ^{1538|} MS:*Opinio*—an <> way *P1869:Opinio,* an
<> way,   ^{1539|} MS:*cordi* heart <> hold. *P1869:cordi,* heart <> hold!
^{1541|} MS:change the style § last word crossed out § name, *P1869:*change their name,

And, *non dicuntur,* are no longer called
His mandatories, *mandatorii,*
But helpmates, *sed auxiliatores;* since
1545   To that degree does honour's sake lend aid,
Adeo honoris causa est efficax,
That not alone, *non solum,* does it pour
Itself out, *se diffundat,* on mere friends
We bring to do our bidding of this sort,
1550   *In mandatorios simplices,* but sucks
Along with it in wide and generous whirl,
Sed etiam assassinii qualitate
Qualificatos, people qualified
By the quality of assassination's self,
1555   Dare I make use of such neologism,
Ut utar verbo.

         Haste we to conclude.
Of the other points that favour, leave some few
For Spreti; such as the delinquents' youth.
One of them falls short, by some months, of age
1560   Fit to be managed by the gallows; two
May plead exemption from our law's award,
Being foreigners, subjects of the Granduke—
I spare that bone to Spreti, and reserve
Myself the juicier breast of argument—
1565   Flinging the breast-blade i' the face o' the Fisc

1542| MS:And *non dicunter* are   *P1869:*And, *non dicunter,* are   1543| MS:mandatories
manditorii   *P1869:*mandatories, *mandatorii,*   1544| MS:helpmates *sed*
*P1869:*helpmates, *sed*   1545| MS:honour' sake § emended to § honour's sake § see
Editorial Notes §   1546| MS:*Honoris* <> *efficax*   *P1869:honoris* <> *efficax,*
1547| MS:alone *non solum* does   *P1869:*alone, *non solum,* does   1548| MS:out *se*
diffundat on mere knaves § crossed out §   *P1869:*out, *se diffundat,* on <> friends,
DC,BrU:friends   *1889:*friends   1549| MS:We pay § crossed out and replaced
above by § bring <> sort   *P1869:*sort,   1551| MS:whirl   *P1869:*whirl,
1553| MS:*Qualificatos*—people   *P1869:Qualificatos,* people   1555| MS:such
barbarous word, § last two words crossed out and replaced above by § neologism—
*P1869:*neologism,   1556| MS:*verbo.* Haste <> conclude—   *P1869:verbo.* § ¶ § Haste
<> conclude: *1889a:*conclude.   1558| MS:For Spreti—such <> youth—   *P1869:*For
Spreti; such <> youth: *1889a:*youth.   1561| MS:law's effect § crossed out § award
C*P1869:*award.   1563| MS:I toss § crossed out and replaced above by § spare <>
Spreti and pick bare   *P1869:*to Spreti and reserve   *1872:*to Spreti, and   1565| MS:And
fling the breast-bone in the <> Fisc,   *P1869:*Flinging the breast-blade i' the

Who furnished me the tid-bit: he must needs
Play off his privilege and rack the clowns,—
And they, at instance of the rack, confess
All four unanimously made resolve,—
1570   The night o' the murder, in brief minute snatched
Behind the back of Guido as he fled,—
That, since he had not kept his promise, paid
The money for the murder on the spot,
So, reaching home again, might please ignore
1575   The pact or pay them in improper coin,—
They one and all resolved, these hopeful friends,
'Twere best inaugurate the morrow's light,
Nature recruited with her due repose,
By killing Guido as he lay asleep
1580   Pillowed on wallet which contained their fee.

I thank the Fisc for knowledge of this fact:
What fact could hope to make more manifest
Their rectitude, Guido's integrity?
For who fails recognize the touching truth
1585   That these poor rustics bore no envy, hate,
Malice nor yet uncharitableness

DC,BrU:the Fisc   *1889:*the Fisc   ¹⁵⁶⁶| MS:he would needs   *P1869:*he must needs
¹⁵⁶⁷| MS:his armoury and   *1872:*his privilege and   ¹⁵⁶⁸| MS:confessed   *1872:*confess
¹⁵⁶⁹| MS:unanimously did resolve,—   *1872:*unanimously made resolve,—
¹⁵⁷⁰| MS:That night < > minutes   *1872:*The night < > minute   ¹⁵⁷²| MS:not kept his
promise, paid § last four words crossed out and original restored §   ¹⁵⁷³| MS:§ crowded
between 1572-74 § And § crossed out § The   ¹⁵⁷⁴| MS:That § crossed out and replaced
in margin by § And reaching home again, § inserted below § might even ignore the pact § last
two words crossed out §   *P1869:*And, reaching   *1872:*So, reaching < > might please
ignore   ¹⁵⁷⁵⁻⁷⁷| MS:pay it in < > coin,/ They would inaugurate   *P1869:*The past < >
coin,/ They one and all resolved, these hopeful friends,/ They   *1872:*The pact or pay them
in < > coin,—// 'Twere best inaugurate   ¹⁵⁷⁸| MS:Taking the necessary rest
meanwhile § line crossed out and replaced above by § Having recruited strength with
needful rest,   *1872:*Nature recruited with her due repose,   ¹⁵⁸⁰| MS:Pillowed by wallet
*1872:*Pillowed on wallet   ¹⁵⁸⁰⁻⁸¹| MS:§ no ¶ §   *P1869:*§ ¶ §   ¹⁵⁸⁰⁻⁸²| MS:fee./
What act could   *P1869:*fee./ § ¶ § I thank the Fisc for knowledge of this fact:/ What fact
could   *CP1869:*fee./   ¹⁵⁸³| MS:rectitude and his integrity?   *P1869:*rectitude, Guido's
integrity?   ¹⁵⁸⁴| MS:recognise apparent here,   *1872:*recognize the touching truth
¹⁵⁸⁵| MS:The harmless § crossed out § silly rustics < > no envy, § inserted above line §

Against the people they had put to death?
In them, did such an act reward itself?
All done was to deserve the simple pay,
1590 Obtain the bread clowns earn by sweat of brow,
And missing which, they missed of everything—
Hence claimed pay, even at expense of life
To their own lord, so little warped (admire!)
By prepossession, such the absolute
1595 Instinct of equity in rustic souls!
Whereas our Count, the cultivated mind,
He, wholly rapt in his serene regard
Of honour, he contemplating the sun
Who hardly marks if taper blink below,—
1600 He, dreaming of no argument for death
Except a vengeance worthy noble hearts,—
Dared not so desecrate the deed, forsooth,
Vulgarize vengeance, as defray its cost
By money dug from out the dirty earth,
1605 Irritant mere, in Ovid's phrase, to ill.
What though he lured base hinds by lucre's hope,—
The only motive they could masticate,
Milk for babes, not strong meat which men require?
The deed done, those coarse hands were soiled enough,
1610 He spared them the pollution of the pay.

---

*P1869:*That these poor rustics   1587| MS:death: *P1869:*death?   1588| MS:them,
the deed reward itself? No, Sirs— *P1869:*them, did such an act reward itself?
1589| MS:deserve their simple *P1872:*deserve the simple   1590| MS:And eat the bread
they gained by <> brow: *P1869:*Obtain the <> they earned by *1872:*bread clowns earn
by <> brow,   1591| MS:Missing of this, they *P1869:*Missing this pay, they
*1872:*And missing which, they   1592| MS:claimed it, even *1872:*claimed pay, even
1593| MS:warped were they *1872:*warped (admire!)   1595| MS:souls. *P1869:*souls!
1596| MS:While he the Count *1872:*Whereas our Count   1598| MS:honor, as who
contemplates the morn *P1869:*honour <> the moon *CP1869:*the sun *1872:*honour, he
contemplating   1599| MS:And little minds what tapers blink beneath, *P1869:*And
hardly minds <> blink below, *1872:*Who hardly marks if taper *1889a:*below,—
1601| MS:Except the vengeance <> hearts, *1872:*Except a vengeance <> hearts,—
1602| MS:Would he so <> deed forsooth *P1869:*forsooth, *1872:*Dared not so <> deed,
forsooth,   1603| MS:vengeance by § crossed out § as *P1869:*vengeance, as
1604| MS:dug out of the earth *P1869:*earth, *1872:*dug from out the   1605| MS:And
irritants, in Maro's phrase, to ill? *P1869:*Mere irritant, in *1872:*Irritant mere, in Ovid's
phrase, to ill.   1606| MS:by lucre's § inserted above § hope of pay,— § last two words

So much for the allegement, thine, my Fisc,
Quo nil absurdius, than which nought more mad,
Excogitari potest, may be squeezed
From out the cogitative brain of thee!

1615 And now, thou excellent the Governor!
(Push to the peroration) *cæterum*
Enixe supplico, I strive in prayer,
Ut dominis meis, that unto the Court,
Benigna fronte, with a gracious brow,
1620 *Et oculis serenis,* and mild eyes,
Perpendere placeat, it may please them weigh,
Quod dominus Guido, that our noble Count,
Occidit, did the killing in dispute,
Ut ejus honor tumulatus, that
1625 The honour of him buried fathom-deep
In infamy, *in infamia,* might arise,
Resurgeret, as ghost breaks sepulchre!
Occidit, for he killed, *uxorem,* wife,
Quia illi fuit, since she was to him,
1630 *Opprobrio,* a disgrace and nothing more!
Et genitores, killed her parents too,

---

crossed out §   1612| MS:*absurdius*—than < > mad— *P1869:absurdius,* than < > mad,
1613| MS:*potest* may squeezed *P1869:potest,* may be squeezed   1614| MS:brain. § ¶ §
And now, *P1869:*brain of thee!   1614-15| MS:§ no ¶ § *P1869:*§ ¶ § *1872:*§ no ¶ §
1889:§ no ¶; emended to restore ¶; see Editorial Notes §   1615| MS:now,—most §
crossed out and replaced above by § thou < > the Governor!— *P1869:*now, thou < > the
Governor!   1616| MS:(Steer, Tully, to thy laurels) § last five words crossed out and
replaced above by four words § Look, § word and comma crossed out and replaced by § Push
to the peroration)   1617| MS:*supplico*—I < > prayer *P1869:supplico,* I < > prayer,
1618| MS:*meis* that < > the Court *P1869:meis,* that < > the Court,   1619| MS:*fronte*
with < > brow *P1869:fronte,* with < > brow,   1620| MS:*serenis* and < > eyes
P1869:serenis, and < > eyes,   1621| MS:*placeat*—it < > they weigh *P1869:placeat,* it
< > them, weigh   1622| MS:*dominus* Guido that < > Count *P1869:dominus Guido,*
that < > Count,   1623| MS:*Occidit*—did < > dispute *P1869:Occidit,* did < > dispute,
1624| MS:*tumalatus* that *P1869:tumalatus,* that   1625| MS:fathom deep
*P1869:*fathom-deep   1626| MS:infamy *in infamia* might arise *P1869:*infamy, *in
infamia,* might arise,   1627| MS:*Resurgeret* as ghosts break *P1869:Resurgeret,* as
1628| MS:*Occidit* killed, I say, *uxorem* wife *P1869:Occidit,* for he killed, *uxorem,* wife,
1629| MS:*fuit* since < > him *P1869:fuit,* since < > him,   1630| MS:*Opprobrio* a < >
more!— *P1869:Opprobrio,* a < > more!   1631| MS:*genitores*—killed < > too

Qui, who, *postposita verecundia*,
Having thrown off all sort of decency,
Filiam repudiarunt, had renounced
1635 Their daughter, *atque declarare non*
Erubuerunt, nor felt blush tinge cheek,
Declaring, *meretricis genitam*
Esse, she was the offspring of a drab,
Ut ipse dehonestaretur, just
1640 That so himself might lose his social rank!
Cujus mentem, and which daughter's heart and soul,
They, *perverterunt*, turned from the right course,
Et ad illicitos amores non
Dumtaxat pellexerunt, and to love
1645 Not simply did alluringly incite,
Sed vi obedientiæ, but by force
O' the duty, *filialis*, daughters owe,
Coegerunt, forced and drove her to the deed:
Occidit, I repeat he killed the clan,
1650 *Ne scilicet amplius in dedecore*,
Lest peradventure longer life might trail,
Viveret, link by link his turpitude,
Invisus consanguineis, hateful so
To kith and kindred, *a nobilibus*
1655 *Notatus*, shunned by men of quality,

P1869:genitores, killed < > too,   1632| MS:*Qui who postposita verecundia*
P1869:Qui, *who*, *postposita verecundia*,   1633| MS:decency *P1869*:decency,
1634| MS:*repudiarunt*—had *P1869:repudiarunt*, had   1635| MS:daughter *atque*
P1869:daughter, *atque*   1636| MS:*Erubuerunt* nor < > cheek *P1869:Erubuerunt*, nor
< > cheek,   1637| MS:*Declaring meretricis* *P1869*:Declaring, *meretricis*
1638| MS:*Esse*—she < > drab *P1869:Esse*, she < > drab,   1639| MS:*dehonestaretur*
just *P1869:dehonestaretur*, just   1641| MS:*mentem*—of § over illegible erasure § which
daughters § final *s* erased § heart § over illegible word § and soul *P1869:mentem*, of < >
daughter, heart and soul, *1869:mentem*, and which daughter's heart   1642| MS:They
perverterunt—turned *P1869*:They, *perverterunt*, turned   1644| MS:to lawless love
CP1869:to love   1645| MS:did alluringly § inserted above § incite *P1869*:incite,
1647| MS:Of the duty *filialis* daughters owe *P1869*:O' the duty, *filialis*, daughters owe,
1648| MS:*Coegerunt* forced < > deed *P1869:Cogerunt*, forced < > deed:
CP1869:Coegerunt   1649| MS:clan *P1869*:clan,   1650| MS:*dedecore*
P1869:dedecore,   1651| MS:might slow. § crossed out § trail *P1869*:trail,
1652| MS:*Viveret* hag-like trail § last two words crossed out and replaced above by three
words § link by link *P1869:Viveret*, link   1653| MS:*consanguineis*—hateful
P1869:consanguineis, hateful   1655| MS:*Notatus* shunned < > of his own § last two

Relictus ab amicis, left i' the lurch
By friends, *ab omnibus derisus*, turned
A common hack-block to try edge of jokes.
Occidit, and he killed them here in Rome,
¹⁶⁶⁰ *In Urbe*, the Eternal City, Sirs,
Nempe quæ alias spectata est,
The appropriate theatre which witnessed once,
Matronam nobilem, Lucretia's self,
Abluere pudicitiæ maculas,
¹⁶⁶⁵ Wash off the spots of her pudicity,
Sanguine proprio, with her own pure blood;
Quæ vidit, and which city also saw,
Patrem, Virginius, *undequaque*, quite,
Impunem, with no sort of punishment,
¹⁶⁷⁰ Nor, *et non illaudatum*, lacking praise,
Sed polluentem parricidio,
Imbrue his hands with butchery, *filiæ*,
Of chaste Virginia, to avoid a rape,
Ne raperetur ad stupra; so to heart,
¹⁶⁷⁵ *Tanti illi cordi fuit*, did he take,
Suspicio, the mere fancy men might have,
Honoris amittendi, of fame's loss,

---

words crossed out § *P1869:Notatus*, shunned ¹⁶⁵⁹| MS:*Occidit*—and he killed these here in Rome *P1869:Occidit*, and he killed them here in Rome, ¹⁶⁶¹| MS:*est* *P1869:est*, ¹⁶⁶²| MS:As the < > theatre witnessed once *P1869:*The < > theatre which witnessed once, ¹⁶⁶³| MS:*nobilem* Lucretia's self *P1869:nobilem*, Lucretia's self, ¹⁶⁶⁴| MS:*maculas* *P1869:maculas*, ¹⁶⁶⁵| MS:pudicity *P1869:*pudicity, ¹⁶⁶⁶| MS:*proprio*—with < > blood:— *P1869:proprio*, with < > blood; ¹⁶⁶⁷| MS:*vidit*—and < > City < > saw *P1869:vidit*, and < > city < > saw, ¹⁶⁶⁷⁻⁶⁸| MS:§ line inserted and then crossed out § (You find it in Valerius Maximus) ¹⁶⁶⁸| MS:Patrem—Virginius *undequaque* quite *P1869:*Patrem, Virginius, *undequaque*, quite, ¹⁶⁶⁹| MS:*Impunem* with < > punishment *P1869:Impunem*, with < > punishment, ¹⁶⁷⁰| MS:§ partly erased, illegible word replaced in margin by § Nor ¹⁶⁷¹| MS:*parricidio* *P1869:pollutum parricidio*, *CP1869:polluentem* ¹⁶⁷²| MS:Pollute § crossed out and replaced in margin by § Imbrue < > with slaughter § crossed out and replaced above by § butchery *filiæ* *P1869:*butchery, *filiæ*, ¹⁶⁷³| MS:chaste Virginia lest she suffer § last three words crossed out and replaced above by three words § to avoid a rape *P1869:*chaste Virginia, to < > rape, ¹⁶⁷⁴| MS:*stupra*, so to heart *CP1869:stupra*; so *1869:*heart, ¹⁶⁷⁵| MS:He took it § last three words crossed out § *tanti* § altered to § *Tanti* < > take *1869:*take, ¹⁶⁷⁶| MS:*Suspicio* the < > have *P1869:Suspicio*, the < > have, ¹⁶⁷⁷| MS:*ammittendi* of honour's loss § crossed out § flight *P1869:ammittendi*, of fames' loss, *1869:ammittendi*, of fame's

300

Ut potius voluerit filia
Orbari, he preferred to lose his child,
1680 *Quam illa incederet,* rather than she walk
The ways an, *inhonesta,* child disgraced,
Licet non sponte, though against her will.
Occidit—killed them, I reiterate—
In propria domo, in their own abode,
1685 *Ut adultera et parentes,* that each wretch,
Conscii agnoscerent, might both see and say,
Nullum locum, there's no place, *nullumque esse*
Asylum, nor yet refuge of escape,
Impenetrabilem, shall serve as bar,
1690 *Honori læso,* to the wounded one
In honour; *neve ibi opprobria*
Continuarentur, killed them on the spot,
Moreover, dreading lest within those walls
The opprobrium peradventure be prolonged,
1695 *Et domus quæ testis fuit turpium,*
And that the domicile which witnessed crime,
Esset et pœnæ, might watch punishment:
Occidit, killed, I round you in the ears,
Quia alio modo, since by other mode,
1700 *Non poterat ejus existimatio,*

1678| MS:*potius filia voluerit* § transposed to § *potius voluerit filia*   1679| MS:*Orbari,*
that he chose to <> child   *P1869:*child,   *1872:Orbari,* he preferred to
1680| MS:*incederet* rather than see walk   *P1869:incederet,* rather than she walk
1681| MS:ways that *inhonesta* child disgraced   *P1869:*ways an, *inhonesta,*
child disgraced,   1684| MS:*domo* in <> abode   *P1869:domo,* in <> abode,
1685| MS:*parentes* that his § altered to § this three § crossed out § guilt   *P1869:parentes,* that
each wretch,   1686| MS:*agnoscerent* might <> say   *P1869:agnoscerent,* might <>
say,   1687| MS:*locum* there's no place *nullumque*   *P1869:locum,* there's no place,
nullumque   1688| MS:*Asylum* nor <> escape   *P1869:Asylum,* nor <> escape,
1689| MS:*Impenetrabilem* shall <> bar   *P1869:Impenetrabilem,* shall <> bar,
1690| MS:*læso* to   *P1869:læso,* to   1691| MS:honour as were § crossed out § we; *neve*
*P1869:*honour; *neve*   1692-94| MS:*Continuarentur,* lest within those walls/ The
opprobrium to that honour be prolonged   *P1869:Continuarentur,* killed them on the spot/
Moreover, dreading lest within those walls/ The opprobrium peradventure were prolonged,
*CP1869:*peradventure be prolonged,   1695| MS:*turpium*   *P1869:turpium,*
1696| MS:crime   *P1869:*crime,   1697| MS:punishment.   *P1869:*punishment:
1699| MS:mode   *P1869:*mode,   1700| MS:*existimatio*   *P1869:existimatio,*

There was no possibility his fame,
Læsa, gashed griesly, *tam enormiter*,
Ducere cicatrices, might be healed:
Occidit ut exemplum præberet
1705 *Uxoribus*, killed her, so to lesson wives
Jura conjugii, that the marriage-oath,
Esse servanda, must be kept henceforth:
Occidit denique, killed her, in a word,
Ut pro posse honestus viveret,
1710 That he, please God, might creditably live,
Sin minus, but if fate willed otherwise,
Proprii honoris, of his outraged fame,
Offensi, by Mannaia, if you please,
Commiseranda victima caderet,
1715 The pitiable victim he should fall!

Done! I' the rough, i' the rough! But done! And, lo,
Landed and stranded lies my very speech,
My miracle, my monster of defence—
Leviathan into the nose whereof
1720 I have put fish-hook, pierced his jaw with thorn,
And given him to my maidens for a play!
I' the rough: to-morrow I review my piece,

1701| MS:fame *P1869:*fame,   1702| MS:*Læsa* gashed griesly *tam*   *P1869:Læsa*,
gashed griesly, *tam*   1703| MS:*cicatrices* get to heal.   *P1869:cicatrices*, might be healed:
1705| MS:her so   *1872:*her, so   1706| MS:*conjugii* that the marriage oath
P1869:conjugii, that the marriage-oath,   1707| MS:*servanda* must < > henceforth.
P1869:servanda, must < > henceforth: 1708| MS:denique—killed   *P1869:denique*,
killed   1710| MS:That if, it might be, he might creditably § inserted above § live—
*P1869:*That he, please God, might < > live   *CP1869:*live,   1711| MS:*minus* but < >
will   *P1869:minus*, but < > willed   1712-14| MS:*honoris offensi* of his own outraged
fame/ *Commiseranda* < > *caderet*   *P1869:honoris*, of his outraged fame,/ *Offensi*, by
Mannaia, if you please,/ *Commiseranda* < > *caderet*,   1715| MS:The pitiable § inserted
above § < > fall.   *P1869:*fall!   1716| MS:Done! I' the rough, i' the rough! But done and,
lo,   *P1869:*Done! I' the rough, i' the rough! But done! And, lo,   1717| MS:very own,
*1872:*very speech,   1718| MS:miracle, nay monster, of § crossed out and replaced above
by § my defence—   *P1869:*miracle, nay monster of defence—   *CP1869:*miracle, my monster
1720| MS:thorn   *P1869:*thorn,   1721| MS:him for § crossed out § < > play.
*P1869:*play!   1722| MS:rough,—to-morrow   *1872:*rough: to-morrow

Tame here and there undue floridity.
It's hard: you have to plead before these priests
1725 And poke at them with Scripture, or you pass
For heathen and, what's worse, for ignorant
O' the quality o' the Court and what it likes
By way of illustration of the law.
To-morrow stick in this, and throw out that,
1730 And, having first ecclesiasticized,
Regularize the whole, next emphasize,
Then latinize, and lastly Cicero-ize,
Giving my Fisc his finish. There's my speech!
And where's my fry, and family and friends?
1735 Where's that huge Hyacinth I mean to hug
Till he cries out, "*Jam satis! Let me breathe!*"
Now, what an evening have I earned to-day!
Hail, ye true pleasures, all the rest are false!
Oh the old mother, oh the fattish wife!
1740 Rogue Hyacinth shall put on paper toque,
And wrap himself around with mamma's veil
Done up to imitate papa's black robe,
(I'm in the secret of the comedy,—
Part of the program leaked out long ago!)
1745 And call himself the Advocate o' the Poor,
Mimic Don father that defends the Count:
And for reward shall have a small full glass
Of manly red rosolio to himself,
—Always provided that he conjugate

1723-30| *P1869:* § these eight lines added §   1723| *P1869:*floridity,—   *1872:*floridity.
1728| *P1869:*law: *1872:*law.   1732| MS:latinize and lastly Ciceroize,
*P1869:*lastly Cicero-ize,   *1889a:*latinize, and   1733| MS:finish—There's my speech—
*P1869:*finish. There's   *1872:*speech!   1734| MS:fry, my § crossed out and replaced by §
and   1735| MS:Where's that old § last two words inserted above line § Hyacinth < >
hug to death? § last two words and question mark crossed out §   *1872:*that huge Hyacinth
1737| MS:Oh, what   *1872:*Now, what   1739| MS:Oh, the old < > oh the
*P1869:*mother, oh, the   *1889a:*Oh the old < > oh the   1740| MS:toque   *P1869:*toque,
1745| MS:the Poor   *P1869:*the Poor,   1746| MS:Mimic the father < > the Count,
*P1869:*Mimic Don father   *1872:*the Count: 1748| MS:himself   *P1869:*himself,

1750   *Bibo,* I drink, correctly—nor be found
      Make the *perfectum, bipsi,* as last year!
      How the ambitious do so harden heart
      As lightly hold by these home-sanctitudes,
      To me is matter of bewilderment—
1755   Bewilderment! Because ambition's range
      Is nowise tethered by domestic tie.
      Am I refused an outlet from my home
      To the world's stage?—whereon a man should play
      The man in public, vigilant for law,
1760   Zealous for truth, a credit to his kind,
      Nay,—since, employing talent so, I yield
      The Lord His own again with usury,—
      A satisfaction, yea, to God Himself!
      Well, I have modelled me by Agur's wish,
1765   "Remove far from me vanity and lies,
      Feed me with food convenient for me!" What
      I' the world should a wise man require beyond?
      Can I but coax the good fat little wife
      To tell her fool of a father the mad prank
1770   His scrapegrace nephew played this time last year
      At Carnival! He could not choose, I think,
      But modify that inconsiderate gift
      O' the cup and cover (somewhere in the will
      Under the pillow, someone seems to guess)
1775   —Correct that clause in favour of a boy
      The trifle ought to grace, with name engraved,

1751| MS:*perfectum bipsi* as   *P1869:perfectum, bipsi,* as   1752| MS:ambitious
can § crossed out and replaced by § do   1753| MS:hold by § inserted above § < >
home sanctitudes *P1869:*home-sanctitudes *CP1869:*home-sanctitudes,
1755| MS:Bewilderment. Because *P1869:*Bewilderment! Because   1756| MS:tie—
*P1869:*tie: *1889a:*tie.   1758| MS:stage, whereon *P1869:*stage?—whereon
1761| MS:Nay,—though the talent so employed it yields *P1869:*employed as yield
*1872:*Nay,—since, employing talent so, I yield   1762| MS:his *1872:*His
1763| MS:satisfaction yea to *P1869:*satisfaction, yea, to   1764| MS:have made my own
wise § last four words crossed out and replaced above by three words § modeled me by < >
wish *P1869:*modelled < > wish,   1765| MS:§ crowded between 1764-66 §
1769| MS:father of the prank *P1872:*father the mad prank   1771| MS:At the § crossed
out § Carnival,—he *P1872:*At carnival! He   1773| MS:cover—somewhere *P1869:*cover
(somewhere   1774| MS:guess— *P1869:*guess)   1775| MS:Correct < > of my boy
*P1869:*of a boy *CP1869:*—Correct   1776| MS:ought to § inserted above § grace with < >

Would look so well, produced in future years
To pledge a memory, when poor papa
Latin and law are long since laid at rest—
1780 *Hyacintho dono dedit avus!* Why,
The wife should get a necklace for her pains,
The very pearls that made Violante proud,
And Pietro pawned for half their value once,—
Redeemable by somebody, *ne sit*
1785 *Marita quæ rotundioribus*
Onusta mammis . . . baccis ambulet:
Her bosom shall display the big round balls,
No braver proudly borne by wedded wife!
With which Horatian promise I conclude.

1790 Into the pigeon-hole with thee, my speech!
Off and away, first work then play, play, play!
Bottini, burn thy books, thou blazing ass!
Sing "Tra-la-la, for, lambkins, we must live!"

engraved   *1872:*grace, with < > engraved,   1777-78| MS:§ crowded between 1776-79 in
continuous line, divided by slash between *come* and *To* §   1777| MS:(Would < > well
produced in feasts § crossed out and replaced above by § years to come   *1872:*Would < >
well, produced in future years   1778| MS:memory when   *1872:*memory, when
1779| MS:§ written in margin with arrow indicating place in text § rest)   *1872:*rest—
1780| MS:*avus,*—why,   *1872:avus!* Why,   1781| MS:wife shall get < > pains
*P1869:*wife should get < > pains,   1783| MS:Which § crossed out and replaced above
by § And   1784| MS:And still § last two words crossed out § redeemable § altered to
§ Redeemable by somebody—*ne*   *1872:*somebody, *ne*   1784-85| MS:§ lines 1787-88
inserted at this point and then crossed out §   1786| MS:*ambulet*   *P1869:ambulet,*
P1872:ambulet: 1787| MS:her bosom shall display § inserted above § those big § crossed
out and replaced above by § brave round balls adorn § crossed out; the entire line crossed out
and rewritten § Her bosom shall display the big round balls   *P1869:*balls,
1788| MS:No bigger borne by wedded wife *ne sit* § entire line crossed out and rewritten § No
braver should be borne by wedded wife,—   *P1869:*wife!   *1872:*braver proudly borne
1789| MS:promise to § crossed out and replaced above by § I conclude § followed by
semi-colon apparently altered to § .   1789-90| MS:§ no ¶ §   *1889a:*§ ¶ §
1792| MS:burn your books, you blazing   *1889a:*burn thy books, thou blazing

THE RING AND THE BOOK, Books 5-8

Emendations to the Text

The following emendations have been made to the 1888-89 text:

5. *Count Guido Franceschini*

5.69: The 1888-89 edition reads *wedding-grown*; the MS-1872 reading *wedding-gown* is restored.

5.469: The 1888-89 edition omits the required punctuation at the end of the line. The MS-1872 comma is restored.

5.989: The 1888-89 edition reads *thoat*; the MS-1872 reading *throat* is restored.

5.1038: The misreading *eaeh* of 1888-89 appears to be a result of a fault in the printing surface of the stereotype plate. The MS-1872 *each* is restored.

5.2027: In MS-1889a *Utopia* is spelled without the *E*. B added the *E* in Dykes Campbell's copy, but the correction was not made in 1889. *Utopia* is emended to *Eutopia* in accordance with B's evident intention.

6. *Giuseppe Caponsacchi*

6.24: The 1888-89 edition omits the required quotation marks at the end of the line. The MS-1872 quotation marks are restored.

6.127: The comma after *Come* is present in the first impression of 1888-89, though missing in the second impression. It was probably lost through type damage, since the space for it remains in 1889. The comma is restored.

6.136: The 1888-89 edition omits the required punctuation at the end of the line. The MS-1872 exclamation mark is restored.

6.594: The quoted sentence requires a period after *elsewhere* rather than the 1888-89 comma. The MS-1872 period is restored.

6.1131: The 1888-89 edition omits the comma added by B to P1868. The CP1868-1872 reading is restored.

6.1171: Although *other wise* is written as two words in MS, it was printed as one in 1868 and the reading was not corrected in subsequent editions. *Wise* here is an archaic noun meaning "way, manner." The adjective *No* is clearly meant to modify a noun and not the adverb "otherwise," and the MS reading has been restored.

6.1499: The word *a-flame* was printed as two words in the 1889a and 1889 texts. *a-flame* suits both rhythm and logic in the line better than *a flame*; the MS-1872 hyphen is restored.

6.1868: The MS-1872 reading is restored to correct the spelling of *dismiss*.

6.1972: MS *slinks* was misread as *shirks* in P1868, and the mistake was not corrected in any printed edition. The emphasis in the passage on disguise and escape, and the idiomatic *away from* of 6.1973, strongly suggest that *shirks* is one of the extremely rare errors that B overlooked throughout all printings of *The Ring and the Book*. The MS reading *slinks* is restored.

7. *Pompilia*

7.523: The 1888-89 edition omits the required quotation marks at the end of the line. The MS-1872 quotation marks are restored.

7.1049: MS *threat* was misread by the printer in 1869 as *thrust*, and the error was not corrected in any subsequent edition. *Threat* refers to the *charge* above at 7.1046, and *charge* refers back to *threatened* at 7.1037. The MS reading *threat* is restored.

7.1125: The 1888-89 edition omits the required punctuation at the end of the line. The MS-1872 exclamation point is restored.

8. *Dominus Hyacinthus de Archangelis*

8.7: MS underlining in this line indicates that *"Quies me"* is parallel with *"Branches me"* above at 8.4. Through printer's error *"me"* was transcribed in italics, as if in Latin, in all printed editions. The MS reading is restored.

8.737: In MS revision of lines 737-38 B eliminated a repetitious *that* at the beginning of 8.738 (see Variants), thus creating an awkwardly elliptical subordinate clause. By later changing *that society of Rome* to *what society of Rome*, and removing the comma after *Rome*, as B indicated in the Dykes Campbell-Brown University revision, he clarified both meaning and syntax, altering the grammatical function of the phrase from simple apposition to a restrictive construction introducing a noun clause, object of the preposition *To* at the beginning of 8.737. These changes seem justified by both sound and sense in the passage, but they were not included in the 1889 text. The corrections have been made to the 1889 text in accordance with B's evident intention.

8.775: The lines of division between the Latin and its English translation in Book 8 are generally clearly indicated by punctuation as well as by parallel construction. Here the comma after *assert*, while grammatically superfluous, may have served originally to indicate that *assert* belongs with the previous Latin quotation, the following words with the following quotation. The comma is removed in the Dykes Campbell-Brown University revision, but the correction was not made in 1889. It seems probable that this correction, like the adjacent changes at 8.737, was intended by B to be made but was not. The 1889 comma has been removed.

8.1035: The logic and syntax of the sentence require a comma at the end of the line rather than the 1888-89 period. The P1869-1872 reading is restored.

8.1545: In MS the *s* after *honour'* does double duty as the possessive and as the first letter of *sake*. The spelling of the possessive of *honour* appeared as *honour'* in all editions. *Honour'* is emended to *honour's*.

In MS B made distinctions between two and three point ellipses which printers often overrode, either regularizing two points to three or on occasion changing three points to two, in order to shorten a line. Where MS uses a two point ellipsis which remained unchanged throughout the printing history of the poem, we retain B's clear intention. Where the two point ellipsis appears only in printed editions, evidently dictated by the width of the line, we have emended to three point ellipses. These emendations have been made at

5.1010
6.1676

B indicated divisions in discourse by line spacing rather than by indentation. During the printing history of *The Ring and the Book* paragraph divisions were occasionally lost when they happened to occur between pages. We have restored all of B's paragraphs. These form a separate class of emendations to the 1888-89 text. Paragraphing is restored at:

5.108-9	7.939-40
5.366-67	7.1036-37
5.1033-34	7.1178-79
5.1234-35	7.1511-12
6.608-9	7.1689-90
6.1228-29	8.73-74
6.1446-47	8.135-36
7.156-57	8.464-65
7.216-17	8.1142-43
7.467-68	8.1193-94
7.705-6	8.1322-23
7.867-68	8.1614-15

In a slightly different class are three instances where paragraphs are omitted from the copy text, but not because of where they fell during typesetting. In each case, the paragraph break suits the rhetoric of the passage, and thus, in the absence of direct evidence of B's intention on the matter, we restore the paragraphing at:

5.396-97
7.1554-55
7.1559-60
8.1042-43

A note on variants:

Since Volume VII was published, we have come to recognize that the documents we labeled *P1872* (i.e., sheets of 1872 with alterations in B's hand in the Beinecke Library at Yale) are in fact unbound sheets of the second edition, not proofs. Furthermore, neither these documents in themselves nor B's alterations to them, lie in the descent of the copy text. Since the printed readings on these sheets are those of the second edition of *The Ring and the Book*, they should have been entered simply as *1872*. The line of the text was accurately recorded; the coding was inexact.

Book 5, Count Guido Franceschini

5] *Velletri* The volcanic soil of Velletri, a town a little S of Rome, produces a wine grape for which the town is famous.

5] *vinegar and gall* The drugging drink customarily given to people about to be crucified was offered to Christ, who tasted and refused it (Matt. 27:34). This reference is the first of Guido's many parallels between himself and the martyred Christ; note that although his drink is wine, he too only takes "one sip" (5.7).

12-13] *Noblemen . . . racking* The normal exemption of the nobility and clergy from torture could be waived by the judge when the presumption of guilt was strong. Torture was decreed for Guido and his accomplices, but according to OYB Guido confessed at the sight of the Vigil (see 1.971-72n.).

25-28] *plied . . . probe* Guido's joke may be the pun on *plied*, or the application of imagery of assault and murder to himself, or both. To *ply* can mean "to urge to take something pleasant or valuable," or "to bend," as he has been bent on the rack. Using a word which ordinarily carries pleasant associations to mean torture is characteristic of Guido's ability to twist meaning and reverse appearances. There is further irony in the similarity of Guido's figure of speech, the *rasp-tooth* and its *probe*, to the jagged murder weapon; see 2.246 and n., and 8.1151-56 and n.; a *rasp* is a coarse file with sharp raised teeth. *Toying* echoes the heavy irony of *plied*, with its suggestions of amorous coaxing reversed to persistent injury, and *toying* in turn is echoed in *play* in the next line. A *probe* is a surgical instrument with a blunt end used to explore wounds.

29] *Four years* Since the marriage in Sept. 1693 (which B thought was in Dec.; see *Chronology*).

30] *tense . . . part* Extended, strained, vulnerable. In the next three ll. Guido indicates the extensions of his spiritual self which have suffered most. His soul, like his body, has been stretched tight and made sensitive in every area, and the equation of soul and concern for appearance is a further ironic stretching of the term.

32] *kindred* A mother, a married sister (4.384n.), and four brothers (of whom B mentions three; see 2.289n.).

36] *Foppishly* Foolishly.

38] *Vigil-torment* See 1.971-72n. An essential part of the Vigil torture was duration, and Guido stresses this element in comparing his mental suffering to the Vigil.

43] *how . . . wears* How poorly rank serves to meet practical needs, and how honor itself becomes threadbare.

46] *The father* From the records we know only that Guido's father's name was Tomaso (OYB, E, 162) and that he died in 1681 (Corrigan, xxii). B has Guido represent him as largely responsible for the decline of the family's fortunes.

48] *cap* Doff cap.

49] *purse . . . spider-webs* A reference to a line in a poem by Gaius Valerius Catullus (c. 84-54 B.C.) which is a mock invitation to dinner. "Nam tui Catulli Plenus sacculus est aranearum" ("But your Catullus' purse is full of spiders") Catullus 13.7-8.

51] *tetchy humour* Irritable disposition.

58] *worthies . . . advice* In spite of the Bishop and the Governor's dismissal of Pompilia's complaints, other citizens of Arezzo are on record as having spoken of Guido's bad behavior both to Guido himself and to Paolo in Rome (OYB, E, 53-54, 245).

63] *sib* See 2.509n.

71] *lamb's . . . purtenance* The word *purtenance* means "entrails." A servant of the Franceschini testified that a suckling lamb bought on a Saturday served the household for a week (OYB, E, 52). Exodus 12:9 describes the way the lamb whose blood was used to mark the Israelites' houses before Passover was to be roasted and eaten, "his head with his legs, and with the purtenance thereof."

73] *wine . . . man* In a parable told by Jotham about his brother Abimelech, who had made himself king, the trees asked the vine to be king over

311

them but the vine answered, "Should I leave my wine, which cheereth God and man, and go to be promoted over the trees?" (Judges 9:13).

74]   *three-parts water* Only a slight exaggeration, according to the testimony of the servant (OYB, E, 52).

83]   *crown* Perhaps an allusion to the crown of thorns placed on Jesus' head before the crucifixion (Matt. 27:29).

84]   *hanged or headed* See 1.124n.

90-91]   *Her . . . style* Following the example of her mother, a prostitute.

93]   *bastard . . . heir* The credibility of Guido's defense of his honor, which he claimed was his motive for the murders, depended on his belief that Caponsacchi fathered Pompilia's child. But should he be acquitted on these grounds, it was then important that the child be legally recognized as his own in order that he inherit the Comparini estate. Here that possibility is treated ironically; at the end of this book (5.2037-47) it is idealized.

118]   *omoplat* Shoulder-blade (see 5.16). Guido is later shown to have a specialized knowledge of anatomical terms through fencing (12.289-90). In 5.119 ("nay clip my speech") he seems to pun on the more familiar *blade*.

121]   *Trinity* An invocation of the Christian doctrine of the one God in three persons, Father, Son, and Holy Spirit, presumes the truth of the confession to follow.

129]   *suzerain* Overlord.

135]   *whealed* Covered with welts.

136]   *eleventh hour* In the parable of the laborers in the vineyard, those villagers who were hired at the eleventh hour were paid the same at the end of the day as those who were hired in the morning (Matt. 20:6-16). Guido, in contrast, has not only worked through the day but is punished.

142]   *ancientest* Arezzo, the old Roman Arretium, is of Etruscan origin and older than its conqueror Florence, which was established in the first century B.C. as a colony for Roman soldiers.

145]   *second* See 1.785n.

149-53]   *Francis . . . Dominic* The rivalry between Franciscan and Dominican monks was strong in the late seventeenth century. St. Francis of Assisi (1182-1226), with whom Guido aligns himself, was born wealthy but took a vow of poverty and founded the order known as the Begging Friars—in clear contrast to Guido, who was poor and determined to enrich himself by marrying Pompilia. St. Domingo de Guzman (1170-1221) founded the Dominican Order, or Preaching Friars. St. Francis was canonized first, in 1228; St. Dominic in 1234.

158]   *Homager . . . Empire* One whose allegiance is directly to the Holy Roman Emperor and not to anyone of lower rank.

164]   *Francis . . . Lord* See 5.145n. and 2 Corinthians 8:9, "For ye know the grace of our Lord Jesus Christ, that, though he was rich, yet for your sakes he became poor, that ye through his poverty might be rich."

170] *lineage . . . pole* Possibly a reference to the distinction between first and second rank above (5.144-45). The first rank was called *Gonfalonière*, which means standard-bearer. A member of Guido's mother's family had in fact held this title (Corrigan, xxii, 125). Though claiming the right to the first rank, Guido realizes he lacks the display which should accompany the title. See also 1.785n.

177] *pricking veins* Hot blood.

182] *merriment . . . late* See 2.652n.

185-87] *Where . . . tower* The parvenu's claim to honored position is as artificial as the showy, non-functional defensive towers he adds to his *purchased pile*.

188-90] *Countess . . . ash* Guido's mother's frugality is described in OYB as one of her ways of tormenting the Comparini, by depriving them of heat (OYB, E, 49-50).

194] *suttler's . . . camp's* Child of a peddler to soldiers or of a hanger-on to troops. The correct spelling is *sutler*.

203] *Molinos* See 1.303-13n.

207] *suum cuique* To each his own (Tacitus, *Annals* 4.35.4).

209] *go, do likewise* After telling a lawyer the parable of the good Samaritan, "Then said Jesus unto him, Go, and do thou likewise" (Luke 10:37).

212] *eldest son* See 2.289n.

217] *gods at home* The ancient Romans recognized special household gods, the lares and penates, and kept individual shrines to them.

227] *porporate* Wearer of purple, cardinal.

228] *Red-stockinged* Cardinals' stockings were red.

230] *Be . . . root* In the parable of the barren fig tree, the dresser of the vineyard asked his lord to "let it alone . . . till I shall dig about it, and dung it" (Luke 13.8).

231] *Be . . . loins* Jesus warned against worldly treasures and advised his followers to "let your loins be girded about" in preparation for the second coming (Luke 12:35).

248-49] *I . . . foot* "And Joses . . . Having land, sold it, and brought the money, and laid it at the apostles' feet" after hearing Peter and John preach (Acts 4:36-37).

252] *villa's* See 2.808n.

259] *sisters* See 4.384n.

263-64] *purse . . . patron* Guido implies an elaborate order and hierarchy in the cardinal's house where he will seek favor, of which bribery is no small part.

264-65] *glove . . . ring* From the earliest times in Europe gloves were a symbolic gift or gage on many occasions. Sixteenth- and seventeenth-century records show that gifts of gloves, one of which might be "lined" with jewelry or money, were customary means of buying favor from a powerful man or from a woman in a privileged position.

269-70] *orders . . . exorcise* The exorcist was the second of the four traditional minor orders. It is first mentioned by Pope Cornelius who died in 253 and it was finally supressed by the Roman Catholic Church in 1872. See also 1.260-62n.

273-75] *loaf . . . friend* When the multitude followed Jesus into the desert he blessed five loaves and two fishes, "And they did all eat, and were filled, and they took up of the fragments that remained twelve baskets full" (Matt. 14:20).

281-83] *Dives . . . repartee* Though he is not named in the Bible, the rich man in the parable of the rich man and the begger Lazarus is popularly called *Dives* (Luke 16:19-31). After death the rich man appeals from hell to heaven for warning to be sent to his living kin in order that they may be spared his punishment. But the answer is, "If they hear not Moses and the prophets, neither will they be persuaded, though one rose from the dead." Guido's determination to be *not immoderate in repartee* may be a reference to such unwelcome warnings.

284] *Utrique sic paratus* "For either thus prepared."

290-91] *sixteen . . . years* See 2.302n.

298] *lacquey's* Footman's.

302-4] *griffin-guarded . . . cypress* The approach to the palace displays conventional symbols of pomp and power, and (ironically) of mortality. A *griffin* in Greek mythology was a winged lion which guarded gold treasure. A *term* is a pillar out of which the bust of a figure sculpted from the same stone appears to emerge. The name comes from Terminus, god of boundaries. The *cypress* tree is symbolic of death and mourning.

306] *varletry* Attendants.

308] *Chamberlain* The highest ranking Cardinal, also called Camerlengo.

312] *Sylla, Marius* Lucius *Sulla* (138-78 B.C.) and Gaius *Marius* (157-86 B.C.), dictators and rival generals. The bust is *noseless* presumably because mutilated by Christian reformers; it is a kind of trophy. The texture of Guido's description of the setting of the Cardinal's palace is consistently ironic in its mixture of pagan and spiritual references; see above 302-4 and n.

313] *hexastitch* A six line verse form.

317] *Purfled* Ornamented.

318] *Peter's-day* The feast day of St. Peter, 29 June.

321] *tittup* Skittish movement.

324] *New . . . Tordinona* See 1.1276n, and 2.1454n.

327] *florins* Gold coins, of Florentine currency.

336] *Matins and vespers* The first and sixth of the seven canonical hours; i.e. continuously.

337] *Monsignor and Eminence* Titles for any distinguished prelate or cardinal.

344] *seventh climacteric* A climacteric is a term of seven years; Guido was in fact not yet forty-nine (see 2.769n.).

346] *fed . . . east-wind* Eliphaz argued with Job, "Should a wise man utter vain knowledge, and fill his belly with the east wind?" (Job 15:2).

347] *Land of Promise* Deut. 9:28; 11:9; 19:8; Heb. 11:9. Guido had been led to expect advancement.

356] *sisters* See 4.384n.

359] *priests* See 1.547n.

359-60] *bat-like . . . fowl* Proverbial for having no definite nature or destiny.

363] *Vittiano . . . thrushes* See 2.808n. Thrushes were a table delicacy, often caught by spreading sticky bird-lime on branches.

377] *cross nor pile* See 3.401n. The phrase means "heads nor tails," i.e., money. The lower piece of the minting mechanism was called the *pile.*

378] *short-casting* Throwing short falls of the dice through timidity.

388] *shagrag* Ragged.

391] *baulked of* Denied, disappointed of (his retaliatory gesture).

401] *sors . . . dip* The Latin word *sors* means "chance" and is here an extension of the gambling image begun above 8.369. *Virgilian sors* refers to the Roman practice of opening Virgil's *Aeneid* at random in search of a helpful quotation. Paul dips into proverb rather than the classics to find "faint heart ne'er won fair lady," but the coincidental appropriateness of the advice makes it a lucky draw.

404] *Camp* The military.

405] *counted* Weighed, accounted.

407] *frieze* Woolen fabric with a coarse nap.

412] *Paul's . . . know* Paul the brother and Paul the apostle, both of whom advised marriage under special circumstances. The apostle Paul said that it was better to marry than to burn (1 Cor. 7:9).

415] *cits . . . stomach* Guido seems to contrast the Comparini's *stomach* (appetite) for more with his own contented *gorge* (5.349). *Cits* is ironic for citizens.

417] *truck* Barter.

456] *prizer* Prize-fighter.

463] *Style and condition* Title and social position.

481] *chaffer* Dicker, haggle.

486-87] *Pietro . . . Ferri* Pietro of Cortona (1597-1669) was a Baroque painter; Ciro Ferri (1634-89) was his pupil.

492] *I falsified* Guido claimed in an inventory of his property given to the Comparini that he had an income of 1700 scudi. He later admitted that this was a gross exaggeration.

501-2] *oil . . . chapmen* A chapman is a peddler or hawker of cheap goods; the *flirted oil* may be figurative for "sales pitch." To have an oily tongue is to employ flattery, just as *flirted* and "coquetry" above (5.495) suggest.

507] *rights of force* If right were might.

516] *qualify* Take on the quality or nature of.

517] *new . . . old* Perhaps an oblique reference to Ephesians 4:22-24, describing the change and renewal of the believer in Christ.

520] *Greatness . . . now* Warning against mere asceticism, St. Paul argued, "Wherefore if ye be dead with Christ from the rudiments of the world, why, as though living in the world, are ye subject to ordinances, (Touch not; taste not; handle not;" (Col. 2:20-21).

521-22] *all . . . describes* "Then I looked on all the works that my hands had wrought . . . and, behold, all was vanity and vexation of spirit" (Eccl. 2:11). Traditionally, Ecclesiastes was ascribed to Solomon, but it is unlikely that Solomon composed it.

526-27] *spoons Fire-new* Fresh from the furnace.

538] *salamander-like . . . flame* The mythical salamander was a lizard supposed to be able to live in fire. *Support* here has the sense of "bear."

540] *baioc* A papal coin worth 1/100 of a scudo.

544] *frizzles* Fries sputteringly; makes kissing noises.

556] *sun and moon* High tragedy.

557-58] *Plautus . . . Tales* Titus Maccius Plautus (c. 254-184 B.C.) and Publius Terentius Afer (c. 190-159 B.C.) were Roman comic dramatists. Giovanni Boccaccio's (1313-75) *Book* was the *Decameron,* a collection of tales, many having to do with deceit and trickery. Franco Sacchetti (c. 1335-1410) was from Florence, not Arezzo; he also wrote tales such as Guido described.

579-80] *Father . . . husband* "Therefore shall a man leave his father and his mother, and shall cleave unto his wife." (Gen. 2:24).

580-81] *weal . . . law* A reference both to the scripture ("Wives, submit yourselves unto your own husband" (Eph. 5:22), and to the marriage vows, which impose fidelity and obedience on the woman "for better or worse" (*weal or woe*).

590] *Epithalamium* Wedding song.

592] *troll* To sing spiritedly as one would a round; a troll is a round.

615] *four months'* See *Chronology.*

623] *soldo* A Tuscan coin of minimal value.

625] *Caligula's* Roman emperor (12-41) whose cruelty, sensuality, and madness became legendary.

630] *Woe worth* OE *weorthan,* becomes; evil will befall (proverbial).

633-34] *lure . . . toad* To cast a spell by use of the tools of a devil.

635-36] *call . . . street* Perhaps a remote allusion to Luke 19:40; see 2.1390-91n.

639] *my . . . priest* See 2.496n.

640] *lenten fare* Priestly celibacy; sexual abstention.

655] *cockatrice* See 1.168n. A fabulous serpent supposedly hatched from a cock's egg. Isaiah spoke of the iniquities separating God and man thus: "They conceive mischief, and bring forth iniquity. They hatch cockatrice' eggs" (Is. 59:4-5).

659] *whetting a sting* A cockatrice had a barbed tail; *sting* here is figurative. The phrase means "getting ready for attack."

662] *plague-prodigy* A *prodigy* is an omen (OED), here an omen of general destruction.

670] *Thyrsis to Neæra* Thyrsis is a shepherd in Virgil's seventh Eclogue; Neæra is a country girl in Eclogues 3 and 5. The names used most frequently in the letters in OYB are Mirtillo and Amaryllis (OYB, E, 99-106).

671] *Provençal roses* Ribbon rosettes. The name is a corruption of Provins, a town near Paris where according to tradition the original double damask roses were brought by the crusaders. Hamlet speaks of "two Provincial roses on my razed shoes" (3.2.288) as appropriate turnout for an actor.

673] *bravo* Hired bodyguard.

698] *true-love-knot* A knot of ornamental design used to symbolize true love.

699] *pigeon . . . pet* The dove is associated with Venus, goddess of love, in Renaissance art.

703] *hawk's service* A bird of prey trained to obey, in contrast to pigeon, dove, bird of peace.

703] *Rotunda* There was a large bird market at the Piazza of the Pantheon, commonly called the Rotunda, in Rome.

707] *hoodwink, starve* Methods used in training hawks. To hoodwink was to blindfold. Of course Guido hoodwinked Pompilia in a figurative sense as well.

708] *haggard* An untrained female hawk which has fully moulted at least once. Also a wild and intractable person.

712-13] *piped . . . finch* Encouraged it to sing by playing music. Finches were often kept as pet song birds.

713] *falcon-gentle* Female hawk.

717] *bile* One of the four humors; thought by ancients to cause ill humor.

721-22] *lords . . . burn* St. Paul advised "I say therefore to the unmarried and widows, It is good for them if they abide even as I. But if they cannot contain, let them marry: for it is better to marry than to burn" (1 Cor. 7:9). Guido is speaking to a court of celibate ecclesiastics.

723-25] *parallel . . . type* See 5.580-81. Marriage signifies the union of Christ with his Church. The priests have given themselves, as it were, to the Church in a marriage relationship, requiring their devotion and obedience. "For the husband is head of the wife, even as Christ is the head of the church" (Eph. 5:23).

726-27] *insubordinate . . . refractory* Guido characteristically claims the same right over Pompilia that the Church has over Priests. Another identification of himself with the Head of the Church, Christ.

727-31] *Monk . . . Bishop* The beginning *Monk*, a novice, and the *Deacon*, lowest order of the ordained ministery, both undergo a probationary period during which they are subject to the severest discipline and possible dismissal. *Claustral* means cloistered. The *rod o' the Bishop* refers to the Crosier, or staff, symbol of the Bishop's office. The crosier is sometimes traced to its derivation from the Roman augurs' divining stick. The rod suggests punishment; the crosier, discipline tempered with mercy.

734] *profess* Take final and lifelong vows, which is done only after a long period of probation.

736] *Francis' . . . quails* The followers of St. Francis took a vow of poverty and were called begging friars. *Manna* seems to refer to the Lord's provision for his own, as when the children of Israel received manna in their flight from Egypt. *Quail* may have a multiple reference; early in the flight from Egypt quails were provided as flesh to eat in the evening, and manna as bread in the morning (Ex. 16:12-15). Later when the quails stopped and the people complained the Lord sent quails again, but this time they brought a plague (Num. 11:18, 31-33). There may be a further ironic reference to St. Francis' special love of animals; he was often painted preaching to the birds.

738] *Levite-rule* In Deuteronomic law the terms priest and Levite were used interchangeably to designate those among the Israelites who served one priestly function. In the post-exilic period, however, the term priest came to mean those in charge of sacrifice at the altar, and the term Levite, those who interpreted the meaning of Israel's faith. In the Middle Ages the title Levite was given to deacons. After many earlier efforts to enforce celibacy upon those in Holy Orders, the Western Church at the Second Lateran Council (1139) made marriage of all clerics unlawful and invalid. A deacon, therefore, could be denied the pleasures of "sweet society."

740] *peccant humours* Sinful inclinations.

748] *pens* Heavy wing feathers. *Pens* means wings, especially in poetic usage; the image here suggests losing the power of flight.

751] *turtle* Turtle-dove, ironic contrast to hawk.

756] *pretty piece* Mistress.

756-57] *save . . . save* The first *save* is a shortened form of "God save," whereas the second *save* is literal.

758] *postulant* A candidate undergoing a period of testing before being admitted as a novitiate in a religious order or to ordained ministry. The line is heavily ironic; a postulant is undergoing a period of instruction in the ways of virtue and is moreover in no position to instruct or tax a Bishop.

764] *Put . . . circulate* Both Spreti, in his defence of Guido, and the pro-Guido anonymous pamphleteer emphasize Pietro's "copious distribution" in Rome and in Arezzo of pamphlets containing "bitter libels" against Guido (see 2.652n.).

768] *by-blow* Bastard.

775] *preferred* Brought forward, formally presented.

800] *proverb . . . by-word* Guido appropriates God's words to Solomon about the punishment of Israel if they should worship other Gods. "This house, which I have hallowed for my name, will I cast out of my sight; and Israel shall be a proverb and a byword among all people" (1 Kings 9:7). Note that Guido has Pompilia refer to him as "my lord" (5.803).

809] *Locusta's* A woman poisoner living during the early Roman Empire, who pretended to nurse her victims, among whom were Claudius and Britannicus.

811] *infectious mistletoe* Mistletoe is a parasite, and the berry is poisonous.

833-34] *speech . . . Abate* The letter to Paolo first referred to in 2.678 (see n.) recounting the Comparini's plots against Guido, claimed by Pompilia to be a forgery.

839, 843] *trick . . . trick* Guido plays on the sense of *trick* as ruse, and as ingenious mechanism (OED), suggesting that both the forged letter and the torture machine were employed in the service of truth.

847] *lathan dagger* Wooden sword. Used figuratively to signify an empty threat. In the old Morality plays the figure of Vice wore a dagger of lath.

848] *Bilboa* Bilbao, a seaport in northern Spain famous for the steel blades made there, was called in English Bilboa, and the name was often used for a weapon itself.

851] *practice* Scheme.

857] *marching . . . rectitude* Within limits permitted by the marriage bond.

868] *Molinist* See 1.303-13n.

874] *coppice* Variation of copse, a thicket or wood of young trees.

876] *many . . . knew* Guido's accusation of repeated adultery by Pompilia is quoted by his lawyers (OYB, E, 135).

877] *cup* Another identification with Jesus: "Let this cup pass" (Matt. 28:39).

895] *hassock . . . lodge* Cushion for kneeling in church; box (Fr. *loge*) in a theatre.

917] *quavering . . . trills* Turns and trills, especially in operatic style, were called quavers.

919-20] *grace . . . uno* The word *grace* here may be a pun on grace note, the decorative embellishment of a melodic line, in extension of 6.917 above and 6.921 below. Guido's elaborate musical metaphors belie his disavowal of artful affectation. *Stans pede in uno*, "standing on one foot," is a proverbial expression signifying the same as "with one hand tied behind my back": it is quoted in Horace, *Satires* 1.4.10.

921] *plainsong* The chants sung in church, called plainsong, were declamatory, unadorned with vocal display.

928] *let . . . alone* A reference to the horns of the cuckold.

929] *mulct of comfits* A fine of sweetmeats—perhaps the same ones that were thrown in her lap when she first saw Caponsacchi (2.793n.).

931] *threatenings . . . slaughter* "Saul, yet breathing out threatenings and slaughter against the disciples of the Lord" (Acts 9:1). This description is given just before the conversion of Saul on the road to Damascus. The phrase *See fate's flare* (5.933) may be a reference to the "light from heaven" which blinded Saul.

934] *dead . . . three* Pompilia died four days after the attack. Here Guido speaks of her as already dead; at 5.1677, he says she is still alive. This inconsistency makes it difficult to determine the exact date of Guido's monologue.

935] *Look . . . this* The line has two possible, if remote, references. At Dante's first vision of Beatrice in the *Purgatory*, standing at the brink of heaven she says, "Look at me well" (30.73). (Guido implies, of course, that the Comparini are in Hell.) A further reference may be the first apostolic miracle, the healing of a lame man by Peter—another clearly ironic contrast to the murders. "And Peter, fastening his eyes upon him with John, said, Look on us" (Acts 3.4).

945] *threatening* Pompilia testified that Guido threatened repeatedly to kill her by sword, pistol, and poison (OYB, E, 91-92).

962] *plaister* Sticking-plaster, bandages.

965] *Malchus* At the arrest of Jesus at Gethsemane, Peter cut off the right ear of the servant of the high priest Malchus (John 18:10).

969] *Potter's Field* The field purchased with the thirty pieces of silver returned to the chief priests by the repentant Judas. It was intended as a burial ground for strangers and the poor. It is not certain that Judas hanged himself in the Potter's Field, an inference based on Peter's statement in Acts 1.18. Matthew says merely, "And he cast down the pieces of silver in the temple, and departed, and went and hanged himself" (Matt. 27:5).

970-71] *Judas . . . thief* At the last supper Jesus gave a sop to Judas as a sign that he knew his betrayer (John 13:26). Judas was at that time still keeper of the bag of the disciples' money even though he was earlier called a thief (John 13:29; 12:6).

974-75] *pricking . . . sampler* Embroidering love designs on cloth.

980] *Malchus'* See 5.965n.

996] *admiring* Wondering.

998] *intelligence* Secret communication.

1004] *villa* See 2.808n.

1005] *husbandry* Industrious thrift, with the ironic second sense that there were possessions closer to home in greater need of husbanding. The line may also be a glance at the Christ role that Guido repeatedly assumes: Christ said, "I am the true vine, and my Father is the husbandman" (John 15:1) to the disciples before Gethsemene.

1010-11] *seventh . . . daybreak* Pompilia said she left at dawn; Caponsacchi said they met at about 7 hours, which would be about 1 a.m. (OYB, E, 93, 96).

1014] *Guillichini* See 2.926n.

1020-27] *They . . . liberty* The road to Perugia and Rome which was taken by the fugitives led from the San Spirito gate at the S side of Arezzo. But the fugitives in fact left the city near the gate at the N side, San Clemente gate, where it was easy to climb the city wall because the hilly ground sloped up nearly to the top of an ancient watch tower (*Torrione*) built into the wall itself. There would have been a drop on the other side of the wall, however. At the Horse Inn outside San Clemente gate the runaways took a light carriage, a calash, around the city to the Perugia road. Pompilia's and Caponsacchi's accounts differ somewhat from the facts, as do also the gossiping neighbors' here.

1029-31] *Flat . . . gods* Guido says both that his fortunes are laid low, and that his fortune (fate) is as plainly written as the sharply patterned mythic images in a *tesselated* (mosaic) floor, which he ingeniously implies has been composed of fragments of all that he held sacred.

1035] *drenched* Given a heavy medicinal dose, with the implications of forcible administration.

1040] *Molinist* See 1.303-13n.

1041-43] *Floundered . . . hell* An echo of lines in Milton's *Paradise Lost* which derived from two Biblical passages: "How art thou fallen from heaven, O Lucifer, son of the morning" (Is. 14:12), and "I saw Satan fall as lightning from heaven" (Luke 10:18). Guido describes the passage of time as a kind of chute, with the discovery of the lovers in the morning as the hellish illumination at the end.

1048] *cavalier confessed* Cavalier has the sense of cavalier-servant, a man who devoted his service to a lady, especially to a married one. *Confessed* is ironic in its sense of brazenly admitted; Caponsacchi has cast off any priestly associations with the word, and by his attire and action confesses his guilt.

1052] *league . . . more* A league is about 3 mi.; Castelnuovo was about 15 mi. from Rome. Castelnuovo was the last station where the fugitives would need to change post-horses.

1072-73] *crime . . . indisputably* The indisputable truth is the birth of the child.

1074-76] *remedy . . . tried* The *remedy* is murder. Guido says that he did not kill Pompilia at the Inn because he lacked positive proof of her adultery. Yet had he killed her then, Law would have regarded him as a *friend* and pardoned the murder. But now, after the decisive proof of adultery in the birth of the child, the same remedy *thrice tried* (the three murders) has proved worse than invalid (*null* in a legal sense)—i.e., punishable by death.

1077-79] *When . . . mine* Now that the shadow of a suspicion which might have proved unfounded (*transient shade*) is confirmed (*Solidifies into a blot*), the indelible *blot* on Guido's name makes the mark or brand of *Hell* look *pale*, peeling and impermanent by comparison.

1101-2] *feet . . . nod* Paul, defending himself in Jerusalem, said he was "brought up in this city at the feet of Gamaliel, and taught according to the perfect manner of the law of the fathers" (Acts 22:3). Gamaliel is more fully characterized in Acts 5:34-39, where he advises tolerance and restraint toward the apostles, "for if this counsel or this word be of man, it will come to nought: But if it be of God, ye cannot overthrow it; lest haply ye be found even to fight against God." Guido speaks figuratively, identifying himself with St. Paul and his "work" with that of God.

1109] *amercement* "Infliction of a penalty left to the 'mercy' of the inflicter; hence the imposition of an arbitrary mulct or fine (originally lighter in amount than fines fixed for specific offences)" (OED).

1118-20] *put . . . conclusions* "To try conclusions" means to experiment; here it conveys more finality. "Pompilia tries my own sword on me, and thus teaches me to be less tentative the (unlikely) next time."

1119] *my own sword* See 2.1023n.

1131-32] *witches' . . . succubus* See 1.564-82n.

1142] *What wine* The letters do discuss the color of Guido's wine (OYB, E, 100-4).

1146] *Somebody forged* They did claim this (OYB, E, 94, 97-8).

1148] *Sacchetti* See 5.557-58n.

1148-56] "Dame . . . more!" A parody of the novella style of Sacchetti's period.

1150] *placket* Pocket or petticoat.

1156] *losel . . . fay* Worthless . . . faith.

1160-69] *I . . . Lazarus* The parable of the rich man and the begger Lazarus, who "was laid at his gate, full of sores" teaches that inequities in earthly life are compensated after death. Lazarus went to heaven; the rich man went to hell. When the rich man appealed to Lazarus for relief, he was answered by Abraham, "Son, remember that thou in thy lifetime receivedst thy good things, and likewise Lazarus evil things; but now he is comforted, and thou art tormented" (Luke 16:19-25). Guido's claim to *Shrink from no probing of the ulcerous part* echoes Lazarus' indignity: "the dogs came and licked his sores" (Luke 16:19-25).

1170] *Cæsar . . . go* Maliciously accused by the Jews of wrongs they could not prove, St. Paul declared that he was willing to die if guilty but that as a Roman citizen he appealed to Caesar for truth and justice. "Hast thou appealed unto Caesar? unto Caesar shalt thou go" (Acts 25:12).

1171] *Rome* Here and in 4.11 Guido is said to have appealed to Rome. In 2.1051 and 6.1557 Caponsacchi makes that appeal. OYB says that it was Guido's idea (OYB, E, 217).

1193] *single . . . strayaway* A reference to the single straying sheep which the shepherd went out to find, leaving ninety-nine others in sheepfold (Matt. 18:12-14; Luke 15:3-7). Guido intends the comparsion of Caponsacchi with the Shepherd to be ironic.

1204-5] *Catullus . . . doctus* Gaius Valerius Catullus (c. 84-c. 54 B.C.) Roman poet. His shorter lyrics were often lively and sensual; his elegiacs, frequently obscene; but his longer, more serious poems earned for him the title *doctus,* meaning learned and celebrated. He became a model for subsequent poets.

1209-20] *Seeing . . . such* Guido embellished the decree of the Court. It passed no sentence upon Pompilia, but rather sent her to the Convent to await further interrogation. Moreover, the meaning of the original decree became unclear when the first presentation which charged Caponsacchi as Guido states was subsequently emended by the Judges so as to suggest that adultery was merely alleged, not proved. The matter became a point of heated contention between the opposing sides during Guido's trial for murder.

1211] *pother* From powder; commotion, such as might raise a choking dust.

1219] *Sisterhood of penitents* See 2.1189-90n.

1229]   *connection* Sexual intercourse.

1230]   *pudency* Modesty. Guido implies that the punishment was castration.

1233]   *Molinists* See 1.303-13n.

1244]   *erred . . . person* According to Canon Law an error "in the individual" did indeed make a marriage void, but not an error "in the quality." Guido's friends argue here that having been deceived as to Pompilia's identity he was deceived in her person; the courts decided it was an error of quality.

1252-72]   *Station . . . sops-in-wine* This passage makes an analogy between Christ's journey to Calvary and his death, and Guido's return home after the trial. *Station by station* invokes the stations of the cross; the sarcasm and insincere sympathy he encounters suggest the mockery addressed to Christ ("Hail, King of the Jews!"); *pelting* ("to assail with reproaches or obloquy" [OED]) may be a reference to the abuse of the soldiers who spit upon and smote Jesus (Matt. 27:29-30); the *sop-in-wine* echoes the sponge soaked in vinegar lifted to Christ on the cross (John 19:17-30) as well as the opiate given to Guido. Other parallels might be the mention of Guido's mother (Christ's meeting with the Virgin), his likeness of his stoical facade to death, and the possible obscure pun of Pilate's disavowal of responsibility (Matt. 27:24) in 5.1270 (*palliate screws?*).

1259-60]   *Helen . . . husband* Casting Pompilia and Caponsacchi as the lovers whose affairs caused the Trojan War by implication casts Guido as Menelaus, King of Sparta, who did indeed enjoy "commiseration" sufficient to prolong the war for ten years.

1262-63]   *underwent . . . street* Guido would have entered Arezzo by the same San Spirito Gate from which the lovers departed. From this gate one can follow a main road directly across the town to the Pieve Church, which was Caponsacchi's church and near which the Franceschini probably lived.

1277-78]   *Ultima . . . Civitas* Farthest Thule . . . nearest town. Thule was the name given to an island reached, according to the ancients, by a six day sail to the N of Britain; it was called Ultima Thule by Virgil (*Georgics*, 1.30) and was associated with the end of the world. Civita Vecchia, where Caponsacchi was sent, was about a six hour ride from Rome (see 2.1171n.)

1295]   *Cancel . . . one* It does not appear from the OYB that Guido did seek a divorce.

1299]   *Abate* Paul was Guido's legal representative in Rome.

1306-8]   *Leah . . . Lot's* Rome reversed Guido's expectations and supported the decision by reference to two OT passages. Laban, after accepting long service from Jacob in exchange for Jacob's marriage to Laban's younger daughter Rachel, tricked Jacob by substituting Leah, the older, on the wedding night (Gen. 29:16-28). Lot was tricked by his daughters into lying with them after the destruction of Sodom (Gen. 19:30-35). Both Jacob and Lot erred in the individual (5.1310), but Guido did not. See also 5.1244 and n.

1326-27] *not . . . Vittoria* See 1.389n.

1337] *three suits* See 3.1661n and *Chronology*.

1341] *vain attempt* On grounds of the prolongation of the litigation, Paul requested the Pope to appoint a special assembly to decide the various causes, but the reply was simply, "The matter rests with the Judges" (OYB, E, 150).

1344] *infallible* The doctrine of Papal infallibility maintains that the Pope, when speaking on faith and morals *ex cathedra* (from the papal throne as successor of St. Peter) is without error. It was not made a dogma to be accepted by the whole Roman Church until 1870. The claim first appeared, however, in the Middle Ages, and remained a continuing issue within the church. During a long period before the French Revolution, the French clergy were required to disavow the belief, but, for the most part, the Papacy and the Jesuits took it for granted. B is thus being neither anachronistic nor prophetic.

1351] *Ovid's art* Ovid's *Art of Love* (1 B.C.) is a burlesque of classical didactic poetry, instructing men and women in the art of wooing.

1352] *Summa* The *Summa Theologia* of St. Thomas Aquinas (1225-1274) was the classical text of students of Roman Catholicism during the Counter-Reformation after the Council of Trent (1545-63).

1353] *Corinna* Ovid celebrated his mistress Julia as Corinna.

1359] *merum sal* Pure salt; savory pinch. Used by Lucretius (c. 96-55 B.C.) in *De Rerum Natura* 4.1162.

1365] *Leaves Rome* Paul did leave Rome over the scandal and did eventually make his fortune in Spain (see F. E. Faverty, "The Absconded Abbot in *The Ring and the Book*," in *Studies in Philology*, 35, 88-104).

1366] *Britain . . . orb* From a phrase in Virgil, *Eclogues* 1.6 expressive of extreme exile: *penitus toto divisos orbe Britannos* (Britain, that place of punishment totally divided from our world).

1369] *bile* According to the ancient theory of the humors, the agitation or increase of bile caused rage.

1382] *toad's-head-squeeze* Toads were thought to be poisonous, and the head especially was considered to have quasi-magical powers for healing or for killing.

1390, 1402, 1404] *nailed/cavern/paving-stone* Perhaps a return to the Christ imagery. After Christ's crucifixion and burial in a cave, a large stone was rolled across the opening of the sepulchre.

1414] *Paynims* Infidels, especially Muslims.

1421] *fifty years* See 2.769n.

1435] *three suits* See 3.166n.

1439] *Loosed . . . loin* Possibly a reference to the chastity belt allegedly fastened on a wife to prevent sexual intercourse in the absence of her husband. It may also be an ironic glance at Eph. 5:14: "Stand therefore, having your loins girt about with truth."

1441] *mulct* A fine or similar punishment.

1444-48] *hap . . . bagpipes* Such sensational events as the murders were often made into ballads and *bawled/At tavern doors*. Peasants playing *bagpipes* at the Christmas season were a familiar sight in Rome. The tradition was ancient but became more associated with drinking and celebration than with religious observation.

1462] *Lawful* A child born in wedlock was by law a legitimate offspring.

1464] *Wednesday* 18 Dec. 1697, Gaetano's birthday, was a Wednesday.

1471] *hidden away* The boy "had been intrusted secretly to a nurse" (OYB, E, 152).

1474] *bantling* Small child, with the connotation of bastard.

1484] *ordure* A pun on order, family device on a crest.

1485] *jakes* Privy.

1497-98] *three-fold . . . pride* A fusion of a passage in Job and one in Ecclesiastes. The *three-fold cord* represents those who have united their efforts in a common cause (Eccl. 4:12)—in this case, Pompilia, Caponsacchi, and the baby. *Leviathan* is an image of God's grandeur and omnipotence, and by extension, Guido's (Job 41). Guido presents himself, paradoxically, as both the invincible and the hooked leviathan. He continues the image in 1514-21.

1507] *spilth* Overflow.

1511] *instil* "To put in by drops" (OED).

1541-42] *No . . . Domino* The Vulgate reads: "*Si quis Dei, jungatur Mihi?*" "Then Moses stood in the gate of the camp, and said, Who is on the Lord's side?" Moses' words were spoken to the faithful after he brought the tables of the law down from the mount and found the people worshipping a golden calf. The quotation has a literal as well as an ironic application to Guido's case: the Levites were instructed to "slay every man his brother, and every man his companion, and every man his neighbor" for their transgression (Ex. 32:37).

1543] *Vittiano* See 2.808n.

1547] *her'hest* Judgement's behest; Justice is often personified as a woman.

1550-52] *brained . . . Duke* Cf. *The Tempest* 3.2.96, where Caliban urges Stephano and Trinculo to help him attack Prospero: "There thou mayst brain him . . . or with a log Batter his skull, or paunch him with a stake."

Guido's servants direct their agricultural skills to murder; just as they dig, dress, prune (5.1548-49), they would have brained, staked, paunched (cut open).

1567-70] *first . . . dust* After Adam and Eve ate the apple and the first knowledge of good and evil (conscience) was born, God said to the serpent, "And I will put enmity between thee and the woman, and between thy seed and her seed; it shall bruise thy head . . ." (Gen. 3:15).

1576] *Joy . . . man* "Glory to God in the highest, and on earth peace, good will toward men" (Luke 2:14). The angel song announcing the birth of Jesus.

1579] *Nine days* from 24 Dec., when Guido arrived in Rome with his accomplices, to 2 Jan., the day of the murders.

1579-80] *pray . . . temptation* "And lead us not into temptation" (Matt. 6:13).

1581] *house . . . once* Paul's, where the five men spent nine days.

1603] *O . . . unavenged* "The souls of them that were slain for the word of God . . . cried with a loud voice, saying, How long, O Lord, holy and true, dost thou not judge and avenge our blood on them that dwell on the earth?" (Rev. 6:10-11)

1606] *death-watch-tick* A beetle which by tapping its head against timber makes a sound like the ticking of a watch; the sound was superstitiously associated with death.

1626] *to Caponsacchi* See 2.1422n.

1631-32] *lamb . . . bosom* "But the poor man had nothing save one little ewe lamb, which . . . lay in his bosom" (2 Sam. 12:3). In the parable the lamb stands for Bathsheba, whom David had taken from Uriah. Presumably this would make Guido the abused Uriah.

1646] *Fury* The three Furies were goddesses of vengence, especially against abuses of kinship. They are represented as death-like and horrifying in appearance.

1651] *serpent's head* See 1567-76n. Here and in lines 1659 and 1668 Guido continues to claim divine sanction for his act, recalling perhaps Jesus' words, "I have given you authority to tread upon the serpents and scorpions, and over all the powers of the enemy and nothing shall hurt you" (Luke 10:19).

1663] *Twenty miles* See 3.1626n.

1673, 1677] *four . . . alive* See 5.934 and n.

1676] *church Lorenzo* See 1.866-67n.

1695] *great Physician* One of the titles given to Jesus.

1698] *eyes . . . hear* Once when his disciples thoroughly misunderstood him, Jesus asked, "Perceived ye not yet, neither understand? have ye your hearts yet hardened? Having eyes, see ye not? and having ears, hear ye not?"

(Mark 8:10:36) Guido's action has been restorative; he now sees and hears clearly.

1713] *warrant* See 3.1621.

1725] *man's . . . house* "And a man's foes shall be those of his own household" (Matt. 10:36).

1727] *acquetta . . . way* See 4.1063n.

1741-49] *brother . . . meos* See 3.1448n. The Latin phrase means "to my judges": *Ad Judices suos* (to his judges) was the Pope's answer to the appeal. (OYB, E, 150).

1770] *Justinian's Pandects* See 1.215-33n.

1774] *confirms* Should confirm, ideally confirms.

1784] *patron . . . Cardinal* See 2.153-55n.

1789-90] *Made . . . deed* The Cardinal who assisted the marriage was Cardinal Lauria, Paolo's patron (OYB, E, 150, 212).

1798] *invalid* See 3.1474n.

1814] *Archbishop . . . Governor* See 3.965-66n.

1827] *Molinists* See 1.303-13n.

1830-32] *Two . . . arm* i.e., the Bishop and the Governor.

1884] *Guilty* See 5.1209-1220n.

1893] *Arezzo* See 5.1501-5n. and *Chronology.*

1902] *Stinche* See 4.1508.

1921] *comfit-pelting* See 2.739n.

1922] *handkerchief* Kerchief in the old sense. A piece of cloth worn over the head or around the neck.

1989] *efficient . . . comminatory* Effective . . . warning.

1990] *terror . . . wicked* "For rulers are not a terror to good works, but to the evil" (Rom. 13:3).

1998-2000] *soldier-bee . . . hive* B's coinage *soldier-bee* surely refers to the worker-bee, a sterile female bee who protects the hive by embedding her stinger in the flesh of the enemy. For this she pays with her life since in attempting to withdraw it she *exenterates*, disembowels, herself by pulling out a vital part of her abdomen to which the stinger is attached.

2006] *fugitive brother* See 5.1365n.

2009] *gibe . . . flung* At the time of the rebellion led by Absalom against his father David, as David was fleeing from Jerusalem, Shimei "came forth, and cursed still as he came. And he cast stones at David, and at all the servants of king David" (2 Sam. 16:5-6).

2010] *youth at home* Girolamo; see 2.289n.

2016] *law . . . mine* See 5.1462n.

2021] *paladin my sire* From Palatine, foremost knight of Charlemagne's court; thus champion, hero. *Sire* means ancestor.

2027] *Eutopia* A Greek word meaning "good place." As first used by Thomas More in 1556, it was a play on *Utopia,* "no place."

2032-33] *Husbands . . . Spouse* "Therefore as the church is subject unto Christ, so let the wives be to their own husbands in everything" (Eph. 5:24).

2034] *Belial* In the Old Testament Belial was not a proper noun but an adjective meaning worthlessness, lawlessness. In the intertestimental literature it was one of the names given to Satan.

2037] *son . . . right-hand* In the position of importance. Luke writes, "This Jesus God raised up, and of that we are all witnesses. Therefore being by the right hand of God exalted . . ." (Acts 2:32-3). The idea recurs frequently in the New Testament where Jesus is seen as the fulfillment of the ancient prophecy: "The Lord said unto my Lord, Sit thou at my right hand, until I make thine enemies my footstool" (Ps. 110:1). Again Guido identifies himself with Deity.

2043] *hand* Cf. 5.15, and 1.971-72n. After his resurrection Jesus said to the doubting apostle Thomas, "Reach hither thy finger, and behold my hands . . . and be not faithless but believing" (John 20:27). These final lines of Book 5 comparing the marks of the crucifixion nails on Jesus's hands and the effects of Guido's torture, complete Guido's reconstruction of his own life so that it becomes an ironic parody of the life, death, and resurrection of Jesus.

Book 6, Giuseppe Caponsacchi

7] *Six months* In the Process of Flight (see *Chronology*), which began eight months earlier (in May) but extended through the summer.

8] *you . . . three* See 1.952n. Rome's sentence in the Process of Flight is not included in OYB but B assumes the judges were the same in both cases.

31] *lounge a little* A reference to his relegation; see 1.1031n.

32] *you summon* There is no indication in OYB of such a summons; at 6.1610 he says he is present "as friend of the court"; see n.

34] *Tommati* See 1.944n.

37] *Three . . . ago* This dating of Caponsacchi's monologue on 5 Jan. is not consistent throughout; see 6.1606.

47] *Pompilia . . . dying* She died on 6 Jan., 1698, four days after the attack.

49-59] *book . . . ago* The story of the casting of lots for Jesus' coat while he was on the cross is told in John 19:23-24.

67] *four . . . earth* ". . . I saw four angels standing on the four corners of the earth." (Rev. 7:1). See also Isa. 11:12 and Ezek. 7:2.

80] *taught you* In the Process of Flight.

87] *fribble . . . coxcomb* A frivolous and vain person.

92] *I held so* I thought one way.

111] *your summons* See 6.32n.

123-24] *solely . . . God* Having pledged himself to the Church and to chastity Caponsacchi was not free to marry.

134] *Chop-fallen* Crestfallen, undone.

144-45] *when . . . judgment-day* "And I saw the dead, small and great, stand before God; and the books were opened . . . and the dead were judged . . ." (Rev. 22:12)

147] *relume . . . flax* A reference to Is. 42:3 (see 1.747n.) and perhaps also to *Othello* 5.2.8-12: "If I quench thee, thou flaming minister,/ I can again thy former light restore,/ Should I repent me. But once put out thy light,/ Thou cunning'st pattern of excelling nature,/ I know not where is that Promethean heat/ That can thy light relume."

150-51] *tares . . . corn* In the parable of the wheat and the tares the master tells his servants not to weed the grain until harvest, which Jesus interprets as the day of judgement. (Matt. 13:24-30, 39).

151] *Molinism* See 1.303-13n.

155] *other potentate* i.e., temporal power, head of state.

166] *gripe* An old spelling for *grip*.

209-10] *rag . . . mock* Perhaps a reference back to the dicing for Christ's coat at 6.59.

225-27] *Fiesole . . . Fiesole* See 2.1240n. Florence conquered Fiesole in 1125 and did indeed ruin it, inflicting wide killing and destruction.

230-31] *Old . . . just* After their move to Florence the Caponsacchi family built a house in the Mercato Vecchio (Old Marketplace), the central square in the town. Their move was sometime between the fall of Fiesole in 1125, and 1147, the date by which they had arrived according to a speaker in Dante's *Paradiso* (16.121-22). Thus it was closer to 550 years earlier than to the 386 Caponsacchi cites that the move was made. Cook speculates that B here confuses two speakers, Dante, who was writing about 1312, or 386 years prior to Caponsacchi in 1698, and Dante's character Cacciaguida, who was killed c. 1148.

232-4] *arms . . . Salviati* Caponsacchi means to suggest the age of his family in saying that its history goes back to the beginnings of Fiesole, one of the most ancient walled villages (until the walls were leveled in the siege by Florence) in Tuscany. A *quartered shield* signifies that different coats of arms (not necessarily four) are combined in one escutcheon to denote descent; presumably this shield contains the arms of Fiesole as well as those of the Caponsacchi and Salviati families. Note too that the colors are reminiscent of St. George (see 1.579n.), already associated with Caponsacchi. The *Salviati* were a noble Roman family with representatives in positions of high rank in the church, but the name survives largely by its association with the Florentine born painter Francisco Rossi Salviati (1510-1563), who adopted the name out of deference to his patron the Cardinal Giovanni Salviati. F. R.

Salviati was a contemporary and close friend from childhood of Vasari (4,54-56), and it is possible that B became aware of the family through his reading in Vasari.

238] *illustration* illustrious person.

245-49] *Granduke . . . father* Arezzo fell to Florence in 1384. The rule of the Florentine Medici family from the fifteenth to the eighteenth centuries was famous both for brilliance and for repressive power. A statue of Ferdinand di Medici (1587-1609, grandfather of Ferdinand II) by Giovanni da Bologna was erected in front of the Cathedral of Arezzo in 1595. The story of the threatened reprisals for pulling down the statue is imagined, but not untypical of Medici rule.

276-78] *Jews . . . superstition* For the Jews, a name expressed the character and identity of a person or a God. The Hebrew name for God YHWH (Yahweh), therefore, was considered so holy that it was avoided in common speech and the word *Adonai* or *Lord* was used in its place. Thus the reluctance of the Jews to utter the Holy Name of God. Contrary to what the Bishop says, the substitution would not have the same meaning as the original. This practice like many other beliefs and customs outside the Christian tradition, appeared superstitious to such a man as the Bishop.

284] *new word* An artificial form derived from an erroneous combination of the consonants YHWH with the vowels of *Adonai* by a Christian in the late 18th century.

290] *Diocletian* Roman emperor and persecutor of Christians, 245-313.

308] *halt . . . blind* See 1.31n.

312] *porphyry* See 2.96n.

313-14] *Saint . . . Onesimus* Onesimus was a runaway slave who had robbed his master Philemon. St. Paul sent him back to Philemon with a letter asking that he be forgiven, not because Paul had "had enough," but because Onesimus had been converted (Philemon 10-11).

315-16] *He . . . Agrippa* In Caesarea Paul was accused by the Jews of being a threat to public order and was brought to trial before a provincial court. He demanded, on grounds of his Roman citizenship, to be tried before the Roman Emperor, as was his right. King Herod Agrippa II was the last colonial Roman official Paul faced before his departure for Rome. Newer translations of the story differ, but according to KJV Agrippa responded to Paul's account of his conversion, "Almost thou persuadest me to be a Christian" (Acts 26:28). The Bishop urges Caponsacchi to seek like-minded equals among the rich and powerful outside the church.

319] *Fénelon* Francois de Salignac de la Mothe-Fénelon (1651-1715) was a French prelate and writer. His book *Explication des maximes des saints sur la vie intérieure* (*Explication of the the Maxims of the Saints concerning the Interior Life*), 1697, defended a woman who herself defended Molinist views (see 1.303-13n.). Partly because of pressure from Louis XIV Fénelon's book was condemned by the Papacy in 1699. These ll. suggest the heated temper of the controversy at the time of Guido's trial, and also implies the Church's attempt to win favor from a reigning monarch, as the speaker suggests Paul did from Agrippa.

321-22]   *meat . . . Friday* Friday is traditionally a day of abstinence.

324]   *swinged* Flogged.

325]   *paste* Composition, mortar, in accord with the imagery begun with rubble-stone, 6.309.

328]   *madrigals* Short love poems or songs.

329]   *Marinesque Adoniad* Giovanni Battista Marino (1569-1625) was so popular for his florid literary style and bawdy content that a school of imitators were know as Martinisti. His long epic poem *Adone*, more than twice the length of *The Ring and the Book*, was his most famous work. Here the flourish of phrase suggests the affected style of the original.

342]   *Pieve* Santa Maria della Pieve, Caponsacchi's church.

344]   *Sub-deacon, Canon* See 1.260-62n. and 1.378n.

345]   *tarocs* A card game which could involve fortune telling.

346]   *fan-mounts* Either the wood or ivory of the frame, or the silk paper of the surface (OED). The line is suggestive of coy flirtation, perhaps connected with the fortune telling that is going on.

350]   *her . . . roast* "To rule the roast" is proverbial for "to have mastery."

352]   *Devoir* Service, respect.

353]   *Passion-week* Holy week, the week before Easter, a time for special prayer and penance.

375]   *tonsure's need* See 1.327-28n.

377]   *his Eminence* A title of honor used in speaking to or of a Cardinal.

380]   *closet-lectures . . . where* Private lessons, perhaps in the confessional.

382]   *body o' Bacchus* An oath, a pagan version of "body o' Christ."

383-84]   *pauses . . . Catullus* The elegiac couplet was a line of dactylic hexameter followed by one of dactylic pentameter, a pattern used for poetry of love and war as well as for elegies. A break or pause in the rhythm of a line was often used for variety or emphasis; it was called a caesura, which may have suggested *chasms* with its added innuendo. The ll. are a series of obvious double entendres mocking the pretense of classical instruction; Bacchus (5.380) is the authority and the libertine *Catullus* (see 5.1204-5n.) the model for the extended interruptions in the stuffy lessons; even *couplet* may be a pun.

385-87]   *break . . . Ovid* Priscianus Caesariensis was a sixth century Latin grammarian who lived in Constantinople. This phrase is proverbial for speaking ungrammatical or unclassical Latin. But there is *Ovid* to fall back

on, both for classical style and for counsel in affairs of love; see 1.1149n. and
2.1212-13n.

391] *Found . . . theatre* The first meeting of Pompilia and Caponsacchi
is described by Pompilia in a deposition made during the Process of Flight
and quoted by the defence in the murder trail. "While we were in a great
crowd at the play one evening, Canon Conti, the brother of the husband of
my sister-in-law, threw me some confetti. My husband, who was near me,
took offence at it—not against Conti, but against Caponsacchi, who was
sitting by the side of the said Conti" (OYB, E 91).

397] *matin-song* A traditional Breviary Office originally performed in the
Roman Catholic Church at midnight or later at 2 AM. After the Middle Ages,
however, it was often anticipated and said on the evening before. Whatever
time B has in mind, Caponsacchi's yawning might seem natural.

398] *facchini* Porters.

402] *Rafael* Presumably a Madonna by Raphael (4.376n.), but there is no
such painting in the cathedral in Arezzo.

404-5] *Canon . . . comfits* See 2.793n.

409] *cousin* In the sense of a relative; Conti was Guido's sister's husband's
brother.

412] *Married . . . since* B dates the first meeting in March, only a month
or so before the flight; OYB does not specify when it was.

433-45] *At . . . Secu-lo-o-o-o-rum* This passage, ostensibly an account of
a Vesper service, contains a series of incoherent Latin fragments. Possibly B
did not understand the service, but more likely, he distorted this account to
satirize the superficiality of the religious life of Caponsacchi and his peers,
and to emphasize the ironic contrast between Conti's asides and the words of
the service. *Vespers* is the early evening office of the Western Church. It con-
sists of lessons, psalms, prayers, and the canticle Magnificat (Luke 1:46-55).
In ex-cel-sis (in the highest) is a phrase from the *Gloria in excelsis Deo,* a
hymn sung during the mass but not ordinarily at Vespers. It seems to be
quoted here to contrast with *louted* (bowed, been obsequious) and *incline.*
Quia sub means "that which under" or "because under." *Jam tu* (now you)
does not appear in the service. *Jam,* however, is the beginning word of the
Vesper hymn *Jam sol recedit ignesis* (Now the light of the sun fades). *In
secula Secu-lo-o-o-o-rum* (From age to age forever) are the last words of the
Gloria Patri (Glory to the Father), which is ordinarily sung at the end of the
Magnificat. Caponsacchi is being advised to engage not in devotion to a
transcendent power but in temporary distractions.

452] *Marino* See 6.329n.

453] *Dante* Dante's love for Beatrice, inspiration for his *Vita Nuova* and
Divina Comedia, was both spiritual and physical.

455-57] *Duomo . . . lancet-windows* The *Duomo* is the cathedral of

Arezzo, not the Pieve Church of which Caponsacchi was a canon. *Lancet-windows* are high and narrow with an arch at the top; the Duomo in Arezzo had a set of such windows made by Guillaume de Marcillat (1467-1529) depicting the life of Christ. *God's robe* is a recurrent metaphor in the Bible for transforming grace (see Rev. 6:11, for example: "and white robes were given to every one of them"). Here the *day's last gleam* and the *skirt of God's own robe* contrast with Light-skirts above (6.448) in the same way that Dante contrasts with Marino to illustrate two kinds of love.

458] *ortolans* Small birds, a delicacy.

462] *canzonet* A light song.

463] *patron* The Bishop of 6.268ff.

468] *Molinist* See 1.303-13n.

473] *strange Pope* Innocent XII; see 1.298n. *Strange* here means both new and different, less worldly than now customary in the Church.

479-97] *Summa . . . word* The *Summa Theologica* of St. Thomas Aquinas (1225-74) is a systematic compendium of Christian theology stressing the importance of rationalism. Its primary method is dialectical, following a question and answer format. It became the official guide to Roman Catholic belief during the Counter-Reformation following the Council of Trent (1545-63). In turning from his *Summa* Caponsacchi expressed his sense that the light of reason is insufficient, and that the new question posed by Pompilia and the grace that she represents has come between him and institutional religion.

513] *patch* Originally a fool or clown, but came to be applied especially to an ill-natured person, as in "cross-patch."

514] *Vittiano* See 2.808n.

515-16] *maid . . . house* See 3.1093-95n. and 3.1103n.

551] *Thyrsis and Myrtilla* See 5.670n. *Myrtillo* (masculine) is the name that appears in the letters (OYB, E, 105); he is the lover in *Il Pastor Fido* (*The Faithful Shepherd*, 1590) by Giovambattista Guarini (1537-1612) whose sweetheart Amaryllis is betrothed to another. One of the letters contains the remark, "I see that you like the Pastor Fido" (OYB, E, 103). The work had enormous popularity and was made into an opera by Handel in the 18th century.

558] *crumbs . . . table* "And there was a certain beggar named Lazarus, which was laid at his gate full of sores, And desiring to be fed with the crumbs which fell from the rich man's table" (Luke 16:20-21).

564] *Concert* Arrange, plan.

566] *Ave* At the time of the evening Angelus (six o'clock), a devotional which began with the recitation of the "Ave Maria" ("Hail Mary") and for this reason popularly called the "Ave" in Italy.

574] *Philomel . . . breast* The name *Philomel* for nightingale comes from the legend of the rape of Philomela by her brother-in-law Tereus, who also cut out her tongue; she was changed by the gods into a nightingale. Another legend about the melancholy of the nightingale's song supposes that it presses its breast against a thorn as it sings. The stories are often combined; see Shakespeare's *The Rape of Lucrece* 1.1135. As Cook points out, "It is, of course, really the male bird that sings" (123).

576] *vespers* See 6.433n.

596-97] *make . . . worm* Cf. Mark 9:43-48. "And if thy hand offend thee, cut it off: it is better for thee to enter into life maimed, than having two hands to go into hell, into the fire that never shall be quenched: Where their worm dieth not, and the fire is not quenched." Mark is paraphrasing Isa. 66:24.

599] *light-of-love* Mistress.

607] *Two . . . spiders* After mating spiders are famished and the female is likely to devour the male unless he escapes immediately. Even if he escapes he is so depleted that he will soon die naturally.

649] *Ave* See 6.566n.

657] *picture . . . church* The Duomo; see 6.402 and n.

658-59] *verger . . . point* A verger is strictly an official who carries a mace or "verge" before a dignitary, but the term is also used, as it is here, for one who takes care of the interior of a church.

662] *venom . . . mouth* See Vol. V, 384 of this edition ("Bishop Blougram's Apology" 1.377n.) for a summary of the mid-nineteenth century controversy in the Roman Catholic church over miracles.

665] *ordure-corner* Scrap heap, or, in light of context ("dung-heap," 6.670), human excrement.

676-78] *heel . . . bruise* God said to the serpent after the temptation, "And I will put enmity between thee and the woman, and between thy seed and her seed; it shall bruise thy head, and thou shalt bruise his heel." (Gen. 3:15).

692-95] *same . . . Sorrows* The seven sorrows of Mary are often represented by seven swords piercing her breast, but the image here seems to be another reference to the Raphael Madonna of 6.398-402. Cf. 6.896.

743] *thought . . . deed* A phrase from the Confiteor (confession said during the mass); the Latin means, "I have sinned exceedingly in thought, word, and deed."

781-83] *they . . . one* "For this cause shall a man leave father and mother, and shall cleave to his wife: and they twain shall be one flesh" (Matt. 19:5).

807-8] *stand . . . go* Jesus said to the palsied man, "Arise, and take up thy bed, and go thy way into thine house" (Mark 2:11).

818-21] *priest . . . Romano* OYB, E, 92.

831-32] *love . . . brother* See 2.496n.

832-33] *idle . . . devil* A reference to the proverb "The devil finds work for idle hands to do."

856] *thief . . . Christ* Luke 23:42. "Lord remember me when thou comest into thy kingdom."

894-899] *simile . . . Babe* See 6.402n. and 6.657n.

926] *bar* Even had Caponsacchi's deposition been in OYB there would have been no bar or witness box; see 1.152n. and *Sources.* Caponsacchi is also referring to anything that would get in the way of a direct relation to God.

931] *first Spring* The first of Spring. The phrase suggest Edenic innocence as well.

933] *In . . . away* "Therefore if any man be in Christ, he is a new creature: old things are passed away; behold, all things are become new" (1 Cor. 5:17); "and there shall be no more death, neither sorrow, nor crying, neither shall there be any more pain: for the former things are passed away. And he that sat upon the throne said, Behold, I make all things new" (Rev. 21:4-5). Being made new is a recurrent theme in this book, and particularly explicit in 6.922-1089.

944-46] *sophist . . . reed* Here *sophist* seems to mean learned teacher, without derogatory connotations; likewise *sinner* means here pre-Christian. Plato's pen is made from a reed grown in the river Cephissus, which flows by Athens. The teachings of St. Thomas (see 6.479-97n.) and Plato (c. 427-347 B.C.) alike are seen as barriers to Caponsacchi's new life through immolation.

951-58] *initiatory . . . pain* In these ll. Caponsacchi makes a mystical leap from language reminiscent of the first sin and the expulsion from Eden (which he feels himself recapitulating by his defiance of both theological and philosophical authority) to reference to the final resurrection. *Initiatory pang* and *felicitous annoy* suggest *felix culpa* (the fortunate fall), and the idea of man's redemption through suffering. *Virgin-band* may echo Rev. 14:4. *Earthly garments* is probably a reference both to Adam and Eve clothing their nakedness (Gen. 3:7) and to the fallen—corruptible and mortal—flesh which must at the resurrection be raised incorruptible and immortal (*immortal nakedness*). *Pain*, like *pang* above may be a transmutation of the Bibical *sting*. "And as we have borne the image of the earthly, we shall also bear the image of the heavenly . . . In a moment, in the twinkling of an eye . . . the dead shall be raised incorruptible, and we shall be changed . . . So when this corruptible shall have put on incorruption, and this mortal shall have put on immortality, then shall be brought to pass the saying that is written, Death is swallowed up in victory. O death, where is thy sting? O grave, where is thy victory? (1 Cor. 15:49, 52-55)

961-63] *church . . . Lamb* The church is imaged as the bride of Christ in Revelation: "And a voice came out of the throne, saying, Praise our God, all ye his servants, and ye that fear him, both small and great. . . . Let us be glad and rejoice, and give honour to him: for the marriage of the Lamb is come, and his wife hath made herself ready (Rev. 19:5,7; see also 21:9).

965-66] *freeze . . . free* In the Roman Catholic Church the priest is required to take a vow of chastity.

973] *corona* Prayer beads.

979] *sheep's . . . faith* The mystic union with the Lamb in 6.962-63 has here become the blind faith of a sheep.

985] *scrannel* Meager. Perhaps, with the reference to sheep of 6.979, an echo of Milton's "Lycidas" 123-25. ". . . their lean and flashy songs / Grate on their scrannel pipes of wretched straw. / The hungry sheep look up, and are not fed."

987-94] *fabled . . . watch* A reference to the myth of the Garden of the Hesperides (see 3.384-85n.) and an inversion of the story of the Garden of Eden. Having mistaken *hips and haws* (rose hips and hawthorne berries) for the golden apples of the Hesperides, the adventurer suddenly comes upon the real thing, but is warned off by the dragon, here both the church and Satan (cf. Rev. 12:1-3: "And there appeared a great wonder in heaven; a woman clothed with the sun, and the moon under her feet, and upon her head a crown of twelve stars: And she being with child cried, travailing in birth, and pained to be delivered. And there appeared another wonder in heaven; and behold a great red dragon, having seven heads and ten horns, and seven crowns upon his head.") The Biblical inversions are complex, and the complexity reflects the struggle of Caponsacchi's intuitive challenge of appearances, duty, convention, safety, and law.

1005] *seals . . . sum* Echoes of Job and Ezekiel. "Then he openeth the ears of men, and sealeth their instruction (Job 33:16). "Thus sayeth the Lord God, thou sealeth up the sum, full of wisdom, and perfect in beauty" (Ezek. 29:12).

1010] *opened . . . Aquinas* See 6.479-97n.

1012] *vespers* See 6.433n.

1033] *Hating . . . lie* An echo of Revelation 22:11, 15: ". . . and he that is righteous, let him be righteous still: and that is holy, let him be holy still . . . For without are . . . whosoever loveth and maketh a lie."

1063] *new moon* B took care about the accuracy of such details as this. In a letter of May 14, 1881 he wrote, "in order to be quite sure of the age of the moon on the occasion of Pompilia's flight, I procured De Morgan's register of lunar risings and settings for the last—I forget how many hundred years." Caponsacchi is speaking on Sunday 21 April. According to the U.S. Naval

1065-69] *Torrione . . . inn* The Torrione was a watch tower in the old city wall. The wall had fallen into ruins at that spot and it was easy to climb over. San Clemente was the gate closest to the Torrione, but it was on the opposite side of the city from the road that they were to take. The carriage was waiting for them at the inn outside the San Clemente gate. The accounts given by Pompilia and Caponsacchi in OYB differ in details of time and meeting place, and the mention of the Torrione appears only in the separate sentence of the court at Florence in the Process of Flight (OYB, E, 93, 96, 5) Cook's note is full on the discrepancies (126-27).

1082] *Summa* See 6.479-97n.

1083-88] *Thomas . . . adieu* The disciple Thomas was known as "doubting Thomas" because he demanded proof that Christ had risen after the crucifixion (John 20:25). According to legend he was also skeptical about the assumption of the Virgin; however, he believed when she dropped him her sash as she rose in the air.

1094-96] *last . . . copes* See 1.579n. A vigil is a service of prayer generally ending with the Eucharistic celebration on the eve of certain of the greater feast days in the church calendar. In the MS B originally had Caponsacchi and Pompilia leaving on 29 April, the Feast of St. Peter Martyr (not the apostle), but in revision changed the departure to 23 April, the Feast of St. George (see also 6.1063n.). The calendar, however, does not provide vigils for either of these feasts and B's ascription of vigils to them is apparently gratuitous. *Copes,* large cape-like vestments worn in the absence of a chasuble, although not prescribed for such occasions, are often worn because of their festive nature.

1097] *Canon Conti* See 2.793n.

1098] *Canon Crispi* Not mentioned in OYB.

1099] *stall* A fixed seat in the choir of a church for the use of the clergy.

1100] *octave* An *octave* is a period of eight days during which a major feast is celebrated. In this case, the Easter octave includes the feast day itself and the seven days following. Proper observance would include additional duties for the priests.

1103] *laic dress* See 2.999n.

1106] *knave* In the older sense of servant.

1128] *San Spirito* The fugitives had to go around the city from the San Clemente gate to the San Spirito gate to take the road S to Perugia and Rome.

1143-44] *God's . . . saints* "And I saw as it were a sea of of glass mingled with fire: and them that had gotten the victory over the beast . . . stand on the sea of glass, having the harps of God" (Rev. 15:2).

1151] *Parian—coprolite* A famous white marble from the island of Paros—fossilized feces of ancient animals.

1159-70]   *Blackness . . . safe* Without direct quotation, this passage draws on the imagery of the prophetic book of Revelation. When the fifth seal of the seven-sealed book was broken, the souls of Christian *martyrs* appeared, "And white robes were given unto every one of them; and it was said unto them, that they should rest yet for a little season" (Rev. 6:11). *Vest* means robe, *dark* here presumably because still symbolic of death. When the seventh seal was broken, seven trumpets appeared and were sounded in turn, each heralding a disaster worse than the preceding one, until finally the seventh *trumpet* announced the final judgment of God.

1183-87]   *Perugia . . . hours* See map for route followed to Rome. The Bs followed this same route on their trips from Florence to Rome, taking, however, five or six days, compared to Caponsacchi's and Pompilia's forty-two hours, to cover the distance. Perugia is 46 mi. from Arezzo, and Treves conjectures that they could not have arrived there before noon (185). Both Perugia and Assisi are on hills, and are bypassed by the main road. Assisi is famous as the birthplace of St. Francis of Assisi (see 5.149-53n.); it is about 11 mi. from Perugia.

1189]   *post-house* On main traveled roads there were post-houses at regular intervals, anywhere from six to seventeen mi. apart, according to Treves, where fresh horses could be obtained. There were fourteen of these stations between Arezzo and Castelnuovo (Treves, 174, 178).

1226]   *blow-ball* The seed of the dandelion.

1229-30]   *smile . . . snakes* A traditional symbol occuring almost universally in folklore. It symbolized in the eagle the triumph of the spirit over the chthonic powers represented by the snake. The smile is evoked by Caponsacchi's awareness of its inappropriateness as a symbol of the present holder of the office of bishop.

1243]   *rocheted and mitred* Traditional vestment and headdress that are part of the insignia of a bishop.

1246]   *angelus* A devotional service repeated three times daily, morning, noon, and evening as a memorial of the Incarnation. The bell rung for the evening service came to be called the angelus bell, or simply the angelus. The evening devotional came at six o'clock.

1247]   *neither . . . write* See 2.1145n.

1251]   *Gabriel's song* The Annunciation (Luke 1:27-35).

1252-53]   *lesson . . . travellers* B seems to be describing the evening service of vespers which does include the Magnificat and lessons. See 6.433-445n. The prayer Pompilia requests comes from the mass for the Feast of St. Raphael the Archangel. It derives from the Book of Tobit in the Apocrypha. The Angel Raphael befriended Tobit's son, Tobias, traveling with him into Media. As they were leaving Tobit said (not knowing to whom he spoke),

"Go with this man; God who dwells in heaven will prosper your way, and may His angels attend you" (Tobit 5:16). The prayer, however, is addressed to God, not Raphael: "O God who didst send the blessed Archangel Raphael to accompany thy servant on his journey, grant that we thy servants may ever be guarded by his care and strengthened by his aid. . . ."

1255] *Foligno* Foligno is only 10 mi. past Assisi. They are averaging 5 mi. per hour (Treves, 177); the delay is not accounted for.

1281] *priest . . . fiends* "And these signs shall follow them that believe; In my name shall they cast out devils" (Mark 16:18). Exorcist was the second of the minor orders (see 1.260-62n), but exorcism was not restricted to a single order. The *Rituale Romanum*, first issued 1614, contains an exorcism rite which might be used by any priest with episcopal permission.

1282-83] *Let . . . scattered* "let God arise, let his enemies be scattered: let them also that hate him flee before him" (Ps. 68:1).

1315-18] *tree . . . mimosa* The mimosa tree known as million-leaved (*millefoliata*) for its fringes of tiny leaflets, is covered with yellow blooms in early spring.

1327] *Lorenzo in Lucina* See 2.6n.

1348] *coil* Fuss, tumult.

1367] *Gaetano* The name Pompilia would give her baby; see *Chronology*.

1373-74] *help . . . carry* "In my distress I called upon the Lord, and cried unto my God. . . . And he rode upon a cherub, and did fly: yea, he did fly upon the wings of the wind" (Ps. 18:6, 10).

1377-78] *Castelnuovo . . . stage* The last post house they will need before Rome, seventeen mi. away.

1381-82] *sky . . . Setting* In OYB Pompilia insisted that they arrived at Castelnuovo at dawn (OYB, E, 94). The time is Tuesday evening 23 April, 1697; they have been traveling for 42 hours.

1403-4] *I . . . grooms* In the Process of Flight Caponsacchi said he was still sleeping when Guido surprised them (OYB, E, 97).

1421] *feminity* Femininity.

1431] *Foligno* See 6.1255n.

1433-38] *halting . . . Force* See 3.1444-49. Vulcan was lame, and in the *Odyssey* he attributed Venus' preference for Mars to this disability. Guido, of course, halts because of the drug he was given. In the story told in the *Odyssey* Vulcan does not pursue the lovers; he traps them in bed and returns home to surprise them. The Cyclopes were servants of Vulcan, but here their *unpoisoned arm* may also refer to the *Cyclops* of *Odyssey* 9.345-94, the one-eyed giant from whose terrible revenge Odysseus was saved by another drugged potion; this Cyclops is not so handicapped.

1451] *gripe* See 6.166n.

1462-65] *Moliere's . . . divine* In Moliere's (1622-73) play *Don Juan* the hero marries and later rejects Donna Elvira, hypocritically justifying himself for the rejection by pretending remorse at having stolen her from a convent. B used Donna Elvira's reproach to Don Juan as the headnote to *Fifine at the Fair* (1872), with his own verse translation.

1482] *priest . . . privileged* Subject to ecclesiastical rather than civil authority. See 6.1548-58n.

1518] *sword* See 2.1023n.

1532] *amorous . . . prose* These letters, allegedly found by Guido, are quoted in OYB, E, 99-106. Caponsacchi and Pompilia said they were forgeries. (See 5.1146 and n.).

1541] *getting . . . countenance* Gaining credibility, and saving face.

1548-58] *nobler . . . shield* As a Tuscan noble, Caponsacchi could refer the case to the jurisdiction of the Duke of Tuscany, but he also has the right both as priest and as current sojourner in the States of the Church, to that appeal. See *Sources* and map. For Guido's rank see 1.785n.

1577-78] *Leap . . . with* For the sword as emblematic of truth, see 2.1022, 1023 and nn.

1579] *you find* MS *you see* was changed to *you find* to avoid repeating *see* (see variants). The sense seems intended to be the same, however.

1594] *paten* The dish on which the blessed bread, the Body of Christ, is carried.

1600] *bravo's dress* Rough clothing appropriate for a *bravo*, a hired killer. The old "crime"—in which Caponsacchi had a hand—was the flight. The new "crime"—in which he disclaims any part—is the murder.

1606] *Two days ago* At 6.37 he said it was three days ago.

1610] *friend . . . Court* A legal phrase meaning that Caponsacchi's presence at the trail is voluntary and that his function there is to implement justice. There is no suggestion in OYB that Caponsacchi was present at the trial.

1618-22] *Noted . . . stays* Caponsacchi's deposition in the Process of Flight and his monologue do vary, however, both in details and in the significance attached to them. Maria's intermediary role in the exchange of the love letters is an invention of the monologue, as is Caponsacchi's indecision and soul-searching about whether or not to take Pompilia to Rome. Details such as how often Pompilia and Caponsacchi spoke together before the flight, and whether Caponsacchi slept at the inn at Castelnuovo, are further discrepancies. See Cook, 291, for fuller discussion. Caponsacchi's language (*jot or tittle*) recalls Jesus' claim that his intention was to "fulfil" the law, not destroy it, by putting it in a larger context (Matt. 5:17). Caponsacchi now sees the flight in light of the new context in which it is placed by the murder.

1633]   *Pasquin* Pasquin, a fifteenth-century Roman tailor, gave his name to *pasquinade*, a vulgar or satirical comment on figures or events of current interest. There was a statue opposite Pasquin's shop in the Piazza Novona, the largest public square in Rome, which became a repository of pasquinades.

1639]   *forgery* OYB, E p. 98.

1640-41]   *Bembo's . . . 'De Tribus'* Pietro Bembo (1470-1547) was known as a scholar and stylist; Caponsacchi says, as well believe the trash of the letter of the letters written by Bembo as by himself. *De Tribus Impostoribus* (Concerning Three Impostors, who were Moses, Christ, and Mohammed) was a blasphemous tract rumored in the sixteenth and seventeenth centuries to have been written in the Middle Ages. It was attributed to various authors but probably never existed. Sir Thomas Browne in *Religio Medici* (1.20) mentions the book. St. John, the beloved disciple, wrote a life of Christ and was at one time considered the author of the book of Revelation. *Quotha* is contemptuous or sarcastic for "quoth he" (OED).

1665-66]   *Sub . . . Laborat* Labored under the suspicion of being a prostitute.

1668]   *Borsi . . . drove* The driver on the first stage of the journey was imprisoned for his participation, and upon release he testified as to his passengers' intimacies. (OYB, E, 249).

1694]   *smack* As in the smacking of lips; appetite.

1701-5]   *name . . . Potiphar* See 2.1105-6n.

1713]   *bravo-hiring* See 6.1600.

1719]   *Civita* See 2.1171n.

1720]   *'De . . . Helenæ'* "Of the Abduction of Helen." A Greek poem written about 500 A.D. by Coluthus of Lycopolis, itself a *travesty*, a poor imitation of Homer's *Iliad*.

1723]   *Vulgar* Common; that is, Italian.

1724]   *Scazons* A scazon is a six foot line of five iambes and a final spondee or trochee.

1739-40]   *Metes . . . now* "Give, and it shall be given unto you; good measure, pressed down, and shaken together, and running over, shall men give into your bosom. For with the same measure that ye mete withal it shall be measured to you again." (Luke 6:38).

1744]   *Saint George* See 1.579n.

1755-56]   *Stand . . . see* "Let them alone: they be blind leaders of the blind" (Matt. 15:14). Cf. also, "Ye blind guides, which strain at a gnat, and swallow a camel" (Matt. 23:24).

1759]   *owl-eyes* The owl is a nocturnal bird whose eyes cannot bear the light.

1761-62]   *Saint . . . Nero* Nero (37-68), persecutor of Christians, cruel and depraved tyrant, is said to have played his lyre while Rome burned in A.D. 64. Because of his fierce persecution he became for the Christians the embodiment of evil. Caponsacchi makes him the prototype of Guido, whose evil is also unmistakable.

1765] *cartulary* Collection or register of charters, deeds, etc.

1766] *head and front* Perhaps a contrast to Aaron, the High Priest, who was commanded by God to wear upon his forehead a plate of Gold bearing the words "Holiness to the Lord." It may also be a reference to the mark of the murderer Cain (Gen. 4:15) or another of the many echoes in this monologue of the book of Revelation, e.g., the mark of the beast (14:9) and the inscription on the forehead of the whore of Babylon (17:5).

1769] *letch* Craving.

1793-94] *Lord . . . Air* As the Father of Lies, Satan is the master of temptation and disguise, from his entering into the "subtil" snake to tempt Eve (Gen. 3:1) to the temptation of Jesus (Matt. 4:1-9). See also 1.561n.

1833] *guiltless . . . deed* See 6.743n.

1846] *Abati* Abbots; see 1.547n.

1848] *silk mask* For clandestine wooing?

1849] *musk* See 1.92n.

1850] *rochet* See 5.1243n.

1869-71] *you . . . Arezzo* MS reading *leaving her* for *leaving you* (see variants) is a clarification of the passage. Caponsacchi's point to the Court is that the Court is as much to blame for Pompilia's death as he is, the one for sending him to Civita Vecchia, the other for not killing Guido in Castelnuovo. By sentencing Caponsacchi to relegation the Court prevented him from staying in Rome to protect Pompilia; the sentence did not keep him from going back to Arezzo when Guido did, which he would not have done in any case, he says.

1888] *cramp* Secure.

1896] *slidders* Dialect for slips.

1907] *discovers* Shows.

1908] *Judas* Dante places the traitors Judas and Brutus in the nethermost ring of hell, each solitarily frozen in ice. The rest of this paragraph is very Dantean.

1915] *Kiss . . . Iscariot* Matt. 26:48, 49.

1916] *smatch* Taste.

1921] *cockatrice . . . basilisk* See 1.168n.

1952] *event* Consequences.

1969] *disfigure* See 2.31n.

1972] *clown's disguise* In the earlier sense of farmer, countryman. The Prosecution argued that Guido's rural garb was indeed a disguise, and thus an aggravation of his crime (OYB, E, 70).

1980-90] *title* . . . *error* The *title* of Caponsacchi's sentence of Relegation in the Process of Flight means the grounds given for the punishment, the language describing these grounds was changed from "complicity in the flight and running away of Francesca Comparini, for carnal knowledge of the same" to "For the reason which is the subject of these proceedings." The meaning of this change in wording was debated by both sides (OYB, E, 66).

1984] *Probationis ob defectum* For want of proof (OYB, E, 66).

1995-96] *Not* . . . *true* I.e., what I wish were true is not true.

1998-99] *Conti* . . . *kinfolk* See 2.793n, 2926n; see OYB, E, 160, 219, 261-62.

2003] *Conti is dead* OYB, E, 219.

2007] *had come* Would have come.

2008-9] *condemned* . . . *galleys* The severe sentence of the Tuscan court in the Process of Flight included five years in the galleys on the island of Elba for Guillichini (OYB, E, 7).

2011] *fortnight* . . . *Governor* The recommendation of the Governor of Arezzo in the case was confirmed by the court at Florence on 24 Dec. 1697, two weeks before Caponsacchi's speech to the court at Rome (OYB, E, 7).

2022] *Vincenzo Marzi-Medici* The Governor of Arezzo.

2027] *Duke* The Grand Duke of Tuscany whose seat was at Florence.

2028] *Rota's* Highest Court's.

2031-32] *Augustinian* . . . *letter* See 3.18n. His letter is dated 10 Jan., however; Caponsacchi is speaking on the 4th or 5th.

2048] *duty* . . . *long* In 1702, four years after the trial, he resigned as canon of the church; what happened to him beyond that we do not know.

2070-71] *Plutarch* . . . *Grecian* Plutarch's (c. 46-c. 120) *Lives*, biographies of the great and famous, are not a parallel to the "imagined life" (6.2052) that Caponsacchi has just sketched for himself, but the contrasts between the imagined and the actual lives of the dreamers are the same.

Book 7, Pompilia

1-2] *seventeen* . . . *weeks* Born on 17 July 1680, Pompilia is speaking 6 Jan. 1698, the day she died.

4] *Lorenzo in Lucina* See 2.6n.

6-7] *Francesca* . . . *Pompilia* Pompilia was called Francesca in OYB. B may have wished to avoid association with the well known Francesca di Rimini, whom Dante immortalized by putting her in her first realm of hell because of her adulterous relation with Paolo.

8-9] *writ* . . . *years* See *Chronology*.

10-11] *insert . . . death* Pompilia's death is recorded in the San Lorenzo Church register with no mention of its circumstances.

12-14] *This . . . weeks* The only recorded date of Pompilia's baby's birth that has been found is a mention in OYB, which gives 18 Dec. 1697, two weeks before the attack (OYB, E, 189).

15] *Curate* See 7.32n.

16-17] *born . . . church* If Gaetano had been born, as B thought, in another parish, he would have been baptized in that parish church. A Vatican MS names San Lorenzo in Damaso as the place of baptism (Corrigan, 12). Violante had been baptized here too.

22-25] *marble . . . door* Pompilia conflates two lion statues outside San Lorenzo Church. The marble half-lions are on either side of the entry. The one on the right represents a lion protectively cradling a human figure; the one on the left has a decapitated beast between its paws. The two figures "symbolize respectively the benignity of the Church towards the neophyte and the docile and her severity towards the impenitent and heretical" (Augustus J. C. Hare, *Walks in Rome* [London: George Allen Co., 1903], 1.45). In a letter to Frederic Leighton requesting details about the church B said that any information about the interior "will be of great use to me." However, he added, "I don't care about the outside" (Oct. 17, 1864; Orr, *Life*, 284).

27] *buried there* The entry for Pompilia's death in the church register records that she was buried there (Treves, 300).

30] *Gaetano . . . reason* See 7.100-107 and n.

31] *Don Celestine* See 3.18n.

32] *Curate Ottoboni* This was the name of the curate at the time of Pompilia's death, not birth. B misread the entry in OYB; see OYB, E, 159. The baptismal record, certified by Ottoboni, reads: "July 23, 1680. I, Bartolomeo Mini, curate, have baptised the infant daughter born on the 17th of this month to Pietro Comparini and Violante Peruzzi, who live in this parish."

37] *Twenty-two dagger-wounds* This figure is in the Secondary Source (OYB, E, 263).

41] *hid away* The child was hidden for a time; see 5.1471n. and 7.203-5.

45] *two . . . born* The customary interval between birth and baptism; see 4.478n.

56] *we . . . where* Since Pompilia and the Comparini are already at the suburban villa (See 1.389n.), this is an obscure reference. See 7.232 and n.

81] *know . . . write* See 2.1145n.

93] *two weeks* The baby was nineteen days old when Pompilia died; see *Chronology*.

100-104] *Gaetano . . . years* St. Gaetano, whose name means "carefree," lived 1480-1547 and was canonized in 1671.

106] *five saints* See 7.6-7. Only four of Pompilia's names are saints' names. St. *Francesca* Romana (1384-1440) was founder of the Oblates of St. Benedict of Tor de' Specchi and was canonized in 1608. St. *Angela* Merici (1474-1540) founded the Ursulines, but was not canonized until 1807. She enjoyed popular reputation long before she was officially recognized. Another *Angela*, of Foligno (1248-1309), was an Umbrian mystic known widely for her visions, which were written down by her confessor and circulated under the title "Liber Visionum et Instructionum." She was beatified by Innocent XI in 1693, but like Angela Merici was a popular figure long before. *Vittoria*, martyr, died in 250 and *Camilla* in 437. We have found no St. *Pompilia*. Perhaps B's revision of MS *four saints* to *five* in 1869 was intended to suggest that Pompilia's sainthood was all her own (see variants).

137] *one . . . ago* See *Chronology*.

154-56] *People . . . wait* The suit for legal separation was brought against Guido in the fall of 1697, about three months before the murders.

164] *priestly vows* See 1.379n.

175-76] *Letters . . . myself* Reproduced in OYB, E, 99-106; forgeries, according to Pompilia and Caponsacchi.

186-88] *With . . . back* Ovid tells the story of the punishment of Acteon, who while hunting, by accident witnessed Diana, virgin goddess of the moon and of the hunt, at her bath. Acteon was turned into a *stag*, then pursued and killed by his own hounds (*Metamorphoses* 3.138-252).

190-93] *green . . . tree* Daphne was turned into a bay tree in answer to her prayer for protection from the pursuing Apollo (Ovid, *Metamorphoses* 1.548-52).

203-4] *they . . . day* See 5.1471n.

215] *lone house* See 1.389n.

227] *cause . . . gained* Neither the dowry nor the suit for separation was settled; Pietro may mean that what was important to them, the return of Pompilia, had been legally accomplished.

232] *other villa* This house is supposedly still more remote than the one in the suburbs where they died (see 1.389n.), but this and 7.56 are the only references in the poem to a third villa of the Comparini.

235] *sincere* Unadulterated; Italian "sincero" is still used in this sense. The porters who carried wine into Rome from the countryside were known for diluting the wine, according to W. W. Story (Story, 25).

259-60] *seven . . . San Giovanni* The number seven refers to the seven hills of ancient Rome; Pietro has been from one end of the city to the other. *San Giovanni*, the Church of St. John Lateran, was first built in 324 A.D. and was the first publicly consecrated basilica in Rome. Its Lateran Palace was the residence of the Popes until the seat of the church was moved to Avignon in 1305. Many Popes were buried there, including the celebrated Formosus of

10.25. The church was rebuilt and restored several times over the centuries, but it has always retained a reputation as among the churches of first importance in Rome. It acquired its Baroque appearance in 1650, not a long time (in Roman terms) before Pietro made his rounds of the city's sights in 1697.

260-63] *There's . . . angel* The scene depicts the adoration of the shepherds (Luke 2:8-10).

284-85] *dying . . . all* There is no indication that Pompilia's mother was dying either at the time of the bargain or of the birth, nor did Violante so claim in the deposition found by Corrigan (26).

308] *Receive . . . die* See 2.210n.

320-21] *Paul . . . me* See 3.250n. and 3.360ff.

325] *God's . . . point* Aaron caused a plague of lice to descend upon Egypt to persuade Pharaoh to let the children of Israel go, but Pharaoh refused to believe that it was a sign from God. "Then the magicians said unto Pharaoh, This is the finger of God; and Pharaoh's heart was hardened, and he harkened not unto them" (Ex. 8:19). Violante's refusal to recognize danger and her insistence on calling the marriage God's will is an ironic echo of the reference.

330] *wife . . . says* "Therefore shall a man leave his father and his mother, and shall cleave unto his wife: and they shall be one flesh" (Gen. 2:24); See also Mark 10:8.

365-68] *sea . . . again* The reference is to Matthew 14:25-32, which describes Peter's attempt to meet Jesus walking on the water, his momentary lapse of faith and consequent sinking, and his rescue by Jesus and the calming of the stormy waters.

367] *Don Celestine* See 3.18n.

375-78] *same . . . tongue* See *Chronology* and 2.69n.

386-89] *slim . . . else* The story of Perseus, rescuer of Andromeda and slayer of the serpent threatening her, is told in Ovid, *Metamorphoses* 4.663-742. In the course of this and other adventures, Perseus flew several times over the whole world. He was a favorite subject of painters and sculptors, who customarily represented him with winged helmet and shoes. For associations of the Perseus and the St. George myths, see 1.579n.

390-92] *old . . . beard* The Secondary Source describes Guido as "low of stature, thin and pallid, with prominent nose, black hair and a heavy beard" (OYB, E, 266).

394] *owl . . . birds* See 3.338n.

419] *Master Malpichi* Marcello Malpichi (1628-94) was famous throughout Europe as a biologist and physician. In 1691 he came from Bologna to Rome to be physician to Pope Innocent XII.

422] *eve . . . day* See *Chronology*.

423-24] *Lion's mouth . . . Corso* The Lion's-mouth, the Via della Bocca di Leone, was part of the route from the Comparini's house to San Lorenzo Church. The Bs spent the winters of 1853-54 and 1858-59 in a flat on the Bocca di Leone.

431] *brother* See 2.358n.

441] *chancel* See 2.20n.

442-46] *Read . . . Christ* "Wives, submit yourselves unto your own husbands, as unto the Lord. For the husband is the head of the wife, even as Christ is the head of the church" (Eph. 5.22-23). The miracle of the turning of water into wine is told in John 2:1-11. The priest's *therefore* is nonsensical, underlining the credulity of the helpless Pompilia: marriage is presented to her as a mixture of cant, hypocrisy, nonsense and exploitation, which she innocently accepts.

455-57] *Violante . . . wetting* To Violante's ear, *wetting* is *wedding*. What a shock she must have had, hearing Pietro announce their secret on the very heels of her warning to Pompilia not to divulge it!

459] *gutter's . . . sea* There were open sewers in the middle of most 17th century Roman streets which would have overflowed with rain, and with the exception of the Corso there were few raised sidewalks for pedestrians.

468] *three weeks* See *Chronology*.

469-71] *Nor . . . house* See 7.444-46.

485] *Pietro . . . angry* Pietro's disapproval and ignorance of the marriage are based on a brief passage in the Second Anonymous Pamphlet (OYB, E, 212).

501] *Since . . . good* Milk is used as a cleanser and polisher of marble.

503] *syllabub* A drink made with milk whipped together with wine or liquor.

535] *wholesome* Both "healthful" and "whole, complete," in contrast to *broken* in the next line.

536] *broken victual* Leftovers, "fragments left after a meal" (OED).

543] *help . . . need* "God is our refuge and strength, a very present help in trouble" (Ps. 46:1).

553] *keep the house* Stay at home.

559] *cast . . . lap* "The lot is cast into the lap; but the whole disposing thereof is of the Lord" (Prov. 16:33).

563] *older far* See 5.142n.

565] *Know . . . Governor* Ironic; she did get to know them but not in the way Violante anticipated (see 2.866-73).

574] *cast* Thrown down.

585-86] *bleat . . . milked* W. W. Story describes the selling of milk "fresh from the udder" of goats herded daily into Rome from the country (Story, 362).

591] *Don Celestine* See 3.18n.

596] *four years* See *Chronology.*

599] *By . . . truths* Caponsacchi, who came to her rescue, and her son. See 7.612-621.

602-3] *Square . . . House* The Spanish Square (Piazza di Spagna) takes its name from the Spanish embassy located there. It is near the Comparini's house.

642] *he . . . first* The deception of pretending that he had an income. The Secondary Source says that "it was then found out that their entire capital did not amount to the total of their income as given in that note" (of initial agreement). OYB, E, 259.

662-63] *blind . . . ways* Light and darkness, vision and blindness are figures for faith and disbelief throughout the Bible, and *worm* is often used to signify man's inferiority and profound humility before God. Here Guido's ways are *wormy* to the *blind* Pompilia because he works in darkness, and because he is devious and base. Cf. 2 Cor. 4:4 and Job 25:6.

672] *lure-owl* See 3.338n.

706-10] *dulness . . . too* Pompilia says in her deposition that Guido's jealousy was associated with her failure to become pregnant (OYB, E, 91). *Dulness* is a secondary spelling of *dullness.*

720] *he . . . God* Since the priest celebrates Mass and hears confession he came increasingly during the Middle Ages to be regarded as the representative of God to the people. This, of course, would have been especially true of an Archbishop.

728] *twelve . . . old* She was thirteen; see *Chronology.*

740-42] *Go . . . house* Pompilia's refusal to have sexual relations with Guido and her appeal to the Archbishop are described in a letter from a gentleman of Arezzo to Pietro Comparini in Rome (OYB, E, 55 and 114). See also 706-10n. and 3.965-6.

742] *he . . . God* See 7.720n.

759-60] *apple . . . Paradise* Against God's command, at the serpent's urging Eve took "the fruit of the tree which is in the midst of the garden" (Gen. 3:3). Expulsion from the garden was the punishment for this disobedience.

761] *qualified* "Legally . . . capable of being" (OED). The Archbishop paraphrases Pompilia's plea in a formal, legalistic way, thus casting her as a true heretic.

763] *blasphemy . . . Molinists'* The Molinist heresy regarding sin is described in 1.303-13n. The Archbishop accuses Pompilia of reversing the meaning of obedience to God and sin against God in a way similar to the paradoxical thinking of Molinism but to her his response is to her sophistical and evasive.

792] *God's Bread* The Holy Sacrament; an oath.

802-3] *priest . . . Girolamo* See 2.496n.

812-13] *child . . . punishment* "The rod and reproof give wisdom: but a child left to himself bringeth his mother to shame" (Prov. 29:15).

815] *Without . . . them* "All these things spake Jesus unto the multitude in parables; and without a parable spake he not unto them:" (Matt. 13:34).

817-37] *flower-fig . . . alike* "And he spake to them a parable: Behold the fig tree, and all the trees; When they now shoot forth, ye see and know of your own selves that summer is now nigh at hand" (Luke 29:30). According to Story, each fig tree bore two crops of figs each year, the first being called flower-figs. He says, however, that they ripened in July rather than in May (*Roba di Roma*, 385).

822-34] *Creator's . . . out* See 7.759-60n. The confusion of the Archbishop's parable, in which the forbidden fruit of Genesis is now under an injunction to be eaten, typifies the inconsistency of *one in authority* (whether husband or bishop), to whom Pompilia is being enjoined to submit. There is further irony in the fact that fig trees are pollinated by wasps.

825] *fig-pecker* Italian "beccafico," a small migratory bird of the genus Sylvia, much esteemed as a dainty in the autumn, when it was fattened of figs and grapes" (OED).

842] *just man* Only man, as proven by his ungodly admonition. Cf. 7.742 "He stands for God."

848-53] *henceforth . . . mankind* Her experience with the Archbishop has taught her, she says, that her former view of the priesthood was erroneous and that, as she now understands, no prelate (mere man) can serve as an intermediary between her and God; in the future she must appeal to Him directly. The passage is reminiscent of the last chapter of Ecclesiastes: "Remember now thy Creator in the days of thy youth. . . . In the day when the keepers of the house shall tremble . . . and those that look out of the windows be darkened. . . . Fear God, and keep his commandments: for this is the whole duty of man. For God shall bring every work into judgment, with every secret thing, whether it be good, or whether it be evil" (Eccl. 12:1, 3, 13, 14).

860] *four years* Of marriage; see *Chronology*.

861-63] *beast . . . murk* Perhaps an echo of "A righteous man falling down before the wicked is as a troubled fountain, and a corrupt spring" (Prov. 25:26). *Murk* is an archaic form of "murky."

905] *tonsure . . . hides* See 1.327-28n.

928] *fond* Foolish.

943] *public play* See 6.391n.

944] *Carnival . . . March* In 1697, Ash Wednesday, the first day of Lent and the day after Carnival week, was 27 Feb.; thus Carnival was actually over before March.

968] *twist of comfits* A paper-twist of candy. See 2.793n.

350

970-72] *As . . . dust-handful* In *Georgics* 4.87, Virgil concludes an extended epic passage relating a battle among bees, by saying that the keepers still the tumult with a single handful of dust.

980-81] *Conti . . . cousin* See 4.384n.

984-85] *psalm . . . flee* "And I said, Oh that I had wings like a dove! for then would I fly away, and be at rest" (Ps. 55:6).

1008] *cornet* The twist (paper-twist) of 7.968.

1022-23] *O . . . thrust* "At the time of the affair of the play told above, as soon as we had returned home, he pointed a pistol at my breast saying: "Oh, Christ! What hinders me from laying you out here?" (OYB, E, 92).

1034] *pink* Pierce.

1039] *God . . . innocent* Perhaps an echo of the self-righteous and dogmatic counselor of Job who argued, "who ever perished, being innocent?" (Job 4:7)

1044] *Margherita* See 3.1093-95n.

1049] *threat . . . shame* MS has *threat*, which was misprinted through every edition of the poem as *thrust*. *Threat and shame* refer to *charge and reply* above (7.1046), Guido's *threat* to Caponsacchi and Pompilia's *shame* for his delusion and cruelty. See variants.

1090-91] *help . . . help* An echo from numerous passages in the Psalms: "My help cometh from the Lord" (Ps. 121:2), "Our help in the name of the Lord" (Ps. 124:8).

1116] *cannot read* See 2.1145n.

1117] *My idol* All the love letters begin with salutations such as "My Beloved Idol" (OYB, E, 104).

1135] *imposthume* Abcess.

1140] *prevent* Act before.

1143] *sonnet . . . Mirtillo* One of the names used in the love letters was *Mirtillo*; see 6.551n. There is no poetry in the letters, but mention is made of "your very gallant verses" (OYB, E, 102).

1162] *Pope . . . Sixth* The last Pope Sextus was the Fifth (1185-90); this claim is obviously that of a mad impostor.

1163] *Twelfth . . . to-day* Pompilia would have been a few days short of eleven years old when Innocent XII was made Pope 12 July 1691.

1175] *Get . . . gone* Pompilia's response to Margherita is an echo of Jesus' answer to Satan after the temptation on the mountain, "Get thee hence, Satan" (Matt. 4:10).

1177] *Saint . . . Ghost* To swear by the Holy Ghost was binding: "Wherefore I say unto you All manner of sin and blasphemy shall be forgiven unto men: but the blasphemy against the Holy Ghost shall not be forgiven unto men" (Matt. 12:31). But in swearing also by Giuseppe Caponsacchi's patron saint—in whose sanctity Margherita clearly believes Caponsacchi does not share—Margherita indicates how unreliable her oath is; see below 7.1195ff.

1192] *cup drained* "Father, if thou be willing, remove this cup from me: nevertheless not my will, but thine be done" (Luke 22:42).

1193] *the over-night* "On the preceding evening" (OED).

1197] *Archbishop . . . Rome* One of "Mirtillo's" letters cites the Archbishop's return to Rome after Easter with three of the available carriages as a reason for Pompilia to leave immediately (OYB, E, 105).

1199] *Even Caponsacchi* Caponsacchi said in his deposition, "I had to go to Rome on my own business" (OYB, E, 105).

1204-8] *Michael's . . . defender* The Archangel Michael was "of celestial armies prince" in Milton's *Paradise Lost* 6.44. His triumphant struggle with the dragon Satan is described in Revelation 12:7-9, and was often depicted by artists.

1224] *building-sparrow* Probably the house-sparrow, which prefers to nest close to human habitation. The attributive *building* means "making a nest."

1256-60] *Though . . . kept* Jewels worth over 400 scudi (about $6,300) are itemized as stolen from Guido in the Sentence of the Court at Florence against the flight (OYB, E, 6). How much of this was part of Pompilia's dowry we do not know. The Governor of Arezzo deposed in a letter that while the Comparini were still in Arezzo "these same Comparini had taken away all her jewellery from the Signora, which I forced them to restore" (OYB, E, 90).

1271-72] *friar . . . Roman* See 3.1013n.

1292] *Augustinian* See 3.1013n.

1295] *Guillichini* See 2.926n.

1296] *flying gout* One that comes and goes; obviously a convenient indisposition.

1298] *Conti* See 4.384n.

1307] *priest and Canon* In addition to being a priest, Conti is a Canon, part of the permanent staff of the Cathedral and responsible, among other duties, for the maintenance of its services. The Second Anonymous Pamphlet suggests that Conti advised Pompilia to seek Caponsacchi's help because of his strength and boldness.

1312-16] *Saint . . . mine* See 1.579n.

1331] *red . . . touch* Torture by red-hot pincers.

1339] *sentry crane* Cook quotes an ancient source: "After companies of cranes fall to the earth, for to rest . . . they ordain watches that they may rest the more surely, and the watches stand upon one foot, and each of them holdeth a little stone in the other foot, high from the earth, that they may be waked by falling of the stone, if it hap that they sleep" (Cook, 154).

1349]   *Peter and Paul* Margherita calls to witness Pompilia's "conversion" two saints famous for conversions or renewals of faith: Paul, who on the road to Damascus was converted to Christianity (Acts 9:3-21), and Peter who on the roof top saw the vision that made him realize that salvation was not for the Jews alone but for all men (Acts 10:9-21).

1356-57]   *force . . . horsehair-springe* Capable of taking the bait without becoming trapped. A springe is "a snare for catching small game, esp. birds" (OED). Cf. Polonius's "springes to catch woodcocks" (*Hamlet* 1.3.115). *Silk* may refer to something fluttering and bright to attract the birds.

1365]   *Ave Maria* See 6.566n.

1367]   *lock of hair* Often exchanged as a love token, which, of course, Pompilia is unwilling to offer.

1371]   *prayer . . . incense* "Let my prayer be set forth in thy sight as incense" (Ps. 141:2).

1378]   *Paynims* Pagans or non-Christians; usually Mohammedans. The reference assigns the story Pompilia is telling to the Crusades and to the same context as the myth of St. George (1.579n.); here she is the St. George figure in her fantasy.

1379-80]   *thunderstone . . . flame* A thunderbolt. It was believed that lightning contained a dart or missile.

1380]   *couch* Hiding place.

1392]   *a star* To lead her to where her child will be born, as the star led the Magi to Bethlehem (Matt. 2:9). See also 7.1133.

1398]   *spectacle* The play where she first saw Caponsacchi; see 6.391n.

1401-2]   *no . . . world* An echo of James 1:17, ". . . with whom is no variableness, neither shadow of turning."

1422]   *I . . . death* Caponsacchi said that Pompilia sent him a letter saying that "as her husband wished to kill her, she had resolved to go to Rome to her father" (OYB, E, 96).

1430]   *first word* According to Pompilia's deposition in OYB she had spoken to him before to warn him to stay away from the house (OYB, E, 92).

1434]   *star* See 7.1392n.

1436]   *House . . . Babe* The stables over which the star shone, where Jesus was born.

1445-47]   *cloud . . . shine* The *cloud* is doubt, momentarily obscuring her faith in Caponsacchi's guiding star. Caponsacchi uses the same imagery for his own passing doubt at a similar moment; cf. 6.908-10, 920-21.

1468-70, 1474-75]   *Jesus . . . devil / I . . . write* Pompilia explicitly compares Caponsacchi and Christ and implicitly compares herself and Christ. When Jesus taught at the feast of tabernacles "the Jews marvelled, saying, How knoweth this man letters, having never learned?" and when

Jesus accused them of breaking the laws of Moses "The People answered and said, Thou hast a devil" (John 7:14-15, 19-20). See also 2.1145n.

1483-89] *mark . . . charter* The passage is a reference to God's promise that the seed of woman shall overcome evil. "And the Lord God said unto the serpent . . . I will put enmity between thee and the woman, and between thy seed and her seed; it shall bruise thy head, and thou shalt bruise his heel:" (Gen. 3:14-15).

1491] *traditionary* Traditional.

1494] *faith . . . so* "(For we walk by faith, not by sight:)" (2 Cor. 5:7)

1495] *Don Celestine* See 3.18n.

1501] *blow* Bloom.

1515-18] *place . . . sank* In her confused memory of the trip Pompilia forgets sequence and times as well as names. For Caponsacchi's more specific but also somewhat inconsistent version of this stage of the journey see 6.1199-1303 and notes. Caponsacchi says, "When we stopped at Foligno it was dark" (6.1274). Treves describes the Plain of Foligno, or the Umbrian Plain, as it is first seen a short distance from where the road crosses the Tiber by an ancient bridge. "A little way beyond the bridge the great Umbrian plain, or Plain of Foligno, breaks into view . . . This plain is very green, since every foot of it is cultivated. . . . Viewed from a height, as from the top of Assisi, the plain is made glorious by its immensity, by its gradations of green, by the beauty of the far-off hills. . . . Many travelers coming towards Rome from the north have fallen into ecstasies over the Plain of Foligno" (196-98). Although the full effect of this paradise luxuriant in spring seems to have been lost on Pompilia, still Treves thinks that she may have noted with encouragement her first glimpse of the Tiber. The river is wide and shallow here: *the small river mitigates its flow*, in contrast to the more familiar—to Pompilia—deep currents of its Roman end (Treves, 197-98). The Bs would have seen all this on their own trips to Rome; see 6.1183-87n.

1522] *grey place* It is impossible to identify this reference with certainty. If we take Pompilia's timing of eve (7.1518) as loosely approximate and relative to her sense that time and strength are running out, we can speculate that the fugitives are at the foot of Assisi at the Church of Saint Mary of the Angels. St. Francis' order, the Franciscans, were called the Grey Friars and there are many legends about the saint; Treves recounts a number of them, estimating that the couple would have been at the shrine about 3 p.m. (Treves, 198-99).

1527-34] *town's . . . self* Foligno, like Arezzo, is a walled town, and the approach to it from the N is across a bridge and through a massive gate. The rock-side of the town and the tiled house-roofs are strikingly evident in Treves' photograph of the entrance to Foligno, and a church and tower are likewise visible on the skyline (plate 72).

1543] *hole . . . heaven* Cf. 1.593-94 and 1.661n.

1550-57] *milky . . . sense* The whole passage is reminiscent of Shelley's ". . . Nor yet exempt, though ruling them like slaves, / From chance, and death, and mutability, / The clogs of that which else might oversoar / The loftiest star of unascended heaven, / Pinnacled dim in the intense inane" (*Prometheus Unbound* 3.3.200-204). B's admiration of Shelley is well documented; see Irvine and Honan, 15-18, and the "Essay on Shelley" (Vol. V, 135-51 and nn.).

1563-66] *you . . . morning* In her deposition Pompilia said, "we journeyed toward Rome, travelling night and day without stopping until we reached Castelnuovo, except for them to take refreshment and to change the horses. We arrived at dawn, and were there overtaken by my husband" (OYB, E, 93-94). This discrepancy with the evidence and with Caponsacchi's account (6.1404-5 and OYB, E, 97), both of which indicate that they arrived at Castelnuovo about 7:30, is explained here and at 3.1189-94 as a consequence of her extreme fatigue.

1624] *truth . . . lies* Cf. 1.1271-73.

1633-36] *judges . . . nuns* See *Chronology.*

1640-54] he . . . ends This man restored my soul closely echoes Psalm 23:3, "He restoreth my soul." But the echo goes beyond the specific line to include all of this passage and the whole of the Psalm, from the pastoral imagery and emphasis on peace in both, to the affirmation of suffering and the promise of life everlasting in both. The soul is sometimes represented as a bird; by saving her son, the *bird-like thing*, Caponsacchi saved her soul as well.

1684] *Carry . . . Lent* Continue to wear the gay costume appropriate for the pre-Lenten carnival celebration after Lent, the somber period of self-denial and penitence, has begun.

1689] *respite* To confess before they died. God will surely forgive them or else he would have prolonged their lives until they, like Pompilia, had opportunity to make a sacramental confession.

1692] *pardon him* Several witnesses confirm that Pompilia movingly pardoned Guido (OYB, E, 57, 59).

1703] *But . . . absent* "Whither shall I go from thy spirit? or whither shall I flee from thy presence? If I ascend up to heaven . . . if I make my bed in hell, behold, thou art there" (Ps. 139:7-8).

1703-4] *In . . . too* "The Lord make his face shine upon thee" (Num. 6:25). "They brought forth the sick into the streets . . . that at the least the shadow of Peter passing by might overshadow some of them . . . and they were healed every one" (Acts 5:15-16).

1711] *evanishment* Vanishing.

1721-22] *saved . . . fire* "If any man's work shall be burned, he shall suffer loss: but he himself shall be saved; yet so as by fire" (1 Cor. 3:15).

1766-67] *with . . . life* By the vow of celibacy.

1776] *Civita* See 1.1031n.

1802] *balsam-tree* The aromatic balsam-tree was used medicinally; "balm" is a contraction of balsam.

1807-9] *Marriage . . . sure* See 7.444-46n.

1810-11] *there . . . angels* "For in the resurrection they neither marry, nor are given in marriage, but are as the angels of God in heaven" (Matt. 22:30).

1816-17] *angels . . . one* A curious echo of 1 Corinthians 13:12: "now I know in part; but then shall I know even as also I am known."

1828] *And I rise* The last line of Pompilia's monologue suggests the Assumption, and thus that it is the moment of her death. The Virgin Mary's corporeal ascent to heaven after her death is a doctrine celebrated by a feast day in the Roman Catholic Church, and it was a favorite subject of religious painters, including Michelangelo and Fra Lippo Lippi.

Book 8, Dominus Hyacinthus de Archangelis

A general note on the Latin in Books 8 and 9: "Dominus Hyacinthus de Archangelis" and "Doctor Johannes-Baptista Bottinius"

The legal Latin in Books 8 and 9 is usually quoted verbatim from OYB and in virtually every case is accompanied by B's line by line translation. While it might be argued in principle that an exact translation of all Latin is useful to the careful reader, we have found that a literal rendering of the legal Latin often raises more problem of interpretation than it solves. B's looser translations are in general both faithful to the sense of the original and easily coordinated with it wherever the reader wishes to make the parallel. We have provided translation with the annotation where the Latin phrase involves a pun, as in 8.113; where the sense of the lines in English requires understanding a grammatical distinction, as in 8.164; in the rare case where B departs from OYB, as in 8.1284; and as always, where the Latin phrase is from a classical source.

Sub-title] *Pauperum Procurator* The official defender of all criminals, and not just those unable to afford a lawyer's fee, as the title might suggest. See also 1.160n. and *Sources*.

1-2] *Giacinto . . . Cinone* Arcangeli's son is named Hyacinth after Arcangeli himself, who refers to the boy by numerous pet names—thus revealing his infatuation not only with his son but also with language and with himself.

4-6] *Branches . . . -aturus* The stem *Am-* of the verb *Amo* (I love) is understood with the branches of the endings for the second person singular present tense, the first person singular past tense, the passive past participle, the infinitive, the present participle and the future participle: you love, I have loved, having been loved, to love, loving, about to love. The conjunction of family tree and verb-tree is characteristic of Arcangeli's mixture of narcissism and pedantry, as is the verb chosen to conjugate.

7]   *Quies . . . cry* The relative pronoun *qui* takes the subjunctive when it introduces certain clauses of a subjective nature, such as "who could cry." In MS the pronoun "me" is not underlined, although in all editions it is in italics; see variants.

8]   *Corderius* The Latin textbooks of the Swiss scholar and teacher Maturin Cordier (John Calvin was one of his pupils) were considered authoritative from the sixteenth century well into the nineteenth. His name became synonymous with Latin scholarship.

11]   *Cinozzo, Cinoncello* See 8.1-2n.

13]   *triturate* A Latinate word meaning "grind, pulp." Arcangeli's oral metaphor for his profession, with here the implication of regurgitation, suggests the connections between his pedantry, his paternal pride, and his self-indulgence, all continuing themes in his monologue.

20]   *Cinuolo's . . . Cinicello's* See 8.1-2n.

30]   *Cinino, Ciniccino* See 8.1-2n.

31-32]   *lands . . . hereditaments* Arcangeli hopes that in a postscript to his will the old grandsire will leave everything without exception to his grandson, from land and all collective assets (*estate*), to property which has a term or tenure of interest or ownership (*tenements*), and anything at all which can be inherited (*hereditaments*).

35]   *Orvieto fuddle* Make drunk with wine; see 4.206.

38]   *smell-feasts* "Greedy spongers" (OED)

41]   *thrid* Archaic form of "thread."

42]   *galligaskin* A corruption of "a la grecque," in the Greek style of full pantaloons. *Galligaskin* in the 16th and 17th centuries was a kind of wide legged pant; in the 19th century the word was dialect for protective leggings.

44]   *Condotti* A street connecting the Piazza di Spagna with the Corso.

45]   *crush cup* An expression meaning "to drink a cup," as in *Romeo and Juliet* 1.2.80, "Come and crush a cup of wine."

45]   *Cinucciatolo* See 8.1-2n.

46]   *camp* The military.

47]   *chambering and wantonness* "Let us walk honestly . . . not in chambering and wantonness, not in strife and envying" (Rom. 13:13); *chambering*: sexual indulgence (OED)

56]   *Nutshell . . . Flaccus* From Horace (Quintus Horatius Flaccus, 65 B.C.-8 B.C.), *Satires* 2.5.36: "A man shall pluck out my eyes before I'll let him rob you of a nutshell."

57]   *Fisc yet bachelor* From B's description of Bottini in 1.1164-1211 he is clearly a bachelor; *yet* has the sense of "still" here. See also 1.160n.

59]   *hour-glass* cf. 8.1427 and n.

60-61]   *saint . . . day* Playing on the tradition of saints' days—which are not the birthdays of saints but days chosen by the church to honor particular saints—Arcangeli confers sainthood for a day on young Hyacinth on the occasion of his birthday.

62-63]   *Cinoncino's . . . Cinarello's* See 8.1-2n.

63]   *dumple* An archaic word meaning "to shape like a dumpling."

66-67]   *Argument . . . defence* Roman legal practice gave the opening plea to the defence; cf. 1.162 and n.

68]   *paper wing* See *Sources.*

70]   *mother-wit* Natural intelligence

72]   *bite his thumb* I.e., take offense and attempt to retaliate in a futile manner. Cf. *Romeo and Juliet* 1.1.42-43, where a Capulet servant says about Montague servants, "I will bite my thumb at them, which is disgrace to them if they bear it."

76]   *Verges on Virgil* As the greatest poet of ancient Rome and the author of the *Aeneid,* Virgil (Publius Virgilius Maro, 70-19 B.C.) is regarded as the crown of the young Latin scholar's efforts.

87-88]   *flower . . . match* Arcangeli's description of the opportunity fallen his way is based on the passage in the Sermon on the Mount contrasting God-given or natural glory, and temporal glory: "Consider the lilies of the field, how they grow; they toil not, neither do they spin: And yet I say unto you, That even Solomon in all his glory was not arrayed like one of these" (Matt. 6:28-29). Arcangeli characteristically spins his own interpretation of the passage and thereby arrays his ambition in hypocritical humility.

89]   *Cinoncino's* See 8.1-2n.

92]   *non . . . laus* "Not to us Lord, but to Thee be the praise." The Latin is a version of the opening of Psalm 115, but not the version which appears in the Vulgate. B has probably done his own translation, perhaps remembering the English version in The Book of Common Prayer: "Not unto us, O Lord, not unto us, but unto thy name give the praise."

93]   *they . . . Fisc* Bottini was appointed to the office of the Fisc subsequent to the Process of Flight, the trial of Pompilia and Caponsacchi in the summer of 1697 (see *Introduction*). Bottini is represented by Arcangeli as ambitious, proud, and pushing.

95]   *Cinotto's* See 8.1-2n.

96]   *'sbuddikins* A variation on "God's bodikin," or "God's dear body."

96]   *Innocent* See 1.298n.

99]   *Pro Milone* "In Behalf of Milo" Milo was clearly guilty and was convicted and exiled for his murder of Clodius, a political rival, in spite of his defense by Cicero. The famous oration here mentioned was written after the trial because Cicero feared the strength of Milo's enemies.

106] *speech . . . white* See *Sources.*

110] *Giacintino* See 8.1-2n.

112] *Procurator Pauperum* Procurator (Guardian) of the Poor. See 1.160n. and *Sources.*

113] *Hortensius Redivivus* "Hortensius come back to life." Quintus Hortensius (115-60 B.C.) was an orator and rival of Cicero. The name means "pertaining to a garden"; Arcangeli puns on his and Hyacinth's name and the botanical system of naming plants, which includes genus and species, in Latin.

114] *Est-est* "It is, it is." The expression means "wine of the best quality" and comes from a popular folk story about a servant who on a journey went in advance of his master tasting the wine at each stop. When the wine was good he wrote *Est* on the door of the inn. At Montefiascone he wrote *Est Est Est.* When the master arrived he stayed there until he died and the inscription *Est Est Est* appears on his tomb in the church of San Flaviano there. There is an Italian wine called Est.

115] *mollifies* Makes tender.

116] *goose-foot . . . cock's-comb* Edible plants so named for the distinctive leaf formation of certain of their species.

125] *pro Guidone et Sociis* "In behalf of Guido and his companions."

127-33] *Duxit . . . prose* Arcangeli rejects "He led for wife" perhaps because it is the phrase that the prosecution uses in OYB. Less literal and therefore less commonplace phrases are "He entered upon, underwent, the marriage torches" (cf. Catullus, 64.300) and "He joined to himself by stable marriage" (cf. Virgil, *Aeneid* 1.73).

133-34] *Virgil . . . Terence* Although Virgil was universally esteemed the greatest Latin poet for his *Aeneid*, the prose comedies of Terence (Publius Terentius Afer, 185-159 B.C.) are of more practical value to a man of the world, according to Arcangeli.

135] *Cinuccino* See 8.1-2n.

138] *owls for augury* Proverbial for bad luck.

139] *Nupserat . . . avibus* Arcangeli's opening words in the first pamphlet in OYB: "He had married, alas, with unfavorable birds" (i.e., ill omens).

140] *one . . . best* See 1.785n.

142] *version* The polished Latin translation.

145] *Farinacci's time* Prosper Farinacci (1544-1613) was highly regarded as an authority on legal matters throughout the seventeenth century. In 1599 he defended Beatrice Cenci in that famous case involving incest and patricide. He is frequently cited in OYB and it is strongly probable from parts of *The*

Ring and the Book, particularly the reference to torture, that B consulted Farinacci's work. Among his several widely read legal treatises is *Variæ Questiones* (*Various Questions*), which is quoted by both Arcangeli and Bottini.

145-46, 149-50] *rule . . . verse / law . . . Latinity* Arcangeli has set (*hitched*) the *rule* to jerky, awkward rhyme: *Latinity* is to be pronounced with a long *i* to rhyme with *fry. Fry* are internal organs such as kidney or liver.

150-52] *Goose-foot . . . idiom* See 8.116n. *Garnish* is probably a legal-culinary pun meaning both "arm or defend," and "decorate." *Idiom* is correct, idomatic "Latinity."

157] *coil* Noisy disturbance.

162-63] *have . . . pate* "To have someone on hip" means "to take or have the advantage of someone" and is probably a term from wrestling. "To break Tully's pate" is another metaphor of attack, meaning to break the rules of Ciceronian Latin (Marcus Tullius Cicero, 106-43 B.C.). Arcangeli puns on several senses of *turn*: as translation (into inferior Latin), as argumentative exchange, and as wrestling move—all inferior to Arcangeli's advantageous position.

164] *Existimandum . . . dog* "It being to be thought." The Latin future passive participle, along with other neologisms, is "freely used in an elliptical manner" in OYB, according to Gest (35-36, 670). Though characteristic of colloquial medieval Latin, such usages break with the classical Latin idiom of Cicero and Virgil (they "break Tully's pate"), and by the standards of classical usage—to which Arcangeli presumes to adhere—they might be considered as barbarous as a *dog* barking. The Latin here and below is very nearly word for word as given in OYB; Hodell gives line by line comparisons in parallel columns in his notes (Hodell, 330ff).

192] *Saint Joseph* Arcangeli causes Pompilia to swear by Joseph, whose belief in the virgin birth of Jesus presumably makes him the patron saint of unlikely stories.

202-6] *Guido . . . popping-piece* All of these florid terms for guns are used by Bottini and others in OYB.

209-10] *I . . . travelling-sword* As indeed the real Arcangeli did; OYB, E, 122. *Own* means here "grant, admit"; *simple* means here "only." A *travelling-sword* was a weapon not included under the bann. Arcangeli anticipates his response to the Fisc's charge that Guido not only killed his wife, but did so under circumstances (aggravating qualities) that compounded the crime, one of which was that he carried prohibited weapons. See 8.1143-80, 8.1178n.

213] *gird* Arcangeli puns on the weapons and his own taunting method of puncturing Bottini's inflated rhetoric.

215-16]   *Venturini . . . law* See 1.944n. and 4.1303-8n.

220]   *hectic . . . fine* Consumptive, thin.

221-22]   *pale-haired . . . ermine* A *ferret* is an albino European polecat, a predator with pale or yellowish fur; the white fur of the *ermine* was worn by high court judges. Arcangeli says, in effect, that Bottini is a dangerous hypocrite.

234-36]   *hoarse . . . all* As at 1.1196, the image is a crowing cock. In Chaucer's "The Nun's Priest's Tale" it is because Chauntecleer the cock crows with head thrown back and eyes closed that the fox (knowing that vanity is blind) catches him. See Arcangeli as the "old fox" below at 8.297. The likeness of Bottini to a cock is of course ironic as well as ridiculing; his *shrill throat* implies that he is emasculate as well as boastful.

239-43]   *cast . . . stroke* References to the game of bowles, played with heavy balls rolled on the ground. A *stroke* is a strong play.

242]   *luck . . . reply* See 1.162n.

244-51]   *You . . . littleness* The *you* of 8.244 is hypothetical, signifying Arcangeli himself, and the third person *cries* agrees with an implied "who" of which the antecedent is *fellow*. Arcangeli paraphrases the strategy that Bottini will adopt in retaliation to Arcangeli's own supposedly ineffectual defense. Mimicking Bottini, Arcangeli characterizes his own defensive subtlety as stopped rat holes on a ship without a pilot. By anticipating this worst-case scenario, Arcangeli is able to annihilate it through his "by-stroke" (8.256) below.

246]   *pilotage* The skill of piloting a ship.

253]   *main . . . death* "The obvious defense (a plea of Not Guilty) has been overworked." *Used to death* has a general rather than a specific sense; the plea of innocence is too hackneyed to have force any longer as a defense. The irony of the cliché *used to death* was apparently deliberate; see variants for B's revision of the original "known by now." That a plea of innocence was out of the question for Guido in any case, his guilt having been confessed, is characteristically of secondary importance to Arcangeli in preparing his defense.

256]   *by-stroke* Counter hit, side hit, answer to the "mortifying stroke" of 8.243.

259]   *Tommati* See 1.944n. and 4.1403-8n.

262-65]   *long . . . head* The image seems to be Tommati as a long-eared donkey who prefers the *amusement* of being tickled by a flea (Arcangeli) to the *instruction* of being cawed at by a crow (*daw*, i.e. Bottini). *Daw* also means simpleton; a jack daw is known especially for its repetitive chattering, an appropriate image for 8.259ff.

270]   *Blunderbore* Jack the Giant Killer tricked the giant Blunderbore into trying to outdo him and then into killing himself.

271-72] *subordinate . . . proof* Arcangeli was the chief defender, the Procurator, and Spreti was the co-defender, the Advocate. See, however, *Sources*; definition of these terms was not rigid. Arcangeli speaks of Spreti as his younger subordinate, but Hodell thinks that the difference between them was one of function and not of age or rank. The Procurator was responsible for determining the facts of the case, and the Advocate for knowing the law, canon and secular, applicable to the situation, a distinction not clearly apparent in the record.

274] *choppy* Chapped.

275] *Cinuzzo* See 8.1-2n.

275] *tippet* Scarf.

278, 280] *Carnival, Carnival-time* Slightly inconsistent with the facts. Carnival is the ten days preceding Ash Wednesday, the beginning of Lent, which in 1698 was on 12 February. Arcangeli is writing in late January (see 8.21 and OYB, E, 12). For *carnival,* see 2.294n.

284] *Cintino* See 8.1-2n.

286] *Rome . . . qualms* Perhaps a reference to Other Half-Rome's prejudice in favor of Pompilia.

288] *topping* Illustrious; here ironic.

290] *Cineruggiolo's* See 8.1-2n.

298] *prints the dew* Leaves tell-tale footprints in the soft and dewy grass.

303] *murder . . . killing* Murder is a technical term of English law meaning killing with malice aforethought. There was no equivalent in Latin; the Latin word for "homicide" simply means "killing" (Gest, 26).

312-13] *noble . . . plebians* See 5.12-13n.

320] *lout* Common.

322-23] *Farinacci . . . Questions* For *Gamaliel* see 5.1101-2n. For *Farinacci* see 8.145n. Since Farinacci died in 1613 it is his *immortal "Questions"* which have instructed Arcangeli.

325] *Vigiliarum* See 1.971-72n.

343-48] *accomplice . . . blood* From the Secondary Source (OYB, E, 265). There were four accomplices: Glasio Agostinelli, Domenico Gambassini, Francesco Pasquini, Alessandro Baldeschi. All were laborers on Guido's estate. *Reclaim* here means "object or appeal," on the grounds of the victim's nearly being killed in order to elicit a confession for a crime not itself punishable by death, i.e. murder in the defense of honor. Spreti used this argument in an attempt to disqualify the confessions (OYB, E, 133).

352-53] *Ah . . . happiness* Virgil's *Georgics* 2.457 reads "Ah, too fortunate the husbandmen, if they but knew their happiness!" Arcangeli has reversed, revised, as well as *reversed,* inverted, the sense of the lines.

358] *proper church* The church of his parish; see 4.148 and 7.17n.

359] *duty* . . . *Christmas-time* Christmas is one of the feasts of obligation, that is, a time when all Christians are obliged to refrain from servile work and to attend mass.

371] *Neither* . . . *peace* Jesus said to the repentant woman taken in adultery, "Neither do I condemn thee: go, and sin no more" (John 8:11).

376] *Is* . . . *good* The words of the householder in the parable of the vineyard to those who complained that he had dealt too generously with some of the laborers (Matt. 20:15).

390-91] *faulty* . . . *truth* A *pipkin* is a small clay or metal pot. Cook gives the explanation that what "faultiness of his apparatus" would be to an alchemist, so the confessions are to Arcangeli's hypothetical claim of Guido's innocence: an inconvenience, but one Arcangeli can avoid by resting his case on grounds less susceptible of either proof or disproof, i.e. the defense of honor (Cook, 168).

394] *Fiscal's cord* The torture of the vigil. See 1.971-72n.

414] *Farinacci* See 8.145n.

416-17] *Vindicatio* . . . *causa* "A vindication . . . for the sake of honor." The gist of Arcangeli's argument here, as in OYB, is that since Guido killed in defense of his honor, the prescribed punishment for murder, death, was not applicable. The lawyers in the OYB give numerous examples from case law to show that under such circumstances husbands have been given a lighter punishment or, in many cases, no punishment at all.

420] *misprision* Misapprehension.

429] *casuists* See 4.1470-75n.

447] *prior case* The case for Guido's innocence that was made awkward by the confession.

464] *To* . . . *end* Virgil, *Aeneid* 1.278-79. The original dominion is that of the Roman Empire.

466] *Cinoncino* See 8.1-2n.

467] *Poscimur* From Horace, *Odes* 1.32.1. "I am called upon." In Horace's case for an ode; in Arcangeli's, for a defense.

474-79] *Theodoric* . . . *interference* The historian and monk Cassiodorus (480-c. 575) served under Theodoric (c. 455-526), conqueror and first Gothic king of Italy. See 1.215-33n. The *apt sentence* cited is a maxim, not a judicial decree, and is mentioned by Spreti in OYB, E, 78-79.

477] *I* . . . *it* A rare admission of Arcangeli's superficial and often erroneous erudition. Examples are 8.474-79, 8.504-10, 8.590-92, 8.672-75; see nn.

481] *Aristotle doubts* In *Of the Generation of Animals* Aristotle says, "There is much difficulty about the generation of bees" (3.10).

483-84] *bee* . . . *Solomon* The author of the book of Proverbs was once thought to have been Solomon. Like the author of that book, bees find unchastity repugnant. "A virtuous woman is a crown to her husband; but she that maketh ashamed is as rottenness in his bones" (Prov. 12:4). See also 8.605-7 and n.

489] *castæ apes* "Chaste bees." Virgil, *Georgics* 4.197-99.

490-91] *Scaliger . . . Table-talk* Both Joseph Justus Scaliger (1640-1609) and his father Julius Caesar Scaliger were Italian physicians and scholars. Joseph's book *Scaligerana* (Sayings by Scaliger), in French, explains the expression "chaste bees" by saying that if bees see a man and wife making love, the next time the man approaches the woman they will sting him.

494] *mind* Call to mind, remember.

495-99] *Idyllist . . . warmth* Perhaps Theocritus, Greek poet of the third century, who did write idylls, "little pictures," is meant, but the citations are either a misunderstanding or a wrong attribution.

504-10] *Ælian . . . admire* See 1.215-33n.

532] *derogate* Degenerate.

534] *Absit* Away with.

546-49] *If . . . man* As Jesus was led to the crucifixion he told the mourners to grieve not for him but for themselves, "For if they do these things in a green tree [to me who am innocent], what shall be done in the dry [to those who are not]?" (Luke 23:31) The lines are another of Arcangeli's ironic inversions of context, imagery and meaning: if guilt went unpunished in pagan times, he says, surely murder should be licensed in the Christian *Autumn dry and ripe.*

551] *Pagan . . . gods* It was widely believed that pagan gods were fallen angels, or Christian devils. St. Paul was often quoted, with dubious applicability, for support: "But I say, that the things which the Gentiles sacrifice, they sacrifice to devils, and not to God: and I would not that ye should have fellowship with devils" (1 Cor. 10:20). Milton lists many of these devils in "On the Morning of Christ's Nativity," 21-24.

559] *minished* Lessened.

562-63] *Athenian . . . Solon's* See 1.215-33n.

564-65] *Laws . . . large* The passage in OYB, E is "This murder indeed was sanctioned . . . even in the rude age of Romulus, law 15, . . . and likewise in the Laws of the Twelve Tables" (page 12). B has conflated parts of two citations here. The Laws of the Twelve Tables were the earliest written code of Roman law. Compiled in 451 B.C. they were engraved on twelve brass tablets and for centuries lawyers learned them by heart. The Roman code itself goes back to Romulus, mythical founder of Rome, according to Plutarch.

566] *Julian . . . Law* See 1.215-33n.

570] *diluculum* "Dawn."

577] *Honour . . . good* Arcangeli's claim is not supported by the Bible;

see, among other passages, Romans 12:2, "And be not conformed to this world: but be ye transformed by the renewing of your mind, that ye may prove what is that good, and acceptable, and perfect, will of God."

578] *Saint Jerome* A priest and scholar of the Church, St. Jerome (c.340-420) is celebrated for his translation of the Bible into Latin (the Vulgate), his Biblical commentaries, and his extensive correspondence. The lines that follow are from a passage in one of his letters and are quoted in the first Anonymous Pamphlet (OYB, E, 155).

590-92] *coerce . . . Dialogue* The word *coerce* has the sense of "restrain" here. Pope Gregory the Great (c. 540-604) was Pope 590-604. He was a great reformer and administrator and a prolific writer. His *Dialogues with Peter the Deacon on the Lives and Miracles of Italian Saints* appealed to the credulity of the middle ages and quickly became a model for later hagiographers. In the quotation above (8.589-91) it was hardly his purpose to justify the wrath simply because it was difficult to control; this is another misleading representation (see 8.477n.).

593-628] *ingenuous . . . ignores* A close paraphrase of a citation in the first Anonymous Pamphlet (OYB, E, 154). The archaic meaning of *ingenuous* was "noble,. . . generous, high-minded" (OED).

605-15] *quia . . . friends* "For jealousy is the rage of a man: therefore he will not spare in the day of vengeance. He will not regard any ransom; neither will he rest content, though thou givest many gifts" (Prov. 6:34-35). The Latin is from the Vulgate. *Zelus*, which Arcangeli translates zeal, is rendered "jealousy" in all the standard translations of the Bible.

618] *consentaneous* Agreeing.

619-20] *St. Bernard . . . nephew* The letter from St. Bernard (1090-1153) is quoted in the first Anonymous Pamphlet (OYB, E, 154), where it is said to be addressed to his nephew, but it may have been to his famous contemporary Robert of Melun (d. 1167), a conservative whose doctrines were opposed to Bernard's; there was much debate between them.

627] *Order . . . mode* Custom and law.

630] *Cavalier Maratta* See 1.58n. Ironically, Maratta was best known for painting the Madonna, not an outraged husband.

632-49] *Samson . . . before* Deceived by Delilah, blinded, enslaved and imprisoned by the Philistines, Samson acted to defend his honor by pulling down the pillars upon which his prison house stood, killing himself and many of his captors (Judg. 16:21-30). A major flaw in the analogy between Guido and Samson is that Samson sacrificed himself with his enemies, thus expiating his violation of Nazarite purity as well as accomplishing his revenge.

635] *Nazarite* One who takes extremely rigorous religious vows. The angel of the Lord said to Samson's mother before his birth: "thou shalt conceive, and bear a son; and no razor shall come on his head: for the child shall be a Nazarite unto God from the womb" (Judg. 13:5).

638] *Gyves* Shackles.

650] *Are . . . example* "Now all these things happened unto them for ensamples: and they are written for our admonition" (1 Cor. 10:11). Ensamples: examples.

652] *mansuetude* Gentleness, meekness.

653] *Sealing . . . up* Not from the Gospels as Arcangeli wishes to imply, but from Ezekiel 29:12, "Thus saith the Lord God; thou sealest up the sum, full of wisdom and perfect in beauty."

654-55] *Opprobrium . . . complaint* A reference to Jesus, who "held his peace" against false witnesses, causing the high priest to ask, "Answerest thou nothing? . . . Then did they spit in his face, and buffeted him; and others smote him with the palms of their hands, Saying, Prophesy unto us, thou Christ, Who is he that smote thee?" (Matt. 26:67-68).

655-59] *but . . . give* It would seem that *Our Lord Himself* refers to Jesus, but the Latin is a distorted quotation from the Old Testament book of Isaiah: "I am the Lord: that is my name; and my glory I will not give to another" (Isa. 42:8). The substitution of *honor* for glory is substantive. There is no parallel statement in the gospel that can be attributed to Jesus. See 8.477n.

665-66] *Paul . . . once* The statement is found in the Epistle of Jude and is not by St. Paul: "It was needful for me to write unto you, and to exhort you that ye should earnestly contend for the faith which was once delivered unto the saints" (Jude 3). See 8.477n.

667-69] *Far . . . void* A misapplication. In 1 Corinthians 9:15, St. Paul writes: "it were better for me to die, than that any man should make my glorying void." His glorying and not his *glory* is in the gospel he has preached; certainly not in the wages he might have received but refused. In Galatians 6:14, he writes, "God forbid that I should glory, save in the cross of our Lord Jesus Christ." See 8.477n.

672-75] *Saint . . . it* The comment by St. Ambrose (340-397), Bishop of Milan, is quoted in Spreti's defense: "For who does not regard a bodily defect or a loss of patrimony more lightly than a defect of soul and a loss of reputation" (OYB, E, 142). See also 8.477n.

677-87] *Revelation . . . wine* Arcangeli's description of the condoning of murder in Innocent XII's millenial high noon is indebted to the description of the coming of Armageddon in Revelation 16 and is thus another of his inversions of meaning and context, Guido being here equated with the God of the Last Judgment (see 8.477n). Revelation describes the pouring out of the seven vials full of the wine of the wrath of God over all the earth, the seventh "cup of the wine of the fullness of his wrath" (Rev. 16:19) being reserved for Babylon; *the chalice teems* means "the cup pours, flows" (OED).

682-83] *flower . . . doctrine* As soon as the appeal to the Pope is resolved by a pardon for Guido.

688-89] *Molinists . . . case* Perhaps a reference to the central paradox of Molinist thought, that the soul in a state of perfect contemplation may render the body unresistant to temptation and sin (here the apparent adultery); see 1.303-13n. The reference is also another of the sweeping condemnations of all non-conformist thinking under the label of one generally acknowledged heresy, Molinism; the *they* of 8.690 seems to refer not only to Molinists but to anyone who has a permissive attitude toward adultery.

690-92] *under . . . law* "the adulterer and the adulteress shall surely be put to death" (Lev. 20:10). "Then ye shall bring them both out unto the city gate of that city, and ye shall stone them with stones that they die" (Deut. 22:4).

692-93] *Nay . . . Lord* Not an accurate statement. Jesus set aside the law requiring stoning in the case of a repentant woman caught in adultery (John 8:3-11), but in Matthew 5:32 he explicitly prohibits divorce except in cases of adultery, an exception not specified in the more rigorous statements reported by Mark (2.2-12) and by Luke (16:18).

694-96] *Nor . . . Christ* In the seventeenth century the Church held to the stricter doctrine that marriage was indissoluble, although an annulment or a legal separation *a mensa et thoro* (from bed and board) was a possibility. *Typifies* refers to the passage "For the husband is the head of the wife, even as Christ is head of the Church" (Eph. 5:23).

697-700] *no . . . pass* The smallest letter, the merest dot. "Till heaven and earth pass, one jot or one tittle shall in no wise pass from the law, till all be fulfilled" (Matt. 5:18). "Heaven and earth shall pass away, but my words shall not pass away" (Matt. 24:35).

703] *infallible* See 5.1344n.

705] *lapidation* Stoning.

706] *Gospel . . . stone* See 8.692n. and 692-93n.

709-10] *fulness . . . dispensation* "That in the dispensation of the fulness of times he might gather together in one all things in Christ" (Eph. 1:10).

714-18] *natural . . . behind* The Jews became discouraged by the hardships of the wilderness and protested to Moses: "Who will give us flesh to eat? We remember the fish, which we did eat in Egypt freely; the cucumbers, and the melons, and the leeks, and the onions, and the garlick: But now our soul is dried away: there is nothing at all, beside this manna, before our eyes" (Num. 11:4-6). Arcangeli's mind is drawn back to food even when the analogy is very remote, as here, where he likens the *natural privilege* of revenge to the manna that God sent the Jews on the journey out of Egypt.

726] *early . . . race* Boethius' (c. 475-525) *Consolation of Philosophy* praises the simple life of the *acorn-eating race*. In the translation by Chaucer,

"Blisful was the firste age of men . . . They weren wont lyghtly to slaken hir hungir at even with accornes of ookes" (2.5.1,5-6). But of course the dish, and the argument, would have an opposite significance for Arcangeli's palate.

727-28] *Behold . . . thereby* "If any man offend not in word, the same is a perfect man, and able also to bridle the whole body. Behold, we put bits in the horses' mouths, that they may obey us; and we turn about their whole body" (James 3:2-3).

734-35] *manners . . . man* The proverb goes back to the fourteenth century.

743-44] *Wherewithal . . . language* "Wherewithal shall a young man cleanse his way? by taking heed thereto according to thy word" (Ps. 119:9).

745] *depicturing* Imagining.

747-49] *Quod . . . leno* "But if the husband in adultery should not complain, he is presumed a pimp." The argument is from Spreti, OYB, E, 32.

754] *Did . . . Paul* In OYB Spreti argues that the adultery of a wife stains not only her husband's reputation but also that of his entire family. Thus, he says, Paul was forced to flee Rome because of the disgrace he had suffered (OYB, E, 32). The same argument is advanced in the Anonymous Pamphlet (OYB, E, 151).

760] *cachinnation* Hooting laughter.

768] *finger-tip* Perhaps a reference to the "finger of God"; see 3.550-51n.

785-86] *ran . . . Deliquit* Neither classical nor medieval Latin attributes B's meaning to *deliquere*, which means "to transgress," not "to run away."

803-14] *Leonardus . . . killing* Leonardus' trial took place in Naples in 1617 and is cited by Spreti (OYB, E, 140). The Two Sicilies was the old name of the Kingdom of Naples.

808] *with commodity* Conveniently.

815-26] *Another . . . exile* Laurentius Matthaeu et Sanz' *Tractatus de Re Criminali* (*Treatise on Criminology*) was published in 1676. It was used extensively by both Arcangeli and Spreti. According to Gest, the author was one of the best legal writers of his time. Gest relates the fuller circumstances and the decision in the case cited in OYB by Spreti (Gest, 659-67). Curiously, the lover in the case was a young cleric whom the wife claimed she had summoned to help her return to her family, and the manner of the killing was repeated stabbing; the wife was found with nineteen knife wounds, but she survived long enough to tell her story. See OYB, E, 140 for Spreti's reference.

826-27] *Enough . . . feast* The proverb goes back to the Greeks.

830] *twinkling . . . eye* An ironic echo of St. Paul's statement, "We shall not all sleep, but we shall all be changed, In a moment, in the twinkling of an eye, at the last trump" (1 Cor. 15:52).

836-37] *Judges . . . testimony* Another attempt to bolster his case by appeal to scripture: "To the law and to the testimony; if they speak not according to this work, it is because there is no light in them" (Isa. 8.20).

837] *Look to it* The wording of the phrase, the trial setting of the passage, and the prevailing theme of the justification of revenge are all reminiscent of Shylock's reiterated threat in Shakespeare's *The Merchant of Venice*, "Let him look to his bond" (3.1.47-50).

853] *votarist . . . mode* Devotee of what is currently fashionable or acceptable.

855] *sciolist* "A superficial pretender to knowledge; a conceited smatterer" (OED)

856-57] *actual . . . virtual* The distinction between *actual* and *virtual* may derive from John Calvin, Protestant reformer (1609-64), who argued that although the eucharistic bread and wine did not become the actual body and blood of Christ (as the Roman Catholic Church held), the faithful communicant did receive along with the elements the virtue or power of the actual body and blood. In any case, here the *virtual wrong* is the more powerful, and certainly equally punishable, evil.

865-71] *Qui . . . worse* For the terms of the Trust see 2.210ff and n.

886] *zeal . . . up* When Jesus drove the money-changers from the temple "his disciples remembered that it was written, the zeal of thine house hath eaten me up" (John 2:17).

888-90] *Crudum . . . phrase* In the Trojan wars Juno, wife of Jupiter, favored the Greek side, while Jupiter was a partisan of the Trojans. In the *Iliad* Jupiter angrily mocks Juno, saying that nothing short of devouring Priam (King of Troy) would satisfy her (*Iliad* 4.35). Cook quotes from a lost Latin translation of the *Iliad* which uses Arcangeli's phrase (Cook, 172).

913] *Dolabella* See 1.215-33n.

921] *Hill of Mars* The Areopagus or Hill of Mars (*Ares* was the Greek name of Mars) is a low hill NW of Athens near the Acropolis; it was the site where the Supreme Court met. By extension the body of judges came to be known by the same title. In legend the Areopagus was the site of the trial of Mars for the death of a son of Neptune.

932] *parricide* See 1.215-33n.

938-39] *Valerius . . . Facts* Valerius Maximus (the Greatest) was a first century Latin author who wrote *Nine Books of Memorable Deeds and Sayings*, intended to be used as a text in schools of rhetoric. The collection of anecdotes, mainly Roman, was very popular during the Middle Ages and even down to the sixteenth century. It includes the story of the double parricide just described.

940] *Cyriacus* A lawyer from Mantua whose book *Forensic Debates* was completed in 1638. He too cites the Dolabella decision.

945] *denegation* Denial.

950] *Temporalem . . . time* Gest says that the term *temporalem* distinguishes temporal from ecclesiastical confinement in a monastery (685).

952-60] *In . . . off* The preposition *in* can take either the accusative or the ablative case in Latin, according to its meaning. The ablative case used here is correct but it jostles Arcangeli's mind once more into young Hyacinth's struggles with Latin grammar. *Villain* is a playful diminutive here. Mrs. Orr tells the story of B's having learned Latin declensions from his father by the same rhyming method he has Arcangeli propose.

962] *just . . . found* Ovid was trained for public service and began his career by holding several minor offices, but he soon discovered that such activity consumed time he would rather devote to writing poetry. He eventually abandoned a public career. See also 2.1212-13n.

975-76] *Brazen . . . peals* According to legend the English philosopher and monk Roger Bacon (1214-94) made a head of brass that could speak. When it spoke it said "Time is," then a half hour later, "Time was," then a half hour later, "Time's past," at which point it fell into fragments.

980-83] *clock . . . days* In answer to the prayer of Hezekiah, King of Judah, God stopped the sun and turned back the clock (sun dial) to save Hezekiah and his city from the Assyrians. In return Hezekiah promised, "I shall go softly all my years in the bitterness of my soul" (Is. 38.8, 15).

991] *ex incontinenti* "Uncontrolled." The legal term had the sense of "immediately, in passion," and signified a mitigation of a crime, a mitigation that the Fisc argued did not hold in Guido's case since he acted only after a considerable lapse of time. The real Arcangeli makes the same distortion of the strict temporal meaning of the term (OYB, E, 14).

1000-1] *Suppose . . . risk* Cited in Bottini's argument, OYB, E, 200.

1019] *brush . . . breast* Graze him at a vulnerable spot.

1042] *gaby . . . goose* A *gaby* is a simpleton. "To shoe a goose" is proverbial for "perform a useless act."

1051] *House of Convertites* See 2.1189-90.

1052] *Villa* See 1.389n.

1058] *You . . . Christmas-eve* From the Secondary Source (OYB, E, 263).

1061-65] *Molinism . . . Time* 1.303-13n. Only in the sense that church ritual was of secondary importance to Molinism would this accusation hold true.

1064-65] *Feasts . . . Time* In addition to the Nativity, there are observances of St. Stephen on 26 December; of St. John, Apostle and Evangelist, on 27 December; of the Holy Innocents on 28 December; and the Circumcision of Jesus on 1 January.

1069-71] *song . . . Camerlengo* The Sistine chapel in the Vatican, with its frescoes by Michelangelo and others, is used only for services at which the

Pope is present. *Song matutinal* would be morning mass. *Camerlengo* means Chamberlain, and is the title of the highest ranking cardinal. He is head of the Apostolic Court and administrator of the properties and revenues of the Holy See. During a vacancy of the Papacy he is responsible for the external affairs of the Church also.

1072-74] *Hat . . . Infidel* The peaked hat and short sword are insignia of the office of Cardinals, who are also called *princes* of the church.

1083-84] *find . . . invent* It clearly matters little which to Arcangeli; see 8.477n.

1086] *lamb's fry* See 8.145-46n.

1094-96] *six . . . crime* See 1.166n. The Latin *qualitas* means "properties, circumstances," here in the sense of incriminating, aggravating circumstances. Against Arcangeli's argument that Guido's murder is pardonable on the grounds of the defense of honor, Bottini's argument will be that the circumstances of the crime, far from excusing it, were such as to render it doubly heinous. The qualities are discussed by both sides in the trial (see for example OYB, E, 16-19, 85, 202-7). The qualities are, in the order that Arcangeli raises them here, 1) the hired accomplices, 2) the use of unlawful arms, 3) the place of the murders (a violation of the sanctity of home), 4) the disguises, 5) the violation of legal supervision (which Guido himself had sought), under which Pompilia remained at the time, and 6) the treason against the state (*Læsa Majestas*) which the flaunting of established law in all the five "qualities" above implied (see 8.1359 and n.).

1099] *skit* Satirical barb.

1101] *fico* A *fico* (fig) is something small and valueless; also a gesture of contempt in which the thumb protrudes from a closed fist or is bitten (see 8.72n.).

1109-11] *Unluckily . . . Rome* See 1.149-55n. It was not this governor, however, who passed bans against assemblies of armed men. Gest suggests that the Latin which both B and Hodell (OYB, E, 68) translate as *Governor* may mean more generally "government" (Gest, 477).

1122] *compassed* "Contrived, proposed," in a bad sense.

1126] *luck* In the sense of fortune, chance.

1129-32] *Make . . . large* The strategy is to get the aggravating circumstances dismissed on the grounds that they are means and not end (the murder of Pompilia), and then to prove that the killing is not really murder since it was committed justifiably in defense of Guido's honor.

1136-38] *Law . . . flag* The example is from Farinacci (OYB, E, 128).

1150] *Pope Alexander* Alexander VIII (1610-91) was responsible for laws prohibiting the carrying or keeping of certain kinds of arms within the Papal State.

1151-56] *Such . . . edge* See 2.146n. The saw-toothed dagger used by

371

Guido was originally a refinement of hand to hand combat, in which a skillful gloved opponent might actually grasp the blade of his enemy to disarm him. In the 16th century sword makers developed a dagger with a double edge or *prong* bearing "little saw-like teeth, set backwards like tiny barbs, the effect of which was to cruelly lacerate the hand that seized it" (Alfred Hutton, *The Sword and the Centuries* [Rutland, Vermont: Charles E. Tuttle Company, 1973], 110). *Glass* here is figurative, meaning "of a brittle, breakable composition."

1152] *Horn-like . . . buck* The number of tines on a stag's horns indicates his age and presumably his strength and fierceness.

1160] *foppery* The artificial invention of a fop.

1166] *Means . . . end* Bearing arms was prohibited because of the "pernicious end which follows it" (OYB, E, 45). Arcangeli begs the question by arguing that given a legitimate motive for murder one means is as good as another.

1168] *Furor . . . arma* "Madness provided weapons" (Virgil, *Aeneid* 1.150).

1169-70] *Unde . . . sagittas* "Where shall I get me a stone,/ Whence arrows?" (Horace, *Satires* 2.7.116-17).

1171] *Eight months* In the Process of Flight.

1178] *sword and blunderbuss* The traveller's sword and long, large bore pistol that Guido had with him at Castelnuovo; see 8.209-13 and notes. A *blunderbuss* is a short range weapon. The size of a weapon, which would determine whether or not it could be concealed, was apparently the decisive legalizing factor; that is, the smaller the weapon the more dangerous it was considered (Gest, 487-88).

1179] *pollent* A Latinism meaning "powerful."

1180] *amasius* Lover. The word is used repeatedly in OYB.

1182] *emprise* Undertaking.

1189-93] *lad . . . full* Reference to the multiplication of the loaves and fishes by which Jesus fed a multitude of people; John 6:8-13. The thought of food again overpowers reason and argument.

1195] *flout* A mocking speech or action.

1214-25] *Panicollus . . . trow* The citation of Caesar de Panimolla (not Panicollus) is adjacent in OYB to the case here described, but refers to a different case (Gest, 325). The ugliness of the revenge in the case of the noblemen of Sicily was "mutilation of the privates" following the murders (OYB, E, 29).

1231] *slur* To render either ugly, or indistinct of speech—or both.

1234] *Objectum . . . corruit* "The charge collapses completely" (OYB, E, 19).

1240-41] *But . . . dwelling-place* By tradition traced back to Cicero, one's home was regarded as a place of safe refuge not to be violated.

1242] *In . . . propria* "In their own home and dwelling place."

1252-53] *We . . . Paolo* In a mandate dated October 7, 1694, Guido gave Paolo power of attorney applicable to all legal suits and decisions, pending or future (OYB, E, 162). Pompilia's move from La Scalette to the Comparini's under "house arrest" was on 12 October 1697.

1255] *commodious* Accommodating, convenient (to Guido).

1260] *jailor . . . hangdog* A series in descending order of dignity or importance. *Turnkey:* subordinate jailor in charge of keys; *hangdog:* person assigned to the most menial duties.

1267] *tipstaff* A staff with a metal cap carried as a badge of office; thus, the sheriff or other official who carried one.

1281-86] *In . . . excusatur* Even in church "in which the King of Kings dwells . . . the one transgressing from a just end is pardoned." The passage is from Spreti, and as Hodell notes, "it contains the only unmistakable error of Browning in the transfer of the book-Latin to his Poem. 'Via' for 'ira' is doubtless a mistake in reading his own written notes" (Hodell, 333). The mistake may have been not B's but the printer's. The word in his MS could be either *ira* (anger) or *via* (way, course); the words are virtually identical in B's script. Although B does not seem to have detected the specific misreading (if there was one), he changed the translation of *Ex justa via* from MS "on fitting cause" to "on ground enough" in the first edition (see textual variants).

1290-91] *hale . . . Sacrament* A reference to the Right of Sanctuary. During the Middle Ages a criminal who had taken refuge within the Church could not be forcibly removed for a period of forty days. At the end of that time, however, he might be taken away for justice. The privilege did not extend to sacrilege or treason. In the Reformation the practice of sanctuary was further curtailed. Arcangeli's point is that even in the church, sanctuary is not absolute.

1293] *Foxes . . . nests* "And Jesus saith unto him, The foxes have holes, and the birds of the air have nests; but the Son of man hath not where to lay his head" (Matt. 8:20).

1298] *Aquinas' word* See 5.1352n. It is probable that Arcangeli's reference is not to a particular phrase in the *Summa Theologica*, but to its supremely rational method. Scholastic argument proposed a question or conclusion which was then proved by defeating a series of objections. Having imagined his defense to the final argumentative coup de grace, Arcangeli claims rank with the acknowledged master of rational discourse, St. Thomas Aquinas. That the *Summa* is a summary of proofs of the existence and nature of God, and that Arcangeli's case against the Fisc is the defense of a murderer, seems to be the irony here.

1300-2] *aggravation . . . wrappage* i.e., to the unaccustomed clothing of a peasant or laborer, thus to a disguise. This aggravation indicated premeditation and weakened the argument that Guido killed in a moment of uncontrollable anger. The use of disguise could even be regarded as similar to an ambush (Gest, 506). The garb that Arcangeli describes is the same that Guido was hanged in (OYB, E 266).

1306] *round . . . ears* See 1.597n.

1309] *travesty* Disguise.

1314-21] *Read . . . Troas* Paul's preaching after his conversion on the road to Damascus led the Jews of Damascus to seek his life. "Then the disciples took him by night, and let him down by the wall in a basket" (Acts 9:25; St. Paul's account of the event is in 2 Corinthians 11:32-33). Paul's cloak is mentioned in a passage written 30 years later near the end of his life (2 Tim. 4:13). Legend has it that the cloak had covered Paul in his escape, but there is no evidence for this belief. Arcangeli's argument that the same evasive methods for use and safety that effected Paul's escape from death should be allowed to serve Guido in his infliction of death, is typically ironic (see 8.477n). Arcangeli says that unlike the governor of Damascus, who failed to believe a prophet (Paul), the Governor of Rome (who presided over Guido's trial; see 1.944n.) will recognize the holy justice of Guido's methods and actions.

1322] *Molinists* See 1.303-13n.

1326] *Protection . . . judge* Pompilia was released from the convent upon the discovery that she was pregnant and permitted to reside with Pietro and Violante in the Via Paolina subject to specified restrictions under the authority of the Judge and a bond of 300 scudi. The official document "Bond given by Pompilia to keep her home as a prison" is printed in OYB, E, 159.

1336] *Corso* See 2.8n.

1340-42] *Tommati . . . big* See 1.944n. *Interest* has the sense of self-interest; should Tommati turn a blind eye to (*blink*) a slur on his own reputation, he would be praised for his unselfishness, but should anyone impede his function as a judge, i.e. his honor, he must defend himself.

1343-44] *My . . . here* Peter, speaking of the Holy Ghost, quoted the words of the Old Testament prophet Joel, "And it shall come to pass in the last days, saith God, I will pour out of my Spirit upon all flesh: and your sons and your daughters shall prophesy" (Acts 2:17). Tommati is represented as feeling that he, his predecessors, and his successors are representatives of the founder of the Vatican (Peter) and that the spirit of the law is a sacred trust of his office.

1359-64] *Læsa . . . criminis* "Wounded majesty/ from hatred of the law-suit/ increases/ the worsening of the crime." This is a slightly different sense of *læsa Majestas*, deriving from Guido's presumed impatience and anger (*envy*) at the slow operation of judicial procedure; see also *læsa Majestas* in 8.1094-96n. *Promoted* means "to set in motion . . . in a criminal suit in an ecclesiastical court" (OED). Two of the three pending suits were civil, those for nullification of the dowry and for divorce, and one was criminal, the suit for adultery (OYB, E, 210). Only in this last was Guido technically the promoter, but he stood to gain from the dropping of the other two.

1365-68] *Yes . . . barbacue* Almost anything serves to remind Arcangeli of his dinner. Does he here associate his own eruptive wrath with the defensive porcupine, or is he stung by the porcupine-like dis*charge* of the prosecution's latest accusation? Probably the latter; Arcangeli implies that it is the defense who is wounded, not majesty (the Pope). The porcupine was popularly believed to be able to dart its quills at an enemy. To *barbacue* was to roast whole. The rather fat meat of the young porcupine was cooked this way.

1369] *jug* An eighteenth century English method for stewing a hare in a jug or crock and serving it in a sauce made of its own blood.

1370] *pine-pips* Pine seeds, pine nuts.

1376] *Our . . . within* Perhaps a reference to Carlyle's "Soul is *not* synonymous with Stomach" (*Sartor Resartus*, "The Everlasting No").

1379-80] *dispel . . . wings* "But unto you that fear my name shall the Sun of righteousness arise with healing in his wings" (Mal. 4:2). *Healing*, as the next line reveals, refers to the appeal to the Pope to pardon Guido; as an argument against *læsa* (wounded) *Majestas*, it begs the question in the extreme.

1381] *prayed . . . self* For the appeal to the Pope see 8.1458-71 and 8.1468n.

1382] *tardy pack* The lawyers and judges, who are slow to arrive at a decision.

1385] *Unisonous* "Of the same pitch for the different voices or instruments; in unison or octaves, not in parts" (OED).

1386] *behoof* Benefit. Usually used with "to" or "for"; used with "in" out of confusion with "behalf" (OED).

1387] *Congregation . . . Court* OYB, E, 150.

1401-5] *Joab's . . . Innocentinopolis* Joab, David's commander in chief, fought against the city of Rabbah, but instead of taking it and claiming glory for himself, he urged David to "encamp against the city and take it; lest I take the city and it be called after my name" (2 Sam. 12:26-29). Before the victory David had been saddened by the mortal illness of his first child by Bathsheba. But his spirits returned after the death, and the Bible does not suggest that

Joab granted David the honor of victory over Rabbah out of concern or pity. Here as elsewhere Arcangeli's analogy suggests meanings unintended by him; the obvious parallel is between David conquering a city of unbelievers and the Pope condemning—not freeing—a murderer (See 8.477n). *Innocentinopolis* means "Innocent's city"; the Pope's name should be his verdict, says Arcangeli.

1409] *Ad . . . Judge* From the first Anonymous Pamphlet, OYB, E, 150.

1411-13] *Why . . . self* Apparently a garbled reference to Matthew 8.14-15: "And when Jesus was come into Peter's house, he saw his wife's mother laid, and sick of a fever. And he touched her hand, and the fever left her." To substitute for Jesus the name of Peter, who office the Pope is said to occupy, is the grossest flattery.

1414] *posed* "To non-plus with a question or problem" (OED).

1415-16] *It . . . it* After Jesus had healed a man born blind, the man's parents were afraid to tell the truth to the Pharisees, who demanded to know who had performed the miracle. The parents' answer to the Pharisees was, "He is of age, ask him" (John 9:21). Arcangeli accuses the Pope of avoiding duty and passing the buck.

1416-17] *inspire . . . Court* "Breathe into, prompt" the Court's reply. In the remaining lines of this stanza Arcangeli imagines or wills the appropriate reply of the Court to the Pope and to his challenge.

1418-37] *Oh . . . doom* Without literally echoing specific verses of the Bible these lines invoke several Biblical passages and themes: the church as God's representative on earth, the all-seeing eye of God, and death as the consequence of sin. Some relevant passages are: for 8.1418-21, "there is nothing covered, that shall not be revealed; and hid, that shall not be known. . . . Are not two sparrows sold for a farthing? and one of them shall not fall on the ground without your Father" (Matt. 10:26,29). For 8.1423, "what doth the Lord require of thee, but to do justly, and to love mercy" (Mic. 6:8). For the whole stanza, "Lift up your eyes to the heavens, and look upon the earth beneath: for the heavens shall vanish away like smoke, and the earth shall wax old like a garment, and they that dwell therein shall die in like manner: but my salvation shall be for ever, and my righteousness shall not be abolished" (Is. 51:6). *Peccable* (8.1425) means "liable to sin." The *father of the flock* (8.1426) is the Pope. The *last faint sands of life*, the *frittered gold* (8.1427) are the beginning of an hour-glass metaphor for life, a figure probably called to mind by the real hour-glass of 8.59, now running out. *Frittered* means "minutely fragmented"; *minim* means "smallest particle" and refers to a grain of sand in the hour-glass. *Let innocence survive* (8.1434) is a play on the Pope's name and age and a calculated, ingenious fusion of the Pope and Guido. The stanza is a carefully executed climax to Arcangeli's defense and in clear ironic contrast to his off-the-record remarks about the Pope's senility below (8.1440-42).

1442] *intellectuals* Mental powers; the implication is that he is *non compos mentis* the rest of the time. See also 12.6-8.

1446] *Hyacinth* See 8.1-2n.

1449-51] *how . . . Writ* "To every thing there is a season, and a time to every purpose under the heaven. . . . A time to weep, and a time to laugh." Ecclesiastes 3:1-8 lists the seasons of life in a stoic tone opposite to Arcangeli's pride and gusto.

1452-53] *cast . . . waters* "Cast thy bread upon the waters: for thou shalt find it after many days" (Eccl. 11:1).

1464] *with safety* With reinforcements and all due precautions against failure.

1472] *fee* Guido did hire and maintain four armed men, a fact which, the Fisc argued, made them hired assassins. See 8.1541-55.

1489] *apprehensive* Understanding.

1492-93] *Tobit . . . dog* Tobit sent his son on his way with the angel Raphael and a dog. Medieval painters often depicted Raphael with the dog. See 6.1252-53n.

1500] *Haud . . . æquis* "With not equal steps!" cf. Virgil, *Aeneid* 2.724.

1508-9] *Pauperum . . . advocate* See 1.174-6n.

1522-37] *Castrensis . . . wrong* The source of the case here described is an eminent fifteenth-century jurist, *Castrensis* (Paolo de Castro), who cites both his fourteenth-century predecessor Giacomo Butringarius and his own judgment in this case, in defense of a wronged husband's use of accomplices (OYB, E, 35). The case is more fully described in Gest, 350.

1538-56] *Opinio . . . verbo* The *mandatories* are assassins hired to kill in the absence of the principal, and an auxiliatory (*helpmate*) is an associate who joins the injured party to help defend his honor. The latter is said to have changed his name and is no longer a murderer. He is deserving, Arcangeli argues, of the same leniency as the principal. *Neologism* (8.1555) refers to the iteration of "qualified by the quality." The legal sense of the word *qualitas* in OYB is "a circumstance which aggravated a crime. Latin *qualitatus* carries the more general sense of "qualified, modified"; in the original Latin of OYB the two words in tandem would not be as redundant as in English.

1559-63] *One . . . Spreti* Spreti actually asserts that both Domenico and Francesco were minors as well as foreigners (not natives of the Papal state; see *Sources*). Gest identifies the accomplices and their backgrounds and ages, 516-17. He conjectures that two were minors (under 25) and that only one was not a foreigner.

1567] *Play . . . clowns* See 8.343-48n.

1568-80] *they . . . fee* From the Secondary Source, OYB, E, 265.

1578] *recruited* Reinforced, renewed.

1581] *I . . . fact* Bottini does not mention the plotted murder of Guido in his argument in Book 9, nor is the plot mentioned in the official records; it is recorded only in the Secondary Source.

1590] *sweat of brow* God said to the disobedient Adam: "In the sweat of thy face shalt thou eat bread" (Gen. 3.19).

1604-5] *money . . . ill* Ovid, *Metamorphoses* 1.138-40.

1608] *Milk . . . require* St. Paul wrote to the immature Churchmen at Corinth, "And I, bretheren, could not speak to you as unto spiritual, but as unto carnal, even as babes in Christ. I have fed you with milk, and not with meat: for hitherto you were not able to bear it" (1 Cor. 3:12). Cf. also Heb. 5:12, 14.

1616-1715] *Push . . . fall* This passage is the concluding peroration of Arcangeli's defense (OYB, E, 130). *Spectata est*, 8.1661, is a passive verb ("was witnessed") rather than the *fuit spectata* ("had witnessed") of the original, an apparent mistranscription by B.

1625-26] *The . . . arise* Another identification of Guido with Jesus, who foretold on several occasions that he would arise from the dead. See 5.5n. and 5.2037n. for other implicit identifications of Guido with Christ.

1660-66] *Eternal . . . blood* See 4.881n. As the legend is told by Livy, 1.58.4, in consequence of a gamble among a group of Roman soldiers about the virtue of their wives, Lucretia, the impeccably virtuous wife of Collatinus, aroused the lust of Sextus Tarquinius, son of the last of the infamous Tarquin Kings of Rome. Tarquin forced Lucretia to submit to him. Afterwards she summoned her husband, her father, and two of their friends, told them her story, and killed herself. According to legend, the Tarquins were the last kings of Rome and this episode contributing to their demise has a special claim to significance in the legendary history of the Eternal City. *Spots of pudicity:* fouled, spotted chastity.

1668-84] *Virginius . . . abode* The Roman centurion Virginius decapitated his daughter Virginia and presented her head to her would-be seducer, the legislator Appius Claudius. The story is told by Livy, by Petrarch, and by Chaucer in the "Physician's Tale."

1698] *round . . . ears* See 4.597n.

1702] *griesly* Archaic spelling of "grisly."

1713] *Mannaia* See 1.1320n.

1717-21] *Landed . . . play* Arcangeli boasts of accomplishing what God proposes to Job as impossible. The famous passage illustrates the wonder and mystery of God's power, and the foolhardiness of the "children of pride." "Canst thou draw out leviathan with an hook . . . Canst thou put an hook into his nose? or bore his jaw through with a thorn?. . . wilt thou bind him for thy maidens? (Job 41:1-2,5). B uses this image in at least two other places, one in Guido's first defense and again in the Pope's monologue; it is given a different meaning in each of the three references. See 5.1497-98 and n. and 10.1097-1105.

1732] *Cicero-ize* Make oratorically effective; Cicero was so famous an orator that his name was later applied to famous speakers in any language; there was a British Cicero, a German Cicero, etc.

1733] *Fisc his finish* Perhaps a pun on Fisc, fish, conclusion, and final fatal stroke (Richard D. Altick and James F. Loucks, II, *Browning's Roman Murder Story* [Chicago: The University of Chicago Press, 1968], 259-60).

1736] *Jam . . . satis* "Enough now!"

1740] *toque* Tall hat.

1748] *rosolio* Alcoholic punch.

1751] *perfectum, bipsi* "The perfect (tense), bipsi." The past tense of *bibo* is *bibi*. Probably young Hyacinth mispronounced the verb because he had the hiccups, not because he could not conjugate it.

1761-62] *yield . . . usury* To the slothful and over-cautious servant in Jesus' parable, his lord said, "Thou oughtest therefore to have put my money to the exchangers and then at my coming I should have received my own with usury" (Matt. 25:27).

1764-66] *Agur's . . . me* "Remove far from me vanity and lies: give me neither poverty nor riches; feed me with food convenient for me" (Prov. 30:8). Arcangeli takes only the advice convenient for him, deleting the inappropriate line about riches.

1768-74] *Can . . . guess* See 8.25-33. *cup and cover*: silver cup and cutlery; a table setting.

1776-80] *trifle . . . avus* The Latin means, "Hyacinth's grandfather gave it to him as a gift!" Engraved with this inscription the *trifle* (gift of the cup) *ought to grace* the grandfather's largesse rather than represent the sum of it.

1784-89] *ne . . . promise* "Lest there be a wife who parades loaded with rounder breast . . . pearls." *Mammis* (breasts) is a slip inserted by Arcangeli into Horace's line in *Epodes* 8.13-14.

1793] *lambkins . . . live* Arcangeli's last words echo another comically pompous misuser of language, Falstaff's friend Pistol. Upon hearing that Falstaff is dying, Pistol says "His heart is fracted and corroborate . . . Let us condole the knight, for, lambkins, we will live" (*Henry V* 2.1.124, 127).